THE WONDER TEAM

To Pete Wonn -
my Centre ROOMMATE AND
FRIEND. HOPE you LEARN A BIT ABOUT
your ALMA MATTER FROM "The Wonder TEAM."

Best wishes!
Bob Albertson
20 JULY '12

'Praying Colonels' Real 'Wonder Team'

By William M Chipman
Staff Correspondent Universal Service

NEW YORK, Dec. 27. –Having visited both the Atlantic and Pacific seaboards this fall and having established beyond the last doubt its prowess on the gridiron, the Centre college football team is even more of a wonder eleven than on that eventful Saturday in November, 1919 when word was flashed across the land that the "Praying Colonels" had vanquished West Virginia 14 to 6 – and West Virginia a victor over Princeton 25 to 0 a week earlier.

The Colonels have been uniformly successful this fall and have suffered only a single touchdown against their record. Harvard, Arizona, Auburn, Tulane, Washington and Lee, Kentucky and Clemson are among the victims of the Danville team.

THE WONDER TEAM

*The Story of the Centre College Praying Colonels
and Their Rise to the Top of the Football World
1917–1924*

Robert W. Robertson, Jr., M.D.

Butler Books
Louisville

To that great fan of the team, and the true inspiration for *The Wonder Team*, I thank my father, Robert Wintersmith Robertson, M.D., Centre '25, 1903-1988. He was there, and his stories over the years about that unique era, and that unique group of young men, gave me the determination to put it all down in writing for future generations to appreciate.

ISBN 978-1-884532-99-3
Printed in Canada

For information write Butler Books
P.O.Box 7311, Louisville, KY 40207
502-897-9393
Bbutler519@aol.com

Visit us online at
www.butlerbooks.com

No book is written alone. *The Wonder Team* is no exception.

There has never been a more dedicated and persistent researcher than Tony Gaier of Versailles, Ohio. Tony, affectionately called Bloodhound, has never felt that a project is impossible, nor that a source can't be unearthed. To him I owe my eternal gratitude.

Bianca and David Lisonbee allowed me to take advantage of that magical term, "residual income," through my association with their nutritional supplement company, 4Life Research, of Sandy, Utah. Without Transfer Factor™ and the company's splendid product line, I would have never had the freedom and resources to spend time in writing.

Ann and Jim McCurry provided me with "Uncle Charlie" Moran's scrapbooks and numerous photographs. Ann's stories about her grandfather, the famous coach of the Centre College "Praying Colonels," helped me understand better the years during and after World War I, and how the team was built. Jim reproduced so much material in so many formats that I have enough to someday, hopefully, do a coffeetable book.

At Centre College, Mike Norris, Diane Johnson and Bob Glass were always willing and able to assist in any way they could. Thanks to them all.

My wife, Dawne, literally gave up her kitchen for two years while material for the book was spread here, there, and everywhere. Her tolerance and understanding went above and beyond the call of normal spousal patience, and to her I give much credit for the completion of my efforts.

As for so many of my age, computer skills are either non-existent or incomplete. My daughter, Brooke, spent hours working me through many "black holes." Both her cheerfulness and aptitude, especially in helping set up files for my illustrations and photographs, were absolutely essential and tremendously appreciated.

Thanks to my son, Rob III, and daughter, McCall, who offered encouragement when I ran stories by them about Centre College football. "Dad, you ought to write a book." Little did they know that, indeed, I would.

TABLE OF CONTENTS

INTRODUCTION

DANVILLE, KENTUCKY

Danville, Kentucky is the county seat of Boyle County and lies within the southern fringe of the famous and beautiful Bluegrass Region in the center of the state. Danville's history is basically Kentucky's history, for it was in Danville that the birth of Kentucky took place.

In 1776, Kentucky was still frontier and was but a county in the western part of Virginia. Daniel Boone led pioneers over what became known as the Wilderness Road which wound through the mountainous Cumberland Gap into the central part of Kentucky.

The prominent location of Danville on the Wilderness Road made it a crossroads for the early settlers coming into the area, and by 1785, the little settlement had become a center for political activity and was chosen as the first seat of government.

A meeting house, courthouse, and jail were built, and over the next eight years, 10 conventions were held in what became known as Constitution Square.

By 1790, the delegates from the county of Kentucky and the government of Virginia had reached an agreement by which Kentucky would become an independent state, and on June 1, 1792, Kentucky County became the Commonwealth of Kentucky, and the 15th state of the Union.

However, having given birth to the baby didn't give custody of the child, and the capital of the newly formed Commonwealth was established some 45 miles north, in Frankfort, on the Kentucky River. Danville's growth, slow but steady throughout the next century plus, never allowed its claim to be more than a small, beautiful, genteel, Kentucky county seat, full of substantial Federal, Greek Revival, Antebellum and later, Victorian homes, and a trading center, surrounded by gently rolling, lush farmland punctuated by limestone fences.

In 1784, the mainly Presbyterian Scots-Irish settlers built the first place of worship in Danville. These same Presbyterians and their descendants were instrumental in establishing Centre College in 1819, using the old English spelling, and so named because of the central location of Danville in the state.

Centre was a men's school, affiliated with the Presbyterian Church. The first building, now known as Old Centre and still in use, was constructed in 1820.

The initial class was comprised of five students. The faculty numbered two. The classes followed the classical curriculum of Greek, Latin, Logic and Rhetoric.

For the next ten years, Centre grew slowly, but in the period from 1830 until just before the Civil War, the college began to develop into a respected institution of higher learning.

The post-Civil War years resulted in several new buildings, but only one of these survived into the twentieth century. However, a construction "binge," beginning around the turn of the century, began to give the campus the appearance that it would have by 1915.

There was still Old Centre. A classroom building, Old Main, was built in 1871. A science building, Young Hall, named after a former president of the college, was erected in 1909. A dormitory, Breckinridge Hall, named for John Cabell Breckinridge, Centre class of 1839, a United States Representative, Senator, and the Vice President under James Buchanan from 1856-60, was completed in 1898, and rebuilt after a fire in 1908. A library, Old Carnegie, was built with a donation of $30,000 by Andrew Carnegie and finished in 1913, and there was a new gymnasium which replaced the original Boyle-Humphrey Gymnasium, and was given the same name when it opened in time for the school year in 1915. Behind the gym and Old Main was a patchy football field with a modest wooden stadium.

Across town, situated on beautiful, tree-lined Lexington Avenue, was a girl's school called the Kentucky College for Women, founded in 1854. K.C.W. was an independent college, becoming a department of Centre in 1926, and formally merged with Centre in 1930. The Lexington Avenue buildings were vacated in1962 when the two campuses consolidated, and the female students took up residence in new dormitories built on Centre's property on West Main Street.

SAN DIEGO, DECEMBER 26, 1921

On December 26, 1921, a group of young men from a little college with just over 200 students was more than 2,000 miles and a week of travel by train from their campus, playing in one of the pioneer, college post-season football games, the Christmas Bowl, in San Diego, California.

After the game was over, a reporter named Robert Edgren asked Bob Evans, who had been the referee during the contest, what his impressions were about the boys wearing the gold jerseys.

"Well," said Mr. Evans, "the thing I noticed most was the cussing. I've refereed a lot of games, but I never heard anything like it before. The University of Arizona was just average at cussing. They had a few novel expressions that they must have learned out there in the desert, but nothing at all startling to the trained ear. I don't know that Stanford or some of the Coast teams couldn't have laid over them in originality and emphasis."

"But Centre! That's what struck me. Not a man in the lineup used a single cuss word. Bo McMillin did all the cussing for the Centre team. I never heard anything like the line that Bo pulled. The strongest word he used was 'Marvelous!' Every time he snapped it out, you could see the entire team quiver as if he'd whip-lashed them. When he wanted variety, he'd use the word, 'Wonderful!'"

"All the cussing I ever heard was mild as milk compared to the way Bo uses the language when his team isn't playing up to their, or his, standards."

"Wonderful, just wonderful!"

"Marvelous, simply marvelous!"

Evans continued, "There isn't a cuss word known that is as insulting to his men than to hear, 'Wonderful!' or 'Marvelous!' Pretty soon they're so mad that they play even harder, if that's possible."

"Bo is some general, I'll say," went on Evans. "He sees everything and he criticizes every man who doesn't play his position. After some plays, he'd yell, 'Marvelous! You didn't play out far enough on that end—you're way up too high—you can't stop them that way.'"

"It was funny, the line of talk that Centre had. They'd call out to each other, 'Take the mail to town, boy,' or 'Take this one up North.'"

"Bo McMillin kept up a line of talk on offense. He say, 'Look out, I'm going around left end this time, and I'm swinging wide.' Then he'd do it."

"In the final period, Bartlett was in for Armstrong. Centre had the ball near Arizona's goal. Bo was calling the plays and signals"

"Bo called out to Red Roberts to take it in, then changed his mind and asked Bartlett if he'd scored yet, and Bartlett said he hadn't."

"So Bo told Red that he should get back in the line because it was Bartlett's turn to score. He hollered to Red to take out the left side of the Arizona line, because that was where Bartlett was going to carry the ball."

"Bartlett made it. Arizona knew he was coming—they clearly heard Bo tell him where to run—and they couldn't stop it. It was that easy! They took turns scoring a touchdown. One each for Bo, Roberts, Armstrong, Covington, Snowday and Bartlett."

Who were these young men? Often, during the years after the Great War, that very question was asked by opponents on the field, and spectators in the stands.

"Who are those guys?"

Let me tell you the story about how a little college named Centre turned out the most popular, and argurably, the best football team during the six years from 1919-1924.

How do I know about Centre's unbelievable history? Because my father was there during the era, along with my uncle, and they followed the team and kept an enormous amount of memorabilia which they passed on to me. Plus, they told me story after story over the years. Much of what they related was hard to believe. Centre played all over the country? Centre beat which teams? How many straight years? Centre produced how many first team All-Americans?

All of the newspaper clippings and photographs which they had hoarded seemed to back up everything they said. So I engaged a researcher, a man I call "Bloodhound," Tony Gaier of Versailles, Ohio, and decided to put the story together, to hopefully bring to life the exploits of a group of young men, led by basically volunteer coaches, who were the most colorful collection of athletes to ever play the game of college football.

To get started, you've got to know something about the man who made it all happen, Robert L. Myers, affectionately called "Chief" by his players.

Bob Myers came to Centre and Danville as a freshman in the fall of 1903. He was born in Atchison, Kansas but his family moved around the country, and he attended high school in Fort Worth, Texas and Philadelphia. Myers was a brilliant young man. He was editor-in-chief of the college newspaper, the "Cento," wrote for the "Eccentric," was secretary of the Deinologian Literary Society, and was voted "brightest man on the campus" when he graduated from Centre in 1907.

After leaving Centre, Myers moved to Chicago where his father had a business that booked talent for Chautauquas which many cities around the country held each summer. Most Americans now don't know what a Chautauqua was, but they certainly knew in the early part of the twentieth century, because these traveling shows, named after the location of their origin, Lake Chautauqua in New York, brought "culture" to rural areas by allowing the locals to hear opera, classical and popular music, great oratory, and to experience Broadway plays. It was a big business in those days, and Bob Myers' father, though his Myers and Trimble Agency, had a very successful company supplying talent on "the circuit."

Young Bob wanted to be more than just a booking agent for Chautauquas. He knew he could make a good living working for his father, but he had a dream—a dream which seemed outrageous to everyone he shared it with, but Bob was a man who didn't let doubters stand in his way.

He lived by a Latin phrase that he had learned at Centre, "Credendo Vides." To believe is to see. "Credendo Vides." To believe is to see.

Bob Myers believed that he could build a national football championship program at his alma mater, little Centre College, and he decided to dedicate his life to doing just that.

There was just one problem. Bob didn't know much about football. He was a scholar, and never had success at any athletic activity. He'd gone out for football one year at Centre, but didn't ever get to play enough to earn the gold "C" cherished by the athletes. So Bob decided to become a student of the game, and in every spare moment that he could break away from his office, he'd journey to the campus of the University of Chicago and watch the famous coach, Amos Alonzo Stagg, put his players through their drills.

Myers took notes. If Stagg was scheduled to give a clinic, Bob Myers was there with pen and pad, ready to take down anything that the coach conveyed. Myers also attended clinics which were conducted by another coach with a big-time reputation, Glenn "Pop" Warner, while Warner led the Carlisle Indians, a famous team which featured the great Jim Thorpe.

By 1912, five years after leaving Centre, Bob Myers was ready to make his move. He heard about a position which was available at North Side High School in Fort Worth. The school needed an English teacher and football coach. Myers knew he was qualified to teach English. He hoped that his resume would be impressive enough to also qualify him as a coach.

Indeed it was. North Side offered him the job, and he worked it out with his father that he was going to Texas for the school year and would return in the summer to help out in the Chautauqua booking business. It was a fateful move, a move which would ultimately allow him to achieve his dream.

"Credendo Vides." To believe is to see. Bob Myers was on his way.

Soon after his arrival in Fort Worth, Myers encountered a young man at a minor league baseball game who was caught trying to get into the ballpark without a ticket. When a security guard began to chase the boy, Myers intervened and said he'd pay for his ticket if the officer wouldn't make a big deal out of the incident.

It was a propitious encounter. The boy was Alvin Nugent McMillin, and his and Myers' lives would forever be joined by that simple act of kindness.

McMillin was called "Bo." It was a nickname given by a cousin. Myers asked the youngster to sit down and to tell him something about himself. Bo said he was 17 and had dropped out of school to help support his family, but that even though his father, Reuben, had died the year before, in 1911, he thought that circumstances were now such that he could go back and continue his education.

It seems that Bo had only completed eight years in school. Myers said it didn't matter. "Come to North Side. I'll help you in school and you can play football. I'm the new coach." Just like that, Coach Myers and Bo McMillin joined forces on a journey which would bring them fame beyond their wildest dreams.

The new coach found that he had quite a lot of athletic talent enrolled at his high school. Rogers Hornsby, later one of the great professional baseball players, and a future Hall-of-Famer, was at North Side. He had played on the team in 1911, and could have returned for the next season, but decided to concentrate on baseball, especially when he saw that Bo was going to be the main gun on the football team in the future. Bo became the natural leader, but there were also other young men who helped North Side High build quite a reputation as a Texas football powerhouse.

James R. "Red" Weaver was a tough-as-nails lineman who stood but 5'7" and only weighed 158 pounds. But he was a great player, made even more so by his determination to excel.

Bill James wasn't much bigger than Red. He also played in the line, and took great pride in opening holes for his backs, and was a tremendous defensive tackle.

Madison "Matty" Bell was only 13 in 1912, but he soon developed into one of the top ends in the state.

Thad McDonnell, Bill Boswell, Bob Mathias and Sully Montgomery were other players who Coach Myers helped develop into stars.

Bo had a brother, Reuben, named after his father, and while he wasn't as talented as Bo, he became a starter for the North Side Steers, which by 1915 were the best team in North Texas, losing only in the state championship game played at the University of Texas stadium against a school from Austin.

Bo starting calling coach Myers "Chief," and the name stuck, and for the rest of his life, Bob Myers was Chief.

From day one on the job, the Chief began to sew the seeds for getting his "boys" to Danville, Kentucky, to play for his beloved school, Centre College, and he began his daily motivational journey to drive his boys to accomplishments that they had never even considered.

"Look what we've achieved in a short time here. We've become part of a winning program. Who would have ever believed it? But you did, you believed."

"Bo, you can be an All-American someday. Red, you can also. Matty, you can become one of the great college ends and with your dedication, you can be a winning college coach."

"Bill James, how would you like to play against the biggest colleges across the country, and win? Sully, Bill Boswell, Bob, Thad, let's stick together. We can do great things!"

"You've got to believe! Believe! Believe! Close you eyes and see the vision."

The Chief wrote on the walls of the football dressing room:

BELIEVE!
ACHIEVE!
SUCCEED!

The boys were constantly told about Centre College, the Chief's great love. He painted word pictures, and asked that they close their eyes and imagine as he spoke.

"It's in a beautiful little town in the Kentucky Bluegrass. It has wonderful facilities, beautiful classical buildings, and great professors. Centre is small, but it turns out more successful men than colleges much greater in size."

"Centre was founded in 1819. This year there probably aren't anywhere near 200 students on the campus. But it produces winners, and you are winners, and if we stick together, we can do great things."

"But you've got to believe!"

Slowly, the Chief talked the stars on the team to eventually head to Kentucky and enroll at Centre. There was one holdout. Roscoe "Cow" Minton, brother of a future Associate Justice of the United States Supreme Court, Sherman Minton, decided at the last moment to enroll at the University of Indiana. His and his teammate's paths would cross some years later.

Here is a list of the Fort Worth North Side Steers who Chief Myers sent to Centre, nearly 900 miles from their home town.

PLAYER	GRADUATED NORTHSIDE	ENTERED CENTRE
MATTY BELL	1916	1916
BOB MATHIAS	1916	1916
RED WEAVER	1916	1917
BO McMILLIN	1916	1917
THAD McDONNELL	1916	1917
BILL JAMES	1917	1917
BILL BOSWELL	1917	1917
SULLY MONTGOMERY	1918	1918

(Bo's older brother, Reuben, also attended Centre and is known to have been on campus in 1916 and 1917, before dropping out of school due to a "family emergency." Doubtless, Reuben was influenced to head to Danville by the Chief.)

An astute reader may have noticed that while five North Side Steers graduated in 1916, only two of them entered Centre the following September. There was a reason for that. The Chief had accompanied Bell, Mathias, Weaver, Bo and Thad McDonnell on the long train journey to Danville with the intent of enrolling each of them at Centre. He also hoped that perhaps he'd be allowed to help in the coaching of the team once he wound up his duties in Chicago.

His plan hit a snag. The transcripts of Weaver, Bo and McDonnell didn't reveal enough credits for them to be accepted into the college. Matty Bell and Bob Mathias were ok. Many people may have been disappointed, but that wasn't the way the Chief operated.

"It's a small setback," he announced. "Let me see what I can work out."

Paul Williams was a friend of the Chief and lived a short distance south of Danville in Somerset, Kentucky. Williams was contacted and asked if he could help "my boys" enroll in high school in Somerset so that they could earn the credits needed.

Myers added a sweetener to the deal. "They are wonderful football players, and the one named Bo is an absolute football playing fool."

Williams called the coach of the Somerset "Briar Jumpers," Paul Dexheimer, and asked him to help find a way to provide the Texans with a place to stay and a way to earn a little money for expenses. Dexheimer knew he already had a team with a good chance to become the Kentucky state champs, and got busy.

Thirty citizens were contacted. "Let's form a Pressing Club. That's what we'll call it. Each of you will send one suit a month to be pressed by the boys, and you'll each pay $1.00 a month, and we can land some great players." The idea took hold. A place was located for the trio to live. A room was found and equipped with the necessary equipment to steam and press the suits.

Again, it was the Chief who found a way to turn a possible disappointment into an opportunity. The year at Somerset allowed the formation of a bond with one of the great players to ever step on the gridiron.

James "Red" Roberts was a huge and talented junior at Somerset High who could play equally well in the line or backfield. The combination of the Texans and the big redhead produced one of the legendary high school teams that few coaches can only hope for.

The Somerset "Briar Jumpers" rolled over all of their opposition by big margins. A memorable game was played in Louisville between Louisville Boys High, a merged school formed by combining Louisville Male and Manual. The Louisvillians had scheduled Somerset as a "breather" between two supposedly tougher opponents.

The heavily favored Boys High team was steamrollered by Bo and his teammates, 51-6. Bo scored three times. Red Roberts kicked a long field goal. Red Weaver was in on every tackle.

In the last game of the season, played in Lexington for the state championship, Somerset dominated Lexington High statistically but couldn't punch the ball over for a score. Bo's team picked up five times the number of yards as the Lexingtonians, but had to settle for a scoreless tie.

The presence of the boys from Fort Worth cemented the relationship between Somerset and Centre College. Seven of the Briar Jumpers of 1916 ended up at Centre. Bo, the two Reds, Weaver and Roberts, John Sherman Cooper, Thad McDonnell, Brinkley Gooch and Herman Lowenthal, all eventually became Centre College Colonels.

Meanwhile, the Chief spent the 1916-17 school year back in Chicago, still attending lectures and still intent on achieving his dream.

Centre had a coach, Orville B. Littick, and he not only directed the football program, but also headed up the basketball and baseball teams. He had some success on the gridiron, running up a 5-1-3 record in 1916. However, while the record wasn't bad, one game had ruined an otherwise respectable showing. Centre's big rival, the "State School," the Kentucky Wildcats, had totally wiped out the Colonels, 68-0.

In the spring of 1917, Coach Littick resigned. He'd been offered a position as football coach at Beloit College in Wisconsin. The Danville "Messenger" had a small announcement about Littick's leaving. The story concluded with the following: Chief Myers will succeed Littick in the fall.

CHAPTER ONE:
THE CHIEF TAKES OVER

The citizens of Danville and the student body eagerly awaited the start of the 1917 football season. There were several regulars returning, and with the reputation of Bo and his Somerset teammates preceding their arrival, everyone felt that good things had to happen on the gridiron.

Dr. William A. Ganfield, the college president, recognized that the possibilities of a successful football program may promote growth in the numbers of the student body as well as the college's endowment. He hired an assistant to help the Chief, and Pitt Green, Centre '07, a classmate of Myers, came over from the University of Missouri to fill the position.

Chief Myers posted some regulations in the locker room in addition to the plaque which had become his mantra:

BELIEVE!
ACHIEVE!
SUCCEED!

There was to be:
    (1) No drinking
    (2) No smoking
    (3) No breaking of curfew
    (4) Attendance of all classes
    (5) Maintenance of passing grades
    (6) No missed practices without a written excuse
    (7) Attendance of daily chapel

There were 60 freshmen entering, a near-record number. The new arrivals included several who were expected to strengthen the football team, in addition to the boys from Somerset.

Norris "Army" Armstrong was a fleet halfback coming up from Fort Smith,

Arkansas, encouraged to enroll by a Centre alumnus who was from Army's home town, and a member of the Centre Board of Trustees. Army would be a big part of the Centre success story for the next five years.

Will "Bill" Boswell and Bill James had graduated and were coming up from Fort Worth. (Eventually, twelve young men from Fort Worth would end up playing football at Centre.)

Practice had hardly gotten under way when there was a crisis. Bo had gone into the gym and seen a senior end, a starter the previous season, putting out a cigarette. At the afternoon session, he called all of the players around him and asked the Chief to join in.

Bo told what he had observed. "The only way that we're going to achieve our dreams, and the dreams of the Chief, is that we all live up to what we had agreed were training rules. Either he leaves, or I do. I won't play on a team that has players who won't keep their word." The senior cleared out his locker that afternoon. Bo's actions set the pattern for the next five years that he was on the team.

The season began with what was essentially an exhibition against the Kentucky Military Institute. A large crowd was on hand, and they weren't disappointed.

The Colonels started the following lineup:

Matty Bell	Left end	Fort Worth, Texas
Bracken Tate*	Left tackle	Danville, Kentucky
Jim Coleman	Left guard	Gracey, Kentucky
Red Weaver	Center	Fort Worth, Texas
Reuben McMillin	Right guard	Fort Worth, Texas
Howard Van Antwerp	Right tackle	Mount Sterling, Kentucky
Frank Allen	Right end	Sharpsburg, Kentucky
Bo McMillin	Quarterback	Fort Worth, Texas
Tom Moran	Right half	Horse Cave, Kentucky
Ed Diddle	Left half	Gradyville, Kentucky
Bob Mathias	Fullback	Fort Worth, Texas

*(Bracken Tate was the team captain during the 1917 season.)

There were six Kentuckians and five Texans from Fort Worth's North Side High School.

The game was a track meet. On the first play, Bo streaked around right end and went 60 yards for a touchdown. Centre lead 28-0 at the end of the first quarter, 48-0 at the half, 69-0 after three quarters and won by a final score of 104-0.

It was an auspicious start, even though everyone knew that KMI didn't offer much in the way of opposition. That changed two weekends later when the Colonels took a train up to Greencastle, Indiana, to play the DePauw Tigers. The game was a disappointment as Centre lost 6-0 when a punt was fumbled by a Colonel deep in his own territory. The ball rolled into the end zone and was recovered for the only score of the game. The loss may have been a disappointment, but it presented an opportunity which no one could have foreseen during the long ride back down the tracks to Danville.

UNCLE CHARLIE ARRIVES ON CAMPUS

A somewhat gruff looking man strolled out onto the practice field on Monday, October 22, 1917 and introduced himself to the Chief. He was Charles B. Moran, known to everyone as "Uncle Charlie," or sometimes just as "Unc." Moran had a son, Tom, on the team, and asked if he could watch the practice.

The Chief knew Moran, because Unc had a very successful coaching career at Texas A&M from 1909-1914, years which overlapped with Myers' tenure in Fort Worth. Moran was 39 years old, and had begun a 23 year career as a National League professional baseball umpire during the just ended 1917 season.

Uncle Charlie compiled a 38-8-4 record during his six years at A&M. He was an offensive genius, and offered some tips to the Chief about how he may want to open up his attack. Moran said that since the baseball season was over, he'd be happy to help out with the team for the rest of the season. And—he'd do it for nothing. No salary. He'd just volunteer his time.

Before the afternoon was over, Centre had a new football coach. The Chief called a meeting and announced that the team was deserving of the best coaching available, and they were fortunate to have a man who could take them to the next level. Even though it had been his long-time goal to head up the program, it was a measure of the man that he stepped aside in a move that he felt was in the best interests of Centre football.

His announcement was met with shouts of protest. The Chief was the man! He'd brought so many of the players to Danville. A compromise was reached that satisfied everyone. The Chief would stay on as Athletic Director. He'd assist in coaching the team. He would accept no salary. Centre had two men at the helm who simply volunteered their time and efforts in their quest to help achieve what everyone in Danville and Centre wanted. They would mold this group of young men into a football machine which would earn the attention and respect of the college football world.

THE PLAN

The Chief and Uncle Charlie drew up a game plan. First, they would become the undisputed champions of college football in Kentucky. In order to accomplish that, they had to gain the upper hand against Transylvania and the University of Kentucky, or "State," both located in Lexington, and Georgetown, situated a few miles outside of Lexington.

Next, they would try to get on the schedules of some big state universities in order to gain more recognition outside of Kentucky. Finally, if they could achieve their first two objectives, they would try to land a big game with one of the powerhouses in the East. Even then, they were beginning to plan a route which would take the Colonels to Cambridge to play Harvard, or perhaps to Princeton, or even to an appearance in New Haven to play the Elis of Yale.

It was an audacious plan. But, as the Chief always said, "You've got to believe!"

THE 1917 SEASON CONTINUES

With just a few days left to prepare for the next game, Uncle Charlie took the helm. The Colonels traveled to Maryville, Tennessee, and totally dominated a pretty good Maryville Fighting Scots team, shutting them out 34-0. Kentucky had only defeated the Scots by a 19-0 score three weeks earlier, so the margin was certainly a confidence builder for the upcoming November 3 contest with the Wildcats.

Uncle Charlie and the Chief then pointed their efforts to the annual battle with Centre's greatest rival, "State." Kentucky was 2-2-1 coming into the Centre Homecoming game. The overall series had Centre leading 12-9, with two ties against its in-state rivals.

Centre adopted the motto, "Right the wrong of 1916," referring to the 68-0 shellacking that the Wildcats had put on the Danvillians the previous year, and placed a huge banner so proclaiming across the back of the Boyle-Humphrey Gymnasium.

It was just before the game was to begin, as the coaches gave their pre-game instructions, that an event took place which ultimately led the Colonels to be called the "Praying Colonels."

Everyone noticed that Reuben McMillin wasn't suiting up. Rube wasn't even in the locker room. Uncle Charlie explained that earlier in the morning, a call had come from Fort Worth that there was some sort of problem in the McMillin family, and one of the brothers needed to go home and help out.

"I am a God-fearing man," Uncle Charlie said. "I may not practice a formal religion, but I believe there is a higher authority that guides us in our lives. Reuben sacrificed himself for the team. He has been here longer that Bo, but Rube came to me and said that he'd return home, because the team needed Bo more. Perhaps we should bow our heads and ask for Divine Guidance from the power above as we enter into this game."

There was a moment of silence, and then Bob Mathias burst out, "Damnit Unc! Let me pray!" It was never revealed exactly what the Centre fullback said, but Howard Van Antwerp related in an interview years later that there wasn't a dry eye in the dressing room as the Colonels jumped to their feet at the final "amen" and raced onto the field.

It was a colorful and festive afternoon. The stands were full, the weather was perfect, the ladies wearing either the blue and white of Kentucky, or yellow chrysanthemums. The goal posts were wrapped in the two school's colors, and most importantly for the Centre College Colonels, they were able to "Right the wrong of 1916."

The only score came on a field goal by Bo in the third quarter. Centre had marched down to the Kentucky 20 yard line after the kick-off starting the second half. Then the Wildcats' defense stiffened. Three plays resulted in no gain. On fourth down, Bo took the center from Red Weaver, stepped back a yard, and calmly kicked a field goal. Later, it was determined that it was the first time that Bo had ever kicked a field goal in a game, high school or college. When asked about why he decided to try the kick rather than have another player with more experience make the effort, he replied, "We had to win. I felt I could make it, and fortunately I did." If self-confidence was called "cocky," Bo may have so qualified. But he was actually a very humble young man. He simply felt he could deliver, and he did just that.

After the win over Kentucky, the Colonels were 3-1 and it looked like they could run the table during the rest of the season and end up at 7-1, which is exactly what they did. Centre shut out their next four opponents, beating Kentucky Wesleyan at Winchester, the University of the South (Sewanee) in Chattanooga, and definitely became the "Champions of Kentucky" after rolling over Transylvania in Lexington and Georgetown in Danville.

A summary of 1917:	Centre	104	KMI	0
	Centre	0	Depauw	6
	Centre	34	Maryville	0
	Centre	3	Kentucky	0
	Centre	37	Kentucky Wesleyan	0
	Centre	28	Sewanee	0
	Centre	28	Transylvania	0
	Centre	13	Georgetown	0

For the season, the Gold and White outscored their opponents 247-6. Even if the KMI game is thrown out, the Colonels scored 143 points to average winning by nearly 20 points per game.

It was obvious that Centre played tough defense. The only score they allowed was the fluke of a touchdown that DePauw got due to a recovered fumble in the end zone, hardly a defensive breakdown.

The Chief and Uncle Charlie were building a team to be reckoned with, and now it was time to ratchet up the program and begin to go after some of the more prominent programs which could put their little school on the map.

At the team banquet after the season ended, 14 gold "C's" were handed out to:

Frank Allen
Army Armstrong
Matty Bell
Bill Boswell
Jim Coleman
Ed Diddle
Bo McMillin
Bob Mathias
Tom Moran
Joe Penn
G.W. Rue
Bracken Tate
Howard Van Antwerp
Red Weaver

After a basketball game on February 15, 1918, Dr. Frank L. Rainey, Chairman of the Athletic Committee, presented small, gold, monogrammed footballs to the lettermen, Chief Myers, Uncle Charlie and Pitt Green. Ann McCurry, Uncle Charlie's granddaughter, proudly wears his gold football on a charm bracelet to this day.

CHAPTER TWO:
THE UNCONTROLLABLE
EVENTS OF 1918

The Chief, Dr. Rainey and Uncle Charlie began working on the schedule for 1918. They knew they were going to be loaded with most of the 1917 team returning. Somerset, Kentucky's Red Roberts had committed to Centre, and he would add tremendously to the strength of the team, plus several other promising prospects had indicated that they planned to enroll.

World War I, the Great War, had a huge impact on college football in 1918. There had been some programs which had been drastically reduced in 1917, but the main impact of the war was felt during the 1918 campaign.

The campuses across the nation literally became military camps under the auspices of a federal organization called the Student Army Training Corp. The S.A.T.C. provided regular Army officers to provide training, and students were provided uniforms, a small monthly stipend, and were readied for future service while maintaining a regular classroom schedule.

Centre was no different. It was reveille in the morning with drilling and exercises, and then to the classroom. In the afternoon, the football team went back on the field, this time in different uniforms, and got ready for the season. The fall of 1918 found that most male students were following a military regimen, and it was only when the war ended in November that campus life returned to normal.

Many of the military bases were filled with ex-college players, and it was decided that it would be good for morale if they fielded football teams. One of the biggest programs originated out of the Great Lakes Naval Training Station north of Chicago. So many applicants turned out for the first day of practice that Great Lakes was able to field several teams and send them across the country to play various colleges.

Camp Zachary Taylor, an army training facility near Louisville, also announced that it would outfit a team for 1918.

Centre planned an intensified schedule which would open with a non-official game with St. Joseph's Prep, located in Bardstown, Kentucky. After the warm-up, the announced opponents were:

Indiana
Georgetown (Ky.)
Transylvania
Kentucky
Camp Zachary Taylor
Sewanee
Vanderbilt
Tennessee

It was clear that Centre wanted to play a tougher schedule by the fact that weaker teams like Kentucky Wesleyan, KMI and Maryville were dropped.

The war changed things, as more and more colleges had their athletes either volunteer for service, or report for duty after being drafted. But equally as disruptive was an epidemic, soon to escalate into a full blown pandemic, mistakenly called the "Spanish Influenza."

The St Joe's Prep game took place in early October as scheduled. Centre wore new gold and white uniforms, and the team was beginning to take on the appearance of a big-time squad. Centre ran all over St. Joe's, and when the little Catholic school ran out of players, Uncle Charlie sent several of the Colonels' reserves across the field to lend a hand to a game but overwhelmed foe.

One of the "loaners" was John Y. Brown who later became one of the premiere legal minds in Kentucky, a United States Congressman, and the father of John Y., Jr., who bought Kentucky Fried Chicken from Colonel Harlan Sanders, and later became Kentucky's governor, serving from 1979-1983.

After the St. Joe's game, the Spanish Flu broke out in Kentucky and throughout the country. The first cases had been in March at Fort Riley in Kansas. The virus was very infectious but seemed to initially be rather benign. However, after it appeared to have run its course, a virulent strain broke out. It infected soldiers who were being shipped eastward to embark from the Atlantic ports on their way to Europe to join the American Expeditionary Force, the AEF, which was fighting alongside the British and French in their battle with Germany and her allies. The virus and soldiers traveled together, and all along the journey to the East, people who came into contact with the servicemen were exposed.

The "outbreak" in Kansas exploded first in the United States, and then spread throughout the world, eventually killing over 50,000,000 people, many millions more than the Great War of 1914-18. Events were cancelled all across the country as the public health authorities forbade the gathering of crowds in an attempt to control the spread of the disease. In July, the virus intensified and became more deadly. By September and into October, the crisis became full-blown. People wore masks. They stayed indoors if at all possible. They looked to the medical profession for answers which were varied, but essentially ineffective.

In October, the United States Public Health Service sent out a bulletin entitled:

HOW TO AVOID INFLUENZA

(1) ALL COLDS, HOWEVER SLIGHT, SHOULD BE TREATED AS POSSIBLE ATTACKS OF INFLUENZA.

(2) AVOID FEEDING OR SPREADING OF THE DISEASE.
(One may wonder what this meant exactly.)

(3) AVOID CROWDS
(Certainly, this meant no football games.)

(4) REGULATE BODILY FUNCTIONS AND KEEP THEM THIS WAY.

(5) WASH OUT NOSE/ THROAT THREE TIMES DAILY WITH SALT WATER.

(6) WEAR A MASK WHEN AROUND THOSE WITH INFLUENZA.

(7) WEAR WARM, DRY CLOTHING. EAT SIMPLE FOOD. DRINK A LOT OF WATER.

The Danville "Messenger" added a local doctor's recommendation to the list.

(8) IF YOU FEEL ILL, TAKE A LAXATIVE—CASTOR OIL—AND GO TO BED AND STAY THERE UNTIL THE DOCTOR ARRIVES.

There was no advice on how one could stay in bed after loading up with a laxative. Children who were allowed outside had to play alone, wearing a mask. A little poem spread across the country which youngsters everywhere repeated while jumping rope.

I have a friend,
His name is Enza.
If you open the window,
In flu Enza.

Centre's football program shut down. There were no games for a month as even little, isolated Danville started reporting cases of the flu which were listed in the two daily papers, the "Messenger" and "Advocate." Finally, Transylvania was allowed to come over on the Southern Railroad for a November 2 game in Danville. Centre crushed the visitors, scoring five touchdowns in the first quarter for a 35 point lead. Uncle Charlie pulled the starters and the second quarter was scoreless. The Colonels added another score shortly after the second half began, Red Weaver kicked his sixth straight extra point for a 42-0 lead, and then a memorable event occurred which was talked about for years.

The game was for all practical purposes over when Centre faced a fourth down at midfield. Red Roberts was sent in to punt, but when he fielded the center pass, he drop-kicked from his own 42 yard line. The crowd watched the ball begin its flight off Red's toe, hearing leather smacking on leather. As the ball shot up toward the goal, all of the players turned and saw the oval flipping end over end. It seemed to literally have wings as it eased over the crossbar.

The official nearest the goal post stood for a few seconds in bewilderment and then thrust his arms into the air.

58 yards! If anyone had ever kicked a longer field goal, it hadn't been recorded. (During this era, the goal post was right on the goal line, unlike now, when it is ten yards back.) Transy kicked a field goal, Centre rang up one final score, Weaver booted another extra point, and the game ended, 52-3.

The Transy game allowed Uncle Charlie to take a look at his new players. Of course, Bo had run the show, but Chick Murphy, an arrival from Columbus, Ohio, showed a lot of speed. Army Armstrong turned in a strong performance at halfback, and was a demon on defense. Ben Cregor, from Springfield, Kentucky, proved why he would be a vital lineman in the coming years.

Red Roberts had a spectacular game. Besides the record-setting field goal, he'd played brilliantly at every position he assumed. The big guy, weighing in at 210 pounds, ran roughshod over the Transy defenders when he was put in at fullback. His interference, whether playing end or tackle, was incredible, opening holes and crunching anyone who opposed him with devastating blocks.

The Centre coaches had to be pleased. The season had been delayed, but things were looking good. So good, as a matter of fact, that Kentucky sent word that it was calling off the next week's game, scheduled for November 9. There was still a degree of quarantine in Lexington. At least that was the message Kentucky sent over to Danville.

Centre called back and said that wasn't a problem. Just hop on a southbound Southern train and come on over. There was no quarantine in Danville. There was no flu. It had run its course, and it would be perfectly safe to play on the Colonels' field.

Kentucky said, "No thanks."

Centre tried repeatedly during the rest of the fall to get UK to play. The Wildcats held their ground, and the two schools didn't meet on the gridiron during 1918.

Uncle Charlie and the Chief placed a call to the Great Lakes Naval Training Station when Kentucky wouldn't play and reached the officer in charge of the base's sports. He agreed to send a team down to Danville.

The squad he sent included several notable college players. Willams and James of Wisconsin, Goggin of Marquette, and Leffler, Whitley and Wetzel of Washington University in St. Louis, were just a few of the collegians who played for the Navy squad.

Centre won easily, 23-0. Red Roberts, Army and little Chick Murphy picked up yardage at will. Bo opened up the attack with an excellent display of passing.

After the Great Lakes game, the Centre staff began to realize that they had a team which was going to make a mark, if not in 1918, certainly in the future. The acclaim may have to wait a year, because the schedule had basically fallen apart.

Indiana, Vandy, Sewanee, and Tennessee all cancelled. (Tennessee didn't even field a team, and it's not certain if the Vandy game had ever been formalized, even if it had been announced earlier.)

Finally, another service team was invited to come to Danville, and on November 22, Camp Zachary Taylor came to town. The Army team, like Great Lakes, was loaded with college players and was heavily favored. It had beaten all of the other service teams that it had played, including a win over Camp Hancock, a team which had walloped a strong Vandy team, 26-0.

Much of the first half was played on Centre's side of the field. Camp Zachary Taylor outweighed the Colonels significantly, especially in the line. Red Roberts continually boomed out long punts after his teammates couldn't mount any significant drives. Finally, Centre got something going, mainly by Bo's passing, and marched to within field goal range, and Red Roberts was good on a kick to put the Colonels up, 3-0.

Zachary Taylor then mounted a counterattack. Line plunge after line plunge carried the ball to Centre's 20, and quarterback Hoffman hit King in the end zone for a touchdown. The extra point failed, and Centre was down 6-3.

As the half wound down, Bo got the Colonels deep in the service team's territory and tried three straight down and out passes to Red Roberts. Each time they were batted down as the defenders were keying on Red.

Bo called a timeout and had the team huddle around him. "Army, they're covering Red with two or three men. Here's what we do. We'll run the same exact play we've been running, but you lag behind Red, and when he cuts out and they cover him, you take off as fast as you can and go straight toward the goal. I'll fake to Red and then hit you."

"If you can imagine it, you can make it come true," the Chief always said.

The play unfolded just like Bo said it would. Army hauled in the perfect spiral and streaked across the goal, unmolested. Red Weaver kicked the extra point and it was 10-6 at the half. And that's the way it ended. The second half was a defensive standoff. The Colonels may have been outweighed, but there was no way they were going to be outfought.

The veteran Zachary Taylor team left Danville with great respect for their opponent, and as the soldiers returned to their campuses in 1919, they helped spread the word that something was happening in Danville, Kentucky.

Centre was 3-0. Only Georgetown (Ky.) was left. No other games could be found despite repeated efforts by Centre's leaders.

The Tigers proved to be Cubs, as they were slaughtered, 83-3. As usual, Bo, Red Roberts and Army led the attack. For the season, Centre scored 168 points while giving up only 13, for an average score of 42-3.

It was an abbreviated season, but everyone had to label it a success. The Colonels had won 10 straight, and things were indeed looking very, very good!

The Great War ended on the eleventh hour of the eleventh day of the eleventh month of 1918. The last pockets of the Spanish Flu, later proven to have no connection to Spain, were in San Francisco, in December, and the virulent illness vanished as quickly as it had appeared.

At the team banquet after the season ended, twenty gold "C's" were handed out.

Army Armstrong
Matty Bell
Ashley Blevins
L. Campbell
John Sherman Cooper
Ben Cregor
Allen Davis
Ed Diddle
Robert C. Ford
Bill James
Bo McMillin
Sully Montgomery
Chick Murphy
A.W. Price
Red Roberts
Bob Walker
Poolie Wayland
Red Weaver
Lefty Whitnell
C.L. Williams

The lettermen then took a vote, privately, after the meal had been served. Unanimously, the team captain for the upcoming season would be Bo McMillin, one of the young men who had followed the Chief to Danville.

CHAPTER THREE:
CENTRE BEGINS THE JOURNEY
TO THE BIG-TIME

It was a wonderful time. The war was over and the flu but a bad memory, and the wild New Year's celebrations found people once again filled with enthusiasm and optimism.

America would begin to flex its industrial might as the vast manufacturing capacity of the country began to shift back to consumer goods. Model T's began rolling off the assembly line at Ford's mammoth Highland Park, Michigan plant—over 750,000 a year, and you could have any color you wanted, as long as it was black.

The first crossing of the Atlantic Ocean by air was completed on June 14 when a United States Navy Curtis seaplane landed on the shore off Lisbon, Portugal. (Charles Lindbergh's 1927 flight was the first nonstop crossing. The Curtis seaplane hopped across the ocean in stages, stopping several times, but made it, finally.)

Film stars Charlie Chaplin, ("The Little Tramp"), Douglas Fairbanks, Mary Pickford, and the legendary director, D.W.Griffith, established United Artists in an attempt to better control their fate in the ever more glamorous world of Hollywood.

Booth Tarkington, a Princeton man, won the Pulitzer prize for his novel, "The Magnificent Ambersons," which traced the declining fortunes of an American family from the end of the Civil War until the early twentieth century, reflecting so accurately how society was changing. F. Scott Fitzgerald finished the rewrite and final version of his first great success, "This Side of Paradise." Dial telephones were introduced for the first time by the telephone monopoly, American Telephone and Telegraph. Einstein's Theory of Relativity, $E=MC^2$, was confirmed when the British Royal Astronomical Society observed, during a solar eclipse, what Albert had predicted. Sir Barton won the Kentucky Derby. America's population exceeded 100,000,000.

Harvard began its quest for a football "National Championship" by fielding one of the strongest Crimson teams yet assembled.

In the small Kentucky town of Danville, plans were materializing for the entrance of a thus far, obscure little college named Centre, to begin its drive to become a football powerhouse—big time.

It was 1919.

In February, the faculty chair of the athletic board, Dr. Frank Rainey, boarded the train and rode the Southern Railroad's "Queen and Crescent" from Danville to New Orleans to attend the annual meeting of the Southern Intercollegiate Athletic Association (S.I.A.A.).

Upon returning to Danville, Professor Rainey wrote a detailed account of what had taken place during the two days he was in attendance, and submitted his report to the Centre "Cento" for publication. A highlight of the proceedings included a ruling on the past football season and how it affected player's eligibility in the future.

A recommendation of the executive committee stated that since the past 1918 football season was under the direction of the Student Army Training Corps, and therefore the normal contests of the colleges were either suspended or altered, the committee in passing of any question arising from the participation of games during the season, should consider them as not being college contests. Therefore the football season is non-existent. This will make for wider liberty among the men who took part in any game this past season.

In other words, "Hey guys, you've got another year of eligibility if you want it! 1918 didn't count!"

A lot of Centre men would use that extra year and come back for a fifth season. It was perfectly legitimate. The season was severely abbreviated at Centre. Many schools had similar effects from the war and the S.A.T.C.

In years to come, after Centre had reached the pinnacle of the college football world, some would question the fact that the school allowed its athletes to play for five years.

Wasn't that some evidence that Centre cheated? The answer is an unequivocal, "No!" The over-30 members of the S.I.A.A. had the same policy. Colleges such as Virginia, Vanderbilt, North Carolina—the list spreads all over the South—allowed their players to come back for a fifth season if they so desired. The season was declared null and void. Centre played entirely within the rules, exactly as so many other colleges did after the S.I.A.A ruling.

Uncle Charlie, Chief Myers, President Ganfield, and Dr. Rainey began holding meetings as soon as the college reopened after the 1918 Christmas vacation.

They had a two-fold plan. (1) Put Kentucky, Georgetown and Transylvania on the schedule so as to firmly establish Centre as the dominant football team in Kentucky; and (2) Contact nearby flagship, state colleges, and try to get them to invite the Colonels to play on their fields.

Centre realized that at this stage there was no way that it could entice a significant football power to come to Danville, but it was felt that some of the larger schools would invite the Colonels to play as a visitor. Perhaps the little Danville college would seem like a nice "breather" for some of the big state college teams, because Centre was virtually unknown. The locals knew that their team was going to be loaded. No one much else did.

Of the twenty lettermen of 1918, thirteen were returning:

Army Armstrong—halfback and end
Matty Bell—end
Ben Cregor—guard
Allen Davis—halfback
Ed Diddle—backfield
Clayton Ford—guard
Bill James—tackle
Bo McMillin—quarterback
Sully Montgomery—tackle
Chick Murphy—halfback
Red Roberts—fullback, tackle, end
Red Weaver—center
Lefty Whitnell—end

In addition, the coaching staff received word that Howard Van Antwerp, who missed the 1918 campaign due to being in the military, was returning to campus.

Now all that was needed was for some of the substitutes from the previous season to contribute after gaining a year of experience, or the arrival of some incoming freshmen who were ready to play at the college level.

Fewer than twenty good men could supply the manpower to play consistent football. The sport during that era wasn't like it is today. Now there are offensive teams, defensive teams, kickoff teams, punting teams, short-yardage lineups, substitutes who are run in when it looks like a passing play is needed—every sort of team.

Centre simply had a team. The box scores of the games after World War I show that except in routs, or if someone sustained a significant injury, substitutions were rare. Players were expected to play both ways, on offense and defense. The spirited defense for which Centre was known indicates there was equal emphasis whether the team was on the attack, or defending.

Bo was quoted in an interview some time after he left Centre that, "Uncle Charlie expected you to play the whole game. You had to get almost killed before he'd take you out."

By spring, the lineup for the 1919 season was pretty well firmed up. Originally, the opener was to be with Kentucky Wesleyan, virtually a warm-up. However, during the summer, Wesleyan was dropped, and Hanover (Indiana) was written into the slot, also seen as a warm-up.

Maryville, for reasons to be explained later, was scheduled to come to Danville, but the game wasn't played.

The local papers printed the schedule:

Sept. 27	Kentucky Wesleyan	Danville
Oct. 4	University of Indiana	Bloomington, In.
Oct. 11	Maryville	Danville
Oct. 18	St. Xavier of Ohio	Danville
Oct. 25	Transylvania	Lexington, Ky.
Nov. 1	University of Virginia	Charlottesville, Va.
Nov. 8	University of West Virginia	Charleston, W.Va.
Nov. 15	University of Kentucky	Lexington, Ky.
Nov. 22	DePauw	Greencastle, In.
Nov. 27	Georgetown (Ky.)	Georgetown

As stated earlier, throughout the years, my father told me stories about his time spent at Centre, and he told them over and over as he got older. People tend to rehash the good times, and many was the evening that we'd sit on our front porch, he in a rocking chair and me on the swing. He'd perhaps have a little bourbon and water, and begin to reminisce.

"Robbie, have I ever told you about how the season ended in 1924?"

"Yes, Dad, it was amazing."

"Amazing hardly describes it. We played Kentucky, Tennessee, Alabama and Georgia, all in November of that year. The first game was with State…….."

Dad was there. He was the team's greatest fan. So throughout the book, from now on, I'm going to let him share his memories with you…

Cousin Ella Welsh had one of the most beautiful homes in Danville. She was married to George Welsh who was one of the owners of the Welsh and Wiseman department store. George was also in a lot of businesses—banking and a savings and loan.

My great-grandfather and Cousin Ella's father were brothers, so that's why we called her Cousin Ella. Her father was one of the richest men in Kentucky. He made his money in the stagecoach business, carrying both passengers and freight between Louisville and Nashville, and later he opened up a line to Atlanta.

His name was Samuel Beale Thomas, and at one time he owned thousands of horses and hundreds of coaches and wagons.

When a railroad was proposed between Louisville and Nashville, he realized what this would mean to his horse-drawn transportation business, so he quite wisely became one the biggest investors in what became the Louisville and Nashville Railroad, the L&N.

His brother, my great-grandfather, was Joshua Howard Thomas, M.D., and he was quite prominent and successful in his own right.

Samuel Thomas built the most beautiful and largest home ever constructed in Elizabethtown, Kentucky, and gave it to one daughter. And he bought a wonderful home for Ella when she married.

The home was right across the street from Old Centre, and when Ella died in 1937, Centre bought it and it became the home for the president of the college, and remains so to this day.

In the late summer of 1919, when I was just 15, Howard and I took the L&N over to Danville. The train actually stopped a couple of miles south of the town, in Junction City. Cousin Ella sent her chauffeur over in her big Maxwell to pick us up, and as soon as we got there, we raced over to watch Centre practicing football.

Dust would fly off the player's uniforms, and Howard and I would think nobody could get up after some of the hits. But they would just get up and laugh and say, "Is that all that you've got?"

We watched till late in the afternoon, and then some of the players came over and asked us where we were from, and our names.

I told them my name was "Red" Robertson. I had red hair then and that's what I was called because Howard went by "Robbie."

So they hollered to this big redhead and asked him to come over, and then they asked me to tell him what my name was.

I said, "Red Robertson, that's my name."

And he said, "Hello son, I'm your dad, Red Roberts."

When I got on the campus in the fall of 1921, I looked up Red Roberts, and he remembered me, and I became sort of the team mascot. Every time I was around Red, he'd introduce me as his son.

As practice began before the first game of 1919, an incident occurred over in Lexington which just about took care of the need for Centre to recruit any more players.

The Kentucky state high school championship for 1917 had been claimed by a team from Owensboro High, and one of the stars, Terry Snowday, enrolled at the University of Kentucky in 1918 and played during UK's war-shortened season.

In 1919, at one of the early practices, Snowday got criticized severely by the UK coach, Andy Gill, who felt that his halfback wasn't "playing tough" when he dropped several passes and missed some tackles.

Snowday packed his bags and took a 50 minute train ride south on the Southern Railroad and told the Centre staff that he was transferring. Kentucky's loss was Centre's gain, as Terry Snowday became a big part of the Colonel's success in 1919, and in the years ahead. Two other Owensboro stars, John Porter "Hump" Tanner and Tom Bartlett followed Snowday to Danville. They were ineligible for 1919, but were vital cogs in the years ahead. Hump played in the opening game, but when it was discovered that he had played at Colorado in 1918, he wasn't allowed to play anymore during the season. Bartlett had played at Missouri. Why was Snowday able to play? Because Kentucky, where he had been in 1918, was a member of the S.I.A.A., and the Wildcats' season was cancelled out or deemed not to have occurred, just as was Centre's. But the same wasn't true at Colorado or Missouri. Transfers from those colleges had to sit out a year before being allowed to play.

We need to clear up a little manner about Terry Snowday's name. Originally, his last name was spelled "Snoddy," but the phonetic pronunciation was "Snow-day." In 1921, he had his name legally changed, and to avoid confusion, we'll use the Snowday spelling.

The 1919 season began on September 27 with the Hanover Panthers at Centre's Cheek Field. Chief Myers handled the team, as Uncle Charlie was still umpiring National League games, and wouldn't be able to get down to Danville until the 29th.

Centre started the following lineup:

NAME	POSITION	HEIGHT	WEIGHT
Gus King	Lt. end	5'9"	170
Red Roberts	Lt. tackle	6'	210
Sully Montgomery	Lt. guard	6'2"	215
Matty Bell	Center	6'	170
Howard Van Antwerp	Rt. guard	5'11"	170
Jim Coleman	Rt. tackle	5'10"	165
Lefty Whitnell	Rt. end	5'9"	163
Bo McMillin	Quarterback	5'10"	175
Joe Murphy	Left half	5'5"	130
Allen Davis	Right half	5'8"	154
Ed Diddle	Fullback	5'10"	165

Red Weaver, Bill James, and Army Armstrong didn't play as they had suffered injuries during practice. It didn't matter. Centre moved the ball at will. Hanover never made a first down, and the only way the Panthers got into the Colonels' territory was due to their recovering a couple of fumbles by the Colonels on the numerous Hanover punts.

Centre got 27 men into the game. Red Roberts played tough at his tackle position, and then was shifted to fullback and just barreled over the outmanned Hanover players. Murph and Bo made several electrifying runs.

Eight Colonels scored a total of 14 touchdowns:

Murphy–	3
Whitnell–	2
Snowday–	2
McMillin–	2
Tanner–	2 (Hump's only game of 1919.)
Roberts–	1
Davis–	1
Diddle–	1

Bo kicked seven extras points. Red Roberts kicked four. The final score was 95-0, not a bad start to the season. Things would get tougher the next weekend.

The University of Indiana was one of those flagship state universities that Centre wanted to play in order to garner more attention around the country. The Hoosiers were members of the Big 10. In 1919, the conference consisted of Chicago, Illinois, Indiana Iowa, Michigan, Minnesota, Northwestern, Ohio State, Purdue and Wisconsin. (The University of Chicago withdrew its football team from the Big 10 after the 1939 season, having gone 1-15 in league play during the preceding four years. Even though there were now only nine teams, the conference was still called the Big 10. In 1953, Michigan State joined, and there were once again 10 teams. In 1993, Penn State joined to make the members number eleven. However, the name remained the Big 10. Go figure.)

Indiana was coached by Ewald O. "Jumbo" Stiehm, who had been at the helm since 1916, having been brought to Bloomington after having compiled a sterling record of 35-2-3 at Nebraska from 1911-15.

The Hoosiers had opened their year at home with a 27-0 win over an in-state school, Wabash College, from Crawfordsville. In the week before the game, the Centre staff had emphasized just how important the Indiana game was. "We have a chance to break out of the small-time. We have a chance to have people out of our area take notice."

Even then, the Chief and Uncle Charlie were talking about the possibility of playing one of the Eastern powers. "Harvard, Yale, Princeton, every year they play colleges like Bates, like Colby; they play Springfield and Williams. There is no reason that we couldn't get a game with one of them if we go undefeated this year."

"We've got to believe!" the Chief shouted.

It was an overcast day on October 4. The Colonels were accompanied by 12 loyal fans on the train ride up to Bloomington. After a light lunch upon arrival, the players dropped their gear off in a visitor's dressing room and toured the beautiful Indiana campus, filled with ivy-clad buildings.

One good thing that the Colonels had going for them was that Bill James, Red Weaver and Army Armstrong were suiting up for the game. James started, Army played but didn't start. Weaver was used sparingly.

The starting line-up was similar to that of the Hanover game, but there were three changes. Gus King didn't start. Max MacCollum, at 5'11" and 160 lbs. took his slot at left end. Bill James at 5'10" and 170 lbs. replaced Jim Coleman. Bill Garrett, at 5'11," 165 lbs., started at center, and Matty Bell was relegated to the bench.

After inspirational speeches and the team prayer, Centre took to the field. Back in Danville, people began to congregate in the newsroom of the Danville "Messenger." The paper had arranged to have the game's results telegraphed to the newspaper. The telegraph operator would write out the message and hand it to a reporter who would shout out the results. Before radio, "a play-by-play" via the wires was the fastest way to get the results of an event out to the public.

Centre took the field first and was followed by the Hoosiers in red jerseys who came onto the turf behind the 75 member Indiana University band playing the school song, "Indiana, Our Indiana."

Indiana, our Indiana,
Indiana, we're all for you!!
We will fight for
The Cream and Crimson,
For the glory of old IU.
Never daunted, we cannot falter,
In a battle, we're tried and true.
Indiana, our Indiana,
Indiana, we're all for you.

As the band headed to the stands, it began to rain. It was a drizzle at first, then a continuous downpour of major proportions.

The Colonels knew that they were going to be outweighed, especially in the line. However, they felt that their speed would counter the weight disadvantage. The rain, if it continued, would make the turf slippery, and would certainly negate some of the speed of their backfield.

Bo won the toss and elected to receive. Neither team could mount a drive in the early going and there were several exchanges of the ball on punts. Finally, Indiana was able to put some points on the board. Red Roberts was lined up to punt, and a crimson-shirted lineman broke through and got a hand on the ball as it came off Red's foot. The ball was recovered on the Colonels' 25 yard line. Centre dug in and stopped Indiana cold on the next three plays. On 4th down, Matheys kicked a 25 yard field goal, and it was 3-0 at the end of the first quarter.

The Gold and White outplayed Indiana during the second quarter. There were effective drives which carried deep into the Hoosiers' territory. Once, the ball was deep enough into Indiana's side of the field that Red Roberts was able to try a field goal, but it was wide, the effort being made more difficult by the wet field. After the missed field goal, Indiana took over on its own 20 and fumbled on the 25. In five plays, Centre marched into the end zone and scored. The little band of supporters from Danville made themselves heard, but they were quickly silenced when the ball was brought back. Centre had a lineman offsides. Again, both teams played tough defense, and the first half ended with the only score being the Hoosier's field goal. Indiana, 3-0.

The Colonels retired to the end of the field, the rain still coming down in sheets. With water dripping off their saturated hats, Uncle Charlie, Chief Myers and Pitt Green told the team that they were pleased with what they had seen during the initial half. They felt their boys had outplayed the Big 10 school. If it weren't for the penalty which called back the touchdown, they'd be ahead.

"You scored. They only got that field goal because of a blocked punt. We don't think they can score on you. We need to play for one break. We can beat this team!"

Bo went over to the stands and borrowed a pocket knife from one of the Centre fans. He cut off the legs of his uniform, leaving just the upper part intact, so that he looked like he was wearing shorts. His soaked stockings and socks came off next, and he wore just his cleats. He later said, "I was so water-soaked, I could hardly run. I had to lighten the load."

Indiana elected to kick to start the second half. Little Chick Murphy fielded the wet ball and returned it 20 yards. The game took on the same pattern as the first half. Centre could move the ball consistently, but couldn't get close to the Indiana goal. The outweighed Colonels' line fought savagely on each play, making the Indiana offense look totally impotent. The third quarter ended with the score still at 3-0, Hoosiers.

As the teams switched sides to start the final period, one of the Indiana players was overheard to say, "Who are those guys, anyway? How do they think they can play with us?" It wasn't the last time that question would be asked. An Indiana fan later stated, "That's the hardest hitting squad I've ever seen." That's who "those guys" were.

Bo took off his helmet and played bareheaded during the last quarter, water pouring off his slicked-down hair. Centre sent in Ben Cregor for Ed Diddle. His fresh uniform stood out, contrasting with the mud-soaked appearance of the rest of the combatants.

The fourth quarter was all Centre. For Indiana, it was three plays and a punt. There was such dominance by the Colonels that later, in analyzing the game, it was pointed out that not one deep back of the Gold and White made a tackle. The front wall and linebackers never allowed one of the Hoosiers to break through their defense. That was dominance.

However, dominated or not, Indiana still led. With only two minutes and 20 seconds left in the game, the Hoosiers once again had to punt the ball away. By now, so late in the contest, with the rain still pouring down, many of their fans had departed, convinced that the final score would be 3-0.

The Colonels took over on their own 15 yard line after the punt. Bo shouted above the howling wind and rain, "Let's go guys! Take it to them. We can beat these guys!"

On the first play, Bo cut over his left tackle for 20 yards. Then Red crashed through for six. Bo picked up five. It was first and 10 on the 46.

Uncle Charlie raised his fist in the air as the officials moved the chain. "Way to go boys! Now take it down the field!" The Chief wiped off his glasses and shouted, "Show them what Centre men are made of!"

Centre was pumped. Bo fought for three and then big Red ran right over the Indiana line and his 10 yards placed the ball across midfield on the Hoosier's 41.

The Chief: "You've got to believe!!!"

On first down, Bo got one hard-earned yard. The next play, he tried to hit Terry Snowday, but his throw fell short. It was third and 10. The game was on the line as the clock ticked.

Bo told Army that he was going to fake a run around the right side, and then pull up. Army was to make a head fake left, and then dart out toward the right flank. The play, probably the most important of the game, worked perfectly. Army hauled in a toss good for 10 yards, and then streaked down the right sideline for another 15 yards before being knocked out of bounds.

The twelve Centre supporters, peering around opened umbrellas, screamed their encouragement as the chains were again moved.

It was first down Centre on the Indiana 16. Red got eight. Bo bucked through for three. First and goal on the Indiana five. Red then took a handoff and barreled through the line, his powerful legs literally carrying what seemed to be half of the red-shirted defenders with him, and he scored!! Touchdown—Centre!! The extra point was no good, but the Colonels had the lead, 6-3.

"Who are those guys, anyway?"

Red boomed a kick deep into Indiana's territory. The game wasn't over. There was still slightly under a minute to play. The desperate Hoosiers tried two end sweeps, hoping to get into at least field goal range, playing for a tie if they were successful. They weren't. Centre shut them down totally.

On third down, the Indiana quarterback, Jewett, faded back and pumped the ball, looking downfield for his left end, Roscoe "Cow" Minton, the team captain, the same young man the Chief had tried to get to enroll at Centre after he graduated from North Side High in Fort Worth. In one of those ironies of life, "Cow" was running stride by stride alongside Bo, his old high school teammate.

Bo had anticipated that the Hoosiers would have to pass, and he played his position perfectly, cutting in front of Minton as the ball was flung, and intercepted the throw. He dodged one defender, straight-armed several more, and skirted down the sidelines, 45 yards for a touchdown. It was Centre, 12-3, after the extra point was missed.

Red Roberts boomed the kickoff deep, and time expired before another play could be run. A contemporary account summed up the game as follows:

Centre turned defeat into victory in two minutes and twenty seconds by speed, brains and fight. This is the story of the Centre—Indiana game. Every man who participated in the game gave his best for Centre. Not only did Bo McMillin prove himself a master strategist and field general, but a line-plunger and interference man of all-star caliber. Unable to run the ends in the mud, he tore through the Indiana line at will. Every man under his leadership deserves the same praise.

Centre picked up 275 yards, a remarkable showing on a muddy, slippery field. Indiana was only able to gain a total of 75 yards all afternoon. The Colonels registered 13 first downs, the Hoosiers only 6.

It was a happy team, along with the twelve stalwart fans, who rode the train back to Danville. The first real test of the season had been successfully negotiated. The Colonels had won twelve straight over the past three seasons.

With the victory over Indiana, Centre College had gained a lot of believers who felt this group of young men had a date with destiny.

MARYVILLE CANCELS

The Maryville Athletic Director wired Centre that its team was so beaten up from the prior week's encounter with Tennessee that it simply couldn't field a team until some of the players recovered. The Volunteers had trounced the Fighting Scots 32-2, and the October 11th game was cancelled.

Uncle Charlie and the Chief tried to line up another game, but on such short notice, they were unsuccessful. In the records, October 11 is listed as an open date, even though Centre could have claimed a victory due to a forfeit, but chose not to.

The Colonels took the train over to Lexington on the free weekend to watch the Kentucky—Indiana game. The result was gratifying. The team that they had beaten the week before, 12-3, shut out the Wildcats, 24-0. It was a confidence builder for their later battle with "State," if such was needed.

One player who wasn't in Lexington was Bo. He'd traveled to Pittsburgh to watch the Pitt Panthers play West Virginia, scouting the Mountaineers, whom the Colonels would meet in four weeks. (West Virginia got off to a terrible start in the contest that Bo watched, fumbling several times, and early on was down, 19-0. The Mountaineers then had to resort to passing to try to get back in the game. They were unsuccessful and lost, 25-0.)

In retrospect, the cancellation of the Maryville game was probably for the best, as it gave Uncle Charlie another week to incorporate his offensive schemes.

ST. XAVIER COMES TO DANVILLE

St. Xavier of Cincinnati, a Jesuit college, came to Danville on October 18th. The Catholics were 2-0, having defeated the hapless Hanover team 65-0, and Kentucky Wesleyan, 35-0.

Centre fielded its regular lineup except that Red Weaver started for the first time during 1919. Jim Coleman, who had started against Hanover and subbed in the Indiana game, watched from the sidelines. He was lost for the season after dislocating his shoulder in practice on the 14th. Ed Diddle played with a broken ring finger. Uncle Charlie had devised a protective cover, and "Mule" played effectively.

There was a large crowd wanting to see the team which had beaten a Big 10 squad. They weren't disappointed. Centre won in a romp, 57-0. Xavier lost two players to injuries in the opening minute.

Centre scored nine touchdowns. Terry Snowday got two. Bo, Red Roberts, Army, Allen Davis, Murphy, and Ed Whitnell each scored once. Uncle Charlie even saw to it that Red Weaver scored by putting his center in at fullback when the Colonels had a short-yardage situation at the goal.

While Centre moved the ball at will, the Catholics hardly moved it at all. They picked up only five first downs all afternoon, with three coming in the third quarter when Centre had a team of subs on the field. Centre was now 3-0 and had won 13 straight since the October 20, 1917 loss to DePauw. The Colonels now had three road games coming up: Transylvania, Virginia, and West Virginia.

TRANSYLVANIA

It was revealing how the Transy-Centre fortunes had changed since Uncle Charlie had taken over. The Crimson had played very competitively with the Colonels from 1910 through 1916, with the series looking like this:

1910	Centre	27	Transylvania	0
1911	Centre	10	Transylvania	6
1912	Centre	13	Transylvania	7
1913	Centre	0	Transylvania	6
1914	Centre	3	Transylvania	53
1915	Centre	0	Transylvania	38
1916	Centre	0	Transylvania	0

After the tie in 1916, Centre took the upper hand and shut out the Crimson 28-0 in 1917, and won 52-3 in 1918. (The Transylvania athletic teams were known as the Crimson during the era of this book. Later, the name was switched to Pioneers, which better reflected the fact that the school was the first college founded in Kentucky, and with its charter dating to 1780, it is the oldest institution of higher learning west of the Allegheny Mountains, and 16th oldest in the United States.)

Centre absolutely had become superior to Transy on the gridiron. To understand the scope of the margin of that superiority, it is best told by a Lexington sportswriter, John R. Marsh:

Centre College defeated Transylvania College this afternoon at League Park by a score of 69-0 in a game featuring the brilliant work of McMillin, Roberts, Davis, Bell, Armstrong, Murphy etc. etc. and others too numerous to mention.

That's the story in a short, condensed form and with the main facts briefly told, according to the best rules of the journalistic schools. It is not for this account to attempt to describe the fine points of the game. It would be too great a strain on the available supply of adjectives to tell adequately of; those countless runs by McMillin for innumerable yards; the punting and plunging of Red Roberts; the runs of Davis, Armstrong, Snowday and Murphy; the cohesiveness of the Danville team and its almost perfect interference that swept the Transy men down and permitted their runners to advance.

Centre has a wonderful team. For the last three years, it has been able to hold together a collection of players which would be dangerous on any gridiron and seems to improve with each season.

Centre took 22 players to Lexington. All played. There were 10 touchdowns. Bo and Allen Davis had three. Snowday scored twice. Army and Murphy each tallied one.

Bo picked up 322 yards rushing and there were eight passes completed for over 200 yards. It had been an excellent afternoon. Now it was time to head east of Kentucky and take on two state universities, one in Virginia, and one from West Virginia.

THE UNIVERSITY OF VIRGINIA

Centre had never played the University of Virginia, but the coaches knew that the Wahoos played excellent football. (Virginia had several nicknames. While the media more often called the athletic teams the "Cavaliers," the "Wahoos" was more frequently used by students and fans of the university during the era.)

For the years, 1913-15, Virginia had a 23-3 record and outscored its opponents, 846-92, for an average margin of victory of 29 points. The three losses were to Harvard, twice, and Yale, both at the pinnacle of their game prior to World War I. Virginia actually beat Yale in New Haven in 1915, 10-0.

Things fell off a bit in 1916, with the Wahoos going 4-5, and losing big time to Yale, 61-3. Then for the next two war years, the Charlottesville school didn't even field a team, one of the few universities to totally shut down its program.

Naturally, 1919 was a rebuilding year. The season began respectably enough.

Virginia 12 Randolph-Macon 2
Virginia 0 Richmond 0
Virginia 0 Maryland 13
Virginia 7 VMI 0

After starting at 2-1-1, the Virginians traveled north across the Mason-Dixon Line and got destroyed by Harvard, 47-0. (Harvard had a great year in 1919. The Crimson's record during the regular season was 8-0-1, having been tied by Princeton, 10-10. They capped off the year by playing in the Rose Bowl and beating Oregon, 7-6, to finish at 9-0-1.)

The fact that Virginia had just gotten beaten by the boys from Cambridge the week before gave the Colonels all the more motivation to win, and to win big. Chief Myers was asked if he had any prediction about how the game would go, and even though it was somewhat out of character for such a modest man, he was quoted as saying, "We're simply going to beat them, and that's all there is to it. We are confidant of victory, and the only thing we want to do is to top Harvard's score of 47-0 against Virginia."

The team rose early on the morning of October 31 and met at Danville's Southern Railroad station for a 6:00 a.m. boarding of a northbound train to Lexington. The entire freshman class was at the station, along with a significant number of the rest of the student body and townspeople. It was a pattern which would be repeated many times over the next several years.

The Colonels had a private, chartered Pullman which was transferred to a regularly scheduled, east-bound Chesapeake and Ohio steamer for the trip to Charlottesville. Fifteen fans were going along.

The team stayed on the Pullman throughout the day and overnight, on the long, 500 mile ride over to central Virginia. They got the rest that only a gently swaying train can provide, the clickety-clack, clickety-clack of the wheels on steel lulling them to sleep.

They were allowed to sleep in on the train once they got to Charlottesville, and then at mid-morning, disembarked and ate at a restaurant near the UVA campus.

During the pre-game talk, Chief Myers reminded the squad that an overwhelming showing against Virginia could be the first step toward securing a date with one of the eastern powers. "People will be watching. Harvard beat this team, 47-0. If we can do as well, or better, it will be an important step in reaching our goal. Take it to them! Bring glory to Old Centre! Believe! Believe! Believe!"

The fans who filled the 8000-seat Lambeth Stadium felt the Colonels looked somewhat lackadaisical as they went through their warm-ups. However, it was just the team's "game-face." They were deadly serious. The Chief and Uncle Charlie wanted them to put on a show and outshine Harvard.

Just like at Indiana, it began to rain as the time for the kick-off approached. The Centre starters remained much the same except that now, with Army totally fit, he was put in the backfield, bumping Terry Snowday to an end position.

Virginia kicked to the Colonels, who began a drive which picked up 43 yards on four plays. However, one of Bo's passes was picked off which gave the Wahoos possession. Centre played its typical tough defense and held. Virginia punted, Centre gained 15 yards before having to punt back, and once again, the defense caused Virginia to kick it back.

The Colonels then began a relentless push toward the goal, running plays with such rapidity that their opponents barely had time to line up before they were exposed to Bo, then Army, Allen Davis and Bo again. Quickly the ball was on the eight, and Davis slid through the line for the first score.

Centre kicked, held the Virginians on downs, and Bo returned their punt 45 yards. Again, the Colonels picked up good yardage on each effort, and Red Roberts was switched to the fullback position and punched it in. Red Weaver kicked his second extra point and it was, just like that, 14-0.

Early in the second quarter, Red Roberts had a poor punt, the slick ball sliding off his foot almost sideways. The good field position, on the Colonels' twenty, allowed Virginia to ring up its only points of the game. Centre was so eager to shut down the Wahoos that linemen jumped offside twice, moving the ball to the ten. It took three plays, but Virginia's fullback, Kuyk, took it in, and he also kicked the extra point. It was Centre, 14-7. Then the races began.

Centre received the kick deep, and Army took it to the 25. On the next play, little Chick Murphy from Columbus, Ohio, subbing for Allen Davis, streaked around the left side for an unmolested 75 yard touchdown. Red Weaver kicked. Centre, 21-7. Another three plays and a punt gave Centre the ball on its own 30. Bo took it 70 yards on the first play from scrimmage, Weaver converted again, and it was 28-7 as the half ended, with Centre driving deep into Virginia territory as the whistle blew.

Rain or no rain, soggy field or dry, Centre was showing the packed stadium both an offense and defense like none they'd ever seen. It was simply an overwhelming display of football by a very talented and determined group of young men from Danville.

The second half was more of the same. Murph broke loose and went 85 yards,

Red Weaver kicked successfully again, and it was 35-7. The Centre sideline urged the team on, hoping to outscore mighty Harvard. Bo sneaked into the end zone just before the 3rd quarter mercifully ended, Weaver kicked, and as the squads lined up to start the last period, it was 42-7. During the last quarter, Army capped a long drive by scoring, Red Weaver made it seven for seven, and the final score was 49-7.

Indiana and Virginia, two flagship state universities, had been beaten. An account from a Virginia sportswriter lauded the Centre College Colonels:

Snowday and Bell were in on every play and demoralized Virginia's offense. Cregor and Van Antwerp cannot receive enough commendation. Their work was superb.

Montgomery and James wrecked the Virginia line, simply wrecked it.

Weaver piled up 100% of his kicks, even with a soggy, spongy ball. He also played his position and bumped off everything that came his way.

McMillin, Davis, Murphy, Armstrong and Roberts simply bewildered Virginia with speed and strength. Together, these men form the greatest backfield south of the Mason-Dixon Line.

Bo alone gained 252 yards. The wet and slick ball kept both team's passing to a minimum. Centre completed one toss for 10 yards. Virginia got two yards on its only successful effort. The afternoon had been an overwhelming display by the Colonels, made even more impressive by the fact that they picked up 34 first downs while holding Virginia to but six for the 60 minutes of play.

Harvard beat Virginia 47-0 on its own home field, the magnificent horseshoe on the Charles River. Centre won on the road, 49-7. For the first time, Centre and Harvard were mentioned together regarding the relative strengths of the two teams. Likewise, for the first time, the term "All-American" was being linked to Centre's players, especially to the young man from Fort Worth North Side, Alvin Nugent "Bo" McMillin. Centre's record was 5-0, and the win streak was now at 15.

The long train ride from Charlottesville, with the transfer again at Lexington, found the team and fans rolling into Danville Sunday night at 11:30. As the train slowed and braked coming into the little railroad station, the Colonels' players were overwhelmed to see a large crowd, several people deep, lined up along the tracks. The entire student body, plus many of the townspeople, had turned out en mass to welcome home their victorious Colonels. After a noisy demonstration in front of the station, led by the school's cheerleaders, the whole throng followed the Gold and White's banner into the town's business section where, "they waked the echoes in the still and almost deserted streets."

After more cheers, the students marched in file to the nearby girl's campus at the Kentucky College for Women where they cheered and sang songs. As the happy throng finally began to drift away, they were applauded by scores of unseen hands in the darkened windows of the school.

CHAPTER FOUR:
THE BREAKTHROUGH GAME—
WEST VIRGINIA

For the initial 50 years after the first college football game in 1869, through the resumption of regular play after the war years of 1917-18, the Eastern schools had been recognized as constantly placing the most talent on the gridiron. This was particularly true of the "Big 3," Harvard, Yale and Princeton.

There was no "Ivy League" as we know it now. That term came into use in the 1930's, and the actual conference didn't exist until 1956. However, the "Big 3" universities reigned supreme for over 50 years. Often their only loss during a season would be to one another, as they would roll over all other competition.

Even though Harvard, Yale and Princeton had played each other for decades before 1900, it is pertinent to see how the Eastern superpowers fared from 1900 through 1916, the last full, normal season prior to the war years.

1900-1916

	WON	LOST	TIED	WINNING %(NO TIES)
Yale	154	19	13	89.0
Harvard	145	20	7	87.9
Princeton	125	25	11	83.3
OVERALL	424	64	31	86.5

Of the 64 losses that the colleges sustained during those years, 36 were to each other, sort of like fratricide. If you exclude those losses in analyzing how the "Big 3" fared against all other programs, again, not counting ties, the overall record is 424-28, for a winning percentage of 93.8.

The "Big 3" dominated. There is simply no other way to interpret their statistics. If a school other than each other beat a "Big 3," it could make their season, and it was big news in sports sections in newspapers all across the country, especially if the loss was by a shutout, and if they were obviously beaten thoroughly.

It was, "Can you believe that?"

"Are you sure that wasn't a misprint?"

That is why people everywhere were so astonished to read about the fact that West Virginia had traveled to Princeton on November 1, 1919, and destroyed, literally destroyed, an excellent Princeton Tigers' squad, 25-0. The Mountaineers led 19-0 after the first 12 minutes, and the game was essentially over.

Uncle Charlie, Chief Myers, Pitt Green and Bo spent much of the time on the train ride home from Charlottesville talking about what Bo had learned on his October 11 trip to scout West Virginia and Pitt. The Centre staff hadn't even wanted to think about West Virginia until Virginia had been played and defeated. "One game at a time," was their philosophy.

West Virginia had beaten itself against Pittsburgh. It fumbled three times early in the game, and got so far behind that Pitt only had to play hard-nosed, conservative football in order to hold onto its large early lead. As the game progressed, the Mountaineers had to try more and more desperate plays in an effort to catch up, and this only led to more errors.

West Virginia bounced back after the Pitt game, shutting out Maryland, Bethany and then Princeton. The cumulative score for those three games was 112-0, and the wins ran its record to 5-1. The star of the Mountaineers was named Ira Errett "Rodg" Rodgers, who stood 5'10" and weighed in at a solid 198 lbs. He was extremely fast for his size. He was also an all-around threat, equally adept at powering through the line or sweeping the ends. It was his pinpoint passing, however, which made him especially dangerous. Even though Rodgers played at the fullback position, he was the Mountaineers' passer, and he could throw a football like most people throw a baseball, straight and hard, with little arc on his toss.

Bo told his coaches that if they could stop Rodgers, they could win the game. Rodgers needed time to set up to pass, so a hard line rush was essential. Also, if the Centre ends could keep him from getting outside of their positions, if they could turn him in, it was felt that Colonels had enough size and quickness in the line to be able to shut him down.

Bill Roper, the Princeton coach, bylined a newspaper column after his team lost to Rodgers and his teammates which described how he felt that West Virginia had revolutionized the passing game:

The West Virginia forward pass attack depends on the deception of the play. The fact is that three men are always sent down the field to act as a "blind" or "barrage," while the man catching the ball remains hidden until a moment before getting the ball.

The West Virginia team lines up with Rodgers about ten yards back, standing alone. Two backs and an end play wide, about fifteen yards out on the extreme wing. One back plays a couple of yards to the right and back of the center to hold the defensive line intact. If the defense spreads too wide, this back can take the pass from the center and plunge through the spread-out defensive line.

The three men on the extreme wing seldom receive a forward pass. They start down the field fast, opening like a fan, attracting the attention of the defensive backfield men. The pass is not made to these men nine out of ten times, but to a man near the line of scrimmage who is unnoticed until he gets the ball.

The West Virginia backs downfield then come back and act as interference. The secret of the forward pass is to send several men in one direction, who, if they are not covered, will prove dangerous. If they are covered, the pass is made to another man.

Getting interference then for a man catching a forward pass is "inside" football, and West Virginia is the first team to use it successfully.

Rodgers is particularly effective in throwing a forward pass. He will stand absolutely unconcerned looking over the backfield and probably pass the opposite way from which he is looking.

*He has a very clever way of backing off from the ends coming through to hurry the pass. I do not think it is possible to stop the West Virginia passing game **without having seen it before.** The only sure way is to hurry Rodgers in passing. He is so shifty, this is hard to do.*

The West Virginia coaching staff didn't know that a little school, at the time so unknown, would have indeed scouted the Mountaineers, and how effective Centre's defense would be against their vaulted offense, **having seen it before.**

The game was to be played in Charleston, West Virginia, at Laidley Field. Kickoff was at 2:30. Dr. Ganfield announced that classes were cancelled for Saturday. Centre had 193 students during the 1919-20 school year. By the time the football team's members were added in, approximately half the student body was going to the game, plus a significant number of the citizens of Danville and the surrounding area had tickets.

The wins over Indiana and Virginia had attracted so much attention that special train cars were lined up to take fans to the game from both Louisville and Lexington. When the whole Kentucky entourage was added up, there were to be 400 supporters of the Colonels in Charleston, quite an impressive showing.

All week prior to the game, Centre had the scrubs out on the practice field running through the West Virginia plays which Bo had brought back from Pittsburgh. The ends, Matty Bell and Terry Snowday, worked out a system to rush Rodgers in order to keep him off balance when he tried to pass. The two developed signals so that they could let each other know how they were going to attack. Rodgers had a way of backing off, and often a defensive end would shoot in short of the big fullback, and not be able to get to him before he fired off a pass. Bell and Snowday decided to alternate their patterns, one going short, in case "Rodg" came forward, and the other going deep in case he faded back, all the while making certain that they were prepared for a possible end-around play.

On the train ride over, the Colonels huddled around their coaches and repeatedly went over their assignments. They also discussed the fact that they were again going to be compared to an Eastern power. They had acquitted themselves well against Virginia, beating the Wahoos as impressively as Harvard had.

Now, with West Virginia having beaten Princeton, there was another perfect opportunity to show the football world that talent existed other than just on the Eastern gridirons.

Even though there was going to be a respectable number of Kentuckians at the game, and even though Charleston was some 150 miles from Morgantown, home of the Mountaineers, there was no way that the game was going to be played on a neutral field. West Virginia had played in Charleston in 1913, '14 and 1916. Also, the city was home to a large alumni group from the school. The capacity crowd of 6,000 would overwhelmingly be for the Blue and Gold.

After the Colonels dressed for what was going to be the most important game the little school had ever played, the dignified school president, Dr. Ganfield, was asked to conduct the pre-game prayer. It was the first time the Centre leader had been asked to offer the prayer, a sign of the significance of the upcoming battle.

He later said, "It seemed perfectly natural. I took off my hat and knelt with the team and asked the Almighty to look after the well-being of the players on each team. I asked that there be no injuries, that both teams play a clean game, and that each of our young men play up to their God-given ability."

It was a fired-up Gold and White that streaked out on the field, ready to give their all for Old Centre. After going through their warm-ups, both teams lined up for the opening kickoff. It was exactly 2:30, a perfect fall day for a football game.

West Virginia won the toss. A murmur went through the Centre supporters as their team broke out of the sideline huddle and ran onto the field. Red Weaver didn't have a helmet. Red Roberts never wore one, but the other Red hadn't ever played bareheaded. He had either failed to pack his headgear, or it had been misplaced on the trip over. It seems unbelievable now, but in 1919, Centre brought only ten helmets when the team traveled. In an important game, Red Roberts played the whole 60 minutes, no matter what. The other players, when a rare substitution was made, simply grabbed the helmet of the man leaving the field. Red Weaver announced that headgear or not, he was playing, and indeed he did.

Early on, it looked like the Mountaineers were going to have an easy time of it. After running back the kickoff, Rodgers completed several passes, and then in one of the rare times that the big fullback was able to go outside, he swept around the right side and was stopped just short of the goal. On the next play he scored, and the home crowd roared. Many of the West Virginians had been so certain of their team's superiority that they had given four to one odds. After the quick score with just four minutes off the clock, their money seemed safe.

"Rodg" missed the extra point conversion even though he had an easy angle. (In this era, the extra point was kicked from the spot where the score took place, unlike now, when the ball is lined up directly in front of the goal post.)

Centre wasn't daunted and came back strong and marched right back down the field and scored. The ball was brought back, however, due to a flag having been thrown for holding.

On the very next play, Bo faded back and hit Red Roberts with a perfect 20 yard spiral and the big guy stepped across the goal for another apparent score. Again, the play was nullified, this time because Bo hadn't been five yards behind the line of scrimmage when he threw the ball. (In this era, a player throwing a pass had to be five yards behind the point where the play began—the line of scrimmage—in order for it to be a legal pass. Now, a player just has to be behind the line, and any distance will suffice.)

The game began to resemble the Indiana contest. Centre had no trouble moving the ball, but couldn't actually score a touchdown that counted, and the initial quarter ended, 6-0.

The second quarter was all Centre. The Colonels' defense, penetrated early, was played to perfection. The linemen began to do some cross-blocking, much as they'd do on offense. Right tackle Montgomery would slant over and take out the defender across from Van Antwerp, allowing his right guard to break free into the backfield toward Rodgers. Ben Cregor and Bill James would do the same. The ends, Matty Bell and Terry Snowday, never again let a Mountaineer back get outside of their position after that one instance on the opening drive.

It seemed that the helmetless Red Weaver was on the bottom of every pile. Red Roberts played primarily at a linebacker position. No one got past him. He plugged every hole that seemed to open up.

Momentum was definitely with the boys from Danville. Even though they couldn't punch it in, they had gained the upper hand during the second period. The score remained 6-0 at the half. Again, players on the field and fans in the stands were wondering, "Who are those guys?"

Centre had a beloved "mascot," Roscoe, who often performed during the half at home games in Danville. He and three other of the "Black Cakewalkers" had their fare paid by Centre alumni and accompanied the Kentuckians to the game. They dressed in formal attire, with gold vests and top hats, and put on a show during the intermission, pigeon-winging, cake-walking, and strutting around the field. The crowd loved it.

Meanwhile, the Colonels had gathered down in the end zone to rest and discuss the first half, and to plan for the rest of the game. The Centre staff was pleased. Their team had outplayed West Virginia. They'd scored twice, even though both of the times they'd crossed the goal had been called back. However, they were worried about Red Weaver. He seemed in a daze, not being able to respond appropriately.

Uncle Charlie spotted a Centre follower in the stands who was known to always carry a silver flask, filled with some good Kentucky bourbon. Moran beckoned him to come onto the field and ran his hand over the fan's overcoat until he felt a container.

"Weaver's been knocked senseless. I need to give him a stimulant."

The Danvillian reached inside his coat and handed Uncle Charlie his flask. Moran had the team line up around Weaver, blocking him from the sight of the crowd in the stands. He knelt down next to Red and said loudly enough for his players to hear,

"Red, you know we don't allow drinking on this team, but sometimes liquor is used for medicinal purposes. This is one of those times. I want you to drink this and see if it won't clear up your head so you can continue in the game. We need you out there."

Weaver did as instructed. He made a face, but swallowed the foul-tasting stuff. Then another sip, and still another. The fan who supplied the "stimulant" looked somewhat dismayed as his nectar disappeared. His sacrifice wasn't in vain. Red began to come around, and by the time the second half began, he was on his feet, raring to go.

Meanwhile, the team manager had gone to the opposite end of the field and explained Centre's problem, and the Mountaineers were gracious enough to loan Weaver a helmet which he used during the rest of the game.

With Red Weaver taken care of, Chief Myers began a rousing halftime speech. He began by relating how so many of those resting in the end zone had been members of championship teams in the past.

"Bo, Bill James, Red Weaver, Sully, Matty, you were the champions of North Texas! Bo, you and Red Weaver and big Red were the best team in Kentucky when you were at Somerset! Terry, your Owensboro team won the Kentucky state championship your senior year!"

"Each of you is a winner! Each of you has been a champion!"

"You've believed! You've achieved! You've succeeded in everything you've ever undertaken!"

"Now, BELIEVE! BELIEVE! BELIEVE!"

"You've outplayed the team that beat Princeton! Remember how you were greeted when you came home after the Virginia game. Let's make the folks back home even more proud! Let's win for Old Centre! Let's win for Danville! Let's win for Kentucky!

"You can do it! BELIEVE! BELIEVE! BELIEVE!"

Tears welled up in the players eyes. They had no doubt how the rest of the game would unfold. They could be champions. The Chief had told them so.

West Virginia kicked off and the Colonels took control of the game. As great as they'd played in the second quarter, it paled in comparison to how they dominated during the rest of the contest.

The first possession of the second half began on Centre's 20 yard line. Bo streaked around his left end for 12. Red Roberts plowed right through the center of the line for 10. It was first down on the 42. Bo fired a quick pass to Army for another first down. The ball was now in the Mountaineers' territory. Bo wiggled through the line for eight. Red crashed ahead for three. It was still another first down. Murph, who was Centre's only substitute during the game, gained seven. Bo hit Terry Snowday, who leaped into the air on a spectacular grab, for a 20 yard gain. It was first and goal on the 10. Bo got two. Army for three. Third and goal on the 5.

"Ok, boys, now we take it in," Bo shouted above the noise from the stands. "Big Red, you have the honors."

Red Roberts fired into the line and Blue and Gold defenders bounced off him as his powerful legs churned over the goal line. Four hundred of the Gold and White's pennants fluttered in the crowd as a huge roar erupted after the score. The rest of the crowd sat in silence.

"Who are those guys, anyway?"

During the drive, Centre's line blocked ferociously. The fleet Colonels' backs had picked up yardage on every run. Bo had completed two passes. It had been a textbook effort, a perfectly executed exhibition of power football. Red Weaver split the uprights. Centre forged ahead, 7-6.

Play resumed after the Centre kickoff with West Virginia unable to gain a first down. Both teams played excellent defense and exchanged punts. Red Weaver was everywhere, playing with seeming recklessness, perhaps benefiting from the "medicinal" that he received during the halftime break.

On still another exchange of punts, the Mountaineers got a break when Centre fumbled a kick and the Blue and Gold recovered deep in the Colonels' territory, on the 20. Rodgers completed a pass for 10 yards and it was first and goal, just inside the ten.

"Hold them, Hold them!" from the Centre rooters was drowned out by:

Take it in,
Take it in,
Blue and Gold,
Blue and Gold.

Take it in,
Take it in,
Blue and Gold,
Blue and Gold.

Centre indeed dug in. West Virginia tried three line bucks. Three yards, two yards and then, no gain. On fourth and goal from the five, Rodgers took the snap and fired into the line. The right side of the Centre front wall, led by Red Weaver, Ben Cregor and Bill James, hit the big fullback and stopped him cold. He made one yard.

It was hand to hand combat on the tuft at Laidley Field that afternoon of November 8, 1919. The boys from Danville weren't to be denied. They truly believed, and their faith in their abilities bore great fruit as they had stopped West Virginia short of the goal. The third quarter ended. The teams changed ends of the field.

It may have been prudent for the Colonels to let Red Roberts boom out one of his towering punts, being so deep in their own territory, and not take a chance of fumbling the ball away. He had averaged 48 yards per boot. Bo and his teammates had other plans. On four successive plays, first Bo, then Army, then Red and finally Murph, gained at least 10 yards on the ground. Uncle Charlie's players were sweeping the Mountaineers out of the way, simply overwhelming them.

The ball was just over the midfield stripe when Terry Snowday cut back from his right end position on a reverse sweep around the left side and racked up 25 yards.

The Centre backs ran their fakes so effectively to the right that each was tackled, the defenders thinking they had the play covered perfectly until they saw Snowday running the other way. Red bulled forward for five. Murph took it to the 10. Bo then took the snap from Weaver and side-stepped his way over the goal. Weaver's kick made it 14-6 for the Centre College Colonels. The Kentuckians in the stands were ecstatic. They could smell victory. Even if the Mountaineers scored, the missed extra point loomed large, as the closest they could get was 14-13. The way that the Colonels had shut down their opponent's high-powered offense made it extremely unlikely that they'd give up two scores so late in the game.

Rodgers fielded the kickoff after the Colonels' touchdown and returned it 35 yards, the longest West Virginia gain of the afternoon. The Mountaineers began a drive with frequent running plays, but they were eating up a lot of the clock.

George Joplin wrote in a story appearing in the Louisville "Herald" that, *The West Virginians were fighting like wild men, and the crowd of over 6,000 was begging for a touchdown, while the Centre partisans were shouting encouragement to their team.*

"Don't let them score!"

"We've got them!"

"Fight! Fight, Gold and White!"

The desperate West Virginians drove to the Centre five yard line, but they were stopped on four straight plays by vicious gang tackles by the Colonels. It was like the Gold and White had erected an impenetrable wall of steel. Don't let them score, indeed.

Red Roberts kicked out of danger. Again, the Mountaineers tried to get something going, but on their second play, they fumbled, and Red Roberts scooped up the ball and ran for 25 yards before being dragged down from behind.

The Colonels were content to simply run out the clock, nothing fancy, knowing that the game belonged to them. Murph went 10, Bo gained eight, and time expired with Centre on the Mountaineers' 12 yard line, threatening to score once again.

The Kentuckians rushed onto the field and embraced their weary warriors, slapping them on the back, hugging them, pumping their fists in the air. Unlike after the win over Virginia, when the celebration began only after the return to Danville, the festivities began immediately, and continued on the train as the team and fans made the journey back through West Virginia, across the state line into Kentucky, on to Lexington, and had hardly died down as the last leg of the trip carried the happy throng to the Danville station.

Word of the victory had been telegraphed ahead. Both of the Danville newspapers printed bold headlines and pasted them onto sandwich boards which were worn all over town by their paperboys, announcing:

CENTRE 14 W.VA. 6 !
TEAM ARRIVES 11:00 p.m.
LET'S MEET OUR BOYS AT THE STATION

And meet them they did. It seemed that the entire city of Danville turned out to greet their returning heroes. Again, the huge crowd cheered and snake-danced up from the station, led by the Gold and White's banner carried on the eagle-tipped flagpole, through the campus, on to Main Street, finally ending up in front of the buildings on the lawn of K.C.W.

It was well past midnight before the delirious fans reached exhaustion and began to filter back to their homes, and the lights at last began to dim all over the small town of Danville.

Little Centre College had beaten the mighty West Virginia Mountaineers. Little Centre College had beaten the conquerors of Princeton. Little Centre College had changed the face of college football.

CENTRE ATTRACTS NOTICE

The win over West Virginia ran the Colonels' record for the season to 6-0, and the winning streak to 16 straight. The little band of warriors was beginning to attract attention not only in Kentucky, but from other points, particularly in what was considered the football capital, the Eastern Seaboard.

The New York "Tribune" sent a telegram to Uncle Charlie and asked him to write some remarks about his team so that the paper could inform its readers about "just exactly what was going on down in Danville, Kentucky." Its sports editors wanted to know "what had allowed such an unknown little college to beat the heavily favored Mountaineers."

Uncle Charlie's reply was printed as soon as it arrived back in New York.

Centre College has at last gotten what it has been seeking for several years—recognition from the larger universities, and from our record, we may get on the schedules of some of the big fellows next year.

The success of the team has been largely due to the influence and playing of our team captain, Bo McMillin. If anyone deserves a place on the All-American team, he certainly does.

Red Roberts, my fullback, has been invaluable to the team, and with Bo and Red in the backfield, there is little worry about the offense. These two are almost a team in themselves.

I must say a word about my center, Red Weaver, who is the pivot of the line in every sense of the word. He is a bear on defense, a slashing, smashing terror on offense, and is in the game every second.

My line is composed of tall, rangy fellows, the real Kentucky type. And how they can fight! I mean in the football sense. When they first came here, they had the physique and the fight but were somewhat awkward in their actions. However, once they were taught the game, my work was practically done.

Then Uncle Charlie told how he and the team felt before the start of the game in Charleston.

The game meant much to us, and I told the boys so. But they took things as a matter of course as they had done in other contests. To them, it was simply another football game, a sort of frolic.

What Moran hadn't said was that the Centre players took the game somewhat in stride because they had such belief in the ultimate victory. Chief Myers had seen to that.

Have a vision and set goals—BELIEVE!
Dedicate yourself and work hard—ACHIEVE!
Now you'll have your reward—SUCCEED!

Uncle Charlie concluded by stressing the importance of a total team effort:

"First we stopped Rodgers, and that meant virtually the checking of the whole West Virginia offense. But while we were stopping Rodgers, they were unable to stop McMillin and Roberts. These two backs gained almost three times what Rodgers did. My other two backs and my ends also gained more ground than the West Virginia star. However, Rodgers is certainly a capable football player and deserves all that has been said of him. I wouldn't object at all to having him on my football team.

"But the point is this. Whereas West Virginia depended almost entirely on Rodgers, my eleven played over every inch of the ground as one man. Stars are a big asset to a team, but stars working in conjunction with the others as one man make what is well nigh an unbeatable combination."

Later in the week, the Centre coach made that point when he began his remarks at chapel.

"Eleven men won the victory over West Virginia last Saturday...." It was the Centre College way.

During the week after the great win over West Virginia, prior to the Homecoming game with Kentucky, the public became more acquainted with Centre College and its football team due to a nationally syndicated story by Fred Turbyville of the Newspaper Enterprise Association, the NEA, which appeared in newspapers across the country. (The NEA was the equivalent of our present Associated Press, United Press, and Reuters syndicated news services.)

Turbyville's reporting appeared under the headline:

HOW CENTRE'S COLONELS ACT BEFORE TROUNCING FOE

Centre College gets down on its knees and cries and then goes out and wins another football game.

But Centre College has something besides a prayer and a headgear when it steps onto the field of battle. It probably has as good a football team—maybe better—than any college in the land today. Its record speaks for itself. The team is unbeaten and probably will finish the season so. How many other teams have such a clean slate at the finish?

The sport world wonders how a little college of less than 200 students can turn out a football team capable of beating Indiana, Virginia and West Virginia. It is because on no other team is there such teamwork and fighting spirit. Every game is a death struggle for Centre College.

They pray before each game and briny tears course down the cheeks of these husky athletes as if this combat they were going into meant the saving of their country. Before the game with West Virginia, they got down on their knees and were led in prayer by Dr. Ganfield, dignified president of the college.

He cried with them, and when they stepped onto the field they had played half of the game.

There is nothing miraculous about Centre's football team. It is a collection of first class football material, good coaching, and splendid spirit. The collection of material is due to the efforts of director of athletics, Bob Myers, and head coach, Charlie Moran. They have been collecting this team for three seasons back. They have eleven regulars who will be back next season. Three of the football players, Howard Van Antwerp, Bill James, and Allen Davis, are among the best students in the school.

The members of the team are not hillbillies as one eastern writer hints. They are products of high schools and prep schools. Most come from well-to-do families in the South. Some come from Ohio, Texas and Arkansas.

Centre College, though small, is not poor financially. It is located in the heart of Kentucky's aristocracy at Danville, one of the oldest cities in the state. Centre is 101 years old and mighty proud of its achievements. Some of the biggest men in the state and nation are products of Centre's learning.

I made quite a long trip to Danville to see this team. I met most of the football squad in the gymnasium before they had changed into their football togs. They looked smaller than most football teams. They looked like high schoolers. But when I saw their well-built legs and shoulders, I knew they were heavier than one would guess. And they looked mighty good on the field—fast and snappy, husky and fighting every minute.

It was this nationally distributed story that entrenched in the public's mind the image of the Centre players kneeling in prayer prior to each game, and resulted in press coverage from that day on increasingly referring to the boys from Danville as the "Praying Colonels."

The Washington "Post" sent sportswriter J.V. Fitzgerald to Danville to do a story on Centre and the football team:

They've got mapmakers down in Kentucky this fall. Eleven football armored youths have put Danville, Kentucky on the charted places and pushed Centre College from obscurity to a place in the gridiron sun. Centre and Danville are basking in an unaccustomed limelight as a result of the prodigious feats of the eleven they jointly claim. Boasting a team that defeated the West Virginia team which had been designated by Walter Camp as the squad of the season, it is no wonder that little Centre is proud, and little Danville mighty cocky.

Fitzgerald then went on to say that the big schools often pat the little schools on the head and say nice things about them, but the little schools rarely get the recognition that they deserve:

Whatever the place Centre is destined to fill at the end of the season, the Danville college has performed one of the most sensational feats in the history of the college game. It has jumped overnight, so to speak, from an unknown school to an institution that is known wherever football is played. Until this year, football followers outside of Kentucky didn't know whether Centre was spelled with the last two letters being "er" or "re." They know now. And they know that Centre has a great eleven.

The St. Louis "Globe-Democrat" requested a 300 word story about Centre from George Joplin, cheerleader and local reporter for the Danville "Messenger," who also filed stories for the Louisville "Herald."

Centre was attracting attention all over the country. It would only get better for the little college.

CHAPTER FIVE:
THE 1919 SEASON CONTINUES

Just as Centre had gained the upper hand over Transylvania and Georgetown since the arrival of the Chief and Uncle Charlie, so were the tables turning against their greatest rival, the Wildcats of the University of Kentucky. Centre had been destroyed in 1916 by that embarrassing 68-0 wipeout. The Colonels had edged the Lexingtonians in 1917 on Bo's third quarter field goal. The war and Spanish Influenza caused the 1918 contest to be cancelled. Now, Centre was the heavy favorite in what was to be the Homecoming game on November 15.

In the week leading up to the UK game, a group of Louisville businessmen took the train over to Danville in an attempt to get Dr. Ganfield to switch the Kentucky game to their city. They pointed out that more sportswriters would be likely to come to Louisville than Danville, and the increased coverage would do worlds for not only promoting the team, but especially Bo, who was beginning to attract enough attention that becoming an All-American seemed a real possibility.

In addition, the Louisvillians said that the largest number of Centre alumni in the country lived in and around their city, and they would make certain that Centre received a royal welcome.

"But gentlemen, while we're honored, it is our Homecoming game. How do you have a Homecoming game if you're not playing at home?"

There was no satisfactory answer for such an obvious fact. However, a compromise was reached. The delegation got Dr. Ganfield to contact DePauw, scheduled to host the Colonels the week after the Kentucky game, and an agreement was made to switch the date from Greencastle, Indiana, to Louisville.

The week before the game with Kentucky saw Danville turn into a town dedicated to the Gold and White. Spoonamore's drug store on Main Street (still in existence), along with several other merchants, sold carloads of gold and white crepe paper. Phone poles were wrapped in gold and white, porch columns were entwined, Centre pennants adorned windows all over town. The K.C.W. campus not only had the columns of their stately buildings turned into gold and white candy canes, but the tree trunks on the lawn were similarly adorned as far up as the girls could reach.

Spoked wheels on automobiles were decorated with the Centre colors. The Centre spirit even caught fire far from Danville. One of the local papers carried a report from an "Eastern writer" who wrote that Mrs. Richard T. Lowndes had a party in her apartment at the Hotel Taft in New Haven, Connecticut, in honor of her son, Richard III, who was a junior at Centre. Attendees were from Princeton, Columbia and Yale. Many had been undergrads at Centre previously. One guest in particular was mentioned, John Sherman Cooper, a star on the Colonels' 1918 squad, who transferred to Yale in 1919. (John Sherman Cooper was a native of Somerset and played on the Somerset High team of 1916 with Bo, the two Reds, Thad McDonnell, and others who eventually ended up in Danville. Cooper had a long and distinguished career, culminating by serving in the United States Senate for many years.) Mrs. Lowndes' apartment was totally transformed by decorating each of the public rooms with gold and white.

Cheek Field had also undergone a transformation. In the four weeks since the last game in Danville, new topsoil had covered the field and a thick tuft of bluegrass had been grown. Additionally, more wooden bleachers had been constructed anywhere there was an open space, so that a crowd of 8,000 could be accommodated if those standing were counted.

The Gilcher and Henson Hotels on Main Street were quickly booked. Mr. McIntyre of the Danville Chamber of Commerce appealed to the citizens of the city to open their homes to visitors who needed a place to stay. The Gilcher's management said its dining room could supply the meals if only rooms for lodging could be located.

Kentucky announced that it had quickly sold the 1,000 tickets allotted to the Wildcats' fans. The city of Somerset sold 200 tickets so that its residents could come up to watch their native sons, and the adoptees, Red Weaver, Thad McDonnell, and Bo.

Uncle Charlie had given the team the day off after the return from Charleston, and for the rest of the week, the practices mainly consisted of refining offensive and defensive formations, with minimal contact. The team had emerged from the West Virginia game with a lot of lumps, bumps and bruises. Chick Murphy had a very tender leg. Red Weaver had recovered from his apparent concussion, but complained upon the arrival back in Danville that he had a headache. Whether it was from his head injury, or the better part of a pint of bourbon, was never determined. Overall, the squad was in good shape going into the game with the Wildcats.

Another reason the coaches lightened up on the practices was that Kentucky wasn't very good. The Wildcats had opened up with a weak showing against an even weaker Georgetown (Ky.) team, squeaking out a 12-0 win. But what little offense they had displayed against the Tigers disappeared almost totally. Their record coming into the Centre game was 2-3-1: Kentucky 12, Georgetown 0; Kentucky 0, Indiana 24; Kentucky 0, Ohio State 49; Kentucky 6, Sewanee 0; Kentucky 0, Vanderbilt 0; Kentucky 0, Cincinnati 7.

The tie with a good Vandy team had heartened the Kentucky fans. Vanderbilt finished 5-1-2 for the year, with the only loss being to Alabama during an 8-1 season for the Crimson Tide. However, the loss to Cincinnati after the Vandy game had been totally dismaying, as the Bearcats had lost to Dennison and tied Wittenberg, hardly powers of the day.

HOMECOMING 1919

On Friday evening and Saturday morning, Danville and the Gilcher Hotel lobby began to fill with many of the returning alumni who had come back for the Homecoming game with Kentucky.

The only time West Virginia and Centre had played before the previous week's game was in 1896. Centre won 6-0 in Danville. Two members of that team were in town and were in great demand amongst the old grads who were swapping yarns.

Quarterback George Colvin and lineman, "Sheep" Harlan, nephew of United States Supreme Court Justice John Harlan, cornered present lineman Ben Cregor and told him about a happening during the game of 24 years ago. "Harlan was playing at guard and I was at quarter. West Virginia had been playing her linemen rather close on the defense, when all of a sudden she opened up her line, setting two men back a few yards away from where Harlan was," Colvin related. "When Harlan lined up, he waved his hand behind him to signal to me that I should run a play over his position."

Harlan picked it up from there.

"I was down in my position when the two West Virginians jumped back up ohn the line, and as our back came runnin' through, they hit me in the sto-mack and our back hit me in the seat of ma pants, and I was rammed fo and aft! I didn't signal foh anything to be run ova my position foh a long time."

One story which had been told for years was that the '96 team had an agreement with Kentucky during that year. The Colonels wouldn't run up the score on the Wildcats, and after they'd scored 35 points, they'd back off.

"Sheep" Harlan said that simply wasn't true. ""No sah, we nevah did that. But we did lend them some playahs in odah to play the game. It was eahly in the season, so we loaned them foh men and them beat 'em, 32-0."

The 1919 Homecoming attracted the largest group of old, veteran Centre athletes to ever find their way back to Danville. Everybody wanted to see the team that had humbled Indiana, Virginia and West Virginia. Old lettermen were everywhere; trackmen, basketball players, baseball stars from the past, and especially those who had been on the gridiron as members of the Gold and White.

Fortunately, the weather cooperated, which only added to the festive atmosphere on that November 15 afternoon. The stadium had never looked better, with Centre's colors decorating one goal post and the blue and white of Kentucky wrapped around the posts on the opposite end of the field.

The largest crowd to ever witness a football game in Kentucky, the largest crowd actually to attend any sporting contest other than the Kentucky Derby, if a horse race can so qualify, began to move en mass toward Cheek Field.

Trainloads of fans from Louisville and Lexington disembarked at the Southern Railroad station and made their way through the campus toward the stadium. The hotel crowd from the Gilcher and Henson struck out from downtown for the five block jaunt. Boarding houses cleared, businesses closed. There was no reason to stay open as everyone would be at the game.

The girls from K.C.W. walked together past the stately homes on Lexington Avenue, each carrying a gold and white pompom, turned left on Second Street and joined the throng which was filling the sidewalks and streets leading through town to the game.

The crowd had been predicted at 8,000, "depending on the weather," and that number seemed to be right on target. In the box with President Ganfield were Governor James D. Black and Governor-Elect Edwin P. Morrow.

By 2:00 in the afternoon, the stands were totally filled, and spectators who couldn't get in lined the wire fence around the field, jockeying for a position where they could see some of the action. The windows of Old Main, behind the field, were full of spectators who actually had a decent view, especially from the upper floors.

A banner across the back of the Boyle-Humphrey Gymnasium again proclaimed "RIGHT THE WRONG OF 1916," a reference to the 68-0 drubbing the Colonels had taken in losing over in Lexington. That humiliation still rankled.

Wagering was rampant, but the Kentucky rooters wanted at least 40 points. As the minutes clicked down toward the kickoff, the margin had climbed to 50. Even at those odds, many Centre fans were so certain of their team's superiority that they were willing to put their money where their faith was.

A cheer greeted the Wildcats when they trotted out on the field at exactly 2:05 for warm-ups. The Kentucky band trumpeted a snappy march, and the crowd joined in, clapping to the rhythm. A huge roar erupted as the Colonels' fans jumped to their feet at the sight of the Gold and White running out onto the turf. George Joplin led the team, waving the big Centre banner back and forth as he sprinted ahead. The alumni from Louisville had hired a brass band and brought it over on the special train that was filled with the fans from the city.

The "Centre Band" alternated songs with UK's musicians, and then as game time neared, the two groups joined in playing "My Old Kentucky Home."

> The sun shines bright in the old Kentucky home
> 'Tis summer, the people are gay;
> The corn top's ripe and the meadow's in the bloom,
> While the birds make music all the day;
> The young folks roll on the little cabin floor,
> All merry, all happy, and bright,
> By'n by hard times comes a-knocking at the door,
> Then my old Kentucky home, good night!
> Weep no more, my lady,
> Oh weep no more today!
> We will sing one song for the old Kentucky home,
> For the old Kentucky home far away.

Centre won the toss and elected to receive. Four minutes later, Red Roberts slammed through the line and scored. Red Weaver kicked. Centre, 7-0. Kentucky couldn't move the ball on its possession and had to punt. Five plays later, Red Roberts once again crashed through the Wildcats, Weaver kicked, and it was 14-0, which is how it stood at the end of the first quarter.

Centre's attack slowed a bit in the second quarter, but this period saw a classic unstoppable drive. Bo failed on a pass to Allen Davis and then ran the exact same play. This time, Davis hauled in a long toss for a big gain. Then, Bo for six, Bo for eight, Red got seven, Bo's pass to Army was good for 10, and Army carried the ball in for a score to make it 21-0 at the half, after Red Weaver again converted.

The Kentucky offense was totally bottled up by the swarming Colonels' defense during the half. The Wildcats picked up but one first down in the entire 30 minutes of action. The students of both schools took to the field, dancing to the music of the bands. Then Roscoe brought down the house with one of his most unique cake walks, ever.

The second half began somewhat slowly and in the first several minutes of play, both teams basically ran three plays and punted. Finally, Kentucky got a little offense going and picked up three straight first downs and got the ball into Centre's territory, but the Colonels toughened, and the 'Cats had to punt. Seven plays later, Bo dashed into the end zone from eight yards out, Weaver was perfect, and the third quarter ended with Centre ahead, 28-0.

Kentucky fans who had gotten 40 points were feeling pretty good. Centre would have to score twice in order for them to lose their bets. Those who had received 50 points were feeling great. In order for them to lose their money, Centre would have to score three times, kick three extra points, and it would still require a field goal for them to come out on the short end.

The Kentucky partisans didn't realize that Centre and Uncle Charlie didn't just want to win. A victory was a foregone conclusion. But Moran and the Colonels wanted more.

Uncle Charlie knew that Ohio State had beaten Kentucky 49-0 back on October 18 in Columbus. Many people across the country were saying that State had the best team in football. The Buckeyes were undefeated and had won impressively.

Ohio State	38	Ohio Wesleyan	0
Ohio State	46	Cincinnati	0
Ohio State	49	Kentucky	0
Ohio State	13	Michigan	3
Ohio State	20	Purdue	0

In addition to wanting to top Ohio State's margin over Kentucky, some of the players later admitted that they knew that many of their supporters had given 50 points on their bets. "We didn't want to see any money go back to Lexington."

Almost unbelievably, Bo and his teammates put 28 points on the board during the last 15 minutes of play. Terry Snowday capped a seven play drive by scoring. Weaver again—Colonels, 35-0.

On the next possession, Kentucky could only pick up four yards, punted, and six plays later, Bo went in from the 12, "Mr. Automatic" kicked, and it was 42-0. Those UK fans who had 40 points suddenly felt much poorer.

After the helpless Wildcats again met the impregnable defense of Centre, Bo passed twice unsuccessfully, then hit Red Roberts for 35, and after another incompletion, decided to just run it in himself, and trucked it eight yards for a TD. Weaver made it 49-0. Centre had matched Ohio State's total against the Wildcats. But there was still some unfinished business.

Kentucky supporters who had 50 points were on their feet, imploring their team to do something, anything, to keep the Colonels from scoring again. They knew the game was long lost. They were pleading for their solvency.

There were just 15 seconds left in the game when Centre once again gained possession of the ball. Bo called time out and had the team huddle around him. All week in practice, he and Lefty Whitnell, a speedy end from Fulton, Kentucky, had worked on perfecting a pass play which depended on pinpoint timing.

Lefty would line up at his left end position and once the ball was snapped, he'd streak down the field at full speed, never even looking back until he'd covered 40 yards. The two had run the play over and over, only stopping when Lefty had his tongue hanging out from near exhaustion.

Bo said, "Lefty, run it just like we did in practice. When you get down 40, look over your right shoulder. The ball will be there. You shouldn't even have to break your stride."

Just as instructed, Whitnell ran at full tilt down the field while Bo waited patiently, the Centre forward wall providing him all of the time that he needed. Then Bo ran up a couple of steps and heaved the ball with all his might, a perfect spiral high in the air.

Lefty glanced over his shoulder and spotted the ball as it came down and reached out and plucked it cleanly out of the air. The play covered 55 yards. Weaver, of course, was perfect, making it 56-0. Centre's fans, all on their feet, roared their approval. A lot of money was going to be left in Danville, Kentucky. The alumni were delirious.

"Did you see that? That's the greatest play I've ever seen!!"

Only once before had Centre beaten its big rival so decisively. The 1894 game's score was 67-0.

"RIGHT THE WRONG OF 1916."

There was no doubt of that. And, there was no doubt in the minds of Centre's fans, of Kentuckians everywhere, and increasingly with football fans throughout the entire country, that the finest team in all of college football represented little Centre College of Kentucky.

That night, after the game, a huge dance was held in the Boyle-Humphrey Gymnasium. The floor was covered by the petals of the gold and white chrysanthemums which fell as the young beauties of K.C.W. danced the evening away with their Praying Colonel heroes.

Centre was 7-0 for the season and had won 17 straight.

WEST VIRGINIA CRIES FOUL

Three events occurred on Saturday, November 22, the week after Centre disposed of Kentucky so handily. The first was cosmic. An eclipse of the sun, which in Kentucky was going to take a crescent shape, began at 6:23 in the morning. The second happening was that Centre was going to meet DePauw in Louisville in the afternoon. The third event was the result of the fact that people back in West Virginia just couldn't, and wouldn't, accept the fact their touted, mighty football team, their team that had routed Princeton, could have possibly lost, at least fairly, to a little unknown school named Centre College.

Major Earl Smith, a West Virginia alumnus, was the editor of the Fairmont "Times." Editor Smith conducted an "investigation" and came up with some accusations which he published in his paper. He sent his expose to the paper in Morgantown, home of the Mountaineers, and the "New Dominion" printed his "findings."

Smith stated that he had determined that Centre's team was riddled with "ringers," some of whom were professional players, and others, ex-collegians, who didn't even go to Centre. His main thrust was that the Colonels who supposedly came from Texas, along with Red Roberts, were actually some of the famous Nesser brothers (there were nine of them) who had played on the Canton, Columbus Panhandle, and Massillon, Ohio, professional teams.

Major Smith sent the results of his "detective work" to Walter Camp who was on the NCAA rules committee. Of course, his accusations were easily refuted. Four hundred Kentuckians, many being prominent citizens from Lexington and Louisville, had been in Charleston, along with locals from Danville. They knew the Reds, they knew Bo, and they instantly stated that Smith's "findings" were pure fantasy.

After being confronted with the facts, the two West Virginia papers printed retractions and Smith sent a letter of apology to Dr. Ganfield, to the coaching staff, and to Bo as team captain, and the other players. The problem was that numerous newspapers across the country had picked up the story and printed it. For many people, it had been one of those "Ahah!" moments.

"So that's how they beat Indiana and Virginia. So that's how they humbled West Virginia. They cheated!"

Scandalous news makes the front page. Retractions are usually buried deep in the paper, if they are run at all. There were those who even decades later felt that Centre had cheated its way to the eminence of the football world. It simply wasn't true, and it was terribly unfair.

LOUISVILLE FALLS IN LOVE WITH THE COLONELS

Louisville was desperate for football. For years the big game had been the annual high school match between Louisville Male and Louisville Manual. The consolidation of the two schools into Louisville Boys High had put an end to the rivalry. (It was this merged school which Bo and his Somerset team, including the two Reds, had so decisively beaten in 1916.)

The University of Louisville began playing football in 1912, but after 1917, didn't even field a team again until 1921. The Centre alumni in Louisville decided to pull out all of the stops for Centre's meeting with DePauw. They flooded the newspapers in town with information about the Colonels. Gold and white was all over the downtown area, especially on Fourth Street, the main commercial street in the city. All of the major stores had pennants in their windows along with team photographs and blown-up photos of the stars.

The Seelbach Hotel at Fourth and Walnut was the premiere lodging spot in the Derby City, having been constructed in 1905 by two Seelbach brothers, Otto and Louis, immigrants from Bavaria. The hotel was literally taken over by the team and its supporters during the weekend of November 22.

Centre traveled over on the Southern Railroad, going through Lexington, where several cars carrying supporters were hooked onto the rolling stock. They arrived on Friday evening and were delighted to see all of the preparations that had taken place to make certain that the Colonels felt not only welcome, but that their every need had been anticipated and covered.

Centre had two objectives going into the DePauw game. No one needed to be reminded that the last loss the Colonels had suffered was that 6-0 loss to the Indiana school back on October 20, 1917. Also, the team was terribly anxious to make a good showing in front of Louisvillians. The city was the metropolis of Kentucky. When Kentuckians from out in the state went to Louisville, they felt they had gone to a large city, and many were nearly overwhelmed by all of the comparative sophistication.

The morning of the game, Centre's team, dressed in ties and wearing overcoats, spent the morning walking around the downtown, mainly spending time down by the Ohio River where Fourth Street ends. All along the way, they were followed by local citizens who wished them well. Many came up to Bo and Red Roberts and asked them to autograph various items. The Centre stars had appeared in so many photographs in the papers that they were instantly recognizable. Always, the Colonels were gracious.

Two years ago, Centre was playing in Winchester, Ky. and Maryville, Tn. Two years ago, Centre was playing in front of small crowds at Transylvania in Lexington, and Greencastle, Indiana. Two years ago, Centre's biggest game was a squeaker, 3-0, over Kentucky.

Now Centre was the hottest ticket in town. The DePauw game was a sell-out. All of the 6,000 seats in the concrete stadium behind Boys High, south of downtown, had been grabbed the minute that the tickets went on sale. Extra boxes had been added anywhere there was a vacant space. The officials in charge of the game stated that they had 10,000 requests from people who wished to attend. Several thousand were to be disappointed. Louisville had totally embraced the Colonels, and it was an eager crowd that awaited the game.

DePauw was coming off a 24-0 loss to Purdue in a game at Lafayette, Indiana. The Tigers were hobbled by several injuries suffered in the contest. Additionally, their coach, Edbert C. Buss, who had been at the helm since 1916, the same man who had guided the Greencastle school to the victory over Centre in 1917, became ill and was hospitalized right before his team was ready to board the train for the trip to Louisville. Buss missed the game, and certainly, DePauw missed its coach.

On the other hand, Centre was in good shape. There was only one player who was hurting. The little speedster, Chick Murphy, had been kicked in the chest during the Kentucky game. An x-ray revealed a non-displaced rib fracture. Uncle Charlie let him make the trip and to suit up, but he told Murph that he'd only see action if he was really needed.

Before the game, there had been discussions amongst Centre's fans about Red Weaver and his accuracy in kicking extra points. Going into the DePauw game, Red had kicked 27 straight, and people were beginning to take notice. More and more press was being devoted to Red in covering his streak.

Saturday afternoon, November 22, was another of those ideal days for a football game. There had been a slight sprinkle the night before, but the field was in excellent shape by game time, certainly an advantage for the Colonels with all of the speed on the squad.

Centre put on an awesome display in Louisville. After an initial exchange of punts, the offensive machine got into gear. The Colonels took over on their own 20 and eight plays later were on the DePauw Tigers' 18. On the next play, Bo fired a perfect pass to Army who stepped over the goal. Red Weaver kicked the first of eight extra points for the afternoon, and it was 7-0 at the end of the first quarter, 21-0 at the half, 35-0 at the end of the third quarter, and 56-0, the same score as the Kentucky game, when the final whistle blew.

The statistics revealed that Centre had totally outclassed a game but overwhelmed DePauw team. Bo gained 286 yards on the ground on 37 carries. Terry Snowday picked up 167 on 14 tries. Red Roberts, running out of the fullback slot, got 113 on 21 efforts, mainly on simple plunges straight through the line.

Army gained 77 on 10 plays, Lefty Whitnell had 78 on seven tries, and Allen Davis carried the ball six times for 80 yards. Uncle Charlie put in Max MacCollum, a Louisville native, near the end of the game so that the locals could see one of their own in action. Max responded by racing for 26 yards on the three times he was given the call. Overall, the Colonels gained an incredible 827 yards in 98 plays, for an average gain of nearly eight and a half yards each time they touched the ball.

Centre played its usual tenacious defense. The only time that DePauw even threatened was when the Tigers' quarterback, "Galloping" Galloway, returned a second quarter kickoff all the way to the Colonels' 10 yard line, but he tried to shift the ball to his opposite arm and fumbled it away. It was indicative of the afternoon for the boys from Greencastle. For the afternoon, they ran 33 plays and picked up a mere 87 yards.

The Louisville "Evening Post" had a headline the night after the game which read, in 1 ½ inch boldface:

CENTRE TOYS WITH DEPAUW

The "Post's" characterization was shared by the crowd. All fall, they'd been reading about the amazing exploits of the Colonels. Now they had seen with their own eyes, and left the stadium marveling at what they had experienced.

DePauw finished the season at 2-5-1, not an impressive record. However, three of those losses were to Big 10 teams. Each was by a much more respectable score than that of the Centre game. Northwestern won, 20-0, and Michigan, 27-0. Purdue came out on top, 24-0. Centre's much more impressive showing certainly reinforced the level of play the Colonels had reached in 1919, but then, this only validated the skill of the team which had already been shown by the wins over Indiana, Virginia, and West Virginia.

Centre's alumni had arranged for a dinner in honor of the team the evening after the game. It was to be held at the exclusive Pendennis Club, located at the time a block down Walnut Street from the Seelbach, in the old Belknap mansion. President Ganfield was in attendance, and his guest was again the newly elected governor, Edwin P. Morrow. Morrow was a native of Somerset, and in his comments, he paid tribute to Red Roberts, also a Somerset native.

"I count it as a great honor to have been elected governor of our great Commonwealth of Kentucky, but after what happened today, I would gladly trade my position for that held tonight by Red Roberts."

The alumni association presented fine, leather suitcases to Uncle Charlie, Chief Myers, and the team captain, Bo. A large contingent had come up to Louisville by train from Owensboro, leaving on the Illinois Central at 4:30 in the morning. T.J. Turley, on behalf of the group, presented a gold watch to their native son, Terry Snowday, who had been a star on the Owensboro High School state championship team of 1917.

Coach Moran, in a short talk at the conclusion of the dinner, acknowledged publicly for the first time that, "Before each game, we say a little prayer. I believe that it is with Divine Assistance that we have what many consider the best football team in the nation."

The evening ended by the team standing and giving lusty cheers for their hosts, which were returned by the grads who proved that they had not lost the ability to give the old college yells.

The Colonels' weekend in Louisville had been a love feast, and their showing both on the field and off, assured that they'd be back in the city annually in the coming years. The Colonels were 8-0. They had an 18 game winning streak.

The little school from Danville had become a machine, running at full speed on all cylinders, approaching the destiny which the Chief had envisioned long ago when he began his great mission.

"You have to BELIEVE!!!"

The Colonels did, indeed.

HOWARD REYNOLDS COMES TO TOWN

Centre now had the most famous and acclaimed football team ever to play in Kentucky. However, the Colonels were also drawing attention outside of the state, and each victory only made the public want to know more. The question, first asked in Bloomington, Indiana, "Who are those guys?" was increasingly being repeated as each week of the season passed.

In the pre-radio world of the era, the only way to achieve more than a state or regional reputation was to grab the attention of major, metropolitan newspapers. Centre's rise to national prominence owed much to the sports editor of the Boston "Post," Howard G. Reynolds, who felt that college football had reached the point where intersectional games should be scheduled. For the most part, schools played other schools in their own geographical area. Harvard, a program that Reynolds had followed closely, had played almost exclusively in the East since its first game in 1874.

Since the turn of the century, the Crimson played Vanderbilt in 1912, Michigan in 1914, and other than getting involved with Virginia and North Carolina, both on the Atlantic Coast, but not truly considered Eastern colleges, that was it. The games with those colleges were all played on Harvard's home field.

Howard Reynolds felt that there was no way to proclaim a college as having been a "National Champion" if that school didn't play more of a national schedule. Of course, he was correct.

The bowl games were in their infancy. There had been a Rose Bowl on January 1, 1902, when Michigan beat Stanford, 49-0. Then there was a gap of 14 years before another Rose Bowl was held on January 1, 1916, when Washington shut out Brown, 14-0. The following year, Oregon beat Pennsylvania, 14-0. The next two years had service teams in the Rose Bowl. (The Orange, Sugar, Sun and Cotton Bowls didn't start until the 1930's.)

Reynolds became intrigued with Centre during 1919 when he saw the scores come in over the wire. He would write that "Centre College, in Danville, Kentucky, wherever that is, beat....." After Centre kept winning, he decided to travel to Danville to see exactly where Centre was, and what was going on regarding the school's football program. Reynolds wanted to see if Centre was for real, if the program was legitimate, and, if everything was on the up and up, to see if he could be the catalyst to get the Colonels on the schedule of the mighty Harvard Crimson.

Eddie Mahan, a three-time All-American (1913-15) at Harvard, considered to be the greatest back ever to play the game for the Crimson, and possibly the greatest back to have ever played anywhere, was invited to go along, and readily agreed. He was of the same opinion as Reynolds regarding the fact that the sport needed to increase its geographical diversity, and he was just as curious about Centre as Reynolds.

The two Bostonians wired Chief Myers that they were coming down by train and would arrive on Sunday evening, November 24. The plan was to look over the campus, take some photographs, interview the players, and then travel with the team to Georgetown, Kentucky, to watch the November 27, Thanksgiving game with the Tigers. All of this was great news to Centre!

The Chief could just envision what he felt would happen. He knew that Centre would make a positive impression on the visitors. "This could be what we've dreamed about. We just let them see what we have here and they have to be, just have to be, in our camp as far as getting on the schedule of one of the big, Eastern programs." Chief

Myers had seen it in his mind for years. He'd truly believed, and now he felt his dream was going to be realized.

Reynolds and Mahan arrived on Sunday night as scheduled and checked into the Gilcher, having taxied up from the station. They arrived early enough to have time to take a little stroll after the long ride from Boston and walked the few blocks to Centre's campus and saw lights on in the basement of the gym. Through unlocked doors, they found a stairwell and descended into the Colonels' small dressing room. Over in the corner was a man bent over a bench, the small naked light from the ceiling augmented by a goose-neck lamp near him. The visitors watched him for a moment and then asked if he knew where coach Moran was.

"You're looking at him."

Uncle Charlie had been working on installing cleats and repairing his player's shoes. There was a sewing machine nearby with a freshly patched jersey draped over it.

The Bostonians introduced themselves, and after the usual pleasantries, they couldn't help but ask, "So tell us, what are you doing down here?"

"Repairing my boys' equipment. Our next game may be played in the mud. Georgetown's field doesn't have a speck of decent grass. We may need these mud cleats if it rains."

The Centre coach could tell by the expressions of Reynolds and Mahan that they were incredulous.

"This isn't Harvard, gentlemen. Down here, we do what we have to do to get along."

The meeting in the basement made its way into the story that Howard Reynolds later filed for his paper. The next morning, Reynolds and Mahan toured the Centre campus and went into each of the college's buildings. It didn't take long as there were but six. They then met with Dr. Ganfield. One of their goals was to become comfortable that the accusations which came out of West Virginia were false.

"We run an honorable program," Ganfield said. He sent his secretary to get the files of the players who were accused of not even being enrolled in the college.

"The article that appeared in those papers over in West Virginia said Red Roberts was a Nesser, that Chick Murphy was some ringer, that Red Weaver wasn't a student here. Nothing could be further from the truth. Here are their transcripts. Here is the letter of apology from Major Smith."

Dr. Ganfield certainly made the Bostonians feel that the accusations from West Virginia weren't true. Had they had any doubt, there was no way that they could later even consider recommending that Centre be given a date to play in the big horseshoe stadium along the Charles.

The visitors met with several of the players and were impressed with each whom they met. Mahan spent a considerable amount of time with Bo.

"You've been getting a lot of favorable press up in the East. Are you aware of that?"

Bo said he knew that there was some interest, "But I wish they'd write about our team and not just me. It's the team Eddie, it's always the team."

Reynolds and Mahan couldn't help but be impressed, and were even more so after attending the practices and watching Uncle Charlie running his charges through one after another perfectly timed play.

"These guys are for real," they agreed. "These guys may well be the greatest collection of football players in the country."

Tuesday night, there was a big dinner at the Gilcher. The guests of honor were the visitors from the East. Centre and Danville wanted to be the most gracious hosts possible. Everyone knew the importance of Howard Reynolds and Eddie Mahan. These two men could open the doors to the royalty of college football—Harvard! Centre and—Harvard! It had seemed impossible to think, just a few months ago, about a game with the most prestigious college in the nation.

The Gilcher's manager pulled out all of the stops for the evening. He invited the officers of the Chamber of Commerce as his guests who in turn had Dr. Ganfield and the Centre team and coaches as their guests. Additionally, 50 of the most prominent citizens, businessmen primarily, were invited. No one turned down the chance to be in attendance.

After dinner, toastmaster C.C. Bagby, president of the Chamber, related how Centre and the fortunes of Danville had been intertwined over the past century. He then introduced Dr. Ganfield who spoke about the prominent graduates which the college had turned out over the years, and then everyone stood and cheered when he announced that "Chief Myers and Charlie Moran will be back next year to lead our team."

While Ganfield praised the work of the coaching staff, he also noted the special Centre spirit which had taken the Gold and White to the heights of the football world.

Toastmaster Bagby then called on Uncle Charlie to make some comments. Again, it was the Centre spirit that was stressed.

"Not one of our men considers himself a star. Each has a part to play, and they play it."

Then it was the time for the players to give a few words.

Bo—"We are all brothers. I love them all. If necessary, I would fight and die for them."

Red Roberts—"I came to Centre not only for the school, but because of the fine men who teach us both in the classroom and on the field."

Lefty Whitnell stood and sang a favorite song, popular at the time, which began, "The world is round, but it's crooked, too."

Bill Garrity, a sub, had the ability to cry just like a baby, and after much prompting, began to wail.

Uncle Charlie introduced the big tackle, Sully Montgomery, and the diminutive Chick Murphy, as "the cow and the calf."

Ben Cregor and Howard Van Antwerp stood and Moran praised them, "…because their great play in the line doesn't receive the attention that it should."

After all of the players had their moment, Howard Reynolds was asked to speak. He said that these young men whom he had met had placed Danville and Centre College on the map, and he related that he had come down from Boston, "to see the best team in the country.

To appreciative laughter, Reynolds said that he'd written stories about the fact that there was a great football team in Danville, Kentucky, "wherever that is." Now he knew its location.

Eddie Mahan declared that he felt Centre had the best team in the country, bar none.

"So Mr. Reynolds and I just had to come to Danville, and we're going to take more pictures of your team and of the Centre campus, and then go to Georgetown for the game on Thanksgiving. And," here Mahan paused, "and then we're going to write about what we saw here, and the readers of the Boston "Post," like Mr. Reynolds said, will know exactly where you are, and what is going on in Danville, Kentucky."

The dinner ended with everyone who filed out of the Gilcher agreeing that the evening had been a wonderful success. They felt they were close to landing a game with Harvard. It would all depend on Howard Reynolds and Eddie Mahan, and they considered that they had two friends in their corner.

To a man, they thought, "Centre and Harvard. Who would have ever believed it!!"

THE 1919 SEASON ENDS

Some of the Colonels' fans had wanted Centre to drop Georgetown off the 1919 schedule after the 83-3 slaughter in 1918. They felt their team's cause would be better served by playing another college with more clout which would be more suited to the greater aspirations for the program.

Dr. Frank Rainey, chairman of the athletic committee, was quoted as saying, "It wouldn't be the gentlemanly thing not to play Georgetown. We have played for years. Sometimes, we may be stronger. Sometimes, they are. Perhaps in a few years, someone may suggest that Georgetown, if they are on the ascendancy, not wish to play us. We must remember that we have a long and friendly rivalry, based on the respect that we both have for each other."

The fans were correct in a way. The two programs had headed in opposite directions in the past few years. Prior to the Great War, the two colleges were competitive on the gridiron. But the last two games had seen Centre victorious by a combined 96-3 margin.

The game witnessed by the visiting Bostonians was a totally one-sided affair. Centre led 21-0 after the first period, 42-0 at the half, 63-7 after the third period, and the final score was 77-7 after the last quarter was shortened by five minutes due to the rout.

Georgetown did manage to score, but it only because of a mix-up on a center pass from Red Weaver. The Colonels' backs were running a play where they were in motion to the left and Red centered to the right. The free ball was picked up by a Tiger lineman named Moss, and he lumbered in, unmolested, for a touchdown.

A highlight for the game for Centre was that Red Weaver was a perfect 11 for 11 on extra points, and his streak now stood at 46.

Bo could have led the nation in scoring in 1919 had he been so inclined. Going into the DePauw game, he trailed West Virginia's Rodgers by just two points. However, twice during that game, he handed off the ball to Red Roberts for easy scores when he himself could have taken it in. Then, in the Georgetown game, Bo called on three seniors playing in their last games, Allen Davis, Matty Bell, and Howard Van Antwerp, and handed them the ball for easy, short plunges over the goal. As it was, Rodgers ended up scoring 146 points, while Bo tallied 122.

Bo reminded people who later asked him about the scoring title that Uncle Charlie had taught them the importance of team play, not of individual honors. Nothing demonstrated the wholehearted acceptance of his coach's philosophy more than Bo's disregard for personal glory. It was the team, for the team, by the team.

Centre easily was the highest scoring team in college football in 1919. The Colonels put 485 points on the board in 535 minutes of play, and were dubbed the "point-a-minute Colonels."

West Virginia finished at 8-2 and scored 326 points to end up a distant second as the most prolific offense.

In reviewing 1919, as impressive as the offense had been, the defensive efforts of the Gold and White were just as amazing. Their opponents scored a grand total of 23 points. The only scoring which was totally the responsibility of the defense was the West Virginia drive early in that contest. Indiana got a field goal after a blocked kick gave the Hoosiers the ball on Centre's 25. Virginia scored only after a shanked punt and two penalties put the ball on the Colonels' 10 yard line. Georgetown scored because of a wrong-way pass from center.

On Friday, Howard Reynolds and Eddie Mahan were bent over typewriters as their train headed back toward Boston. They had been terribly impressed by their stay in Danville, and by watching Centre overpower Georgetown. They spent a lot of the trip comparing notes and planning how each was going to relate to the people back home what they had experienced.

Reynolds, as the reporter, wanted to let his readers have a feel for what was happening in the world of college football out of their area. Mahan was also going to write a short article for the "Post," but his main mission had been to gather facts about Centre that he could report to Harvard, and hopefully influence his alma mater to consider placing the Colonels on the schedule during 1920.

While the New York Central train was crossing from Albany across the Hudson into Massachusetts, Centre was holding its post-season football banquet for the team at a downtown restaurant called the "New York." The Danville "Messenger" had a reporter at the event. He wrote that the players broke training for the first time in months, and some of the boys had a smoke after the turkey dinner. None would have dared smoke during the season.

Uncle Charlie was a benevolent dictator. He was much loved by his team, but they knew their limits. An article had just appeared in the Louisville "Herald," written by Bruce Dudley:

OH, NO, "RED" ROBERTS ISN'T SCARED
ONE BIT OF "UNC" CHARLIE MORAN

The door of the City Restaurant swung wide tonight and Red Roberts, followed by Tom Bartlett, strode through.

"Start cooking, Mike, start cooking," bellowed Red. "I'm on the warpath for food and I don't care who knows it."

Red plunked himself down on a chair which squeaked beneath his weight.

"What do I want? I want food. Something. Anything. Give me the nearest thing you can reach. Maybe you better make it a bacon sandwich with no grease. And a glass of milk," Red added after a moment's thought.

"That'll do for me, too," Bartlett informed.

"Hush up, Bartlett, you know you're broke," reminded Red.

"Didn't you invite me in here as your guest?"

"Guest? Guest, you have another guess coming. Hush up now. Didn't Uncle Charlie tell you to be in bed in ten minutes?"

Red's food came and he began to eat with gusto, ordering a second glass of milk.

"I hate to see you sitting around not eating, Bartlett," remarked Red between swallows.

"You show it, and I'm all the time giving you quarters and half dollars, too," replied Bartlett.

"That's so funny it's worth a glass of milk. Give the boy a glass of milk, Mike."

The milk was brought. Tom drank it.

"Don't let me find you here in five minutes," warned Tom, as he left to go to the post office to mail a letter.

Mike asked, "Didn't Uncle Charlie tell you to be in bed at this time?"

"Yes, but Unc and I are old buddies. I call him Charlie and he calls me by my real name, James. That's just how thick we are. Why if he walked in here right now, I'd probably ask him to have a hot dog. Why, I wouldn't bat an eye if he'd walk through that door this minute. Uncle Charlie knows that I'm always in good shape. I never limp around and whine and ask for time out. He wouldn't care anything about me not being in bed right now. What's ten minutes? Nothing. I tell you I'd greet him like a long lost brother if he'd come in right now. I'd say, 'Unc, doggone your old hide, how's tricks,' and then I'd...."

Red was interrupted by Peck Mannini who strolled in and told Mike that Uncle Charlie wanted a club sandwich, and he'd call for it in a half minute.

Red knocked over a table and two chairs getting out the back door.

After the meal at the New York, the group walked over to the Elk's Club where Uncle Charlie presided over the rest of the evening's events.

Eighteen letter winners were awarded the coveted, gold "C."

Army Armstrong
Matty Bell
Jim Coleman
Ben Cregor

Allen Davis
Ed Diddle
Robert Clayton Ford
Bill Garrett
Bill James
Max MacCollum
Bo McMillin
Sully Montgomery
Chick Murphy
Red Roberts
Terry Snowday
Howard Van Antwerp
Red Weaver
Lefty Whitnell

The letter winners then retired to a side room to elect a captain for the upcoming 1920 season. It just took a minute as Bo was re-elected unanimously.

The only starters who weren't returning for the next season were the three seniors Bo had made certain scored in the final game of the season—Howard Van Antwerp, Matty Bell, and Allen Davis.

THE BOSTON "POST" DECEMBER 1, 1919

Howard Reynolds took his copy straight to the "Post" when he disembarked from the train at Boston's South Station. He was determined that it be printed as soon as possible and spent Sunday in his office, getting it ready for the Monday, December 1, edition. His story appeared in a double column form, under a three deck headline, covering the whole of the front page of the sport section. It was a long story, and excerpts pertinent to our understanding about how Centre hit the big time need to be included. Reynolds quickly got busy by debunking the claims that came out of West Virginia.

Incensed gossip coming in from the outside world that a team previously unknown except in limited circles could have such a brilliant record, and win such national importance without the aid of professionals, semi-professionals or ineligibles from other colleges, has caused the Danville Chamber of Commerce to take action. There is money deposited in a local bank here waiting for anyone to collect on producing evidence to the honorable C. C. Bagby, President of the Chamber, regarding the accusations made after the West Virginia game.

After nearly a week of investigation and observation in the little Kentucky town, I have returned convinced that I never had a chance to earn that reward, that every man on the Centre College team is as eligible as any man who ever represented Harvard or Yale on November 22. (Harvard and Yale met on November 22 at Harvard Stadium with the Crimson coming out on top, 10-3.) *It is my feeling that Centre College has the championship eleven of the year on its record.*

Immediately, Reynolds had addressed and debunked the charges that Centre wasn't legitimate. He then followed up by boldly stating the Colonels were the best team in the country in 1919. Centre certainly had an advocate in its corner.

Next, Reynolds made the case for Centre being in the same class as Harvard.

I am convinced that Centre College would have made it extremely uncomfortable for the Crimson gridiron warriors in their final game of the year, and beaten it in some of its earlier contests. In my opinion, Harvard's defense would not be able to keep Centre from scoring.

With less than 200 students, Centre has produced a team that has rolled up 485 points to its opponents 23, which is the high total for the year. In doing so, it has on its schedule not only faced teams similar to those of Harvard, like Bates, Colby and Wesleyan, up New England way, but teams of much tougher fiber as well. For Centre College, owing to its strenuous schedule, paved the way to nail the championship from two roads. By one route, it defeated the University of West Virginia after the Mountaineers had administered a 25-0 defeat to Princeton, and then Princeton proceeded to tie both Harvard and Yale.

On the other road, Centre took into camp, 12-3, Indiana University, an eleven that defeated Syracuse. Syracuse defeated Colgate and tied Dartmouth. Everyone must admit that Colgate was in the line for the leading honors of the year until the Syracusans spoiled its record, as was Dartmouth until Brown administered that bitter dose to the "Big Green" on November 15.

How did such a little school as Centre do it? How was it possible for this previously obscure eleven to accomplish this remarkable feat? After all, the entire student body does not equal the numbers that Harvard, Yale and Princeton are able to draw out for the early practice drill of the season.

The answer seems to be a combination of various ingredients that mixed together make a winning formula.

Down in Danville, folks will tell you first it is the material, then the coach, and finally the spirit. But I believe to solve the secret you have to dig deeper than that.

First—There is the faith in themselves, not born of overconfidence.

Second—Coach Charles Moran.

Third—The material.

Fourth—The firm belief of the material in, and its almost filial affection for, that coach.

Fifth—The complete absorption of the fact that no matter when or where they play, there has to be eleven men in it. That a play can't go wrong if every man is where he belongs and does his duty.

Sixth—Every man knows that no matter how good he is, he is bound by honor to strict training.

Seventh—The possession of three great players in McMillin, Roberts and Weaver.

Eighth—The hammering home of the idea that clean play is the only kind of play.

There is a play in every game that Centre takes part in that precedes the kickoff. In a very large manner, it may account for the faith and spirit. It is a prayer offered either by the president of the college, or Captain McMillin.

Not a prayer asking for great accomplishments, but a quiet, earnest prayer, a prayer for guidance and direction that the sons of Old Centre may live up to the glorious and worthy traditions of the past.

It is a prayer that sends every man out of the locker room onto the field crying and weeping, determined to play a man's part in a man's game, from first to last. A prayer that fills him with faith that all he has to do is perform his part, and all will be well for Old Centre.

Every one of them seems to be iron men and able to go through grueling games at top speed. In two important contests, only two substitutions were made, and only one in the West Virginia contest.

They are as fine a lot of clean-cut athletes as one ever sees on a college gridiron. One look at them and any idea that there are "ringers" among them is squelched in your thoughts.

Howard Reynolds then pointed out the contrast of the program in Danville with that of Harvard.

On Thanksgiving, Centre played its final game against its traditional rival, Georgetown College, which is located a short distance from Lexington. To them it is their Harvard and Yale contest.

The day before, Moran had been busy from 8:00 in the morning until noon at the athletic office. In the afternoon, he gave his squad its final workout on a rain-soaked field.

At 10:00 that night, I heard that he was in the gymnasium, and out of curiosity, went to see what he was doing at such an hour.

There he was, down in the basement locker room hard at work. Uniforms had been drenched and muddied in that last practice, and owing to the fact that uniforms, like all other equipment at Centre College, do not exceed the number of players, had to be washed and dried out as best they could and packed that evening.

The tenders of this drying-out process and the packers of the equipment were none other than team captain, Bo McMillin, and Terry Snowday, a starting end. Can you imagine at Harvard, Coach Bob Fisher, assisted by Eddie Casey (an All-American on the 1919 Crimson team) packing up the gridiron wearing apparel on the night before the game with Yale?

Moran is chief cook and bottle washer here. He is the trainer and masseur. He is the custodian of the equipment and keeps the head gears, the shoulder gears and foot gears in order.

Moran's big asset as a coach in my opinion is that outside of the boy's time in the classroom and sleeping hours, he lives with his players. He makes them all love and respect him. He knows when to praise and when to call down, and is lavish in both. He allows no one to get a swelled head because he is a star. The player is made to understand from the start that he is only able to shine because there are 10 other men working with him. It they were not, his efforts would not be successful.

Centre has three brilliant stars in Bo McMillin, Red Roberts, and Red Weaver.

McMillin is a savvy leader on the field, an excellent passer, and runs much like Jim Thorpe, except lower. Roberts is one of the premier line buckers in the country, much like Gillo of Colgate. Weaver is an excellent passer of the ball from the center position, and a terror on defense.

All of the Colonels hope to invade the East, and it would be a shame if football fans in our area don't have a chance to see this remarkable group of young men in action.

Howard Reynolds had truly done everything in his power to promote Centre in his quest to have the Crimson play more of an intersectional schedule.

Eddie Mahan did the same.

CENTRE PLAY IS IMPRESSIVE
UNDEFEATED KENTUCKY COLLEGE
BEST RECORD OF SEASON SAYS MAHAN

Mahan's story took up two columns in the same issue of the "Post."

If you go by the records of college football, Centre College of Kentucky's undefeated eleven has more of a right to claim to be the championship team in 1919 then any other program.

Perhaps even more important than his proclamation about Centre's strength on the gridiron was Eddie Mahan's intervention on behalf of the Colonels with the Harvard athletic authorities.

Mahan, the greatest of the Harvard football players, captain of the 1915 team, three-time All-American (1913-15), advisory coach of the present team, author of a book entitled, "How to Play Halfback," personally met with the Harvard staff and assured them that Centre had a clean program, and that there was absolutely no chance that they cheated in any way on their rise to the top.

"McMillin is McMillin, and the Reds are the Reds-Roberts and Weaver."

CENTRE WAITS TO HEAR FROM CAMBRIDGE

On Monday, December 1, Uncle Charlie, Chief Myers, Dr. Ganfield, and the faculty representative on the athletic committee, Dr. Frank Rainey, began to work on the schedule for the upcoming 1920 season. While they knew they needed to get some commitments, and to make some commitments, they didn't want to firm anything up until they heard from Harvard. The meteoric rise of the Colonels into the hierarchy of the college football world had caught the attention of colleges all over the country. Suddenly, everyone wanted to play the little school which just two years previously had difficulty in getting anyone to take notice.

The University of Illinois invited Centre to come to Champaign to play in its 17,000 seat Illinois Field. (Memorial Stadium wouldn't be completed until 1923.) Washington and Lee, at the time a football power, contacted the Chief and Dr. Rainey. Pittsburgh, the only school other than Centre to beat West Virginia in 1919, sent a letter that the Panthers would like the Colonels to come up for a game. Boston College's graduate manager, Frank Reynolds, said his team wanted a game. Lehigh, of Bethlehem, Pennsylvania, said it could guarantee a nice payday for Centre from what was predicted would be an attendance in the 14,000 range due to the great interest that the Colonels were generating.

While the offers continued to pour in and were gratifying, Centre waited for one, hopefully, from Cambridge. All week—nothing. By the weekend, the Chief had to go to Chicago to attend to some business. As the athletic director, he would be the person to contact regarding scheduling. Chief Myers sent a telegram to Harvard advising them of his whereabouts for the next few days.

Monday, December 8. Again—nothing. Tuesday, December 9. Silence.

On Wednesday, December 10, a telegram was delivered by a young courier to the office of Myers and Trimble, Suite 911, on 624 South Michigan Boulevard.

The Chief nervously opened it and then let out an uncharacteristic, "Whoop!"

"We're going to play Harvard! We're going to play Harvard! Can you believe it?"

"I guess that's swell."

"Harvard! We're going to play Harvard!"

The Chief began the arduous process of calling long distance to Danville. First he had to contact a local operator who would take down the information and then pass it on to a long distance operator who would get the various circuits connected necessary to complete the call. Meanwhile, he sat impatiently, waiting for the AT&T operator to call back with his connection.

Dr. Ganfield knew when he picked up the phone and heard that he had a call from Chicago that it had to be Chief Myers. And he knew that it had to be about Harvard.

"Chief? We've been put on Harvard's schedule! We're going to play Harvard!"

The Chief couldn't restrain himself, nor could the dignified Dr. Ganfield. They both jumped around their offices, congratulating each other about the wonderful news.

"Harvard!" they would say over and over. "Can you imagine, we're going to play Harvard!!

Kentuckians throughout the state were as thrilled as Dr. Ganfield and the Chief had been when they heard that Harvard had put Centre on its schedule.

The Louisville "Times," afternoon partner of the Bingham's morning the "Courier-Journal" published a story after the Harvard game was announced which predicted what it would be like when Centre arrived in Cambridge.

When the Centre College football eleven trots out onto the gridiron at Cambridge, Mass. at 1:45 o'clock on the afternoon of October 23, 1920, there will be a delegation from Kentucky, a mass waving the Gold and White's banners, sitting down near the front. This band of rooters will immediately go into convulsions as the Colonels take the field and start running through their signals.

The bowl will be filled because the strength and power of the Centre eleven have been cast upon the waters and are returning. Eastern newspapers have published a world of information about Charlie Moran and his boys, and the Easterners are curious to know just what sort of team can stir up such a noise way down in Kentucky.

Nobody in the East had ever heard of Centre until well along in the season of 1919. The first news that trickled up there was the score of a game showing that some insignificant eleven called Centre had beaten Indiana. Must be some fluke. Later, a score bobbed up that Centre had hopped over to Virginia and trimmed Virginia by a large score. Then everything was quiet. People saw where West Virginia had taken on Centre for a practice game. Well,

West Virginia would show the Centre crowd some tricks. They'd knock some of the cocky air out of the Southerners. But alas and alack—and a couple more of them, Centre lambasted West Virginia. Then it was that the East said that it would have to find out where Centre College was and publish some dope on it. The news contained a lot of interesting stuff.

Harvard invited Centre to play in 1920, and Centre accepted. And that's how little insignificant Centre accomplished in one year what it has taken other teams years to do. And that's how it happened that Centre trotted onto this field on this day in October. As we said, the delegation from Kentucky went wild when the "Praying, Fighting Colonels" lined up for the first scrimmage.

In three years, the Chief and Uncle Charlie had scaled the mountain. They were near the pinnacle. The Chief's longtime ambition had nearly been fulfilled. His beloved Centre College was poised to become known anywhere there was a fan who cared about football, and to gain recognition and fame far beyond what anyone other than the Chief and Uncle Charlie could have imagined even in their most outlandish dreams.

"Centre and Harvard. Who would have ever believed it!"

"Credendo Vides."

"To believe," the Chief would say, "To believe, is to see."

THE 1920 SCHEDULE TAKES SHAPE

Harvard wanted to play on October 23. Any date was fine with Centre and that slot was filled in. Now, the Centre athletic committee began to round out the next year's lineup.

One aspect for getting on the schedule of the Crimson was the understanding that Centre would arrive in the East undefeated. There was nothing in writing, but there was definitely an implied agreement. Harvard knew that if Centre lost an early game prior to their contest, it would take some of the luster off the intersectional battle.

Centre made certain that it would be unblemished by scheduling three easy home games prior to the Harvard contest. It couldn't get much easier than Morris Harvey from Barboursville, West Virginia, Howard College from Birmingham, Alabama, and old foe, Transylvania, which had lost to the Colonels the last three years by a combined score of 149-0.

Georgia Tech was going to be played in Atlanta following the Harvard game. After Tech, Centre felt it owed DePauw for switching the previous year's game to Louisville, so agreed to go to Indianapolis to take on the Tigers. Kentucky was, of course, going to be penned in, and the 1920 game was to be an away date in Lexington.

Louisville had been such a great host when Centre played DePauw there the year before that the college wanted to make it an annual tradition to play in the state's biggest market. Virginia Polytechnic (VPI) from Blacksburg would be a worthy opponent for that venue.

The annual Thanksgiving game was going to take place with Georgetown even though the folks who ran Georgetown's program were having doubts about playing after being drubbed the last three years by a total score of 173-10.

1920 SCHEDULE

Oct. 2	Morris Harvey	Danville
Oct. 9	Howard	Danville
Oct. 16	Transylvania	Danville
Oct. 23	Harvard	Cambridge
Oct. 30	Georgia Tech	Atlanta
Nov. 6	DePauw	Indianapolis
Nov. 13	Kentucky	Lexington
Nov. 20	Virginia Tech	Louisville
Nov. 25	Georgetown	Danville

WALTER CAMP AND THE "ALL-AMERICA" TEAM

Walter Camp is considered the "Father of American Football." He was born in New Britain, Connecticut on April 7, 1859, ten years before the first contest between Princeton and Rutgers which would evolve into the sport that we call football. Camp helped guide the game from the English rugby to the American game as we know it. He entered Yale in 1875 and played in the college's first game with Harvard that fall, won by the Crimson, 4-0.

In 1880, Camp graduated from Yale and entered medical school there. However, the sight of blood made him faint, hardly conducive to a career as a physician, and he went into the clock business, becoming president of the New Haven Clock Company by 1902.

Camp's love of football led him to devote many hours as the advisor to a succession of coaches at his alma mater. By 1906, football had become so rough, with an ever increasing number of injuries, some fatal, that President Theodore Roosevelt invited a group of football devotees to attend a meeting in the White House, and out of the old "Rough Rider's" intervention, changes in the game's rules were proposed to make the sport safer.

Walter Camp was at the meeting in Washington, and as one of the founding members of what became the National Collegiate Athletic Association, the NCAA, he was in the forefront in decisions which determined that plays would be run from a line of scrimmage, along with the standardization of points awarded for touchdowns, extra points and field goals.

He was instrumental in designating that eleven players make a team, influenced and defined what constituted a penalty, and how many yards should be forfeited for an infraction, along with other concepts which make the game what it is today.

Camp not only served on the NCAA rules committee from its inception, but was its chairman from 1911 until his death from a heart attack while attending the committee's annual meeting in 1925.

However many were Walter Camp's accomplishments and contributions to college football, it was his designation of what became known as the "All-American" football team that he is best known.

The first All-American team was announced in 1889, comprised of players who had competed in 1888. There is no definite agreement if the idea was Camp's or that of an individual named Casper Whitney who was the editor of a short-lived magazine named "This Week's Sport." However, Camp definitely took over the naming of the team after that first year.

Obviously, Camp couldn't attend every game played each week, so he devised a system where he would ask sportswriters, officials of games, and trusted athletic figures, to be his "eyes and ears," taking notes during or after games and reporting back to him.

During the important game between West Virginia and Centre, the referee was listed as "Sudgens from Harvard." It was later announced that besides officiating, he was going to report back to Walter Camp regarding the player's skills and importance to their respective teams.

There were several All-American teams announced each year. So-called "football experts" would be chosen by various papers to pick a team, or the paper's own staff in the sports department would announce their selections. However, the only team that was universally recognized as THE All-American team was that chosen by Walter Camp.

The make-up of Camp's team was kept a secret until it was announced each fall in "Collier's," a nationally distributed weekly publication. The December 13, 1919 "Collier's" was eagerly awaited all across the country, and especially in Kentucky. Uncle Charlie and Chief Myers had stated in several interviews that they felt Centre had the best team in the country, and that Centre had talent which would rate with any program, anywhere.

The Centre mentors weren't bragging. They were simply expressing what they considered to be factual, but they realized that tradition was against the possibility of the smaller, non-Eastern teams and their players gaining the recognition that they deserved. At the same time, they were encouraged that Walter Camp had recently been quoted as saying that Centre deserved to be labeled the "National Champions" for 1919, and by the fact that in the 1919 "Spalding's Football Guide," Camp had recognized the skills of Bo, Red Roberts, and Red Weaver for their play displayed during the 1918 season.

Centre's concern about its players being recognized, however, was justified by the facts. In analyzing the first team All-Americans as chosen by Camp from 1900-1918 (there was no 1917 team due to the war) the Eastern schools and larger state colleges outside of the East had landed by far the most slots.

Of the 18 teams and 198 first team selections, the breakdown was as follows:

(1) Yale	47
(2) Harvard	39
(3) Princeton	21
Total	107

Thus, the "Big 3" had 54% of the total selected. This was understandable. The "Big 3" dominated football during this period, and that domination meant that these schools had the best material.

The rest of the selections were heavily weighed toward the East.

(4) Pennsylvania	14
(5) Army	9
(6) Dartmouth	8
(7) Brown	6
(8) Navy	5
(9) Cornell	4
(10) Pittsburgh	4
(11) Syracuse	4
(12) Colgate	4
(13) Carlisle (Pa.)	3
(14) Columbia	3
(15) Amherst	1
(16) Penn State	1
(17) Rutgers	1
Total	67

These additional programs, added to the "Big 3," meant that the Eastern colleges had grabbed 174 positions, or 88% of the All-American selections.

All of the other programs outside of the East which had players who made the All-American squad were larger colleges.

(1) Michigan	8
(2) Chicago	6
(3) Minnesota	4
(4) Illinois	2
(5) Ohio State	1
(6) Wisconsin	1
(7) Georgia Tech	1
(8) Notre Dame	1
Total	24

It didn't take much analysis to see that a small college, especially a small Southern college like Centre, would have a very tough time placing any of its players on Walter Camp's All-American team. The only Southern player named since 1900 was 1918's Bill Fincher of Georgia Tech., and of course, Georgia Tech, with an enrollment of nearly 2,500, was no small college like Centre with its student body of under 200.

81

My brother Howard and I had followed Centre's football team ever since we'd seen the practice when we visited Cousin Ella just before the 1919 season. We had a paper route and would meet the L&N train from Louisville and get the morning "Courier-Journal" off the train and read the sports section before we'd start our delivery.

Everybody knew that "Collier's" weekly magazine put out the All-American team each season. Our family didn't subscribe, but there were several people in town who did, and one of them was the Montgomery family. They knew how interested we were about Centre because Howard was going to be a freshman there in the fall of 1920, and I hoped to go the next year.

Mrs. Montgomery rang us one morning and said she thought we'd be excited to come over and see who made All-American. So Howard and I raced over to her house as fast as we could run, and she gave us the magazine which I have to this day.

We flipped through the pages and there was a full page which said, "The All-American Team." There were pictures of all of the first team, and right there were Bo McMillin and Red Weaver, both of them on the first team.

And then we saw that Red Roberts, my "father," was on the third team! You just can't imagine how big that was. Two first team All-Americans, and one on the third team. And Howard was going to enroll there next year!

THE SELECTIONS FOR THE FIRST, SECOND AND THIRD TEAM ALL-AMERICANS FOR 1919

POSITION	FIRST TEAM	SECOND TEAM	THIRD TEAM
End	Higgins, Penn State	Weston, Wisconsin	Blaik, Army
Tackle	West, Colgate	Ingwersen, Illinois	Slater, Iowa
Guard	Alexander, Syracuse	Dinfield, Annapolis	Clark, Harvard
Center	**Weaver, Centre**	Bailey, West Virginia	Callahan, Yale
Guard	Youngstrom, Dartmouth	Depler, Illinois	Pixley, Ohio State
Tackle	Henry, Wash. & Jeff.	Grimm, Washington	Cody, Vanderbilt
End	H. Miller, Pennsylvania	Dumoe, Lafayette	**Roberts, Centre**
Q-Back	**McMillin, Centre**	Strubing, Princeton	Boynton, Williams
Half	Casey, Harvard	Trimble, Princeton	Steers, Oregon
Half	Harley, Ohio State	Oss, Minnesota	Gillo, Colgate
Full	Rodgers, West Virginia	Braden, Yale	Robertson, Dartmouth

Camp had still included members of the "Big 3" in his selections, for a total of six from Harvard, Yale, and Princeton among the 33. But for the first time, three first team All-Americans were from small schools, two from Centre, and one from

Washington & Jefferson which is located in Pennsylvania, and like Centre during this era, played a big-time schedule with a small-time enrollment.

It was truly a breakthrough year for Camp's team. For the first time ever, a small, Southern college had gained recognition. Huge recognition! Centre was the only school to have three members chosen on the first three teams. Harvard, Yale and Princeton each had but two.

As football fans across the United States studied the December 13, 1919 "Collier's" and the All-American teams, again people were increasingly asking, "Who are those guys, anyway?"

Somerset, Kentucky was bursting with pride. The three Centre All-Americans had been members of the Briar Jumpers' team in 1916. There may have been Eastern high and prep schools in the past which had been so honored, but if that was true, no one in Kentucky was aware of it. Also, those who had followed Fort Worth North Side's gridiron heroes in 1915 were excited to see that two of their graduates, Bo and Red Weaver, were first team picks.

It wouldn't do justice to the analysis of the 1919 All-American team without paying tribute to that official who worked the Centre-West Virginia game, "Sudgens from Harvard." Sudgens must have sent a glowing report to Camp about the participants in the November 8 game played in Charleston.

West Virginia landed two men on the All-American teams of 1919. Errett Rodgers was on the first team at fullback, and Russ Bailey was on the second team at the center position. Therefore, five of the players in that game caught the attention of Sudgens, and it is to him that Centre and West Virginia must have felt a debt of gratitude.

Typical of how the news was greeted across Kentucky about Centre being honored was the headline in the Louisville "Herald" for its Sunday, December 14 issue:

McMILLIN and WEAVER ON CAMP'S ALL-AMERICAN
CENTRE ONLY COLLEGE WITH TWO ON FIRST TEAM
ELEVEN BEST FOOTBALL PLAYERS IN AMERICA
BO AND RED OWE MUCH TO COACHES
MYERS FIRST INSTRUCTED, MORAN PROVIDED POLISH
ARE 100% MEN

Besides the All-American awards, Bo and the two Reds were named on the All-Southern team. In 1919, there was a conference called the Southern Intercollegiate Athletic Association (S.I.A.A.) comprised of 30 colleges in Alabama, Florida, Georgia, Kentucky, Louisiana, Maryland, Mississippi, North Carolina, South Carolina, Tennessee, and Virginia. Fourteen of the schools represented were designated "minor colleges," and Centre fit into this category.

"Minor" may have been the category, but "major" was the recognition given the Colonels' players when the All-S.I.A.A. team was announced. Seven of the squad made the first team. Montgomery, Snowday, Van Antwerp and Weaver were placed in the line. Army,

Bo, and Red Roberts were picked for the backfield. Matty Bell was on the second team as an end. To round off the honors, 11 of the Centre players were named to the All-Kentucky team. Bo, both Reds, Snowday, Army, Van Antwerp and Montgomery were on the first team. Ben Cregor, Bill James, Matty Bell, and Lefty Whitnell were on the second team.

As the campus shut down for the Christmas vacation, the fame and appreciation of Centre College was truly spreading all across the land. "On to Harvard!" became Centre's battle cry. An example of how seriously Centre took the upcoming season was the fact that the college introduced the first ever spring training practice sessions which began on March 24, 1920. Bo was put in charge. The school newspaper, the "Cento," covered the innovation.

Spring football, in vogue in Eastern universities, was introduced by Uncle Charlie Moran who is anxious to round his men into shape early for a season that will be the most strenuous in the history of Centre College football.

The Centre College year traditionally ended each spring with the Carnival, a formal evening during which a King from Centre and Queen from Danville were crowned, followed by a dance with full orchestra, usually brought over from Louisville.

The Boyle-Humphrey Gymnasium was beautifully decorated. It was black tie for the men and long gowns for the ladies. There was great applause when the name of the King was announced by Dr. Ganfield. In what became a pattern as the team gained prominence, a player was elected.

"Ladies and gentlemen, it is my great pleasure to present the King of the 1920 Carnival, Mr. Matty Bell."

CENTRE CLAIMS THE NATIONAL CHAMPIONSHIP

So who was the best college football team in 1919? It would seem reasonable that the best team should be undefeated, even if tied. If this is a criterion, only five teams met the standard.

Texas A&M	10-0-0
Notre Dame	9-0-0
Centre	9-0-0
Harvard	9-0-1
Tulsa	8-0-1

Sorry Tulsa fans, but the "Yellow Jackets," as the Tulsans were known then, really can't be seriously considered due to the weakness of their schedule which included Oklahoma Baptist, East Central Oklahoma, Central Oklahoma State, Northwest Oklahoma, Trinity, and Burleson. The tie came against a so-so 3-3-2 Oklahoma A&M (State) team.

Texas A&M had a great year. The Aggies were not only undefeated, but they didn't give up a point.

Texas A&M	77	Sam Houston State	0
Texas A&M	28	Texas State	0
Texas A&M	16	SMU	0
Texas A&M	12	Howard Payne	0
Texas A&M	42	Trinity	0
Texas A&M	28	Oklahoma A&M	0
Texas A&M	10	Baylor	0
Texas A&M	48	TCU	0
Texas A&M	7	Southwestern	0
Texas A&M	7	Texas	0

Notre Dame, coached by the soon-to-be, legendary Knute Rockne, in his second season, had a legitimate case to claim the top spot. Notre Dame and Centre had one common opponent, Indiana. The Irish beat the Hoosiers in Indianapolis, 16-3. The Colonels won 12-3 in Bloomington. Certainly, on that basis, the two teams would have seemed to be equal.

Notre Dame	14	Kalamazoo	0
Notre Dame	60	Mt. Union	7
Notre Dame	14	Nebraska	9
Notre Dame	53	Western Michigan	0
Notre Dame	16	Indiana	3
Notre Dame	12	Army	9
Notre Dame	13	Michigan State	0
Notre Dame	33	Purdue	13
Notre Dame	14	Morningside	6

Harvard had a marvelous year. The Crimson capped off their year by playing in the Rose Bowl on January 1, 1920, beating the Oregon Ducks, 7-6.

Harvard and Centre had a common foe in Virginia. Both schools pasted the Virginians, Harvard winning on its own field, 47-0, while the Colonels were victorious over in Charlottesville, 49-7. So like Notre Dame and Centre with their common foe, Indiana, Harvard and Centre would appear to be a toss-up based on their games with Virginia.

Harvard	53	Bates	0
Harvard	17	Boston College	0
Harvard	35	Colby	0
Harvard	7	Brown	0
Harvard	20	Springfield	0
Harvard	10	Princeton	10
Harvard	23	Tufts	0
Harvard	10	Yale	3
Harvard	7	Oregon	6

So which college should be declared the best of 1919 on the gridiron? One of the reasons that Howard Reynolds was promoting more intersectional games was to help in the determination of such questions.

Each of the teams, Centre, Harvard, Texas A&M. and Notre Dame, had reason to feel they were the champions. However, there was no doubt in Danville, Kentucky. The Centre College Colonels were number one. Of this, there was absolute certainty. And even more importantly, Centre was going to play Harvard. Who would have ever believed it?

HOLD UP A MOMENT ABOUT THE NATIONAL CHAMPION

You might remember at the onset of this book that the statement was made that Centre College had the overall number one ranked football program in the country during the six years, 1919-1924, following the end of World War I.

We need to lay a little ground work here. Of course, there were no national polls. Now we have polls determined by various "experts," or by computerized programs.

There is, however, a retroactive computerized ranking which has been developed by James Howell who has a degree in computer science. You can see Mr. Howell's system, which is available at *http://www.jhowell.net/* by clicking on "College Football Power Ratings."

Basically, the system ranks teams based on their performance against an opponent (50% of the ranking) with the power rating being modified by the strength of the team's schedule, and whether a team was playing at home or on the road.

At the end of this book, we'll average out the yearly rankings of the top thirty teams during our time frame to see who was ranked, and where they landed in the top 30 programs of the time. We'll get into this more later, but meanwhile, if you're so inclined, go to the site. If you're not so inclined, we'll catch you up at the end of the book.

CHAPTER 6:
WARMING UP FOR HARVARD—1920

The Chief put many members of the team to work on the Chautauqua circuit for the summer. It was a perfect type of job, especially for someone like Bo. The now All-American could parley his national fame to fit in with his duties going around the country publicizing an up-and-coming Myers and Trimble show which was due in town.

A local citizen would hear that Bo, "Bo McMillin, the All-American," was going to be in town to put up some posters and speak to various groups about the coming attraction. The Centre star didn't have to nail up any posters. There were always eager young boys who would jump at the chance to help out, and every group was eager to have him speak so they could say that they'd been in the presence of, "the greatest football player in the whole country."

"Bo McMillin? Of course I know Bo. He's a buddy of mine."

Bo was an excellent pool player, and in every community, he'd head to the local parlor and relieve some of the locals of several dollars.

"Bo McMillin? Of course, I know Bo. We're pool playing friends."

Bo said later in life that if there had been one thing that best prepared him for life after college, it was the experience and confidence that he gained in dealing with the public as an ambassador of the Chief's Chautauqua company.

Red Roberts couldn't wait for the upcoming season to start. One day, late in the summer, he traveled to Louisville and went to the Spalding's sporting goods store and picked up his new uniform which Centre had ordered. He had a couple of footballs and headed to Cherokee Park to practice his kicking.

My aunt, Mary Robertson, was my father's sister. She married Theodore Wintersmith who was on my mother's side of the family. Uncle Theo had a company called Wintersmith Chemical Company which made Wintersmith's Chill Tonic which had quinine in it, and was effective against malaria which was pretty prevalent in those days, especially in the South. His company did quite well, especially when prohibition became the law of the land, because they upped the alcohol content to 10%, which made it quite popular, because you could buy it

legally. A lot of people decided that they needed to PREVENT malaria, even in the winter when there weren't any mosquitoes around.

Anyway, Aunt Mary's home was a beautiful place on Cherokee Parkway which was right across from Cherokee Park. Howard and I were visiting there, and we saw this big, red haired guy over in the park kicking a football We ran over to see him, and it was Red Roberts who instantly recognized me and said, "Hey, my son, why don't you and your brother go down and catch my kicks and get the ball back to me.

So, of course we did. We stood at least 50 yards away and he boomed a kick out that sailed totally over my head.

Red hollored, "Son, you better back up a little. I'm hitting the ball awfully well today."

Howard and I just looked at each other. Later we agreed that we could understand why he was an All-American. Red could just kick the heck out of a football.

The fall semester was to begin on September 15, but football practice began nine days earlier, on the 6th. Uncle Charlie was still umpiring, so the Chief came down from Chicago to assume the coaching duties, with the able assistance of Bo.

"Boys, let's get busy," was the first thing Chief Myers said on opening day. "We can't lose a minute between now and October 23. It's going to be a mighty hard season, and it's up to every player to keep in the best condition and report regularly and on time for practice."

Myers stated that when all of the members returned, and with the new men showing up, who couldn't join the team until classes actually began because of S.I.A.A. restrictions, he expected 60 men to try out for football.

"We have good men coming in from Seattle to Long Island, with Kentucky in the lead and Texas coming on strong. Boys, I know we'll lay all of their heads down. We'll miss nobody. They'll all go Titanic," a reference to the 1912 tragedy in the North Atlantic when over 1500 people perished when the great ship hit an iceberg and sank.

What a difference a great season can make in a school's football prospects. Centre had 210 students during the 1920-21 academic year. There was a huge freshman class (for Centre) arriving on campus. Where there had been 76 newcomers in 1919, there were now 99, an increase of 30%.

THE STUDENT BODY FOR 1920-21

Seniors	25
Juniors	36
Sophomores	51
Freshmen	99
Total	211

Centre had been hard-pressed to put 22 men on the practice field in order to scrimmage just a few short years ago. Now, nearly 30% of the young men attending the college wanted to be members of the Gold and White. Interest was such that the two local papers announced daily who had gotten in from the summer hiatus and was out on the field.

"Gus King will arrive on the morning train on the 8th."

"Chick Murphy and Lefty Whitnell sent a wire that they couldn't get to Danville until the 13th."

"Big Sully Montgomery and Bill James can't get away from their jobs down in Texas until the 21st."

One interesting route of travel to Centre was the canoe trip that an incoming freshman, Stanley Robb, took from Pittsburgh. Robb embarked on the Ohio River from his home town and paddled down-river for several days until he came to the mouth of the Kentucky River where he took a left, heading south. After navigating up the Kentucky, he entered the Dix River and finally pulled his trusty little boat out of the water and walked the few miles into Danville.

Twenty freshmen were introduced at the first chapel who were going out for football. Most of the regulars from the 1919 season were returning, with only Allen Davis, Matty Bell, and Howard Van Antwerp lost to graduation.

Two great players who had been on the campus during 1919, but weren't eligible to play, were John Porter "Hump" Tanner and Tom Bartlett from Owensboro. Hump, a little fireplug, and "Long Tom," a great back and defensive man, would play vital roles in the upcoming campaign.

Centre's "Press Day" in the past was attended by the two local papers, the "Advocate" and "Messenger," with perhaps a reporter, if one could be spared, coming over from one of Lexington's papers. Certainly things had changed. All of the weekly papers from Central Kentucky sent their representatives. The wire services were represented by the NEA. The Lexington "Leader" and "Herald" had their men in Danville. The Louisville papers, the "Courier-Journal", the "Times," and the "Herald," each had their reporters interviewing the Colonels and taking pictures. Naturally, Danville's "Advocate" and "Messenger" showed up.

Photographs were taken of the whole team and then of individuals, posing in their new uniforms which had been shipped over from Louisville. The two Reds were posed together. Murph was snapped running back punts. Bo was shown firing passes, and then the three All-Americans, Bo and the Reds, were lined up for multiple shots.

Ed Danforth of the Atlanta "Journal" took the train up to spend the day with the team. Each year, Danforth made the circuit to various colleges to size up their prospects for the upcoming football season. He hadn't come to Danville previously, but now the little school was gaining such fame that he wanted to let his readers know exactly what they could expect from this previously unknown program which had reached such heights as to attract the attention of mighty Harvard.

The halo of the supernatural that has surrounded the Centre team has been dispelled as far as I am concerned. They unite in prayer before every game, but otherwise this football team that plunged Danville and the college into a flood of pleasurable publicity last year by scoring 485 points to their opponents 23 is composed of human beings and not cantors or holy rollers. In fact, the only difference between Centre College and any other team in the South is about five touchdowns.

Twenty eight men followed Captain McMillin through the gate of Cheek Field for the first practice of the 1920 season. (Several returning regulars were still to report, and freshmen couldn't begin practice until the official opening of the school.)

The crew .trotted around the field and pulled up huffing and puffing, listened to McMillin caution them against straining themselves, did a few starts from a charging position, went through some setting up exercises, circled the field several times more, straggled into the gym, found the water cold, complained about the lack of towels and uncomfortable shoes, and foregathered again down in front of the pool hall, just like regular guys everywhere.

Clever press agenting and the mystery that surrounds the overnight champions have given the public a distorted view of this football team. One comes expecting to see men with pale, drawn faces filled with holy enthusiasm and eyes lit with the lurid light of the zealot fighting like crusaders of old. But instead, one finds a normal, clean cut gang of college boys who smoke cigarettes in the summer, but not during the season, hang out around cigar stands when off duty, and are out of uniform if they leave that frat pin at home on the bureau.

Charlie Moran was not here on Monday. He is still wearing the blue serge of a National League umpire and won't take over the directorial reins until September 15. Uncle Charlie has coached the Centre team since after the DePauw game in 1917, and they have not lost since.

Talk about personal attention! These fighting, crying, praying Colonels get more petting and pampering from Charlie Moran than any string of trotters on the Grand Circuit receive from a veteran trainer. Not that Moran is easy on the boys—quite to the contrary. Bo McMillin has been jerked out of a game for missing one tackle. Uncle Charlie takes the boys fast, but he looks after their physical well-being with his own eyes and hands.

Moran has a sewing machine which he operates in person. He sews up rips in pants and rents in jerseys. He repairs their shoes and smooths out rough places on the inner soles. And before every game, he bandages their ankles, arms and ribs. As a result, he loses few men through injuries. The famous Bo has never been out of play but three minutes due to "injury," and even then, it was only because he was so hoarse that he couldn't call signals.

A full game scrimmage was scheduled for September 23 with Uncle Charlie having been on the campus for the last four days. Even though it was just a glorified practice, there was a large crowd which wanted to see this edition of the Colonels in action. Bo was to quarterback the newcomers and Hump Tanner the regulars. Bo's value was further demonstrated by the fact that his relatively inexperienced group was able to hold their own while he ran their plays, but when he was switched to the veterans, he led a determined drive which marched the ball down for a quick score, highlighted by his 50 yard sprint. Fans on the sidelines noted that the veterans "whole countenance" changed when Bo switched to their team.

After the scrimmage, Uncle Charlie announced that from now on, until after the Harvard game, practices would be closed to "strangers." It was obvious that Centre wanted to perfect its attack away from the prying eyes of any scouts who may wish to size up the Colonels, especially if their reports may be sent back to Harvard, or even to Georgia Tech.

Thad McDonnell, one of the Fort Worth North Side boys, decided that he wasn't good enough to play and became the team's manager. He was asked by the two local papers to report on any injuries or to provide any other information which could be related to the team's fans. Fortunately, the only casualty that he reported was the shoulder injury suffered by Terry Snowday which kept him out of any of the drills requiring contact for much of September.

McDonnell related an interesting tidbit about Chick Murphy which was reported in both papers.

Murph, fleet little star, stepped out in a brand new pair of shoes. They had to be made to order because Chick's feet are so small. They are size 4½. He took a couple of laps in them and pronounced them to be fine.

The local papers also felt it necessary to carry any bit of news that they could pick up over the wire services about Harvard. The "Messenger" ran a front page story on September 20 under the headline:

HARVARD OPENS SEASON THIS SATURDAY

The story related that the Crimson coaches were satisfied with their team's progress and expected a big season. It was revealed that the line would average 185 pounds in the opener with Holy Cross on September 24.

The day before Harvard's first game, H.C. King, district passenger agent for the Southern Railroad, came down from Lexington to complete arrangements for a special train to take the team and fans to the October 23 game in Cambridge. The round trip ticket was to cost $110.00 which would include not only the train fare, but the Pullman tariff and all meals. (On a regularly scheduled, non-special, passenger train of the day, there was a fare charged just for the transportation to a destination. If someone wanted to ride in a sleeper car, a separate tariff was paid to the Pullman Company which owned and staffed the cars. The railroad operated the dining cars and charged for any meals served.)

The "Harvard Special" was going to be parked in the South Boston Terminal yard upon arrival. The train would be kept intact until the return trip so that those who wished could return to their car each night and avoid any extra lodging charges while in Boston. The team's headquarters was going to be at the Arlington Hotel at Tremont and Arlington, just a short cab ride from South Station, or a walk of several blocks.

Shortly after the arrangements for the "Special" were completed, Chief Myers received the welcome news that Harvard was holding 600 seats for Centre's fans on the 50 yard line, seats which were considered the prime location in Harvard Stadium. The ticket's price was $2, which put to rest the rumor that an exorbitant amount was going to be charged.

Meanwhile, even though all eyes were on Harvard, one month away, there was the matter of three games to be played before the momentous journey to the East. The Colonels knew that much of the luster would be removed if they didn't arrive in Cambridge undefeated. If they could sweep and go 3-0, they would be riding a 22 game winning streak when they went up against the Crimson. Likewise, if Harvard opened 4-0, their squad wouldn't have lost during their last 14 contests, the only blemish being the 10-10 tie with Princeton on the previous November 8.

Army was quoted as saying, "We're cheering for Harvard. We want to be the team that hopefully hands them their first defeat since 1916." (It must be remembered that Harvard didn't consider the war years' records as "official," and therefore didn't include any games during 1917-18 when compiling statistics.)

The Colonels' opening opponent was basically unknown regarding its strength. Morris Harvey (now the University of Charleston, in West Virginia) and Centre had played but once before, with the Mountaineers winning big in 1912.

In order to get ready for 1920, the student bodies of Centre and K.C.W. had spent several afternoons being trained in the cheers of the Gold and White. It was felt that the "Old Centre" spirit would never be more important than during the upcoming season.

MORRIS HARVEY OCTOBER 2, 1920

Morris Harvey, located in 1920 in Barbourville, West Virginia, took a west bound C&O train to Lexington, switched to a Southern Railroad car, and its 20 man team arrived in Danville late Friday afternoon, October 1.

Centre's starting lineup was as follows:

Left end	Stanley Robb	Pittsburgh, Pa.	6'	180 lbs.
Left tackle	Sully Montgomery	Fort Worth, Tx.	6'2"	215 lbs.
Left guard	Clayton Ford	Danville, Ky.	6'	193 lbs.
Center	Red Weaver	Fort Worth, Tx.	5'10"	162 lbs.
Right guard	Ben Cregor	Springfield, Ky.	5'10"	178 lbs.
Right tackle	Bill James	Fort Worth, Tx.	5'9.5"	170 lbs.
Right end	George Chinn	Harrodsburg, Ky.	5'11"	183 lbs.
Quarterback	Bo McMillin	Fort Worth, Tx.	5'9.5"	165 lbs.
Left half	Tom Bartlett	Owensboro, Ky.	5'10.5"	154 lbs.
Fullback	Red Roberts	Somerset, Ky.	6'	210 lbs.
Right half	Army Armstrong	Fort Smith, Ar.	5'10"	162 lbs.

The only regular who was on the sidelines was Terry Snowday, who still had his arm in a sling due to his sprained shoulder.

Centre's line averaged 183 lbs. The backfield, helped by big Red's 210 lbs., came in at 173 lbs., and the overall team average was just over 179 lbs., which was pretty respectable for the era. There were four starters from Fort Worth, five Kentuckians, and one each from Arkansas and Pennsylvania.

The 1920 edition of the Centre College Colonels went into action for the first time on October 2, at 2:45 in the afternoon. The team sported their new gold and white uniforms and their neat looking, green blankets with a gold "Centre" stitched across them.

Uncle Charlie kept it simple. Only five plays were used on offense. There were runs over the left or right tackle, sweeps around either end, and one forward pass formation. Moran wasn't going to reveal anymore than was needed. He knew there were scouts in the stands.

Five plays were adequate. The season was but three minutes old when Red Roberts plunged across the goal for the first points of 1920. By the end of the first quarter, it was 28-0.

With only three regulars in the lineup in the second quarter, the only score was a 30 yard field goal by Roberts to make it 31-0. During the third quarter, Centre scored twice to go up 45-0. In the last quarter, the Colonels added another 21 points to make it 66-0. The last score was a touchdown by Bill James who picked up a fumble and ran it in from the 20.

Morris Harvey tallied only two first downs all afternoon. Centre played 30 men, with only Bo and Red Roberts playing the entire 60 minutes. Uncle Charlie even let Sully Montgomery play in the backfield and the big tackle rumbled in for a score late in the game.

Touchdowns were spread evenly:

Bo	2
Army	2
Roberts	2
Whitnell	1
James	1
Montgomery	1

Red Weaver kicked nine extra points to run his consecutive string to 55. Centre now had won 20 straight.

HOWARD COLLEGE OCTOBER 9, 1920

If Morris Harvey came to Danville unknown, Howard College (now part of Samford University in Birmingham) was even more of a mystery. The Centre staff knew that in 1919, Howard had played tough against an excellent 8-1 Auburn team whose only loss was 7-6 to a tough Vanderbilt squad. Howard went down to Auburn by a respectable 19-6, and it was assumed that Howard would field a good team in 1920.

Centre was still holding its cards close to the chest. Practices remained closed.

Uncle Charlie wanted to trim the squad's numbers and pitted the third team against the fourth in order to determine who would be cut. A typical practice for the first two teams was a three hour workout, followed by six laps.

Everyone was healthy. Terry Snowday's arm was out of his sling. He was expected to see some action, but not to start.

Howard arrived on Friday morning, October 8. The team was led out on Cheek Field by captain "Bunny" Acton who had received special mention in the "Spalding's Official Football Guide" for his play the previous year. After a three hour workout, one of their young men was quoted as saying, "Just wait, you'll see a better battle, and the Colonels will realize that they're not up against another Morris Harvey."

It was hardly a prophetic comment. Centre played 31 men, scored 16 touchdowns, kicked three field goals, was good on 15 extra points, and crushed hapless Howard, 120-0.

Touchdowns were again spread throughout the team.

Bo	4
Chinn	4
Murphy	2
Snowday	2
Tanner	1
Roberts	1
Army	1
J.M. Liggett	1

Red Roberts kicked two field goals. Bo booted the other one. Red Weaver kicked 10 straight extra points to run his streak to 65, then turned the kicking over to Bo, who got four, and Roberts, who was good on one attempt.

Howard never registered a single first down. Centre was 2-0, and had now won 21 straight.

Uncle Charlie and the Chief had always taught their players that you prepared for the upcoming game, not for some opponent in the future. They abandoned that philosophy now that Harvard was only two weeks away. All plans were now being made with Harvard in mind. Even though Transylvania was next, the last three games had seen Centre win by a cumulative score of 149-3. The boys from Lexington were not in Centre's league now, and the coaches felt that they could concentrate on the Crimson from Cambridge, and not the Crimson from Transy.

To emphasize how seriously Centre took the Harvard game, Dr. Ganfield and the athletic committee authorized Uncle Charlie to hire two new line coaches prior to the Transylvania game. The Chief was a great help, but now Moran needed more specialized coaching, especially in the line, and a former University of Pittsburgh, All-American guard (1916), Claude "Tiny" Thornhill, arrived on campus along with a former Georgetown (D.C.) lineman and team captain, Daniel G. O'Connor, class of 1917, who had been recommended to Uncle Charlie by the legendary Jim Thorpe.

The arrival of the new line coaches allowed Uncle Charlie the time that he needed to expand the offensive arsenal. The team worked on running interference after a pass, with the goal to have at least seven men downfield after a completion, each with an assigned player to block. On Tuesday, October 12, the second team was equipped with crimson jerseys and simulated the Harvard attack. Uncle Charlie had received reports that Harvard had utilized a formation called the "revolving shift," and wanted to prepare his team so that the unusual lineup wouldn't catch his defense off guard.

The "shift" consisted of a Harvard lineman coming to the line of scrimmage and suddenly shifting to the opposite side of his line, resulting in unbalanced line, with four players to either the left or right of their center, while two men remained on the opposite side. The Colonels' defenders were placed according to whether the "shift" was to the left or right, and they quickly caught on to their positioning, shifting with their opponent's line shift.

"Shift left," Moran would instruct the Colonels, and his linemen would hop quickly over to the left of center. "Ben, you and Bill, slide over to your right if they shift in the opposite direction."

Then the second team went on the defense, and Bo took over the offense. Uncle Charlie had the team go into its passing drills, with several new patterns introduced. Lefty Whitnell was going to sub at halfback, and he and Bo worked on some plays, particularly new timing routes.

Lefty would dash down exactly 15 yards and cut sharply left. Bo would throw a bullet just as Whitnell cut out and the halfback would haul it in. Then, they'd run the same pattern but Lefty would do a little head fake like he was going to cut out, then would fly as fast as he could and Bo would hurl a high spiral, and again, his fleet back would reach out and pull it in. It was the same play that Bo and Lefty had combined on for that last touchdown against Kentucky the year before, which had eased the margin over the 50 point spread.

The only difference this year was that, "We'll set up the long pass first by running the cut-left before we go deep," said Uncle Charlie.

When the rest of the team had left the field after a hard, three hour practice, Lefty and Bo ran the two plays over and over until they were confidant that they had the timing down perfectly.

"We can put some points on the board with that combination," Bo said as they finally trotted off the field to the dressing room.

During the week prior to the Transy game, there was a diversion which interrupted practice. It had to be awfully important for Uncle Charlie to let it take any time away from the team's preparations, and was.

United States Senator Warren Harding, Ohio Republican, was running for president against another Ohioan, Governor James M. Cox. Harding was heavily favored nationally, but the race in Kentucky was neck and neck, and Harding's advisors felt it would be politically astute if their man were to come to Danville and do a little campaigning, mainly consisting of having a photograph made with the Colonels, the biggest attraction in the Commonwealth.

Harding, and his wife, along with Republican United States Congressman King Swope of Danville, and a large contingent of reporters and photographers, disembarked from the Southern Railroad station and were transported to Cheek Field where a platform had been constructed for the event.

The Colonels had suited up in their game uniforms and clustered around the candidate as he effusively praised "the Wonder Team, the best football team in all of America." On cue, the players let out a "Hip, hip, hooray, hip, hip, hooray for Harding." When the cheer ended, the students sitting in the wooden bleachers opened up with, "Hip, hip hooray, hip, hip, hooray for Cox."

As Harding tried to give his speech about a return to "normalcy," he was again interrupted by the students who cheered for Cox. Harding stopped in mid-sentence and admonished the students for their behavior. The team seemed greatly amused by the whole spectacle. The next day's "Advocate" defended the student's behavior, feeling that they had acted "in a gentlemanly way."

Kentucky was indeed a toss-up state. Cox garnered 456,497 votes to Harding's 452,400, and King Swope was voted out of office in the eighth distract, losing to Ralph Gilbert by a margin of slightly over 3000 ballots cast.

Of even more importance than a mere presidential candidate traveling to Danville was the return of Howard Reynolds, the Boston "Post" sports editor, who had sent a telegram to the Chief advising him that he planned to come to Danville as soon as the World Series between Brooklyn and Cleveland, which he was covering, concluded in Cleveland.

Reynolds boarded a train after the Indians won the seventh game on October 12, and headed south. He switched from the New York Central to the Southern in Cincinnati, came through Lexington, and arrived in Danville the morning of the 13th.

Howard Reynolds had a lot invested professionally in the upcoming October 23 game between Centre and Harvard. It was he who had first promoted intersectional games, and Reynolds and Eddie Mahan had personally validated Centre as a worthy foe for the Crimson, not only athletically, but as a college which ran a clean and honorable program.

Reynolds planned on sending daily stories back to his paper in order to build even more interest in the upcoming contest. Ticket sales had been brisk. It didn't appear that more publicity was really needed, such was the public's desire to see the little David appear against the Goliath of college football in its big horseshoe stadium.

However, Reynolds didn't just want the game to draw a big crowd. He wanted it to be an absolute sellout, and to that end, he was willing to spend 10 days promoting the Colonels. Reynolds felt that if Harvard had a big payday from the Centre game, it would make other Eastern programs see that at least from a financial standpoint, intersectional games were attractive, and the athletic committees of Yale and Princeton would want to get on board, as well as colleges such as Brown, Dartmouth , Columbia and Pennsylvania. Reynolds was on a mission, but no more so than the Centre College Colonels, the student body, and the fans throughout the state.

The "Harvard Special" was taking shape. Dr. Ganfield announced that all students who wished to go to the game would be excused from classes. They would have to make up the work missed, but they wouldn't have any penalties from their absences. Also, the Monday after the game was announced as an official school holiday.

Reports started coming in from Lexington and Louisville about special Pullmans which were going to be connected to the train originating in Danville. People wondered just how that whole enterprise was going to be run. Explanations were printed in various Kentucky papers.

The Southern Railroad was to be in charge. The rolling stock was to include the engine and coal car which would be owned by the Southern. The railroad was going to hook on two baggage cars. The "Special" was to be an all-sleeper train so those cars would be supplied by the Pullman Company. The dining car was operated by the railroad, not by the Pullman Company, even though it was built by Pullman.

The Southern would operate the train from Danville to Lexington where cars from Lexington and those brought over from Louisville would be connected. The "Special" would then be hauled to Cincinnati, still under Southern steam, where the New York Central tracks originated. The Southern engine and coal car would be disconnected and the NYC would take over. The entire trip from Cincinnati to Boston would be over the New York Central's tracks, or one of its subsidiary lines.

The number of Pullmans originating in Danville was eight, so with the baggage cars and dining car, there were eleven units. Two more Pullmans were going to be added in Lexington, one full of Lexingtonians and another which was going to be brought over carrying Louisvillians. The Pullmans were 14 or 16 section cars. A section could sleep up to four people. During the day, the seats would be in a daytime configuration. At night, a porter would slide the two lower seats together to make a lower bunk, comfortable for a couple, and pull an upper bunk down which would have been folded into the wall during the day. Then he'd draw curtains down so that each section would have some privacy.

The total number of passengers on the "Harvard Special" was right at 400, so an average of 40 passengers would occupy each car, with many of the sections having only two occupants.

Besides the "Special," plans were being made in New York City by the Centre Alumni Association to get the college's fans to Boston. Rooms were reserved at the team's hotel, the Arlington, and special cars were booked on the "Merchant's Express" of the New Haven Railroad, which was to leave New York at 4:00 p.m. and pull into Boston at 9:10 p.m., allowing the alumni time to hustle to the Arlington to meet friends for a late dinner and perhaps some bootleg libations. (Prohibition, due to the Eighteenth Amendment to the United States Constitution, went into effect on January 16, 1920.)

Besides the New Haven Railroad, plans for other modes of transportation were being firmed up. The Eastern Steamship Line's "Great Northern," was to leave the dock in New York late in the afternoon on Friday, October 22, and tie up the next day at Boston's harbor in plenty of time for the afternoon game.

For those who wished to be transported from New York by automobile, it was announced that several "touring cars" were going to be made available which could carry seven passengers each. The vehicles were going to take the Old Boston Post Road which went through New Haven and Providence. The distance was 226 miles. The drive time was 9-10 hours, if there were no flats.

With all of the excitement about the upcoming Harvard game, it was almost forgotten that the Colonels had a game with Transylvania on October 16. The last scrimmage which contained any contact was held on the 14th. The few locals who were allowed to watch noticed a significant change in the lineup. Bo was nowhere to be seen, and Hump Tanner was running the offense.

Uncle Charlie announced that Bo "has a little bit of a cold. Nothing serious, but I gave him the day off." Actually, Bo had gone to Cambridge to watch Harvard play Williams. Uncle Charlie knew that Bo wasn't needed in the Transy game. The Centre coach knew that nobody in the country was more astute about sizing up an opponent than Bo.

From now till the game with Harvard, it was going to be more mental preparation than physical. The Centre staff planned to run plays, but the players were told "absolutely no contact!"

There were long chalkboard sessions. Thornhill and O'Connor had played multiple times against Eastern teams and understood their style. A board was set up outside so that the players could sit in the stands and watch as formations were drawn up, and defensive or offensive plays were devised, hopefully for every Harvard strategy.

"We can't fumble and win."
"We can't have penalties and win."
"We have to not only be tougher physically, we have to be tougher mentally."
"We have to play smart."
"We can't make mistakes. We have to play a perfect game."

The Chief continuously fired up the team with stories about his Fort Worth North Side teams.

"We were better each year. The boys and I had a dream. We saw it. We envisioned it. We willed ourselves to be the best team in North Texas because we believed! No group of young men ever worked as hard as our team. We worked and we achieved! I've told you over and over—if you work—and you have—you'll become something. You'll become the champions of all football. You can go up there and beat Harvard. I know it!" Then the Chief spoke from his heart, his voice now much more subdued.

"But boys, no matter how the game comes out, I'll be as proud of you as anyone could possibly be. Because, I'll know you gave it your all. You fought for Old Centre. You fought for all of Kentucky. You fought for the pride of football players all over the South."

If the weather gods had wanted to design a perfect day for a football game, Saturday, October 16, in Danville, Kentucky, could forever serve as a model. There was just a slight chill, a gentle breeze, and only a wisp of an occasional cloud in the blue sky. The trees around the campus were barely beginning to turn, and soon there would be a palette of colors which made the fall so beautiful and anticipated in the Bluegrass.

While the weather was perfect, so was the Colonels' performance against an outgunned Transylvania squad. Many in the stands had come from the surrounding counties to see the team that was going to meet Harvard seven days hence. Some had never seen a game and didn't really understand what was taking place on the field below. But they cheered when others cheered, certain that something good had happened for the Gold and White, their team now.

Also sitting in the stands, marveling at how a team with such a rickety wooden stadium had become so accomplished, was Harvard quarterback coach, W.B. Felton, who hoped to see exactly what the Crimson could expect to see in Cambridge the following Saturday afternoon.

Later, Coach Felton went to the Centre dressing room and thanked Uncle Charlie and Chief Myers for the hospitality that had been extended to him during his stay in Danville.

"But I expected to see a football game," he said, as he shook Moran's hand. Of course, Felton knew that Centre wasn't going to show but basic football. The Colonels didn't need to play any other way in dealing with Transy. Centre had been such an overwhelming favorite that bettors couldn't find anyone to cover their wagers no matter how many points were given. The only bets during the afternoon were on how many first downs Transy may make.

Hump started at quarterback in Bo's absence. The game wasn't as close as the 55-0 margin would indicate. Centre played 26 men and led 17-0 after the first quarter, 24-0 at the half, ran it up to 38-0 after three periods, and then tallied two touchdowns and a field goal during the final quarter to end up, 55-0.

Again, the Colonels were very democratic in their scoring with Roberts, Army, Snowday, Hump, Uncle Charlie's son, Tom, Whitnell, and Allen, all crossing the goal. Red Roberts and Tom Moran each made good on a field goal.

The fans were really getting into Red Weaver's steak. The All-American was a perfect seven for seven, and now he had extended his consecutive string to 70. After each kick, the crowd would shout out the total:

64! 65! 66! 67! 68! 69! And finally, 70!!

For a period of the game, Moran instructed his team not to even try for a first down, but to run two plays into the line and punt so that the Colonels could practice their defensive formations.

Transy didn't register one first down. There were many who took money home, so certain were they that the Crimson couldn't move the ball against the Colonels even once for the needed 10 yards for a first down.

The only time Transylvania was able to get the ball into Centre's territory was when their quarterback, A.B. "Happy" Chandler, intercepted a pass and got it back past midfield. However, on the very next play, Chandler himself was intercepted and the Colonels again had possession. ("Happy" Chandler had quite a career. He was a United States senator, twice Kentucky's governor, and served as Commissioner of Major League Baseball, helping integrate the game by championing the Brooklyn Dodgers' efforts to add Jackie Robinson to their roster.)

Centre was now 3-0, the record that they wanted going into the Harvard contest. The winning streak reached 22. The Colonels' tough defense had given up only the two first downs that Morris Harvey picked up on passes. The combined score of the three opening games was 241-0. Not a bad start, but of course, everyone knew that the opponents hadn't been major powers.

PREPARATIONS FOR HARVARD INTENSIFY

Bo had seen Harvard beat Williams 38-0 while his teammates were toying with Transy. It was the first time he had ever experienced the vastness and grandeur of the beautiful, classical, horseshoe stadium across the Charles from the Harvard campus.

Williams had a quarterback named Ben Boynton who was a Walter Camp third team All-American the previous year. It was interesting for Bo to see a rival for honors in action, but the Crimson bottled up Boynton and the "Ephs'" offense. (The unusual nickname of the Williams' teams was derived from a shortening of the first name of Ephraim Williams who first had the idea for founding a college in western Massachusetts.)

The win over Williams made Harvard 4-0, and interestingly, neither the Crimson nor the Colonels had given up a point. Obviously, it seemed that something had to give.

Harvard	3	Holy Cross	0
Harvard	41	Maine	0
Harvard	21	Valparaiso	0
Harvard	38	Williams	0

Harvard was 9-0-1 in 1919 and had won four straight during the present season. Thus the stage was set. Harvard hadn't lost in the last 14 games. Centre had won 22 straight. As the week of Monday, October 18 began, an article in the "Messenger" conveyed to its readers how the team and Danville were facing the upcoming contest.

COLONELS BEING GROOMED FOR EASTERN TILT

Man o' War could not have been groomed any more carefully before his race with Sir Barton last week than the Centre Colonels in preparation for the Harvard game Saturday. (Man o' War beat Triple Crown winner, Sir Barton, by seven lengths in the Kenilworth Park Gold Cup in Windsor, Ontario. It was the great champion's final race, his 20th win in 21 starts, after which he was retired to stud at Faraway farm in Lexington, Kentucky.)

Hour after hour, Coach Moran, Chief Myers and assistants Thornhill and O'Connor, along with trainers McDonnell and Caudill, are making every effort to prime the eleven for the greatest intersectional battle in the history of college football.

The team is progressing nicely and though members are saying little, their thoughts could not be bound in a thousand volume library. The new assistants, both 200 pounders, know their football as well as Dr. Redd, Centre professor of languages since 1881, knows his Greek, which in the polite verbiage of the bystander, is "sure covering a lot of territory."

The coming game is being played on every street corner every hour of the day. Interest in the presidential race had been completely switched to Centre's chances against the Harvard Crimson. Enthusiasm is not confined to Danville and Boyle County, for reports from all over the state indicate that Kentucky athletic lovers are running on high and find it hard to wait for game time. "Play by play" will be called at Somerset, Lexington, Louisville, Franklin, Carlisle, Georgetown, Owensboro, Henderson, Ashland, and many other cities.

A quiz session was held last evening in the gym with mentors Moran and Myers at the blackboard. Plays were minutely detailed and each man was questioned as to his part in the formation. Skull practice is again scheduled for the next two days.

It is the tradition with Centre's teams to fight to the bitter end. That spirit was never manifested more than at Charleston, W.Va. last November. It is a general belief that Saturday's performance will eclipse even that record. The eyes of Kentucky and the South are leveled on the wearers of the Gold and White, and when the referee sounds the following interrogation—, "Are you ready Captain Horween? Are you ready Captain McMillin?"—there will be many who will spasmodically hold their breaths for the first return.

When it was mentioned that there was to be "play by play" regarding sporting events of the era, further explanation is in order. Prior to radio coverage, which was soon to come, the telegraph lines were utilized to pass on information. For sports such as football, there was a system in which a chalkboard was set up with the yard markers painted in white. Various businesses such as brokerage houses or newspapers, which already had regular telegraphic wire service connected, or even businesses which set up a wire just for a particular event, would receive a short summary of each play from an operator at the site of the contest, such as "Roberts runs 5," or "McMillin pass— Snowday 4." The operator on the receiving end would jot down each message and hand it to an "announcer" who would shout out the results. Meanwhile, an individual would be standing next to the chalkboard and draw a line to indicate what yard marker had now been reached.

Some "announcers" added a flourish to their telling of the results. "Roberts fights his way through the line and picks up a tough five yards!" "McMillin fires a bullet to Snowday who is tripped up after a quick four yard gainer."

In Danville, both the "Messenger" and "Advocate" announced that they were going to offer "play by play." The chief of police, George T. Thurmond, said he'd approved roping off Main Street between Third and Fourth to accommodate the crowds. The two biggest hotels in Lexington, the Phoenix and Lafayette, advertised in the local papers that they were "wired." In Louisville, there was to be a "broadcast" from in front of the

Hay hardware store, and from the stages of both the Strand and Ben Ali theaters.

Besides the skull sessions held by the coaching staff, captain and traveler Bo was given considerable time to describe what he had seen at the game between Harvard and Williams. Bo had a notebook in which he'd constantly written while sitting up in Harvard Stadium and refined on the long train ride from Boston. He would draw an offensive lineup and the resultant play on the board, and the coaches would discuss how to defense it. Another, and still another play—"Sully, if they line up like this, you…."

"Bill, what should you expect if you see this formation?"

Bo would draw different Harvard defensive schemes. "Here's where they may have a weakness if they spread out like this. It would be a good time to take it right over the left tackle. We've got to play smart. We can't beat ourselves. We have to constantly think, to analyze."

Other than doing laps in order to stay in shape, there was little time spent on the field. It was skull session after skull session. It was pep talk after pep talk. It was a time once again to believe. It was a time to achieve. It was a time to succeed in the greatest event that anyone connected to the team and to Centre College had ever experienced.

Ticket sales were far beyond the greatest expectations as the game day approached. As immense as Harvard Stadium was, it was announced that an additional 4,000 seats were being constructed in the north end zone which wasn't closed, to be sold for $1.50.

The end zone seats had been present in 1919 because Yale was playing in Cambridge that year. With the game with the Elis scheduled for the big bowl in New Haven in 1920, it wasn't felt that the temporary bleachers would be needed again until 1921, and they were removed and stored. Now, with the huge demand for seats, the wooden bleachers were trucked to the Stadium and workers were reassembling them. Additionally, box seats, five rows deep, were being constructed on the west side of the field below the permanent, concrete part of the horseshoe.

The gate receipts were announced at $72,000, and major numbers of orders were still coming in. One newspaper reported that an individual in the Harvard athletic department stated that 75,000 tickets could be sold if they were available.

Other than Yale and Princeton, and sometimes Dartmouth, no school had come close to having the appeal as Centre in Boston. Brown, Penn State, Virginia, and North Carolina couldn't come close to filling the Stadium. In the last intersectional game for the Crimson, the 1914 game with an excellent Michigan team, only 23,213 fans were in attendance, respectable, but just half the capacity of the Stadium.

Centre had been guaranteed $6,000.00. The game was going to be a huge financial success for Harvard. Certainly this was important to Howard Reynolds. His goal of having intersectional games become regular parts of the schedules of the Eastern colleges didn't have a chance to fly if it wasn't shown that such contests could be big money makers.

The Boston papers began giving major coverage to the game. Unlike today, when many metropolitan areas have perhaps one, or two major dailies, Boston was the home of multiple papers in 1920. There was the "Post," the "Globe," and "Herald." There was also the Boston "American," the "Traveler," and the "Daily Advertiser."

The "Post" published a large cartoon by Collier, a noted Eastern artist. Centre's team was depicted as an animal that "eats them alive," chewing up the Harvard squad. Another panel had the Colonels in circus-like wagons being transported from the train to the football field. The players were represented as having long, shaggy hair, with big mouths and prominent teeth able to chew up anything in sight. Still another area in the cartoon had a mother who was trying to get her child to quit crying. As a final resort, she threatened to send for a Centre player and the chap immediately goes silent.

Wednesday, October 20, was the last day of practice. The team actually took to the field in sweat suits and ran through some plays, perfecting timing, showered, broke for dinner, and then it was back to the drawing board for one more session. After the last diagram had been reviewed, the players walked the few blocks to the downtown, Boyle County courthouse.

It was a cool, clear night as a huge throng made its way to the plaza around the 1862 government building, its architecture inspired by studying the great buildings designed by Christopher Wren. Spotlights flooded the area. All of the students and faculty from K.C.W. were in attendance, as were the faculty members and students of Centre. Local citizens of Danville and from out in the county swelled the crowd to over 1,000. At exactly 7:30, cheerleaders George Swinebroad and Edwin Thomas began the pep rally by leading the cheers.

The members of the team were brought up on the wooden stage which had been constructed on the courthouse steps and asked to make a speech, and when each finished, a cheer resonated through the downtown, echoing off the walls of the nearby buildings. Many of the players ended their comments by assuring the onlookers that they had every intention of representing Centre and Danville by fighting as hard as they could, and—"We intend on winning!" The Chief and Uncle Charlie gave brief speeches, thanking everyone for the loyalty shown to "our boys."

Both Myers and Moran praised the spirit of the team. "They have great fellowship and conduct themselves as brothers."

After the pep rally wound down, the coaches led the players back to the gym to make certain that each member had packed all of their necessary equipment. Several of the Colonels came over to Red Weaver and pretended to search his bag to make certain that he had included his helmet. Other than ribbing Weaver, the expressions of each of the Colonels reflected a calm determination.

Then it was back to the dorm or their rooms in town for one last night's sleep before beginning the venture which each of the wearers of the Gold and White, which each of the coaches and faculty members, that all of Danville and so much of Kentucky, had dreamed about and made plans for since the telegram arrived from Harvard the previous December 10th.

It was, "ON TO HARVARD!!"

CHAPTER 7
CENTRE VS. HARVARD—1920

Boyle County had a population of 14,998 in the 1920 census, of which 6,000 lived within the city limits of Danville. Over 4,000 people were at the Southern Railroad's little brick station to see the team off on Thursday morning. Classes were delayed at Centre and K.C.W. so that the faculties and students could be at the station. The public schools were likewise closed for the morning. Businesses had signs on the doors and in the windows that they'd open after the "Harvard Special" pulled out, because, "We are at the station, and you should be, too!"

Many were seen running through town to get down to the tracks. One older man said, "I thought I may have caused a heart attack, but I knew for certain I'd have one if I didn't get here on time."

The Centre cheerleaders, waving the large Gold and White pennant presented to the school by the citizens of Danville at the halftime of the 1917 Georgetown game, led the team on the walk from the campus to the station. A deafening roar erupted as the players came into view. Several of the Colonels were seen to have glistening eyes when they saw such a mass of cheering humanity. The crowd slowly separated and allowed the players to walk toward the train.

"Go, Bo!"

"Red, Red! Win for Old Centre!"

The cheerleaders climbed up on top of one of the Pullmans and led the crowd in:

Centre, Centre, Fight! Fight! Fight!
Centre—Fight with all your might!

Then it was:

Fight, Gold and White!
Fight, Gold and White!
Fight, Gold and White!
Fight, Gold and White!
Fight! Fight! Fight! Fight!

Everybody wanted to just touch the players, to reach out and pat them on the back, to grab and shake their hands. There were constant shouts of encouragement.

"Good luck!"
"Go get 'em, guys!"

Two little twin, blond girls came up and handed a gold and white floral arrangement to Bo, and as he bent down to thank and hug them, one was heard to say, "Captain Bo, my mom and dad said they are so proud of you and your team."

The players made their way to the last Pullman which would be their private home for more than 24 hours. The travel squad was made up of 27 players. The 16-section sleeper was set up for 32 passengers, with coaches Moran and Myers and their wives, and team manager/trainer, Thad McDonnell, rounding out the number to full capacity.

One of the well-wishers at the station was Lucien Becker from Winchester, Kentucky. He had pulled up, covered with dirt, in front of the Gilcher at midnight, "after driving over the dustiest roads in all Kentucky." He was Centre, class of 1892, and, "I just had to be here boys. I'd have gotten here if I'd had to crawl."

The Colonels were dressed in their "travel togs" which Bo had designated. Bo had certain superstitions. He decided after the West Virginia game, when he had worn a soft blue shirt, tie and khakis, and things had gone so well, that this attire was the team's "good luck" outfit, and so while on the train, this was what everybody wore under their sportcoats. Ever conscious of their image, they would change into proper white shirts, ties and suits before disembarking in Boston.

The train began to fill with the fans who were boarding in Danville. The travelers would hook up with those from Lexington and Louisville which would swell the entourage to 400.

Then it was "all aboard." The bell on the front of the big steam engine was ringing, the whistle announced the departure, and the "Harvard Special" slowly churned out of the station at exactly 8:00 a.m., right on schedule, heading north toward Lexington.

Included in the departing passengers were 50 Centre students. When the team members were added, it meant that one third of the student body was heading to the East.

Howard Reynolds had booked a berth on one of the Pullmans, but was going to ride in the team's car until the seats were converted to beds for the evening. Paul Dexheimer, who had coached Bo, Red Weaver, and Red Roberts at Somerset High, made the trip, as did Red Roberts' mother and sister. George Chinn, Sr. from Harrodsburg was going to watch his son, George, Jr., play. Bruce Dudley, sports editor of the Louisville

"Herald," was on the train. Hump Tanner's and Clayton "Paps" Ford's fathers were along. Of course, the two Danville papers had their representatives aboard.

As the train neared High Bridge outside of Danville, the passengers noticed a large crowd which had gathered just past the span which crosses the Kentucky River. Some children were holding a sizable, white banner painted with gold letters which said, "GO GOLD AND WHITE." Another said, "BEAT HARVARD!" Everyone along the tracks waved and blew kisses as the "Special" steamed by, whistle blowing.

Further along, the train slowed as it moved through Nicholasville. At the town's station, scores of people were lined along both sides of the track, cheering and smiling as they exchanged waves with those peering out of the Pullmans.

At 8:55, the engine braked as the "Special" pulled into Lexington. The "Leader" and "Herald" had both publicized the arrival time, and the platform in front of the station was lined many deep with proud residents who had come out to greet the team. The University of Kentucky and Centre may have been rivals, but now everyone was a Kentuckian and brimming with pride that their own people were on the way to meet the "Giant of the East."

The entire Kentucky football team and their coaches had come to the station to cheer the Colonels. Bruce Dudley of Louisville's "Herald" filed stories along the way as the train headed east. Every station had a Western Union office, and he would type out his impressions and hand them to an operator to wire back to his Louisville paper.

Of the Lexington experience, he wrote:

Tears came to the eyes of the Centre men at Lexington, where the University of Kentucky team, Centre's oldest and severest rival, met the train and gave dozens of rousing cheers for the Centre warriors.

"This is one time we are with you Centre fellows, heart and soul," yelled a big Kentucky halfback. "Go get 'em Centre, and tear 'em to shreds."

Uncle Charlie turned to me and said that the Wildcats' action was one of the most generous things he'd ever experienced in all of his coaching career.

At 9:08, the switch-engine had completed its work, hooking on the Pullmans filled with passengers from Lexington and Louisville. The whistle blew and the train chugged out of the station, heading north toward Cincinnati, sent on its way by the cheering crowd.

During the layover in Cincinnati, while the Southern engine was disengaged and the New York Central's was connected, one of the passengers jumped off the train and picked up a copy of the Cincinnati "Times Star" because he noticed a headline which read:

FOOTBALL CAPITAL
IS DANVILLE THE FOOTBALL CAPITAL
OF THE UNITED STATES?

On Saturday, Centre College will carry the banner of Southern football onto Soldiers Field. That banner may not stay there. Retreat, honorable retreat, may become necessary. But Harvard will know there has been a football game.

Last year, Centre was the champion of America according to the rather unsatisfactory method of determining the championship, comparative scores. Centre badly defeated West Virginia, West Virginia decisively defeated Princeton, and Princeton played Harvard to a tie. Unfortunately, Centre had no games with the East that could give her a title not "once removed." But her successes of last year have given her an honored place on Harvard's schedule this fall. We shall soon know if Danville, Kentucky is the football capital of America, as was claimed by Centre's partisans last year. Here's hoping that it is.

The train left Cincinnati on the "Big Four" (Cleveland, Cincinnati, Chicago and St. Louis Railroad) tracks, part of the New York Central system, and headed northeast across the length of Ohio toward Cleveland. At every stop in Ohio, Centre alumni and friends met the "Special" and came aboard to greet old friends before being hurried off so the journey could commence once again.

A Danville "Advocate" reporter, W.V. Richardson, sent a story back to his paper when he jumped off the train in Cleveland and handed his typed report to the Western Union operator at the terminal.

As the "Old Centre Special" pulled out of Dayton, Ohio, on the New York Central line's double track, a fast passenger train raced for half an hour with our train, first one pulling slightly ahead, then the other. The crowded train had discovered on their last stop that our train carried the Centre College gladiators, and a great demonstration was given. Word had gone forth that the Centre football squad would pass through Ohio and crowds had gathered at each of the stations to give cheers. People in Danville little realize how popular the team is away from home, and how well posted the people are about the Old Centre "Wonder Team."

Two Boston newspapers, the "Herald" and the "American" had sent sports writers to Cleveland where they joined Centre's train for the rest of the trip east. The writers brought the cheering news that Harvard was taking the upcoming game "very seriously."

Heading east out of Cleveland, the "Special" continued on the New York Central's tracks and entered Pennsylvania, stopping at Erie, where "Advocate" reporter Richardson once again hopped off at the station and turned over another dispatch to be sent back to his paper.

Our train has been running on schedule all the way. Everyone is happy. The trip is a veritable house party. Old Centre men have met the train at every stop and the greatest enthusiasm was shown at all of the stations in Ohio. The Boston "Herald" and "American" reporters said every seat had been sold for the game and another 4,000 seats had been constructed which sold out quickly.

Along the way, every Ohio newspaper which I could find was full of news about the "Special" and about the Harvard-Centre game.

With the large passenger load, meals were served quickly. The dining car had ample seating so that the team and family members could all be accommodated together. The team's Pullman was the last car, and as the members walked through the other cars to the diner, they were treated like the celebrities they had become.

It was, "Hey champs, let's show those Harvard boys the way Kentuckians play the game."

"Bo, Bo, will you sign this newspaper?"

It was midnight before most of the travelers got into their berths. The "Special" ran through the northwest corner of Pennsylvania and into New York. The Colonels slept through most of the Empire State as the train passed through Buffalo, Rochester, and Syracuse. After a stop in Albany, the team was in the dining car for breakfast as they crossed the Hudson River just east of Albany, and by doing so, entered the Commonwealth of Massachusetts.

BOSTON

The "Special" pulled into Boston's South Station 28 ½ hours after it had steamed out of Danville, at 1:30 Friday afternoon, Boston time, which was an hour ahead of Danville, as Boston was still on Eastern daylight time. Five hundred people, mainly Centre alumni from throughout the Northeast, met the train and gave rousing cheers as the players and fans disembarked. Buses were waiting which carried the entourage to Centre's headquarters, the Arlington Hotel.

As the players entered the lobby of their hotel, they noticed posters placed near the desk advertising the "Harvard-Center" game. (The "Center" spelling was also used on the official programs and tickets for the game.) After checking in at the Arlington, the Colonels gathered up their gear and led by their captain, Bo, reboarded the buses at 2:30 for the trip to Harvard Stadium. Only Bo, who had been in Boston the week before to scout the Harvard-Williams game, had ever seen the big horseshoe. Despite his efforts to describe it, and despite photographs which had been shown back in Danville, no one, including Uncle Charlie and the Chief, was prepared for the beauty and magnificence of Harvard Stadium.

Head football Coach Robert Fisher and Harvard team manager W.P. Belknap, Jr., waited outside the stadium as the team filed off the buses. Fisher and Belknap welcomed Uncle Charlie and Chief Myers, and then impressed the Centre players by shaking hands with each of the Colonels, warmly welcoming them. They called Bo and the two Reds by name, and asked each of the other team members to introduce himself. (Robert Fisher was a 1910 and 1911, Walter Camp All-American at Harvard, in a guard position. He became the head coach in 1919 after serving as an assistant under

Percy Haughton, his coach during his playing days. Fisher's 1919 team was 9-0-1, the last win being a 7-6 win over Oregon in the January 1, 1920, Rose Bowl. Going into the Centre game, Harvard was 4-0, giving Fisher a record at the time of 13-0-1, the tie being with Princeton, 10-10, in the seventh game of the 1919 campaign.)

The two Harvard men led their guests to the visiting team's locker room which was in a separate building at the north end of the stadium. Along the way, Moran and Myers were assured that no one other than those approved by Centre would be allowed to watch their practice, that Harvard students were guarding the gates, and that the Colonels could be certain that they were going to be able to work out in total privacy.

The way that Centre was welcomed and treated made quite an impression on the Kentuckians, and the courtesies shown that afternoon were the first of many that their gracious hosts bestowed.

After suiting up and getting some last minute instructions, the Colonels walked out of the locker room toward the stadium and came around the end of the horseshoe to the opening separating the new end zone seats from the concrete structure. As they entered, they were, to a man, awestruck.

Harvard Stadium was constructed on land south of the Charles River, in Boston's Allston neighborhood, across the river from Cambridge. The acreage, called Soldiers Field, had been vacant, and the school was able to purchase it thanks to bequests made by Henry Wadsworth Longfellow, his family, and Henry Lee Higginson.

Construction of the large, concrete stadium took place during 1902-03, and the first football game was played there on November 14, 1903, an 11-0 loss to Dartmouth.

The building of the stadium literally changed the way the game is played to this day. Due to the increasing number and severity of injuries (which resulted in President "Teddy" Roosevelt getting involved), the rules committee, chaired by Walter Camp, was set to recommend that the playing field be widened 40 yards to give players more room to maneuver. However, Harvard Stadium would have had to undergo reconstruction if such a widening took place, and the committee adopted the legalization of the forward pass instead in order to more open up the game.

The stadium was bathed in sunshine as the team trotted out on the perfectly manicured turf. The wooden, north end zone bleachers had just been completed, and the boxes along the sideline were finished, bringing the capacity to 45,000 seats. The open area above the colonnade would allow another two to three thousand spectators to watch the game.

Uncle Charlie and the Chief gave the players time to walk around the field, allowing the magnitude and magnificence of the facility to sink in. They didn't want the Colonels to act stunned or overwhelmed on tomorrow's game day. It was acclimation time.

The stadium combined the features of a Roman circus and a Greek amphitheatre. The colonnade was added in 1910, circling the entire upper level of the horseshoe, creating the feeling of being thrown back into the classical styles of Rome and Athens. Several of the team climbed up into the stands and sat silently, trying to absorb the scene and permanently burn it into their consciousness. Centre was used to playing sometimes before crowds of as few as 1,500. A great crowd was several thousand. Over 45,000 was hardly fathomable.

Bruce Dudley accompanied the team to the workout. He captured some of the emotion when he wrote:

George Chinn, the youngest player on the Centre team, is barely 18. He had not been out of the state of Kentucky until this epochal offensive was launched. Today we trod the sacred soil at Harvard. Chinn walked within the huge horseshoe which surrounds nine-tenths of the field. Removing his headgear, he gazed heavenward and raising his hand as if taking an oath, declared, "This time tomorrow we'll show them what Centre men are made of. We will win, or else..."

Dudley continued:

Such is the spirit with which Centre hopes to batten down the last obstacle in its path to football pre-eminence. "Or else..." Every Colonel vows he will do his utmost to bring honor and glory to Centre and Kentucky, "Or else..."

The sentence has never been finished. They are only living for tomorrow and victory. They care naught what happens to them unless the triumph is gained. The triumph will open to Centre and Kentucky a new world. The Centre spirit is the spirit that turned back the foe at Chateau-Thierry. The battle cry is, "They shall not pass."

Dudley spoke to Bo and Uncle Charlie:

Bo McMillin quietly said that the team shall fight until consciousness is lost. "We will show them nerve like they've never seen before."

"We are ready," said Uncle Charlie. "If we lose, we can have no alibi. No courageous team ever needs an alibi. The old guard may die, but never surrenders. My boys have that kind of stuff in them. It is for Centre, and it is for the entire state of Kentucky."

After some minutes had passed, Uncle Charlie called for the team to gather around him. "Bo, set up the offense. Second eleven, get into defensive position like Harvard does. Let's spend 30 minutes on offense and then reverse the roles. Be sharp! No mistakes!"

The team looked crisp, running their plays with precise timing. Halfway through the offensive drills, Bo signaled to Lefty Whitnell with a wink and the Fulton, Kentucky speedster took over the position at left half. After Bo called the signals, Lefty streaked out as he had done so many times during practice back in Danville, gave a little head fake, and turned it on straight down the field. Bo heaved the ball as far as he could, and just like they had done against Kentucky in 1919, Lefty hauled in the ball, never breaking stride, and ran like a rabbit toward the end zone. When he got back to the huddle, Bo winked again. "We can score on that play tomorrow. Just wait and see."

When the practice session was over, the stadium was opened to reporters and photographers. The Colonels were lined up in their starting formation and numerous shots were taken. President Ganfield, Bo and Uncle Charlie were photographed, Bo with his helmet on, looking very serious and determined. Ganfield expressed confidence but made no predictions. He simply repeated that Centre "should make it an interesting game."

Sports reporters from the newspapers then converged on Coach Moran. It was stated that there had never been as many news organizations covering a Harvard game as there were on the tuft that day. All of the numerous Boston papers were there. New York had reporters from the "Times," the "Daily News," the "World," and "Herald," around Uncle Charlie.

The Providence "Journal" was represented, and reporters from New Haven, Hartford, and many other northeastern cities were covering the game for their readers, as were the various wire services which would send their coverage to newspapers all across the country. Of course, the Danville papers had their men on the field, as did the papers from Lexington and Louisville.

The importance of the Centre-Harvard game was emphasized by the fact that standing in the group circling Uncle Charlie were the two most famous sportswriters of their day, Grantland Rice and Damon Runyon, plus there was an even more distinguished gentleman on the field.

Walter Camp, selector of the All-America team each year, the same man who had bestowed the ultimate college football recognition to Bo and Red Weaver by placing them on his first team, and to Red Roberts, a third team selection, listened intently to the Centre coach as he began to speak.

"The boys are in good fighting form. We now figure we are like an Eastern college because we have gotten so much attention from you here in this part of the country."

"Football is a man's game. We play it hard and clean. I am a stickler for clean sport and insist on it. We feel that in meeting Harvard we will be tackling a worthy foe, but that it will know that it has been in a struggle before the game is over. Centre has confidence in its men. They will battle to the end, and when the game is over, no matter who wins, it will be said that Centre played a clean game, and we are from a college that Harvard will have no regrets about putting on its schedule."

"I am not in the habit of making predictions or claiming anything. Experience has taught me that lesson. All I can say is that it is going to be a football game worthy of the name in every word."

It was significant that Uncle Charlie stressed that Centre would play hard but cleanly. "I am a stickler for clean sport and insist on it." It was something the Centre mentor stressed everyday in his discussions with "his boys." Uncle Charlie often emphasized that the way one conducts oneself on the field is the way that life will later be conducted once college days are long past. It was characteristic of Centre's teams during this era that no matter how the game ended on the scoreboard, every rival felt that they had played a foe that was above reproach regarding sportsmanship.

Moran fielded a few questions as his team ran three laps and then headed to the dressing room to shower and dress to re-board the bus. The Harvard team manager told the Colonels that they could leave their equipment in the dressing room and would find that their uniforms had been washed and dried and put back in their lockers when they returned for the game the next day.

"Can you believe that? They're going to wash our uniforms!"

It was a long way from Danville, they all had to agree. The water was hot, the soap and towels bountiful, and the uniforms were going to be washed, even though they had just run through drills with no contact.

Instead of heading back to the Arlington, the bus drivers steered over the Anderson Memorial Bridge, often referred to as the Larz Anderson bridge because its construction was funded by a donation from Larz in honor of his father, Nicholas Longworth Anderson.

The Chief had been anxious for the team to see Harvard's campus during the daylight hours, and the buses parked at a kiosk on Harvard Square where the players bought ice cream and then walked through the Class of 1875 Gate into Harvard Yard.

Across the Yard was the massive Widener Library, completed just five years previously. One Colonel walked around the huge building and announced that all of the buildings on Centre's campus would fit within the massive edifice, and there'd be plenty of room to spare. They contrasted the buildings around Harvard Yard to those of Centre.

"It's no prettier, just bigger," and to a man, they agreed that they wouldn't trade their little college for all of the monumental structures on all of the campuses anywhere in the world.

"We are Centre men."

The Colonels climbed the steps up toward the Widener's colonnade and sat down, finishing their cones and watching the students come and go. After a while of just sitting in silence, the Chief beckoned and it was back on the buses and to the hotel to get ready to come back to the campus, and the Harvard Union, which was holding a dance in honor of the team and all of the Kentuckians who had come to the East for the big contest the next day.

The dance featured an orchestra made up of Harvard men and young ladies from Radcliffe. The invitation stated that the visitors would be taught the "Touchdown Dance," and they were also invited to a pre-game buffet and another dance to be held Saturday night after the game.

The Colonels were treated like kings at the party. Red Roberts was the star Colonel in the "Touchdown Dance," in which after several dance steps, the music would suddenly stop and the participants would thrust their arms in the air like an official would during a football game after a score, and shout—

"Touchdown!"
"Touchdown!"
"Touchdown!"

The players made it an early evening.

"It was a long trip up here, and we have a football game tomorrow."

They left the Union in good spirits. No one could have been treated more nicely than the Gold and White.

It was estimated there were more than 700 fans of the Colonels in the city, many wearing badges and some carrying Centre pennants. A group of Centre rooters had gone to the stadium to watch the workout. A supporter stood at the gate and identified "non-strangers" who were allowed to sit up in the stands. Most found the seats they would occupy the next day.

Those who didn't make their way to the practice session took in the sights of Boston and the surrounding area. More than 45 climbed the Bunker Hill Monument, and well over 100 hit the long trail to Lexington to see where the "Minute Men" fired, "The shot which was heard around the world."

The Boston "Globe" reported:

It was a gay gathering of tourists that invaded the Boston theaters last night. More than a month ago a theatre not far from the Boston Common reserved scores of seats for the "sons and daughters" of the Bluegrass Country, and if anyone thinks that blazing red makes color, they should note what Kentucky's gold and white can make for scenic effect when combined with enthusiasm and a chance for a good time.

Every Kentuckian who had the price, and dozens of past and present Centre students, accompanied their team. For them, there can only be one result of the game—victory. The visitors needed no badge to show who they were, and they were welcomed everywhere they ventured.

The arrival of the Centre team had every newspaper in Boston printing big, boldly headlined stories. The "American," "Globe," "Herald," "Post," and "Transcript" all ran front page coverage about, "The Wonder Team from Kentucky." Interest was enhanced by emphasizing the disparities between the two colleges. Always, it was the numbers which made good reading.

Little Centre College with only 200 students while Harvard has more than 6,000… Centre, with only six buildings on its campus, while there are hundreds at the Cambridge school… Centre has only 14 professors. Harvard has more deans, 18, than Centre has faculty members, and its 222 professors are a greater number than the little Danville college has in its entire student body.

The differences in numbers of students, buildings and faculty weren't pointed out to ridicule Centre. On the contrary, they were stressed with a sense of wonderment. It was basically, "How can such a small, unknown college from Kentucky accomplish so much?"

All of the publicity pushed the prices for the game to levels unheard of since Harvard began playing football. First it was reported that some people were selling their tickets for twice what they paid. Then four, eight, twelve times—if anyone could be found who would even consider selling one.

Betting was brisk. Harvard supporters wanted 10 to 6 odds, while Centre wanted 4 to 10. (This meant that Harvard bettors would be willing to risk $10.00 in order to win $6.00, while Centre supporters would only risk $4.00 to win $10.00.)

GAME DAY—OCTOBER 23, 1920

The Centre team and fans awoke to a pleasing forecast on Saturday morning. The papers reported there would be a moderate, fresh wind from the north, just enough to set the clouds drifting and flooding the stadium with sunshine, and, *The man with a heavy coat and sweater will perhaps be following the calendar rather than the actual weather conditions.*

The team had an 8:00 breakfast together in the Arlington dining room. Uncle Charlie wanted his players to relax before the ride out to the stadium, so the Colonels walked as a group to the Boston Common and then through the 50 acre park toward Beacon Street. Along the way, they were stopped frequently by Bostonians who wished them well in the upcoming game. It seemed that every occupant of the city knew about the team and why they were there.

On leaving the Common, the Colonels turned left onto Beacon and strolled past the rows of town homes which lined the beautiful street on the Back Bay. After walking seven blocks, they turned left on Gloucester and in another two blocks, headed back east on Commonwealth Avenue, a boulevard lined with four and five story Victorian, Classical Revival and Renaissance-styled townhouses with arched windows, wonderful fanlights and rusticated stonework. Even though their minds were focused on the game, they couldn't help but marvel at the beauty of the great architecture that graced the wonderful neighborhoods of Boston.

"It's a little different than Danville," they all agreed.

Then it was back to the Arlington. A light lunch was served and the squad retired to a meeting room for one more chalkboard session. Thad McDonnell taped the player's ankles using the special technique that Coach Moran had used so successfully over the years.

Chief Myers had written the team's creed in big letters across the top of the chalkboard.

BELIEVE! ACHIEVE! SUCCEED!

The room was quiet as the Chief began to speak.

"Men, within the hour, we will board our buses and travel to the most wonderful stadium in the country to play the famous Harvard Crimson football team. For many of you, this journey started when you were but boys from Fort Worth."

"For others, the mission truly began when we beat Kentucky State in 1917, a team that had beaten us 68-0 the year preceding. After that game, we began to truly believe that we could accomplish great things. Still others of you have been on our team but for the three games played this season. But no matter how long you have been members of the Centre College football family, each of you will forever remember this day."

"We ask only one thing of you. Play hard. Play clean. Remember that not only the eyes of those in the Stadium will be on you, but the eyes of all of Danville, of the state of Kentucky, of the hundreds of thousands of fans from all over the country who each week have followed your successes."

"On every play, remember that you are Centre men. Play accordingly. Give it all that you have, and no matter what the final outcome, walk off the field with your head held high, for you will be victorious no matter what the final score."

The Chief had never given a more heart-felt, eloquent, pre-game speech. He then turned the time over to Uncle Charlie who gave a few last minute instructions, drawing the sequence of the first series of offensive plays on the board.

"From then on Bo, you'll have to call the signals from what you feel and see out there on the field. But let's start this way to get into the flow."

It was then to the team buses for the ride to Harvard Stadium. The vehicles were led by two motorcycle policemen with sirens blaring. The buses had gold and white banners taped to the sides—CENTRE COLLEGE COLONELS. It seemed that everyone who turned to look at the escorting 'cycles quickly smiled and waved and gave the universal thumbs up-good luck!-sign. The players could hear the many shouts of encouragement through the open windows.

"All the way, Colonels!"

"Take it to them boys!"

"You can do it, Colonels!"

And the one that they didn't really understand.

"Beat Harvard!"

M.I.T. students or grads, or those who were from Boston College, or Boston University, or even Holy Cross, would have liked nothing better to see the Crimson beaten.

It was a matter of wanting to see the college that they perhaps hadn't been able to enter, for whatever reason, brought down to earth, especially if that leveling could be accomplished by a little school from Kentucky.

As the team buses were carrying the squad to the stadium, the crowds were already beginning to find their way to Soldiers Field. The Boston elevated was running extra trains from the Andrew to Stadium Station. The Harvard student body and Radcliffe girls walked from their campuses over the Anderson Memorial Bridge which took them right onto North Harvard Street and into Soldiers Field.

The open field around the stadium began to be dotted with cars, though most fans arrived by mass transit or by foot. Slowly, the seats began to fill. Those who wished to see the game, but didn't have an assigned seat, first filled the temporary, general admission, end zone seats. After they were taken , the five story towers which anchored the open end of the stadium provided stairwells for fans to climb to the top of the colonnade where they first occupied the area opposite the 50 yard line, and then filled the roof all of the way around the stadium.

Centre's buses ground to a halt outside of the locker room. A cheer went up as the team stepped off. The Colonels smiled but made no comments as they filed into the building. The demeanor of the team was deadly serious. Each member knew that they were about to embark on the most important day in their young lives.

After everyone suited up, their cleaned uniforms removed from the hooks in their lockers, the quietness was broken as the speeches began. The Chief again exhorted the Colonels to "go out and win one for Old Centre."

Uncle Charlie reminded his players that they were now about to step out on the field "where the greatest moment that Centre has ever experienced is about to unfold."

"You're going to see over 45,000 people in the great Harvard Stadium. The impression that you make will forever remind each of them about your college, about Centre men. Play hard. Play clean. Show each and everyone what Centre men are made of."

"You can do it, men! You can do it."

Chief Myers leaped to his feet.

"Believe! Believe! Believe!"

Moran pulled a large number of telegrams from his leather briefcase.

"These are from all over Kentucky, all over the South. Each of them is wishing you success on the field this afternoon. Let me read one in particular, the message from Governor Morrow of our great Commonwealth.

"Today you will bring honor and glory to all of Kentucky by your actions on the field against Harvard. On behalf of our citizens, I wish you great success in your historic undertaking. I shall not be there in person, but I shall be there in spirit, as will all of Kentucky."

Bo then asked the Colonels, the Praying Colonels, to kneel. It was his honor and duty as the team captain to offer the prayer before this, the most important game that he or anyone else had ever played.

Once again, it wasn't a prayer for victory. During the previous day's session with the press, one player had been asked by a curious reporter just exactly what was said during the pregame ritual.

"It is a private prayer. We know that God doesn't favor one team over another. We simply pray that we play with courage. We pray for each other. We pray for our opponents. We pray that there are no injuries, that we play with honor. And we give thanks to the Almighty that we have been given the ability to represent Old Centre. It gets pretty emotional at times, I guess. But it's part of our spirit, and I consider myself fortunate to play for a team that feels that prayer is an important part of our lives."

Bo gave a long and emotional benediction. There wasn't a dry eye in the locker room when he finished with, "May God grant the blessing of the Almighty on our endeavor today. Amen, and amen."

Then there was the blur of the Gold and White as they streaked out of the dressing room and came around the temporary bleachers and onto the field. A huge, spontaneous roar erupted as the crowd saw the Colonels emerge. It was 2:30, just 30 minutes till the kickoff.

Every Centre fan who had been at the Arlington had been given a yard long, gold and white streamer prior to leaving for the game. Extra ones had been brought to the stadium for those who were arriving from other locations and were sitting in the Centre section, directly on the 50 yard line. The Colonels' fans were on their feet, waving their streamers wildly, cheering for their boys from Kentucky.

Another roar drowned out the Centre partisans as the Crimson of Harvard, 38 strong, led by captain Arnold Horween, trotted out on the turf and jogged to the opposite end of the field. The Crimson band, formed the year before to bring spirit and enthusiasm to the school's football games, marched in behind their team, playing the college's fight song, "Soldiers Field."

O're the stands in flaming Crimson
Harvard banners fly.
Cheer on cheer like volleyed thunder
Echoes to the sky.
See! The Crimson tide is turning—
Gaining more and more.
Then, Fight! Fight! Fight!
For we win tonight!
Old Harvard, forevermore!

Harvard head coach, Robert T. Fisher, led nine assistant coaches, all Harvard alumni, onto the field, trailed by the Crimson team manager, assistant manager, and the veteran trainer, "Pooch" Donovan. It was quite a contrast to Uncle Charlie, Chief Myers, and trainer/manager, Thad McDonnell.

"Can you believe this?" Bo shouted to Army, pointing to the stadium. "Did you ever think we'd be playing in front of all these people?"

"Look sharp, boys! Look sharp," Uncle Charlie said as the offense ran through its drills."

George Swinebroad, Jr., from Lancaster, Kentucky, led the Centre faithful in cheers. He was dressed in all-white down to his white shoes, with flannel slacks, and a wool sweater with a gold "C," shouting into a gold megaphone with a white painted "C."

Fight, Centre Fight!
Fight, Centre Fight!
Fight, Centre Fight!
Fight, Centre Fight!
Fight! Fight! Fight! Fight!
Fight! Fight! Fight!

As the scene was unfolding in Harvard Stadium, crowds were forming all over Kentucky to listen to the re-creation of the game that was going to be sent telegraphically throughout the Commonwealth of Kentucky. With Main Street roped off, it seemed that the entire population of Danville and Boyle County was massed in the street.

At 2:55, referee Robert W. "Tiny" Maxwell called for the team's captains, Arnold Horween and Bo, to join him at midfield for the toss of the coin to determine who would kick. As the shiny Morgan silver dollar flipped in the air, Bo called "heads" and the coin landed obverse up in the grass.

"We will receive," Bo said.

A cheer arose from the crowd when the huge, 300 pound plus Maxwell placed Horween's back toward the open end of the horseshoe, lined Bo across from him, and then stood beside the Harvard captain and carried out a kicking motion.

"They kick—we receive—great start!"

GAME TIME! THE FIRST HALF

H.H. Faxon, a burly Crimson tackle, boomed a kick down to the 10 yard line where it was fielded cleanly by Bo and returned to his own 22.

As Centre set up for its first play from scrimmage, the lineup was as follows:

POSITION	PLAYER	WEIGHT
Left end	George Chinn	180
Left tackle	Sully Montgomery	210
Left guard	Clayton Ford	180
Center	Red Weaver	158
Right guard	Stanley Robb	176
Right tackle	Bill James	170
Right end	Terry Snowday	173
Quarterback	Bo McMillin	168
Left halfback	Army Armstrong	157
Right halfback	Tom Moran	155
Fullback	Red Roberts	210

Across the line was a Harvard squad that substantially outweighed the Colonels. Centre's line averaged 178 pounds, while the Crimson front wall weighed in at an average of 192. There was an equal discrepancy in height, with Centre having only Sully Montgomery who topped six feet. Everyone in the trenches for Harvard was at least six feet tall, with five starters exceeding 6'1".

Centre opened with three line plunges which went nowhere and punted to the Harvard 35. The Crimson then began a seven play drive right through the Colonels' defense which looked helpless to stop the attack.

The Harvard backfield was composed of little "Fitzie" Fitzgerald, the quarterback, George Owen, a talented 179 pounder at left half, "Winnie" Churchill, a speedster at 155 pounds at right half, and Captain Arnold Horween, a hard charging, solid, 194 pound fullback.

Gaining consistently on each play, running off advances of from seven to 20 yards, Horween plunged over from the seven, the extra point was converted, and it looked like a rout was in store.

The Colonels huddled up after the score and Bo shouted encouragement.

"We are Centre! We are Centre! Tighten Up! We can take it to them!"

"We are Centre!"

"Line. Charge hard, keep low, take them to their knees. Tom, you and Army and Red, find the holes. Make a hole if there isn't one!"

"Remember, we are Centre!"

The gold and white streamers moved in a wave from the middle of the stadium.

Fight, Centre Fight!
Fight, Centre Fight!
Fight, Centre Fight!
Fight, Centre Fight!
Fight! Fight! Fight! Fight!
Fight! Fight! Fight!

Over and over, the same refrain.

Harvard kicked off and Centre returned to its own 20.

"Remember, we are Centre!"

Bo raced around Harvard's right end for 20. Two line bucks picked up only a yard. On third and nine, Bo hit Ed "Lefty" Whitnell, who had come in for Tom Moran, on a perfectly thrown 30 yard pass.

The Colonels had the ball in Harvard territory with first and 10 on the Crimson's 29. Successive runs by Red Roberts, Army, Lefty Whitnell and Bo moved the ball to the 15 where it was another first down for the fired up Gold and White.

The Centre fans were all on their feet, cheering wildly, led by George Swinebroad.

Harvard stiffened. Three straight runs, two over tackle and one over a guard position, were met by a charging Harvard front wall. The Crimson hadn't given up a point during the 1920 season. Over their last 14 games, they had only 19 points scored against them. They were determined that Centre wouldn't take it in.

On fourth down, Bo barked out the signals and headed on an end sweep around his right side, led by a line of gold jerseys. The Crimson defenders cut down the Centre interference and Bo, seeing his way blocked, instinctively pivoted around 180 degrees and began a wide reverse around the opposite side.

The entire Harvard eleven was caught off guard. Only a quick response by "Winnie" Churchill, who was playing back near the goal line, kept Bo from crossing into the end zone untouched. Churchill tripped up the Colonels' quarterback on the three yard line.

First and goal! All over Kentucky, fans eagerly awaited the next telegraphic message from Harvard Stadium. The chalkboards had the ball X'ed on the three. The "announcers," standing with megaphones, shouted, "Roberts, no gain."

"Roberts, no gain."

Then finally, "Roberts scores! Roberts bucks over! Roberts crashes over the goal!" An enormous roar filled Main Street in Danville as the touchdown was called out. Likewise, Centre's fans in Lexington, Louisville, Somerset—so many cities and towns throughout the Bluegrass and beyond—erupted with spontaneous shouts and pats on the back.

"We scored! Red took it in!"

Even though the stadium was filled with mainly Crimson partisans, there seemed to be as much appreciation for Centre's successful drive as was being demonstrated in section six, where the Colonels' fans were dancing about, waving their streamers frantically, hugging and twirling around in a frenzy of celebration.

Their happiness was further intensified as Red Weaver calmly booted the extra point, bring his consecutive streak to 71.

It was 7-7. After the quick Harvard score, the Colonels had fought back!

Centre kicked off and held Harvard on the next series of downs. The boys from Danville were pumped! Pumped!

"Atta boy Sully. Great hit!"

"Army—Way to turn 'em in."

After receiving the Crimson's punt, the Colonels had good field position on their own 35, but a 15 yard penalty on the first play carried the ball back to the 20.

Lefty Whitnell had remained in the lineup for Tom Moran at right half, and he carried the ball twice for virtually no gain. As the team huddled, Bo looked over to Lefty and winked, and Lefty and Army changed positions as the Colonels came up to the line of scrimmage. Grantland Rice described the next play for his readers all over the country.

Facing a punting situation, McMillin dropped back within a few yards of his own goal line and whipped a forward pass straight down the field. Whitnell, running like a greyhound, was under way. Around the midfield, with two tacklers at his elbow, he took the forty yard pass over his shoulder with a spectacular catch and then out-sprinted his two Crimson rivals for a 45 yard dash across the line, and after Weaver kicked his 72nd straight goal, Centre was leading, 14-7. The play will stand as one of greatest ever seen on any field, and for a moment the big New England crowd was stunned, with the Kentuckians in the stands making enough noise to rattle the bridge across the Charles.

Again, the impossible had happened. Centre, without surrendering the ball, had rushed and passed her way for 170 yards and a pair of touchdowns against a defense that was supposed to be impregnable. It was an amazing turn, all the more amazing because of the way the game had appeared to be heading during the first five minutes of play.

The Bo to Lefty pass, the same play that the two had practiced over and over, the same play that they had used to beat the oddsmakers in the Kentucky game the previous season, had been pulled off with perfection.

The crowd was still buzzing as Whitnell came back up the field. Bo ran over to join his teammates in congratulating his receiver.

"Told you we could score on that play," Bo said, patting Lefty on his helmet.

"Great pass, Bo. Like you've said, I never had to break stride. All I had to do was reach out and pull it in."

Harvard came back strongly after Centre's second touchdown. The Crimson's weight advantage began to take its toll. The Colonels didn't help themselves with two 15 yard penalties being marched off against them for holding. Centre's linemen fought furiously, contesting every play with all of their strength, but Harvard was relentless, moving the ball with a power running game featuring Arnold Horween and George Owen.

Near the end of the first half, as the clock ticked down to the two minute mark, the Crimson had the ball just inside of Centre's 10. It was first and goal. The Colonels dug in. Bo was back and forth behind his crouched down linemen, hollering encouragement.

It was a virtual war in the trenches, the outmanned Kentuckians making Harvard fight for every inch. But on the fourth rush into the line, George Owen finally broke through the defense and fell into the end zone. The extra point was good. It was 14-14. The whistle blew shortly afterward, and the first half of a classic battle was over.

14-14 at the half! What had initially looked like a runaway for Harvard had turned into an extremely competitive game. Followers of the Crimson's fortunes on the gridiron realized that they had witnessed something truly unique.

Harvard traditionally played hard-nosed, tough defense. Since the turn of the century, through the first four games of the season, Harvard had played 176 games (remembering the war years of 1917-18 weren't official) and shut out its opponents 118 times, or 67% of the contests played. Only seven times had a foe scored 14 or more points as Centre had done. The Colonels had accomplished what, on average, only one team every 25 games was able to do, and they had done it in just one half—30 minutes—of play.

The Centre team retired to the end zone nearest the temporary bleachers rather than go to the locker room. They were a hurting group. George Chinn had so much soreness in his shoulder that he could hardly raise him arm. Red Weaver had chronically painful knees, and was noticeably limping after having been blocked late in the second quarter.

But the really worrisome injury was that sustained by Red Roberts. The big fellow had been twisted when several of the Crimson linemen hit him as he plunged through on a short-yardage gainer. His foot was planted, cleats dug into the turf, when he was turned halfway around by the hits and felt a sudden severe pain in his left knee. He got up and continued to play, but his effectiveness in the last half of the second quarter was severely limited.

Trainer/team manager Thad McDonnell took a look at Red's knee during the halftime break and knew it was trouble. There was already a considerable amount of swelling.

"What do you think, Red? Can you play?"

"Of course," Red replied. "I can play, and I will play." But Red's tone gave away his obvious concern. Later, Red was quoted as saying that he knew he was hurt, and he knew that his play would be affected in the second half.

"But it was Harvard. We'd been pointing at Harvard for nearly a year. Do you think there was any way that I was going to be on the sideline?"

Several other Colonels had various bumps and bruises, but the most serious concerns were about young George Chinn, and the two Reds.

A Centre fan hollered to Sully Montgomery, "Hey Sully, do you think we can hold them?"

"I don't know. They block and hold us out so well. They're stronger, but we'll fight them to the end, you know that."

Harvard hadn't escaped unscathed. "Winnie" Churchill was slowed by the knee that he twisted on the play where he brought Bo down on the three yard line before Centre's first touchdown. Tackle Wynant Hubbard strained his leg, and after the game, left the locker room on crutches. Right end John Gaston sprained his ankle. "Tarzan" Tolbert, a 6' 2" guard, strained his shoulder.

John Crocker, a junior, replaced Gaston. Eastman replaced Hubbard. A.D. Hamilton took over for Churchill, even though the starter was able to play intermittently. Tolbert was hampered but was able to start the second half.

There were two main differences in the teams. Harvard was heavier, and Harvard was deeper, especially in the line. Losing a player, or having one slowed by an injury, was sustainable by the Crimson, but not by the Colonels.

Halftime found the Easterners and Kentuckians engaged in a songfest. First from the Centre section, "My Old Kentucky Home," then from the Bostonians, "Yankee Doodle Dandy." In return, the Southerners lively rendition of "Dixie" echoed through the horseshoe.

> I wish I was in the land of cotton,
> Old times there are not forgotten,
> Look away, look away, look away, Dixie land.
> In Dixie land where I was born in, early on a frosty mornin'
> Look away, look away, look away, Dixie land.
> Then I wish I was in Dixie, hooray! Hooray!
> In Dixie land I'll take my stand, to live and die in Dixie.
> Away, away, away down south in Dixie.
> Away, away, away down south in Dixie.

In genuine appreciation for all the courtesies that the visitors from Kentucky were shown, George Swinebroad led the Gold and White supporters in a hardy, and heartfelt, "Hooray for Harvard" cheer.

I went to Centre in the fall of 1921 and pledged Phi Delt because my brother Howard, who had enrolled in 1920, was a member of that fraternity. Red Roberts

was a Phi Delt also, so when I had a chance, I always talked football with him. Red was always real friendly, not just with me, but maybe even more with me because I was his "son." Naturally, I asked him about the Harvard game and how he felt at the half with the score tied at 14-14.

Red said that he knew they were in trouble. He could hardly walk, much less run. Several other of the fellows were banged up. Harvard was tough, Red said. They may have been from elite prep schools, but the Harvard boys were tough as nails. They ran hard, they hit hard, and there was no quit in them.

Red said Bo kept telling everybody that they could still win. But even Bo knew that without Red being able to play up to full strength, the attack would be hurt. Red was not only a powerful runner, but he was one of the greatest blockers who ever played the game.

And Red Weaver was limping badly. When you have a first and third team All-American hurt, you know that your chances of winning are really hindered.

THE SECOND HALF

Harvard had the option of either kicking or receiving to start the second half, and chose to kick. Bo brought it back to the 20, but Lefty Whitnell was shaken up on the return and had to leave the action. He was replaced by Chick Murphy. Bo called Murph's number twice but he only picked up a yard. Bo's third down pass was incomplete.

Whitnell had been doing the punting after Red Roberts hurt his knee, but as he was on the sidelines, Murph took over the kicking, and a full Harvard rush caused him to hurry his effort and the ball went off the side of his size 4½ shoe, nearly sideways into the stands.

Harvard had the ball, first and 10 on the Centre 30, not a good way to start the second half. The Crimson scored three minutes into the second half in seven plays, kicked the extra point, and just like that, it was 21-14.

George Chinn had to come out after the Harvard score. He simply was in too much pain to continue. Jack Converse replaced him, and Centre lost a considerable amount of weight in the exchange, as Converse was 6' tall, but only weighed 158, compared to Chinn's solid 180 lbs.

After the score, there were two exchanges of punts and Horween put the Colonels back on their own four with a booming kick. Bo gathered his teammates around him, bucking them up as only a captain, and as only Bo, could do. Uncle Charlie had always said that his quarterback was a virtual coach on the field.

"Let's go guys. We're still in this thing. They had us down 7-0 and we came back." And then Bo said what he repeated over and over.

"Remember, we are Centre!"

Bo then brought the crowd to its feet as he took the center pass and raced around his right end for 30 yards before being brought down. Red Roberts was still game, and bucked through for two. The big redhead could go forward, but was unable to make any sharp cuts to either his left or right.

On second down, Bo faded back to pass and fired a bullet toward Terry Snowday. The Crimson's captain, Arnold Horween, cut in front of Snowday and intercepted the pass and was tripped up on the Colonels' 30.

Centre went back on the defensive. Bo cheered his teammates on even more.

"Let's hold them guys and get it back. Show them what we're made of."

The outweighed Centre line did hold. Three Harvard rushes into the line were met with savage hits by the boys from Danville, the popping of leather hitting leather resonating throughout the stadium. On fourth down, Horween took the pass from center and kicked a 37 yard field goal, splitting the uprights with plenty of distance to spare. It was 24-14.

Army hauled in the ensuing kickoff and returned it to the 30. Bo went off tackle for five, Red rumbled over the right tackle for 10, and it was first down for the Colonels on their own 45. There was still a lot of fight in the Gold and White, but the mini-drive was halted and Red Roberts punted to the Harvard 28. Harvard lost four on a running play, and the quarter ended.

After switching ends of the field, Centre proved her fighting spirit by totally shutting down the Harvard attack and the Crimson had to punt. The Colonels took over on their 30, but Bo realized that he had to get something going quickly, and after a slight gain on a run, he had another pass picked off. Harvard had first down in great field position on the Centre 35.

No one in the Centre section had given up. They were still very much into the game, and George Swinebroad had no trouble getting them on their feet, where they all shouted—

Hold that line,
Hold that line,
Hold it, hold it.

Hold that line,
Hold that line,
Hold it, hold it.

The Colonels heeded their fans exhortations. If they were going down, they were going down fighting to the last play, and fight they did. Harvard gained three, lost two, gained back two, and attempted a field goal which was wide.

Centre had indeed, again, held that line.

Cheers went up all over Kentucky as the play was announced.

"Field goal wide. Centre holds."

"Centre from its own 20."

There was still time for Centre to come back. Bo and Uncle Charlie knew that their team needed two scores—a touchdown (with Red Weaver's automatic) and a field goal would tie it at 24-24. Two touchdowns would win.

From the 20 after the missed field goal, Bo ran the ball three straight times, getting three, another three, and then four for a first down. With time on the side of the Crimson, Bo called a pass play in an attempt to move the ball quickly down the field, but again, Harvard was alert, knowing that the Colonels had to put the ball in the air, and Havemeyer intercepted, returning the ball to Centre's 20 before he was knocked out of bounds.

Horween, running with power and determination all day, now put the game away. He punched forward for five. A Centre penalty moved it to the 10. Then it was Horween for six, Horween for the final four and another TD, and after the extra point, the score stood 31-14.

If the Centre fans were dispirited, they didn't show it. Even thought they knew time was running out, they still screamed for their team as enthusiastically as when the game began.

Fight, Centre Fight!
Fight, Centre Fight!
Fight, Fight, Fight!
Fight with all your Might!

Bo gathered his team around him and shouted above the noise of the crowd, "Do you hear what they're saying? They're saying—fight! They're saying—fight! They're saying—fight!"

Faxon, the big Harvard tackle, kicked to Army, who returned it to the 22. Bo knew he had to go to the air. Gus King came in for Jack Converse at left end and Bo hit the Dallas native for a 25 yard gain. Harvard was penalized 15 yards on the next play, and then Bo carried the ball to the Crimson's 35. A flag was thrown for what was deemed a late hit. Suddenly the Colonels had the ball deep in Harvard's territory, on the 20.

Bo hit King again on a perfect spiral and his end wasn't stopped until he had bulled his way to the five yard line where it was first and goal. Centre had moved the ball quickly down the field, driving 73 yards (30 of which were due to penalties) to run up their total offense for the afternoon to well over 250 yards against a defense which was felt by many to be the best in the East, if not in the country.

Everyone was on their feet, not only the Centre supporters, but even those who backed the Crimson. The grit of the little band of warriors was infectious. It was recognized that the Colonels couldn't pull it out—they couldn't win. Yet still they fought on, determined to take it to the Crimson until the last tick of the clock, realizing that even if they couldn't win, they were going to end the game hitting as hard, driving as hard, fighting as hard, as they had on the initial contact of the contest.

On first and goal, Red Roberts hit the line hard but was thrown back. Bo tried to sneak around his left end but was cut down for no gain. Bo tried a quick hitter to Terry Snowday, but a Crimson hand was flicked out and timed perfectly, and the pass fell incomplete to the turf.

On fourth down, Bo fired to Tom Bartlett on a short pass as he cut toward the goal. The toss was completed, but the Harvard linebackers gang-tackled Bartlett, and he fell just short, by less than a foot, from the goal.

After taking the ball back over, Horween made a long run out to the Harvard 42. Centre was penalized 15 yards on the next play, and the Crimson was on the Colonels' 43. Still, Centre hung tough, and on three straight rushes, held the Easterners to four hard earned yards. On fourth down, Harvard passed and Tom Bartlett intercepted.

"Hurry! Hurry!" Bo shouted, trying to get his team lined up for one more play. But before Red Weaver could snap the ball, Tiny Maxwell trotted over, blowing his whistle, and announced it was over, time had expired.

Centre had lost, but Centre hadn't been outfought. Each of the over 45,000 spectators and the scores of sportswriters knew that they had seen a special group of young men play a great game, and despite the loss, the afternoon of October 23, 1920 only resulted in further fame and acclaim for the "Wonder Team" from little Centre College in Danville, Kentucky, "wherever that is," as Howard Reynolds had written.

Bo raced over and congratulated Arnold Horween, captain to captain. There were tears in his eyes.

"We fought you as hard as we could. You have a great squad, and we got beaten by a better team." He wanted to say more, but the crowd streaming onto the field kept the two stars from talking further. Horween patted Bo on the helmet as the mass of fans forced them apart.

Bruce Dudley of the Louisville "Herald" watched from the press box as the two teams, surrounded by their adoring admirers, began to wind around the north side, end zone bleachers toward the locker room. He hustled down the stairs, weaving in and out, and barely beat the first arrivals as they came through the door.

Later, in the early evening, Dudley bent over his typewriter and then wired his impressions back to Louisville for publication.

Boston, Mass. Oct. 23
Success is not so much in winning, but in playing well the hand you have.
The truth of this assertion never was more emphasized than in the Centre-Harvard conflict which Centre numerically lost by 31-14, but in which Centre, by its exhibition of courageous manliness, won the hearts of all and merited everlasting gridiron glory.
The little college in the Kentucky Bluegrass which President Wilson told a meeting of the Princeton alumni "has turned out more men who have reached fame than Princeton, with all its years and members," is triumphant in defeat. It won everything today but the game, and the game was lost because courage could not overcome such a number of superior physiques which Coach Fisher had in his Crimson hoard. But Centre kept the faith. It fought a heroic fight which roused the sold out stadium crowd to the heights of enthusiastic admiration. It heightened Kentucky's star in the Grand Old Flag. It upheld the fine traditions of Kentucky's manhood. It battled as nobly as any band ever led by Daniel Boone. But why yearn for victory when Centre's triumph over hearts is more lasting and more to be desired?

At the conclusion of the contest, Harvard men remained on the field to shake hands and praise every Centre man, and as soon as the Crimson players redeemed their street clothing, they impulsively hastened to the Centre dressing room and again praised the men individually for their lion-hearted work. Arnold Horween, a very big factor in Harvard's success, carried the game ball to Bo McMillin and asked him to accept it with the admiration of Harvard.

Bo, with eyes bubbling with tears, thanked the Harvard captain for such an unprecedented spirit of sportsmanship, but said he could not accept a ball that Centre hadn't won.

"Well, let me tell you this then," said Horween, placing his arm around McMillin. "You are the best quarterback who ever walked into that stadium."

"If you hadn't been in the Harvard line-up, we might have won," Bo replied.

Prominent Harvard men and football officials flocked into the Centre locker room to shower praise on the athletes.

Coach Bob Fisher was one of the first to arrive.

"Boys," he said to the Kentuckians, "I consider you at the fore of the greatest football players who ever trod a gridiron. I want to tell you that you had me worried sick throughout the contest. I want to express the appreciation of all Harvard for your worth. You have shown Harvard that you are true-blue gentlemen and a foe of the rarest merit. Harvard invites you to an annual date on its football calendar. This is how much Harvard thinks of you."

Fisher shook hands with Bo. "You are the greatest quarterback I've ever seen. I hope to see you up here next year."

"This is my one hope," replied Bo. "And next year, we'll give you a better fight."

"It was plenty hard enough for me today," vouched the great mentor.

Tiny Maxwell, who weighs about two tons, puffed into the dressing room. "Boys, I want you to know you played the cleanest, squarest, fightingest game I ever refereed," he said. "I'm for you and for you strong. Today's game will live as one of the most courageous struggles in football."

Percy Haughton, the great, former coach of the Crimson, rushed in and asked for McMillin.

"You are the greatest quarterback in the world," he told Bo. "In no battle did Napoleon handle his men more brilliantly than you handled Centre today. Centre has the greatest offensive team that ever launched an attack against Harvard."

"Pooch" Donovan, the legendary trainer for Harvard, who had been associated with the sport of football for over two decades, came in and heaped compliments on the team.

"I've seen nearly every great squad over the years, and this team ranks up there with the very best. I congratulate you, each and every one of you, for your fine showing."

A great crowd of Harvard students massed outside of the Centre locker room and stood patiently for almost an hour to pay their respects to the beloved warriors. When the Kentuckians came out, they were given an ovation never before paralleled in college athletics. All were deeply affected by such a touching and unusual tribute. How many times in the history of athletics have hundreds and hundreds of victorious students been so impressed with the merits of the losing team that they have stood for an hour to cheer the defeated?

It was late in the afternoon, the sun setting behind the locker room, when the weary Colonels carried their duffle bags of equipment to the team buses. Just before Uncle Charlie boarded, he saw Coach Fisher rushing up, accompanied by a distinguished looking gentleman.

"Coach Moran, I want you to meet Mr. Frederick Moore. Mr. Moore is a Harvard man and quite a supporter of our football team."

Moore was a wealthy businessman who served as the graduate manager of the Harvard Athletic Association. The 50-year old Moore could hardly contain himself.

"Harvard wants to play Centre next year, even if we have to go to Danville for the game."

Uncle Charlie could only imagine what any team from Harvard would think when they ran onto a scruffy field and saw the patched together wooden bleachers which contrasted so starkly with the classic lines of Harvard Stadium.

"Don't fail to reserve a date for us," continued Moore. "We want to see more of the Centre College team. If Centre doesn't come back next season, we'll be sick at heart. We'll give you a choice contract and if necessary, Harvard will travel to Danville for the game. We must play your boys again. They've won our admiration and respect, and furthermore, they've taught us a lot about football."

Coach Fisher continued the conversation. "Mr. Moore is correct. Our game with you has made our team. We are right on edge now for any eleven in the country. The game was a wonderful experience for us and we must play you again. We will come to Danville if you'd like, or we'll play you here if that's what you wish. But we must have another contest."

The Harvard men's comments were extraordinary. Harvard just didn't venture far from home when it played. Since 1900, the Crimson team had taken the field 187 times, and only 28 of those games were on the road, and of those, the only trip of any distance was the January 1, 1920, Rose Bowl game.

Harvard's other games away from home were:

OPPONENT	LOCATION	GAMES
Army	West Point, NY	9
Yale	New Haven, CT	9
Princeton	Princeton, NJ	4
Penn	Philadelphia, PA	3
Navy	Annapolis, MD	2

To be willing to travel all of the way to Danville, Kentucky, demonstrated just how seriously Harvard wanted to meet Centre again, and the degree to which the college was willing to go in order to assure that Centre would put the Crimson on the schedule.

Uncle Charlie later told the Chief about the conversation with Frederick Moore and Coach Fisher. They both had to chuckle at the thought of Harvard and the team's fans rolling into Danville.

But while that possibility may have amused the two, what they found gratifying was that Centre would be back. An offer had been made, and from that moment on, the Colonels' mentors began to envision how the next visit could result in victory for the Gold and White.

The evening after the game the Centre team members were the guests of the Harvard Club for dinner. They changed into their best attire and most walked the several blocks to the club, a four story brick structure built in 1912, on Commonwealth Avenue.

One bus ferried the coaches and their wives, Dr. Ganfield, and the cripples from the game. The two Reds were on the bus. Red Weaver's knees were terribly tender. Red Roberts was walking with a cane borrowed from a fan at the Arlington. George Chinn had his injured shoulder protected by using a sling. As the Kentuckians entered the foyer, they were met by the club manager and led into the elegant foyer, and then into the most beautiful room any of them had ever seen, Harvard Hall, a four story banquet and dining room with mahogany paneling halfway up the height of the walls, exquisite marble fireplaces, and majestic silver chandeliers.

The Colonels were met by spontaneous applause by over 400 members who were standing as they entered. Soon they were surrounded by Harvard alumni who wanted to shake each of the player's hands and know their names. What followed was a night the entourage from Danville would never forget. The menu included oysters, clam chowder, Caesar salad, prime rib, asparagus, corn pudding, and wonderful, freshly baked breads, topped off by bowls of ice cream and chocolate éclairs.

Following dinner, a welcoming speech was made by the Harvard Club president who spoke about how the Colonels had gained the admiration of, "all of the Northeast for your quality of play and sportsmanship." Then the members stood and belted out a hardy, "Hip, hip, hooray for Centre."

Dr. Ganfield rose and thanked the hosts for having invited the team to the Club for such a wonderful evening. "From the minute we left the train, until this very moment, we have been treated with courtesies by everyone in Boston."

Bo was asked to say a few words, but instead, beckoned to his teammates to stand and together they returned the member's cheer with a "Hip, hip, hooray for Harvard." It seemed an appropriate way to end the evening. After another round of handshakes, the team filed out of the Harvard Club, returned to the Arlington and packed for the return to South Station. It was a weary group of young men who made their way to their Pullman. They were saddened by their loss, gratified by their play, and absolutely in awe of the reception that they had received during their 34 ½ hours in Boston.

The "Special" pulled out of the station at midnight. Most of the travelers headed for their berths. A few made their way to the dining car and recounted the events of the day.

The train retraced its earlier route, back through Massachusetts, past Albany, Utica, Syracuse, Rochester, Buffalo, and finally braked to a halt the next morning on a siding on the tracks of a New York Central subsidiary, the Buffalo and Niagara Railroad.

Sunday, October 24, was spent at Niagara Falls, first climbing up to the observation deck overlooking the American Falls, and then later taking a boat ride which came so close to the falling, roaring waters that the passengers were covered with mist. Several of the more adventurous players took a gondola ride across the Falls, transported by a dangling cable.

Five hours after leaving the "Special," following lunch and the obligatory purchasing of souvenirs and postcards, the Colonels re-boarded in the early afternoon and the big steamer pulled the train back onto the main line for the ride back toward Kentucky.

It was during the evening that Uncle Charlie and the Chief finally had time to analyze the statistics from the game. Thad McDonnell had gotten them from the official scorer prior to leaving the stadium.

Centre gained 133 yards through the air to only 13 for Harvard, but Harvard had a big advantage on the ground, running for 276 yards to only 129 for the Colonels. The overall offensive total for Harvard was 289 yards while Centre picked up 262, a mere 27 yard advantage for the Crimson.

It was in penalties that Centre had a definite, unfortunate margin over Harvard. The Colonels were penalized a total of 129 yards to only 48 for their opponents. There were no infractions for roughness. Centre played a clean game. Rather, the penalties were for holding and, due to the eagerness of the Colonels, many yards were marched off for jumping offsides.

Howard Reynolds and Grantland Rice wrote that the difference in the two teams was in the line play, particularly from the tackles. Sully Montgomery and Bill James had played their hearts out, both going the entire 60 minutes without any substitutes to give them a breather. They were worn down as the second half progressed, and many of the Crimson gains were power runs right over their positions. They were simply outmanned, not outfought.

Both Reynolds and Rice had ventured that if the tackles on the two teams had switched sides, the game may very well have had the score reversed, with the Colonels coming out on top. Certainly the skill positions in the backfield and at the ends found comparable talent on both squads.

All in all, Moran and Myers were proud of their team's performance. They felt it had been a great football game and their boys had handled themselves well both on and off the field. They had reacted as they had been taught. They had lived up to their responsibilities as Centre men.

The Kentuckians slept through the state of Ohio, had breakfast in the dining car between Cincinnati and Lexington and were eager to complete the last leg of their marathon adventure, the less than hour run from Lexington to Danville's Southern Railroad station. The players and fans were no more eager for the "Special" to arrive than those who were waiting at the station.

THE ARRIVAL IN DANVILLE

Members of the Danville Chamber of Commerce had been in communication with stations along the route home, both by telephone and by wire. Their purpose was to let the townspeople know when the "Special" would roll back into town. There were conflicting reports, some of which were incorrect due to the time differential between Boston and Danville. Similarly, since the "Special" was just that, a special, non-scheduled train, there were delays from time to time when the Kentuckians' train had to pull off onto a siding in order to let a regularly scheduled "Express" pass so that it could stick to its timetable.

At first it was announced that the train would arrive at 6:00 in the morning, then 8:00. Finally at 9:25, the huge crowd at the little brick station heard the whistle in the distance and peered down the tracks for the first glimpse of their returning heroes.

The Danville "Advocate" had a reporter in the crowd who wrote about the morning's events for publication in the afternoon paper. His story ran under a ¾ inch headline:

GLORIOUS WELCOME!

Long before the time for the special train bearing the football team and rooters to arrive at the station, a throng of 4,000 people crowded the station platform and overflowed on the tracks. College yells were given and cheering was joined in enthusiastically by the townspeople, the girls from K.C.W., and the pupils of the public schools, all of whom were present to see the return of the football heroes who have made the name of Centre so famous. The Danville town band played the college airs and "Hail! Hail! The Gangs All Here!" which served as sort of an outlet for the overflowing spirits of the enormous gathering.

When the train finally braked to a stop at 9:25, a mighty tide of cheering drowned out the roar of the engine, and when the football men stepped down from the train, they were seized by eager students and carried to automobiles which brought them to town.

The scores of machines that were parked at the station then fell in behind the procession that came to the business center of town. The band took its stand at Third and Main and played until it was purple in the face. The college students gathered in front of the Shop Perfect store and were led by George Swinebroad and Arthur Williams, who, taking their position in a second floor window, gave mighty cheers for the team. The college part of the demonstration was then concluded by a monster snake dance which wound its unerring way to the K.C.W. campus.

Business virtually suspended for three hours this morning while the town celebrated. The college was dismissed just before the train rolled in, and then all classes were cancelled for the rest of the day. Groups everywhere were fighting the game all over again, congratulating the returned heroes and greeting their friends who made the trip.

The team and fans had been gone four days, one hour and twenty-five minutes. Everywhere they went, when asked about the trip to Boston, they invariably started out by saying, "These were the most exciting, unforgettable days that I've ever spent!"

In the week following the game, Uncle Charlie received a hand-written latter from William T. "Bill" Reid, coach of the Harvard football team in 1901, and during the 1905 and 1906 seasons. Coach Reid's record was 30-3-1.

The Centre coach was very pleased to read what the former Crimson leader had written:

Dear Mr. Moran,

As a former head coach of the Harvard football team, I write to offer you and your fine team my heartiest congratulations on the bully, clean-cut, sportsmanlike game played here Saturday. In making two touchdowns in one half, you accomplished more than any team has done here in many years against Harvard. Most teams that come here to play shoot their fireworks in the first quarter, and then they flicker out. Your boys blazed brightly clear through. They played hard, clean, steady football, and Harvard men, had the game gone the other way, would have been proud to take their hats off—as we do anyway—to a team of thoroughbreds. Your whole trainload played the game, too, and we like you. We are glad to know that you will be back next year, and you may be confident that no team on our schedule will be more welcome.

Shake!

William T. Reid

CHAPTER 8:
GEORGIA TECH IN ATLANTA

It was a mistake to schedule Georgia Tech after the Harvard game, and the Centre staff knew it. However, when the 1920 schedule was made, Centre found itself in a bind. The "understanding" with Harvard was that the Colonels would arrive in the East undefeated. So the first three games had to be against opponents which would best guarantee no blemishes on the Colonels' record. Certainly, Morris Harvey, Howard and Transy fit that particular bill, as they were crushed by a combined score of 241-0.

DePauw had been so accommodating about relocating the 1919 game to Louisville that the return engagement in Indianapolis simply couldn't be avoided. It was DePauw's call, and it set the date for November 6. The arrangement with Kentucky was such that the Wildcats could name the Saturday when they were hosting the game, as they were in 1920. So there was no way to get out of that November 13 date, since that was when Kentucky wanted the game played.

Louisville had to be included on the schedule. Centre was determined to cement its great relationship with the citizens of the major metropolitan area in the state, and the best date for the Louisvillians and Virginia Tech was November 20. And the traditional Thanksgiving game with Georgetown was just that—traditional—and a Thanksgiving game has to be played on, of course, Thanksgiving.

So the only date open for Georgia Tech was the Saturday after the Harvard game, a most unfortunate development indeed. Another unfortunate but unavoidable fact was that the game was to be played in Atlanta. Centre had been gone for over four days on the Harvard venture, and nearly 60 hours had been spent on the train. Now the team faced another journey, even though this time, instead of over 1000 miles, the destination was at least only a little over 400 miles by rail from Danville.

But the really unfortunate fact, added to all of the other unfortunates, was that the Centre College Colonels were a wounded bunch of guys. The Harvard game had taken its toll, big time.

The team was so beaten up that Uncle Charlie decided not to even hold a practice on Monday, October 25. Instead, along with Dudley, the official trainer, and Thad McDonnell, he had a "sick and injured" day in order to evaluate each of those who had participated in the Harvard game.

George Chinn presumably had a shoulder separation. When Uncle Charlie, a very astute diagnostician regarding sports injuries, palpated the area on the top part of Chinn's shoulder, the freshman end grimaced. When Chinn tried to raise his arm out away from his body, he couldn't even begin to move it without considerable pain. Chinn was out. There was no way he could play in the Tech game, even though he protested the decision.

Red Weaver was next. Red had chronic problems with his knees, dating back to his playing days at Fort Worth's North Side High. Uncle Charlie had rigged up some metal braces which helped, but now the All-American center's knees needed time, not just bracing. Both were swollen, and he walked with difficulty. Running and cutting was out of the question.

"No way, Red. I don't even want you to practice this week."

Again, the decision was met with a protest, but Weaver knew he couldn't be effective on the field. As devastating as the loss of the two starters would be, their not being able to play was nowhere near as big a blow to Centre as was the prospect of facing future opponents without the services of Red Roberts.

Red had twisted his knee during the second quarter of the Harvard game. By Monday, the swelling was so severe that he could hardly bend it, and he walked stiffly, only able to get around by using a cane.

In 1977, Reggie Jackson, upon signing on with the New York Yankees, famously and correctly, if somewhat immodestly, stated that his abilities made him "the straw that stirs the drink." Decades earlier, Bo fit that category, though he was far too modest to utter such.

If Bo was the straw, Red Roberts was the drink itself. Much credit for the Colonels' success went to Bo, justifiably so. But the "man behind the man," actually, more correctly, the man in front of the man, leading interference, opening holes, brushing aside the opposition so the shining star, Bo McMillin, could dazzle with his brilliance, was Red Roberts.

Now, there was simply no way Red could be a factor against an excellent Georgia Tech team. Uncle Charlie told him he could make the trip, but to not even think about playing. Several other Colonels had lumps, bumps and bruises. But after examining each, Moran declared them fit enough to play.

On Tuesday, October 26, Centre had a light workout. During the afternoon, a local men's clothing store, Bruce-Martin and Company, presented Red Roberts with a new suit, fulfilling a pledge made prior to the trip to Boston that the first player to score for Centre would receive an outfit of his choice. Also, the Piggly Wiggly at Third and Main presented $10.00 certificates for groceries to Red and Lefty Whitnell for their scores.

Uncle Charlie planned to start two Owensboro natives, Tom Bartlett at end, in place of Chinn, and Hump Tanner at fullback, in place of Roberts. Terry Snowday, also from Owensboro, would give the city from western Kentucky three starters. Filling in for Red Weaver was a Texan from Dallas, Harry "Shanks" Lipscomb, who was 5'11" and weighed 155 lbs.

The upcoming foe, Georgia Tech, was playing excellent football. The program had been under the direction of John Heisman (for whom college football's most prestigious honor, the Heisman Memorial Trophy is named) from 1904 until the year preceding the Tech-Centre game. From 1904 through 1919, Heisman's teams had a record of 102-29-7. During a run from 1914-18, the Yellow Jackets had an undefeated streak which reached 32 (there were two ties) before it was broken on November 23, 1918, against Pittsburgh.

Heisman left Georgia Tech after the 1919 season because he and his wife had divorced and he wanted to spare her the embarrassment of living in the same town. He finished his career at Pennsylvania, Washington and Jefferson, and finally, Rice, retiring from coaching after the 1927 season.

John Heisman's assistant for seven years had been William Alexander, a 1912 Tech graduate, and Alexander took over the program in 1920. (Alexander was the Tech coach from 1920-44, and during 25 seasons, his record was 134-95-15. One of Alexander's assistants, Bobby Dodd, became head coach in 1945 and in 22 years at the helm, compiled a record of 165-64-8. Therefore, Georgia Tech had only three coaches from 1904 through 1966, quite a remarkable record for consistency and continuity.)

Georgia Tech was 4-1 when Centre traveled to Atlanta. The record was marred only by a tough loss at Pittsburgh, 10-3, to a "Pop" Warner coached Panther team that finished the 1920 season, 6-0-2.

Georgia Tech	44	Wake Forest	0
Georgia Tech	55	Oglethorpe	0
Georgia Tech	66	Davidson	0
Georgia Tech	44	Vanderbilt	0
Georgia Tech	3	Pittsburgh	10

Thursday night at 11:00 pm, the Centre entourage boarded an overnight Southern Railroad train for the ride down to Atlanta. They slept all night as their Pullman was pulled south down through Central Kentucky, on to and through Chattanooga, where it traveled across the Tennessee-Georgia state line, and arrived at the ornate Atlanta terminal somewhat after noon on Friday.

As was becoming the norm, the Colonels were met by a large crowd of supporters, photographers and reporters. The next morning's Atlanta "Constitution" published a six inch high photograph which was spread across all the columns under the caption, "The Praying Colonels Come to Town."

Headquarters for the team was the Kimball House Hotel. After checking in, the players were transported in cars owned by local fans to the campus of Marist College on Ivy Street where they held a two hour practice, watched by a large crowd which not only included Centre alumni and supporters, but spectators from Atlanta and Fulton County.

Centre had brought pride to the South by its play at Harvard. The Georgians wanted to see the Colonels up close, and even though most of the hundreds who watched the team go through its drills at Marist had tickets for the next day's game, they wanted to see the team in a more intimate setting.

The local papers reported on the injuries suffered during the Harvard game. With two All-Americans and the stoutest end, Chinn, severely crippled, the "dope" about which team would be favored was up in the air.

The uncertainty was explored by a local pundit.

THE QUESTION OF THE HOUR
(OR, THE ADVICE OF THE OUIJA BOARD
TO TECH & CENTRE FANS)

Which will it be—
Centre or Tech?
You tell 'em brother
My mind is a wreck.

I've gone 'round the circle
And all the way back.
I've worked it by algebra
Calculus, trig;
But the dope's as elusive
As any greased pig.
I've even asked the Ouija
Which team is the best?
But the board said, "You've given me
Too hard of a test."

The spirits that guide me
And by whom I swear,
Are quite flabbergasted
And up in the air.

You ask me, my young friend
Just what you should do—
I find by my magic
Just one tip for you—

Go out to the ball game
And have a fine time.
But take my advice, kid,
And don't bet a dime.

Centre wasn't the only team that was afflicted by injuries. Tech had taken some hard hits during the Pittsburgh game and actually was planning to start a halfback named Frank Ferst at quarterback since the first and second stringers, Jack McDonald and Bill Gaiver, weren't able to play.

Depth was where the Yellow Jackets had the advantage. Coach Alexander was often able to substitute a whole eleven at a time, a luxury certainly foreign to Uncle Charlie.

It is important to understand just how vital Red Weaver was to the Colonels' single wing offense. So many of the plays depended on pinpoint passing back from the center, and perfect timing. Red was a master. "Shanks" Lipscomb was put into the starting lineup on short notice, and the abbreviated time for practice prior to the Tech game gave him little chance to prepare for the contest. Weaver's absence would be felt, big time.

The Saturday afternoon game was to take place at Grant Field on the Georgia Tech campus a few blocks west of Peachtree Street. The stadium was built by student volunteers during the summer of 1913, funded by a grant of $15,000 from the High Inman Grant family. The original capacity in the concrete part of Grant Field was 5,600. Wooden bleachers added later stretched the seating to 15,000 plus, and with standing room spectators added in, it was felt that there would be 20,000 at the game, the greatest crowd ever to watch a football game in the South. Such was the interest that Centre had garnered in its meteoric rise to the upper echelons of college football.

Fans came up to the game from New Orleans. The Southern Railroad ran a special train which carried 400 people the 150 miles from Birmingham to attend. Cars were added to regularly scheduled trains to accommodate fans from Mobile and Montgomery. Georgians from Macon, Augusta and Decatur flocked to Grant Field. Greenville, South Carolina was represented by a crowd of 100. Groups came from Nashville, Chattanooga, and Memphis.

Game time was 2:00. The gates were opened at 12:30. The predicted 20,000 in attendance was later revised upwards to closer to 25,000 by reporters covering the game. Many were able to only get fleeting glances of the play as they peered over and between those standing in front.

Referee Mike Thompson flipped the coin at midfield. Bo won the toss, and Centre chose to receive. It was the high point of the Colonels' afternoon.

The Atlanta "Journal" featured the Centre-Tech game in its Sunday morning, October 31 paper. Besides "Yellow Jackets," Tech was often called the "Golden Tornado."

TORNADO DOWNS GALLANT CENTRE 24-0
FLAG OF TECH FLOATS FROM HIGHEST PINNACLE

The flag of Tech now floats from the highest pinnacle it has ever known. The Golden Tornado of 1920 placed it there yesterday.

A bombshell exploded above the Mason and Dixon Line when the wires carried the news to the North that Georgia Tech had triumphed over Centre College by a margin of seven points more than the great Harvard team, and held the Kentuckians scoreless for the first time in four years.

The game was very controversial. Bruce Dudley of the Louisville "Herald" wrote that Georgia Tech was the dirtiest playing team that he had ever witnessed. Dudley was incensed at what he had observed. He had been in attendance at the Harvard game and contrasted the sportsmanship shown that prior week with what he had seen take place on Grant Field.

Dudley wrote that, *Centre despises alibis, as do all lovers of clean sport, but the mess that I saw during the game besmirched the name of the country's greatest college sport.*

Dudley told about an incident soon after the opening kickoff. On the first series of plays, Bo was tackled, and as he lay on the ground, with the ball blown dead, and all but Bo back on their feet, "Red" Barron stepped over and deliberately kicked Bo in the head.

This startling violation so incensed the Centre men that for a few minutes, they threatened to call off the game rather than engage in a free-for-all fight. Bo was so stunned that for the first time in his football career, he had to be helped to his feet. His head was bathed while half a dozen Colonels rushed over to the sidelines and demonstrated to Coach Moran how McMillin had been fouled.

Tech was penalized half the distance to the goal for unnecessary roughness. Dudley recounted multiple other instances of "brutality" by the Georgia Tech players.

Centre simply wasn't used to, or had ever engaged in, such play. Uncle Charlie had stated repeatedly to his team and to the press, "We play hard. We play to win. But we play fair, and we play as gentlemen." Dudley's report, wired back to Louisville, continued.

Sully Montgomery was kicked two or three times on his forehead and beneath both eyes. A kick by Fincher cut a gash in his face and Dr. May had to sew it up with several stitches. Tom Moran, Bartlett, Tanner, Lipscomb, James and Snowday were each kicked in the face. Every Colonel who played was fouled at least once.

After the game, Bo was asked if he felt that Centre would have been able to beat Tech if it have played the Atlantans before the Harvard game, before having suffered so many injuries and his team had been at full strength.

Bo answered, "After seeing the type of football Tech plays, I doubt it. I don't see how any team in the world could hope to beat Tech at Grant Field if Tech used the kind of tactics that they used today."

One point of contention was about the noise coming from the stands when Centre was on offense. Uncle Charlie was particularly incensed in his post-game comments in the dressing room.

"We're not going to squeal one bit. We came down here to play football, but everything but football unfolded. This is the first town where the coach and captain of the team and college officials would permit its student body and band to unite in screams to prevent the visiting team from hearing its signals. When Tech had the ball, you could hear a pin drop. When Centre had the ball, the noise was so deafening that our center couldn't hear the signals."

Moran continued, "Bo went to the Tech captain, Flowers, three times and requested that he, in the interest of fair sport, stop the band and shouting, but the tumult seemed to increase with each request. Last week when we played Harvard and they had the ball at a critical time, three fourths of the crowd of over 45,000 were hollering, 'Hold them, Centre!' and Bo held up his arms requesting silence, and every voice was hushed. Unsuccessful efforts to have this courtesy shown today resulted in several fumbles and missed signals."

Harry "Shanks" Lipscomb didn't have the experience of Red Weaver. He was game, but the noise and his having been put into a starting position on such short notice, certainly played a role in Centre's relative inability to get its offense in gear.

Uncle Charlie and Bo both stated that they'd like to have another shot at Georgia Tech, but never again in Atlanta.

"I know my boys will never be content until another date is arranged, but you can tell the world that the game will not be played in Atlanta. Our college would never consent. We'd play on any neutral field, Louisville, Nashville, or anywhere. But we'll not come back to Atlanta."

Centre was good to its word. The Centre College Colonels and Georgia Tech Yellow Jackets never met on the gridiron again. Instead, Centre shifted to Birmingham the next four years, playing Auburn three times and Alabama once.

Bruce Dudley had the final word. He admitted that Centre probably wouldn't have won the game even if Tech had played fairly. The Colonels were too tired and battered after two successive road trips and the toughness of the Harvard squad.

But Tech sacrificed honor in winning. Centre refused to lose both honor and the game, so all that Centre lost was the game.

A poem was published in the Danville "Messenger" on Monday, November 1. There was additional resentment that Tech hadn't offered to let the Colonels practice on Grant Field after the team's arrival in Atlanta, necessitating the workout at Marist College.

WHEN CENTRE PLAYED TECH

Did Georgia Tech meet Centre's men,
Offer the field for practice?
Then their hospitality extend?
Oh! No! Not Tech!

And when our signals Bo would call,
And then upon the drums they'd fall,
But for their own? No noise at all,
To favor Tech.

Our Centre men were wounded more
Than in the Harvard game, just o're.
Such dirty sport we do deplore,
And scorn this Tech!

For Bo was kicked upon the head,
Completely dazed, by his men led;
And they too, kicked on mouth, 'tis said!
Oh ! Brutal play by Tech !

What of this foe, so like a Hun?
Where is the glory tho' they won?
For much disgraceful work was done
That day, by Tech!

All glory be to Harvard's name!
All shame to Tech's! May critics blame
Your play that day—who wants your fame?
Dishonored Tech!

CHAPTER 9:
BO PULLS THE TEAM TOGETHER—
THE SEASON CONTINUES

An interesting tidbit appeared in the Danville "Advocate" on November 2, ten days after the Harvard game.

Mr. and Mrs. Rufus Lipps have returned from Boston, Massachusetts. They saw the Old Centre and Harvard football game. Mr. Lipps states they made the entire trip in a Ford automobile and did not have a single puncture and that it was not necessary on a single occasion to even add additional inflation to a tire.

Meanwhile, there was a football season to complete after the debacle in Atlanta. DePauw, Kentucky, Virginia Tech and Georgetown (Ky.) remained on the schedule, with only Georgetown being a home game.

Once again, Uncle Charlie and his trainers used the Monday after returning to Danville to evaluate the players who were still suffering from the injuries sustained at Harvard and the many new ones received during the Georgia Tech game.

Bo felt that the team had reached a critical juncture and used the day off from practice to call a late afternoon team meeting held in the Boyle-Humphrey gym. He knew that his squad was down both physically and mentally. The injuries would heal. What he wanted to make certain was that the emotional state of his teammates wouldn't hamper the rest of the season. The team needed bucking up. It was a meeting that only a team captain, and only a player as well respected as Bo, could conduct. Bo recounted the events of the last two weeks and how great teams and great players bounce back from adversity. Over and over he reminded his teammates that, "We are Centre!"

Bo said that if the Colonels won the last four games, the season could still be a success. He told the team that now was the time that separated the men from the boys, that separated those who would be winners in life from those who would be mere spectators.

"It's easy to be on top, when everything is going good. But the test of the man is to come back when he's been dealt a blow. Will you roll over, or will you work even harder and show what type of character you have?"

My brother Howard was at Centre, and he was on the team as a scrub in 1920. He didn't even suit up for games, but he practiced and he knew what was going on. Howard happened to be in the gym when Bo called the meeting after the loss to Georgia Tech. He said the most amazing thing happened.

Bo kept repeating, over and over, "We are Centre! We are Centre!"

And then, one by one, a player would stand up and begin to join in.

"We are Centre! We are Centre!"

Pretty soon, they were all on their feet yelling, "We are Centre! We are Centre!" It just went on and on.

"We are Centre! We are Centre!"

"We are Centre! We are Centre!"

"We are Centre! We are Centre!"

Howard said that whatever doubts the team may have had after the two tough losses just disappeared. The team walked out of that meeting more convinced than ever that they had a great destiny, and they were going to fulfill their dreams, and soon they began talking about playing Harvard the next year.

DePauw in Indianapolis was next, with the game to be played on November 6. During the 1919 game between the two schools in Louisville, the Tigers had been handled easily by the Colonels who won 56-0. Uncle Charlie reminded the team that DePauw could be tougher than expected.

His reasoning was based on the Harvard-Valparaiso game of October 9. Harvard won 21-0. DePauw and Valpo had been tied 0-0 in the fourth quarter of their game on October 29 when there was a disputed play and Valparaiso walked off the field in protest. (DePauw was declared the winner by forfeit, and the game is listed in the records as DePauw 1—Valparaiso 0.)

"So that means that DePauw and Valpo are basically equal. They were tied, and Harvard scored 10 less points, 21, against Valpo, than they did against us."

The players had to think about that for a moment. It was somewhat of a convoluted type of reasoning, but Moran's point was well taken.

"We've got to take this team seriously, especially because we still have a lot of injuries."

Indianapolis certainly was taking the game seriously. DePauw was having a good year, winning four straight after losing its opener against Purdue, 10-0. Centre was Centre, and everyone was anxious to see what was still being referred to as the "Wonder Team," despite the loss of the last two games.

The highway from Greencastle, Indiana to Indianapolis wasn't great, and the college secured a special "Big Four" day train to take 1,000 students to the game on the Vandalia Line, even though the distance was only approximately 40 miles.

The school newspaper, "The DePauw," had built up the contest with articles about the Colonels accompanied by photographs of Red Roberts and Bo. The editor of "The DePauw" arranged for an article to be sent from Centre's school paper, the "Cento," containing the Centre viewpoint of the upcoming game. Walter Brashear, the

"Cento's" editor, wrote that Centre looked forward to the contest in Indianapolis, and somewhat undiplomatically reminded the readers that Centre had won by a decisive 56-0 margin the pervious year. However, Brashear did point out that DePauw had beaten the Colonels in 1917, the last loss prior to the Harvard and Georgia Tech defeats.

During the week, Uncle Charlie again didn't let the team have any contact. They mainly jogged and worked on their timing. One diversion was when the team went to the Colonial movie theater on Main Street to watch films of the Harvard game which were being shown all over the country. M.G.Weisinger, the theater manager, roped off the front two rows with gold ribbons and invited the Colonels to watch not only the scenes from Harvard Stadium, but the featured film, "The Lone Wolf's Daughter," starring Louise Glaum.

The audience stood and cheered for several minutes when the players came into the theater. When the lights went out, they were thrilled by the coverage of the game.

There were several shots of the fans filing into the stadium, a panning inside the big horseshoe of the capacity crowd, and several series of plays on the field were shown, including Red Roberts scoring and Lefty Whitnell hauling in Bo's long pass for the second touchdown.

Whistles, clapping, and foot stomping seemed like they'd never let up as Lefty crossed the goal. The theater resonated with the crowd chanting, "Lefty, Lefty, Lefty," until the Centre star stood and took a bow. The films were shown in Boston at a downtown theater, and a reviewer wrote that, "The photography is excellent and there are plenty of scenes which make this great viewing."

Centre left for Indianapolis at 5:35 Friday afternoon, traveling through Lexington and Cincinnati. The team's overnight journey found them arriving at their destination at 7:00 a.m., Saturday, the day of the game.

As the Colonels were transported to their hotel, the Claypool, they were impressed by the extensive preparations which had taken place in the city for the game. The entire area was decorated in the gold and white of Centre, and the gold and black of DePauw. In the lounge of the Claypool, Indianapolis Mayor Charles W. Jewett and representatives of DePauw formed a reception line and shook the hands of the Colonels as they filed into the big reception room. Mayor Jewett then read a proclamation in which he declared the day, "Gold Day," in honor of both school's colors.

Photographs were taken, interviews conducted, and then the Colonels retired to the dining room for breakfast, after which they strolled around downtown Indianapolis prior to heading to Washington Park for the game.

Uncle Charlie had to scrape together a lineup. He took 25 men to the game, and hoped to play most of them, saving his team for the following week's important game with Kentucky. Stanley Robb was penciled in at fullback. Not only was Red Roberts still hobbled, but Hump Tanner, who started in the Tech game, had taken such a beating that he was also going to ride the bench, at least at the start. Red Weaver was going to Indianapolis, but once again, "Shanks" Lipscomb would be over the ball at center. Lefty Whitnell was to be replaced by Tom Moran, and Uncle Charlie planned to give Ashley Blevins, who only weighed 158 lbs., considerable time in the line in order to spell Bill James and Ben Cregor.

Centre entered Washington Park to a huge ovation. The facility held 16,000, and an additional thousand standing room tickets had been sold. With the 45,000 plus at the Harvard game, 20,000-25,000 in Atlanta, and the crowd of 17,000 in Indianapolis, it meant that the Colonels would have played in front of somewhere around 85,000 fans the past three weeks!

The Centre College Colonels could generate more excitement and interest than any team in the country, and the games which sold out everywhere they played certainly attested to that fact.

Centre got back on track in Indianapolis. The first quarter was scoreless, but the Colonels racked up six first downs. DePauw didn't get one. In the second quarter, Lefty Whitnell came in for Tom Moran, carried for 24 yards on two wide, end-sweeps, and Bo took it in from the 23. Red Weaver could still kick and made it 7-0.

Later in the quarter, Bo ran for 24, threw a 30 yarder to Terry Snowday, and had the ball on the DePauw 15 but couldn't move it over the goal, so he kicked a field goal and it was 10-0 at the half. Army had played well, running once for 30 yards and hauling in a pass for similar yardage. Bill James and Ben Cregor led the defense in shutting down DePauw's attack. Centre was marching again when the half ended.

The Colonels offense looked like its old self in the second half. Bo intercepted a pass and ran the ball back for 15 yards, then gained 18 around end, hit Terry Snowday on a 20 yard pass, and Terry stiff-armed and faked and twisted down the field through five defenders for another 22 yards and scored. Weaver kicked number 74 to put the Colonels up, 17-0.

Hump got into the game and Bo called his number four straight times and the coal-haired fireplug picked up 30 yards. Bo hit Jack Converse for 20, and then Army plunged over from seven yards out. Red Weaver's 75th, naturally, made it 24-0 as the 3rd quarter ended.

Tom Bartlett moved to the fullback position and scored from the 24, Bo hit the extra point as Red Weaver's knees were stiffening. Bo booted a 17 yard field goal, and the Colonels walked off the field with a very workman-like, 34-0 victory.

Uncle Charlie put Red Roberts in near the end of the game after the crowd had begun to chant his name. The big guy got a standing ovation, stayed in for a couple of plays in the line, and received an even greater cheer when he trotted back off the field, waving and smiling at the appreciative fans.

After the game, the DePauw alumni association hosted a banquet at the city's finest hotel, the Severin, a luxurious, brick, high rise built seven years earlier at 40 West Jackson. Mayor Jewett praised the clean play of both teams, and everyone at the event who was familiar with what had transpired in Atlanta was gratified that Indianapolis and DePauw had stepped up and displayed the sportsmanship which Centre had become both known for, and to which the Colonels were accustomed.

After the banquet, the Kentuckians returned to the Claypool for a dance hosted by DePauw's Delta Tau Delta fraternity, and it was late before the Colonels retired upstairs to their rooms, with even the sore-legged two Reds taking part in some of the less lively dances.

An article written the weekend of the game concluded by stating:

It was indeed a great day for the Colonels and they can only hope that next year they can in some degree extend the same welcome and same courtesies to the gentlemen of DePauw. Games of Saturday's caliber may be termed jewels in gridiron history where the teams throw aside sectional differences and meet on the same level with only one idea in mind—to play their best and give the victor his due.

BO GETS COMMITMENTS FOR 1921

Before the Kentucky game, Bo held another team meeting. He had been thinking a lot about Harvard and the next season. However, it was important to him, and to Centre's chances, that the team stick together in order for the Colonels to be able to challenge the Crimson in 1921.

Everyone knew that due to the S.I.A.A.'s having declared the 1918 season as not having occurred, Bo and many of the seniors would be able to play in 1921, and Bo, in particular, wanted to get a head count about who planned to return for a 5th year of eligibility. Also, for the others who weren't affected by the 1918 ruling, were they coming back?

Bo unloaded a bombshell in the meeting held in the lounge of Breck Hall.

"I've been offered $50,000 over the next five years to turn pro. I can't tell you who made the offer, but you can believe me when I tell you that the offer was for real, and I have received a contract that they want me to sign."

There were several whistles and gasps.

"Bo, how can you turn that type of money down?"

It was a legitimate question. Bo and Marie, his long-time love, were determined to get married, eventually. They had decided to hold off until Bo either graduated, or until he got a good job offer, hopefully associated with football. The $10,000 yearly certainly was "a good job offer." To understand exactly how good, it needs to be pointed out exactly what $10,000 would buy in 1920 dollars. A Ford Model T cost $350.00. A nice home could be bought for $2,500 to $3,000. You could stay in a good hotel with private bath for $2.00-$3.00 nightly. A movie cost 25 to 50 cents. A gallon of gasoline was 30 cents. Milk was 58 cents/gallon. But the really impressive statistic regarding the offer that Bo received was that the average annual salary in 1920 was less that $1,500. $10,000 a year was big time money for a young man from North Side High in Fort Worth! $10,000 would allow him to marry his childhood sweetheart.

"But I'm going to turn it down, if," and Bo paused, "I'm going to turn it down if you'll all come back next year, especially those of you who could graduate but who have another year of eligibility, because," and again Bo paused, "because, I know we can beat Harvard. I know we can beat Harvard."

One by one, Bo asked for commitments, almost like a drill sergeant.

"Army?"

Army had received an offer of a job which would guarantee him a good salary. "I'll be back."

"Sully?"

Sully wasn't certain, but he said he'd try.

"Red Weaver?"

"Bo, you know how financially stressed out I am. If I can afford to come back, I will. But I can't make a commitment."

"Red Roberts?"

Like Bo, big Red had received pro offers, but his loyalty was to Bo and his teammates. "I'll be back, and I'll be in the best shape I've ever been in."

"Bill James?"

"You couldn't drag me away. Count me in."

"Owensboro—Hump, Terry and Tom?"

Tanner, Snowday, Bartlett, all answered, "We'll be here, Bo."

"Baldy?"

Ben Cregor replied in the affirmative.

Bo closed the meeting after getting several more positive answers by saying, "Then I'll be back, because I'm telling you, we can beat Harvard. I know it, we can beat Harvard."

HOMECOMING AT KENTUCKY

The University of Kentucky was Centre's next foe. It was to be the Homecoming for the Wildcats. Centre was a huge draw, and the Colonels coming over to Lexington, plus the fact that it was to be Homecoming, guaranteed a sellout. Kentucky had started the season well but had hit some bumps along the way, so that going into the game with Centre, it was 3-2-1.

Kentucky	62	Southwestern	0
Kentucky	31	Maryville	0
Kentucky	0	Miami (Oh.)	14
Kentucky	6	Sewanee	6
Kentucky	0	Vanderbilt	20
Kentucky	7	Cincinnati	6

Once again, the annual battle between the old rivals was attracting interest all across the state. So many fans from the Danville area wanted to attend that Howard King, the Southern Railroad's district passenger agent, came to Danville to make arrangements for a special train consisting of day coaches to carry the fans and students on the 50 minute ride to Lexington. Dr. Ganfield had cancelled Centre's Saturday morning classes, K.C.W. had done likewise, so that the entire student bodies of both schools bought $2.70 round trip tickets for the trip. The team occupied the last car, and the train consisted of 15 day coaches for the students and townspeople, each carrying 70 passengers.

Danville High scheduled a game with Lexington Model School for Friday afternoon, and arrangements were made for the players to stay overnight in Lexington so that they could take in the next day's contest.

All week preceding the game, Centre held a brief pep rally following chapel where the cheerleaders fired up the students by trying to get one side of the church to shout louder than the other.

Over in Lexington, similar events were taking place. A big pep rally was to take place at noon prior to the game. A special Homecoming edition of the college's newspaper, the "Kernel," would be published and distributed to everyone at the rally, and additional copies were to be handed out at the Southern station for arriving passengers, and outside of Stoll Field. After the game, the Kentucky team and coaches were to be guests of honor at a reception at the Armory, and all out of town visitors were invited.

The game was played on a crisp, sunny afternoon in front of a crowd of 10,000, absolutely capacity and then some. Bo ran the offense rather conservatively, sticking mainly to the ground, and spread out the rushes over several backs. The Colonels won easily, 49-0.

The highlight for Kentucky and the team's fans was the halftime performance by the school's band and students. The band took the field first and white clad girls came out of the stands and formed a big "U" as the musicians struck up the Kentucky fight song. Then the cheerleaders led blue clad male students out who formed a big "K." After the "UK" was assembled, the band played "My Old Kentucky Home," and everyone in the stadium stood and sang along. The halftime ended with a spirited rendition of "Dixie."

Hump Tanner, running from the fullback position, had quite a game, scoring three times and never failing to pick up yardage on his numerous efforts. Bo tallied three touchdowns also, on short runs, and Lefty Whitnell rounded out the scoring on a six yard burst right over the left tackle. Red Weaver was a perfect seven for seven to run his streak to 82.

Uncle Charlie let Red Roberts play a couple of series in the line, but Red limped off the field and was mainly a spectator for the afternoon. It was obvious that his knee hadn't healed.

A measure of how totally Centre had dominated was the fact that Kentucky was virtually helpless in stopping the relentless Colonel attack as the Gold and White had 34 first downs. The Wildcats had but three, their offense being totally shut down.

From a 68-0 drubbing in 1916, Centre had established itself as the class of the Commonwealth, winning three straight from Kentucky, with the last two by a combined margin of 105-0. It was quite a turn-around.

There was no doubt who was the "Champion of Kentucky."

BACK TO LOUISVILLE

Centre had bounced back nicely from Harvard and Georgia Tech and now stood 5-2, with Virginia Tech and Georgetown still to play.

Uncle Charlie and the Chief spoke in chapel Monday after the Kentucky game and thanked the students and faculty for their support of the team, especially the showing they made in Lexington. "It may have been Homecoming in Lexington, but from the sidelines, we heard as much support for our team as was given Kentucky."

Then the Chief made an announcement that even the players hadn't known about. "We have been in contact with the Texas Christian University in Fort Worth and a committee of prominent citizens and are pleased to report that we've been invited to play a bowl game in that city on January 1, 1921."

Most of those in chapel that morning had never heard of Texas Christian, so the Chief gave a little history about the college and added, "Their football team is undefeated. They will be a worthy foe, and the game will give Old Centre even more recognition. I think we have become known in the Northeast because of the Harvard game. Now we have a chance to let people know more about our college in the Southwest."

First Harvard! Now a bowl game! Who would have ever believed it? However, there was a regular season to complete. After the wonderful reception the previous year in Louisville, the Centre administration was anxious to cement the relationship between the college and Louisville, so the Colonels were to travel to the Derby City on November 20 to take on Virginia Tech.

Virginia Polytechnic Institute, VPI or Virginia Tech, and Centre had never played before. VPI was founded in 1872 and was located in the far western part of Virginia, in Blacksburg. The college had gone through an evolutionary process in coming up with a name for itself. It was first Virginia Agricultural and Mechanical College, and in 1896, Polytechnic Institute was added, giving the school the rather awkward mouthful, Virginia Agricultural and Mechanical Polytechnic Institute, with the initials VAMPI, certainly a less that desired acronym. It would have naturally followed that in any sporting contests, VPI's teams would have been referred to as "Vamps," and since one of the definitions of the word was "a woman who uses her sex appeal to entrap and exploit men," a hastily called meeting resulted in shortening the name to Virginia Polytechnic Institute.

After the name of the college was determined, the school officials decided it would be nice to have a new nickname and cheer. A contest was held and a senior, O.M. Stull, won the competition when he submitted the "Hokie Yell."

Hokie, Hokie, Hokie, Hi!
Tech, Tech, VPI
Sol-a-rex, Sol-a-rah
Poly Tech Vir-gin-ia
Ray Rah VPI
Team! Team! Team!

Stull admitted later that he had no inkling what "Hokie" meant, but rather, "It was a product of my imagination, and was an attention-getter for my yell." Whatever the reason, the cheer caught on, and the school's nickname, "Hokies," is now well into its second century of use.

As the Louisvillians were getting ready to welcome the Colonels, they were pleased to read about the team during the week preceeding the VPI game when they opened the November 13 issue of the "Literary Digest," a weekly news magazine. The "Digest" had a circulation of 2,000,000 copies. (The magazine was merged with another newsweekly, "Time," in 1938.)

There was a significant article under the heading, "Centre College Gives Harvard a Tussle."

Twenty-seven husky youths from Danville, Kentucky, clad in weird gold jerseys, and led by a wise and valiant coach from Horse Cave, in the same state, a few days ago swarmed into Harvard Stadium and met the powerful Crimson eleven in a football game variously described as "one of the most spectatular games ever fought in the Stadium," and as "one of the most dramatic moments in football history."

The long story then recreated the game in vivid prose. Above the article was a two column photograph of the starting eleven, with Uncle Charlie in an overcoat and wearing his fedora. The picture was captioned, "Kentucky stalwarts who almost defeated Harvard."

The Harvard game had generated such excitement in Louisville that it was decided the high school facility used in the 1919 DePauw game wouldn't come close to handling the crowd expected for the VPI game. The stadium with the greatest capacity in Louisville was Eclipse Park at Seventh and Kentucky Avenue, just a few blocks south of the downtown area. Eclipse Park was named for Louisville's original professional baseball team, and could hold 15,000 people when used for football. From pregame ticket sales, it was realized that the demand was going to exceed the seats available, and an additional 2,000 temporary seats were constructed on the east side of the field.

The game was going to be a moneymaker for Centre. VPI was guaranteed $1,500, the stadium expenses would be $1,200, and Centre figured that $2,000 would cover the team's travel, lodging and meals plus any promotional expenses and incidentals incurred in putting on the game. With ticket sales generating close to $30,000, Centre would have a very profitable weekend.

VPI began its football program in 1892. The school had mainly played a regional schedule over the years with opponents primarily being from within Virginia or from the neighboring states of Tennessee and the Carolinas. When the Hokies traveled to the East, they had met no success, losing to Princeton three times, Yale twice, and once each to Bucknell, Cornell, and Rutgers.

VPI had started out the season with three straight wins over weaker teams, but then lost three straight against better competition to go 3-3, beat Richmond, lost to North Carolina State, and came to Louisville with a 4-4 record.

VPI	35	Hampden-Sydney	0
VPI	21	William and Mary	0
VPI	75	Emory and Henry	6
VPI	6	Rutgers	19
VPI	0	Maryland	7
VPI	0	Washington and Lee	13
VPI	21	Richmond	0
VPI	6	North Carolina State	14

There were some interesting sidelights to the Centre-VPI game. Uncle Charlie had been a star halfback on the University of Tennessee team that defeated the Hokies in 1897, 18-0. Tech had some unique players. Tex Tilson and Red Deer Tilson were full-blooded Indians from Texas. In the days of less sensitive journalism, the Danville "Advocate" stated, "It will be worth the time and then some to journey to Louisville to see these aboriginals in action."

There was a tackle named Henry Crisp who had but one hand, having suffered an accident while a child. And there was George Washington who claimed to be a descendant of George, the original.

Centre was taking VPI quite seriously. Bo was cornered by a reporter and quoted as saying, "We know Virginia Poly lost to North Carolina State last week, but Poly has not been beaten badly in any of its losses. They've played tough, and we expect a tough game."

Slowly, Centre was getting back into shape. Red Roberts was only going to be used in the line, but he would start. George Chinn would play only if absolutely necessary. His end position was going to be filled by Stanley Robb. Hump was going to start at fullback. One complication occurred just before the team was to head to Louisville. Ben Cregor had been diagnosed with the mumps. "Baldy" was going to be left behind in Danville.

The Centre alumni in Louisville had again been extremely active in getting Louisville ready for the game. Gold and white was all over the downtown. Banners adorned various structures and were draped across intersections, proclaiming that "LOUISVILLE WELCOMES THE CENTRE COLLEGE WONDER TEAM!" Pennants of the Gold and White were seen fluttering from light poles and decorated windows of businesses all over the downtown area.

Meanwhile, a smaller but no less enthusiastic group of local VPI alumni was making certain that their team would feel welcome. They had the area around their team's hotel, the Watterson, decorated with the maroon and orange school colors.

A large contingent of Danvillians was coming over to the game on a Southern Railroad special train which was going to pick up several carloads of fans from Lexington en route.

Governor Edwin Morrow was bringing his entire family over from Frankfort. Louisville's mayor, George Weissinger Smith, was going to be in attendance, as were several other local and state politicians. To emphasize how big Centre's following was,

Kentucky's two United States senators, John C. Beckham and Augustus O. Stanley, were coming down from Washington just for the game.

The Colonels left Danville in a private car on the Southern at 5:25 Friday afternoon. They ate in the dining car and were met by a boisterous crowd at Louisville's Central Station along the Ohio River at 9:10 p.m. The alumni had arranged for a caravan of cars to get the Kentuckians shuttled to the Seelbach Hotel which had been taken over by Centre as headquarters for the team and fans.

Saturday, November 20, was a perfect day for a football game. There wasn't a cloud in the sky, the temperature was in the mid 50's with a minimal breeze, and it was an excited crowd that filled Eclipse Park. An unusual event took place prior to the kickoff.

Dr. Ganfield and the Centre team and coaches had been so upset by what they considered unsportsman-like conduct that was experienced during the Georgia Tech game in Atlanta that they got together and vowed that it would never happen again in any game in which they participated. VPI had brought no cheerleaders, and Centre decided that it would forego any organized cheers during the game. If fans wished to cheer after individual plays for either team, so be it. But the Centre cheerleaders were instructed not to involve the fans in any organized cheering.

"None at all," Dr. Ganfield explained later. "It was the decent thing to do."

The newspapers dubbed the VPI contest, "The cheerless game." It may have been "cheerless," but the play, especially by Bo, was enthusiastically appreciated by the crowd.

Bruce Dudley of the Louisville "Herald" led off his coverage by writing about Bo's humility and dedication to teamwork for the Sunday morning edition of his newspaper.

Very frequently, Bo McMillin has called the press down for heaping so much praise of the success of the "Wonder Team" to himself individually. He does not like it at all, for he believes like Kipling:

> *It ain't the individual,*
> *Or the army as a whole,*
> *But the everlastin' teamwork*
> *Of every bloomin' soul.*

But it must be said that Alvin Nugent McMillin gave a sparkling exhibition of his super greatness against the heroic Virginia Polytechnic Institute at Eclipse Park. The largest crowd that ever witnessed a football contest in Louisville was elevated repeatedly by the dazzling advances of the Kentuckians and the courageous defense of the Virginians.

Centre was denied a score in the opening period, but McMillin crashed through for two touchdowns in the second period, and in the third, he stupefied the Virginians with his aerial attack and registered two more bell ringers. The visitors won unstinted admiration in the final quarter by refusing to yield to the Gold and White onslaughts. Only the stoutest hearted of teams, beaten 28-0 after three quarters, could have come back as the Virginians did and hold the opposition scoreless in the last period.

The game was one of the cleanest ever contested. Not a single penalty was called on the boys from Blacksburg, and only three on the Colonels, all for offsides.

The statistics for the game told the tale. Centre had three and one half times the yardage gained by VPI, 458-131. The Colonels had 19 first downs. VPI had but four, two in each half, and one was helped along by an offsides penalty. The closest that Tech got to the Centre goal was the 33 yard line when the Hokies recovered a fumble. The one-handed Crisp tried a field goal from that position but it failed.

Bo hit on 8 of 15 pass attempts for 135 yards which included TD's to Lefty Whitnell and Stanley Robb. Red Weaver was four for four and ran his streak to 86. Centre was now 6-2 on the season.

Centre's alumni put on quite a feast after the game in the Seelbach's Red Room. The place was hopping as a jazz band belted out lively tunes while the team and alumni hosts went through a buffet packed with every conceivable type of food.

After the dinner, the chairman of the Louisville alumni club, Nick Dosker, asked Dr. Ganfield to speak. He reviewed the progress that Centre's athletic program had made over the last few years.

"And finally, by the courageous, clean fight displayed in the Harvard game, there came the satisfaction of winning the great enthusiasm and devotion throughout the nation for a small college, and now everyone knows who and where we are," a reference to Howard Reynold's comments about "Centre College in Danville, Kentucky, wherever that is."

Uncle Charlie spoke about the team. "I love them, fuss at them, fight with them and sometimes even agree with them. The one thing I never do is lie to them. Whenever a coach does that, he immediately loses the confidence of his team."

Bo was called on to say a few words and his comments were met by a standing roar of approval when he said, "Everyone who can, is coming back to play another year, with our goal being to beat Harvard. We had a meeting and I got commitments, and I made a commitment. I'll be back. Red Roberts will be back. Army and Ben Cregor and Bill James will be back. All of our guys from Owensboro have made a pledge. We have gotten nearly everyone to agree. We will go to Harvard and….."

Bo stopped in mid-sentence. It didn't need to be said, because his grin said it all.

The room echoed with a spontaneous—BEAT HARVARD! BEAT HARVARD! BEAT HARVARD! BEAT HARVARD!

The jazz band picked it up and would play a few chords, and then—BEAT HARVARD! BEAT HARVARD! BEAT HARVARD! BEAT HARVARD!

The dignified Red Room of the Seelbach had never seen such a demonstration. BEAT HARVARD! BEAT HARVARD! BEAT HARVARD! BEAT HARVARD!

When the Colonels got in their private day coach the next morning for the return trip to Danville, they had to agree that their reception in Louisville had been wonderful. But then, that's what they had said about Boston and Indianapolis. That was what they said about their treatment in Lexington. It was what they were experiencing everywhere they went. There is no doubt that the Centre College Colonels had quickly become one of the most loved groups of athletes anywhere, of any time, in any sport.

"WE ARE CENTRE!" was beginning to be the slogan of people everywhere.

THE 1920 REGULAR SEASON ENDS

Georgetown simply couldn't play with Centre anymore. The two colleges had gone their separate ways in the last few years. Georgetown was respectable in 1917, losing by just 13-0. Things had changed dramatically since then with Centre pounding the Tigers 83-3 in 1918 and 77-7 in 1919.

The main interest of the fans in the 1920 Thanksgiving game was whether Red Weaver would get his 100th straight extra point. He had 86. Could the Colonels score 14 touchdowns?

There was no betting on the outcome. A few wagers were made on whether Georgetown would get a first down, or how many, if any. There were few who were willing to put any money on the possibility that the Tigers would score.

The Lexington "Herald" ran a story on the day before the game with the headline:

GEORGETOWN READY FOR SLAUGHTERING

Georgetown goes to Danville Thursday to supply the turkey day feast for the Colonels. It is surely the lamb led to the slaughter this year, for it is conceded that Centre will run up just as many points as she desires.

To accommodate the Colonels in their exhibition, Georgetown will furnish every thrill possible. Their whole play will be directed to slipping over a score of some sort, and every chance will be taken. Their rules in the game will be to take a risk in every play in hope of scoring any way possible, despite the diasterous consequences which may follow.

The capacity crowd which packed Cheek Field on Thanksgiving, 1920, couldn't complain about there being a lack of action. Centre beat the hapless Georgetown team 103-0. The last three contests had a cumulative point total of 263-10. It wasn't a pretty picture.

The Colonels scored 15 touchdowns, averaging a TD every four minutes. Nine men for Centre scored. Each Gold and White who suited up got into the game. The regulars played only the first and third quarters. It didn't really matter who was on the field as Centre scored 28 points in the first quarter and 14 in the second, to lead 42-0 at the break.

The regulars scored 33 points in the third quarter to make it 75-0. The reserves put another 28 on the board in the final period. Uncle Charlie did his best to hold the score down. Once he sent in big Sully Montgomery to fill the quarterback position.

"Red Weaver, do you want to run the ball some? Go in there for Lefty and tell Sully to let you run an end sweep."

Georgetown made two first downs in the entire game, neither against the starters. In their desperation to score, late in the fourth quarter, the Tigers tried a field goal from

155

the impossible range of 50 yards. They used a holder and he knelt down a good 12 yards from the center. The kicker got running start, like he was kicking off to start a game. He gave it his all, but the "Messenger" reported that his effort, "lacked force and direction." It was a sensitive way to say the ball was, "way short and really wide."

At the end of the first half, Uncle Charlie didn't even let the team rest but rather entertained the crowd by having his players line up in offensive and defensive positions to compare how plays were run in the early days of football, and how they were run now, since coaches such as himself had opened up the game.

"You see, it was a couple of yards and a cloud of dust," he'd yell into a megaphone when his team ran an old-fashioned, rugby-like play.

Then the coach would have his players line up in a similar formation, but Bo would send his ends and a couple of backs down the field and he'd fire a pass to one of them.

"What kind of football is more fun to watch?" Uncle Charlie would ask the crowd.

"Yours, Uncle Charlie! Yours, Uncle Charlie!"

Later, a reporter asked the Centre mentor about the rather different type of halftime entertainment. Uncle Charlie explained.

"There's an effort afoot to try to take the forward pass out of football, or at least effectively kill it."

Moran explained that some of the old traditional coaches in the East felt that football had become more like basketball. "They say that we just run the ball up and down the field like they do in the hoops game. They want a pass, if it isn't completed, to be a free ball, so that anyone can recover it and take possession. Of course, no one would dare pass under those circumstances."

Uncle Charlie continued, "It would ruin the game. It would really ruin Centre. Our attack is built on a wide open attack. I just wanted the people to see the difference. That's why I held my little drill."

Fortunately, Uncle Charlie was in the majority. Percy Haughton, the legendary Harvard coach from 1908-16, who in his nine seasons had a 71-7-5 record, was pushing to change the rule about the forward pass, but the NCAA rules committee, chaired by Walter Camp, voted him down, much to the relief of everyone who appreciated that a wide open game was what had made college football the most exciting and well attended sport in the nation.

The only disappointing aspect of the game was that Red Weaver's toe was only used four times. Uncle Charlie let Red do the kicking after the first four touchdowns, and he was good on each effort to run his consecutive streak to 90.

There was some talk that the coach had been in communication with some of his old friends in Texas, and they had told him that Centre could score at will against TCU, and he wanted Red to hit 100 in front of his home town supporters in Fort Worth. Of course, we'll never know, but that was the talk at the time.

Even though Uncle Charlie and Dr. Ganfield had vowed to always include old traditional opponent and friend, Georgetown, on the Colonels' schedule, the last three games were so one-sided that the Georgetown administration wisely decided to take a breather, and the two colleges didn't meet again on the gridiron until 1925, when Centre, even after the school's glory years, still was too much for the Tigers, and won, 34-6.

LOOKING FORWARD TO TCU AND THE NEXT SEASON

The Colonels were 7-2. They had lost two tough games on the road, but in reality, the Harvard and Georgia Tech games had assured the team that the next year, 1921, would be great.

Bo had pulled his teammates together after the return from Atlanta when his meeting in the Boyle-Humphrey Gymnasium had resulted in each player standing and shouting, "WE ARE CENTRE!" over and over. If there was a special spirit prior to that moment, and there was, it was now almost a supernatural force, dedicated to just one goal.

"WE ARE CENTRE!"

"BEAT HARVARD!"

"WE ARE CENTRE!"

"BEAT HARVARD!"

"WE ARE CENTRE!"

"BEAT HARVARD!"

"WE ARE CENTRE!"

"BEAT HARVARD!"

Offers and requests to play Centre were coming in from all over the country. Centre was the hottest ticket, by far, of any team in the country. Everybody wanted a piece of the action!

Columbia University wanted the Colonels to come to New York on October 29, 1921, to play at the Polo Grounds. The prediction was that the game would draw 65.000 fans. Centre had to reluctantly wire back that the date proposed was already filled by the rematch with Harvard.

Interest in the "Wonder Team" was further promoted by a piece put out by the Publishers Autocaster Service, a company which supplied inserts for papers to include in their regular distribution. On Sunday, November 21, readers all across the country found that the featured subject of their insert was, "The Praying Colonels of Centre College."

On that same Sunday, the Louisville "Courier-Journal" published an editorial about Centre.

CENTRE AS UNIFIER

The echoes of the Centre–Harvard game are still reverberating. It has been the wonder game of the football season, but its effects transcend even its importance as a sporting event. The great reputation of Centre preceded the team to Boston and the Praying Colonels found more that 45,000 people in the Crimson stands, with 10,000 more outside the great stadium to see the eleven men from an insular Kentucky college do battle with the giants of the East.

The editorial recounted at length the wonderful way that Centre and all of the fans from Kentucky had been treated.

If the Harvard faculty and the men and women of Boston and Cambridge could hear all that has been said in Kentucky about Harvard's hospitality and broadmindedness, they would realize that Harvard has taken a new hold on the South. The Centre College boys, when they came home, were outspoken and unreserved in their praise of the sportsmanlike conduct, the unexpected welcome, the generous cheers, and testified that no Southern hospitality could ever be greater then that which they had felt and known in Yankee land.

The moral of the event is the oneness of America and lack of provincial jealousies. It is true that people who live in the large cities often effect to look down on the rural population as being less sophisticated, but even this feeling is almost always good natured, and the great number of boys from the country who have become important figures in Chicago and New York belies the right of superiority of metropolitian citizens.

The press, the railroad, the telegraph, and the telephone have often been given the credit for the unity between different sections of the country. Now a football team has shown itself a valuable factor in the nationalizing process.

A November 27 article appeared in the "Advocate" stating a reader had a dream that Bo, on October 29, 1921, crossed the Harvard goal line for the winning score.

That same paper reprinted a story which had appeared in the Lexington "Herald" which exemplified how the Centre-Kentucky rivalry had gone from Wildcat domination to the overwhelming superiority of the Colonels.

BEAT CENTRE, 1921 BATTLE CRY OF WILDCATS

What will be the battle cry of the Kentucky Wildcats in 1921?
Beat Centre!
What words are on the lips of every member of old State?
Beat Centre!
What is the ambition, hope and prayer of the Blue and White?
Beat Centre!!

The tables had totally turned. From a 68-0 massacre in 1916, Centre was now to Kentucky what Harvard had become to Centre—an obsession to meet their rival on the gridiron and to emerge victorious.

POST SEASON HONORS

Bo was the only Colonel to make Walter Camp's 1920 All-American team which was announced in "Collier's Weekly" in December. He was placed on the second team at the quarterback position. Princeton's Donald Lourie led the Tigers to a 6-0-1 record, the tie being with Harvard, 14-14, and he was picked as the first team quarterback. Ben Boynton of Williams was the third team pick. Camp mentioned Red

Weaver in his "honorable mention" classification.

Bo was the first team selection on the Boston "Telegram" All-American eleven, and Walter Eckersall, who was a three-time Walter Camp honoree from 1904-06, put Bo on his first team in his Chicago "Tribune" squad.

Bo made first team All-American on the Newspaper Enterprise Association (NEA) team, as well as on the team picked by Frank G. Menke (1885-1954), noted sports authority who wrote "The Encyclopedia of Sports."

Harvard had three selections on Camp's team. Tom Woods was a first team tackle, and Arnold Horween and Charles Havemeyer were on the third team at fullback and center, respectively. William Fincher of Georgia Tech, the same Fincher who reportedly kicked Sully Montgomery in the face in the game in Atlanta, was placed on the first team, at end.

Much more recognition was gained by the Colonels as eight All-Southern teams were announced by various newspapers below the Mason-Dixon Line. Bo made five of the teams, Red Weaver and Terry Snowday each made three, and Bill James and Sully Montgomery were selected on two of the newspaper elevens.

The "All-Southern, All-Southern" team was announced on November 29. It was composed by taking all of the selections and compiling the "best of the best." Centre had three men, Bo, Red Weaver and Bill James, on the first team. Georgia Tech also had three, Auburn and Georgia had two, and the eleventh spot went to an Alabama player.

Of course, Centre dominated the All-Kentucky team, taking each of the positions. Robb and Snowday were the ends, James and Montgomery, the tackles, Cregor and Roberts were the guards, and Weaver was at the center slot. Bo, Army, Whitnell and Hump made up the backfield. There was no doubt who ruled in the Bluegrass. Centre College was the undisputed "Champion of Kentucky."

On the last night of November, the Centre football team banquet was held at the Gilcher. There were 125 people in attendance. The coveted gold "C" was awarded to 24 players and team manager, Thad McDonnell. Letter winners were:

Army Armstrong
Tom Bartlett
Blink Bedford
Ashley Blevins
Fred Caudill
George Chinn
Ben Cregor
Jack Converse
Clayton Ford
Bill James
Henry "Shanks" Lipscomb
George Maver
Lee McGregor

Bo McMillin
Sully Montgomery
Tom Moran
Chick Murphy
Carlton Rice
Stanley Robb
Red Roberts
Terry Snowday
Hump Tanner
Red Weaver
Lefty Whitnell
Thad McDonnell — manager

Senators, Governor Morrow, sportswriters including Damon Runyon, Grantland Rice and Howard Reynolds, prominent businessmen and civic leaders from all over the country, and alumni from various locations, sent telegrams and letters which literally filled a basket placed at the head table.

Of note, Walter Camp's wire was read at the banquet and published in the local paper.

"I want to congratulate Centre College and its football team, as well as the residents of Danville, not as I did last year upon such remarkable victories, but upon the fine football spirit displayed, and the real success of the team's trip to the East, and the sportsmanlike way in which Centre represented Kentucky."

Arnold Horween, the Harvard captain and third team All-American, sent his regrets and said that college duties prevented his attending, "but I should like to take part in honoring a team which has proved itself such a worthy opponent for any team in the country. Harvard football men will not soon forget the Centre College team of 1920, not only on account of the high caliber of football it played, but also on account of the gentlemanliness and true sportsmanship of its members who played the hard, clean game that everyone admires. I sincerely hope that athletic relations will continue between Centre and Harvard for the benefit of both colleges. Sincere personal regards to Captain McMillin and his men."

Harvard Coach Robert Fisher sent a letter which was read at the banquet.

"The game between Centre and Harvard certainly has caused favorable comment in this part of the country. We can truthfully say that we have never met a team that displayed cleaner sportsmanship that Centre, and it is just such contests that will help the great game of college football. I look forward to meeting you again next fall."

Uncle Charlie introduced each member of the team and asked them to say a few words. When it was Bo's turn, he was asked to come forward and the head of the Chamber of Commerce reached under the table and pulled out a framed certificate signed by Governor Morrow.

Captain Bo McMillin had been promoted to Colonel Bo McMillin. Governor Morrow had made Bo a Kentucky Colonel, and a letter accompanying the certificate stated, "…and you Sir, have been promoted from the Captain of the Wonder Team of Kentucky to a Colonel on my staff."

After receiving the honor, Bo spoke, and his comments concentrated on Harvard. It was always, Harvard.

"The Eastern papers said we would have stage-fright before the large Harvard crowd. The only time I have stage-fright is when I have to give a speech."

"I'm not really certain why we didn't defeat Harvard this year. We really felt we could win. Next year, we expect the score will be on the right side of the ledger. If each man on the squad makes up his mind, right now, at this very moment that we can beat Harvard, we will."

"We must make sacrifices. We must continuously train. The ambition of my life has been to play some Eastern eleven and beat them. The Chief began telling us more than seven years ago that we could achieve that goal if we had the belief that we were capable. I believe it! I believe that we can beat Harvard! And I ask that each man begin to prepare for the game with Harvard in 1921."

Bo got teary eyed talking about the Chief, the man who had meant so much to him in shaping his life. The Chief was back in Chicago, but Bo wanted everyone to know how much he felf that the team owed the man who first had the dream.

"I love the Chief as a son loves his father. The measure of the man was shown when he pulled me aside early in 1917 and said we need a bigger man than he was to coach the Centre team, and that man was Charlie Moran."

The final event of the banquet was to announce the team captain for 1921. Bo had announced that he didn't want to be considered. He had held the position for the past two years, and he wanted someone else to assume the position. He wanted to concentrate all of his energies on Harvard.

As was the custom, only letter-winners could vote, and they retired to an adjoining room. Bo said he wasn't going to vote, that he felt there were too many who were qualified. The first ballot had Army and Bill James with eight votes each, Red Weaver got five, and Sully Montgomery and Tom Bartlett each received a single vote.

It was decided to narrow the candidates to the top two, and Army was elected in a 13-10 tally. The guests and team stood and cheered when Bo introduced, "Captain Norris 'Army' Armstrong, from Fort Smith, Arkansas!"

It had been a memorable night at the Gilcher Hotel. After all of the honors and all of the accolades, there was one last selection that thrilled everyone who followed the Colonels, perhaps more than all of the others combined. Each year, the Harvard "Crimson," the university publication since 1873, selected the greatest players to appear in games played by the Crimson during the previous season. The "Crimson" billed those chosen as the "Mythical eleven picked from all of the brilliant players who have thrilled gridiron lovers with their play."

There were four from Harvard, four from Princeton, two from Yale, and but one player from other than the "Big 3." Bo McMillin rounded out the squad.

CHAPTER 10:
POST-SEASON BOWL—
THE FORT WORTH CLASSIC

Uncle Charlie gave the team some well deserved time off after the Thanksgiving rout of Georgetown. The players kept in shape by jogging, but they didn't put the pads back on until December 13, a chilly, sunny, Monday afternoon. The plan was to have an intensive week of workouts, culminating in one last "walk-through" and skull session on the following Monday. The Texans were to leave for home on Tuesday, December 21, and the rest of the team would scatter to their homes for Christmas and then head to Texas on the 26th.

Uncle Charlie announced that the travel squad would include the 24 letter winners, manager Thad McDonnell, and himself, and some non-letter winners who were from Texas and were going to be allowed to suit-up.

A reporter dug up some interesting information in writing a story about the upcoming Centre-TCU game. Bill Driver, the TCU mentor, had been at the helm of the University of Mississippi program during the 1913-14 seasons. In the closing game of the 1914 campaign, his Ole Miss team went down to defeat, 14-7, in the last game that Uncle Charlie coached at Texas A&M.

Centre's fans began to research TCU in order to learn more about the Colonels' upcoming opponent. Texas Christian University, founded in 1873, was located in Fort Worth, which had a 1920 population of 106,000. The college began playing football in 1896. The Horned Frogs got their nickname due to the fact that the practice field was overrun by fierce looking reptiles.

The founders of the school were Addison and Randolph Clark, two brothers associated with the Campbellite movement, the ancestor of the present day Disciples of Christ Church. TCU was first called Addran University, then Addran Christian University, and finally, in 1902, Texas Christian University, TCU. It was associated with, but never governed by, the church.

The original plan was to locate the campus on five city blocks that the brothers had purchased in Fort Worth. However, about the time that the Clarks were ready to begin putting up some buildings, their plans were disrupted by the fact that the

Chisholm Trail, the main route for driving cattle from Texas to the railroads in Kansas, ran right through their property.

It seemed that the influx of cows, cowhands, and money had turned sleepy little Fort Worth into a brawling "Cowtown," and the proposed campus site was smack in the center of a huge swath of bordellos, saloons, and gambling and dance halls which catered to the "baser instincts" of the bawdy cowboys and gamblers.

It didn't take long for the brothers to realize that building a school right in the center of a vice district probably wasn't going to allow them to attract the type of students they were after, especially since they were progressive enough to plan to admit females as well as males.

The Clarks made a hastly retreat to Thorp Spring, a stagecoach stop 40 miles to the southwest of Fort Worth, which they felt now, "should be renamed—HELL!"

In 1895, the school relocated to Waco. After a fire in 1910, inducements from the citizens of Fort Worth, which included $200,000 and 50 acres for a campus, resulted in TCU moving to Fort Worth, back where it had been envisioned to be situated in the first place.

TCU played in the Texas Intercollegiate Athletic Association. The Frogs were the undefeated champions of the T.I.A.A. at 9-0.

TCU	20	S.E. Oklahoma	0
TCU	9	Austin College	7
TCU	19	Arkansas	2
TCU	20	Trinity	7
TCU	3	Phillips	0
TCU	19	Missouri O's	3
TCU	21	Baylor	9
TCU	31	Hardin-Simmons	2
TCU	21	Southwestern	16

TCU's strength of schedule had to be somewhat suspect, but they had only given up an average of less than seven points per game and would be playing in their own home town.

Uncle Charlie and the Colonels had to take TCU seriously, and they had another incentive. Centre's players were coming home, as nearly half of them had a definite Texas connection. Bo, Red Weaver, Bill James, Sully Montgomery, Lee McGregor, and the team manager, Thad McDonnell, were all from Fort Worth. Harry Lipscomb, Gus King, Blink Bedford, and Bryan Allen, all hailed from Dallas, just 20 miles to the east. Of course, Uncle Charlie had not only coached at Texas A&M, but played baseball and umpired in Texas for several years.

TCU's home games were played at Clark Field which had two wooden stands with 25 rows of seats. The facility was adequate for the number of fans who attended TCU's games with regional foes. However, the Centre game was attracting such interest that the school's administration and the game's promoters decided that a much larger stadium was needed, and an agreement was reached with the management of the Fort Worth Panthers, a "AA" baseball team in the Texas League, to play in the team's Panther Park.

Panther Park was a state-of-the-art ballpark. It was built in 1911 and located north of downtown Fort Worth on the west side of Main Street. It held 8,000 spectators, but even that capacity was considered too small, and like so many venues where Centre played, a hurried construction project added 2,000 seats in the outfield, assuring that the crowd would be the greatest ever assembled for a football game in the area.

When tickets went on sale, orders were brisk. TCU decided to call the contest a Homecoming game and encouraged all alumni to support the Horned Frogs by attending. Centre's alumni associations in neighboring states did the same, and Colonels' fans from Oklahoma, Arkansas, Louisiana, along with Texas, made arrangements to head to Fort Worth.

TCU held a huge pep rally on December 16, prior to heading into its Christmas vacation. Colvin Renfro, sports editor of the Fort Worth "Star-Telegram," attended and was asked to make a few comments.

"The Horned Frogs will win because Centre is a one-man team, while TCU is a machine, and every time such a combination meets, the machine will always triumph."

Coach William L. "Bill" Driver then took the podium and went through his starting line which he predicted would present an impregnable wall to Bo and the other Colonels' backs.

"Centre hasn't run up against the likes of "Doug" Douglas at center, "Big Pete" Fulcher and "Leviticus" Levy at guards, "Uncle Billy" Acker and "Red" Spiller at our tackle positions, and our ends, "Dutch" Meyer and "Hootch" Houtchens."

("Dutch" Meyer later became the legendary coach of the Horned Frogs, taking over the program in 1934. During his 19 seasons at SMU, his teams were 109-79-13, and he was, and remains so to this day, the winningest coach in the school's history.)

Coach Driver then spoke of his backfield, getting cheers as he mentioned each starter's name.

"Boob" Fowler is anything but a "boob" when he runs the ball. If "Ponzi" Rowson is declared eligible, he'll more than offset McMillin. McSweeny Ryan, the man with the "depth-bomb" plunge, has scored two-thirds of our touchdowns, and "Jack" Jackson is not only a great runner, but one of the top receivers in the Southwest!"

"Ponzi" Rowson had been declared ineligible late in the season when it was discovered he had taken a correspondence course from Texas A&M. Bo and Uncle Charlie went to bat for "Ponzi" by pointing out that whatever he had done happened in 1920, and since the game was to be played on the first day of 1921, he should be allowed to play. "Ponzi" was declared eligible and indeed did play.

After Coach Driver's colorful introduction of his team, Bailey Diffie, "The greatest pep leader the school has ever had," according to the school newspaper, the "Horned Frog," worked the crowd into a frenzy as he led the "rah, rahs" and "rip, rams" which echoed throughout the gymnasium.

Centre's Texans came to their homes in Fort Worth and Dallas earlier than the rest of team in order to be with their families during the Christmas vacation. In the December 23 issue of the Fort Worth "Record," reporter "Pop" Boone asked Bo how it felt to be home.

Bo said he'd been in Boston and other cities all over the country, but there was no place like home, "because here is where I have so many friends."

Bo was holding court at his home, and Boone stayed with him throughout the day.

Bo had a busy day, taking a minute with 600 friends yesterday. He arrived home after the long train ride from Danville in the morning and planned to just laze around the house until Christmas. But it wasn't long before the word got out that Bo was in town. The phone got busy and Fords, Buicks, Cadillacs and Packards got busy also. It was reception day at the McMillin home out on North Houston Street, and Bo saw them all.

When the Colonels arrived in Fort Worth, they headquartered at the Westbrook Hotel at Fourth and Main Streets. The arrival of the team members was somewhat chaotic, but by the morning of the 28th, everyone who was coming was present, and the first workout took place on that afternoon at League Park. Uncle Charlie held an open session and several hundred spectators lined the field, anxious to get a glimpse of the Wonder Team.

Uncle Charlie had the team up early on the 29th, where they held a closed door session at Panther Park. The Centre coach was reported to have said to Red Roberts, Terry Snowday, Hump Tanner and Jack Converse, "All right, you four, you look like you must have eaten all day and night during the holidays. Ten laps for each of you, and I've got your buddy Thaddeus (McDonnell) to do the counting."

"Aw, Unc, this trip is supposed to be a reward for a good season," as they grinned and began to trot off.

The incident demonstrated the great bond between the coach and his players. Uncle Charlie could have told any of the four to start running and not stop until they reached Danville, and they would have said, "Which way do I head?"

After the morning practice, the former Fort Worth North Side Steers, Bo, Red Weaver, Bill James, Sully Montgomery, and Thad McDonnell, headed to their old school where there was a special assembly of the students in the auditorium. A local report said, "A thousand pairs of eyes were turned in worship on the gridiron heroes."

After the Colonels were introduced and they were praised by the principle and North Side coaching staff, Bo was asked to speak, and his theme was that the students should pay more attention to studies than to athletics.

"Honor in sports is alright, but when you finish school, sports become but a memory, and unless you've studied hard, the time that you spend in high school or college is sheer waste."

After the North Side visit, it was back to Panther Park for another workout.

Centre was feeling confident, and one of the main reasons was that Red Roberts was back. The big guy had totally recovered from the knee injury suffered during the Harvard game. He was running at full speed and cutting and slashing his way down the field just as he used to do. When Red was right, Centre was right. And, "Red's back."

The attitude and confidence of TCU wasn't quite so positive if you read between the lines when reviewing an article which was published quoting the team captain, Astyanax "Doug" Douglas. (You read correctly. Astyanax was derived from Greek mythology, and meant "prince of the city.)

It is said that opportunity comes to a man but once in a lifetime. If such be so, then our opportunity has arrived. To beat Centre would place our school among the greater institutions of America and bring us to world-wide fame. To this end we have worked, and worked hard, with nothing in view but to beat Centre if it is possible to do so. The Horned Frogs will not be the same team that has gone through an undefeated season with that care-free spirit of never trying to run up a large score, only enough to win, but a team that is backed to the last ditch with odds staring them square in the face, but determined to win, and not until every mother's son is battered down to where he is unable to go another inch will we admit we are beaten.

It was a determined by hardly inspiring message from Astyanax.

Coach Driver had contacted several of the coaches of teams Centre had played, and his goal after hearing back from them was not to let Bo and the Colonels set the tone of the game with their passing attck. Most of the drilling of his team concentrated on passing defense. Bo had heard that fact from some of his local friends. He simply replied, "If they line up to cover against the pass, we'll run. If they try to stop our running game, we'll pass."

Game day, January 1, 1921, the day of the "Fort Worth Classic," was indeed classic football weather. The sun shone brightly, there was just a nip in the air, and Panther Park was decorated with the purple and white of the Horned Frogs and the gold and white of the Colonels. The crowd began to file into the permanent seats, then the temporary bleachers in the outfield began to fill, and soon there was standing room only, and hundreds of disappointed fans had to be turned away.

Unce Charlie had written an article for the Fort Worth "Record" in which he described the pre-game ritual.

We are now getting ready to play the great game. Just before going to the field, the coach gives his club the last heart-to-heart talk. To the critical observer, this scene would appear to be heart-breaking, for it seldom that a club that has a chance to win such honor and glory can listen to this great master's instructions without shedding tears – but the tears are only the tears of scorching impatience to get into the game and get started. When the referee's whistle blows, however, all of this nervousness disappears and the men settle down to play the game as they have been coached and as they are capable of playing.

Centre won the toss and elected to receive. "Uncle Billy" Acker, a tackle weighing in at 180 lbs., kicked off for TCU and the "Fort Worth Classic" was underway. It was a deep kick which Bo brought back to the 20.

Centre lined up and went to work. Bo got five through the line, another six on the same play and Centre, looking good, had a first down. TCU was penalized five, Army got two, a pass to Terry Snowday was batted down, and Bo gained eight for another first down.

Centre looked sharp. Bo was directing the first drive with his usual confidence. On a first down play, Hump streaked ahead for eight, and then Bo looped around the left end for 20 before being brought down. It was another first down, the Colonels running with machine-like precision.

Tom Bartlett got the call next and picked up eight, however Centre was penalized five for being off sides on the next play. Hump got four of the five back, Bo was racked up for no gain, and on the next play, the Centre quarterback fired a long pass toward Stanley Robb.

"Jack" Jackson, a fleet 150 lb. halfback for the Horned Toads, had been playing deep, and he timed his move correctly, picking off the toss at his own 10 yard line, and he streaked 90 yards down the field for a touchdown.

The stands erupted with, "Did you see that?"

"Way to go, Toads!"

"Atta boy, Jack!"

The cheering only intensified as Acker booted the extra point and it was TCU, 7-0.

The Centre sideline remained absolutely calm. The Colonels had moved the ball easily on the drive before the pass was intercepted. Uncle Charlie was later quoted as saying that he could see from the onset that TCU was no match for his team. He simply hollered out once, "That's ok boys. Now, take it back to them."

The Colonels scored easily on the next possession. Bo alternated plays with his backs, first one and then the other. It was Hump, then Bo. Army, then Bo. It was relentless.

Coach Driver was determined not to get beaten by Centre's passing attack.

"That's was fine with me," Bo later said. "We knew we could run if they spread out their defense, or we could pass if they tightened up to protect against the run."

On the tenth consecutive run, each for a gain, Hump scored from five yards out, Red Weaver booted his 91st, and it was 7-7.

After a booming Red Roberts kickoff, TCU had poor field position and had to punt, running up against a smacking Gold and White defense. Stanley Robb broke through, blocked the kick and followed it into the end zone where he smothered it for a touchdown. Red for 92, and just like that, the Colonels were up 14-7.

Red Roberts really got into the next kickoff and boomed it totally over and out of the end zone, bringing a collective "whoa!" from the crowd.

The game was beginning to enter into a pattern which would continue all afternoon. This time, the Horned Frogs ran three plays for no gain and then couldn't even get a punt off, fumbling the ball around in the backfield where the Colonels covered the loose ball on the eight yard line.

Bo carried it over on the first play after the recovery, and it was 21-7 after Red's number 93. TCU was looking something more than bewildered. The most points that the boys from Fort Worth had given up all season was the 16 scored by Southwestern in the last game of the regular season. Centre had 21, and the first quarter wasn't even over!

Finally, somewhat mercifully, the initial period ended, with the Colonels driving again and on the Toad's 10 yard line. After switching ends of the field, two straight five yard plunges, the last by Army, brought the score to 28-7 after Red split the uprights for his 94th.

After the interception by TCU early in the game, it hadn't been able to get even one first down, with the Colonels swarming and gang tackling on every play. The game was essentially over. Now it was just a matter of the final score.

The Fort Worth papers had given native son, North Side grad, Red Weaver, a lot of pre-game publicity about his streak of consecutive extra points. Every fan who had any inkling about football records knew that Red had started the day at 90, and there was speculation whether he could reach 100 during the game.

Now, with the four quick scores, and Red on target each time, the crowd began to get behind the Centre kicker and his streak. After the 94th, the fans began to chant, "100! 100! 100!"

During the second quarter, the TCU offense began to pick up a bit, and got four first downs, but never moved closer that the Colonels' 30. Uncle Charlie was running in subs left and right, especially being sensitive to getting all of the Texans on the field who hadn't started.

The Colonels from Dallas, Gus King, Harry "Shanks" Lipscomb, Bryan Allen, and Blink Bedford, all saw action. Lee McGregor from Fort Worth got in the game. Uncle Charlie put in his son, Tom, at halfback. Jack Converse from Somerset went in for Terry Snowday, and at one point, Red Roberts took over for Tom Bartlett in the backfield. The half ended at 28-7.

The third quarter saw the Colonels pick up the tempo as the starting lineup returned to action intact.

Red Roberts kicked off and on the first play, TCU tried to get some offense going by passing. Tom Bartlett intercepted and six plays later, Centre scored. The big play was a 40 yard Bo to Robb pass. Weaver for 95. 35-7.

"100! 100! 100!"

In desperation, TCU again passed. Again, Bartlett plucked it out of the air, this time taking it in for a score. Red for his 96th. 42-7

"100! 100! 100!"

Another futile series followed for the Toads. A hard hit by the left side of the Colonels' front wall caused a fumble. For once, Centre was held and had to punt and TCU actually got a first down, but that was all. After kicking back to Centre, the Colonels marched right down the field and Bo capped off the drive by twisting and cutting the final 30 yards. Red for 97. Centre 49-7.

"100! 100! 100!"

The crowd could only watch in astonishment. TCU had only given up 46 points during the entire season. Fans in the Fort Worth remembered Coach Driver's comments about his line and how Centre hadn't run up against the likes of "Uncle Billy," "Big Pete," "Dutch" and "Hootch," "Red" and "Leviticus," and "Doug" Douglas.

It was still in the third quarter and Centre had scored 49 points!

"What in the world is going on?"

Once again, the question was being asked, "Who are those guys, anyway?"

After the third quarter wound down, the teams changed ends of the field and there was another series in which the Horned Toads couldn't even pick up a yard and had to punt.

Bo caught the ball on the run on his own 40 and ran right through the befuddled Texans for a 60 yard, unmolested sprint. Red Weaver was on the sidelines, having been replaced by "Shanks" Lipscomb. Uncle Charlie motioned to Red to get back out on the field and the crowd shouted "100! 100! 100!" as he trotted down toward the end zone. It was 98 as he returned to the Colonels' bench, with the score now at 56-7.

Uncle Charlie was constantly running players in and out of the contest. In "Pop's Palaver," a sports column in the Fort Worth "Record," written by "Pop" Boone, an incident was reported which indicated how frantically Uncle Charlie was rotating his line-up.

Along in the final quarter, when Moran was shooting players in so fast that they couldn't keep up with the procession themselves, Bo hollered over to the bench and said, "Unc, we've only got 10 players out here." Charlie looked around for a minute. Then he said, "Where's Bill James? I never took him out of the game." Bill was sitting back in the box with the mothers of the Centre team and, of course, couldn't get back as he had left the field. Unc scratched his head and found someone who hadn't played much and sent him in."

After Bo's long touchdown run, the pattern of the game continued. TCU threw two passes which were way off the mark. Centre intercepted the third throw and went back on the attack. Bo hit Red Roberts for 20 yards, missed on his next two efforts, so just ran it in from the 22. Red Weaver booted his 99th. The crowd was energized, shouting for Centre to hurry up and score again so that Red could reach the milestone.

"100! 100! 100!"

It was 63-7 as darkness began to envelop the field. After two punt exchanges, Uncle Charlie sent his first stringers back in. He certainly wasn't trying to further embarrass TCU, but was hearing the crowd cheering for Red, and he felt that he owed it to his great kicker to try to make that last extra point.

It was so dark that Bo kept it on the ground. He was afraid that his receivers couldn't pick up the ball with so little light.

"100! 100! 100!"

But it wasn't to be. Centre was moving and on the TCU 35 when the final whistle blew. Red fell one short, but what a run he had!

The "Record" carried a little boxed story the next day.

RED WEAVER HAD TOUGH LUCK; ONLY KICKS NINE

.....Red went into the game with 90 boots to his credit without a miss. The crowd became greatly interested in whether he could make it to 100 or not. Nobody doubted his ability to run the string just as high as his teammates would let him.

Someday, Texas may go Republican. Someday, Iowa or Kansas may go "wet." Someday, New York may admit that Chicago is the better town. Someday, someone may give me a million dollars. But Red Weaver miss a goal? Never!

The fans had seen a team play like they hadn't witnessed before. The TCU Horned Frogs walked off the field with a new understanding of the game of football. They had played hard and clean, but they were simply totally outclassed, going from an undefeated season to being completely dominated, 63-7.

TCU paid dearly for concentrating on shutting down the Colonels' aerial attack. They were successful in that endeavor, with Bo and his mates completing only three of 20 all afternoon. But by being so determined to play good pass defense, they had left themselves wide open to Centre's unrelenting ground attack. Centre simply had too much in its offensive arsenal, too much skill and power, for TCU to be able to shut down the Colonels both in the air and on the ground.

After the game, as the players mingled around on the field, accepting hugs and kisses from the many family members and friends who were present, several Horned Frogs drew individual Colonels aside and asked, "How in this world did you guys ever lose? How could anybody even stay close to you the way you play the game?"

When Bo was asked that question, he replied that he really didn't know. It was a question he had asked himself repeatedly.

"How could we have lost?"

Bo didn't give an answer. But he was determined it wasn't going to happen again, at least not in Cambridge, Massachusetts.

Even as the team reveled with the fans at Panther Park that New Year's Day in 1921, it was still—Harvard. It was always—Harvard.

The "Daily Skiff," the TCU student newspaper first published in 1902, ran a story in the first edition put out after the students returned from Christmas vacation.

MORAN'S GANG DEALS ROUGHLY WITH HORNIES

They came. We saw. They conquered.

We had heard about the famous praying, fighting, wonder thoroughbred, the Kentucky Colonels from Centre College, until it seemed that the whole world judged a football team by what it could do against these super-men.

We got all ambitious and decided that the best team in Texas could beat the best team in Kentucky. They did not think so. They were right. We have no alibis to offer. We gave them the best we had. It was not enough. They played hard but clean, and they won.

The writer made the best that he could of the situation. He recounted that the Horned Frogs had shut down the fabled Centre passing attack. He was correct. What he didn't mention was how costly that effort had been. Centre had run at will, rolling up several hundred yards on the ground.

The final point made in the article was that TCU was hitting as hard at the end of the game as at the onset.

This only shows that TCU fights just as hard when the score is 63-7 against us as when it is reversed. No school need be ashamed of a team that fights until the end, even if it loses.

The significance of the "Fort Worth Classic" of January 1, 1921 can't be overly emphasized. Bowl games, now so common, were in their infancy.

The first ever post-season college football game was the Rose Bowl of January 1, 1902. Michigan took a train from Ann Arbor and met the Stanford Cardinal at Pasadena's Tournament Park and won, 49-0.

After that game, there were no more Bowl games until 1916. As unbelievable as it may seem, the organizers of the Rose Bowl decided to have chariot races to entertain the masses, and these throwbacks to Roman times prevailed for the next 13 years.

However, when only 2,000 spectators showed up for the 1915 races, it was decided that perhaps people had tired of the dusty event, and football was seen as a better draw, which it certainly proved to be.

The second New Year's game in Pasadena featured Washington State and Brown, with State coming out on top, 14-0.

That was the same score in the 1917 game, this time with Oregon beating Pennsylvania. 1918 and 1919 had service teams facing each other, and colleges returned on January 1, 1920, with Harvard coming to the West and edging Oregon, 7-6.

The "Fort Worth Classic" was the first Bowl game to be played besides the Rose Bowl, and for that reason, it is recognized by football historians as a major event in the evolution of college football.

A REVIEW OF CENTRE COLLEGE FOOTBALL, 1917-1920

The Colonels returned to campus after the trip to Fort Worth and were met by an enthusiastic crowd at the Southern station. One member of the team who had difficulty leaving his home town was Bo, for departing Fort Worth meant he was leaving behind the only girl he had ever loved, Maude Marie Miers.

Marie told him he had to go back and not only finish his education, but also to complete his dream, the dream whose seeds had first been planted by the Chief back at North Side High School.

"Bo, you'll never be happy until you have beaten Harvard. You know that's true. You've told me so many times. And if you're not happy, we can't be. I'll wait. I'll wait."

Bo knew Marie was right. But it was so hard. It was so very hard to leave her.

What Bo and Centre had accomplished was truly remarkable. Since he had become a starter, Centre had won 28 games and lost but three, a winning record of 90.3 %.

YEAR	RECORD	POINTS-CENTRE	POINTS-OPPONENTS
1917	7-1	24	6
1918	4-0	168	13
1919	9-0	485	23
1920	8-2	532	62
Totals	28-3	1432	104

Centre had run up an average score of 46-3, rounded off, during the last four seasons. It had shut out its opponents in 20 of the 31 games played. The only losses had been on the road, out of the state of Kentucky; DePauw in Indiana, Harvard in Massachusetts, and Georgia Tech in Georgia.

There was no doubt that the Colonels had become the most storied team in college football. They played to standing-room-only crowds everywhere that they went. They were the darlings of the sporting media, garnering headlines and photo spreads all over the country.

In the last four years, Centre College, little Centre College of Kentucky, had truly become America's "Wonder Team," and the best was yet to come.

CHAPTER 11:
MORE POST-SEASON EVENTS

With its small student body, Centre had to have men who could play multiple sports in order to field teams other than that on the gridiron. During the era of this book, the little school not only played football, but basketball, baseball, competed in track, and in the early twenties, began to put together a tennis and golf team, even though the latter two sports weren't "official."

During the 1920-21 school year, the Colonels had quite a basketball team.

Charles Rice McDowell, a native of Danville, and a 1915 graduate of Centre, took over the basketball coaching job in the winter of 1920. Before coming back to Danville, Rice had done graduate work at the University of Chicago and Columbia, ending up with a master's in history and education. Besides becoming the hoopster's coach, he taught history and political science at the college. Rice had been quite a player of the sport in his days at Centre, and was young enough to not only coach the team, but able to be a buddy of the players, and to mix it up on the court.

(According to the official Washington and Lee School of Law website, Rice later "was the most beloved professor ever" at the Lexington, Virginia school. He was on the faculty there from 1927-68.)

Army was the basketball team captain. Besides Army, Bo, Blink Bedford, George Maver, Red Roberts, Royce Flippin and Stanley Robb, all played football. A non-football player, William Julian "Judy" Walden, was a starter and quite a player. While "Judy" may not have played football, he was a star on the track team.

Centre opened the season successfully by winning eight of its first nine games.

Centre	46	Kentucky Wesleyan	14
Centre	34	University of Louisville	20
Centre	42	Auburn	24
Centre	29	University of Kentucky	27
Centre	62	Georgetown (Ky.)	23
Centre	55	Transylvania	23
Centre	13	University of Kentucky	20
Centre	44	Vanderbilt	18
Centre	69	Georgetown (Ky.)	20

After the last Georgetown game, the team took off by train on a several day trip to the East. Harvard had invited Centre to come up and play its basketball team, so Coach McDowell and the athletic department plotted out a route that could make a loop around the area, playing four different colleges.

The first game was against the University of Buffalo in the Bulls' Clark Gymnasium. Centre wasn't used to the tighter officiating in basketball "up East," got into foul trouble and lost, 40-28.

The next stop was Harvard as the Colonels took the New York Central to Albany and switched to a Central subsidiary, the Boston and Albany, just as the football team's "Harvard Special" had done the previous October.

It was like a reunion when the Colonels returned to the Boston area. The local papers played up the game because of the tremendously positive reception that Centre had received in the fall.

Harvard had just resurrected its basketball program. The college played an intercollegiate schedule from 1900 through 1908. From 1909 to 1920, the program was shut down and only an informal team was put on the court, almost a pick-up game situation, where students who were interested in playing on the courts would challenge other organizations to play.

In 1920, the athletic department decided to once again sponsor an official Crimson team. A coach, Edward A. Wachter, was hired, and Harvard took to the court.

The game with Harvard was played on the night of March 7 in the Hemenway Gymnasium on the Harvard campus. The gym, designed by architect Robert Peabody, was built with funds supplied by August Hemenway, Jr., son of a successful Boston merchant, who made a fortune trading with countries on the west coast of South America, particularly Chile. When it was completed in 1878, it was the largest such facility in North America.

Peabody designed Hemenway Gymnasium with a large assortment of gables, wings, dormers, chimneys and cupolas, along with an entrance which resembled a porte cochere. The building really wasn't set up for basketball as it had mainly been used to develop one of the premiere physical education programs during the period when Harvard didn't play an intercollegiate basketball schedule.

Like everywhere Centre played football, new bleachers were rapidly installed so that the capacity exceeded 1,000. When the Colonels ran onto the court for pre-game warm-ups, they were met with a loud cheer from the overflowing crowd which was swelled by a story in the "Harvard Crimson" publicizing "the return of the Gold and White lads who had played so brilliantly the previous fall in the Stadium."

The entire Crimson football squad turned out to meet their rivals on the gridiron who, "had left behind a reputation for clean play and sportsmanship that has earned them a lasting welcome at Harvard."

The game lived up to the excitement it had generated. Centre played but five men, four of whom had been on the football team that traveled to Boston. Army and Bo lined up at the guard positions, George Maver played center, and Blink Bedford and

"Judy" Walden, the non-footballer, were the forwards. (Red Roberts was on the team but didn't make the trip to the East.)

The Colonels got off to a fast start and led by six at the half. During the second half, Harvard regrouped and forged into the lead for a short time, but Centre fought back and regained a five point lead with a little over five minutes left and managed to hold onto that margin until the final whistle, walking off the court victorious, 41-36.

As the 1921 "Old Centre" yearbook later stated, "Hemenway Gymnasium was kept in an uproar throughout the hotly contested event." After the game, the players retired to Harvard Square for refreshments and to rehash not only the basketball game, but many of the Crimson football players sought out the Colonels to again wish them well and to let them know how much they looked forward to their return in October.

The Centre roundballers were driven to South Station by members of the football team for an overnight Pullman journey to Providence, Rhode Island, where a game was scheduled the next night against Brown University.

Centre again played before a sold-out crowd against the Brown Bears. The Colonels had an easier time than against the Crimson, winning 40-28. Coach McDowell managed to get Chas McCall, Royce Flippin and Stanley Robb into the game, in addition to the starters. George Maver, with 24 points, almost outscored the entire Brown team.

The win put the Colonels' record at 10-2. After another Pullman overnight, Centre was in Baltimore to take on Johns Hopkins. The game was a nip and tuck, lead-changing affair until the last seconds. Centre was ahead as time expired and won, 26-23.

The Hopkins game ended a very successful season with the Colonels finishing 11-2. With the three wins on the trip to the East, big wins over Vandy and Auburn, and a split with Kentucky, Centre had proven that in basketball, as in football, the little school could play with the "big boys."

MORE RECOGNITION

On April 9, 1921, the Syracuse University Athletic Association held its annual Block "S" dinner at the Archbold Gymnasium. Following the usual custom, "S" insignias and medal awards were made to the athletes of the various major sports.

The "Orange" had a successful season in 1920, going 6-2-1. Their two losses were to Holy Cross, 3-0, which had lost to Harvard by a field goal, 3-0, and to a 7-2 Maryland team, 10-7. Their tie was to an undefeated but twice tied Pitt team. A total of nine points could have produced an undefeated season. So Syracuse was playing good football.

The banquet featured guest speakers representing each of the five sports whose athletes were to receive letters and other awards. The speakers were:

Captain John W. Thomas, Annapolis, 1901, for rowing, or crew.
Jack Moakley, Cornell track coach, for track.
G. Edwin Brown, Syracuse, 1920, for baseball.
William C. Schmeisser, Johns Hopkins, 1900, for lacrosse.

The master of ceremonies, Hurlburt W. Smith, introduced, "the famous All-American, Bo McMillin of the Wonder Team, the Centre College Colonels, who will now represent the sport of college football in our honors program tonight. I present to you, from Danville, Kentucky, the Centre team captain, and Kentucky Colonel—Mr. Alvin Nugent "Bo" McMillin."

Bo strode to the podium. "I want to thank you for inviting me up here to take part in this wonderful….."

How far from North Side High. And it all had begun with the Chief painting word pictures in the minds of the members of his Steers' football team about a wonderful little college in the Bluegrass of Kentucky.

Not too long after Bo returned from Syracuse, a novelist named Ralph D. Paine arrived on the Centre campus. Paine (1871-1925) was an author who already had published many books, mainly with maritime themes, but he had also written "Campus Days" with a college setting, and had published several articles on sports.

Paine was intrigued with Centre and Bo and how the little college, previously so obscure, had vaulted to the top of the college football world. He thought there was a story to tell, so came down to Danville, checked into the Gilcher, and spent several weeks absorbing the atmosphere of the college and Danville, and interviewing members of the team and local Danvillians. Paine also caught Uncle Charlie in the summer while the Centre Coach was umpiring in Boston and interviewed him there.

The book that resulted was named "First Down, Kentucky." It was a very thinly disguised "biography" of Bowman McMurray, "a quarterback on the Centre College football team," and followed the exploits of Bowman and his teammates, culminating in the trip to Boston and the loss to Harvard.

"The Popular Magazine," published every other week, serialized the book in five segments, beginning with the August 20, 1921 issue, and ran the last installment on October 20, just in time for its readers to finish before the real-life, October 29 rematch with Harvard. After the serialization, the actual hardcover book would hit the bookstores, again coincident with the Centre-Harvard rematch. The book proved to be so popular that it went through several reprints, and it was another vehicle for introducing Centre College and the Colonels to an ever adoring public. Nearly everyone in Danville and the surrounding area went to Spoonamore's Drug store and the Shop Perfect and put their names on a list in order to make certain that they received the next five issues of "The Popular Magazine."

WHO WAS THE BEST TEAM IN 1920?

Centre certainly had a fair claim to being the top team in 1919, and Walter Camp and Eddie Mahan had both stated that they felt the Colonels were the best squad in the country that year. So what about 1920?

The undefeated, untied teams were:

Virginia Military Institute	9-0
Texas	9-0
California	9-0
Notre Dame	9-0

Undefeated, with one tie:

Harvard	8-0-1
Georgia	8-0-1
Princeton	6-0-1
Oklahoma	6-0-1

Undefeated, with two ties:

Penn State	7-0-2
Pittsburgh	6-0-2

You can take your pick. If you want to see how Mr. Howell ranked the teams in his retroactive computerized system, mentioned briefly when discussing the top team in 1919, go to *http://www.jhowell.net/cf/* and you'll see the annual rankings. Click on 1920. And let the discussions, civilized of course, begin.

CHAPTER 12:
1921—A HUGE YEAR FOR THE COLONELS

Uncle Charlie returned to his farm and home in Horse Cave, Kentucky, after the return from Fort Worth. He was a great hunter, had a dairy herd which he and his wife, Pearl (McGee), used to augment their income by producing milk, and he farmed a bit. Uncle Charlie led a busy life, trying to juggle his responsibilities at home, his seven months of National League umpiring, and his job as head coach of what was now a nationally recognized, college football program.

It wasn't long before Unc had to take the L&N back up to Danville to work on the 1921 schedule with Dr. Rainey and the Chief, who'd come down from Chicago. Obviously, the scheduling had to be built around the October 29 game with Harvard. There was a lot of discussion about the early contests to be played prior to the trip to the East.

In 1920, Centre had scheduled teams before the Harvard game in order to make certain that it arrived undefeated so as to assure maximal interest, and therefore, maximal attendance, at the October 23 game in Cambridge.

"We probably hurt ourselves," said Uncle Charlie. "We were undefeated, but we weren't game-tough. This year we need to put some teams on the schedule that will give us more of a challenge before taking on Harvard."

The Chief and Dr. Rainey agreed, and they got to work on finding some teams who would come to Danville, or who were located close enough to Danville so that even if the Colonels went on the road, they wouldn't get worn out by extended travel.

Before Uncle Charlie returned to Horse Cave, he met with Bo and Army to size up Centre's prospects for the upcoming season. The trio met for coffee in the Gilcher Hotel restaurant where Uncle Charlie had a favorite, corner table.

"Unc, you and the two of us know that last year, we got beat in the line. Our guys gave it their all, but we got worn down in the second half. We just got beaten physically." Uncle Charlie had to agree.

Bo told his coach about a recent letter he'd received.

"Eddie Mahan (the great Harvard back who came to Danville with Howard Reynolds in 1919) wrote me about a fellow named Bill Shadoan. He said he was a tough-as-nails lineman who played service ball with Eddie, and he had recently gotten

181

out of the service and returned home. Eddie said he thought this Shadoan wanted to go to college."

Uncle Charlie looked interested.

"Guess where his home town is. Somerset."

Uncle Charlie looked more interested.

"I'm going to run down there and talk to him," Bo said.

Uncle Charlie looked even more interested.

"Get him to come here, Bo. If Eddie Mahan says he's good, that's enough for me."

Bo, Army and Uncle Charlie continued analyzing the prospects for 1921.

Bo continued. "We worry about losing a couple of the guys. Red Weaver is sounding like he can't come back. He's got real financial pressures, plus he doesn't know if his knees can take another year of pounding."

Army jumped in. "Here's the good news. There's a cracker-jack of a center in my home town back in Fort Smith named Ed Kubale. I know him, and if anyone can replace Red, Kube can, and I think I can get him here."

Uncle Charlie had perfect confidence in Army and Bo.

"Get him, Army."

Bo told Uncle Charlie about Sully Montgomery.

"Sully says he's 'taken a wife.' That's how he calls it. And he doesn't know if he can get her to come to Danville, or afford to have her come, even if she's willing."

Bo took over. "Big Red says he's going to be in his best shape ever. The way Tom Bartlett and Hump have developed at fullback, we can put Red in the line where his size will make a lot of difference, especially if Sully doesn't return."

Army continued, "Bill James is coming back. Baldy Cregor is committed. We've got Terry Snowday back at end. Tom Bartlett can play at end if needed. We've heard about some really promising fellows who are coming in as freshmen, guys who've got size and are tough."

"We're set in the backfield. Everybody is coming back. I'll be back. Army will, of course. Chick Murphy is committed. We can always put Red in if needed for short yardage. We're going to be good," Bo said.

"Actually," Army continued, "we've got the players to be great."

Army was a very modest guy. When he said Centre was going to be great, you could go to the bank on it. Centre was going to be loaded in 1921. Things were indeed looking not just good, but great, in Danville, Kentucky.

Bo did go to Somerset and met with Shadoan. They had dinner at a local restaurant and by the time the evening was over and Bo grabbed a late train back to Danville, the ex-Marine was in the fold. Bo knew he'd landed his prize when he leaned over the table and said, "We can beat Harvard next year if you come to Centre. How would you like to be a part of that?"

Shadoan was 27 years old at the time. He was battle-hardened, stood an even six feet tall, was big-boned, and weighed 192, without an ounce of fat on his body.

"I'd like that a lot. Count me in."

The schedule was announced just as January ended.

Oct.	1	Centre-Clemson	Danville
Oct.	8	Centre-VPI	Danville
Oct.	15	Centre-St. Xavier (Oh.)	Cincinnati
Oct.	22	Centre-Transylvania	Lexington
Oct.	29	Centre-Harvard	Cambridge
Nov.	5	Centre-Kentucky	Danville
Nov.	12	Centre-Auburn	Birmingham
Nov.	19	Centre-Washington & Lee	Louisville
Nov.	24	Centre-Georgetown	Georgetown

Georgetown signed on reluctantly, and as the season approached, the Tigers decided that they really weren't capable of competing with the Colonels. The annual Thanksgiving game was called off, and the Chief starting looking around for another foe. The replacement wasn't announced until after the season was well underway.

Of interest in looking at the 1921 schedule is the game scheduled after the October 29th Harvard game. Centre had vowed after the debacle in Atlanta with Georgia Tech that the game in 1921, the week after returning from Cambridge, would be with an easier opponent. The school didn't want a repetition of 1920.

So what school did Centre think would fit the bill for a breather the week after returning from Cambridge? None other than old rival, Kentucky! Centre felt that the Wildcats were now a breather! How the tables had turned!

In May, another vital cog in the Centre plans was the agreement by the administration to offer a full-time coaching position to Claude "Tiny" Thornhill, the same Thornhill who had come down from Pittsburgh in 1920 to assist Uncle Charlie and the Chief the week before the Harvard game. Thornhill had been a star performer on Pitt's undefeated 8-0-0 team in 1916, and had been one of the top linemen in the country, having earned his letter four straight years.

Every Centre player spent the summer after the school year ended preparing for the fall campaign. Army held a team meeting just before the summer vacation began and stressed just how important the upcoming season was going to be.

"We need to arrive back in the best shape we've ever been in. Of course, we're pointing for Harvard. But we've got some good teams to go against from day one. Clemson and Virginia Poly aren't Morris Harvey and Howard. They're not Transy. They're good programs, and we have to go to Cambridge with a spotless record."

Clemson had lost to Georgia Tech in 1920 by the close score of 7-0, so Army was certainly correct when he said the South Carolinians weren't Morris Harvey.

Red Roberts stood up and made a vow.

"Boys, look at me. I have a job on the Southern Railroad, stoking coal all summer. I'm going to be ready!"

One by one, each Colonel made a vow.

"I'm going to be ready!"

The Chief got many of the players summer jobs with his booming Chautauqua business. Myers and Trimble booked the talent for more than 300 Chautauquas all over the country during the summer of 1921, and there was plenty of work for "my boys."

Everywhere they traveled, when the Colonels weren't helping the locals with the publicity and setting up of the tents and stages necessary for the events, they were out jogging, always carrying their togs along so that they could get in their daily exercise.

During the summer, Centre found that indeed, Red Weaver wasn't going to be able to return due to "financial pressures." Sully Montgomery's marriage kept him in Fort Worth. Clayton "Pap" Ford from Danville had another year of eligibility, but he decided not to come back. Stanley Robb, the young man who took the canoe ride down from Pittsburgh, sent word that he couldn't return.

While there was great anticipation in Danville, in Kentucky, and increasingly all over the country, particularly in the South, about how Centre would fare in 1921, there was a somewhat similar interest about TCU's prospects for the upcoming season.

The "Daily Skiff" summarized who the returning players were and how they had fared against the Colonels in the January 1, 1921, Fort Worth Classic game. The "Skiff" reported that the Centre game was still the talk of the campus. Mention was made that the only time Centre's 63 points had been exceeded against the Horned Frogs in all of its 24 years of playing football, over 172 games, was when the University of Texas racked up 72 points in 1915.

Jackson, who scored the touchdown against Centre....
Alexander, who showed up well in the Centre game....
Leviticus Levy, who demonstrated his prowess in the Centre....
"Walter" Camp, substitute fullback, is another Humpty Tanner....
Loren "Hootch" Houtchens, one of the three who survived the full four quarters of the New Year's game with Centre....

SEPTEMBER, 1921

Centre's school year, and therefore football practice, would begin on September 12. The Chief and Tiny Thornhill planned to arrive in Danville that very morning. Uncle Charlie wouldn't arrive until the date of the first game, if by then. It depended upon his umpiring duties as to when he could get to Danville. Meanwhile, things were different in Cambridge.

Harvard began practice three weeks prior to a rather unusual opening doubleheader with Middlebury and Boston University. The Crimson planned to play both teams on the same day, September 24, and felt confidant they had sufficient depth to perform double-duty against the two schools felt to be the "soft" part of their schedule.

They were correct about the depth. 87 men showed up for the first day of practice, and late arrivals boosted the total to 92 the next day. When six more players returned from a trip to the West, there were 98 varsity candidates.

These totals were only for the varsity team. The freshman team had 136 candidates competing for what would eventually be pared down to 34 slots. The breakdown of the first year men was 34 trying out for end, 32 tackles, 14 guards, six centers, and 50 backs, of whom 20 were vying for a quarterback position.

Therefore, 234 young men were trying out for the freshman and varsity squads, just 28 less than the Centre's total enrollment of 262 in the fall of 1921.

Centre, under S.I.A.A rules, was allowed to play freshmen, and if this hadn't been the case, would have been hard pressed to field a team. There were only 137 sophomores, juniors and seniors on the Danville campus.

Harvard, in contrast, adhered to the custom in the East of allowing only three years of varsity play. While this may have seemed unfair at first glance, it actually gave the Eastern schools the advantage of turning their first year men into better candidates for the varsity by more concentrated coaching and a regular schedule of games which gave them valuable experience going into their sophomore year.

Coach Fisher, in his third year at the helm, had a policy of hiring only former Harvard players as "active assistants" who had been on varsity teams from his own time, 1911, to the present. This assured continuity in how the program was run. An "active assistant" position was in addition to what was termed a "daily coach."

Fisher wanted to better coordinate the coaching techniques of the freshman and varsity staffs. He hired a new freshman coach in 1921, Tommy Campbell, Harvard 1912, who had actually been the head coach at North Carolina.

Campbell was assigned four "active assistants" when he took over coaching the first year men. Therefore, the freshman team had five coaches, two more than Centre's entire staff of Uncle Charlie, the Chief, and Tiny Thornhill. (It was really a bit of a stretch to call the Chief a coach. He was the Athletic Director, and helped with coaching when he could.)

Fisher retained three "active assistants" for the varsity. And then he had a "daily coach" for the centers, one for the guards, one for the tackles, and an end coach.

The Harvard varsity thus had four line coaches. Centre had Tiny Thornhill. Harvard had a backfield coach, assisted by a coach who just worked with the quarterbacks. Eddie Mahan was also to work with the backs. To cap off the coaching staff, there was a full time coach in charge of the varsity's second team.

In summary, Harvard had five coaches for the freshmen, 11 for the varsity, and this didn't even include Coach Fisher, who rounded out the staff at a total of 17. In addition, there were numerous student managers, assistant student managers, assistant trainers and locker room attendants, all overseen by the veteran head trainer, "Pooch" Donovan.

The Crimson had an abundance of skilled backs and excellent returning ends. They had lost the interior of their line from tackle to tackle, and the main concern of Coach Fisher and his staff was to rebuild that portion of the forward wall.

Harvard had a difficult schedule lined up. All of the games were scheduled for the big horseshoe except the Princeton contest, to be played at the Tigers' Palmer Stadium.

Sept. 24	Boston University
	Middlebury
Oct. 1	Holy Cross
Oct. 8	Indiana
Oct. 15	Georgia
Oct. 22	Penn State
Oct. 29	Centre
Nov. 5	Princeton
Nov. 12	Brown
Nov. 19	Yale

(The excellent "ESPN Football Encyclopedia" lists the game with Boston University as being played on September 17, but in fact, both BU and Middlebury were played on September 24.)

Harvard was coming off two great seasons, going 9-0-1 in 1919, including the Rose Bowl victory over Oregon, 7-6, and 8-0-1 in 1920. Both ties were with Princeton.

As practice began, despite the loss of key linemen, the Harvard coaches and team felt they could reload and continue in their winning ways.

Meanwhile, in Danville, the strongest freshman group which Centre had yet attracted was due to report in the fall of 1921. Certainly the group that came to Danville in 1917, which included Bo, Red Weaver, Army and other future stars, was impressive, but it was far fewer in numbers.

The 19 freshmen on the Centre team in 1921 were from nine states, and seven had attended prep schools, listed in bold face.

KENTUCKY

MAYFIELD
Herbert "Herb," or "Covey" Covington—5'6" 150 Quarterback
Castle Heights Military Academy
Clifton "Hennie" Lemon—5'10" 165 End
Mayfield High School

LAWRENCEBURG
Ted "Tubby" Johnson—6'1" 185 Guard
Lawrenceburg High School

LEXINGTON
Leslie "Les" Combs II—5'11" 156 End
Swarthmore Preparatory School, Morgan Park Military Academy

LOUISVILLE
Richard "Dick" Gibson—6'1" 180 Tackle
Louisville High School

MILLERSBURG
Proctor "Proc" Wood—5'8" 170 Center
Millersburg Military Institute

NEWPORT
Robert L. "Case" Thomasson—6' 175 Fullback/End
Newport High School

SOMERSET
William "Bill" Shadoan—6' 192 Guard
Somerset High School

ARKANSAS

FORT SMITH
Edwin "Kube" Kubale—6' 175 Center
Fort Smith High School

ILLINOIS

JACKSONVILLE
Edwin "Alex" Alexander—5'10" 163 Halfback
Missouri Military Academy

LOUISIANA

ABBEVILLE

Minos "Cajun" Gordy—5'10" 180
Peoples-Tucker Academy—Springfield, Tennessee

MICHIGAN

DETROIT
John "Johnny" Hunter—5'8" 155 Halfback
San Diego High School, California (Hunter's family moved to Detroit.)

OHIO

MIDDLETOWN

> Ray Class—5'10" 169 Halfback
> Middletown High School

PENNSYLVANIA

PITTSBURGH

> Don Beane—5'7" 175 Guard
> Peabody High School

TEXAS

AMARILLO

> Howard "Bull" Lynch—5'10" 180 Tackle
> Amarillo High School
> Hope Hudgins—5'7" 150 Halfback
> **Missouri Military Academy**

DALLAS

> George "Buck" Jones—5'9" 213 Guard
> Forrest High School

GATESVILLE

> Frank "Rube" Rubarth—5'11" 175 Guard
> Gatesville High School

WISCONSIN

RACINE

> Jack Rowland—5'8" 150 Halfback
> **Tennessee Military Institute**

Centre's freshman class would add considerable strength to the Colonels during the 1921 season. Red Weaver, Sully Montgomery, Stanley Robb, and "Pap" Ford would be missed, but the newcomers arriving would more than make up for those not returning.

Centre received a blow shortly after classes began when Dr. Ganfield, the college president and great supporter of the school's athletic programs, announced that he was resigning and returning to Carroll College. Dr. Ganfield had received a doctorate of divinity from Carroll in 1912, and it had always been understood by those who were close to him that he wished someday to return to the Waukesha, Wisconsin college.

Dr. Ganfield made one vow when he announced that he was reluctantly leaving. He had made it part of his contract with Carroll.

"I will not leave Danville and Old Centre until after the Harvard game. I'll be on the sidelines."

Meanwhile, up in Cambridge, things were clipping along. On September 14, Coach Fisher posted the names of 64 varsity men on a bulletin board in the locker room. There were 34 young men who read the list with disappointment.

Centre began the 1921-22 school year with "the highest enrollment it has ever had," according to accounts in the two local papers, even though actual numbers weren't supplied. True enrollment figures for the college have always been a little difficult to determine in the era after the Great War. Totals like "the little college with less than 200 students," or, "last year there were 225 at the start of the year, and this fall, there appears to be more on campus," were reported throughout this period.

One way to calculate a total is to count the members of each class as they appear in the "Old Centre" yearbooks.

In the 1922 yearbook, there were:

32 seniors
33 juniors
72 sophomores
125 freshmen
262 Total

That number was considerably higher than the preceding three years.

(1918-19) 141
(1919-20) 183
(1920-21) 205

Dr. Ganfield had felt that the exposure of Centre's athletic teams, particularly football, could boost the college's enrollment. His belief is born out by the growth in the freshman class during the years when the Colonels began to attract big-time attention.

In 1918-19, there were 77, and by 1921-22, the freshman class had grown to 125, a bit over a 60% increase.

By comparison, the 1922 Harvard yearbook has photographs of 714 graduating seniors in the undergraduate school. According to a September 27, 1920, New York "Times" article, the total enrollment at Harvard was 6,000, approximately the population of Danville, Kentucky.

The Danville "Messenger" subscribed to the United Press news service and began to carry stories about anything that came across the wires regarding Harvard and its football team. Danvillians scoured every word, trying to divine how the Colonels and

Crimson would stack up.

After the first week of practice in Cambridge, the "Messenger" notified its readers that:

Line problems are the only football problems faced by Harvard as the Crimson gets ready for its biggest season in years.

Coach Fisher is frank in saying that much of the success of the Crimson team depends on the development of good linemen to replace the heavy forwards graduated last year.

The "Messenger" also reviewed the big intersectional games which were scheduled for the upcoming season:

Centre vs. Harvard
Georgia Tech vs. Penn State
Indiana vs. Harvard
Georgia Tech vs. Rutgers
Georgia vs. Harvard
Tennessee vs. Dartmouth

By September 20, Centre was ready to scrimmage. Bo and Chick Murphy led one team while Army and freshman Herb Covington led the other.

Covington was from Mayfield, Kentucky and came from a prominent family in the far-western Kentucky town. He was often called "Rabbit" or "Flash," because he could simply fly and was almost impossible to catch when he got open.

"Covey" had a lot of confidence in his ability, confidence which was shown to be justified during his career as a Colonel.

When he arrived in Danville, he headed to the City Barber Shop on Main Street for a touch-up prior to a fraternity rush party. While he was being trimmed, another patron asked him if was going to play football and he replied that he was, and he was a quarterback.

"Don't you know who the quarterback is? Bo McMillin holds down that position. And anyway, what makes you think you can play football?"

It was obvious that Covington's 5'6, 150 lb. frame didn't make him appear to be much of a threat on the gridiron.

Covington pulled a crisp $50.00 bill out of his pocket and said calmly, "I'll wager this with anyone who wants to bet that I won't earn my letter this year."

There were no takers. Had there been, Covey would have collected.

The City Barbershop was a black-owned and operated shop patronized by most of the townspeople and students. There was a young barber there named E.O. Richardson who had gotten his name in a rather unusual way. His mother had a difficult labor, and when E.O. finally emerged, she was totally exhausted. The person who brought E.O. into the world needed to know what name to put on the birth certificate.

"Do you have a name?"

"No."

"How about Frank, or maybe Richard."

"I don't care. Just name him either one."

On the wall at the City Barber Shop was a barber's license issued to Either One Richardson, always known as "E.O."

It was apparent that the freshmen were going to play a big role in the upcoming season. Ed Kubale took over Red Weaver's position at center, and even though it seemed impossible for anyone to outshine the 1919, All-American, it appeared Kubale may just do that. Covington ran with skill and great speed. Minos Gordy, who had been recruited heavily by Vanderbilt, was a bull at the fullback position and a hard hitting tackle when moved into the line. It was obvious that Bill Shadoan was going to measure up to what Eddie Mahan had said about the Somerset native.

On September 24, the veterans and freshmen (Colts) went at it in a full-fledged scrimmage. Several hundred fans paid a quarter to watch. The papers had said that it should be a very evenly balanced game, but they were wrong.

Bo stood out and the vets showed the new men what Centre football was all about, racking up a 38-0 win. Hump crashed through for two scores. Tom Bartlett hit Terry Snowday for a score and then Bo hit Bartlett for a TD. Chick Murphy broke loose on an end-around and put six on the board on a nice bit of broken field running. Bartlett kicked five extra points and Red Roberts, who played both in the line and backfield, booted a 35 yard field goal.

The "Messenger" summarized the game.

Bo worked in his usual scintillating form and appears even faster than he was last year. The spirit and general morale evidenced Saturday afternoon convinced followers that the team was returning to the level of the 1919 championship squad.

I enrolled at Centre in September of 1921. I was 17 and didn't turn 18 until December. My brother Howard was over a year older than me, and he enrolled the year before.

We went to the game between the varsity and freshmen. Of course, I was sort of pulling for the freshmen because a lot of them lived in Breckinridge Hall where I roomed. What I remember was that it was just like the time before, when Howard and I were visiting Cousin Ella. I've never seen such hitting. At our high school in Elizabethtown, it seemed like most of the time, tackles were made by just grabbing someone and flinging them to the ground.

People remember Bo because of his passing and running, but he was like all of the rest of the team. When Bo hit somebody, they knew they'd been hit. He loved contact, just like all of the guys did. Red Roberts did, too. He'd take on anyone, and I never saw him wear a helmet.

Everyone used to talk about the great offensive teams that Centre had, and we indeed did have a wonderful offense.
But Centre played a ferocious defense.

While Centre was having an intra-squad game, Harvard was putting on the doubleheader with Boston University and Middlebury before a decent, but nowhere near, capacity crowd.

The Crimson played over 50 men in the two contests. The starters were in the line-up at the beginning of the Boston U. game, but one of the reasons that the two games had been paired on the same Saturday was to give the Harvard coaches plenty of opportunity to evaluate their personnel in game conditions.

Substitutions were frequent. The Crimson beat Boston U. 10-0, and then Middlebury went down 16-0. Little Middlebury fought to the end, and the crowd cheered them on near the end of the contest when Harvard had first and goal on the Panthers' five yard line, and the boys from Vermont stopped four straight rushes and regained possession.

Winnie Churchill, the same Churchill who had tackled Bo just short of the goal line during Centre's first scoring drive in 1920, scored both of the TD's against Middlebury.

Winthrop Hallowell Churchill prepped at Milton Academy and was a member of the class of 1923. During Christmas vacation the previous year, he had visited a friend in Louisville and said he couldn't be so close to Danville and not come see the school. His friend drove him down on the several hour trip, and when it was discovered who he was, the "Messenger" reported:

A crowd of men and boys followed the great gridiron star as though he was a conquering hero from the field of battle. Churchill walked over to Cheek Field and tore a large splinter off the stands and carried back a bag of soil from the field. He said the people of Boston were electrified by the wonderful play of the Centre team and were delighted with the sportsmanship of the players and the entire Centre delegation, and that the Crimson team was highly pleased that they were going to play Centre again in the Stadium in the fall.

OCTOBER 1, 1921
CENTRE-CLEMSON / HARVARD-HOLY CROSS

Centre was to open against Clemson at home on Saturday, October 1. The old wooden stadium had been spruced up as best possible while the team prepared for the Tigers. Ticket sales were so strong that the athletic department again conducted a crash program to try to add more seats, since many of the temporary seats from the previous years had to be dismantled due to safety concerns. Crews managed to get enough built that the capacity of the old lady was just a bit over 6,000 if you counted standing-room fans.

Clemson was coming off a 4-6-1 season. The four victories were over the weaker teams on the schedule—Erskine, Newberry, Wofford, and The Citadel. Presbyterian and Clemson tied, 7-7.

Auburn, Tennessee, South Carolina, Georgia, Furman and Georgia Tech all beat the Tigers, but as has been pointed out, and as the Centre players were constantly reminded, "Boys, this team got beaten by Georgia Tech, 7-0. They played Tech evenly. You know what happened to us against Tech."

An article appeared under the headline, "Clemson Confident of Trouncing Centre," in a Charleston, South Carolina paper on September 28. A summary of the article was telegraphed to the Chief, and it was tacked onto a bulletin board in the gym so all of the Colonels could read it.

Uncle Charlie managed to get released from his umpiring duties a few days early and arrived in Danville on Tuesday morning, September 28. His arrival had been publicized in both Danville papers and in chapel. He was met by many of the faculty, every member of the team, and most of the students, all of whom gave a lusty cheer when he stepped off the train, a big smile on his face.

Amongst Uncle Charlie's baggage which was transported to the Gilcher was a canvas bag containing several wooden-shafted golf clubs. The Centre mentor had decided to take up golf at age 42, and later said that any free time he had on the baseball circuit, he hit the links.

"I hit the links. I didn't say I hit the ball!"

After settling in at the Gilcher, Uncle Charlie headed to the campus. The "Messenger" reported that:

"...the newcomers thought a cyclone had hit the field. Unc slipped into his moleskins shortly after noon and trotted out onto Cheek Field with all of the pep of a two-year old. Danville is mighty glad to welcome him home and believes another "Wonder Team" will be turned out in the fall." (The term "moleskins" was often used to signify a football uniform. It was understood to mean a heavy-napped, cotton twill fabric, often used to make clothing, especially trousers.)

There were but three practice days before the opening game with Clemson. In Cambridge, Coach Fisher and his staff were preparing for the Holy Cross game. With the double-header under their belts, the Crimson players knew they had a much greater challenge than had been presented the previous week.

Holy Cross was a Jesuit college founded in 1843, situated in Worchester, Massachusetts, 25 miles west of Boston. The "Crusaders," an appropriate name for a Catholic school, first played Harvard in 1904, and then three straight years, 1911-13. Harvard won all four of those contests by a combined score of 102-12.

The 1920 game proved to be a tougher affair. Holy Cross was playing good football and Harvard won by a field goal, 3-0. (Holy Cross went on to defeat an excellent Syracuse team in 1920.)

With many of the starters returning from the 1920 squad, Holy Cross expected to give the Crimson all they could handle, and did. Once again, Harvard eked out a 3-0 win. Even though his team won, Coach Bob Fisher was dissatisfied with his offense, and particularly with the line play. Changes in the line-up were expected when practice took place the following Monday.

Uncle Charlie had the luxury of devoting his full time to the backfield now that he had the fulltime assistance of Tiny Thornhill. Tiny was pleased at the skill and toughness of the freshmen who had come to Centre. Ed Kubale was a spectacular talent and would fill the center slot for the foreseeable future. Bill Shadoan would eventually more than adequately replace Sully Montgomery. Minos Gordy, the "Cajun" from Abbeville, Louisiana, looked good in practice, as did "Buck" Jones, a 213 pounder from Dallas.

Centre had a scare during the practice when Bo was hit in the nose. Uncle Charlie reached into his bag of tricks and devised a nose-guard of sorts. (It wasn't until the late 1940's and early 50's that nose guards or face masks began to appear on helmets. The first was a single metal bar, and over the years they evolved into a very effective protective device. The introduction of the face mask necessitated that a new penalty be added to the game, five yards for unintentionally or accidentally grabbing a mask, and 15 yards if the infraction were to be intentional or flagrant.)

George Swinebroad led a spirited pep rally in chapel Friday morning, Centre held a non-contact workout that afternoon, and the Colonels were ready to open the 1921 season. Clemson had taken an overnight Pullman to Lexington, leaving Wednesday afternoon. They disembarked and spent Thursday in Lexington, working out during a closed door session on Kentucky's Stoll Field. Friday, the Tigers journeyed on the Southern to Danville and had another private workout on Cheek Field in Danville.

Clemson was coached by E.J. "Doc" Stewart who was head coach at Oregon State during 1913-15, going 15-5-5. Stewart went to Nebraska during 1916-17 and compiled an 11-4 record before his career was interrupted by the War.

Over 6,000 fans came to the October 1 game. They watched a very workmanlike effort by the Colonels. Uncle Charlie had Bo run a very conservative game plan. He and Tiny Thornhill were mainly concerned with making certain that the Colonels could play defensively with an intensity which could win against Harvard.

Bo and Army had said, "We know we have the offense to score against anybody. What we want to do this season is to shut out every opponent." It was an ambitious goal. Not only the players, but the Centre coaches felt it was achievable.

Centre lead 7-0 at the half after the Colonels put together a sustained drive late in the second quarter. Clemson had to punt and Bo called out the first play from his own 35. Hump went over right tackle for 20, Bo skirted around his left end for 12, and it was first down on the Tigers' 33.

The game had been rather unspectacular to that point, but the Centre partisans sensed that their team was on the move and cheered them on, wanting to take the lead going into the locker room for the halftime break.

Army got three, Tom Bartlett plunged ahead for five, and Bo picked up the first down when he went around the left side for 10.

The ball was on the Clemson 15. Hump was brought down after picking up three. Tom Bartlett burst through and went 12 yards for the first score of 1921. Bartlett's extra point was the 100th straight. Red Weaver didn't get it, but Centre did.

During the third quarter, Centre picked up another score, set up by a Terry Snowday interception.

Bo picked up nine. Uncle Charlie had sent in Minos Gordy at fullback and he picked up a first down, going six. Centre confused Clemson with a cross-buck play as Bartlett gained 15. A 15 yard penalty gave the Colonels the ball on the 18. Bo swept around the right end as his line pulled out and led the way, totally clearing the Clemson defenders out. He scored untouched, and Tom Bartlett kicked to make the final margin 14-0.

Centre played 23 men. Uncle Charlie just didn't play 23 men in a relatively close contest! Like Bo had been quoted—"You had to nearly get killed to have a substitute sent in."

1921 was going to be different. Centre had been outmanned against Harvard in 1920 as the Coach Fisher was able to substitute frequently and effectively.

"It won't happen again," was the vow that the Colonels' coaches had made as the season began. They were determined to have the depth to play at Harvard's level. The games preceding the trip East were designed to develop the depth which would be needed.

"We don't intend to run up any big scores early in the season. We will win, we feel confidant of that. But we will also give our men game experience, as much as necessary, to have them ready for Harvard." It was Harvard. It was always—Harvard.

Centre played nine freshmen against Clemson. Tiny Thornhill felt confident about his line. Uncle Charlie felt that same level of confidence about his backfield.

Bo, Army, Hump Tanner, Tom Bartlett, Chick Murphy, Hennie Lemon, Herb Covington, Red Roberts if needed. Centre could just keep rotating backs in all afternoon without losing one bit of speed or skill. They were tough. They played intelligently. Each of the backs at Centre could play for any team in the country. The little school had the greatest collection of backfield talent of any team in the country in 1921.

George Chinn, Terry Snowday, and Case Thomasson were all excellent ends. Hennie Lemon could also play end, and later in his career, that was his best position. Red Roberts was a fixture. Bill James was back for his 5th year at tackle. Ben "Baldy" Cregor had filled out to a solid 180 and was a 4th year man. Buck Jones, Dick Gibson, Minos Gordy, Frank Rubarth and Bill Shadoan were all freshmen with enough bulk and talent to be able to contribute immediately in the interior of the line.

Ed Kubale was able to perform at the level both offensively and defensively where he left no doubt that he was one of the best centers ever to be a member of the Gold and White. There simply wasn't any weakness on the Centre team of 1921.

OCTOBER 8, 1921
CENTRE-VIRGINIA TECH / HARVARD-INDIANA
Centre took the upcoming game with VPI very seriously. Bo had planned to take a train to Chicago for his brother Reuben's wedding on Wednesday before the game. He cancelled his plans and when asked why, stated, "VPI."

The Hokies looked to have a good team in 1921. They had eight starters back from the team which the Colonels beat in Louisville, 28-0. The relationship between Centre and VPI was excellent due to the sportsmanship shown by both teams in the previous year's contest.

VPI had a new coach named Ben Cubbage and had joined the newly formed Southern Conference in 1921. The conference was composed of the larger schools which left the S.I.A.A., of which Centre, as one of the smaller colleges, remained a member.

(The charter members of the Southern Conference in 1921 were: Alabama, **Auburn**, **Clemson**, Florida, Georgia, Georgia Tech, **Kentucky**, Louisiana State, Maryland, Mississippi, Mississippi State, North Carolina, North Carolina State, Sewanee, South Carolina, Tennessee, **Tulane**, Vanderbilt, Virginia, **Virginia Tech**, and **Washington & Lee**. Centre played those in bold face in 1921.)

VPI had started the season with wins over Hampden-Sydney, 14-6, and William and Mary, 14-0.

While Centre was preparing for VPI, Harvard was getting ready for Indiana, a member of the Big 10. The Hoosiers had opened their season with two rather minor challenges and disposed of them handily, winning over Franklin, 47-0, and Kalamazoo, 29-0.

Coach Fisher was worried about his offense. In the first three victories, the Crimson had only scored 29 points, and the toughest part of the schedule was still to be played. During the first three games in 1919, the Fisher-led Crimson scored 105 points. In 1920, the first three games resulted in 65 points. The lack of offense had the huge coaching staff in Cambridge working overtime trying to get some spark in the attack.

"We're playing well on defense," Fisher said. "We've yet to find our stride on offense."

Down in Danville, offensive production wasn't the worry. Uncle Charlie and Tiny Thornhill, helped by Chief Myers, constantly emphasized defense.

"Gentlemen, we are going to be the toughest team in the country this year to score on. We want 11 men in on each play. We want you to swarm, to gang tackle, to play smart, play clean, but play with ferocity. We want you to feel that if you give up a first down, you have failed. It is defense which is going to help us win the national championship. Defense!"

Uncle Charlie could be infectious.

Soon, every Colonel became "infected."

"Defense! Defense! Defense!"

Interest in football in Blacksburg was high. With a new coach and a step up to a new conference, the Hokies had their greatest fan base yet. The college engaged a special, all-Pullman train to carry the team and a large contingent of fans to Danville, leaving on Thursday night, October 6, and riding all night on the Chesapeake and Ohio tracks through Virginia, into West Virginia, and entering Kentucky by skirting just south of the Ohio River to Ashland. Then it was westward to Lexington where the "Special" was connected to a Southern steamer for the final 50 minute run to Danville.

The team and as many of the fans who could be accommodated filled the Gilcher and Henson. Local boarding houses and citizens of Danville took in the rest. The Hokies held a closed-door session at Cheek Field on Friday morning. The 33 member Colonel squad had a non-contact session in the afternoon.

VPI gave Centre all it could handle on a breezy Saturday afternoon. The Colonels moved the ball constantly in the first quarter, but as the end of the period neared, Bo was knocked to the ground after a vicious tackle and didn't get up. There was absolute silence as players and officials huddled around him. Finally, the Centre star began to respond to some smelling salts administered by team manager, Johnnie McGee, and he was able to get to his feet and walk under his own power, but with assistance, to the sidelines.

Many on the Colonels' bench and in the stands were naturally worried about Bo, and also couldn't help but be concerned about the season. It was certainly true when it was said that, "As Bo goes, Centre goes." Not that there weren't other great players on the Gold and White, but Bo was the one indispensable performer.

Bo's absence was felt on both offense and defense. Herb Covington, the little freshman "Flash" from Mayfield, Kentucky, took over at quarterback and performed well. But it was a lot to expect a young man with little college experience to fill the big shoes of a Bo McMillin.

Red Roberts took over the calling of the signals.

The second quarter was evenly played, but VPI made four first downs during the period that Bo was trying to shake the cobwebs out of his well-rung head.

"Who are we playing?" Bo would ask. "Virginia? Are we winning?" (The game has certainly changed. Red Weaver obviously had a rather significant concussion during the 1919 West Virginia game. A little Kentucky bourbon and he was a tiger in the second half. Bo came around as Johnnie McGee kept putting the smelling salts under his nose where he had to inhale them.)

The half ended with no score.

The crowd roared as the Colonels, and Bo, returned to the field to start the second half. The whole demeanor of the team changed. Bo later said, "I was still in a fog, and don't really remember much about the third quarter. But things seemed to clear up as the period went on."

At the half, Uncle Charlie had again emphasized defense

"If a team can't score, they can't win. Pure and simple. Defense! Defense! Defense!" Defense it was. VPI got only one first down during the second half. Still, it was 0-0 as the whistle ended the third quarter.

Uncle Charlie reached into his bag of tricks and out came little Chick Murphy, the speedster with the size four and a half shoe who weighed 130 pounds after a good meal.

VPI had just punted and Centre found itself in good field position as Murph replaced Tom Bartlett. On his first play, Murph got 10 on a lightening dash around the left end. After the yard markers were moved, he darted around the right end for 18. The Centre fans were on their feet, led by cheerleader George Swinebroad.

Take it in, Take it in,
Gold and White, Gold and White.
Take it in, Take it in,
Gold and White, Gold and White.

Bo cut through the center of the line for seven. Hump got two and was hit hard. Bo got the yard needed for the first down. It was first and goal on the 10. In the huddle, Bo said to Murph, "Chick, I'm going to let you be the hero and take it in like they're saying."

Murph took the handoff and fired toward the left side of the line and was crunched by two determined Hokies. He crumbled to the ground and lay motionless. It was several moments before he could be assisted off the field. It was never said the game was for those who were not stout of heart.

Army gathered his mates around him. "Now we win it for Murph. We score and we win. They can't move it. Now, let's win it for Murph!"

Bo told Buck Jones, at 213 lbs. and Red Roberts at 215 lbs., that he was going to have Hump run right behind them for the score. "Drive 'em back. Humpty will be running up your backsides."

It was going to be simple, power football, a fireplug behind two bulls. The two big men lined up at right guard and right tackle. Bo called the signals and the VPI defenders were knocked back and Hump got five. VPI knew that Centre was going to run the exact same play again but was powerless to stop it. Buck and Red fired out, sent the defenders up and then back where they landed sprawled in the end zone. Hump, running low, hurdled the last couple of yards and rolled over the goal.

It was a savage display with neither team giving ground. But Centre was just too strong. After that series, Tiny Thornhill knew that he had the horses to take on Harvard. The Colonels were tough.

The crowd whistled, cheered, clapped, shouted and at the same time breathed a collective sigh of relief. VPI was good. The Hokies were a worthy opponent, and for a while, there was some doubt about going to Harvard undefeated. Hump kicked the extra point, the 102nd in a row. Two minutes later, Centre scored again, the touchdown being set up by a poor punt that gave the Colonels the ball on the VPI 45 yard line.

Bo ran for 30, a five yard penalty and seven yard loss moved the ball back to the 27. Bo then hit Army with a perfectly thrown spiral and the captain hauled it in and scored. Hump kicked Centre's 103rd straight, and it was 14-0. The game ended shortly afterward with Centre in possession and on the Hokies' three yard line. Overall, the Colonels not only won on the scoreboard but statistically, running up12 first downs to five for VPI.

A dance was held in the Boyle-Humphrey Gymnasium, attended by all of the Virginians and the Centre team and student bodies from Centre and KCW. There was great camaraderie between the two squads and schools, and already there was talk of another game in 1922, this time hopefully somewhere in Virginia. While the Colonels were having a tough but successful outing with VPI on Saturday afternoon, October 8, Harvard was taking on Indiana.

Coach Fisher and his staff had made several switches in the team's lineup in the week leading up to the game with the Hoosiers trying to find the right combination. Team captain, Richmond Keith Kane was moved to tackle from end. C.A. "McCaw" Tierney, at 6'1/2" and 186 lbs., formerly a center, was going to start at the other tackle. C.C. Macomber was slotted to replace Kane at end, and a sophomore named Fleming Bradford was to replace Tierney at center.

In the backfield, Vinton Chapin and R.W. Fitts were demoted to the second team, and two sophomores, Burke Gehrke and Wilkens Jenkins, were moved up to the starting lineup.

It was unusual for the Crimson to be entering into the fourth game of the year with so much juggling of the starting eleven, but as Fisher explained, "We just have to get some offensive production. We haven't really moved the ball consistently at all."

Harvard shut out the Hoosiers, 19-0. The score looked fairly promising, as it was the most points scored yet by the Crimson. Yet, when analyzing the game, it was very apparent that the offense hadn't yet arrived.

The Crimson jumped out to a 3-0 lead on a 32 yard dropkick by quarterback Charles C. Buell just as the first quarter ended. The second points were registered not by the offense, but by a good defensive play when Gehrke blocked Captain John Kyle's punt and scooped it up and raced in for a score. As the second quarter wound down, K.S. Pfaffman kicked a 31 yard field goal and Harvard led 13-0 at the end of the first two periods. Rain began to come down hard when the Crimson marching band, making their first appearance of the season, was marching off the field after the halftime performance.

The last score came when R.W. Fitts returned a Kyle punt 76 yards for a TD, the extra point was no good, and the final score was 19-0.

Coach Fisher had to be concerned. It was great to be 4-0. It was great to have registered four straight shutouts. But in the game with the Hoosiers, once again, the Crimson never really put together any significant drives. They scored because of field goals, a blocked punt, and a punt return, and things were definitely going to get tougher in the weeks ahead.

A review of the Harvard season after the Indiana game, and a look ahead, revealed the following:

Sept.	24	Harvard	10	Boston U.	0
		Harvard	16	Middlebury	0
Oct.	1	Harvard	3	Holy Cross	0
Oct.	8	Harvard	19	Indiana	0
Oct.	15	Harvard		Georgia	
Oct.	22	Harvard		Penn State	
Oct.	29	Harvard		Centre	
Nov.	5	Harvard		Princeton	
Nov.	12	Harvard		Brown	
Nov.	19	Harvard		Yale	

If there was a silver lining in Cambridge, it was that Harvard was playing defense like the college had done in years past. Since the resumption of "official" football following the War, Harvard had played 23 games and given up only 47 points, and during that period, the Crimson had shut out their opponents 18 times.

OCTOBER 15, 1921
CENTRE-ST. XAVIER / HARVARD-GEORGIA

On the Monday after the VPI game, the Chief received a telegram from Howard Reynolds, the sports editor of the Boston "Post" who had been so influential in getting Centre on Harvard's schedule in 1920 after he and Eddie Mahan had visited Danville in 1919.

Reynolds was coming down the week before the Harvard game to take some photographs, interview the coaches and players, and to make certain that his readers knew everything that he could report about Centre's preparations for the October 29 contest.

Centre now had two relatively easy games coming up prior to going back to the East. It may have been a bit of a gamble to play Clemson and VPI so early, and before the Harvard game, but Uncle Charlie wanted his team to have sufficient competition so that the Colonels would be battle-tested. It had worked out as planned—two victories, then two less skilled foes, and then on to Harvard.

Harvard had a harder row to hoe, with a good Georgia team coming to Cambridge the weekend that Centre was journeying up to Cincinnati.

Georgia had an excellent year in 1920, going 8-0-1.

Georgia	40	The Citadel	0
Georgia	37	South Carolina	0
Georgia	7	Furman	0
Georgia	27	Oglethorpe	3
Georgia	7	Auburn	0
Georgia	0	Virginia	0
Georgia	56	Florida	0
Georgia	21	Alabama	14
Georgia	55	Clemson	0

The tie with Virginia was a road game in Charlottesville.

During the present 1921 season, the Bulldogs were 2-0 with wins over Mercer, 28-0, and Furman, 27-7.

Certainly, Harvard was bringing some decent programs into the Stadium, and Georgia was one of the better ones.

Centre's game the weekend of the Harvard-Georgia contest was with St. Xavier of Cincinnati, later called Xavier of Ohio. The two schools had played only once before when the Colonels pasted the Saints 57-0 in 1919 on Cheek Field. The match-up was ideal for Uncle Charlie's purposes. The game wouldn't tax his team too greatly, and the travel was very manageable—just a little over 100 miles up the Southern tracks through Lexington and into Cincinnati.

Centre had one worry going into the St. Xavier game. Bo hadn't fully recovered from the hard hit that he took in the first half against VPI. In retrospect, it was probable that he had suffered a broken nose. He was having trouble breathing, and on Sunday and Monday after the game with the Hokies, he spent the nights in the local hospital where he received a sedative to help him sleep.

Uncle Charlie decided that he had to provide his quarterback some facial protection. He called a friend in Lexington and had him procure an actual World War I gas mask from an Army surplus store in Lexington and send it down on the train.

Bo tried out the apparatus during practice on Tuesday. It worked well for him, but not for his teammates.

"Unc, it sounds like he's in a cave somewhere. We can't hear him call the signals."

Moran cut a hole in the front of the mask, and Bo used it the rest of the week. The Centre staff was so concerned about Bo that they sent him to Cincinnati on Friday before the game and had him check into a hotel so that he didn't have to get up early Saturday morning to travel to Cincinnati with the team.

Tickets to the Harvard game arrived in Danville during the week. The Shop Perfect was going to handle the sales, and once again, Harvard had sent some of the best seats in the big horseshoe, a block directly on the 50 yard line.

The Danville "Advocate" announced plans for travel to Cincinnati. The team, including coaches and manager Johnnie McGee, would occupy a private day coach for the trip. There would be 41 going. The team's car, along with several additional ones for fans, would be brought down from Lexington the night before and left on a siding so that they could be occupied Saturday morning and connected to the regularly scheduled "Carolina Special" which came through heading north each morning at 7:25 a.m.

The train would arrive in Cincinnati before noon and leave plenty of time for the travelers to grab some lunch and head to Redland Field for the 2:00 game. The round trip would be $7.13, game tickets were $1.25 for the grandstand and $2.00 for a box, so that even if one were to spend $1.50 each for lunch and dinner, the whole day wouldn't cost more than $11.00-$12.00, assuring that many of the students could afford to make the trip.

The "New Orleans Limited" pulled out of Cincinnati each evening and the Danville cars would be hooked onto it for the 8:00 p.m. departure, arriving back in Danville at 11:20. (The reason that a little detail is being given about the trip to Cincinnati is to show how passenger train service so totally dominated travel in the United States during this era. If you wanted to go someplace, even such a relatively short distance as from Danville to Cincinnati, you hopped on a train. Trains went literally everywhere. They came through frequently. They were reliable, and, an important consideration in relation to our present predicament, they ran on an abundant and seemingly inexhaustible fuel supply. All that was needed was some high grade coal and water which resulted in steam, and you were good to go. One can only wonder if the money that was poured into highways, culminating with the Interstate Highway System begun in the Eisenhower era, had instead been used to underwrite high-speed rail travel, where we would be now regarding energy independence.)

The Cincinnati school had won its last nine games during which it gave up only 14 points. The St. Xavier game was memorable because of the fact that the Saints scored, which was a major disappointment to the Colonels. The players had really felt they could go through the season without giving up a point.

There were over 8,000 fans in attendance. The Saints' score came early in the game, and it wasn't really due to a defensive breakdown. There was a Colonels' fumble deep in their own territory. In their eagerness to keep St. Xavier out of the end zone, Centre's limemen jumped offsides twice, moving the ball closer to a score. Then, a hard hit caused a Saints' runner to cough up the ball and it went up in the air, took a big bounce forward, and rolled over the goal line where it was recovered by an alert St. Xavier player for a touchdown.

Centre played conservatively all afternoon, aware that there were scouts in the stands. Hump scored in the first quarter after the fluke touchdown by St. Xavier and then kicked the extra point, the Colonels 104th straight.

The second quarter was scoreless, and the first half ended, Centre 7-6.

Freshman Robert "Case" Thomasson was alternating with Herb Covington in the backfield in the second half, relieving either Terry Snowday or Army. "Case" scored the only TD in the third quarter, Hump kicked number 105, and it was 14-6 at the end of the period.

Tom Bartlett scored on a 25 yard run early in the fourth quarter, stiff-arming several defenders along the way. Bo kicked the 106th. Bo closed out the scoring near the end of the game on a six yard run, kicked for the 107th straight, and the final margin was 28-6.

The game wasn't really as close as the score. The Colonels ran at will, picking up 24 first downs while giving up only six. It wasn't an overly spectacular display, but served its purpose. Uncle Charlie and Tiny Thornhill got 25 men into the game, and Tiny sent nine subs into the line at various times. It was depth that Centre was seeking, and the game in Cincinnati provided playing time for many men who may be needed two weeks hence.

The Cincinnati "Star-Times" made special mention of Red Roberts play.

Although McMillin featured in carrying the ball, the shining light of the whole game, and the man most effective on the defensive, was Roberts, third team All-American in 1919, who is playing tackle for Centre. Time after time he broke up the Saints' plays, and on one occasion, he lifted up a Saint bodily and set him back. Coach Moran seems to have made a clever move when he shifted Roberts and his 225 pounds of beef, backed by plenty of football sense, from the backfield to the line. It was almost impossible for the Saints to make anything through the line with Roberts on the job.

After the game, the team attended a dinner given by the Cincinnati alumni club, hustled to the station and was on the train for the 8:00 departure. On the way back, Herb Covington introduced a new version of an old song which everyone thought appropriate and joined along in singing.

It was good for Uncle Charlie,
It was good for Uncle Charlie,
It was good for Uncle Charlie,
And it's good enough for me.

The Chorus

'Tis the old-timey football,
'Tis the old-timey football,
'Tis the old-timey football,
And it's good enough for me.

And—

Good enough for Captain Armstrong....

And then—*For the whole darned crew.*

Team favorite Roscoe made the trip and then entertained by playing music on a bottle as the train pulled into the Danville station late in the evening. It had been a successful day, but there was some disappointment about having given up a score. Bo and Army spoke on the platform to several students who were there when they disembarked.

"Yes, we won. We're always glad to win. We sure wish they hadn't scored. But you know, we'll just work that much harder to keep anybody else from scoring again."

Meanwhile in Cambridge, Harvard had the same goal going into the Georgia game. The Crimson knew they had to play tough defense since their attack had been so impotent.

Once again, Harvard's offense performed poorly and without precision, losing the ball five times due to fumbles. Georgia scored the first points of the season against the Crimson. It took a 28 yard field goal by K.S. Pfaffman for Harvard to eke out a 10-7 victory. (Perhaps it is being a little tough on the Crimson to downplay their win over Georgia. After all, as pointed out, Georgia was 8-0-1 in 1920, and in 1921, ended up 7-2-1. Besides the loss to Harvard, the Bulldogs dropped a 7-0 decision to a strong Dartmouth team (6-2-1), and played an excellent Vanderbilt team (8-0-1) to a 7-7 tie.)

After the game with St. Xavier, Centre was 3-0. Harvard was 5-0 after squeezing by the Bulldogs. Things were looking good for both the Colonels and Crimson to be undefeated when they ran out onto Harvard Stadium's turf on October 29.

OCTOBER 22, 1921
CENTRE-TRANSYLVANIA / HARVARD-PENN STATE

Transylvania had to at least be credited for stepping up to the plate again. The school had found itself going south in the relationship with Centre, just like Georgetown and their fellow Lexingtonians, the University of Kentucky.

In 1915, Transy put a 38-0 defeat on Centre. The Colonels managed a 0-0 tie the following year, and then the tables not only tilted, but literally turned over on the Crimson, and Centre began a major domination.

1917   Centre 28   Transylvania 0
1918   Centre 52   Transylvania 3
1919   Centre 69   Transylvania 0
1920   Centre 55   Transylvania 0

The last four years had Centre winning by a cumulative score of 204-3, which along with the big wins over Kentucky and Georgetown, established without debate who was the kingpin of football in the Commonwealth of Kentucky.

The 1921 game was to be played in Lexington, and since it was to be the last Lexington appearance of the famous Kentucky Colonel, Bo, a sell-out crowd was expected, and extra bleachers were thrown up at Transy's stadium to accommodate the crowd. (It was also to be the last appearance of Army, Tom Moran, Bill James, and possibly Ben Cregor and Chick Murphy. But it has to be accepted that it was Bo who was the big draw, even though Uncle Charlie constantly drilled into the Colonels that it was a team game, and no one individual was more important than the team as a whole.)

Just as in 1920, the week before the Transy game wasn't spent preparing for the Crimson from Lexington, but rather the Crimson from Cambridge.

It was getting intense. There had been a year's mental preparation, and the early season's games had been designed with the October 29 showdown always in mind. Now the time was near, just two weeks away.

Monday, October 17, Uncle Charlie's son, Tom Moran, took the third team and other scrubs over to the baseball diamond behind the stadium. Red jerseys had been ordered from Sutcliffe's on 4th Street in Louisville and were worn by the subs who were to run anticipated Harvard plays against the first two teams. Tom Moran spent the day teaching the Crimson formations to his charges.

Meanwhile, Uncle Charlie, Tiny and the Chief, held a chalkboard session in which new plays to be used against Harvard were diagramed, and then walk-through sessions were held out on the field.

"No, Hump. First do a stutter-step left and then pivot and sweep wide right."

"That's right, Army. You take out the left side linebacker."

Nothing was to be left to chance. It was game time, even though the actual date was still 12 days away.

On Tuesday, a full scrimmage of four 15 minute periods was held with the first and second teams against the scrubs decked out in their crimson jerseys. First the reserves ran the Harvard plays against the starter's defense, then the second team took over for the next period and defensed the anticipated attack. Back and forth it went, and then the first and second teams went on the offensive and ran against what it was felt would be the Harvard defensive formations. Red Roberts was switched to the backfield and ran some power plays designed for short-yardage situations, when just a yard or even less was needed.

The same type of vigorous practice took place on Wednesday, attended by George Joplin who wrote a piece for the Danville "Messenger" which appeared in the paper on Thursday, October 20.

While the Sunday papers give glowing accounts of the varsity football team, mention is never made of the squad of scrubs who went out day after day and got the livin' daylights kicked out of them by this same crowd of varsity performers. They knew it was coming, day after day—nothing but kicks and bruises. It was, and is today, this heroic gang of third stringers that fit the varsity for the test.

When the list is made out, the day before the team is to make a trip, they huddle up in the corner of the dressing room and nurse some forlorn hope that maybe—maybe their name will be on the list. It seldom is. Yet they never utter a complaint. A regular halfback or lineman may let out a loud squawk when he is removed from a game. He never considers that there are a dozen men back home who would have given his right arm to have played as long as he.

When Jack Dempsey knocked out George Carpentier last July, there was nothing said of his sparring partners. Week after week, these lads faced and gamely took their medicine. It was this crowd who fitted Jack for the acid test. Jack got the money and credit—they got the air.

Out on Cheek Field every afternoon the spectators will see a crowd of red-jerseyed youths fight for all they are worth to check the dynamic assaults of the first and second teams. The first team will have their turn smashing into the mass of red. Then the second team, all fresh, will open up their guns. When the powder has cleared away, and the scrimmage is over, one will find a battered, bleeding, weary, heavy-footed gang still holding the fort. Their goal line may have been crossed a dozen times during the afternoon, but they have battled and are inwardly proud of their showing.

When the train to Harvard pulls out to Boston next Wednesday morning, this red-sweatered clan will be down at the station. They won't board the train, but they will join in with the rooters in giving the team a rousing send-off. They will envision the Harvard game here at home, play by play, as it comes in over the wires, and they will be thrilled by the achievements of their big brothers. No finer spirits can be found anywhere, and in perhaps another year or two, their names will find a place in the streamers that run across the city sports pages.

Scrubs, our hats are off to you!

Whether it was due to George Joplin's piece or not, Centre took every player who had a uniform, 41 in all, on the train over to Lexington The Colonels outweighed the overmatched Transy team by 21 lbs. per man. Centre slaughtered the Crimson, 98-

0. Uncle Charlie played everyone who made the trip, all 41.

Red Weaver came over from Montgomery, West Virginia, where he was coaching the West Virginia Trade School football team. He watched the game from the sidelines. It seemed appropriate that he was in attendance when Centre's amazing extra point streak finally ended. After the Colonels' third touchdown, Bo's kick was wide. The miss ended the successful boots at 109 straight. It was 26-0 at the end of the first quarter, 60-0 at the half, and 88-0 after three quarters.

Army and Transy's captain decided to lop five minutes off the final period, and Centre still scored a TD and kicked a field goal to reach the 98 points total, achieved with 14 touchdowns, 11 extra points, and the field goal. When the last of the Colonels' subs ran out onto the field, George Joplin must have felt good about his column two days earlier. (The 98-0 win meant that in the last five years, Centre had outscored its old Kentucky rival by a combined 302-3. The five contests were played over a total of 290 minutes, so Centre averaged over a point per minute during the run. Transylvania tossed a white flag onto the turf, and the two colleges didn't meet again until 1924.)

While Centre was enjoying a romp, things weren't so easy in Cambridge.

Harvard was understandably quite confident when the schedule was made out for 1921. And why not? The Crimson had enjoyed so much success in the past that it was just understood that the winning ways would continue. However, in scheduling Indiana, Georgia and now Penn State on consecutive weekends, and then with Centre to follow the Nittany Lions, the Crimson had packed the middle of their season with some real, quality opponents, and the games with their arch rivals, Princeton, Brown and Yale, would still remain. (The "Nittany Lion" nickname of the Penn State athletic teams had an origin somewhat like that of Virginia Tech's "Hokies" in that both were the products of a student's imagination. Penn State was playing Princeton in baseball in 1904, and a Penn State student, Harrison D. "Joe" Mason, was shown a statue of Princeton's famous Bengal tiger, an example of the ferociousness of the Princeton athletic teams. Joe Mason replied that a Nittany Lion was the fiercest of all animals, and would overcome any "mere tiger." The instant fabrication stuck, and the Nittany Lions and Penn State have been synonymous since.)

Hugo Bezdek had taken over the Penn State program during the war-shortened 1918 season and jump-started the program the following year. Penn State was tough. The Pennsylvanians were 7-1 in 1919, losing only to Dartmouth in Hanover, 19-13, and went 7-0-2 in 1920, the ties being with Lehigh and Pittsburgh, both on the road.

Thus far in 1921, Penn State was undefeated at 4-0.

Penn State	53	Lebanon Valley	0
Penn State	24	Gettysburg	0
Penn State	35	North Carolina State	0
Penn State	28	Lehigh	7

Coach Fisher and his staff spent the week prior to the Penn State game once again shuffling the starting line-up. In the practice sessions, seven players who hadn't started against Georgia were put on the first unit.

The only back who had started against Georgia who was still on the first string was George Owen, the fullback. Jewett Johnson was to replace Charles Buell at quarterback, Winnie Churchill, the Crimson who had visited Danville over the past Christmas vacation, was starting at halfback along with Vinton Chapin. Several linemen were moved in and out of starting positions during the week, with the Harvard coaches determined to get an eleven on the field who could put some points on the board.

In addition to the offensive woes which were worrisome, Harvard was going to be outweighed one of the few times in its long gridiron history, with Penn State having a seven pound weight advantage per man.

35,000 people attended the Penn State game in the Stadium, more than had attended the Georgia game, but far from capacity. The Nittany Lions showed the crowd that their growing reputation was well deserved.

The Crimson jumped out to a 7-0 lead after driving 70 yards on their first possession. Harvard then scored a second time to go up, 14-0, and it looked like business as usual. However, Penn State's defense tightened up and their offense came alive and suddenly the Crimson looked out of sync. A score by the Nittany Lions made it 14-7 at the half.

Percy Haughton, the former Harvard coach (1908-16) scampered out of the press box just before the half ended and hustled to the Crimson locker room. A reporter watched Haughton rushing out of the end zone, obviously heading to the locker room.

The squad looked like it had been talked to a bit, quite a serious array as it walked slowly back into the stadium after the half, especially as compared to the dashing way it introduced itself to the crowd before the game.

Penn State scored once in the third quarter to knot it at 14-14 going into the final period. Certainly the momentum had changed, and its power offense brushed right by, over, and around the Crimson defenders as suddenly the Nittany Lions took it in again to go up 21-14. The Pennsylvanians had put 21 unanswered points on the board, and things were looking quite serious in the big horseshoe.

Preceding the "12th Man" legend at Texas A&M (which we'll get into later) was an event which could have achieved the same status as the Texas happening had someone promoted it.

It was unbelievable with the depth of the Crimson squad, but Coach Robert Fisher had run out of backs! Fisher got one of his backfield coaches to contact an "H" sweatered cheerleader named Bayard Wharton, a senior from Philadelphia who had prepped at Chestnut Hill Academy. Wharton had been on the football team the previous two years, but decided to concentrate on track and became a cheerleader in the fall of 1921.

Bayard Wharton was told that he may be needed and he raced to the locker room and suited up. As darkness fell over the playing field, the Crimson regained possession at midfield. Coach Fisher had a quartet comprised of two quarterbacks, a guard, and Winnie Churchill in the backfield.

The crowd was on its feet, cheering on their team. Methodically, junior Charles Buell directed what everyone knew would be the last drive of the game. Buell kept the ball on the ground, and by picking up 4-5 yards per carry, managed to take his team to the Nittany Lion 15. Two line plunges moved the ball to the 10, where it was 3rd and 5.

On the next play, Buell took the snap and drifted slightly left where he spotted Churchill out near the left sideline. Buell pulled up, fired a bullet, Churchill grabbed it, and danced across the goal. Charles Buell calmly put the extra point boot squarely through the uprights to tie the game at 21-21. Harvard had escaped, but just barely.

Penn State won the battle of the statistics, rushing for 330 yards while holding Harvard to only 130. The Crimson passed for 67 yards. Penn State got 57 through the air. Only five times since 1900, a period stretching over 206 games, had a team scored 21 or more points against Harvard. Coach Fisher used 25 men in the game. He didn't put cheerleader Wharton in, but the young man stood by if needed. (Doubtless, Wharton would performed well if he'd been sent out onto the field. He had proven himself under fire during the Great War, being awarded the Order of the British Empire, the OBE, and the Italian Silver Medal of Valor, for his service in France and Italy.)

Upon returning back onto the Penn State campus, the Nittany Lions were met by the school band and the entire student body as they disembarked off the train. The whole throng made its way to the athletic field where speeches were made by Coach Bezdek and the players.

One member of the team, Captain George Snell, hadn't been able to make the trip as he was in the infirmary with a throat infection. Captain Richmond Keith Kane of Harvard sent the game ball back to State College where it was presented to Snell with a warm note wishing him a speedy recovery. It was the Harvard way.

When members of the Colonels received the results of the Penn State game, they were greatly relieved.

"We loved the Harvard players," Army was quoted as saying years later. "We always cheered for them except, of course, when they were playing us. And then, we wanted to be the ones to beat them. We wanted to go to Harvard and be the first team in many games to defeat what we considered the greatest college, and greatest bunch of guys."

CHAPTER 13:
THE BIG WEEK ARRIVES!
CENTRE-HARVARD—1921

So the scene was set. Centre was undefeated. Harvard was undefeated, even though tied. Centre had won 32 and lost three since 1917. Harvard, which didn't count 1917-18 as "official," had a record of 23-0-3 since 1919. Two great teams were barreling toward each other, two programs that were at the top of the mountain in college football's hierarchy. Something had to give, and sports fans all over the country collectively held their breaths, as "Centre-Harvard" dominated the interest and conversations of anyone who had any knowledge at all of the sport.

On Friday, October 21, Howard Reynolds of the "Post" arrived in Danville. He was going to stay at the Gilcher and return to Boston with the team, sending back stories to his paper in the week leading up to the game. Reynolds had become such a confidant of Uncle Charlie's that Centre let him in on everything the team planned regarding the tactics and plans for the Harvard game. Uncle Charlie knew that Reynolds would never betray the Colonels, and indeed, he never did.

The "Messenger" reported that a Mr. Lemuel McHenry of Louisville was hoping to get a ticket to the game through Centre. He had a son in Boston who had tried every angle to secure a ticket and couldn't find one anywhere.

Other than the Princeton, Dartmouth and Yale games, no other team could fill the Stadium except Centre, attesting to how popular the Colonels had become, and how the team had captured the hearts of fans everywhere they appeared.

George Joplin was put in charge of the "Harvard Special" which was going to carry the team and several hundred fans on an all-Pullman train to the game. Joplin got the arrangements made and then there was a wrench thrown into his plan.

Centre announced that students wouldn't be excused from classes in order to go to the game. The college had received word from the Southern Intercollegiate Athletic Association that it would be in violation of the rules of the S.I.A.A if excuses were given to attend an athletic event. There was a huge protest at the news. Even Howard Reynolds jumped into the fray and wrote a long article in support of the students which was first published in the "Post," and then in the local Danville papers.

Reynolds pointed out that the previous week, Ohio State had engaged special trains to take the entire student body, numbering some 5,000, to Ann Arbor to the Michigan game. The students were excused from their Friday and Saturday classes, and, "Ohio State is what everyone would call a fairly regulated institution."

Nothing that was said could change the decision of the faculty. The fact was that even though Dr. Ganfield was still on the campus, his resignation made him powerless to intercede. It was the impression that there were certain professors who felt that perhaps Centre's athletic prowess was getting more attention than its academic reputation, and maybe there was a need to pull in the reins a bit.

Whatever the reason, the "Harvard Special" had to be cancelled, because the student's numbers were necessary to reach the quota set by the Southern Railroad to make the whole affair possible. Now there would be special cars hooked onto regular trains. It was a setback, but not a deal-breaker.

What was more serious as a threat to the trip to the East was the possibility of a national railroad strike. The Federal Railroad Board ordered the five big unions representing railway workers not to strike until October 30 in order to give the unions and negotiators time to work out an agreement. However, there was no guarantee that arbitration would be successful.

The October 30 date was critical. If a strike were to occur, trains would stop running when the clock struck 12:00 on Saturday night the 29th. The Colonels and fans would find themselves stuck somewhere between Boston and Albany, New York, as they didn't plan on leaving until Saturday night after the game.

"No problem," came the word out of Cambridge.

At least there would be no problem in getting the team back to Danville. As for the fans, that was another situation.

A headline in the Danville "Advocate" announced a solution if a strike indeed was called. The story was a reprint from the Boston "Evening Transcript."

SPLENDID GENEROUS HARVARD

A less intrepid band of warriors than that of Danville, Kentucky might hesitate to stray so far from the Bluegrass as Boston with a railroad strike impending. It is certain, however, that the Kentuckians will appear in the Stadium Saturday, and that the Harvard Athletic Association will furnish a fleet of fast automobiles to get the Centre football squad back to Danville. This statement was authorized by Major Fred W. Moore, graduate treasurer of athletics at Harvard.

Centre will get to Harvard before the threatened "walkout." Harvard will see to it that Bo McMillin and his teammates get back to their Southern campus.

As it was, the strike was averted at the last moment, but the offer to actually drive the team back to Danville was greatly appreciated by the Colonels and the coaching staff. It would have been a major undertaking of over 1700 miles roundtrip, and the roads would have gotten progressively worse as the caravan had driven south, with a lot of the "highways" being little more than dirt. An average of 15 miles an hour would be all that could be achieved along many stretches, and it was estimated that the trip would have taken several days each way, with stops at various hotels along the route as darkness approached.

Nonetheless, Major Moore said he had more volunteers than he would need. "They are lined up and will be ready to go if they are called."

"Amazing, simply amazing," was the sentiment in Danville.

Kentuckians began lining up outings and securing tickets for events besides the Harvard game. The Ziegfeld Follies, a musical comedy named "The Rose Girl," a light comedy, "Little Old New York," and the Harvard Glee Club with Mary Garden at Symphony Hall, were all playing in Boston. Mr. Joseph Burkes, at the Adams House in the theatre district, was "reserving an ample number of seats to accommodate the Centre delegation," according to newspaper reports in local Kentucky papers.

In addition to the theatrical opportunities, plans were being drawn up for tours around Boston with the Royal Blue Lines Coach Company. For $2.50, a four hour round trip could be made between Concord and Lexington.

"The tour is through the territory of the Revolutionary War where 'the shot heard round the world' occurred, which was 'the first Declaration of Independence.'"

"In the course of the four hour spin, one will visit historic scenes and houses that are of poignant interest to all Americans: the Trinity Church, the Fenway, John Harvard's statue, Cooper's Tavern, Harrington Elm, Monroe Tavern, Lexington Green, the scene of the Battle of Lexington, Pulpit Rock, Old Revolutionary Monument, Parker Boulder, the Old Northbridge, Hawthorne's Wayside, Grape Vine Cottage, The Old Manse, where Emerson wrote "Nature," and the Concord Battle Ground." It would have been a whirlwind event with so many places to be visited.

Other possible trips were offered and outlined by the Blue Line; Boston to Salem and Marblehead, Boston to Plymouth, Boston to "quaint" Gloucester via Ocean Boulevard, or one could simply go on one of the coaches for a city wide tour of Boston.

Multiple sportswriters in Kentucky were going to Boston. The Louisville "Herald" was sending Bruce Dudley and a staff photographer, Al Piers. The Louisville "Courier-Journal" was to be represented by Sam McMeekin who was taking along his wife. The sports editor of the Louisville "Times," Bob Dundon, was going. The Louisville "Evening Post" sent Lawrence Caudill. The editor of the Kentucky "Advocate", Vernon Richardson, made plans to go, and the Danville "Messenger" signed up to send both editor J. Curtis Alcock and reporter George Joplin.

Both the Lexington "Herald" and "Leader" had reporters assigned to go to Boston. Most importantly, of course, was that Howard Reynolds was going to accompany the team to Boston, filing stories along the way.

The University Club telegraphed the Centre "5" that they would guarantee the group $500.00 if they would perform at a dance on Friday night, October 28, and the Southern Club wanted the group to perform Saturday night after the game

The Jazz group was able to secure excuses from classes, as they were told, "You are going on a business trip, not an athletic venture, and naturally, we wouldn't want to interfere." After being assured of no penalty for missing classes, the "5" wired back— "Will be there with bells on."

On Monday, after the romp over Transylvania, Centre began holding practices that were closed to all except well-known supporters of the team, and Howard Reynolds. Reynolds was even able to sit in on a meeting with Uncle Charlie, Bo and Army.

Bo and Army set up the session with their coach to discuss Centre's game plan for Harvard in the Gilcher's dining room on Sunday night, October 23. Uncle Charlie had a table which was reserved for him when he was in town, and he often held court there while smoking a cigar and drinking coffee.

Bo began the conversation, "Unc, you know I've been quoted as saying I know why we lost to Harvard."

"Tell me about it! I heard from all over the country when you gave that interview."

Bo had been in New York City late in the summer, invited by some local alumni to speak at a fund raising dinner for the college. While there, he was cornered by a reporter. The next day, there was a story that hit not only New York, but was carried by a wire service to papers all over the country. Even out in Denver, the story hit the paper with the headline:

BO KNOWS WHY HARVARD WON

Bo was so well known nationally that there was only one name used, like Babe. There was only one Ruth. There was only one Bo.

"Unc, I didn't tell that guy why we lost. I just told him that I knew why we lost, but I didn't supply him any details."

Army picked up the conversation.

"That's what we want to talk to you about. Bo and I have thought about it a lot, and we want to make a suggestion about how we play against Harvard."

Uncle Charlie had great respect for his team captain and Bo. He knew that both of them were not only great talents, but great students of the game as well. Both Bo and Army planned to get into college coaching after leaving Centre.

Howard Reynolds asked Uncle Charlie if he wanted him to leave so that he could talk to his players privately.

"Absolutely not! You're here to get some slants on the game. You know we trust you like no other."

"Here's what Bo meant when he told that reporter he knew why we lost last year," Army said. "We played a great half, but we showed them our whole attack in the first two quarters. And then they went in at the break, and with all those coaches, they came up with a plan to shut us down in the second half, and they did."

Bo jumped back in.

"They beat us down, sure. We were physically beaten, but even if we were hurting, we had some plays that should have been big gainers, and they weren't. They had us figured out."

"So what do you suggest?"

"Army and I think that we should play a very conservative game, especially in the first half. You know how we dedicated ourselves to not let anyone score on us this year. The Saint Xavier score was a fluke. We don't think anyone can score on us again."

"Bo is right. We think if we play conservatively, we can wait for one break and win. We want to primarily stick to the ground. Punt if we have third down and long yardage."

It was an unusual request and it was asking a lot for Uncle Charlie to agree to his star's plan. He was an offensive genius who took great pride in keeping his opponents befuddled by his wide open attack. But it was even more unusual for Bo to be advocating such a toned down attack. Bo was the shooting star, made famous by his offensive brilliance. It was like having a gunslinger go to a duel, leaving his six-shooter behind.

"We can score on them, I'm confidant of that," Bo said. "We don't think they can score on us. Let's not show them anything, at least in the first half." Uncle Charlie slowly came around the more Bo and Army talked. What really convinced him was that it would be a surprise. Uncle Charlie liked to spring the unexpected on his foes.

"Ok, we run, we punt, we wait for a break. I'm confidant you guys can pull it off. We play exactly the game they won't expect. That's a great idea! I like it!"

Howard Reynolds filed his daily stories with generalities, and in no way did he betray Centre's confidence. One story spoke of a different style of play, but didn't divulge just what that style would be.

When Centre College goes on the playing field at Cambridge this Saturday against Harvard, several changes in the playing style will be used from the system adopted in swamping Transylvania, and which was viewed by Harvard's scouts. Some trick plays may be used, but what these may be has so far been concealed by Coach Charles Moran. Bo McMillin will take full charge of the team when the battle begins.

Certainly nothing new there except that some new plays will be used, and as usual, Bo will be running the team.

On the next day, Reynolds wrote:

The Praying Colonels of Centre College, 33 strong, tonight are resting preparatory to starting for Cambridge Wednesday for the game with Harvard Saturday. Coach Moran put his men through a grueling practice in secret this afternoon, and will give them a light workout tomorrow.

Wednesday at 8:00 a.m., the train will pull out for Boston with about 100 Kentuckians and the Centre squad aboard. Many of these travelers will be Old Centre men from the West and South. Centre's alumni in the East will go direct from their homes to Boston. President W.A. Ganfield will see his last football game with Centre as he has become the president of a Wisconsin college.

Centre will have a much stronger team to throw against Harvard than last year. When the season began, the motto was "win 'em all." The team and its supporters actually believe that the team will indeed "win them all."

Centre points out that its players are better than those of the previous teams, and that it is playing better and stronger this year. Kentuckians speak of going to Cambridge and Boston as the Southerner speaks of "going home." They remember the warm reception given last year by the New Englanders when Centre played Harvard.

In Boston, the Harvard coaching staff was faced with a real dilemma. The Centre game was important. It was drawing interest from all corners of the country. It was going to be played in front of an absolutely jammed stadium. There was excitement being generated which was even greater than the year before.

However, it was a simple fact that the games with the Crimson's traditional rivals, Princeton and Yale, were the critical dates on the schedule each year. A season's success was measured by the results of games between the "Big 3."

Melville Webb, a sportswriter for the Boston "Globe," summarized the Harvard situation in an article appearing in the October 24th paper.

This week against Centre, Harvard will not be able to muster its full strength. The Kentuckians are not expected to have such surprises up their sleeves as they did last fall, and Harvard will doubtless move as straight as possible for the Princeton game, now two weeks away.

Owen and Captain Kane, both injured, easily can stand a rest, and both must need one as they were hit hard in the Penn State game, as was Fitts, whose knee has been bothering him since the early going. Crocker is also nursing an injury, and it is absolutely necessary that he be ready for the Princeton game.

So while Harvard respected Centre, it must be remembered that Harvard was Harvard, seemingly invincible, and Coach Fisher and his staff were understandingly perhaps pointing more toward the Princeton game of November 5, and the season ending game with Yale.

There was no such ambivalence back in Danville. It was Harvard. It was always—Harvard.

Howard Reynolds read the installments from "First Down, Kentucky" that were published in "The Popular Magazine" with great interest while he was in Danville and sent back an excerpt for his readers.

Here is the way that Ralph Paine describes what Bo and Uncle Charlie thought about Harvard and Boston before they ever thought they had a chance to play the Crimson. They were already thinking about Harvard even before they had played West Virginia in the break-through game of 1919.

"We've got to show them," said Bo. "This is the first chance we've ever had to get a line on what we could do against one of the great Eastern colleges. Beyond the Alps lie Italy and Harvard."

"Your aims are lofty and you're afflicted with imagination, as usual," said the coach, who had umpired many a league game in Boston. "You whip these West Virginia mountain

men and Harvard may condescend to notice your existence. If you asked 'em right now for a game next year, they might take it as an insult."

"I reckon Harvard is in an unfortunate mental attitude," observed Bowman. "Does it wear off later in life?"

"If they get out into the United States, it does, Bo. But it doesn't, if they stay in Boston. Of course, they know who Princeton is. The wilderness begins west of New Jersey, but for little colleges like us away out in no man's land, they'd be liable to ask if we graduated barbers, stenographers, or banjo players."

Then when they entered the stadium a year ago, Paine writes:

They trotted out on the field and dispersed for a quick rehearsal. A glance at the crowded slopes of the Stadium, all flecked with Crimson flags, and the nervousness tautened again. But now there came down to them a tremendous outburst of applause. It was not the courageous cheer of a few hundred partisans from Kentucky, but the voices of many thousands. Bowman McMurray flashed a smile at Len Garretson and slapped him on the back as he shouted above the crowd, "Would you believe it? Where did all these friends of ours come from? And they call it cold roast Boston."

We all read the installments of "First Down, Kentucky." There were several copies of the magazine each week in the dorm, and they were passed around. I think that everybody at Centre and Danville read them. It was like they were reading about themselves because even though the author used fake names, all the facts were true.

Bo was always really friendly, even to a freshman like me. We were in the lounge on the first floor of Breck Hall, just before the 1921 Harvard game. There were some of the magazines lying around, so I asked Bo what he thought about what had been published.

He said he thought it was great for the school and the team, but he wished it had been written a year later, because Centre lost to Harvard, and that's how the story ended.

Bo told me that if the book were to be written after the rematch with Harvard, it would have a better ending, because it would have Centre winning.

The way he said it, I really felt that we'd beat Harvard. Bo didn't make comments like that if he didn't really believe what he said.

There were simply no more tickets for the Centre-Harvard game available. Just like in 1920, it had become a scalper's market, and up to 10 times and more of the price printed on the ticket was the going rate. It was reported that with the Centre sell-out included, 150,000 people would have seen the Crimson play during the year thus far. The papers were stating that offers were being made to pay $50.00, the equivalent of $500.00 in today's money, for a seat anywhere near the 50 yard line.

The fact that Indiana, Georgia and Penn State couldn't come near filling Harvard Stadium reinforced just how huge a draw the Colonels were. The Harvard athletic officials said it was felt that over 75,000 tickets could have been sold had the capacity of the Stadium been that great.

Howard Reynolds was much appreciated in Danville, and on Monday night, the 24th, the Chamber of Commerce gave a dinner in his honor to thank him for all he had done in publicizing and promoting Centre.

The Boston sportswriter was asked to say a few words after the meal, and he stood and said that if Centre won, "and I feel there is an excellent chance that it will, I'll be coming back with the team, because I wouldn't miss the celebration for anything in the world."

Reynolds' comments were met with a standing ovation, and many of those present told him, "We'll see you Howard, when you get back into town."

Tiny Thornhill had used the first four games of the season to experiment with various combinations of starters in the line. The backfield talent was so deep that Uncle Charlie could substitute freely without weakening the team. But the situation with the line was vital if Centre were to pull off the unexpected. It would be the performance of the front wall which would be critical.

In the week leading up to the game, Tiny finalized his lineup. The addition of Red Roberts to the line was made possible by the strong showing of Tom Bartlett and Hump Tanner at the fullback slot. Unless Red was needed for a short-yardage plunge, the big fellow would play end.

Bill Shadoan had worked his way into a starting position at guard. It was only his 5th game as a member of the Gold and White, but his prior experience of playing service ball had allowed him to quickly learn Tiny's system.

Thornhill moved Bill James out from tackle to end. James had filled out to a solid 180 pounds, and his speed was essential to keep Harvard from successfully running end sweeps. The steady Ben Cregor would play in his regular position at right tackle and Minos Gordy would start at the other tackle position.

George "Buck" Jones and Ed Kubale would round out the starting lineup at guard and center.

POSITION	STARTER	WEIGHT
Left end	Bill James	180
Left tackle	Minos Gordy	182
Left guard	Bill Shadoan	196
Center	Ed Kubale	177
Right guard	George "Buck" Jones	213
Right tackle	Ben Cregor	180
Right end	Red Roberts	215

Centre's line would average 191 ½ pounds which would be the equal of Harvard's. Tiny was confident that he could send in Frank Rubarth, who weighed 175, or Richard Gibson, at 180, and they could adequately hold their own in the trenches. (The various accounts of the line-ups had varying weights listed, but they were just a few pounds off.

For instance, Red Roberts was noted to weigh anywhere from 215 to 219, and "Buck" Jones from 200 to 213.)

The only question mark about how the line would perform was due to experience. Gordy, Jones, Kubale and Shadoan were all freshmen, as were Rubarth and Gibson. Could a team with four freshman starters in the line, as well as the top two subs, be expected to play competitively, and what would their reaction be when they ran out onto the field and saw 50,000 people in the stands?

Tiny Thornhill said simply, "Time will tell, I suppose. But I have all the confidence in the world in my men." Tiny later said that the fact that Red Roberts and Ben Cregor were in their fourth year at Centre, and Bill James his fifth, "will have a steadying influence on my first year men."

The movement of Red Roberts into the line allowed Terry Snowday, who had alternated between end and the backfield, to play halfback full-time. Of course, Bo was a permanent fixture at quarterback. Army was just as permanent at left half, and Bartlett and Hump gave the fullback position great depth.

This was the lineup which would start. It was powerful. It had speed. But even more importantly, it was on a mission.

"We are Centre!" was the spirit that this group of young men constantly repeated.

"We are Centre!"
"We are Centre!"
"We are Centre!"

And Centre planned on making the journey to Boston and this time, coming home the winner. Because it was Harvard, as always. It was—Harvard.

The last Centre practice on Cheek Field was begun at 2:00 in the afternoon of the 25th. The session lasted until it was literally too dark to carry on, and then, after showers, the team assembled in the gym for a marathon skull session. Every conceivable Harvard formation was diagrammed. Moran drilled and drilled, as did the Chief, who had just gotten in from Chicago, and Tiny Thornhill. They wanted the Colonels to be so sharp that they could anticipate the upcoming Crimson plays from the way their opponents lined up.

Only after the skull session was over did the squad learn who was going to be on the trip to Cambridge. George Joplin captured the moment when he wrote:

Twenty-six players will be taken on the big jaunt, but as yet, the names of the lucky ones have not been announced by Coach Moran. The official party will consist of thirty-two. Tonight, after the final preparations, the names of those men who will make the trip will be posted in the dressing room. Many a valiant warrior's heart will be cast into the deepest gloom when he fails to see his name on the honor roll, while others will secretly rejoice. The lucky ones will sympathize with the less fortunate, and the one who stays at home will smile bravely and say that he is glad the other is going. Not a man of them but would give anything to battle for Old Centre.

One player who knew he wouldn't be going was Lefty Whitnell who had caught the pass which resulted in the second touchdown for the Colonels in the 1920 Harvard game. Lefty had run into some problems with his studies which had made him ineligible to play. He'd continued attending practice, hoping that he could pull up his grades enough to be able to get back into the action. It wasn't to be. The faculty, just as in the issue of allowing the students to be excused from classes to make the trip, wouldn't budge regarding Lefty. It was a major disappointment for the speedster from Fulton, Kentucky.

The travel squad was posted after the skull session. Most already knew they were going and were packed and ready for the early Wednesday morning departure.

Norris "Army" Armstrong—Fort Smith, Arkansas
Thomas G. Bartlett—Owensboro, Kentucky
Don Beane—Pittsburgh, Pennsylvania
George Chinn—Harrodsburg, Kentucky
Ray Class—Middletown, Ohio
Herbert "Covey" Covington—Mayfield, Kentucky
Ben W. "Baldy" Cregor—Springfield, Kentucky
Royce N. "Andy" Flippin—Somerset, Kentucky
Richard "Dick" Gibson—Louisville, Kentucky
Minos T. "Cajun" Gordy—Abbeville, Louisiana
James E. "Jimmy" Green—Louisville, Kentucky
A. Hope Hudgins—Amarillo, Texas
William N. "Bill" James—Fort Worth, Texas
George R. "Buck" Jones—Dallas, Texas
Dewey Kimbel—Louisville, Kentucky
Edwin Kubale—Fort Smith, Arkansas
Clifton W. "Hennie" Lemon—Mayfield, Kentucky
Alvin Nugent "Bo" McMillin—Fort Worth, Texas
Joseph "Chick" Murphy—Columbus, Ohio
Slim Newell—Dallas, Texas
James B. "Red" Roberts—Somerset, Kentucky
Robert Frank Rubarth—Gatesville, Texas
Hall Terry Snowday—Owensboro, Kentucky
John Porter "Hump" Tanner—Owensboro, Kentucky
William P. "Bill" Shadoan—Somerset, Kentucky
Robert L. "Case" Thomasson—Newport, Kentucky

In multiple contemporary articles in the Danville, Louisville and Lexington papers, these are the 26 players who were listed as being in the group which went to Boston on the train. Also, in the official program for the game, only these 26 are listed.

Yet, there is a photograph taken in Fenway Park, published in the Boston "Post" pictorial section on October 28, with 28 players dressed out in uniform. In the photo, Weldon Bradley from Dallas and Leslie Combs II from Lexington, Kentucky are shown, and listed in the caption.

Also, on October 27, an article in the Boston "Herald" named 28 players, and Bradley and Combs are included. Since they weren't in the original list, it must be concluded that they were last minute additions, or paid their own way, brought their gear, and were allowed to suit up. Whatever. When the players are mentioned as being in uniform for this historic game, Combs and Bradley should be listed, because they were definitely there.

Along with the team, others in the official party were the Chief and his wife, Uncle Charlie, Tiny Thornhill, Swede Anderson, the team trainer, and the student manager, John McGee. Also going along was Roscoe Breckinridge Conklin. (It was 1950 before the United States Supreme Court ruled that segregated dining cars on railroads—the Southern Railroad in particular—were illegal. Roscoe was known to travel with the team to various locations. Apparently, there was no problem once the train crossed over the Ohio River. The ride from Danville to Cincinnati would have been made under the segregation policies of the Southern Railroad.)

In Cambridge, Coach Fisher was telling the press that his team was "shot to pieces." A story was published in the Lexington "Herald" with the dateline, Cambridge, Mass, October 24.

When Coach Fisher surveyed his team to see who was available for the Centre game, he found Captain Kane, Owen, Fitts and Gehrke just out of the "infirmary," and several others convalescing. The Crimson team, with a wealth of backfield material early in the season, was so reduced by the Penn State contest that linemen were sent into the backfield, and a cheerleader was sent to the clubhouse to change from white flannels to moleskins. It was such a stop-gap combination that went into the last period and tied the score when the game appeared lost.

The Danville "Messenger" picked up the story and added a sports editor's comment:

Take the above like Rube Goldberg would say in one of his cartoons, "It's terrible, but it don't mean anything."

Despite Fisher's professed worries, in actuality, Harvard felt confident in the week leading up to the Centre game. A big headline in the Boston "Globe" stated:

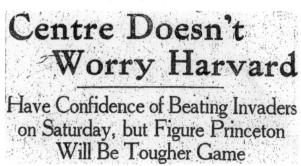

Centre Doesn't Worry Harvard

Have Confidence of Beating Invaders on Saturday, but Figure Princeton Will Be Tougher Game

Captain Keith Kane and "Tobby" Grew were back in the Harvard varsity lineup yesterday afternoon with the result that the "A" team went through the workout with more "pep" and confidence of any of the sessions thus far this week.

At present, the Crimson coaches are worrying more about the Princeton encounter next week than about Saturday's battle with McMillin and his confreres. The Kentucky Colonels have a reinforced line and are expected to put up a stiffer defense than they did last year, but out at Harvard, there is confidence that the daring visitors will be sent back to the Bluegrass on the short end of the score.

Harvard isn't expected to try to run up the score against the Danville invaders. Coach Fisher and his assistants are anxious to have every man ready for the trip to Princeton. The Kentucky boys are sure to be putting up their best every minute of the game, and if the Crimson regulars can get a respectable lead in the first half, the second sting men will be given the opportunity to get their bruises of the fray during the second half.

Back in Danville and throughout the state, plans were again being made to "broadcast" the game. Stout's movie theater was "running in a wire" and planned to charge 25 cents. Dr. Stout, the owner, had Lefty Whitnell lined up to call out the plays from the stage.

Louis Mannini was going to describe the plays from the front of his news stand on Main, and his service was free. The brokerage house, W.L. Lyons, planned to have the game come in over its ticker-tape, and again, there would be no charge to "listen" to the action. Similar arrangements were made all over Kentucky, with both Louisville and Lexington planning several locations to "carry" the game.

On Tuesday night, October 25, there was a huge and enthusiastic pep rally beginning at 7:30 at the courthouse on Main Street in Danville. Like the previous year, there was a makeshift stage and the whole area was flooded with spotlights. The crowd was estimated as exceeding 1,000. The girls from K.C.W. were there along with the Centre student body and a considerable number of the citizens of Danville and Boyle County.

George Swinebroad, Jr. led the cheers.

Fight! Gold and White.
Fight! Gold and White.
Fight! Gold and White.
Fight! Fight! Fight! Fight! Fight! Fight! Fight!

Old Centre Fight!
Old Centre Fight!
Old Centre Fight!
Fight with all your might!

Halfway through the pep rally, an enormous cheer began at the back of the crowd and then resonated throughout the entire throng as the Centre team walked en mass toward the stage. Uncle Charlie, the Chief, and Tiny Thornhill followed Army, with Bo walking behind the team captain, and the rest of the squad trailing Bo.

The team had left the skull session and walked the few blocks to spend a few moments at the rally. There was so much enthusiasm that they could hear the cheers floating through the cool night air toward the campus as they left the Boyle-Humphrey Gymnasium.

As the players stood on the courthouse steps and waved to the crowd, the chant, "Speech, Speech, Speech," rang out. No one stepped forward. Those on the steps who had been there the year before remembered the predictions of how they were going to beat Harvard.

Chief Myers motioned to George Swinebroad to come over and shouted in his ear, and the cheerleader put a finger to his lips to quiet the crowd. Swinebroad hollered into his megaphone, "The Chief said the team would save their speeches until they've returned from Boston," and after a pause, "until they've beaten Harvard!" The roar was deafening, echoing off the walls of the buildings around the old courthouse.

In Boston and the surrounding area, the odds given on the game were anywhere from 3-1 to 10-6 in Harvard's favor. Writers from all of the Boston papers predicted a Crimson win. Those same columnists predicted a wide open game like the battle of 1920, just as Centre hoped the Harvard coaching staff would expect.

A story in the "Post" was typical.

Reverting once more to the dope, it can be said that the crowd will again expect the following things to take place. There will be a current of forward passes by Centre—long ones, middle-sized ones, and short, sharp ones over the line. There will be a wonderful open field showing by Bo McMillin once he gets clear of the Harvard ends. There will be a series of trick plays by Centre that are designed to catch the Harvard front wall unawares. And there will be some first class line bucking by Armstrong and Snowday when Centre effects to play the orthodox game.

At least the last sentence was factual.

Another story again related how the crowd would feel about the Colonels when they entered the Stadium.

Of the sell-out crowd which will watch the game, one half will be for the Bluegrass boys, not because they love Harvard less, but because they love Centre more. The reasons are multiple. Centre is perhaps the smallest college that has ever attacked a member of the "Big 3." Its entire team is absolutely the salt of the earth. In Bo McMillin, they have in their lineup a young man who transcends any star since the days of Eddie Mahan. He is surrounded by plucky, intrepid chaps who would take broken bones for the honor to win. That is why this hostile team finds welcome in the heart of the cold, codfish zone.

In his opinion of how the teams compared and how the game may unfold, another writer analyzed what he expected to see on the field.

221

Centre is rated to achieve about as much as it did against Harvard a year ago. The Colonels scored on the Crimson twice and had the Fishermen netted for the entire first half. But in the second half of the game, their power curled up before the Harvard drive because the team was well worn out from so gallant a battle in the first half.

Centre is better equipped for Harvard in the matter of substitutes. The entire first string will not have to fight against fresh understudies from the Harvard bench, and Centre has no doubt learned a lot about the principles of defense that was their downfall last year. They were buzzards for scoring, but not so good at checking an assault.

Allowing, however, for Centre's improvement in its power of resistance; allowing also for the flash of its stars and the fervor that animates those boys when they step out for a gridiron conflict; allowing for all those increased virtues, the chances for Centre are still below par. The reason is that Harvard "arrived" in its game with Penn State last week.

ON TO HARVARD !

The "Harvard Special," which had to be cancelled due the inability of the students to be excused from classes, was to have departed from Danville's station at 8:00 AM on Wednesday, October 26. Now that the Pullmans were going to be connected to a regularly scheduled Southern passenger train, the "Queen City, Crescent City Special," the team and fans would pull out at 6:00 AM.

Despite the early hour, a large and enthusiastic crowd had already gathered on the station's platform and all around the building when the players arrived to board. Howard Reynolds carried his well used typewriter to the lounge car and pounded out a story as the train chugged out of Danville. He had less than an hour to complete it, as he wanted to jump off in Lexington and hand it to the Western Union operator at the Southern station there.

Even if the sun had hardly gotten out of bed, the entire student body and it seemed like all of Danville flocked to the station to give the team a send off only equaled by that which it received a year ago.

There is no getting away from this Kentucky spirit. There is no thought of failure on Saturday left behind in Danville, any more than there is in the minds of those who are making the trip. Such a spirit cannot help but cause admiration. To think that such a little college can possess it after those defeats administered last year by Harvard and Georgia Tech is truly inspiring.

The Centre team of 1919 had run over such opponents as Indiana, the conquerors of Syracuse, and West Virginia, an eleven that had beaten Princeton when Harvard had been held to a tie by those same Tigers.

After the two defeats of last year, these boys showed they had learned the lesson to "carry on." These boys, particularly McMillin, had hammered it to the younger set that no matter how hard you get handled in football, as long as your opponent does it in a legitimate manner, you take it without batting an eye, and that no man knows how good he really is until he has received a wallop. To show how good he really is, all that was needed was to show he could recover from such a wallop.

The efforts of Uncle Charlie, Bo and Captain Armstrong were concentrated on the gospel of "carrying on," that the real man and the real team was the one which could smile under a hard jolt and recover the faith, and that Centre indeed had the "stuff," and was able to move on.

The Centre cheerleaders were again leading the crowd in shouting their encouragement. The Southern Railroad had allowed the Colonels' fans to chalk messages on the sides of the Pullmans, unlike the year before.

31-14—1920
1921—CENTRE VICTORIOUS
TO HARVARD—YEA CENTRE !
CENTRE COLLEGE

Howard Reynolds wrote about an incident which happened just before the train left the station.

An aged native of the foothills stepped to the door of the Pullman and handed Moran a package.
He whispered, "It is for the boys. It is cold and rainy up there."
The package when opened proved to be a quart jar of moonshine. A sweet potato was plugged in the broad mouth of the jar to hold the contents in.

The team settled into their chartered car, the last Pullman which had been connected to the "Queen City, Crescent City Special," and waved from the windows as the big steamer slowly pulled out of the station. Someone mentioned that Red Roberts wasn't aboard. Uncle Charlie sent out a search party which looked through the train. No sight of Red was found. The Centre contingent was getting more than a little concerned.

"Did anybody see Red get on for certain?"

"Here's his suitcase. I know he must be here somewhere."

It wasn't until they stopped in Lexington that Red was located, along with Roscoe. Red and his helper had been in the engine, stoking coal. When the train stopped, Red hopped down, wearing the engineer's hat and had his picture taken which appeared in the Lexington papers under the headline:

"RED" ROBERTS IS DISCOVERED IN ENGINE CAB; FIERY-HAIRED
STAR, HOWEVER, LETS EBONY VALET HANDLE SHOVEL

Uncle Charlie greeted his star when he finally returned to the team's Pullman.

"Redhead, you big lug. You put a scare in us. We thought we'd left you behind. You pull another stunt like that, and we'll put you in a Railway Express car and ship you back to Somerset, collect."

"Aw, Unc….."

The crowd greeting the Colonels in Lexington wasn't as large as the previous

223

year because many of the Lexingtonians had expected the "Harvard Special" to arrive at 9:00 AM rather than 7:00. But those who had gotten word when the team would arrive made up in enthusiasm what they lacked in numbers. At the layover, another Pullman was hooked in front of the Colonels', to be occupied by fans from Lexington and Louisville.

A long banner was attached to one side of the car which said:

OCTOBER 23, 1920 31-14
OCTOBER 29, 1921
REVERSE THAT SCORE!!

On the other side:

THE PRAYING, FIGHTING COLONELS FROM DANVILLE TO BOSTON

As the train slowly pulled away from the Lexington station, shouts were heard from the waving fans on the platform.

"Get 'em this year guys!"

"We're behind you all the way!"

Then it was north bound, over the tracks to Cincinnati where once again the New York Central's tracks were joined. There was a one hour layover in the Queen City, and the Colonels hiked to a nearby diner for lunch.

The Chief was quoted as saying that, "If those boys consume many more meals like they did this noon, we'll have to correct our weight average when we get to Boston."

From Cincinnati north, the Centre "5" went through the cars and entertained the team and passengers. Thomas Mercer and John Eads with their saxophones, J.B. Lusk, the drummer, and Tuttle, known as a "banjo artist," were greatly appreciated as they circulated throughout the Pullmans. J.W. Randall, the pianist, could also play the mandolin, and joined in.

When the train pulled into Columbus, Ohio, over 500 people were at the station, the crowd swelled by fans who came out to see a local member of the team, Joe "Chick" Murphy. A similar reception occurred at a stop in Middletown, Ohio, where the added attraction was native son, Ray Class, a drop-kicker. At Middletown, the Centre "5" quickly got organized on the station platform, and "romped to the delight of the crowd."

At 6:00 PM, the travelers pulled into Cleveland to connect to the 20th Century Limited for the express run east. The 20th Century Limited had two sections which were separated in Albany, New York, with one part continuing to Boston, and the other proceeding into Grand Central Terminal in New York City. Several of the reporters jumped off while the cars were being hooked up and sent stories back to their papers, with the dateline being, "Oct. 26, Cleveland, O.—aboard the Centre Special."

CENTRE
COLONEL

CENTRE COLLEGE BUILDINGS, 1920

OLD CENTRE- 1920

OLD MAIN- 1920

YOUNG SCIENCE HALL- 1920

BRECKINRIDGE HALL- 1920

CARNEGIE LIBRARY- 1920

BOYLE-HUMPHREY GYMNASIUM- 1920

KENTUCKY COLLEGE FOR WOMEN
Danville, Kentucky

LEXINGTON AVENUE, DANVILLE, KENTUCKY- 1920

NORTH FORT WORTH HIGH SCHOOL

ROBERT LEE MYERS, A. B.

Born September 1, 1887, at Atchison, Kan. Prepared at the Ft. Worth (Texas) High School and the Central High School of Philadelphia. Class Football Team. Reserves, '05. Manager of "Tush Hogs." '06. Cento-News Staff. Ec-Centric Staff. Editor-in-Chief of Cento. Secretary of Deinologian, '05. Brightest man in college. Deinologian. A. B. C.

R. L. MYERS
FOOTBALL
BASEBALL.

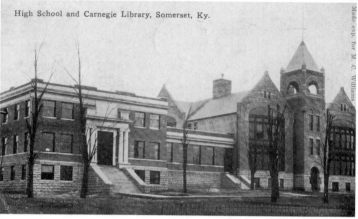

High School and Carnegie Library, Somerset, Ky.

Made exp. for M. C. Williams

(Below) 1917 CENTRE COLLEGE FOOTBALL TEAM. BOLD FACE INDICATES FORT WORTH NORTH SIDE ASSOCIATION.

LT. TO RT.- FRONT ROW- McMILLIN, ARMSTRONG, CAPTAIN TATE, MORAN, **MATHIAS**, BOSWELL

SECOND ROW- BELL, WEAVER, ALLEN, COLEMAN, VAN ANTWERP, DIDDLE, PENN

UNCLE CHARLIE, TOP LEFT. **CHIEF MYERS**, TOP RIGHT

The Somerset Idea

VOLUME XIV, NUMBER 5.   SOMERSET, KENTUCKY   NOVEMBER 15, 1916

Somerset Shows No Mercy to the Blue Clad Team of Louisville

The "Mountain Wool" of "Briar Jumpers" Was Not Seriously Disturbed by Metropolitan Warriors.

Louisville Thought Somerset's Line Wasn't "Such-a.- Much." They Have Been Converted!

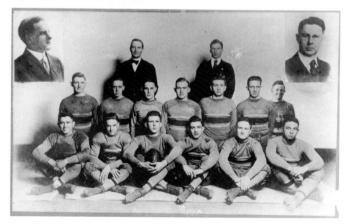

(Left) 1915 NORTH SIDE HIGH TEAM WHICH WAS THE NORTH TEXAS STATE CHAMPIONS.

MASCOT AND MAN UPPER RIGHT, UNKNOWN. BOLD FACE INDICATES CENTRE ASSOCIATION.

LT.TO RT.- FRONT ROW-RALPH HOPKINS, **BILL JAMES**, J. STEGALL, ROSCOE MINTON.

SECOND ROW-**BILL BOSWELL**, KENNETH NORTON, MOD OVERTON, **MADISON BELL**, CLARENCE BROWN

THIRD ROW- **CHIEF MYERS**, BO McMILLIN, PAUL WATHALL, JACK FARMER, **RED WEAVER**, THAD McDONNELL

(Left) SOMERSET HIGH "BRIAR JUMP-ERS" AGAINST HEAVILY-FAVORED LOUISVILLE HIGH, 1916. THREE FUTURE FIRST-TEAM WALTER CAMP ALL-AMERICANS ARE SHOWN PLAY-ING FOR SOMERSET. RED WEAVER (WHITE SCARF, LEFT); RED ROBERTS (WHITE SCARF, CROUCHED); AND BO MCMILLIN (CENTER OF PICTURE, CHARGING FORWARD). SOMERSET WON, 51-6.

(Below) FALL, 1916. SOMERSER "BRIAR JUMPERS" WITH THREE FUTURE ALL-AMERICANS SHOWN: 1) BO MCMIL-LIN, 2) RED WEAVER, 3) RED ROBERTS.

Dropkick from McMillin's toe going between bars November 3rd, 1917

(Right) 1918 CENTRE COLLEGE FOOTBALL TEAM. BOLD FACE INDICATES FORT WORTH NORTH SIDE ASSOCIATION

FRONT ROW- WAYLAND, **MONTGOMERY,** CREGOR, **BELL, WEAVER,** BLEVINS, **JAMES**

SECOND ROW- WHITNELL, MURPHY, DAVIS, ROBERTS, **McMILLIN,** ARMSTRONG, MORAN, COOPER

THIRD ROW- WILLIAMS, LANCASTER, FORD, PRICE, WALKER

TOP ROW- LT. CURTIS, COACH MORAN, LT. WILSON

1919 TEAM

STANDING—Moran, Coach; McMillin, Capt.; Montgomery, Van Antwerp, Roberts, Bell, Garrett, McDonnell, Trainer; Ford, Weaver, Cregor, Armstrong, Myers, Athletic Director.
SITTING—Whitnell, King, McCullum, Snoddy, James, Diddle, Davis, Murphy.

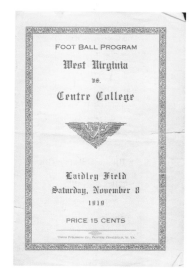

FOOT BALL PROGRAM

West Virginia
vs.
Centre College

Laidley Field
Saturday, November 8
1919

PRICE 15 CENTS

(Above) BACKFIELD AGAINST WEST VIRGINIA- BO McMILLIN, ALLEN DAVIS, RED ROBERTS, ARMY ARMSTRONG

STANDING IN THE END ZONE AT THE WEST VIRGINIA GAME- LT. TO RT. – BILL JAMES, BEN CREGOR, ARMY ARMSTRONG, CHICK MURPHY, UNCLE CHARLIE

THE BOYS FROM FORT WORTH NORTH SIDE WHO PLAYED AGAINST WEST VIRGINIA- LT. TO RT.- BILL JAMES, BO McMILLIN, SULLY MONTGOMERY, MATTY BELL, RED WEAVER

Pulls Biggest Surprise In Gridiron History By Busting West Virginia

With 6 To 0 Score Staring Them In Face And Two Tough Breaks Against Them, Kentuckians Grit Teeth And Start Unstoppable March To Victory—Win By 14 To 6—Mighty Rodgers And Great Bayley Outshone By McMillan, Roberts And Weaver.

THE ALL-AMERICA TEAM
Selected for Collier's by WALTER CAMP

McMillan and Weaver On Walter Camp's All American; Centre College Eleven Pronounced Nation's Best

NEW YORK, Dec. 8.—For the first time in the history of football, Walter Camp has selected two Southern players on his all-American football team. They are "Bo" McMillin and "Red" Weaver, of Centre College, Danville, Ky. It is understood also that in his resume of the season which will be made public in Collier's Weekly tomorrow, Mr Camp credits Centre College with being the strongest eleven in the United States. If true, this will be the first time a Southern eleven has ever gained such a distinction. Roberts, of Centre College, also was picked as an end on the third team.

ALL-AMERICAN FOOTBALL STARS

"Bo" McMILLIN Quarterback on Walter Camp's First All-American Team, 1919.

"Red" WEAVER Center on Walter Camp's First All-American Team, 1919.

"Red" ROBERTS Fullback on Walter Camp's Third All-American Team, 1919.

1920 Team

TOM BARTLETT, BO MCMILLIN, HUMP TANNER, AND ARMY ARMSTRONG

1920 CENTRE COLLEGE FOOTBALL TEAM- WHEN COMPARING THE 1919 TEAM PHOTOGRAPHS WITH THE 1920 PICTURE, IT BECOMES OBVIOUS WHAT A YEAR OF SUCCESS BRINGS. IN 1919, CENTRE SUITED UP 19 TO 20 PLAYERS. IN 1920, THE NUMBER WAS 30.

RED ROBERTS, A GIANT FOR HIS TIME. WEIGHED UP TO 235 LBS. DURING HIS CAREER.

PRACTICE 1920- BO RUNNING WITH RED ROBERTS LEADING THE WAY.

HOWARD G. REYNOLDS OF THE BOSTON "POST," CENTRE'S GREAT FRIEND

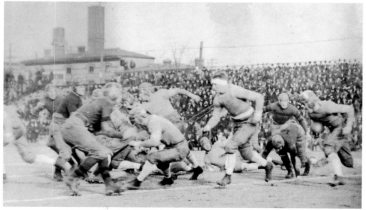

A FAMILIAR SCENE—RED ROBERTS, WITHOUT HELMET, LEADING BO. DEPAUW GAME IN LOUISVILLE, 1919.

TWO NEW COACHES BROUGHT IN TO HELP BEFORE THE 1920 HARVARD GAME. DANIEL G. O'CONNOR, LEFT, AND CLAUDE " TINY " THORNHILL, TOP. THE CHIEF IS IN THE MIDDLE AND UNCLE CHARLIE IS ON THE RIGHT.

PRESIDENTIAL CANDIDATE, WARREN HARDING, CENTER, HANDS FOLDED. SILVER-HAIRED CENTRE PRESIDENT, DR. GANFIELD IS LEFT OF HARDING, WITH HUMP TANNER TO HARDING'S RIGHT. ON FAR LEFT ARE RED WEAVER, BO, WEARING HIS HELMET, AND TERRY SNOWDAY. UNCLE CHARLIE IS BEHIND THE LADY WITH THE WIDE-BRIMMED HAT. TOM MORAN IS TO THE RIGHT OF UNCLE CHARLIE.

CENTRE'S PLAYERS START FOR BOSTON

Big Crowd at Lexington, Ky, to See Them Off

Plenty of Halfbacks to Shoot at Harvard in the Squad

All Danville Turns Out In Inspiring Send-Off; Cheered At Every Stop

(Left and Below) IN 1920, IT WAS "CENTER"— NOT CENTRE

HARVARD

CENTER COLLEGE

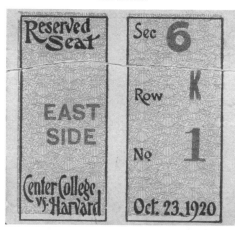

Reserved Seat

Sec 6

Row K

EAST SIDE

No 1

Center College vs Harvard

Oct. 23. 1920

HARVARD VS Center College

OFFICIAL PROGRAM

IRWIN SCORE BOARD

FOOTBALL GAME

HARVARD

VS.

Center College

SOLDIERS FIELD

Saturday, Oct. 23, 1920

HARVARD COACHES—LT. TO RT.—TIERNEY, EDDIE MAHAN, LEO LEARY, BOB FISHER, CHARLES DALEY

UNCLE CHARLIE AT THE STADIUM

Boston Daily Globe (1872-1922); Oct 22, 1920; ProQuest Historical Newspapers Boston Globe (1872 - 1923) pg. 10

W. D. SULLIVAN

will write his personal impressions of the

HARVARD-CENTER COLLEGE GAME

IN THE STADIUM FOR THE

SUNDAY GLOBE

Mr Sullivan, City Editor of the Globe, saw the Crimson football players in their classic contest with Oregon last year, when Eastern football met the Pacific Coast brand—and won out.

Now he will watch the Cambridge style of play pitted against the whirlwind brand of the Middle West, so that he may tell Globe readers the real significance of what promises to be the most interesting game in the Harvard Stadium this Fall.

The only way to be sure of your copy is to tell your newsdealer tonight to

"SAVE ME A SUNDAY GLOBE"

FACTS ABOUT KENTUCKY STARS WHO FACE HARVARD TOMORROW

Years on Squad	Name	Position	Weight	Height	Age	Home
3.	A N McMillin	Quarter	168	5-10	23	Ft Worth, Tex
3.	James P Weaver	Center	158	5-10	22	Ft Worth, Tex
2.	James B Roberts	Fullback	200	5-11	20	Somerset, Ky
3.	Norris Armstrong	Halfback	157	5-10	21	Ft Smith, Ark
2.	R C Ford	Guard	180	5-11	19	Danville, Ky
2.	Ben W Cregor	Guard	176	5-10	22	Springfield, Ky
2.	Edwin A Whittnell	Halfback	160	5-9	20	Fulton, Ky
3.	William N James	Tackle	168	5-9	20	Ft Worth, Tex
2.	Ralph Montgomery	Tackle	210	6-2	19	Ft Worth, Tex
1.	Gus King	End	137	5-9	21	Dallas, Tex
2.	Terry Snoddy	End	173	5-10	21	Owensboro, Ky
1.	J H Tanner	Halfback	158	5-4	22	Owensboro, Ky
2.	Eugene Bedford	End	164	5-9	20	Dallas, Tex
1.	Ashby Blevins	Guard	162	5-10	21	Mt Sterling, Ky
1.	George Chinn	Halfback	180	5-10	18	Harrodsburg, Ky
1.	James Liggett	Halfback	160	5-10	19	Pittsburg, Penn
2.	Thomas M Moran	Halfback	152	5-9	20	Horse Cave, Ky
1.	Carlton Rice	Tackle	180	6	19	Seattle, Wash
1.	Stanley Robb	End	176	5-11	19	Pittsburg, Penn
1.	H V Lipscomb	Center	152	5-11	22	Dallas, Tex
1.	Thomas G Bartlett	Half and Quarter	150	5-10	21	Owensboro, Ky
2.	Joseph Murphy	Halfback	128	5-5	21	Columbus, O
1.	George Maver	Halfback	158	5-10	19	Freeport, L I
1.	Lee McGregor	Guard	189	5-11	21	Ft Worth, Tex
1.	George Converse	End	145	5-7	21	Somerset, Ky

IF CENTRE DEFEATS HARVARD - - - - - - By Donelan

STARTERS AGAINST HARVARD, 1920.
IN THE LINE—LT. TO RT.—TERRY SNOWDAY, BILL JAMES, STANLEY ROBB, RED WEAVER, CLAYTON FORD, SULLY MONTGOMERY, GEORGE CHINN.

IN THE BACKFIELD—LT. TO RT.—TOM MORAN, RED ROBERTS, BO McMILLIN, ARMY ARMSTRONG, AND COACH MORAN.

DANVILLE IS ALL HET UP OVER GAME

BY HOWARD G. REYNOLDS

New England Aroused Over Old Centre Team

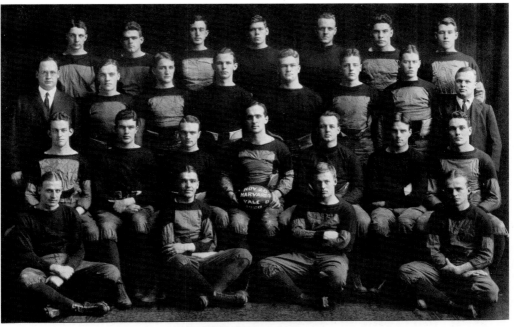

UNIVERSITY FOOTBALL TEAM (1920)

A. D. Hamilton   C. C. Macomber   C. A. Tierney   J. F. Brown   W. G. Brocker   R. W. Fitts   G. Owen
R. T. Fisher (Coach)   R. L. Finley   J. Crocker   H. H. Faxon   J. R. Tolbert   M. Gratwick   J. Gaston   J. A. Sessions (Manager)
R. S. Humphrey   R. M. Sedgwick   R. K. Kane   A. Horween (Captain)   T. S. Woods   W. Hubbard   C. F. Havemeyer
J. Johnson   J. J. Fitzgerald   W. H. Churchill   C. C. Buell

Forces Crimsons To One Of Hardest Tests In Stadium's History

Courageous Squad From Little Kentucky Town, After Being Scored On In First Five Minutes Of Play, Crushes Easterners In Two Dramatic Marches To Touchdowns— Mystic Spell Of Huge Bowl Has Its Effect—Score 31-14.

By GRANTLAND RICE

(Right) BO RUNNING OFF TACKLE. RED ROBERTS WITHOUT HELMET.

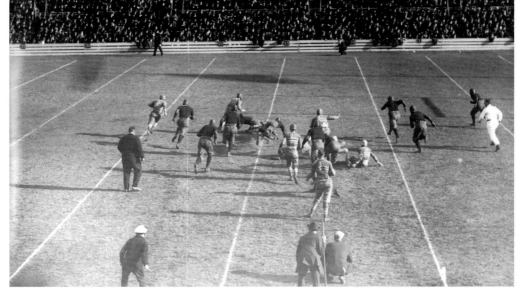

ACTION DURING THE 1920 CENTRE-HARVARD GAME. ED WHITNELL (1) RUNNING AROUND LEFT END. OTHER IDENTIFIABLE COLONELS ARE MCMILLIN (11), ROBERTS (8), ROBB (21), AND WEAVER (7) WHO IS ON THE GROUND.

The Horned Frog--Colonel
Announcer

New Year's Day Football Classic
Texas Christian University
Undefeated Champions T. I. A. A.
vs.
Centre College
Fort Worth, Texas   The Wonder Team of the United States   January 1, 1921

NEWLY ELECTED CAPTAIN FOR 1921, NORRIS "ARMY" ARMSTRONG FROM FORT SMITH, ARKANSAS.

(Above) A COLD ,THANKSGIVING DAY, NOVEMBER 25, 1920, AT CHEEK FIELD IN DANVILLE. UNCLE CHARLIE IS CONSULTING WITH CHIEF MYERS WHO IS HOLDING THE PLAY CARD. HUMP TANNER IS NUMBER 46. CENTRE CRUSHED GEORGETOWN, 103-0.

SPECTATORS AT CENTRE-TCU FORT WORTH CLASSIC BOWL GAME

CENTRE-GEORGIA TECH AT A PACKED GRANT FIELD IN ATLANTA. THE TECH TEAM RUNNING ONTO THE FIELD—1920

BO McMILLIN HERE AGAIN

Centre College Football
Star Will Play
Against
Harvard in Final
Basket-Ball Game
Tomorrow

BO McMILLIN

"BO" McMILLIN AND HIS CENTRE COLLEGE MATES PIN A DEFEAT ON HARVARD, 41-36

Crimson Five Misses Chances to Score, But Makes It a Real Battle From the Start in the Hemenway Gymnasium

RED ROBERTS

TOM BARTLETT

BO, RED, AND ARMY

CHICK MURPHY

HUMP TANNER

TERRY SNOWDAY

BILL SHADOAN

ED KUBALE

BILL JAMES AND BUCK JONES

MINOS GORDY AND HUMP TANNER

HERB COVINGTON

DICK GIBSON AND FRANK RUBARTH

BEN CREGOR

THE LEXINGTON AUTOMOBILE COMPANY MANUFACTURED CARS IN CONNERSVILLE, INDIANA FROM 1910-1927. THERE WAS NO BETTER ENDORSEMENT THAN TO FEATURE BO IN A NEW LEXINGTON R-19 "MINUTE MAN" SIX TOURING CONVERTIBLE.

BO WORE HIS HELMET WHEN DRIVING BUT REMOVED IT WHEN HE REACHED HIS "WORKPLACE," CENTRE'S FOOTBALL FIELD.

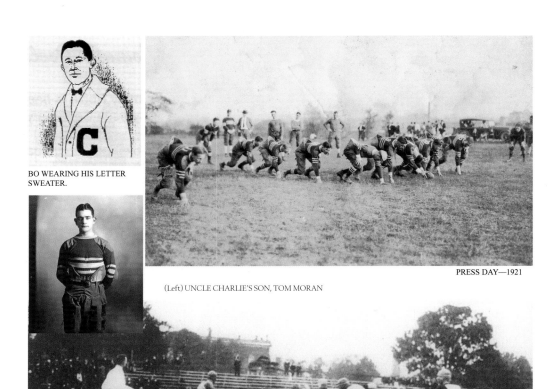

BO WEARING HIS LETTER SWEATER.

(Left) UNCLE CHARLIE'S SON, TOM MORAN

PRESS DAY—1921

SCRIMMAGE BETWEEN VETERANS AND "COLTS"—SEPTEMBER 24, 1921. BO RUNNING THE BALL.

ADMIT ONE
CENTRE VETS Vs. COLTS
Saturday, Sept. 24th
Cheek Field
25c.   3:00 P. M.

THE CENTRE "5"

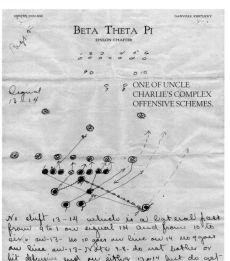

ONE OF UNCLE CHARLIE'S COMPLEX OFFENSIVE SCHEMES.

BETA THETA PI
EPSILON CHAPTER

CENTRE COLLEGE   DANVILLE, KENTUCKY

BAYARD WHARTON '22
University quarter-miler, who aids in leading the cheers.

HARVARD'S 12TH MAN.

RAY CLASS

Centre Doesn't Worry Harvard

Have Confidence of Beating Invaders on Saturday, but Figure Princeton Will Be Tougher Game

The Harvard--Centre Game

Play by Play

Will Be Received By Wire at

THE FARMERS BANK & TRUST CO.

Saturday 1:30 P. M.   Come--Enjoy The Game--Come

GEORGETOWN HI

vs

SOMERSET HI

FOOT BALL - - HINTON FIELD

Oct 28, 1921   2:30 P. M.

City Meat Market

THE HOME OF GOOD MEATS AND CHEAP PRICES

GIVE US A TRIAL AND BE CONVINCED

Give Us a Call   Phone 175

GEORGETOWN BATTERY STATION

CHAIN STORAGE BATTERIES

VICTOR SPRING TIRES, TUBES AND ACCESSORIES

PHONE 83

A NOTICE ANNOUNCING THAT THE CENTRE-HARVARD GAME
WOULD BE "CARRIED" IN GEORGETOWN, KENTUCKY.

BO HAS BEEN PRESENTED A BOUTONNIERE AND IS TALKING TO FANS AT THE DANVILLE STATION PRIOR TO EMBARKING FOR THE HARVARD GAME.

THE CROWD SEEING THE COLONELS OFF FOR THE 1921 HARVARD GAME.

TEAM MANAGER, JOHNNIE McGEE, FLIRTS WITH PRETTY LUCY COVINGTON AT A STOPOVER ON THE WAY TO BOSTON.

(Above) BO DURING PRACTICE AT HARVARD STADIUM—OCTOBER 28, 1921

RED ROBERTS AT THE STATION

"ON TO HARVARD—YEA CENTRE"

A STOP ON THE WAY EAST. THE CENTRE "5" ON A BAGGAGE CART ENTERTAINING THE CROWD. RED ROBERTS IS IN THE CENTER, LOOKING OVER HIS SHOULDER.

"RED" ROBERTS IS DISCOVERED IN ENGINE CAB

Fiery-Haired Star, However, Lets Ebony Valet Handle Shovel.

APPETITES OF PLAYERS TAX PURSE OF CHIEF

RED AND ROSCOE

COLONELS GIVEN WARM WELCOME IN EASTERN CITY

Bostonians Again Receive Team From Danville With Enthusiasm.

SEAT DEMAND EXCEEDS THAT FOR YALE GAME

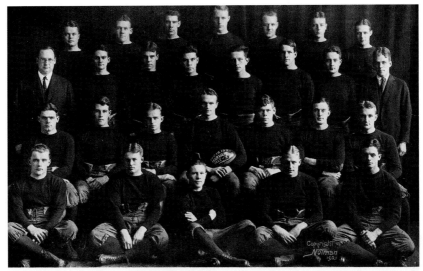

UNIVERSITY FOOTBALL TEAM (1921)

D. Angier P. F. Coburn H. C. Janin B. Lockwood W. G. Brocker M. Gratwick F. H. Hovey
Coach R. Fisher D. S. Holder A. H. Ladd R. Fitts H. W. Clark C. J. Hubbard H. S. Grew R. R. Higgins (Manager)
C. C. Macomber G. Owen, Jr. C. C. Buell R. K. Kane (Captain) J. F. Brown C. A. Tierney J. Crocker
J. M. Hartley W. H. Churchill A. J. Conlon F. J. Johnson V. Chapin

The LENOX

THREE "PRAYING COLONELS"

"BO" McMILLIN

McMILLIN'S NEVER TO BE FORGOTTEN PASS TO WHITNELL IN THE 1920 GAME

"RED" ROBERTS LAST YEAR'S FAVORITE IS PLAYING IN THE LINE

GENE MACK

DIXIE

CAPT. ARMSTRONG

THREE PLAYERS WHO MAY FIGURE PROMINENTLY THIS AFTERNOON.

W. H. CHURCHILL '23.
Who scored the tying touchdown in the Penn State game.

K. S. PFAFFMAN '24.
His drop-kick was the margin of victory against Georgia.

VINTON CHAPIN '23.
An early season regular, who has been hampered by injuries.

(Above) CENTRE TEAM MEMBERS AND FANS POSE OUTSIDE OF THE LENOX HOTEL AFTER ARRIVAL. HUMP TANNER IS SEATED, FAR LEFT. UNCLE CHARLIE HAS HANDS CLASPED, FRONT ROW. LUCY AND HERB COVINGTON FLANK JOHNNIE McGEE WHO IS SQUATTING IN CENTER. RED ROBERTS IS SEATED FAR RIGHT. THE TALLEST MAN STANDING IS DR. GANFIELD. BO IS THE 3RD LEFT FROM DR. GANFIELD.

PRACTICE IN HARVARD
STADIUM—OCTOBER 28TH

TAKEN OUTSIDE HARVARD STADIUM, OCTOBER 28TH.
TERRY SNOWDAY, HOLDING BLANKET, UNCLE CHARLIE
IN PASSENGER SEAT IN CAR, BO ON THE FENDER AND
GEORGE JOPLIN, WEARING HAT AND LEANING ON THE
HEADLIGHT

OFFICIAL PROGRAM
IRWIN SCORE BOARD

FOOTBALL GAME

HARVARD
VS.
CENTRE

SOLDIERS FIELD

Saturday, October 29,1921

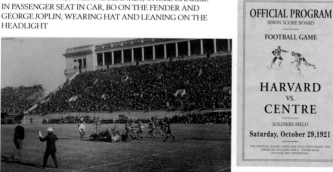

ACTION NEAR MIDFIELD. BO IS COLONEL
STANDING. ED KUBALE IS NUMBER 8. BILL
JAMES IS NUMBER 10. RED ROBERTS IS
STANDING, WITHOUT HELMET. NOTE HOW
CENTRE HAS NEARLY THE ENTIRE TEAM
IN ON THE DEFENSIVE PLAY, TYPICAL FOR
THE COLONELS' SWARMING EFFORT ALL
AFTERNOON AGAINST HARVARD.

FOR THE 1921 CENTRE-
HARVARD GAME, THE
PROGRAM HAD CENTRE
SPELLED CORRECTLY

THE HARVARD MARCHING BAND MAKING
ITS FIRST APPEARANCE IN 1921 PLAYING "ON
SOLDIER'S FIELD."

(Below) THE NEW YORK NEWSBOY BAND
MARCHES INTO THE STADIUM.

CENTRE FANS ON THE
SIDELINE. LUCY COVINGTON
IS SMILING, FRONT ROW,
CENTER.

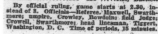

(Above) HARVARD'S VINTON CHAPIN RUNNING. CENTRE'S DEFENSIVE
BACKS ARE—LT. TO RT.—ARMY ARMSTRONG, BO AND TERRY SNOWDAY.
TINY MAXWELL, THE HUGE REFEREE, IS FAR RIGHT.

MORE MIDFIELD ACTION.
CENTRE PLAYING
TENACIOUS DEFENSE.

HUMP TRUCKING IT.
SHADOAN (17), BO (11),
AND SNOWDAY (12) ARE
IDENTIFIABLE COLONELS.

CENTRE-HARVARD 1921. ROSCOE CAKE-WALKED, PIGEON-WINGED, AND PRANCED AROUND THE FIELD AT THE HALF.

CENTRE-HARVARD 1921—BO WITH ARROW. MINOS GORDY IN FRONT OF BO, HEADING TO TAKE OUT HARVARD'S CLARK MACOMBER.

McMILLIN SCORED DRAMATICALLY WHEN HE ELUDED HARVARD'S GEHRKE AND JOHNSON, WHO CHASED HIM VAINLY TO GOAL LINE

(Above) ONE OF THE MOST DRAMATIC MOMENTS EVER IN COLLEGE FOOTBALL. BO TAKES IT IN !

TOM BARTLETT, FAR RIGHT, ON HIS 32 YARD RUN. IDENTIFIABLE CENTRE PLAYERS—RUBARTH (9), KUBALE (8), AND JAMES (10)—1921

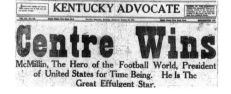

KENTUCKY ADVOCATE

Centre Wins

McMillin, The Hero of the Football World, President of United States for Time Being. He Is The Great Effulgent Star.

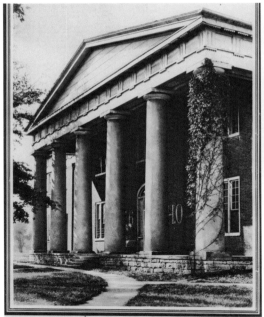

"Old Centre." Centre College. Danville, Ky. This building was erected 'n 1820

NOTE C6 H0 ON FRONT OF OLD CENTRE.

ARMY, UNCLE CHARLIE, AND BO AT THE STATION BEFORE BOARDING THE TRAIN LATE SATURDAY NIGHT AFTER THE GAME.

McMILLIN HEADING FOR HOME WITH BALL

Gets Treasure He Missed in Game a Year Ago

Victors Have Celebration After Stadium Triumph

DANVILLE MOTOR COMPANY—READY FOR PARADE—
TO HONOR CENTRE FOOTBALL TEAM.

(Below) DANVILLE WELCOMING VICTORIOUS COLONELS BACK TO OLD CENTRE.

BO, STANDING ON THE FIRETRUCK, HOLDING BALL

(Right) ON THE FIRETRUCK—(1) BO, (2) HERB COVINGTON, (3) ARMY, WITH THE COVETED BALL, (4) BILL JAMES, (5) BEN CREGOR, (6) THE CHIEF, (7) UNCLE CHARLIE, (8) HOPE HUDGINS, (9) FRANK RUBARTH, (10) HENNIE LEMON, (11) TINY THORNHILL, (12) BUCK JONES, (13) ED KUBALE, (14) GEORGE CHINN, (15) TERRY SNOWDAY, (16) TOM BARTLETT, (17) HUMP TANNER, (18) JIM PRIEST, (19) DEWEY KIMBELL, (20) DICK GIBSON, (21) BILL SHADOAN. THE ONLY PLAYERS WHO GOT INTO THE GAME WHO AREN'T IDENTIFIED ARE RED ROBERTS, MINOS GORDY AND RAY CLASS.

The Centre team that upset Harvard in 1921 is shown after returning from the game to Danville to celebrate with their fans. The players: (1) Bo McMillin; (2) Herb Covington; (3) Norris Armstrong; (5) Ben Cregor; (8) Hope Hudgins; (10) Hennie Lemon; (12) Buck Jones; (13) Ed Kubale; (14) Major George Chinn; (15) Terry Snowday; (17) John "Hump" Tanner; (18) Jim Priest; (20) Dick Gibson. Others: (6) Chief Myers (behind wheel); (7) Coach "Uncle" Charley Moran (deceased); (11) Line Coach Tiny Thornhill; (9) Frank Ruhartz; (16) Tom Bartlett; (4) Bill James and (19) Dewey Kimbell.

THE RECEPTION AT THE COURTHOUSE.
LT. TO RT.—UNCLE CHARLIE, ARMY, LUCY COVINGTON, BO, MRS.
COVINGTON—OCTOBER 31, 1921

Boston Sunday Post

CENTRE TRIUMPHS OVER HARVARD, 6-0

McMillin's Spectacular Dodging Run for a Touchdown Defeats the Crimson Before 45,000 Spectators—Southerners Clearly Outplay Cambridge Team—McMillin, Roberts and James Star for Kentucky

Offside Play Upon Successful Forward Pass Spoils Harvard's Chances

McMillin Carried Off Field by Admirers When Final Whistle Is Blown

PARTICIPANTS-1921 HARVARD GAME

(1) ARMY ARMSTRONG, (2) RAY CLASS, (3) BILL JAMES, (4) TOM BARTLETT, (5) MINOS GORDY, (6) ED KUBALE, (7) BO McMILLIN, (8) BEN CREGOR, (9) BUCK JONES, (10) DICK GIBSON, (11) HERB COVINGTON, (12) BILL SHADOAN, (13) HUMP TANNER, (14) RED ROBERTS, (15) FRANK RUBARTH, (16) TERRY SNOWDAY, (A) UNCLE CHARLIE MORAN, (B) CHIEF MYERS, (C) ROSCOE CONKLIN BRECKINRIDGE

Harvard Coach Pays Tribute to the Centre College Colonels

Sewanee Triumphs Over Kentucky Eleven In Hard-Fought Game

Where "Bo" McMillin and His Kentucky Cohorts Learned the Art of Football

(Right) TEAM PHOTOGRAPH TAKEN AFTER THE HARVARD GAME. LT. TO RT. – FRONT ROW: KIMBEL, TANNER, CLASS, THOMASSON, BARTLETT, CAPTAIN ARMSTRONG, SNOWDAY, McMILLIN, MURPHY, GREEN. SECOND ROW: GORDY, CREGOR, BEAN, BUCK JONES, DICK GIBSON, KUBALE, CHINN, SHADOAN, RUBARTH, JAMES. THIRD ROW: BRADLEY, BILLIS, PRIEST, NEWELL, JOHNSON, RICE, CLARENCE JONES, G. GIBSON, LYNCH, INGERTON, COMBS. TOP ROW: LINE COACH THORNHILL, TOM MORAN, HUNTER, TRAINER ANDERSON, BROOKS, SANVITO, COACH MORAN

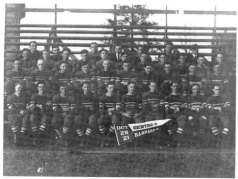

THE TEAM RUNNING THROUGH DRILLS AT ECLIPSE PARK PRIOR TO THE W&L GAME—1921

RED ROBERTS AND HIS JENNY. BEN CREGOR BEHIND THE "6." HUMP BEHIND THE "H." UNCLE CHARLIE, FAR RIGHT. CASE THOMASSON OVER MORAN'S RIGHT SHOULDER. W&L GAME— LOUISVILLE 1921

(Left) RED ROBERTSON IN SOUTHERN RAILROAD YARD, READY TO GO TO THE AUBURN GAME IN BIRMINGHAM—1921

RED ROBERTSON BOARDING—1921

BO (11) FIRES A PASS IN W&L GAME—1921

THOROUGHBRED BO McMILLIN

UNIQUE RECORD SET UP BY "BO" M'MILLIN, CENTRE STAR

Scored Enough Points to Win Games For Team in Ohio, Massachusetts, Louisiana, Alabama and California

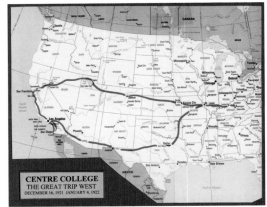

CENTRE COLLEGE
THE GREAT TRIP WEST
DECEMBER 16, 1921 JANUARY 4, 1922

Coronado, California, *Dec 23,* 1921

The Management of the Hotel del Coronado
Introduces to the
Coronado Country Club

Mr. *John Tanner*

Room No. *15*

W. A. Turgmand

THE LOUISVILLE HERALD, FRIDAY MORNING, DECEMBER 16, 1921.

Moran's Colonels Leave Today On Long Jaunt to the Coast

THE WONDERFUL HOTEL del CORONADO.

SQUAD'S SPIRIT EARNS PRAISE OF SCHOOL'S GRADS

McMillin Weeps As He Speaks Of Team And His Last Game On Home Soil.

MORAN SAYS KUBALE IS GREATEST CENTER IN U.S.

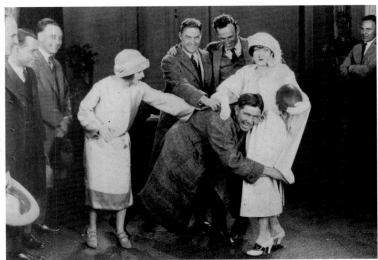

(Right) BO TACKLING ACTRESS
GLORIA SWANSON.
LT. TO RT.—UNCLE CHARLIE,
JOHNNIE McGEE, UNKNOWN,
MAY McAVOY, ARMY, SAM
WOODS, BO AND SWANSON.

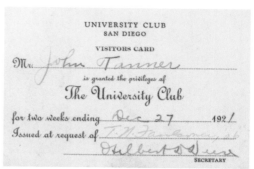

CHRISTMAS BOWL—BO RUNNING, RED ROBERTS SEEN UNDER REF'S ARM. NOTE REFLECTIONS FROM WATER ON FIELD.

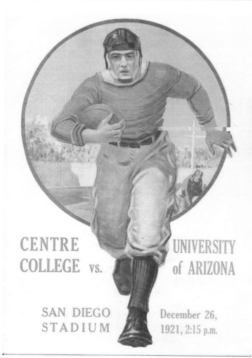

CENTRE
COLLEGE vs. of ARIZONA

SAN DIEGO
STADIUM

December 26,
1921, 2:15 p.m.

RED ON THE GROUND WITH BALL. HUMP TANNER, STANDING ON ONE LEG, WITHOUT HELMET—CENTRE-ARIZONA, DECEMBER 26, 1921

BO McMILLIN MARRIED.

Centre College Football Star Weds Miss Miers at Fort Worth.

FORT WORTH, Texas, Jan. 2.—Alvin (Bo) McMillin, Centre College football star, and Miss Maude Marie Miers, sweethearts of his high-school days, were married here this morning. They left by motor for Dallas, where McMillin this afternoon played against the Texas A. and M. eleven.

CENTRE ON OFFENSE AT TEXAS A&M GAME.

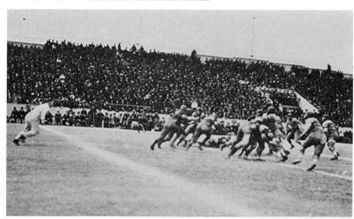

CENTRE-TEXAS A&M—NOTE PACKED STADIUM.

(Left) A DAY AT THE RACES—
DECEMBER 25, 1921

ACTION SHOTS DURING THE DIXIE
CLASSIC BOWL GAME—
JANUARY 2, 1922

The Farmers Defeat the Praying Colonels

BO SWEEPS RIGHT IN DURING TEXAS A&M GAME.

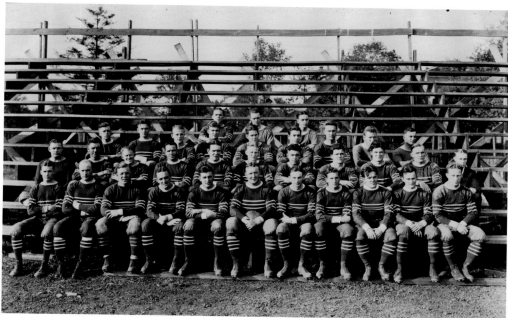

1922 CENTRE COLLEGE FOOTBALL TEAM

FRONT ROW- LT. TO RT. – HOWARD ROBERTSON, CREGOR, GEORGE JONES, COVINGTON, LEMON, CAPTAIN ROBERTS, BARTLETT, HUDGINS, TANNER, GREEN, SNOWDAY
SECOND ROW- LT. TO RT. - ASST. COACH BOND, RUBARTH, KIMBEL, GORDY, BRADLEY, COMBS, THOMASSON (?), CECIL, ALEXANDER, GIBSON, BERRYMAN, STUDENT MANAGER
THIRD ROW- LT.TO RT. – WOOD, KUBALE, ROLAND, SHARON, LYNCH, KAGIN, PRIEST, SHEARER, INGERTON
TOP ROW- LT. TO RT. – CLARENCE JONES, BAXTER, MOORE

HOWARD ROBERTSON WAS THE BROTHER OF ROBERT WINTERSMITH ROBERTSON.
—NOTE THE CONSTRUCTION OF THE OLD WOODEN BLEACHERS.

HUMP TANNER RUNS AGAINST CARSON-NEWMAN—SEPTEMBER 23, 1922

NOTABLE FOOTBALL PLAYS THIS SEASON

THE LOCK-STEP OR CHAIN GANG FORMATION USED BY
CENTRE IN THE 1922 HARVARD GAME.

PROGRAMS FOR TODAY

STATION WGI, MEDFORD HILLSIDE

7 A M Radio health school.
10 A M—Musical program.
10 30 A M—Official weather forecast (485 meters).
1 30 P M—Weather forecast (485 meters) Produce market report.
2 30 P M—Harvard-Centre football returns
5 P M—Market reports.
6 30 P M—Police reports, early sports, late news
8 P M—Evening program, "Science up to date"; concert by male quartet.

PUBLISHED RADIO SCHEDULE VERIFYING CENTRE-
HARVARD 1922 CONTEST WAS THE FIRST FOOTBALL
GAME EVER BROADCAST.

THE TEAM SUITED UP AT THE LENOX BEFORE
HEADING TO THE STADIUM FOR PRACTICE.

RED ROBERTS OUTSIDE OF THE LENOX, FRIDAY
AFTERNOON—OCTOBER 20, 1922.

BEST HARVARD TEAM TO OPPOSE CENTRE

Crimson Determined to Get Revenge For Defeat of a Year Ago—Crowd of 50,000 to See Struggle in Stadium —Cambridge Team 3-1 Favorite

SOMETHING DOING? YOU SAID IT.

THE CENTRE "SIX." HOWARD ROBERTSON, BROTHER
OF RED ROBERTSON, AND THE AUTHOR'S UNCLE, IS
FAR LEFT.

CENTRE SIX, from famous old Centre College of Kentucky, sensation of the football world. A crack singing orchestra, featuring classic and popular novelty music and songs. Has played all over the South, also in exclusive hotels and clubs of Boston and New York, and at Wellesley and Harvard.

WESTERN UNION TELEGRAM

Rob goes to see Centre-Harvard game
Mr. Hilford Bibertson, a student at Centre College, accompanied the Centre football team to New York, where they played West Virginia.

RECEIVED AT

10K MY 12 COLLECT

UK BOSTON MASS 1159A OCT 20 1922

W H ROBERTSON

ELIZABETHTOWN KY.

SAFE IN BOSTON HAVE HEAVY OVERCOAT SAW EVELYN STAYING WITH HAYS

ROB

1122A

"Red" Robertson Gave Press Box Writers a Hand

There was a young man in the press box at the Harvard Stadium last Saturday, who announced all of the Centre plays.
His name is "Red" Robertson, and to beat his way from Danville to the big game on the strength of his name. Because of the similarity of his and the Centre captain's name the boys down in Danville call him "Red" Roberts' son.

STUDENT-PRODUCED MAGAZINES DURING CENTRE'S GOLDEN AGE OF FOOTBALL

Smashing Attacks, Spectacular Runs and Furious Scrimmages in Recent Football Games

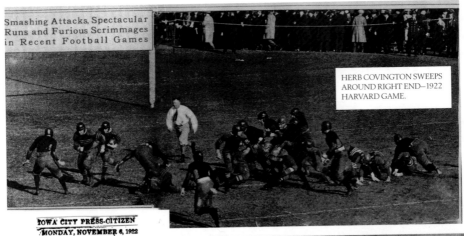

HERB COVINGTON SWEEPS AROUND RIGHT END—1922 HARVARD GAME.

IOWA CITY PRESS-CITIZEN
MONDAY, NOVEMBER 6, 1922

"Flash" Sets New Drop-Kick Mark

Herbert "Flash" Covington, successor to "Bo" McMillin as quarterback at Centre college, made six successful drop kicks in a football game at Danville, Ky., with the University of Louisville. In performing such a feat, Covington established a world's record for drop kicking. The best previous record was five successful drop kicks, held jointly by B. W. Trafford of Harvard and Walter Eckersall.

Trafford made his record in 1890 in a game with Cornell. Eckersall twice turned the trick while at Chicago, first against Illinois in 1905 and the following year against Nebraska.

Of the six successful field goals made by Covington, the longest one was from the 40-yard line and two from the 30-yard mark. Back in 1900, E. C. Robertson of Purdue is credited with seven goals from placement in a game with Rose Poly.

"Red" Roberts, captain of the Centre College team, leading the way for Covington in the game with Washington and Lee University. NOVEMBER 11, 1922
"HUMP" TANNER IS THROWING THE BLOCK ON THE GROUND.

Eastern Colleges Want Centre Date

NEW YORK, Oct. 23.—Centre College, which ended a three-year engagement with Harvard Saturday by losing by a gallant fight against the Crimson, may play either Cornell or Columbia, in New York next fall.

Danville, Boyle County, Kentucky, Saturday, March 10, 1923

How Centre's Proposed Athletic Fields and Stadium Will Look When Completed

Sports of 1923

FAMOUS FOOTBALL COACHES

CHARLEY MORAN OF CENTRE

KNUTE ROCKNE OF NOTRE DAME

Knuts Rockne and Charley Moran

AS THE ARTICLE IN THE "MESSENGER" STATED—"TWENTY LOCAL, COLORED FOOTBALL ENTHUSIASTS HAVE VOLUNTEERED.....'

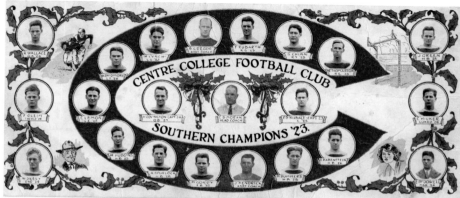

CENTRE COLLEGE FOOTBALL CLUB
SOUTHERN CHAMPIONS '23

THE ANDERSON NEWS.

CAMPAIGN WILL BE STARTED THIS WEEK TO RAISE $140,000 FOR KENTUCKY STADIUM

(Left) THE UNIVERSITY OF KENTUCKY CAN'T LET CENTRE GET AHEAD.

(Right) JIMMIE GREEN, A TEAM AND CROWD FAVORITE.

(Below) SOLD OUT, STANDING ROOM ONLY AT THE NEW STADIUM.

COVINGTON PASSING AGAINST W&L. MINOS GORDY IS IN CENTER OF THE PHOTOGRAPH, LOOKING DOWNFIELD—1923

UNCLE CHARLIE'S 1919 CONTRACT—SALARY $500

(Left) CENTRE COLLEGE FOOTBALL TEAM, 1924

(1) PRIEST, (2) McCLURE, (3) SUMMERS,
(4) DURHAM, (5) WALLACE, (6) GRUBBS,
(7) KAGIN, (8) HEAD COACH, CHIEF MYERS,
(9) ASST. COACH, HAROLD OFSTIE,
(10) ASST. COACH, A.B. "HAPPY" CHANDLER

(11) LYNCH, (12) SKIDMORE,
(13) RABENSTEIN, (14) LEMON,
(15) KUBALE, (16) CAPTAIN COVINGTON,
(17) THOMASSON, (18) BUSH,
(19) ASST. COACH AND FRESHMAN COACH,
RED ROBERTS

(20) WILSON, (21) GORDY, (22) RUBARTH,
(23) HILKER, (24) PRICE, (25) MORROW

(26) DUDLEY DONEGHY, TRAINER

(Right) THE "SEVEN IMMORTALS."
LT. TO RT.—THE TOP 5 ARE: ED
KUBALE, HOWARD LYNCH, HERB
COVINGTON, MINOS GORDY AND
CASE THOMASSON. BOTTOM—
HENNIE LEMON AND ED RUBARTH.

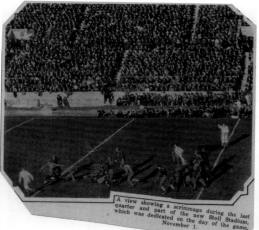

A view showing a scrimmage during the last quarter and part of the new Stoll Stadium, which was dedicated on the day of the game, November 1.

(Right) FRANK RUBARTH COMES OUT OF THE GAME HOLDING HIS ARM. HE WAS OBVIOUSLY IN PAIN FROM HIS BROKEN COLLAR BONE, BUT PLAYED ON. WEST VIRGINIA GAME—1924

(Left) ACTION BEFORE A PACKED STADIUM AT THE STADIUM DEDICATION GAME AT UK— NOVEMBER 1, 1924

(Below) NOT AN EMPTY SEAT IN THE HOUSE. THE COLONELS COULD PACK THEM IN.

Centre Provides for Both Work and Play

Old Centre, Erected 1820—Restored 1929. Now used as an Administration Building.

Airplane view of Centre College Athletic Field and Stadium.

Boyle-Humphrey Gymnasium at Centre College.

This picture was taken on that memorable day in Danville history when the Centre College team returned home after defeating Harvard in 1921.

GRAYIN' COLONELS—The famous 1921 Centre team poses in full uniform at its reunion. From left, front row—James "Lefty" Whitnell, Bill James, Ben Cregor, Dick Gibson, Major George Chinn, Ed Kubale, George "Buck" Jones, Minos Gordy, and Hennie Lemon. Second row—Case Thomasson, Herb Covington, Hope Hudgins, Terry Snowday, Norris Armstrong, Alvin "Bo" McMillin, John "Hump" Tanner, Joe Murphy, Clarence L. Jones, James Priest, Marshall Shearer. Back—R. L. "Chief" Myers, John McGhee, Carl "Swede" Anderson, Dudley Doneghy.

IT WAS LIKE THIS—James "Red" Weaver (left) and Alvin "Bo" McMillin of Centre College football fame, talk over old times at the reunion yesterday at Danville.

(Left) THE 1920 AHRENS-FOX FIRETRUCK AS IT LOOKS TODAY. IT WAS BOUGHT IN 1973 FOR $1500 BY JERRY VOISINET WHO IS SHOWN SITTING ON IT. THE PHOTO WAS TAKEN IN 2006. THE PERFECTLY RESTORED FIRETRUCK IS NOW VALUED AT OVER $100,000.

THE WEST STANDS TODAY. UNCLE CHARLIE GOT THE STADIUM BUILT. WOULDN'T IT BE WONDERFUL TO REDEDICATE IT IN HIS NAME?

It may not have been the "Special" that had originally been envisioned, but from the great time everyone was having, no one seemed to really care. The trip east took a little longer than the year before, with several stops that hadn't been made in 1920 on the "Harvard Special," but the squad couldn't really tell any difference, as they had a private Pullman.

It was after dinner on Wednesday evening when Uncle Charlie, Tiny and the Chief, outlined the game plan that Army and Bo had promoted.

"We've discussed it with Captain Armstrong and Bo," the coaches explained. "We're going to run the ball. We're going to play for field position. It's defense that's going to win this game."

Tiny Thornhill had confidence that he had the horses in the line to play Harvard evenly. Much had been written over the last few years about the Centre offense. It was indeed a marvelous machine. But the defense was just as important a part of the team's great success.

The first four games of 1921 were actually contests in which defensive play was emphasized. Centre's coaches knew exactly what they were doing in the two 14-0 wins over Clemson and VPI. They had scheduled teams with enough of an attack to challenge their defense. Now, that part of the team's game was going to either win or lose the upcoming contest with the Crimson.

"We may not pass in the first half."

"We may punt on third down unless we have a short-yardage situation. And even if we have short yardage, we may still punt on third down if we're deep in our own territory."

"We won't show them anything but our basic offense in the first half. Nothing fancy at all. If we can get to the half by holding them scoreless, we'll have a great chance to win. As a matter of fact, we will win."

"We must swarm on defense. Go in low. Protect your position. If you see that a play is definitely going the other way, cut them off by running laterally. But make certain first that they're not running a reverse."

"Ends. Don't let them get outside of you. Turn them in. The rest of that side of the line, and linebackers, will bring them down."

"Make them pay for every yard."

"Eleven men in on every play."

"Play hard, but play clean. Remember that you are Centre, and you are representing Old Centre." The Chief later went to his boys from North Side High in Fort Worth, Bo and Bill James.

"We've come a long way together, haven't we? You remember what we used to talk about years ago?"

"Of course, Chief. We talked about beating one of the big Eastern colleges. We talked about that way back in 1915, and even before."

"You remember that motto we had in our dressing room? 'Credendo vides.' To believe is to see."

"Yes," Bo replied. "We had to look it up in an old Latin book. It's always stuck with me. It's the only Latin I know.'"

"And you remember our other motto. 'Believe. Achieve. Succeed.'"

"How could we forget it, Chief.? You've always written it on the walls of our dressing room," Bill James said, laughing.

"You men have lived by our ideals and philosophy," the Chief said, his eyes glistening. "And I want you to know that I'm so very proud of both of you."

"You said it, Chief. We've come a long way together," said Bo "And now we're on way to make our dream and hard work come true. We're on our way to beat Harvard."

As Centre's team was rolling toward Boston, Bob Dunbar, Boston "Herald" sports columnist, revealed some "inside information" about the Harvard team that pointed out some of the differences in playing for the Crimson verses being on the Colonels' squad.

Harvard takes exceptional care of the physical being of its football men. The Crimson spares no expense. Take the shoulder pads the Harvard men wear. Each player must have one of these specially molded leather pads, made from special individual molds of each shoulder, and they fit perfectly to the contour of the player's body. That is why there are so few shoulder injuries at Cambridge. These pads are expensive, more so than the average paraphernalia, or the cost of even better than regular, but non-custom pads, for they cost $30.00 each, a lot of money for such a little article. But it saves the players and the team. The daily reports from other colleges are replete with the sad details of cracked collar bones and shoulder blades. This is a vital and characteristic bit of the "System" across the Charles. (Centre, by contrast, was buying shoulder pads from A.G. Spalding. The college was billed $2.50 a pair for "Moran style shoulder pads.")

In the same column, Bob Dunbar wrote about a phone call he had received. A young lady called to ask Centre's colors.

When I told her yellow and white, I hope she did not misunderstand me. Bo McMillin's personal color is a blue streak. (Centre's colors were actually gold and white.)

After dinner had been served, the Centre "5" got permission to perform in the dining car and set up to play. Several of the Kentuckians danced the evening away, as the 20th Century Limited crossed northern Ohio, cut through the northwest corner of Pennsylvania, and hugged the south shore of Lake Erie, heading east across New York.

The team turned in early. They would dance later, but now were conserving every bit of their energy for the game.

At Albany, the Pullmans filled with the team and fans were disconnected along with the Boston-bound section of the Limited, and hooked onto train # 25 of the Boston and Albany, a subsidiary of the New York Central.

The train steamed into Boston's Back Bay Station at 1:00 PM, some 31 hours after they had left Danville. They were met by over 1,000 enthusiastic supporters, including native Bostonians who wanted to welcome the Colonels back after their showing of the previous October. Howard Reynolds caught up with Bo as the great quarterback was shaking hands with everyone who could get near him.

"Wonderful reception, Bo. What do I tell my readers about how you feel your chances are when I write my next story?"

"You can tell them I, and the whole team, wouldn't be here if we didn't think we were going to win."

The Centre entourage was staying at the Lenox Hotel, built in 1900 at the cost of $1,100,000. It was located at Exeter and Boylston in the Back Bay. The Lenox was close enough to where the Pullmans were uncoupled that those who wanted to use their berths the next two nights would only have a short walk to the hotel if they wished to convene at Centre's Boston headquarters.

The original plan, when the "Harvard Special" was to be the mode of transportation, was to have the team arrive after breakfast, check into the hotel, and head out to the Stadium for practice. Now, the later arrival necessitated a change in plans. Uncle Charlie got on the phone with Larry Graver of the Boston Red Sox who was expecting his call, and was gratified that the baseball executive was extremely accommodating, agreeing to go to Fenway Park, just a mile from the Lenox, and open it up immediately.

The Colonels ate a quick lunch specially rushed by the hotel's kitchen, gathered up their gear, hustled onto chartered buses, and amazingly, were on their way to the ball park within an hour of stepping off the train.

After dressing in the home team's quarters, the Colonels walked around the interior of the 1912 built stadium. Here was where the great Babe Ruth played from 1914 until he was traded to the Yankees after the 1919 season. Tris Speaker spent some of his greatest years at the Fenway. (During Babe Ruth's years playing at Fenway Park, he was actually one of the premier pitchers in the American League. His record on the mound there, from 1914-19, was 89-46. His best year was 1916, when he compiled a 23-12 record, with an ERA of 1.75. The "Bambino" became the game's greatest slugger when he began playing full time in the outfield as a Yankee starting in 1920, and became known everywhere as, "Babe".)

Uncle Charlie let the squad stroll around a few moments and then called for them to huddle around him. There were some reporters and others who had heard about the practice and were allowed to watch, without restrictions.

With the team squeezed in close, the coach almost whispered, "We have some eyes in the stands. We know that Harvard would never send out spies, but there may be some spectators who will tell others about what we plan on offense. Bo, open it up. Call every trick play we've ever run."

Bo did just that. He called reverses which had the back coming around suddenly stop and fire a long pass back across the field to James, who would have uncharacteristically gone deep. Or, on the same play, the reverse would go from a simple reverse to a double reverse, or even a triple reverse, in which four backs would handle the ball. If a wide open play had ever been in the arsenal, Bo ran it.

After the offensive display, Uncle Charlie acted like he was surprised that he had discovered anyone in the stands and beckoned to team manager McGee to go up and ask everyone to leave. Then, in privacy, Centre began its defensive drills, lining up in formations that the team actually planned on using on Saturday.

Tiny, then Uncle Charlie, would call out predicted Harvard formations and plays, again having the defense assume the proper positions, again drilling their team to "divine" how the upcoming play would develop.

Centre had prepped mentally and physically for a year for the upcoming battle. The Centre coaches felt that the mental preparations were no less important than the physical.

"We must make no mistakes."

"We must out think them."

"Every man in on every play."

Shadows were rapidly covering the field when a kick-off drill was held, and after a few runs-through, Uncle Charlie blew a whistle and signaled the end of what had been a vigorous, but no contact, three hour session.

The team had a quick shower and boarded the buses for the return to the Lenox, grabbed a bite, went to their rooms for proper attire, and then it was off to the Colonial Theatre to see the Ziegfeld Follies. (The Ziegfeld Follies staged a new production each year in New York City. The Follies was a combination of vaudeville and a musical stage show. After a few weeks in New York, the show would go on the road, and one of the stops was in Boston. The most famous star of the 1921 presentation was none other than W.C. Fields.)

The Colonial, built in 1900 (and still operating) was seven blocks down Boylston Street from the Lenox, across from the Boston Common, and the team walked en mass from the hotel to the theatre. Like everywhere they went, many strollers recognized that they were from Centre, certainly prompted by the stories and photographs in the numerous Boston newspapers about the upcoming game.

It was, "Bo McMillin, good luck on Saturday!"

"Red, you can win this year!"

Bo, always conscious that Army was the team captain, would rarely fail to introduce his good friend to the well-wishers.

"I want you to meet our leader, the captain of the team, Mr. Army Armstrong."

At the theatre, everyone sat together except for Hump, Red Roberts, and Terry Snowday, according to George Joplin, who was sending stories back to the "Messenger."

The three pulled a string somewhere and drew front row seats.

As the Colonels found their seats, a murmur went through the crowd.

Howard was there. He said that people began to whisper and nod, and sort of point when the guys came in, and he could hear, "Centre" and "football."

Pretty soon, it became obvious that everyone knew who was there. The performance was ready to start and the lights went off and it was a great show. Howard was a banjo and mandolin player who was later in the Centre "Six," and he knew music and appreciated it. (The Centre "5" was expanded to six members the next year and was called the Centre "Six.")

At the intermission, W.C. Fields came out onto the stage and asked the crowd—Howard said it was a full house—to remain seated, that there were some special guests there that night, and said he was pleased to introduce the famous football team, the Centre College Colonels from Danville, Kentucky.

And he signaled to the team to come forward, and everyone, everyone stood and cheered as the players went up on the stage.

Howard said he'd never been so proud to be a part of Centre College. People whistled and clapped and he said you could just tell how much they loved the team.

After the show was over, people lined up along the sidewalk and street and cheered the team as they left the theatre to walk back to the hotel. Everyone, team and fans alike, was smiling and waving to each other.

The Boston papers seemed to be in a major contest to see which could provide more information about the October 29 game, and especially to provide their readers insight into the colorful aspects of the Colonels.

The "Post" ran a four column cartoon of "Danville's Alexander the Great, Bo McMillin."

In different poses, the following inscriptions appeared:

(1)   A famed novelist has written a novel about Bo.
(2)   As a disciplinarian, Mr. J. Caesar had nothing on Bo.
(3)   As he plunges through the line, it has Bo shouting, "Outa the way."
(4)   As he plunges through the crowd, it reads, "Bo on the way to his first football game, and he's been going through the opposition like that ever since."

The "Post" ran a little filler which said that Bo made Frank Merrill, a famous National Champion gymnastic legend, look like a "piker."

The "Post" had a sports columnist who had been writing bits all week preceding the game.

About the most cruel cut of all from a Harvard standpoint would be for Centre to trim Harvard Saturday—but not a chance, say the Crimson rooters.

Talk with any Harvard man nowadays and all you get is what the Crimson is going to do with the Tigers and Elis in the upcoming games, but the way that the fans are warming up to the Centre College game Saturday, one would hardly think that there are any such contests as the Harvard-Princeton and Harvard-Yale games.

Despite Harvard being an odds-on favorite to beat the Praying Colonels, there are not a few who are grabbing up all the short-end wagers. They figure that Bo McMillin and his crowd are going to have a better chance than many will admit for them to win the game.

Another cartoon in the "Post," making a point about the darkness that engulfed the Stadium at the end of the previous week's Penn State game, showed a football player holding a lantern, and under the figure, it read: "One if by end, and two if by Centre." There were several entries written by Bob Dunbar, a sports columnist in the Boston "Herald."

Wonder how Bo McMillin feels when he reads about himself in Ralph D. Paine's "First Down, Kentucky?" The book is published by Houghton Mifflin Company, and is delightful reading for anyone who cares about quick, lively and colorful gridiron romance. Bo's the hero, and if he wants to increase the sale a few thousand per cent, let him lead his Colonels to victory.

Uncle Charlie Moran, the National League umpire, would feel more at home if they played the Harvard-Centre game at Braves Field.

I know of several of my friends who quite foolishly told that they have tickets for the Centre game. They are traveling around in alleys or taxicabs to keep clear of acquaintances who want to go to the game but can't get a ticket.

On October 28, the "Herald" ran a four column wide photograph of the Colonels taken at Fenway Park, with the team lined up as they would start the game. In the backfield, hands behind their backs, were Terry Snowday at right half, Bo at quarterback, Uncle Charlie wearing his ever present hat, standing between Bo and his left half, Army, and Tom Bartlett at fullback. The line, crouched in position, had Bill James at right end, Ben Cregor at right tackle, Bill Shadoan, right guard, Ed Kubale at center, George Jones, left guard, Minos Gordy, left tackle, and Red Roberts, left end. Bo was smiling, a confident smile actually, while the rest had a rather serious demeanor.

Bob Dunbar, again writing in the "Herald."

What do you think? Has Centre a chance? Will Harvard take a beating in preference to using some of the men they want to save for the Princeton game? These and a lot of other questions are winging their way through a host of autumnal haze today as they have been for the last week. The analysts of the game tell us that Centre is an over-rated team, and that a Harvard system, which refused to deviate a bit from its general plan to win the Princeton and Yale games, regardless of the results, just naturally will flatten the Praying Colonels. I will tell you what I think about that in the Monday "Herald."

The newsprint continued, providing unparalleled coverage for a little previously unknown college in Danville, Kentucky, "wherever that is."

The "Post" had three photographs in its Pictorial Section on October 28. There was a full-width picture of the entire Centre team taken at Fenway Park, a photograph of the starting eleven and Uncle Charlie, and a wonderful picture of some of the smartly dressed Centre fans, posing in front of the Lenox.

On that same day, the "Herald" turned over nearly the complete page 16 of the sports section to the Centre-Harvard game. There was a general headline:

CENTRE GETS ANOTHER WHIFF OF STADIUM AIR TOMORROW
KENTUCKIANS HIT TOWN ARMED WITH A "BO"
TO HUNT BIG GAME

A column-wide cartoon at the top of the page, "By Collier," had a caption over it which read, *"NOT RIPE UNTIL TOMORROW."* Bo was drawn buried in a garden with just his head and a couple of curling vines sticking out of the "Centre College Patch." Looking down on him, sitting on the side of the Harvard Stadium horseshoe, is John Harvard, rubbing his chin, saying, *"He's not as green as last year, and he may be harder to pick."*

Uncle Charlie was interviewed as the team was changing after the practice session at Fenway Park. Amongst his comments printed, were:

We have a stronger team than last year. Our line is improved considerably, and this was a department where we were weak in 1920. Many of the boys are playing together through another season, and this means they are more experienced and cooperate better in team play.

I am indebted to Eddie Mahan for Bill Shadoan, one of our new linemen. Eddie told Bo about Shadoan playing tackle on his service team over in France and that the youngster lived in Somerset, the home town of Red Roberts, and the town where Bo played before enrolling at Centre. Of course, there was only one college for him to attend, so he came to Centre and has worked himself into a starting position in our line. He's a good one.

Bo was cornered as he dressed after the Fenway workout by one of the many reporters who had been assigned to get any tidbit available regarding the Colonels. He was asked about the additional weight he carried when compared to when he was last in Cambridge, for the 1920 game.

I wasn't well when I came up to play last year. I had been captain of the team for two years and worried so much about things in general that my weight went down to 152 pounds. I don't have the cares of the captaincy this year. My great friend Army is our captain. I am weighing 170 and feeling considerably better now. This is my last year at Centre and I want to make it a good one. I just love to play football, and I plan to follow it up after I graduate by taking up coaching.

Ed Cunningham of the "Herald" wrote about "4 Cubs" in the Centre line.

There are quite a few changes in the Centre team. Four freshmen are playing in the line, and they are shoulder to shoulder—Bill Shadoan at right guard, Ed Kubale at center, George Jones at left guard, and Minos Gordy at left tackle. They have replaced the veterans who were lost—Red Weaver, the All-American center, Montgomery, a tackle, Robb, a guard, and King, an end.

Red Roberts was asked about the knee injury which had hampered him in the 1920 game.

"It's just a memory. I'm in fine condition."
Cunningham stated: *The big redhead looks great after spending the summer shoveling coal on a Southern Railroad freight engine.*

The cartoonist for the "Post" was featured across the whole eight columns of page 24 in the sports section of the paper on October 28, the day prior to the game. There were two panels. Both emphasized how popular Centre had become by focusing on the fact that there were no tickets to be had. The first had several men, one with a butterfly net, chasing after a little stick-legged character with "TICKET" written on him. The caption—*There's few of them loose.* The second showed a Princeton Tiger and Yale Bulldog perched atop a hill watching what looked like explosions going off in the distance. Near the fireworks was written—*Rah, Rah, Rah, Rah, Harvard,* and then, *Rah, Rah, Rah, Rah, Centre.* A character was asking, *Can't anyone get me a ticket?*
The Tiger and Bulldog say, *"Those 'Centres' are stealing our stuff."*
The Boston "Evening Transcript" had nothing but coverage of the game on an entire page of their sports section on the afternoon before the contest. There was a six column composite photograph under the title:

NEW FACES AND OLD IN CENTRE'S LINEUP AGAINST HARVARD

Minos Gordy and Ed Kubale were in their crouching line positions, Hump Tanner was punting, and close-ups of Army, Bo, and Terry Snowday completed the picture.
Another "Evening Transcript" cartoon, by Gene Mack, occupied three columns and featured Bo running. There was a drawing of Red Roberts captioned: *Last year's favorite is playing the line,* and a great head portrait of—*"Capt." Armstrong.* In the lower right hand corner, Mack had drawn a little square replete with a band blasting out, "Dixie."
Much had been written about how Harvard was going to hold out its starters and save them for the next week's Princeton game. Perhaps the Crimson supporters expected Coach Fisher to do exactly that, especially due to the fact that his team had so dominated a beaten down Colonels squad in the second half of the 1920 game. The fact is that Harvard took Centre quite seriously. The changes that were going to take place in the Crimson line-up were secondary to injuries suffered during the Penn State game, and not from the fact that Fisher and his staff were looking past Centre. Also, the

Harvard coaches were still shifting their lineup in an attempt to provide more offensive punch. Even though the Crimson had managed to tie a good Penn State team, their significant deficit statistically showed that the offense simply wasn't where it was felt it should be.

Harvard planned on starting seven of the same players against Centre as had begun the game with the Nittany Lions. New starters are in boldface.

HARVARD LINEUP vs. PENN STATE		HARVARD LINEUP vs. CENTRE
Clark Macomber	Left end	Clark Macomber
Keith Kane	Left tackle	Alexander Ladd
Friske Brown	Left guard	Friske Brown
Henry Clark	Center	**Francis Kernan**
Charles Hubbard	Right guard	Charles Hubbard
Alexander Ladd	Right tackle	**Philip Kunhardt**
Covington Janin	Right end	Covington Janin
Jewett Johnson	Quarterback	Jewett Johnson
George Owen	Left half	**Frank Rouillard**
Winthrop Churchill	Right half	Vinton Chapin
Vinton Chapin	Fullback	**Edwin Gehrke**

Other than a change in the center position, and one tackle, the line remained the same. Henry Clark was being replaced by Francis Kernan who was heavier and, as Melville E. Webb, Jr. stated in a story in the Boston "Evening Transcript," *Kernan is a pretty rugged customer.*

Keith Kane, the team captain, had been shaken up in the Penn State game and was replaced by Alexander Ladd, who was switched from right to left tackle. Philip Kunhardt was slipped into Ladd's former position at right tackle. In the backfield, two starters against State remained in starting positions against Centre, Jewett Johnson at quarterback, and Vinton Chapin, even though Chapin was moved from fullback to halfback.

Winnie Churchill and George Owen weren't starting, but Coach Fisher stated that they were ready if needed. Owen wasn't 100% after the State game, and Churchill was being replaced by Edwin Gehrke who had been getting a lot of personal instruction from Eddie Mahan. Gehrke hadn't started the game against the Nittany Lions because of nagging injuries, not lack of ability.

Overall, the Harvard lineup announced the day before the game reflected that the Colonels were indeed being shown respect, and the assertion that the Crimson held back their stars for future contests simply wasn't true.

George Joplin of the Danville "Messenger" spent the 28th with the team and filed a story that afternoon. Joplin was privy to everything that the team did, as he was a Centre graduate, former cheerleader, and one of the greatest boosters the Colonels ever had.

There is a wonderful October 28 photograph of Joplin leaning with his hand on a brass-rimmed headlight of a convertible automobile, top up. He is dressed in a suit with vest, wearing a topcoat and a coachman hat. The photo was taken outside of the Stadium. Sitting on the fender is Bo, dressed in his uniform but with no helmet. Terry Snowday is standing along the side of the car, similarly with no headgear, displaying one of the green blankets with the gold "Centre" monogram clearly displayed. Uncle Charlie is sitting in the right front passenger seat.

Of the day's events, Joplin wrote:

The Colonels answered reveille at 6:30 this morning and were on the way to the Stadium at 8:30. They shook the Danville turf out of their uniforms and put in three and one-half hours at practice. The weather was ideal today. The air was crisp and only a mild wind was blowing over the Stadium.

After the noon meal back at the Lenox, team headquarters, the Colonels remained in the dining room for an hour and a half of skull practice. The three Centre tutors, Moran, Myers, and Thornhill, took turn-about in chalk-talking to the boys.

While Joplin was wiring his reports back to Danville, Arthur Duffy of the Boston "Post" was writing in his "Sport Comment" column.

Danger signals are being shown all along the Atlantic Coast, from Danville, Kentucky to the Stadium in Cambridge, to watch Centre in the big Harvard game tomorrow—but whatever storms might be brewing, Harvard appears to be able to take care of the best that Uncle Charlie Moran's "Praying Colonels" may have to offer in the big contest.

Joplin:

One thing is sure. Harvard will not romp to the goal line this year because the Centre warriors this time will have no stage fright. Last year, the Crimson waded through the Kentuckians before they could come to earth, but when they did land on terra ferma, they swept the Crimson off their feet until injuries and exhaustion so weakened them that they could not stem the tide in the second half.

Centre will miss Red Weaver, but Kubale has come as close to anyone could to replace him, and despite the loss of Montgomery at tackle, the line should be stronger with the addition of the new men in the front.

Duffy:

You cannot beat those "Praying Colonels" for having their nerve with 'em. They still think they are going to lick Harvard Saturday. A more cocky little group of footballers never hit these diggings. They argue that Centre is stronger than it was last year, and that Harvard is not tuned to the same pitch as it was last season. But if some of those Centre players had seen that Penn State game of last Saturday, probably they would have another think coming their way.

Joplin:

Centre will fight every inch of the way tomorrow. The great physical condition of every man on the squad has given the boys a lot of confidence, and they will have no alibi if defeat camps with them. They place little faith in the stories relative to Harvard's crippled condition, for they know that Harvard has a squad of 40 first-string men of real ability.

The old war cry, "Centre fights!" will ring out and the boys will be off.

May the best team win!

Duffy:

Yet, whether Harvard or Centre wins, there are not a few who are giving the Kentuckians a chance to win. Yesterday, I heard one football fan offer 100 to 60 that Harvard would win and the bet was taken so quickly that it almost took his breath away. Centre is going to try to defy the old illusion about Harvard getting the "breaks" in the game. They contend that they will get the "breaks" this time simply because they will create them.

Uncle Charlie was asked after the practice Friday evening how the reception given the Kentuckians thus far compared to the attention given during the 1920 visit. A reporter quoted him as saying it was like a landlord who awakened his quests every half hour to make certain they were enjoying themselves, and, *Southern hospitality is set a very hot pace by Bostonians.*

After the skull session in the Lenox dining room, the team left in two buses of the Royal Blue Line and headed toward Cambridge. The football players, Uncle Charlie, Chief Myers and his wife, Tiny Thornhill, trainer Carl "Swede" Anderson, and manager Johnnie McGee were in the vehicles. The Chief had instructed the drivers to journey along the Charles and cross over to the Harvard campus, the big Harvard horseshoe on their left, as they turned toward the (Larz) Anderson Memorial Bridge.

Several new team members hadn't had the opportunity to experience the campus itself. The Centre coaching staff felt it was important for all of the team, even those who had been along in 1920, to "feel" the magnificence and beauty of the greatest university in the country, to be able to appreciate how important Harvard was, and how huge a victory would be when winning against a team representing the best that America had to offer.

Bo and Army wanted the team to see the Hemenway Gymnasium where their basketball exploits had taken place earlier in the year, so the buses drove up Massachusetts Avenue, past the red brick athletic building.

"That's where we beat a good Harvard team," Army said. "Let's make it two for two for 1921."

The buses turned back toward Harvard Square and went left onto Peabody Street, parking so the occupants could disembark. The campus was entered by walking through the Johnson Gate, constructed in 1890. On the left was Harvard Hall, built in 1766, and on their right, the even older Massachusetts Hall, circa 1720.

The Chief had a map and pointed out the buildings which fronted the Old Yard and when they were built. The group turned left in front of, "Hollis Hall, 1763," and Myers continued identifying the historic structures.

"Stoughton Hall, 1805."

"Holworthy Hall, 1812."

"Thayer Hall, 1870."

"Chief, that's not as old as our Old Centre," said one of the players.

"University Hall, 1815."

"Weld Hall, 1872."

"Grays Hall, 1867, over there," the Chief said, "but let's turn here into what is called Harvard Yard." As they entered Harvard Yard, they saw the massive Widener Library, "built just a few years ago, in 1915." By the time the team was reaching the library, they were beginning to draw attention from students who were walking around the Yard. Several came up and told various team members that they would be at the game tomorrow, "as will everybody," and wished them luck.

"These are just a few of the buildings that make up the campus," the Chief said as the group sat on the steps of the library.

"Harvard dates back to 1636. Massachusetts was founded only a few years earlier, when the Pilgrims landed at Plymouth Rock in 1620. Education was important, and I have always found it to be remarkable that only 16 years after the landing, it was seen as necessary to establish an institution of higher learning."

The Chief continued.

"Centre was founded early in the history of Kentucky. Harvard has a magnificence heritage. You too, come from an institute with a wonderful heritage, on a lesser scale. It is only fitting that these two colleges, so beloved by their students and alumni alike, should meet on the field of battle, at Harvard Stadium on Soldiers Field, and engage in a game as only true sportsmen can play." It was Harvard. It was always—Harvard.

After leaving Cambridge, the two buses slowly eased back into Boston and wound through the city. The coaches wanted to find some remote spot where the team could spend the rest of the day, away from the hustle and bustle of the city. They went east toward the coast and then headed north, out of the city limits, hugging the shore, and crossed over the Saugus River into Essex County and Lynn. After driving eastward through Lynn, they turned south down Nahant Road and traversed the narrow strip of land which connected the mainland with the resort city of Nahant, situated on a rocky coast jutting out into Massachusetts Bay and the Atlantic.

The buses stopped at Bass Point and the team disembarked and spent the afternoon walking around the streets which were lined with summer homes, now mostly closed until the following spring. It was a quiet group, the members of the squad walking alone or in twos and threes, each player lost in his own thoughts as to how he would meet the challenge, now just 24 hours away, in Harvard Stadium. It was late afternoon before the buses pulled back out of Nahant and began the 15 mile journey back to the Lenox.

At the same time the Colonels were in Nahant, there was a surge to buy an additional 5,000 "rush" tickets that the Harvard Athletic Association had decided to make available. The term came from the fact that the tickets carried no assigned seats and were sold at the last moment. A holder, when admitted, literally had to "rush" to either the newly constructed end zone bleachers, or climb up to the parapet on the roof above the colonnade. It was "first come, first served" type of seating.

When these seats were added, it guaranteed a crowd of over 50,000, and still many more could have been sold. Such was the demand. George Trevor, writing in the New York "Sun," offered his thoughts on why Centre attracted so much attention, and why there was such true affection by Bostonians and people throughout the East for the Kentuckians.

There is Uncle Charlie, coach, umpire, psychologist, revivalist, shoemaker, tailor, and Father Confessor, now devising original plays, now bandaging limbs, now patching helmets, now darning jerseys; there is the "Kentucky Colonel" stuff, the bands blaring "Dixie," the mint-julep background, the aroma of bluegrass, the Southern Belles waving gold and white pennants; there is the elemental lure of the Kentucky hills, of picturesque moonshiners, who have no connection with the college; beyond all of these is the never-failing religious appeal— the anecdotes concerning pre-game prayers in the dressing room, the Centre warriors kneeling with bowed heads as they sought Divine Guidance.

The Louisville "Courier-Journal" devoted an editorial to the Colonels on the morning before the game.

WHERE'S CENTRE GOING?

Centre is in Boston today. That much could be gleaned by reading its railroad tickets. But this doesn't denote the real destination of the boys. Their long trip to the East terminates on a few square yards of soil in Harvard Stadium. Centre will be treated to handshakes, receptions, and team parties. But its heart will lie in that little patch of green behind the goalposts in the big Harvard horseshoe.

Geographically speaking, the hinterland of the Harvard goalpost has often been discovered, but it never has endured a permanent settlement. Penn State camped there last Saturday several times, and our own Centre made two distinct voyages there last October. But the land has never become common property. Some of the brave alumni of Harvard claim it is consecrated ground, as brave alumni will do. But Kentucky expects to see Army Armstrong's explorers plant the Centre flag there tomorrow.

Centre learned much at Cambridge last year, notably that eleven men cannot play four quarters of hard football successfully against a team that is constantly reinforced and refreshed by substitutes. Harvard wore Centre down last year with its flow of "subs." It is heartening to see that Centre has a solid twenty-five man squad this year, and to see that the second string compares favorably with the first line.

This year has been particularly rich in classical sporting events, and the Centre-Harvard game is a fitting climax. Somehow or other, the West and South delight in the prospect of a Harvard trimming. When the team expected to do it comes from a remote and Lilliputian College in Kentucky, the joy is equal to that in Israel when David's forward pass decided the game against Goliath.

Kentucky hopes that Centre never stops until it reaches the green, back of the Harvard goalpost, and that it makes a permanent settlement in that jealously guarded territory.

The Boston "Herald" published a cartoon which implied that all of the Harvard talk about the team being weakened by injuries was overblown. A Crimson coach is telling the trainer, *Have the team report in full splints and bandages! There's a photographer from one of papers outside.*

The trainer replies, *We better wheel the fullback out on a cot, hadn't we?*

Regarding injuries to the Harvard team, Bo was asked by a reporter what he felt about the reports being circulated.

You won't hear any Centre men saying that he hopes those reports are true. We pray otherwise that they aren't. Outside of the feeling of keen sympathy that we should have for the injured, let us consider that there is more credit and glory in playing the game right and being beaten by a physically fit Harvard eleven than there would be in defeating a maimed and crippled opponent.

Much was made about the fact that Centre was going to start four freshmen in the line. Sportswriters just couldn't believe that any team would come into the Stadium with four "cubs" in the trenches and have any hope of emerging victorious. George C. Carens, writing in the "Evening Transcript," was typical.

It is inconceivable that Centre can win tomorrow. Harvard has a sound defense for forward passes. It appears that an aerial attack is the only hope of the Southerners, for their opponents will be better versed in gridiron knowledge, which should prove advantageous.

Take the Kentucky team's line, for example. There are four freshmen slated to start. The middle section of the country is notoriously weak in line play. That is the link that may be unable to hold the Crimson surge. It doubtless has prevented any undue elation on the part of the Centre veterans at the prospect of facing Harvard tomorrow.

If Centre's line outmatches Harvard's, then the Crimson may bow, but it is difficult to imagine Harvard losing to Centre.

Arthur Duffy, in his "Post" column, "Sport Comment," reported the results of a poll that he had taken in the sports department of his paper.

Harvard	14	Centre	0
Harvard	10	Centre	3
Harvard	21	Centre	7
Harvard	31	Centre	14

Duffy also reported on the results of the Friday workout at the Stadium, and how Uncle Charlie had let several Harvard supporters watch the team's practice.

When someone asked Uncle Charlie if he wasn't afraid that some Harvard scouts would be around, Uncle Charlie answered in his usual customary drawl, "Oh, we're not worried about Harvard scouts. Harvard has regular fellows. They wouldn't resort to such tactics on the eve of the game, and we expect them to be miles away."

The truth, of course, was that Centre hoped that Harvard would indeed receive reports of their practice session. The Colonels signal drills contained multiple passing formations that morning. It was exactly what Centre planned to avoid the next day, especially in the first half. Centre hoped the Crimson defense would always be set up to prevent a passing attack. The Colonels would run, and run again, and punt if necessary. It was going to be a different game plan, different in what Centre was capable of, but as Uncle Charlie had said in his conversation with Army and Bo at the Gilcher, "I like it! It's exactly the opposite of what they will expect. I love to spring a surprise on our opponents! I like it!"

After returning to the Lenox from Nahant, the players changed into suits and walked the several blocks from the hotel to the University Club, located in the old Whittier House at 270 Beacon Street. (The Club moved from 270 Beacon to 426 Stuart in 1926.) The Club was hosting a party for the Centre visitors and had the Centre "5" set up to entertain. The Colonels were nearly overwhelmed with the pats on the back, hands out-stretched to shake, and the sincere, "Best wishes" and "Good luck" from their gracious hosts.

Meanwhile, another party was being held at the Belmont Springs Country Club, hosted by Howard Reynolds, Centre's great advocate. Reynolds had invited the Centre and Harvard coaching staffs, Dr. Ganfield, and others in the administration and on the faculty of Centre. An honored guest was Ralph D. Paine who handed out copies of his just printed hardcover edition of "First Down, Kentucky."

GAME DAY, OCTOBER 29, 1921

The Colonels were allowed to sleep in relatively late on the morning of the game. It wasn't until 9:30 that they assembled in the dining room for breakfast. The weather forecast in the previous evening's papers had called for rain, but there wasn't a cloud in the sky, and the air was crisp with barely a breeze. It looked like it was going to be a perfect fall day for a football game.

After breakfast, the dining room was sealed off for another skull session. Once again, the coaching staff emphasized the game plan.

"It's going to be simple. We'll run."

"Nothing fancy. None of our trick plays. We'll hold our cards close to our chest the first half."

"Defense will win this game. We'll play typical hard-nosed Centre defense."

"We'll substitute in the line. If you get taken out, it will be to rest you for later."

"They won't wear us down this year."

"All of our student body, all of Danville, all of Kentucky, all of the South, will be following this game. We are playing for football fans all over the country."

Again, the coaches drilled that, "Centre plays like gentlemen. We play hard, but we play clean, just as our opponents will play." The Chief wrote in big, bold letters on the chalkboard, speaking the words as he wrote.

BELIEVE!
ACHIEVE!
SUCCEED!

Then the session broke up and the members of the team were free to spend the rest of the morning strolling around the city. There was no particular destination, just a chance to unwind before heading to the Stadium. The Colonels had that look like they had before the 1919 game with Virginia in Charlottesville. It was their "game face."

Howard said there were a lot of Centre people and sportswriters in the Lenox lobby, but as the team came out of the dining room, the fans and writers seemed to sense that this wasn't the time to be chummy, or to ask questions. They clapped politely and let the guys leave the hotel.

Howard trailed along behind them but stayed about half a block back. Most of the members walked to a big park down the street which I found out the next year is the Boston Common.

They found benches and sat, or just milled around. Occasionally, a few of them would gather together and say a few words. But there was no laughter or horsing around.

Uncle Charlie, Chief Myers and Tiny Thornhill came on down to the park, but the three of them stayed alone, and they talked awhile, like they were making plans, but they left the players with their thoughts.

Army, the captain, walked around, huddling with a couple of the guys and they'd talk a moment, and then he would seek out some of the other players, and say a few words, and move on again.

It was obvious, Howard said, that each member of the squad was simply concentrating on the game which was just a few hours away. He told me later that he felt if quiet determination would win a game, Centre would have to be victorious. He'd been around the team for over a year, and he'd never seen them, or anyone for that matter, so serious and intent on winning.

I told him what I had felt when Bo spoke about "First Down, Kentucky." How Bo had said he wished the book had been written a year later, because then it would end with Centre winning. Howard said he had that same feeling when he watched the team in the park. He felt that there was no way they could lose the game.

Around noon, the team stopped again in the Lenox dining room for a light lunch of roast beef, dry toast and hot tea, ordered by the Chief. Red Roberts said, "Chief, you trying to starve us? How are we going to beat Harvard being all hungry and stuff?" The meal was the favorite pre-game menu of the Chief.

"Red, you can eat after the game. I want you to be so hungry that you'll eat up Harvard."

"Aw, Chief, geeze-louise."

After the meal, everyone gathered up their gear and headed to the buses. Unlike last year, there was no police escort, no banners draped on the sides of the buses, and no attention from Bostonians as they drove west toward the Stadium.

Game time was 2:30 even though the tickets had 3:00 printed on them. The previous week's Penn State game had ended in near darkness, and the Harvard Athletic Association had moved the kickoff up by half an hour. Every newspaper in Boston had repeatedly printed the new starting time, and from the size of the crowd beginning to converge on the Stadium by 1:00, it was obvious that the word had gotten out. This year, the tickets being used and programs being sold had "Centre" as Harvard's opponent rather than the "Center" spelling used in 1920.

As the big horseshoe began to fill, the air was filled with the sounds of music from the three bands which occupied different sections of the Stadium. The New York Newsboy's Band, 200 strong, had been brought up on an overnight boat by the Harvard Athletic Association and occupied a section of the newly constructed end zone bleachers. The 50 member Harvard Crimson band marched into the Stadium wearing red sweaters, white flannels, and sailor hats. As they entered onto the field, they struck up, "Soldiers Field." Many of the Crimson fans, old grads and students alike, stood and sang the familiar lyrics.

O'er the stands in flaming Crimson,
Harvard banners fly.
Cheer on cheer like volleyed thunder
Echoes to the sky.
See the Crimson tide is turning
Gaining more and more,
Then fight! Fight! Fight! For we win tonight
Old Harvard forevermore.

The Centre "5" marched in playing "Dixie," and their peppy jazz rendition brought a quickened pace to the crowd filing into the huge facility.

Daniel, who used only the one name in his bylined articles, penned his impressions for the New York "Herald."

It was a crowd which in size, brilliance, color, and enthusiasm, rivaled that seen at one of the "Big 3" contests. Nearly half were women, and they gave to the assemblage a prismatic quality which only feminine attire and floral splendor can give.

The reds and blues and greens of the prevailing fashion in feminine millinery made those thousands look like fields of colorful poppies and of waving rhododendrons.

It was a perfect afternoon as could be for a football game, with just a bit of tang in the air, and for the onlookers, the afternoon was ideal—perfect.

Not a cloud flecked the blue. Across the Charles, back on the distant horizon, there lay the lazy haze of Indian summer, wisps of smoke curled here and there in the calm of a glorious afternoon.

The Colonels hauled their duffle bags filled with gear out of the buses when they pulled up to the locker room. A throng of fans, many wearing gold and white chrysanthemums, cheered them on as they made their way into the building.

The visitor's dressing room was spotless. It smelled a bit like tincture of benzoin, a solution applied to the skin to make tape used on ankles more adhesive. The wire lockers were opened with each of their doors standing at the exact same angle. Inside, folded on a shelf at the top, was a large, fluffy, white cotton towel with a small bar of soap placed on top of it. It was quite a contrast to the haphazard appearance of the Colonels' locker room back in Danville, even after Uncle Charlie had urged his players to "tidy up the place."

The team stripped off their clothes and began their pre-game ritual. Nearly all had some superstition-fed manner of getting into their uniforms. A couple put on their undershirt, shoulder pads and jersey before getting to their stockings. If they'd dressed a certain way and had a great game, they'd try to follow the same pattern, gaining just that bit of confidence that the repetition might give them. One player had to put on his left stocking first, then right. He had reversed the sequence once and felt he'd performed poorly, and vowed never to make that mistake again. Red Roberts always finished his preparation by standing in front of a mirror and carefully wrapping a white silk scarf, ordered by the team from A.G. Spalding, around his head, getting it just right so that his ears would be covered and protected.

There were guys on the team who had some real superstitions. Bo was known to be one of the most.

There was a big water tower between Breck Hall and the train tracks. Before going to the Harvard game, Bo decided that he had to climb up the ladder to the top where there was this ledge, or walkway, and leave something on it. I've forgotten what it was that he felt he had to place there, maybe just a rock or something.

When he came back down, he said everything would be ok, because he'd done whatever he was supposed to do.

It wasn't like he'd been drinking or anything. I don't think Bo ever had a drop, but he was sort of superstitious about some things.

As the Colonels were suiting up, the Harvard players were doing the same. The coaches were circulating around the locker room, reminding their men to be alert for trick plays, certain that Uncle Charlie had a wide-open game plan in mind.

"Pooch" Donovan, the longtime trainer at Harvard, had his assistants going around the room rubbing water on the Crimson's moleskins once they had gotten into uniform. As the water dried, the material would harden, giving added protection, plus make opponents pay a little more of a price when they made a hit below the waist.

Just as in 1920, Uncle Charlie and the Chief had received multiple telegrams from Kentucky and from alumni and fans throughout the country wishing the team success. Occasionally, a wire would be personalized, and the coaches would walk over to the recipient and read it to him.

"Captain Army—Lead the Colonels to victory on the field of battle."

"Bill James—Friends in Fort Worth will follow heroic Centre. Wish you best."

After the team was totally suited up, it was time for the speeches to begin. However, there were few of the "rah, rah" types of addresses that usually preceded a game. Uncle Charlie was fairly subdued in reminding the team that several of the players who could have graduated had instead returned specifically for this opportunity, and now, "the time has come."

The Chief again gave a short history of his quest since arriving in Danville in September of 1903.

"I dreamed from the first moment I came on the Danville campus that someday I'd be involved in making Centre be known not only in Kentucky, but all across the South and now all over the nation, as the home of the finest young men, and the greatest, fightingest group of football players who have ever played the game. Today, we're going to prove to the world what Centre men are made of." Army stood up and began the chant.

"WE ARE CENTRE! WE ARE CENTRE!
WE ARE CENTRE! WE ARE CENTRE!"

Over and over, the same refrain.

"WE ARE CENTRE! WE ARE CENTRE!
WE ARE CENTRE! WE ARE CENTRE!"

Finally, the captain motioned for silence.

"We all know our assignments. We all know that if all eleven of us play as one, as we have been taught to play, we can win."

Army continued, "Here's what I'm telling you, and you can be certain of it. If we hold them scoreless in the first quarter, we will win." As Army was speaking, the officials for the game were in a nearby room getting dressed.

W. R. Crowley from Bowdoin was the umpire. The head linesman was E.C. Taggert from Rochester, and the field judge was W.J. Crowell from Swarthmore. Also from Swarthmore was Robert J. "Tiny" Maxwell, working as the head official, the referee.

Maxwell's nickname was the antithesis of his actual physical dimensions. He was a giant of a man, standing 6'4" and weighing in at well over 300 pounds. Despite his immense size, he was nimble on the field and one of the most respected football officials of his time. Maxwell had played football first at the University of Chicago under Alonzo Stagg, and later transferred to Swarthmore in Philadelphia where he was a star guard. "Tiny" had been the editor of the sports page of the Philadelphia "Public Ledger" since 1916.

After dressing, Maxwell walked toward the Centre locker room and heard a loud voice as he neared the door. He stopped and heard one of the Colonels, in good form, giving the pre-game benediction. The huge referee signaled for his fellow officials to come near, and they listened as the prayer ended with a loud "amen" shouted in unison, and then they were nearly bowled over as the team, led by Army, came barreling through the door, tears streaming down every face , pumping their fists in the air, and screaming, "Go Colonels!"

Maxwell turned to the members of his crew and said, "Well, I guess that proves it. They really do pray before a game. There's no denying it."

The Crimson had been met with a loud cheer from the Harvard student body and fans as they sprinted out onto the field right at 2:00 for their warm-up. An equally enthusiastic greeting erupted when the Gold and White, wiping away tears, trotted to the far end of the field to go through their drills.

The fan situation for Harvard was rather complicated. The Stadium was universally filled with spectators who pulled for the Crimson when they played Princeton or Yale. But the loyalties were somewhat clouded when other teams came to Soldiers Field, especially when the opponent was a decided underdog. There were students from many of the numerous local colleges, especially Massachusetts Institute of Technology, Boston College and Boston University, who cheered for anyone other than Harvard. There were also Harvard graduate students who had come to Cambridge and never felt they were really part of the Harvard "family." And finally, there were many in the stands who had grown quite attached to the Centre College Colonels in 1920 due to the little school's audacious, clean and courageous play.

Centre lined up and began running pass plays. The coaches wanted Harvard to feel that the Colonels would play as they had the year before. Bo would fling passes left and right, short and long, passes to the flanks, passes across the middle. Uncle Charlie couldn't help but to glance down toward the Harvard end of the field and observe some of the Crimson coaches watching his team's drill.

Army kept telling anyone close enough to hear, "Hold them scoreless in the first quarter and we'll win this game."

At 2:27, Tiny Maxwell asked the team captains to come to the 50 yard line for the flip of the coin.

Army and Richmond Keith Kane were both natural leaders who had the respect not only of their teammates, but also the coaching staffs of their colleges. Army had a more humble, but no less impressive, background than Keith Kane. He was from Fort Smith, Arkansas and went to the public high school there. Army was a four-sport man at Centre, having played football from 1917-21, baseball from 1918-21, basketball during 1918-21, and ran track in 1918 and 1920. He was class president in 1917-18 and was on the social committee in 1920. His fraternity was Beta Theta Pi.

Kane was the quintessential Harvard man. Handsome, just as Army was, he was born on July 3, 1900, in San Francisco. He prepped at St. George's in Middletown, Rhode Island and listed his home address as 5 Champion Street, an appropriate address indeed, in Newport. During his first year at Harvard, he had been on the freshman football team and crew, and was on the varsity football team in 1919-21. Kane was crew captain in 1920-21, class president during his junior year, and First Marshall of the class of 1922, analogous to the class president.

Kane was vice president of the Harvard Union 1921-22, and involved in the Institute of 1770, the umbrella organization for the social and performing activities of the Hasty Pudding Club, of which he was a member. His fraternity was Delta Kappa Epsilon. During the war year of 1918, Kane had been stationed at the Great Lakes Naval Training Station from July 29, 1918 until September 6, 1918.

In Danville, Lexington, Somerset, Louisville, Georgetown, and other cities across the state, the first announcement that the game was ready to start for the "play by play" was greeted with cheers. Over the wires came the starting line-ups dutifully written down on the pre-prepared boards in each Kentucky city which was "carrying" the game from the Western Union wires. The positions were down the center of the rectangle and there were columns for the names of the starters and their weights.

HARVARD			CENTRE	
Macomber	(178)	Left end	Roberts	(219)
Ladd	(184)	Left tackle	Gordy	(182)
Hubbard	(190)	Left guard	Jones	(200)
Kernan	(185)	Center	Kubale	(177)
Brown	(205)	Right guard	Shadoan	(196)
Kunhardt	(190)	Right tackle	Cregor	(179)
Janin	(185)	Right end	James	(176)
Johnson	(167)	Quarterback	McMillin	(170)
Chapin	(166)	Left halfback	Armstrong	(158)
Gehrke	(170)	Right halfback	Snowday	(172)
Rouillard	(170)	Fullback	Bartlett	(155)

Centre's line averaged 189 lbs. and backfield weighed in at 164, for a team average of 180. Harvard's line averaged 188, the Crimson backfield, 168. Overall, the team was comparable to the Colonels at 181 lbs. Certainly, there was parity regarding size, and it was felt that Centre may have a bit more speed.

The two captains shook hands and referee Maxwell showed them a shiny, 1921 uncirculated Morgan silver dollar, obtained specially by Tiny to use in starting the game. (The Morgan was reintroduced for just one year, 1921, after having been produced annually from 1878 to 1904.)

"This is heads. This is tails. I'm going to ask you, Captain Armstrong, to state your preference, and I'm going to flip the coin and let it fall on the ground."

"Heads."

"Heads it is. Do you choose to kick or receive?"

"We'll receive."

In all of the cities across Kentucky carrying the game by wire, the news was greeted with cheers as the announcers shouted, "Centre receives."

"We receive!"

"They have to kick to us!"

People who until the last couple of years had never heard of Centre, or knew little about the college, now referred to the Gold and White as "we," or "us."

The entire block on Main Street from Third to Fourth Streets in Danville was filled with excited fans who had congregated to hear the play by play. They met the news that the Colonels had won the toss with shouts, and many patted others on the back.

"It's a good start!"

"Bo will have the first shot!"

Centre was to defend the north end of the field, with their backs to the wooden bleachers that filled the end of the horseshoe. At exactly 2:30, Harvard teed up the ball on its own 40 yard line. It was game time, the culmination of a year's planning by the Centre coaching staff and players.

FIRST QUARTER

Clark Hubbard, the Crimson's starting left guard, got his foot into the ball and booted a high, end over end kick which landed on the 10 yard line and bounced into the end zone for a touchback. The officials moved the pigskin out to the Centre 20 yard line, and the Colonels lined up on offense. Bo started the game just as planned, sticking to the ground. He picked up two on a plunge through the line and then Terry Snowday went for nine off tackle, and it was 1st down Centre on its own 31.

The Colonels then ran three straight plays into the line, netting only five yards and had to punt. Red Roberts got off a decent kick and Frank Rouillard hauled it in on his 35 and returned for six before being hit with a crunching tackle by Army. Centre took great pride in covering punts, and the team's speed often allowed a defender to reach an opponent as soon as the ball came down, resulting in no run-back at all.

First down Harvard on its own 41. Rouilland picked up one yard, then nine for a 1st down. Bo and Army were up and down the line, exhorting their line to charge hard. They knew it was important for the freshmen to have success early, gaining confidence on each play.

The "cubs" responded and hit Vinton Chapin hard on the next play, causing the Harvard halfback to cough up the ball and Bill James, the 5th year lineman from North Side High in Fort Worth, smothered it.

There was no way that the Colonels were going to let Harvard get off to a start like it did the previous year and score on the first possession. Army and Bo and their teammates didn't plan on Harvard scoring at all, much less early-on, as they had before. The Colonels were playing with confidence and determination.

Centre took over on the Harvard 49. Terry Snowday ran two straight plays off tackle, picking up five and then six. First down Centre on the Harvard 38. Bo shot over the left guard position but could get only two. Snowday got another three, and it was 3rd and five on the 33. Bo had called nothing but simple runs through the line, and hadn't even tried an end sweep. It was as conservative an attack as Centre had ever used in a game as long as Bo and Uncle Charlie had been in the spotlight over the last five years. However, on the next play, Bo attempted a little of the razzle-dazzle that had so captivated the crowd in 1920.

The Colonel quarterback barked out the signals and took the center pass from Ed Kubale and flipped a short pass out to Army who had had stepped two paces back. Army fired a perfect strike to Tom Bartlett, but the Crimson backfield was alert and was able to get a hand on the ball just before it hit Bartlett's outstretched hands.

During the pre-game warm-ups, the Centre coaches had watched 19 year old Ray Class, a 169 lb. freshman halfback from Middletown, Ohio, kick several field goals from as far out as 45 yards. With the upright being on the goal line, as opposed to the present day's 10 yards back, an attempt for three points would be within, but stretching, the young man's range. The eight or so yards back from the line of scrimmage where Class would receive the center pass from Kubale would make the effort be from just over 40 yards. Uncle Charlie, the Chief and Tiny Thornhill conferred and hollered down the bench, "Raymond, get in there and get us 3!"

Class replaced Tom Bartlett and gave it his best, but the ball fell considerably short. It was the only play for Class during the afternoon. Hump replaced him, and he didn't get back into the game as Centre didn't try another field goal during the contest.

Actually, the field goal attempt made sense. Had Centre punted, by all odds the ball would have ended going into the end zone, resulting in a touchback and 1st and 10 for Harvard on its own 20. As it was, the result was the same because the missed field goal also resulted in a touchback.

The Colonels' eagerness caused them to jump off sides and be penalized five yards on the next play. Chapin then got the call and swept around left end for 23 yards, and Harvard had a 1st down on its own 48. Again, the Colonels jumped off sides, fired up and trying to get the edge, and the ball was moved across midfield to the Centre 47. First down and five.

Army and Bo ran back and forth, slapping backsides and shouting encouragement. "You can do it, Cajun!" to Abbeville, Louisiana's Minos Gordy. "Go low, Shad. Go in low and fire!"

Harvard gained two, then was met by the pumped up line and had no gain, lost four on the 3rd down play and the Crimson now found themselves in a punting position with 4th down and seven on the Colonels' 49. Harvard punted and Hump snagged the ball, pivoted, avoiding a hard charging Crimson player, and made a nice run of 20 yards to get it out to the 30 before being brought down.

"Humpty," as the little fullback was affectionately known, was a fireplug, not much over 5'5". He was all muscle and ran with abandonment. When you hit Hump, you paid, and the Harvard defender who brought him down was slow to get up. From the bench, "Great run! Way to take it to them!" Bo kept to the ground, and Centre had to punt.

Harvard did the same, failing to pick up a 1st down, and the Crimson punted it back. The Colonels stuck with their game plan, and again had to punt it back to the Crimson. The 1st quarter ended with Harvard in possession on its own 45 yard line.

It had been a most uncharacteristic quarter for the Colonels. Bo had tried the one pass, the toss to Army who tried unsuccessfully to hit Tom Bartlett. The rest of the plays were simple runs. The Colonels were pleased however. They hadn't shown the Crimson anything. They'd given as good as they'd gotten. And they could hear their captain, Army Armstrong, who said over and over, "If we can hold them scoreless in the 1st quarter, we can win. As a matter of fact, we will win."

One person was tremendously pleased with the team's efforts. Tiny Thornhill felt his linemen had played as well as they possibly could. They'd played with strength. Tiny knew they were tough. But the really gratifying aspect of their performance was that they'd played smart. They had held their positions like they'd been taught. They hadn't fallen for any fakes. And they had constantly boosted each other's morale.

Red Roberts, Bill James and Ben Cregor had played flawlessly, like the veterans they were. Ed Kubale, Minos Gordy, Buck Jones and Bill Shadoan were playing like veterans also. Tiny had confidence as the teams changed ends of the field after the initial quarter that his boys would continue to acquit themselves well.

As Tiny Maxwell marched the ball across midfield and carefully placed it on the opposite 45 yard line, a open cockpit biplane was seen to be banking around Harvard Stadium, a photographer leaning out and taking shots of the packed horseshoe, preserving the event for posterity. (Robert W. Robertson, M.D., Red Roberts' "son," had a copy of the photograph taken that afternoon hanging on his office wall for years, and now it is in the possession of R.W.R., Jr., M.D.)

SECOND QUARTER

Harvard began the 2nd quarter with a running play and Terry Snowday read it precisely and crashed through and tripped up the Crimson back four yards behind the line of scrimmage. It was 2nd and 14.

On the next play, Jewett Johnson, the Crimson quarterback, floated a pass out to Clark Macomber who pulled it in right in front of Army, would made the tackle, but not before a 15 yard gain.

It was first down on the Centre 44. Despite the gain, Army had picked up on a trait of Macomber that would later prove valuable. It was Army's 5th year of college football, and he was one of the most savvy Colonels to ever wear the uniform.

Macomber planted his feet in the direction that the play was to unfold. It was a subtle thing, but Army studied his feet each time Macomber lined up, and the slight foot variance was noticed every time the Harvard player assumed his right end position.

On 1st down, Edwin Gehrke broke through the Centre line and gained seven yards before he was brought down by Bo. On 2nd and three, Philip Coburn gained one yard before Red Roberts literally lifted him off his feet and drove him back. Coburn tried the opposite side of the line and Ben Cregor made a similarly savage tackle. No gain.

"Atta way, Red!"

"Great hit, Baldy!"

On 4th and two, Gehrke bucked through the line after the Colonels felt it was an obvious punting situation. It was one of the few unexpected plays called all afternoon by the Crimson, and while it caught Centre off guard, the middle of the Gold and White line, led by Bill Shadoan, reacted quickly and stopped the run. However Gehrke managed to get the two yards needed, and it was 1st down on the Colonels' 33.

Harvard was driving and seemed content to stay on the ground. Coburn got four before Red tackled him. Coburn again for three. Bo hit him solidly. Bill Shadoan was shaken up on the play and Dick Gibson, another freshman who carried 180 lbs. on a 6'1" frame, reported in to Tiny Maxwell. The Louisville native had played three years at Louisville High and had progressed well under the tutelage of Tiny Thornhill. Unlike last year, the Colonels could substitute in the line and keep the relative strength of the team intact.

It was 3rd and three on the Centre 26. Coburn got the call again and ran over his left tackle. Ben Cregor fought off blocks by Ladd and Hubbard and made the hit, and Coburn came up one yard short. The Centre line was determined to hold. Harvard was just three feet away from getting a 1st down which would give the Crimson a great shot of putting some points on the board.

"We've got to hold them! Give it your all!"

Coburn took the snap for the 4th straight time and crashed directly behind his center, the forward wall of the Crimson trying to move the Colonels back enough for their halfback to get the needed yardage. It was a massive pileup, and the stands were quiet, not knowing if Coburn had been successful, or the Colonels had held. The officials untangled the mass of players, determined to spot the ball just where Coburn's forward motion had carried it. Tiny Maxwell signaled for the chain gang to come out for a measurement, and when the chain was stretched out, the big referee turned and signaled, shouting, "First down, Harvard."

The ball was on the Centre 23. The Crimson lined up and kept Coburn as the attacker. He ran over his right tackle, and Bo raced over from his position and hit him cleanly, driving him back, holding him to two yards gained. It was a leather smacking hit heard all over the Stadium.

Harvard again ran right into the line, this time with Gehrke testing the Colonels. Ben Cregor hit the Crimson back solidly, and the run gained only two yards. On 3rd and six, the Crimson ran a play off of a pass formation, but after feigning a pass, Chapin ran for three before Bo threw the streaking back to the ground.

The Harvard rooters were really getting into the game, urging their team on. They screamed for their boys, while the Kentuckians followed George Swinebroad's repeated, "Hold them, Colonels. Hold them, Colonels."

On 4th and three, on the 16, the Colonels lined up suspecting a pass. Chapin took the center toss and ran right over his right interior line, with Friske Brown and Philip Kunhardt providing excellent interference, and when the officials again peeled the players off the pile, the ball rested on the Centre 11 yard line.

Again, Tiny Maxwell shouted, "First down, Harvard."

The Crimson supporters erupted in a loud, spontaneous cheer as the yard markers once again were moved down the sidelines toward the goal. Harvard was on the move. It was 11 yards to a score.

The drive had now reached 14 straight plays and covered 44 yards, and those in the stands who had been in the Stadium during the previous year's contest saw some similarity with how the game unfolded in 1920. Harvard had opened up with a successful drive then, and seemed to be following the same exact pattern now, even though it was much later in the game.

With a deafening roar from the crowd, the Crimson lined up with the intent of taking the lead. The Colonels dug in, each man intent that, "They shall not pass." Coburn fired through the right side and Red Roberts hit him so hard that he literally was knocked backwards, and then crumpled to the ground, the wind knocked out of him. He managed to get up, but was visibly shaken.

"Great hit, Red!" Army hollered as the officials marked the ball a yard back from the line of scrimmage.

The Centre coaching staff and reserves on the bench hollored encouragement. Gehrke tried the opposite side of the Centre line, away from Red, and Bill James drove his shoulder into the stomach of the Crimson back, stopping him for no gain with a tackle as vicious as Red's on the previous play.

The Colonels cheered each other on.

"You can do it! Fire out! Go low, take them to their knees."

Chapin took a perfect pass from center and ran hard into the left side of Centre's defenders. The Colonels' front wall submarined under the blockers, bringing them down, and Bo, ever alert, raced forward, leaping over his linemen, and planted a solid hit, chest high, on the Crimson runner, stopping him at the line of scrimmage.

Three plays and a net loss of one yard! The Colonels were pumped! The Centre bench screamed encouragement and the little flock of Kentuckians, standing in their section on the 50 yard line, waved their streamers and danced around, shouting, "Hold them! Hold them!"

The Gold and White had shut down the Harvard attack. Coach Bob Fisher motioned to quarterback and field goal kicker, Charles Buell, to go in for Johnson to attempt a kick. As Buell was reporting to Tiny Maxwell, the Colonels huddled up and decided to put such a rush on Buell that he wouldn't have time to pass, if that's what Fisher had in mind. Also, a full rush may result in a hurried kick. Either way, Centre planned to go for broke.

If Buell had time to get a boot off cleanly, it would be a rather routine shot of 22 yards. The little quarterback had been a perfect three for three in extra points the prior week against Penn State, and all three had more than enough distance to exceed 22 yards.

Harvard broke from the huddle and the entire 11 man Centre squad spread across the line of scrimmage. The effect was to catch the Crimson off guard, as the blocking assignments would be different with an 11 man rush. As the ball was snapped back to Buell, two Colonels peeled back off to cover against a possible pass. The other nine barreled through toward the Harvard place kicker. Buell rushed his kick in the face of the crashing Colonels and hit the ball imperfectly, sending it just over the linemen and under the goal posts. Centre had held! The drive had been stopped!

There was applause throughout the horseshoe. Harvard's supporters were showing their appreciation for an excellent effort. It was different in the Centre section. It wasn't just applause. There was absolute joy—jumping, shouting, patting each other on the back. It was delirium, pandemonium!

"We held! Way to go Colonels! We held!"

Throughout Kentucky as the announcers shouted, "The kick misses!" cheers rang out everywhere crowds were gathered to follow the account coming from the Stadium. The Colonels took over on their own 20 after the touchback. Bo kept to the ground, with Terry Snowday picking up two. Bo then ran around left end and had gained five yards when he was hit. The ball popped out of his grip, and an alert Clark Macomber recovered for the Crimson. Once again, Harvard had excellent field position. Once again, Centre dug in, determined to hold.

Chapin tried to skirt around his right end but was stopped for no gain by Red Roberts. The big redhead's position was impregnable. Buell, who had stayed in the game after the missed field goal, then tried two short passes, but they were knocked down by the Colonels' secondary. Once again, Harvard found itself with a 4th down. The Crimson decided again to try a field goal. This time, the ball would have to carry 37 yards to clear the crossbar. It was still within Buell's range.

Once again, the Colonels lined up with the intent of trying to block the attempt, and again, they were successful by actually having one of the charging players get a hand on the ball, blunting its trajectory so that the effort was far short.

Another touchback! The Gold and White had held again!

The ball was again marched out to the 20. There were just a few seconds left in the half, and the Colonels were content to simply run out the clock, being extra careful to hold onto the ball. Bo took the center pass and ran sideways, taking a five yard loss as Tiny Maxwell blew his whistle, signaling that the half was over. The score was 0 to 0.

The Colonels were extremely pleased. They had played conservatively, exactly as Army and Bo had said they should in order to win. They hadn't shown their big plays, and were still even with the Crimson after 30 minutes of hard-fought football.

The little school from Danville, Kentucky, was close to accomplishing its mission, a mission to which it had been totally dedicated during the last year. Thirty more minutes! The Colonels felt good as they trotted off the field toward the locker room.

After the teams left the field, an influx of "husky youths wearing red caps" marched into the stadium and knelt down behind the Centre bench.

"Are they the Centre porters?" a lady was heard to ask. They were actually members of the University of Pennsylvania soccer team which had been over on the

Harvard practice field.

As soon as the teams had cleared the field, the Centre "5" fired up and onto the turf went no one other than Roscoe Breckinridge Conklin, the Colonels' all-around helper, great supporter, and a person the players affectionately called, their "mascot." It was Roscoe who had been photographed with Red Roberts when the train had reached Lexington, the two of them riding in the engine.

Roscoe was wearing a tall, silk hat and was dressed in a black, swallow-tail coat, gold vest, white flannels and white shoes. He cakewalked, pigeon-winged, and pranced all over the field, waving the Gold and White's pennant on a shaft. The crowd, except for the Kentuckians, had never seen anything like it.

As Roscoe would near one part of the Stadium, the crowd closest would stand and cheer, and as he circled the field, it was like a modern-day "wave," as section after section stood and cheered the smiling performer. It may have actually been the original "wave," as there was only one Roscoe, and no one had performed similarly as far as has been recorded.

After Roscoe finished his circumference, it was time for the New York Newsboy's Band to play, and the halftime entertainment was capped off by the Crimson band playing the Harvard songs, finishing with "Soldiers Field." Everyone agreed that there had never been a halftime to match what they had witnessed, even when Princeton or Yale came to the Stadium.

Meanwhile, Uncle Charlie was praising the Colonels' play.

"It's been a great half. Each of you played perfectly. You know how we've said we didn't think Harvard could score on you? It hasn't! You've played tough! You've played smart! Now we take it to them! If we score, we win!!"

The Chief jumped to his feet.

"Believe! Believe! Believe!"

THIRD QUARTER

As the teams lined up to start the 3rd quarter, Tom Bartlett was back at fullback, having replaced Hump Tanner, and Dick Gibson continued at the left guard position as Bill Shadoan's injury during the 2nd quarter kept him out of the action for the rest of the afternoon. Jewett Johnson was in at the Crimson quarterback position, and Charles Buell was on the sidelines.

The crowd was on its feet as Red Roberts kicked off for Centre. It was a low but long effort and scooted all of the way to the goal line where it was picked up by Chapin who returned it to the 15.

Harvard ran a fake punt play, thinking that Centre may fall for it with the Crimson being so deep in their own territory, but when Gehrke ran instead of kicking, the Colonels held their ground and the play only netted two yards.

"Play tough! Play smart!"

Each of the Colonels could hear Uncle Charlie's words as they lined up.

On 2nd down and eight, the Crimson quick-kicked and Bartlett fielded the ball on his own 48 and returned it to the Crimson 47 where he was tackled by Macomber. Two Harvard players piled on top of Bartlett and the refs threw a flag. It was 15 yards for unnecessary roughness, as unintentional as the infraction may have been. Harvard was playing for keeps, just as Centre was. Uncle Charlie often said, "It is a manly game."

The Colonels had excellent field position, with a 1st down on the Harvard 32. The ball was positioned toward the right sideline.

Centre had been practicing a play back in Danville which Uncle Charlie planned to use in just such a circumstance as the Colonels now found themselves. The play was designed so that Bo would begin a run to his right, then briefly pull up to fake a pass to Terry Snowday who was to dart down the right side, hopefully causing the left-side linebacker and halfback to follow him in order to protect against a pass. (Perhaps, it should be pointed out that the right side of Centre's formations would be facing the left side of Harvard's.) Of course, if Snowday wasn't covered, Bo would hit him, but the expectation was that Harvard was too well drilled to leave a man wide open downfield.

Red Roberts was switched from his left end position to right end, and his assignment was to take out the left side of the Harvard front wall, protecting Bo while he was running right. The Centre coaches had faith in Red's ability to take out more than one defender. The redhead would be the only interference needed on that side of the line.

Meanwhile, the rest of the Centre line, while starting right, was to then double back and begin to mow down the Harvard linemen. Bo, after the quick little faked pass to Snowday, was then to cut back and follow the wall of interference leading him on his run.

It was a designed play. A play that the Colonels had run many times in the week leading up to the game, but which there had been no evidence of in the practices in Fenway Park on Thursday, or at the Stadium on Friday.

It has been hinted at many times, but never conclusively proven, that Centre had a way to "send in" a play by the coaches. During this era, coaching from the sidelines was prohibited, unlike now, when nearly every offensive and defensive play is dictated by an offensive or defensive coordinator. If one were caught, a penalty would be marched off, and it was understood that any coaching from the sidelines just wouldn't occur.

Centre had a water bucket which was white, identified by widely spaced letters, C-E-N- T- R- E, painted in gold. Roscoe was in charge of the water bucket, and it was inferred that he would hear a whisper from Uncle Charlie instructing him to turn the bucket so that a certain letter pointed directly out in the direction where the Colonels were standing. "N" may mean an end sweep. "C" might indicate a pass. Whether the first play that Centre ran to start the 2nd half, after Centre had the ball on the Crimson 32, was called or not, will never be known for sure. But the possibility has entered into the lore of what happened next.

As the penalty was marched off, Bo got in a little "gamesmanship" by saying loudly enough for the Harvard squad to hear, "Now's our chance, be ready Terry," to his right halfback before turning back to huddle up.

When the Colonels were in the huddle, Bo said, "We've been playing our game. Everything's gone according to plan. Now it's time to spring the play, #17, the left cut-back."

The Boston "Advertiser" had a reporter sitting in the Centre section in the

Stadium. He heard a girl's voice say, "Oh Lord, give him speed!"

Up in the cement stand, a pale little bundle of nerves, yes blazing with excitement, gasped her plea for the success of the mighty McMillin.

Pretty Helen James of "down there in Danville," a typical Southern Belle with soft, drawny voice, did her bit as she tried to pray her team to victory.

Helen had no monopoly on the praying. She was joined by Mrs. Gus Covington, wife of the "Majah," and her daughter, Lucy.

"Oh Lord, give them courage." Mrs. Covington repeated the refrain as she grasped tightly the hand of her husband, or turned and embraced her daughter.

The girl, twisting and squirming, kept up a rapid-fire comment, punctuating her talk with a gasping "aha" or "oh," and wee little shrieks scarcely audible to her mother or to her handsome father.

"Oh Lord, give him speed!" prayed Helen James again. "Oh Lord, give him speed!"

The Gold and White lined up in an unbalanced line right, meaning that there were four men to the right of Ed Kubale, and two to his left, and Bo barked out the signals. A perfect Kubale center pass was fielded by Bo and he ran to his right, seeing Red Roberts take out the Crimson's left end and tackle, crumbling them both to the ground with a massive hit. Red then headed toward his next assignment, the Crimson safety, and batted him onto his back.

The Centre line brush-blocked the Harvard front wall, slanting right. Bo ran parallel to the line and pulled up for a splint second, looking at Terry Snowday who was running down and out, taking the Harvard secondary with him as planned.

Bo feigned a pass to Snowday and quickly reversed his field, now running to his left, again parallel to the line. At the same moment, the Colonels' linemen abruptly stopped their rightward drift and shifted their direction to the left, forming a wall for Bo to run behind.

Red had taken care of the Crimson's left end and tackle. Now Cregor, Gibson, Kubale, Jones and James began picking off Crimson linemen, one by one.

Bo was streaking toward the left side of the field, running at breakneck speed. He circled the Harvard right side, still heading toward the sideline, when his freshman right tackle, Minos Gordy, threw a block which brought the final Harvard lineman to the ground, and Bo broke right behind Gordy and the flattened Clark Macomber.

Bo had clear sailing! But he wasn't yet home free.

Two Crimson defenders had figured out the play and were running to their right, trying to cut Bo off before he could swing his run directly toward the goal. Bo shifted the ball to his left arm, freeing up his right to use as a stiff-arm if needed. As he got to the 10 yard line, he pulled up for a split second and stiff-armed Edwin Gehrke, and the hard-charging Jewett Johnson slightly overshot the Colonel quarterback who then turned on his speed, streaking just inches inside the out of bounds marker toward the coveted end zone.

Just as Bo reached the goal line, he was hit from behind by Gehrke and Johnson, but his forward motion carried him safely over the chalk mark.

Centre had scored! Bo and his teammates had done it!

As Bo's run unfolded, every spectator in the stands had stood in near silence as the Colonels executed the perfect play. When they saw that he hadn't stepped out of bounds, and saw the officials with their arms in the air signaling a touchdown, a thunderous roar began which lasted a full four minutes. The little Centre throng danced in the aisles, but there was equal celebration throughout the stands. Even in the Harvard student body section, they were clapping appreciatively.

Herb Covington, from Mayfield, Kentucky, a freshman substitute on the Colonels' team, looked up in the stands where he knew his mother, father and sister, Lucy, were sitting. He saw them bouncing up and down, waving their pom-poms and screaming with joy.

Roscoe, on the Centre sideline, did a little strut, not a full blown cakewalk, but a spontaneous two steps forward, and two steps back— a strut, that's all you could call it.

Later, when Howard got back home, I asked him to tell me everything about the game, and especially about the play when Bo scored.

Howard told it so perfectly that I felt I was actually there. One thing I've always remembered was what he said about Roscoe.

The Centre bench was wild, with everyone jumping around and slapping each other on the back, pumping their fists in the air, and Howard said he just kept on concentrating on Roscoe who had this huge smile, and he was just strutting, back and forth, back and forth.

There wasn't a person there that day who was any happier than Roscoe. He was the greatest fellow, and the greatest fan that Centre could ever have.

I was on Main Street in front of Louis Mannini's newsstand, nervous as I could be. I couldn't stand still. I'd watch the board and listen to the call of the plays, and then have to try to walk down the street for a few minutes, especially if things weren't going well, but it wasn't easy to move around.

There must have been well over three or four thousand people filling the block of Main that was roped off. People were constantly trying to get closer to the chalk board so they could see better, and also so they could hear the results of the plays being called out.

When Centre scored, the street became one mass of cheering, clapping, whistling, nearly hysterical people.

Everybody was shouting, "We scored! Bo scored!"

I was as happy as everyone else, but also, I remembered that we had led the year before, and then Harvard got going and beat us, and there was still a lot of time left.

When Bo fell into the end zone, only 48 seconds had elapsed in the 3rd quarter.

There were still 29 minutes and 12 seconds of action left. The Colonels lined up for the extra point. It was going to be a kick with a holder, not a drop kick. Bo was to be the holder, and Tom Bartlett the kicker.

Ed Kubale centered perfectly to Bo who was so full of adrenaline after his touchdown run that his hands were visibly shaking as he tried to get the ball in position. The poor placement resulted in Bartlett hitting the ball off-center, and the kick wasn't close. It was 6-0.

The stands were still buzzing, everyone still on their feet, as the Colonels put the ball on their 40 for the kick-off to the Crimson.

The team could hear Army's words in their minds.

"If they don't score in the 1st quarter, we will win."

Indeed, Harvard hadn't scored. Now, with a 6-0 lead, would the team's captain have been prophetic?

Red Roberts made excellent contact and his kick was picked up by Chapin who was brought down at his own 25.

On the initial play, the fired-up Colonels gang-tackled the Crimson runner, Coburn, for a two yard loss. Chapin tried the right side of the Centre line and was brought down by "Baldy" Cregor, who fought off a block by Harvard's Kunhardt. The play resulted in a hard earned one yard.

The Centre contingent was joined by over half of the Stadium crowd in cheers for the Colonels' defensive play. Gehrke took a center pass from Frances Kernan and ran right up the middle, only to be brought down by a solid hit from Ed Kubale after a one yard gain. Three plays and the ball was exactly where it had started, with the Crimson now having 4th and 10 on their 25, and Harvard had to punt.

Chapin's boot was an excellent 45 yard effort and it was covered well. Centre ended up with the ball on its own 30. Snowday got the call and bucked ahead for one yard, but a flag was thrown for holding, and the penalty moved it back to the 15. Bartlett picked up five. Gehrke was injured on the play and replaced by Mitchell Gatwick.

Second down and 20 on the Colonels' 20. Bartlett picked up another eight. Third down and 12 on the 28. Bo then lined up the team to kick but instead sprinted around his right end for nine. He ended up three yards short of a 1st down, and Red Roberts had to punt it away.

Roberts got off a decent boot, good for 35 yards. Jewett Johnson caught the ball but couldn't advance it as Army was all over him.

Harvard had 1st down on its own 28. Centre was pumped sky high. Every member of the Gold and White was fighting with all of his strength, and cheering each other on.

"Hold them line," Bo shouted.

Army hollered to Baldy Cregor, "Play tough! Play tough! Play tough!"

The Crimson tried line plunges. Chapin got four over his right tackle. Coburn got another four before Ed Kubale brought him down. Kernan, the Harvard center, was shaken up on the play and Coach Fisher replaced him with Bradford.

While the substitution was being made, Centre huddled briefly. "It's 3rd and two. Give it everything you have. We've got to hold them!"

"Go in low, under the interference. We'll plug the holes. Let's go!"

The Colonels were so eager to stop the Harvard attack that a lineman jumped offside, giving the Crimson a first down on their own 41.

Tiny Maxwell shouted it out. "First down, Harvard!"

Chapin picked up five and Harvard had 2nd and five on its own 46. As the Crimson lined up, Army glanced down at Macomber's feet. The right end had his shoes pointing outward, and Army felt the play would come his way. Macomber indeed headed toward Army and turned, ready to haul in a pass from Jewett Johnson. Army cut in front of Macomber, timing his move perfectly, and picked off the toss, returning it to the 50 before he was tripped up. Another five yards was paced off for what was termed an illegal block, and the Colonels had the ball on the Harvard 45, first and 10.

Centre had stopped the mini-drive of the Crimson, and the tide really seemed to be turning in favor of the Colonels. Many had felt that the Centre score would wake up Harvard and the boys from Cambridge would now begin to turn it on as they had the previous year. The Crimson fans had great belief in the Harvard "System," which had produced such consistent results. Percy Haughton, the greatest coach in the history of Harvard football, had introduced a systematic approach to produce winning teams, and Coach Robert Fisher had continued the evolution of what Haughton had begun in 1908. The two men had a combined record of 93-7-7 going into the Centre game.

The famous sports writer, Grantland Rice, spoke of "The System" in his "Sportlight" column.

In the first place, just what is this mysterious ingredient that is known as the "Harvard System?"

It is the winning menu which Percy Haughton devised over 10 years ago, and which, because of its inherent soundness, had endured under the capable direction of Coach Robert Fisher.

Its main groups follow—

(1)   The development of quarterback generalship to a high degree.

(2)   The complete use of the quarterback for putting the generalship into effect upon the field, where the day's strategy may be almost his permanent assignment.

(3)   Almost perfect use of every moment of practice for the development of fundamentals and team play. All waste has been removed.

(4)   Special preparation for the kicking and passing game.

(5)   A mixture of deception with power and speed.

(6)   The type of preparation that doesn't over train, but leaves each man keen for the contest, rather than weary of work.

In this way, Harvard comes as close to getting 100% out of its material as any university in the land.

It is all perfect organization, psychologically and instructively in the soundest manner.

Individual Harvard material may at times be ordinary, but there have been no ordinary Harvard teams for over 10 years.

When Harvard is beaten, it is by a better team. She has developed no habit of beating herself.

Excluding ties, Harvard had a 93% winning record during the Haughton-Fisher years. Crimson fans had come to expect a victory when they entered the Stadium. The fact that Centre had scored and was up 6-0 wasn't really that alarming, at least not yet.

With the penalty marked off, play resumed with Centre having 1st and 10 on its own 45. On the first play, with several defenders clutching at him, Bo evaded the rush and hit Terry Snowday over the middle. Snowday leaped high in the air and snagged the ball and fell to the ground on the 37. Red Roberts was shifted to fullback and plowed forward for seven yards, easily getting the 1st down. The Crimson defenders never got Red to the ground, but the whistle was blown when they stopped his forward motion.

It was 1st down on the Harvard 30.

The small Centre contingent danced around the stands as the Centre "5" played a snappy march in short segments. Each time the little jazz band stopped, the Colonels' fans would shout, "Fight!" Then a couple more bars and, "Fight!"

Soon it appeared that half the Stadium crowd was joining in.

Fight!
Fight!
Fight!

The Crimson team tried to regroup as time was called for a moment to get Frank Rubarth into the line, replacing Dick Gibson. It was third freshman that Tiny Thornhill and Uncle Charlie had used at right guard. Bill Shadoan had started. He was replaced by Gibson, and now Rubarth reported in to Tiny Maxwell.

Bo shouted out the signals above the roar of the crowd and a quick charging Friske Brown broke through from his right guard position and cut Bo down three yards behind the line of scrimmage. A flag was thrown for offensive holding and the ball was marched all the way back to the 48.

It was now 2nd and 28. Bo tried to get the lost yardage back by going to the air. He ran right and pulled up and fired a pass toward Tom Bartlett, but Bradford cut in front of the receiver and intercepted the throw. He was brought down on his own 35, but another penalty on the Colonels, this time for five yards, resulted in the ball being placed on the Harvard 40 yard line, 1st and 10, Crimson.

Harvard now sent in Henry Grew to replace left guard Charles Hubbard, the coaches wanting fresh legs across from Frank Rubarth.

Centre played even more ferocious defense as Harvard tried to mount a drive. Gatwick was hit hard and could only pick up two. Coburn fired toward a hole between his center and left guard. Rubarth and Kubale, two freshmen, brought him down after another hard-earned two yards. Coburn took the snap again and Bill James rushed over from his right end position and tackled him after still another two yard gain.

It was 4th and four. Centre had held, and held convincingly. The crowd now seemed to sense that they were seeing something special. The little band of Gold and White warriors was playing with emotion and confidence. Harvard, mighty Harvard, had been stopped and momentum definitely seemed to be with the Colonels.

Later, Bo was quoted as saying, "We could just feel it. After we stopped them cold, after the interception and penalty, we felt we could keep them off the scoreboard. To a man, we just had that conviction that we were going to win."

Harvard lined up on its own 46 and Chapin got off an excellent punt. Centre wasn't able to make any yardage on the return, and the Colonels found themselves deep in their own territory, on the 17. Army had been hit hard on the punt, and got up slowly with a pronounced limp. Time was called. The Centre captain tried to stay in the game, but he was having such pain in his hip that he couldn't continue. The officials conferred with the Centre bench, and it was determined that Bo would be acting captain until, or if, Army could return.

Freshman Herb Covington, a fast 5'6" halfback weighing 155 lbs., from Mayfield, in Western Kentucky, also Bo's backup at quarterback, reported into the Centre lineup. Uncle Charlie had the choice of several experienced backs to send in for the injured Colonels' captain. However, he saw that Covington was already warming up as Army was being helped from the field. Later, the Centre coach stated, "I picked Covington because I could see how much he wanted to go in. He was warming up and ready. It just seemed like the smart thing to do."

Covington's parents and beautiful sister Lucy had taken the Illinois Central Railroad from Mayfield to Louisville, and then came over to Danville through Lexington on the Southern Railroad to get on the train carrying the team and fans to Boston.

Herb Covington was appearing in only his 3rd college game, and now he was in the most important contest that Centre had ever played. There were 50,000 people who watched him sprint out onto the field. No one was more nervous and excited than his sister, Lucy.

Lucy had become somewhat of a celebrity in Boston since her arrival. A photograph of her taken with one of the green Centre blankets wrapped around her, with the gold letters clearly spelling Centre, appeared in the Boston "Post." Lucy had her gloved arm raised and was smiling into the camera.

The caption read, "Who wouldn't play football for a maid like her?"

Another "Post" photograph appeared on the front page, under "Dixie Day at the Stadium," on Saturday morning before the game. Lucy was standing next to her mother and two other ladies, all decked out and ready to go to the big event.

The "Post" also published a photograph of the Centre fans in that same edition. The Kentuckians were posed in front of the Lenox, and of course, Lucy was right in there with the crowd. Not to be outdone, the Boston "Herald" had a composite photo, four columns wide, with the Centre eleven and Uncle Charlie at the top and Lucy, below, smiling and holding a spread-out Centre blanket. The heading above the picture was, "Centre's Lineup, and One of the Incentives."

Lucy had almost cheered herself hoarse since the game began. She stood nearly constantly, if jumping about can be called standing. Her voice was raspy, but sometimes she could get out a loud squeal. With Army out, it would be up to her brother, "Herbie" to his sister, to pick up the slack.

Army hadn't run up a lot of impressive statistics. He'd only carried the ball a couple of times, neither time for significant yardage. His defense and intercepted pass had been important, but it was in his overall quiet, confident leadership where he excelled.

Army played without any desire for glory. It was always for the team. If a hole needed to be plugged on defense, Army would plug it. If a block needed to be made, Army would get it done. Often it was said of the team's captain that he did more with less apparent effort than any man who had ever worn a Centre uniform.

Now, it was expecting a lot to send a freshman out into the big horseshoe and hope that he was up to the task of replacing Army Armstrong.

On the first play from Centre's own 17, Herb Covington stepped up to the plate. The little speedster streaked around the left end for 10 yards, just enough to pick up a 1st down. On the next play, Covington's number was called again and he raced around the opposite end for seven before being tripped up. It was 2nd and three, on the Colonels' 34. Lucy Covington squealed, danced, jumped and hugged anyone she could reach.

"Herbie! Herbie! Go, Herbie!"

A 3rd straight effort by "Herbie" picked up one yard. Third down and two.

Bo called a play with a fake to Covington, but this time Bartlett took the ball and hurled himself at the Crimson defenders. The Centre fullback wasn't to be denied and got the two yards with just inches to spare after the chains were brought out for measurement. It was 1st and 10 near the Colonels' 38 yard line.

Bo brought his team out of the huddle, having observed that Harvard still seemed to be employing a spread-out defense, always continuing to protect against the possible pass. Bo lined up the Colonels in a passing formation but instead sent Tom Bartlett through the left side of the line, through a big hole opened by crunching blocks by Minos Gordy and Red Roberts.

Bartlett wasn't touched as he raced over the Colonels' 40, cut slightly left and crossed midfield, then avoided a Crimson defender with a slight shift to his right. It looked like he was going all the way to the goal when a last gasp, diving tackle by a Harvard defensive back brought the Owensboro, Kentucky native down on the Harvard 30.

The run had been good for 32 yards. Covington picked up a quick five yards on the next play, and Centre had 2nd down on the 25. Coach Fisher and the Harvard staff ran in some substitutes. Their team had been on the defensive most of the 3rd quarter, and it was decided to get a couple of linemen replaced. Richard Fields came in for left end Henry Covington Janin, and Benont Lockwood relieved Philip Kunhardt.

On the next play, Bo called one of the few trick plays of the afternoon for his team. Again, there was speculation that Uncle Charlie may have called the play with Roscoe sending in the signal via a turn of the water bucket, but no one ever knew for certain.

Bo took the center from Ed Kubale and Tom Bartlett faded out to the left flank. Bo hit Bartlett who never took another step but rather turned and faced downfield, spotting Terry Snowday 10 yards down on the right side. The Harvard secondary had momentarily headed toward Bartlett, expecting him to run after having caught the pass, and Snowday was left open.

Bartlett fired a bullet across the field. Snowday caught it and tucked it in safely and streaked toward the goal. Philip Coburn raced over from his halfback position, dove under Snowday, and brought him down on the 11.

Everyone was on their feet when Tiny Maxwell, sounding like the title of the Ralph Paine novel, placed the ball a yard back from the 10 yard marker and shouted, "First down, Centre!" The whistle blew to end the 3rd quarter.

Centre had totally dominated during the period. People were buzzing. How could this be happening? Centre wasn't expected to be able to play competitively with Harvard. The pre-game predictions had been that Harvard would win easily, and even be able to rest the starters in the second half, saving then for the upcoming Princeton game. But the Colonels were not only playing equally, they were somewhat manhandling the Crimson.

Harvard had never been able to get past midfield in the entire 15 minutes. The Colonels had gained 139 yards during the quarter, Harvard, a mere 21.

Centre picked up four first downs. Harvard had but one, and that was aided by a penalty. But most importantly, Centre had scored, and after 45 minutes of play, the score stood 6-0. Again, the question was being asked, "Who are those guys, anyway?"

Howard said it was the greatest quarter of football he'd ever seen. Both teams fought with all of their might. There were no easy tackles. Even with all of the cheering going on, you could hear leather on leather popping as pads hit pads.

One thing that Howard said really stuck with me, and has to this day. Whenever a Colonel was tackled, a Harvard hand was there to help him off the ground. Whenever a Harvard player was tackled, a Colonel was there to help him to his feet.

If someone was slow in getting up, the players on the other team wouldn't just stare off into space like most teams do when an opponent is injured. Instead, they'd gather around, as close as the refs would let them, hoping that the injury wasn't too serious.

When Army had to leave the game, several Harvard players came over as he was limping off the field and patted him on the back and told him how well he had played.

It was that kind of game, and both teams were made up of those kinds of guys.

261

FOURTH QUARTER

Harvard used the break between quarters to send in more fresh players. For the first time, Captain Keith Kane got into the action, replacing Alexander Ladd at left tackle. Winnie Churchill subbed for Mitchell Gatwick in the backfield. Charles Buell replaced the quarterback, Jewett Johnson.

Since the second half had begun, Harvard had made eight substitutions. Centre made but two, Rubarth for Gibson in the line, and Covington for the injured Armstrong. The Centre coaches later said they felt their team was so well conditioned that their starters could play another full quarter just as well as they had played the first three. Unless there was an injury, the Centre team on the turf would end the game with the same eleven which was now switching ends of the field in order to start the final 15 minutes of play.

Tiny Thornhill's line had been well-served by the rotation of first Bill Shadoan, then Richard Gibson, and finally Frank Rubarth at the right guard position. The rest of the front wall looked as fresh as it had on the opening play of the game.

Bill James was everywhere, as was Ben Cregor. George "Buck" Jones showed no sign of slowing down, nor did Minos Gordy. Ed Kubale was not only having an excellent game on offense at the important center slot, but he was holding his position on defense, and had come up with several unassisted tackles.

Fans always appreciated Terry Snowday for his addition to the Colonels' offense, whether in the backfield or at end. However, like Army, his play was almost effortless, and it would be after the game, when an analysis was made, that coaches and fans alike would realize that the Owensboro native had played his position perfectly, and it was a rare end sweep that was able to get outside of Snowday due to his speed.

And then there was Red Roberts. If there ever was an example of a "man amongst boys," it was true regarding Red during the second Centre-Harvard game. During the 1920 contest, fans and writers felt he had been oversold insofar as his abilities on the gridiron. They had felt he was "fat;" it was written that he was "slow;" it was said he was "sluggish." The truth was that Red had suffered such a severe knee injury early in the game that his real abilities were never displayed. The very fact that he was able to continue at all was due to his dedication to the team. Red had no doubt torn a cartilage, and had probably strained, if not torn, ligaments. His knee had so much internal bleeding that he could hardly bend it, yet despite the pain and despite his relative immobility, he continued to play, and actually didn't miss a minute.

Now, it was different. It was a totally fit Red who was on the field. He was a horse when Centre had the ball, taking two or even three defenders out on each play. On defense, whether he lined up at end or tackle, runners came his way at their peril.

Red loved to hit. He played cleanly, never getting a penalty. But when he hit somebody, they knew they had run into the best that Kentucky had to offer.

Red took off his white silk scarf after the first few plays of the game, and his flaming red hair was even more prominent. It seemed that every time there was a pile-up, as the players got to their feet, Red would usually be the one on the bottom as they untangled.

Tiny Maxwell blew the whistle to begin the last quarter. There were but 15 minutes to play, 15 minutes between the Centre College "Praying Colonels" reaching the goal that they had dedicated themselves to since leaving Soldiers Field on that late afternoon of October 23, 1920.

The ball was on the 11 yard line. The Colonels were facing the permanent, enclosed portion of the horseshoe. They had moved the ball from their own 17, the drive now having eaten up 72 yards.

Bo, now Captain McMillin, with Army still on the sidelines, brought his team up to the line of scrimmage to begin the 4th quarter. Bo was caught by the Crimson's Bradford as he tried to slice through the left side of the line. Second and nine on the 10. Terry Snowday could only get one additional yard on the next play. It was 3rd and eight on the nine. Centre had two plays left. The Colonels had to move eight yards, just inside the one yard line, for a 1st down. Of course, nine yards would have resulted in a touchdown.

Bo thought he could get inside the minds of the Harvard defensemen. He knew exactly what would have been expected of him on his next call. The obvious tactic would have been to play conservatively, hoping to pop a runner through the line for a score. If the run was not successful, there would still be a down left to attempt what should be a simple, chip-shot of a field goal, which would make it 9-0, Centre.

Harvard would then have to score, kick the extra point, and add a field goal to go up 10-9. Bo made probably his only unwise decision during what was an otherwise perfectly called game, and again, it is possible that Uncle Charlie, through Roscoe, actually "sent in" the play. With Harvard lined up to stop the expected run, Bo called out the signals for a quick pass to Terry Snowday as his end cut behind the Crimson linebackers who were stunted close behind their front wall. The pass was wide and fell into the end zone, untouched.

It was the worse possible outcome for the Colonels. The referee signaled a touchback, and Centre lost possession of the ball. Harvard now had the ball, 1st and 10 on its own 20. (It is necessary to clearly understand the rules regarding touchbacks that were used in the era of the Centre-Harvard game. Here is exactly how Rule VI, Section XV, read regarding the pass that fell into the end zone: *It is a touchback when a forward pass crosses either the end line (goal line) or side line extended; when it strikes the goal posts or cross bar, or when it touches the ground within the end zone.*)

Bo's pass crossed the goal line and touched the ground within the end zone, thus clearly being a touchback. Present day rules would have made the incompletion simply be just that, and the Colonels would have 4th down, and they could have attempted the field goal.

Bo felt that the Crimson would see that a pass was so unlikely because it could (and did) result in a touchback, that he could surprise his opponents and score. He knew the math. If Centre settled for the field goal, Harvard might still have life since there was still enough time left in the last quarter, and a 9-0 lead could have been overcome by a TD, extra point, and field goal. He had to remember how the Crimson had fought back against Penn State.

However, the way the Colonels were playing defense, 9-0 would have looked awfully good.

When play resumed, Harvard went on the attack, cheered on by their many fans. It was beginning to get serious out there, with their team still down and the game into the final period.

Meanwhile, Centre's little group of fans was constantly growing as more and more of the 50,000 plus in the Stadium were developing even greater appreciation of the boys from Kentucky.

On the first play after the touchback, Chapin went through the center of the line and was met hard by Ben Cregor. Chapin got only one yard. Winnie Churchill then drove over his right tackle for seven before Terry Snowday brought him down. It was 3rd and two on the Crimson 28. Buell then picked up the 1st down by hitting Churchill on a short pass and the ball was marked just over the 30.

Harvard had decided to open up its attack with Buell and Churchill in the backfield. On the 1st down play, Buell hit Churchill on the left flank but the swarming Centre defense immediately engulfed him and threw him for a yard loss.

"Way to cover," Army hollered from the sidelines. The Centre captain wanted desperately to get back in the game, but he was noticeably limping as he followed the action from the sidelines. Eager or not, Army was through for the afternoon.

Churchill got the call on the 2nd down play but bobbled the center pass and just made it to the line of scrimmage before he disappeared under a mass of gold jerseys. It was 3rd and 11, right on the 30.

Buell then completed a short pass to Churchill, but Red Roberts raced over from his end position and hit the Crimson back hard, and he fell to the ground, fortunate to hold onto the ball. Red helped the stunned little thoroughbred up, and patted him on the helmet. Churchill had gotten only six very hard-earned yards, and the ball was five yards short from a first down.

The Crimson had to punt. Centre had held! It was an important possession. After the disappointment of not putting even a field goal on the board, and after the touchback, it may have seemed natural to let up a bit. But instead, the Colonels played all the harder.

As Uncle Charlie repeated constantly when speaking to his team, "It is a manly game."

Churchill put his punt high in the air and it was caught cleanly by Covington on his 30 yard line. Centre was setting up a wall of interference to lead little Covey down the right side of the field and he cut back to the 28, attempting to fall in behind his blockers, but a streaking Harvard defender broke through, caught Covington on the 28, and brought him down. It was 1st down for the Colonels on their own 28.

"Herbie! Herbie!" Lucy Covington squealed when her brother fired around his left end and brought the ball up to the 36. However, his eight yard gain was negated by a holding penalty and the ball was marched back 15 yards from the line of scrimmage, and the Colonels were dangerously deep in their own territory at the 13.

Again, it was Covington who had his number called and he got back nine of the 15 yard penalty.

"Herbie! Herbie!"

Coach Fisher sent in Joseph Hartley for right end Clark Macomber, the 9th substitution of the half by the Crimson.

Red Roberts quick-kicked on 2nd down hoping to get a good roll and put Harvard back well into its own territory. The punt only traveled to the Crimson 45 and took a high bounce and an alert Buell hauled it in, pivoted, and picked up 10 yards before Covington wrestled him to the ground.

"Herbie! Herbie!"

The Centre fans picked up on the cheer and it was, "Herbie! Herbie!" all around Lucy.

The Crimson had good field position as they lined up on the Colonels' 45. Bo was all over the field, shouting to his teammates.

"We've got to hold! Go Cajun! Go Baldy! Fight, Bill James! Fight!"

If there was one man Bo knew would die in the trenches, fighting with his last ounce of strength, it was Bill James. The two had begun their football careers together at North Side High in Fort Worth and both had the dream which the Chief had instilled in them back in Fort Worth.

"You can be somebody. You can achieve great things. But you've got to believe. Believe! Believe!"

Now it was Bo shouting to his teammates.

"Believe! Believe! We are Centre!"

The Crimson began their attack and Winnie Churchill got two before Tom Bartlett cut him down. A 2nd attempt got three and it was 3rd and five on the Colonels' 40.

Henry Clark came in for Bradford, the 10th Harvard substitution of the 2nd half. It was as if Harvard was determined to wear down Centre by sheer numbers.

Uncle Charlie stuck with his men. It was a football variation of, "You dance with the one who brought you." The players on the field had brought the team this far, and unless there was an injury, those same Colonels would be on the field when the final whistle blew.

Centre was penalized five yards on the next play for having jumped offsides, and after the measurement, Tiny Maxwell signaled that the Crimson had a 1st down, with the ball now resting on the 35. Coburn ran for four and after he was brought down, Harvard sent in Wesley Goodwin Blocker for Fiske Brown, the 11th substitute. It was 2nd and six on the Colonels' 31.

Vinton Chapin got the center pass and tried to go through Centre's right side. Bill James fought off a block and he and Terry Snowday threw him for a yard loss. Now it was 3rd and seven on the 32. Time was running down. Harvard had two plays to pick up seven yards for a 1st down, 32 yards to score.

Buell led his team out of the huddle and called the signals. After the center toss, the Crimson quarterback ran a couple of steps right and then reversed and fired a perfect pass back across the field to Winnie Churchill, who had drifted out in the left flank. The Harvard back tucked the ball under his left arm and instantly saw that his field was blocked by converging gold jerseys. Churchill headed right, diagonally across the field, racing toward Centre's goal.

Over the 30, past the 25, then the 20, the little back turning on the speed.

When Churchill reached the 10, it looked like he would score. Bo was frantically chasing him, trying to cut him off, having a slight angle. Bo desperately lunged at the five and barely wrapped his outstretched arms around Churchill's ankles, and the effort brought him down on the 3.

Bo had saved the day, at least for a moment. But there was plenty of time for Harvard to score, and as Bo lay sprawled on the ground, he bowed his head and pounded his fists into the grass.

There wasn't a spectator in the Stadium who wasn't on their feet, cheering for their team. The Harvard supporters were certain that their team could take it in. The fans in the Centre section were screaming their encouragement, but there was sudden doubt and despair at the turn of events.

"Hold them! Hold Them!"

Just as suddenly as the tide had seemed to turn, everyone watched with a bit of confusion as Bo suddenly jumped to his feet and ran up the field to the line of scrimmage, where the play had begun. Bo slumped down on his knees on the grass, his arms thrust into the air as if to be saluting the Almighty. There was a flag on the play!

Head linesman E.C. Taggert had been focusing on the front wall of the two teams, looking for any infraction, looking for any false starts on either side of the line of scrimmage. Taggert saw a Crimson lineman lunge forward just a split second before the ball was centered, and threw his flag.

Tiny Maxwell trotted over to Taggert and the two consulted briefly. Then the giant referee lumbered down to the three yard line, picked up the ball, ran it back to the 32, and marched off a five yard penalty for Harvard's offsides play.

The huge roar from the stands which erupted after Churchill's great run had died down, but an even greater outbreak of cheers, screams, and whistles echoed throughout the packed horseshoe as Maxwell marched off the penalty.

The Centre fans were delirious. It had been a roller-coaster moment, going from, "Hold them!" to "Oh, no!" to "They're marching it back!"

Harvard still maintained possession of the ball, but instead of 1st and goal on the three, it was 3rd and 12 on the 37. The fans continued a deafening roar, still on their feet. Both benches had every player cheering their team on to an even greater effort.

"Hold them, Colonels!"

"Go Crimson! Go!"

After the penalty, Harvard had no recourse but to continue passing. The Crimson needed 12 quick yards, and time was getting short. Buell again went to Churchill, but the Centre secondary was expecting a pass, and batted down the throw.

"One more play!"

"Let's go guys! Be alert!"

"They have to pass! They have to throw it! One more play!"

Bo said later that he was literally trembling with excitement.

"Could this actually be happening?"

He looked up in the stands and tried to capture the moment so that he could relive it later by just closing his eyes and seeing the images again, and again; the 50,000 spectators standing and screaming, the sounds of the Centre "5" once again blasting out little segments and hearing the fans shout, "Fight!"

Bo looked at his teammates, all wide-eyed, all caught up in the moment, and he shouted as loudly as he could, "One more play! One more play! One more play!" Charles Buell and Harvard still had one last chance.

On 4th down, Buell heaved the ball toward the Colonels' goal, sort of a "Hail Mary" type effort, hoping against hope that it would find the hands of a Crimson receiver. Tom Bartlett was determined that the pass wouldn't connect. He was playing deep and was perfectly positioned to grab the spiral out of the air and safely hold onto it, his goal to simply return it without fumbling.

The Crimson was still giving it every effort, and several raced over and downed Bartlett, but not before Tom got out to the 23.

"Ok," Bo shouted as the Colonels huddled to go on the offense. "We need a couple of 1st downs, and we should be able to run out the clock. No fumbles! Hold onto the ball! No fumbles!"

Bo decided to run the next three plays himself. He got five, then two, and on 3rd and three, he barely picked up the 1st down. The clock continued to run. It was 1st and 10 just over the Colonels' own 33. Bo knew that Harvard was keying on him so decided to mix it up and called Terry Snowday's number. Terry sliced through the left side of the Colonels' line, as Red Roberts, Minos Gordy and "Buck" Jones led the way. The effort was good for nine yards, and the ball was placed on the 42. Bo hollered out to Red. "Big fellow, you get us a 1st down and the game is ours!"

Red and Bartlett swapped positions. Red ran right up the center of the line and crashed into Richard Fields. Harvard was still playing tough, but Fields couldn't keep Red from picking up the yard needed, and it was another 1st down for Centre on the 43. The Colonels were driving, just as hard as they had at the beginning of the game.

Herb Covington ran right, holding carefully onto the ball, being careful not to cough it up. Keith Kane made the tackle. The run picked up a yard, but just as importantly, it ate up some clock. Bo gained another yard over left tackle, again, clutching the ball tightly. The clock ticked on.

It seemed appropriate that it was Covington who got the assignment on the next call. He skirted around the right end for five yards, and after being brought down he placed the ball near the midfield line.

Tiny Maxwell trotted over, blowing his whistle, and picked up the ball and turned to Bo. Tiny had been in the dressing room the year before when Arnold Horween, the Harvard captain, tried to give the game ball to Bo, and Bo had said he couldn't accept it, but would rather come back and earn it by winning.

"Mr. McMillin, here is your ball!"

Bo didn't exactly understand. His heart was pounding as he glanced up at the ponderous referee.

"The game is over," Maxwell said. He had a big smile on his face.

"As I said, Mr. McMillin, here is your ball!" And he handed the ball to—"Mr. McMillin." Bo hugged the ball and began to run in circles, jumping and whooping and hollering to his teammates.

"We did it! We did it! We beat Harvard! We did it!"

Lucy Covington and her parents headed for the field along with the rest of the Kentuckians. They were almost knocked over as swarms of fans raced onto the turf. The first group headed for Bo and soon had him on their shoulders. He held the ball high with both hands and continued to shout, "We won! We beat Harvard!"

Bo's cheers were drowned out by thousands of voices.

"You did it! You did it! Hey Bo, you did it! You beat Harvard!"

Lucy ran around the field looking for her brother and finally spotted him where a group of admirers had elevated him up on their shoulders, hollering, "Herbie! Herbie!"

There are moments in your life, maybe not so many, but certain moments which are so defining that they are just seared into your memory—made permanent-distant memories, perhaps, but they seem like they happened just yesterday. You can close your eyes and see the scenes and hear the voices clearly. You can actually feel the emotions again, like they were just occurring.

Every time I think about Centre beating Harvard, it's like I was on Main Street again on that October afternoon in 1921.

The ticker tape at W.L. Lyons was in their office over the Shop Perfect. It was sort of a contest to see who could get the results out on the street first.

Louis Mannini would be ahead for awhile, and then the brokerage house would take the lead. Toward when everybody knew it must be near the end of the game, the fellow getting the results at W.L. Lyons was a play ahead of Louis Mannini's announcer.

A big cheer went up from those who were closest to the Shop Perfect, and people began to shout, "We won! We won!"

But those of us who were in front of the newsstand down the block wanted to hear the next play. It was like, "Did we win, really?"

And how did the game end?

So we all pushed forward a little, really squeezed in, straining to see, straining to hear, so excited I was literally shaking.

I remember it so well.

"Bo gains."

"Covington gains."

"The game is over! Centre wins!"

And the place went crazy. I mean—crazy!

Ten thousand people massed on the turf in the Stadium. The Centre players had no chance to get to the locker room. Soon every one of the Colonels who had played was riding on a mass of humanity, being carried around the field.

It was a demonstration like Bostonians had never seen. It was a demonstration unique in the history of the Stadium. Never had a team been treated with such enthusiasm and love.

It was pandemonium, a wild, non-stop celebration. People were screaming, whistling. clapping, jumping up and down, spinning around, trying to get to each of the Colonels to touch them and shout their congratulations.

The Harvard student body section sat quietly, watching the bedlam on the field. After a few minutes, even the Crimson's most ardent supporters joined the throng out on the grass. It wasn't that they hadn't appreciated Centre. It was just that they didn't know how to act. Most of them hadn't even been enrolled the last time that their team had suffered a defeat.

Slowly, the mass of humanity, with the Centre players aloft, wound out of the field, around the openings at the ends of the wooden bleachers, toward the locker room. Behind them the goal posts were being rocked back and forth by M.I.T. students and finally brought to the ground.

Lucy Covington and her parents finally caught up with the group carrying "Herbie" and he managed to work his way over to his family where they embraced, all with tears filling their eyes.

"We love you son, and are so proud of you," his parents shouted.

Lucy couldn't speak but just hugged her brother until he finally had to break away and head to the dressing room. As Covington darted in and out of the admiring crowd, he received innumerable pats on the back, shaking hands as he ran, hardly believing that he had been a part, a big part actually, of the great Centre victory.

The locker room was full of sportswriters who were trying to get a quote for their stories. Bo kept saying that his winning touchdown run had only been made possible by his teammates.

"It was a set play. Everybody did their job. Did you see the blocking I got? Red, Army, Terry, all of the line, and you see that freshman over there, Minos T. Gordy, Abbeville, Louisiana? He took out the end. All I did was run the play like Unc designed it."

It was typical Bo, and it was typical Centre. Eleven men play as one, and nobody can beat you. As the writers continued to question Bo, one asked him, "Exactly how do you feel right at this moment?"

Bo replied, "I am the happiest man in the world."

It was a quote that made its way into the write-ups about the game in newspapers all across the country.

Bob Fisher came in, just as the Crimson leader had done the year before when his team was victorious. Fisher had been at the helm for 25 games prior to meeting the Colonels for the second time. His record was 22-0-3. The loss to Uncle Charlie and Centre was the first time he had ever experienced a defeat in his coaching career.

Fisher showed his class, typical of the entire Harvard staff. He was as gracious in defeat as he had been in victory.

"I want to congratulate you Coach Moran. You're team played wonderful ball. They outplayed us all the way, and furthermore, they played clean and hard all the way."

Later, Bob Fisher handed out a statement.

"I extend my heartiest congratulations to the Centre College team. They played a clean game, a good game, and showed that they were a well-drilled team. In Bo McMillin, Centre had a man who was probably the hardest in the country to stop. The Harvard men in today's game gave the very best they had."

Eddie Mahan came into the dressing room and sought out Uncle Charlie. The two had gotten close enough that they were on a first name basis.

"I want to congratulate you Charlie. It is the biggest thing in the world for Centre College." The former Harvard superstar also went around complimenting the individual Colonels on their outstanding play.

The sports editor of the New York "Tribune" said to Army that it was the most spectacular game he had ever covered, and Army asked that the men on the sidelines who hadn't gotten into the game not be forgotten.

"And please say something about the men back home who didn't get to make the trip, the red-shirted third squad that took their punishment out on the practice field each day. They were down at the Danville station when the train pulled out, and they were the leaders in the cheering, yet people wonder why Centre turns out a team like we have. It is because we pray and fight and love each other like brothers, and it is this spirit that gets us over even the biggest barriers."

Graduate Manager Fred Moore, Harvard class of 1894, came into the locker room, and after going around the room congratulating Uncle Charlie, Tiny Thornhill and the players, sought out the Chief.

"We want to play your team next year. Of course, McMillin will be gone, but that line of yours will be back."

It was good news obviously, but the next thing that Moore did was nearly as pleasing. He pulled out the check for $8,000 that Centre had been guaranteed, and then produced a blank check and paid Centre another $2,000. Certainly Harvard could afford to be generous. The game had been a huge moneymaker, but the additional payout wasn't part of the contract, and further cemented the great relationship between the two schools.

It was difficult with all of the writers and well-wishers in the locker room, but the squad finally was able to shower and dress for the return to the Lenox. They stuffed their duffel bags full of their equipment. Several of the reserves didn't have a jersey to stuff. They had literally sold the shirts off their backs to people massed around them after the game. Offers of up to $50.00 were hard to turn down, and money and jerseys changed hands as the players made their way to the locker room.

When the team was finally able to clear the dressing room, they weren't prepared for what awaited them. It seemed that hardly any of the crowd had dispersed. A huge mass of cheering fans surrounded the two team buses, and it was difficult to get through the crowd in order to board. Several members of the Harvard team were next to the buses, clapping as the Colonels came near.

Hump Tanner and I were Phi Delts. He was a couple of years ahead of me. Once, when we were sitting around talking, he told me that the Harvard game was the greatest moment of his life. He said that as much as he and all of the team wanted to beat Harvard, and they had certainly worked for a year to win that game, as much as they wanted to win, they were also sorry that Harvard had to lose. They had developed such a respect for the Harvard boys that it seemed a shame that they couldn't have won also. Our boys always cheered for Harvard when they were playing anybody else.

The bus drivers had to inch along. Howard Reynolds joined the team on one of the buses. It seemed to take forever to make just a few feet of progress. When the buses finally got going, nobody could believe what they saw out on the Anderson Memorial Bridge that crossed the Charles. People were lined shoulder to shoulder, several deep, waving and cheering as the buses turned right, heading back into Boston. All along the road for several blocks, waving hands and smiling faces greeted the team as they drove along.

Never, it was reported, had a team been so captivating, and never had a team so captivated, the supposedly reserved citizens of Boston. The team was so emotionally overwhelmed that most just sat silently, waving to the crowds, holding back tears, as they slowly made their way back to the Lenox.

Howard Reynolds, writing under the pseudonym, Mona Mour, attempted to get his readers to understand exactly how the crowd had embraced the Colonels. His story was wired back to the Louisville "Courier-Journal", and appeared under the headline:

"YOU-ALLS," 99% STRONG, SUCCUMB TO "WE-ALLS"

Boston, Mass., Oct. 29—In the manner of speaking deemed characteristic by a certain Boston newspaperman who came North on the train with the Centre team, the crowd at the Harvard Stadium was made up of "you-alls" and "we-alls."

The "you-alls" comprised 99% of the crowd, pure Boston born, bred and buttered within the scent of Cambridge's glass flowers. The "we-alls" consisted of the remaining 1%, Kentuckians brought up with, perhaps, a more pungent aroma.

Be that as it may, a "wee drop" has more potency than a silver goblet of shaved ice. Not that the temper of the crowd was altogether frigid; rather, it was temperate, ready to cheer dutifully for the Crimson or, if the tide should turn, glad (even anxious) to yell for the plucky little Kentucky college which in a spirit of what to them was sheer bravado, seemed to think it could triumph over the incomparable majesty, sanguine Harvard.

It was the case of Carpentier and Dempsey all over again. Of course, both common sense and loyalty bade all good descendants of the Mayflower's passenger list to be for the upholder of power and patriotism; obviously, one was for the native born, and yet—

That "yet" grew more and more positive as the game progressed. After the victory, one

271

woman was overheard to remark to her neighbor: "Say Mary, I thought you were for Harvard."

"Well, I was in the beginning," responded Mary. "But now I just can't help being for Centre."

So sentiment grew and grew until the "Boston Tea Party" forgot themselves and behaved like a good old Kentucky Jubilee. Spectacled professors and feminine blue-stockings cheered in an altogether non-puritanical fashion as Roscoe cake-walked and pigeon-winged around the Stadium. Banners waved and hitherto scholastically pitched voices shouted themselves hoarse as the victors wrapped themselves in blankets whose emerald hue gave a false impression of barbaric ignorance.

Outside the gate, the small stock of chrysanthemums was sold at a premium while the larger supply of crimson carnations fell carelessly into the gutters. The peddlers gold armbands were quickly snatched and pinned on with the remark, "Aw, I was only bluffing. I knew all of the time that Centre was going to win. Why? Bo McMillin!"

Golden balloons fluttered triumphantly above the heads of the crowd. On the lips and in the hearts of all Boston was praise and glory of "we-alls."

When the final play was called out and we heard that Centre had won, Main Street just exploded and went crazy.

I remember the celebration back in Elizabethtown when the Great War ended. It didn't even come close to what happened in Danville.

The first thing I recall, besides all of the hollering and cheering and hugging and dancing around, was the sound of firecrackers. Someone started shooting them off and you could hear the "pop-pop-pops" and "booms" above the yelling of the crowd.

The people who had been inside Stout's Theater came running out and joined everyone else in celebrating.

Then it seemed like every church bell starting ringing. All of the churches were within a couple of blocks of Main Street. The Episcopal Church was near where we were standing, and the First Presbyterian was just two blocks down on Main, toward the campus. That's where we had chapel.

Soon there was "clang-clang, clang-clang" all over the area. I'll never forget how the bells just went on and on, and just when it seemed that one church would quit, someone else must have taken over the ropes because they never stopped ringing.

It seemed like everyone who owned a car started driving around honking their horns. Some people just sat by the curb and left their motors running and honked and honked.

The Danville fire station was just a block up from where Main Street was roped off, and here came the big, new, red Ahrens Fox #772 Model K fire truck which everyone was so proud of. Its siren was vigorously cranked and its bell was ringing. It couldn't get through because of all the people massed in the street, so it just drove around the rest of the downtown, siren blaring, and the firemen who were on it helped some of the K.C.W. girls get up on the truck and let them ride around with them.

There was a run on any stores which sold paint, and it seemed that everyone wanted to paint the score all over Danville. C6-H0 was everywhere, on store windows, on the curbs, on the sides of buildings, everywhere.

The water tower across from Breck Hall had C6-H0 painted in big figures on it. The front of the gym, and even Old Centre, had the score painted on the bricks, and when I took my son to Centre in the fall of 1959, I walked him over to the gym and showed him the score which was still there nearly 40 years later.

The strangest thing that I remember was that a cow had C6-H0 painted on both of its sides. It was an old dairy cow, and there was a boy riding it up and down the street.

The celebration went on into the night. People continued milling around. A bunch of us waited in front of the "Messenger" office to get the first papers that were printed.

When we saw one of the newsboys come out carrying a stack of papers, we all rushed to buy a copy. I still have my paper after all of these years. It had a big, bold headline:

CENTRE,6   HARVARD,0

The whole front page was a play-by-play of the game, just like it had come over the wires. I took my copy back to my room and read every line over and over, just imagining how the game was played. I could hear the bells ringing, far into the night.

In Somerset, Kentucky, an equally boisterous celebration began. Somerset had quite a personal interest in the Colonels. Red Weaver had played there, along with Bo. Red Roberts was born and played there, and now was a star in Danville, and Bill Shadoan was a native. Royce Flippin, another Somerset boy, hadn't played against Harvard, but was on the travel squad, and watched the game from the sidelines.

The "Messenger" had a correspondent in Somerset who sent newsworthy items to the paper.

Doubtless since my last wire, many events of interest have taken place in our city. Naturally, we suppose there have been the usual deaths, births, marriages and accidents, and further more, we presume that our prominent citizens have come and gone, entertaining and suffering themselves to be entertained.

But why would an obscure social or local item–hunter go asking for news after Centre battled Harvard and won?

Somerset absolutely refuses to speak to you about anything else.

Somerset is hoarse from the shouting about it. Ribs and shoulders are black and blue from the great thrust punctuated thereon.

Some of them are Somerset boys, and Bo used to attend school here. Yes—we all know it and would shout some more, but we are too hoarse.

Here's to our boys from the Dixie land;
Our heroes of the Gold and White,
Who tore from Harvard with a clean, strong hand,
Each laurel long held by might.

And some of those heroes are our own boys—
Somerset's very own.
Ah, Centre, your joys are our joys,
We join you in the welcome home!

When the team buses finally made it back to the Lenox, the players saw people lined several deep out onto Exeter and Boylston Streets. The drivers pulled up in front of the Exeter Street entrance, just crawling along so as to not run over any of those who were cheering and pounding on the buses, welcoming the Colonels back to the team headquarters.

It was with some real difficulty that they were able to ease toward the entrance. Everyone wanted a piece of any Colonel they could reach out and touch.

As the team finally entered the lobby, the Centre "5" began to play "Old Centre," and many of those who knew the words joined in.

Old Centre marches ever on,
On to victory, on to glory,
Loud cheers ring out, huzzars resound,
To proclaim the same old story.
Ever bold, as of old, guard her honor;
On the field, never yield, win her fame.
For Centre now be bold,
The Gold and White unfold.
Our heads we bare,
Our pledge renew,
Old Centre we'll be true.

At the end of the song, everyone joined in with:

Rah, Rah!
Rah, Rah, Rah!
Rah, Rah!
Rah, Rah, Rah!

The players could still hear the cheering as they rode up the two elevators to stow their gear.

George Joplin filed a story which he sent back to his paper, the Danville "Messenger."

Back at the Lenox Hotel gathered the "Jazz Babies," five syncopating youths who whooped it up in a manner suggestive of college victories of the departed wet days.

The team began straggling back down from their rooms. First came "rugged" Red Roberts, his bright-hued locks marking him in the crowded lobby.

"Oh, my dear Red," Mrs. Covington fairly shrieked the greeting, flung her arms around him and smacked him full on the lips.

The two-fisted Colonel blushed and mumbled something and attempted to edge to the outside, when up came the Chief's wife, Mrs. Robert Myers, and Red was greeted again. The girls, Herb Covington's sister, and Helen James, took courage and followed the example set by the older women.

Red shyly worked his way to the door when there came into the picture, Bo McMillin.

Bo was greeted as his teammate. He appeared to take the kisses with the nonchalance of a veteran, though he did blush a bit once.

"Impressions? Oh, I had so many, really, I am too excited to talk," said Miss James as she turned to devote her full attention to watch Bo working his way through the encircling throng.

"My impressions? My dear boy, just at this moment, I am too excited to tell you or anyone else. It was so wonderfully, wonderfully, wonderful." And Miss Lucy Covington looked about as though seeking others to reward with kisses.

The buzz of talk, frequent cheers and singing, and the wailing of saxophones filled the lobby.

Outside, John Dempsey, taxi starter, grunted, "Beats hell. Never would have thought it."

While the celebrations were continuing, the team filed into the Lenox dining room for a specially prepared dinner by the chef. Steaks, pork chops, even lamb chops with mint sauce were available, along with multiple vegetables, salads, breads, and desserts. It was the first no-holds-barred meal since the stopover in Cincinnati, with the Chief having dictated the selections since Wednesday's lunch.

Red Roberts couldn't wait as orders were taken. He strolled back into the kitchen and found a refrigerator where milk was stored and pulled out a quart, glass bottle, and downed it, then decided that wasn't enough and polished off another quart.

Meanwhile, Uncle Charlie was holding court upstairs in his room. He was puffing on a long Cuban Madura, a gift from an appreciative fan. Asked how it felt to beat Harvard, Moran smiled and said, "It feels better than when I was here in the summer."

"How's that, Charlie?"

"I nearly had my head taken off by a pop bottle when I made an unpopular call here at Braves Field."

Uncle Charlie continued, "It's not so tough to be a coach of a football team that beat Harvard."

Ed Cunningham, of the Boston "Herald," was one of many reporters in the room, and recorded many of Uncle Charlie's comments for his paper.

"I certainly am proud," Charlie continued between puffs, "to be coach of a football team produced by a little college of just over 200 students down in Kentucky, and have that eleven beat Harvard. And I don't think that such a feat would have been possible without the capable cooperation of Claude Thornhill, our line coach."

"He is,"—"Why you old bearcat, Charlie"—shouted a wild-eyed Southerner who burst into the room and threw his arms around Moran's neck. Charlie had to accept a hardy kiss on the cheek before he was released.

"As I was saying," Charlie continued, "Thornhill made the line. He gave Centre seven men on the forward wall who worked as an offensive and defensive unit, and consequently, our backs had a chance when we had the ball."

"I am a great advocate of having eleven men figure in a football game. You can't win with one man. If all eleven wearing Centre's colors had not played together, we would not have won."

"Wasn't Red Roberts great? I believe that football critics will say, Tom, see that some kerosene is taken upstairs for those boys. They'll need to take those bandages off. As I was saying, I believe that football critics will give him consideration when they pick the All-American teams at the end of the season."

"Red played offensive end, defensive tackle. He played fullback and carried the ball when we needed tough yardage. He was our punter and kicker. He was always doing something."

"The way that Snowday, McMillin, Bartlett, Tanner, Covington and our captain, Army Armstrong, ran the ball was glorious."

"Hey, Charlie, you certainly played a great game today!"

It was Bill Roper, coach of the Princeton team, who interrupted. Roper had been in the press box, scouting Harvard, his next week's opponent, and had left his assistants in charge against Virginia. His team won easily, 34-0.

"I sure am strong for that redheaded end, Roberts," Roper said, and Moran beamed acknowledgement and pleasure. "You have a wonderful machine and the fightingest squad I've ever seen. Your men are conditioned to the minute and outplayed Harvard at every angle."

"Thanks, Bill." Moran continued, "Those backs of ours can do anything, either run the ball or catch forward passes. That kid, Herb Covington, from Mayfield, Kentucky, was great. This was only the third game he'd gotten in for Centre, and he played like he'd been there for three years. He's been Bo's understudy this year and will take over quarterback next year."

"Ed Kubale's passing from center was on target all afternoon. He played wonderfully on both offense and defense."

"Jones, Shadoan, Rubarth and Gibson at guards and Roberts and Cregor at tackles gave us a staunch line from tackle to tackle."

"Gordy and James certainly strengthened our wings. James had been a tackle, but he is so fast that Tiny Thornhill moved him to end, and he played a whale of a game, as did Gordy, who is just a freshman."

"In my long experience in football," Moran continued, "I have never met such sportsmen as Bob Fisher, Fred Moore, and the Harvard assistant coaches, especially Eddie Mahan."

"I want to say a couple more things. The attitude of the Harvard team, even when it

looked like it was going to be defeated, continued to play hard and clean. Captain Kane and his men played clean football. They played manly football."

"The people of Boston have once again treated all of us wonderfully. I'm certainly glad that we came back to Boston. We're always glad to come here, and I must say, this is the most pleasant visit I've ever had."

Before the team had left the dressing room and boarded the buses, a statistician had brought some papers down from the press box and given them to Uncle Charlie who had placed them in his inside suit pocket. The Centre coach finally had a chance to go over them while he was in his room back at the Lenox.

Centre had picked up 10 first downs to eight for Harvard. The Colonels had out-gained the Crimson, 219 yards to 187.

Uncle Charlie handed the papers to Bill Roper. "It wasn't one of those fluke scores when one team wins on everything but the score." Roper said. "Your team won on the scoreboard and the field. It was a wonderful effort, Charlie, an effort which will long be remembered by anyone who loves the game of football."

Howard said that no one wanted to leave the hotel and head for the train which was scheduled to pull out at 11:00 p.m.

Everyone felt that they just wanted a few more moments of the magic they had felt in Boston. The Centre "5" was still playing when Howard brought his bag down from the room which he had occupied with three other Centre students, but they packed their instruments quickly and hailed a cab.

Howard walked to the station and got there about the same time that the buses pulled up with the team. The Chief felt that the players deserved to ride after the effort they'd put into the game.

Howard wasn't sure what was happening when he got there. He wondered if some King or Queen or even a movie star had just come in by train. There were some 2,000 people cheering, but they weren't cheering for some member of royalty or movie star. They were cheering the Centre College Colonels.

Howard said it was the most wonderful thing. It was like at the Ziegfeld Follies. Everybody just loved the team, and just as much as the fact that no one wanted to leave Boston, it was just as obvious that no one in Boston wanted to see the team leave.

Eddie Mahan had come to the station. He stood by the steps at the door of the Pullman, waiting to shake each Colonels' hand as they boarded. Everyone was shouting to the players and the rest of the smiling Kentuckians.

"Have a safe trip!"

"God speed!"

"Come back next year!"

A cab sped up while the players were weaving through the crowd and screeched to a halt.

A very tipsy Roscoe was helped to the train by several M.I.T. students who had grabbed him after the game and begun a fraternity house to fraternity house jaunt, staying just long enough in each to down some bootleg gin before moving on. Roscoe was intact but minus his prized top hat and coat. They were left in the Beta Theta Pi house, and hung there for years under a sign that read, "Roscoe's hat and coat." That was all of the identification needed. After all, there was only one, "Roscoe."

After a thousand pats on the back, handshakes, and more "Great game!" salutations than they could count, the players approached the Pullman's door. The car had been covered with signs.

"CHAMPIONS OF THE WORLD!"

"THIS CAR CARRIES A CHIEF, AN UNCLE, ONE KENTUCKY COLONEL, AND 26 COLONELS FROM CENTRE COLLEGE."

"C6 H0"

"PLEASE RETURN THIS PULLMAN TO DANVILLE, KENTUCKY, HOME OF THE CENTRE COLLEGE COLONELS"

Eddie Mahan shook hands with each of the Colonels as they climbed up the steps. He embraced Army and Red Roberts, and then held Bo for what seemed at least a minute, patting him on the back and finally running his hand through Bo's hair as they broke apart. It was a feeling that only two All-Americans could have for each other.

"You did it, guy, you really did it," Mahan said, as Bo climbed the steps.

Bo turned. "We did it Eddie. We did it—the team."

It was the team, as Uncle Charlie had constantly preached. It was always—the team.

The Colonels were weary, even those who hadn't gotten into the game, but rather had hollered so constantly that they also felt drained. There is no better feeling of tiredness than that produced by triumph after a total physical and emotional effort. Adrenaline has been pumped to the max, and then the body pays, but it is a wonderful exhaustion.

A few of the players drifted up to the fan's Pullman and talked for a few moments, but didn't stay long. The big steam engine slowly wound through the city, picking up speed as it reached the outskirts and headed due west. Most of the team were already in their pajamas and under the covers drifting off to sleep, still hearing the roar of the crowd, still seeing Bo cross the goal line, still seeing Tiny Maxwell running over to Bo, still hearing the big referee say, "Mr. McMillin, here is your ball."

The whistle blowing in the night, far ahead, was the last thing they heard until morning came, and the sun rose in the East behind the racing train as it steamed toward Buffalo.

THE DAY AFTER THE GREAT VICTORY

Bill James, who had a job outside of Danville milking cows in order to help pay his way through school, was used to getting up as the darkness began to give way to morning. He was awake at 6:00 and headed to breakfast, trying not to awaken sleeping passengers as he eased through the Pullmans to the dining car.

When he opened the door connecting the diner, he saw George Joplin sitting in the otherwise empty car, smoking a cigarette and drinking a cup of coffee. Joplin, ever the fan, but also ever the reporter for his newspaper back in Danville, pulled out his notepad and began to write as James ordered from the menu which he had lifted from the wire-loop holder next to the window.

The white-jacketed waiter held his pre-printed order form and began to check off items.

"Three eggs over light."

"Two orders of bacon, crisp."

"Grits? No sir, we don't have grits on this train."

"A double order of sausage."

"Toast? White, wheat or rye?"

"Plain white bread, yes sir. Six pieces, yes sir."

"Coffee? Yes sir."

"Two orange juices, coming up."

"Milk, just two glasses?"

James looked up at Joplin and said, "Jop, I was so keyed up when we got back to the Lenox that I couldn't even think about eating. I'm going to make up for it all the way home."

While the waiter bought the silver coffee pot over and filled the two cups, James said, "You know, Bo said he was the happiest man in the world. If he's staked out a claim to be the happiest, then I want you to write it down and tell everybody back in Danville that I'm the second happiest man in the whole wide world, and that includes Texas."

Bill James had been there the whole way to the top. He had been at North Side and heard the Chief paint those word pictures so eloquently that he followed the Chief to Kentucky, not having any idea where he was heading, only that he was going to the college that the Chief had attended.

"Jop, I got on that train, carrying a cardboard suitcase with all my possessions, because I would have jumped right off a cliff if the Chief had said to jump. We all loved him. We all still do. He's the finest man I've ever known."

"I stayed the extra year that we got due to the war because of the Chief. He told us we could be champions. We were just a bunch of boys down there in Texas, trying to make something out of ourselves, not having any idea how we would ever amount to anything, and the Chief…."

There was a pause as Bill James, the same young man who had been an absolute warrior in the Stadium the afternoon before, the same young man who'd played the entire 60 minutes of the great victory, composed himself.

"The Chief made us believe. He wrote the words—you've seen them in the dressing room—Believe, Achieve, Succeed. But they first appeared back in our little locker room in Fort Worth—Believe, Achieve, Succeed."

"He made us believe in ourselves. He told us if we could see in our minds what we wanted to make of ourselves, we'd achieve what our vision was. And Jop, I don't think that anyone could deny that by beating Harvard, we've had some success. We've succeeded. The Chief told us we had, and if the Chief said it, you can write it down."

The rest of the team slept in as the train neared its regularly scheduled stop in Buffalo. They barely had time to finish breakfast when they had to hurry back to their Pullman. A switch engine was disconnecting the cars carrying the Kentuckians so that they could be pulled on the Buffalo and Niagara Falls Railroad tracks to the Falls.

It had been arranged for those who hadn't been to the Falls the year before to spend the day at what many felt was the most spectacular sight in North America. Others who didn't want to go to Niagara had the opportunity to go with Tiny Thornhill to watch a professional football game between the local Buffalo team which Tiny had played for briefly, and the Massillon Tigers, coincidentally, a team which Uncle Charlie had been a part of during the early 1900's.

Going to Niagara Falls in those days was a dream come true. It was where many people went on their honeymoon, and if they couldn't afford to go when they were young, they'd make it a goal to go sometime later in their lives.

Howard went to the Falls and said it was almost as thrilling as the game. Red Roberts went too, even though he'd been there the year before.

Howard was standing next to Red when the big guy said he had so much energy that he felt he could jump in the water and swim over to Canada.

Uncle Charlie told him he better not, because the water may wash the red out of his hair, and that's what made him so appealing to the girls.

Howard bought a big pennant while he was at the Falls. It said, "Niagara Falls, New York" and had this ribbon across it that said, "1921."

He brought it back to Danville and gave it to me and told me that he wanted me to save it forever as a memory of when Centre beat Harvard.

I have it to this day.

(The pennant is now in the possession of R.W.R., Jr., M.D. and looks almost new after all of these years.)

The Centre team and Kentuckians returned to the Buffalo station following their afternoon stopover and were surprised to find a large crowd along with several reporters and photographers awaiting them on the platform. The fact that the famous Colonels were in town had gotten around, and there were many who just wanted to see and talk to the most publicized football team in the country.

The Pullmans were hooked to a westbound New York Central train and the Colonels and their fans were underway on their memorable journey once again. The

Chief had picked up a large stack of telegrams just before leaving the Lenox the previous evening and stuffed them in his leather briefcase. There hadn't been time to read them before, but now there was, and he, Uncle Charlie and Tiny Thornhill, began opening the envelopes and reading them aloud while many of the players stood around.

The Reverend James Richards, Centre 1866, and a graduate of the Princeton Theological Seminary — *My warmest congratulations to the Centre College Praying Colonels…*

From Somerset—*Red, Shad, Andy, Bo—way to go Briar Jumpers.*
From Owensboro—*Tom, Hump, Terry—All Owensboro sends…*
From R.B. Waddle—*Will be in Danville for celebration. Glory.*
From Louisville—*Old Centre has brought glory to herself and Kentucky. Accept our congratulations—Louisville Board of Trade*
From Louisville—*Members of Merchants and Manufacturing Association mighty proud…*

The coaches kept reading and passing the telegrams around and then gathered them up and they were carried forward to the fan's cars for them to read and enjoy.

In the middle of the night, the Pullmans were hooked onto a southbound New York Central passenger train at Cleveland and by early morning, they had reached Cincinnati. Again, hundreds of fans were at the station to greet and cheer the team as the cars were disconnected and then hooked onto the Southern Railroad's "Royal Palm."

They traveled south to Lexington where the Pullman carrying those from Lexington and Louisville was uncoupled. As was everywhere, the station platform was loaded with people who were ready to pour out their gratitude for what the Colonels had done, not only for Centre, but for all of Kentucky.

Hump Tanner was interviewed while standing with a group of admirers.

"We beat them at their own game. We played solid, conservative football. They expected us all afternoon to open it up. We thought we could hold them scoreless and could win with just our running game, and we did."

Governor Morrow and his wife had motored the 30 miles from Frankfort and boarded the train, getting on the team's car for the last leg from Lexington into Danville. The governor was effusive in his praise, walking up and down the aisle, shaking hands and then telling everyone in a little speech, "You have made every citizen, from the Mississippi in the far West of our state to the mountains of Appalachia in the East, so proud to be called a Kentuckian."

Even before the train had gotten to Lexington, Danville had begun to overflow with people eager to welcome the team back home. Both of the Danville papers, the "Advocate" and "Messenger," had publicized the time that the "Royal Palm" would arrive, and urged their readers to turn out and "welcome the boys back home."

They need not have worried about the reception.

I got up early, grabbed a roll and milk, and raced down to the station. I thought I'd be one of the first ones there, but a big crowd was already beginning to gather. There were no classes scheduled. The public schools and K.C.W. had also cancelled their classes. Even the school for the deaf and the school for negroes were closed.

The Danville brass band came down early and started playing and entertaining everybody. There were vendors selling candied apples and gold and white pom-poms. Cars were decorated with gold and white crepe paper. Old letter winners from Centre were wearing their letter-sweaters, and there were several of them, members of the "C" club.

Children were sitting on their father's shoulders. Everyone had to make way for the fire truck which came down Walnut Street, ringing its bell.

Someone stood up on a wagon and hollered that the station master had gotten a wire from the Lexington station that the train was pulling out. We all knew that it was only about a 50 minute ride over, so word went through the crowd that the team was on its way.

People were literally everywhere. I know there couldn't have been more than a few old people and babies and their mothers who hadn't come down to meet the train.

I remember hearing someone joke that it would be a good time to rob a bank, because you could dynamite the safe and clean out the money and nobody would know about it until the next day.

The "Royal Palm" wound through Nicholasville and local citizens along the tracks waved to the team members who sat at the windows and smiled and waved back. The same thing occurred at High Bridge. New signs and banners had been made which reflected the success in Cambridge.

COLONELS WINNERS—YEA!
WAY TO GO, BO!

The engineers who drove the "Royal Palm" south out of Lexington knew exactly who they were pulling toward Danville. They had worked their whistle nearly constantly during the trip, and a couple of miles outside of Danville, they never let up, alerting everyone along the track that they were conveying a special group home.

We were straining to hear, but there was so much noise at the station that we really couldn't be certain if we were going to be able to hear the train or not. There was a building up from the track and some people had climbed up on the roof to watch for the train.

Since I'd gotten there pretty early, I was down near the tracks and all of a sudden, I saw people up there on the roof jumping up and down and pointing. And even over the noise, I could hear the whistle, and then see the smoke, and I knew and soon everybody knew that the team had come home, they'd gotten back to Danville.

The engineers were waving their hats and smiling out of the cab as they slowly brought the train to a halt, pulling up so that the cars with the fans and the team were even with the station.

The whistle kept blasting, three times, two times, and then no more.

Members of the Danville Chamber of Commerce had taken over the planning for the reception, but there was no way for an orderly procession to even be attempted because of the delirium and pandemonium at the sight of the Pullmans. The Southern yardmen had difficulty getting to the cars which were to be uncoupled and left in Danville, and there was no way that they could signal the engineer that the cars had been unhooked.

Finally, one of the workers climbed up on the fan's car and waved his cap toward the engine to indicate the unhooking had been successful. Again, the whistle began to blow to warn everyone that the "Royal Palm" was going to proceed south, and very slowly the big steamer pulled the train away from Danville.

The brass band was playing as loudly as the members could blow, but even the musicians were drowned out by the spontaneous eruption of cheers as the Colonels began to descend from their Pullman's steps and into the crowd.

I had never seen and never will see a happier group of people. Every player was smothered with kisses and several people at a time tried to hug each of them. Pretty soon, the members of the team, even the big linemen, was riding on a mass of shoulders away from the station toward where the Chamber was trying to get the parade to begin.

It was just confusion. The plan was to get everybody lined up on the block of Walnut Street which connected the station to where the campus began. George Joplin was there, and it is fitting to read his description of the reception that the Colonels received.

With hearts full of gratitude, the entire populace of Danville and hundreds of Kentuckians from every section of the state met the "Wonder Team" at the station this morning. There was nothing but a "we-are-proud-of-you-boys" spirit in the minds and hearts of all who were in Danville today. And the Centre College Colonels were met in a befitting manner as conquering heroes, not unlike the Romans of old who, as victors from their triumphant battles, were greeted by their admiring fellow citizens.

When the Chamber members finally got everything sorted out, the last act was to locate Roscoe and put him at the front of the parade. Roscoe was without his top hat and coat, but still looked snappy in his gold vest, and he hadn't left his smile in Boston. The procession began to move slowly up Walnut. Roscoe carried the Centre banner, waving it as he walked, and behind Roscoe marched the brass band, each member playing his heart out.

Every member of the team was on the fire truck, including the coaches and the Chief's wife. Each member was dressed in a suit and tie. Several wore overcoats. Bo wore a belted trench coat. Captain Army clutched the coveted ball which was handed to Bo by Tiny Maxwell. Everybody was smiling and waving to the crowd, and hollering back to familiar faces which were shouting congratulations. Many students and children were skipping along behind the slowly moving fire wagon.

Behind the truck and those skipping along were two goats on leashes being led by young boys. On one goat was a gold blanket with "6" sewn on in white. On the other was a red blanket with a white "0."

George Joplin:

Next came an old car with the terribly dilapidated figure of "Old John Harvard." He was impersonated by a "bean" whose makeup was a classic.

Immediately following was the car with Governor Morrow and his wife, George Colvin, the superintendent of public instruction for the state, and Mr. and Mrs. Howard Reynolds of Boston.

Behind Governor Morrow's car came the justly celebrated Centre "5" wearing their gold and white clown suits.

A local motor car company placed in line 12 beautifully decorated cars which were filled with Centre enthusiasts. In the rear of the dozen came one Ford which was battered and worn, being one of the first made, and it represented the defeated warriors of the East, and an effigy named "Coach Fisher" was aboard.

Back of this car came hundreds of gaily decorated cars bearing banners of praise, all honking their horns, and people by the hundreds on foot, which included many members of the Centre and K.C.W. student bodies, and the local Danville school children including those from the Bate School for the colored.

The parade proceeded up Walnut Street, through the heart of the Centre campus. Breckenridge Hall, Young Hall, Old Main, the gym and Carnegie Library were on the right. Old Centre was on the left.

Once the library was passed, Roscoe turned left and led everybody the block down College Street where he turned right, onto Main Street. A block down Main was the First Presbyterian Church where the bells were being worked in the tower, clanging almost in rhythm with the brass band and the "5." Two more blocks found the assemblage at the courthouse.

Joplin:

The south side of Main Street was occupied by the faculty and students from the Kentucky School for the Deaf, and they all waved a warm welcome to the victorious players as they rode in their triumphant glory.

The fire truck arrived at the courthouse where a platform had been made, and after Dr. Ganfield, Governor Morrow and Mrs. Morrow, Honorable George Colvin, the Centre coaches and Mrs. Myers and other members of the party had taken positions on one end, the team climbed up and took places on the other.

Then the jam of struggling humanity began to get as close around the platform as possible. The Centre "5" was posted off just a few feet, and it was called on and made good, playing the "Centre Swing."

Cheerleader George Swinebroad had his boys closely banded together and he gave many of the yells, and one was for the vanquished giant of the East—Harvard.

Senator J.W. Harlan was chairman of the ceremonies and made a splendid and well received introductory speech on behalf of the Chamber of Commerce and citizens of Danville. Senator Harlan said in part, "Napoleon met his Waterloo; Harvard met Centre."

"The Romans of old never welcomed with more exciting pride its Caesar than we today welcome back the victorious sons of Centre. We write upon the tablets of our memory with the same pride and appreciation as did they upon their triumphant arches: 'They came. They saw. They conquered.'"

"Every heart in Danville, yea, Kentucky and the whole Southland, throbs with pride over the splendid and well-merited victory last Saturday. With intense expectation we saw the grid sons of David humble the football Goliath of the East. We welcome you back today with heartfelt praise not only because of what you have done, but also because of what you are. We are for you, with you, and back of you, as you continue your march of conquest."

On behalf of the Commonwealth of Kentucky, Governor Morrow gave a ringing address. It was obvious as he spoke, smiling over and over as he addressed the boys, that no one was more proud of the victory than he is.

Morrow turned to the team and said, "I'd gladly trade places with Captain Armstrong, Bo McMillin, Red Roberts, or any member of the Centre College Praying Colonels' team."

Dr. Ganfield, with tears in his eyes, told of the wonderful reception that the East had given the team and its supporters, and told how nothing had been left undone to make the stay pleasant in Boston.

The next to be called on was Centre's staunch friend, the sporting editor of the Boston "Post," but Howard Reynolds was at the telegraph office wiring a story for his paper, and Mrs. Reynolds responded in his behalf and was met with wild cheers.

Chief Myers received a loud cheer when he closed his brief remarks. It is always troublesome to keep Chief from conflicting in one's mind as a coach. While he is not exactly a coach in name, he is the "pop" artist and combs the kinks out of the personnel and knows just how to smooth the brows of the boys who love him.

Uncle Charlie Moran, the greatest coach in the country, and line coach, Tiny Thornhill, both gave wonderful talks.

The chairman called on Captain Armstrong, who is the happiest captain of any team in the country, and he was given a thunderous ovation before and after his words.

Army, in turn, called on his great friend to speak next.

Bo, overcome by emotion, teams streaming down his face, magnanimously asked that the team be praised as a unit, and not any one player individually.

"My only regret," said Bo, "is that my dear mother is not here to take part in this celebration. Oh, if she could only see this! She thought as much of me as Danville and Boyle County think of our team."

The peerless quarterback broke down here, but regained his composure in a minute's time. Mrs. McMillin was killed in an automobile accident this past June.

Each Colonel who appeared in the game, even Ray Class who had only been involved in one play, the missed field goal attempt, was asked to speak and the crowd hung on every word, giving each of them a resounding ovation after they finished.

Maybe it's hard now to realize just how much love everyone felt for that team. In today's world, with television and more of a professional bent to sports, even in college, people just don't get so emotionally attached to the players, and the players don't interact with the rest of the school, like our guys did.

Bo gave me an autographed photograph which I hung in my room all four years I was at Centre. My parents came over to Danville and took Howard and me, along with my "dad," Red Roberts, over to the Beaumont Inn in Harrodsburg for dinner, and Red gave my parents a photograph which said, "To the Robertsons, 'Red' Roberts." I have both photographs to this day. Wouldn't give them up for anything.

We worshipped each and every one of them, and it wasn't just because they were such great athletes. It was also because they were such great guys. We all wanted to be like them, and I know that their examples made every student a better man, because they were the perfect role models, especially for someone like me who was only 17 years old during that great season.

The night, after the big welcome home, the Chief's aunt, Lizzie Sheers, gave the team a dinner. She had decorated in gold and white, and after the meal was over, the Colonels "made the dining room ring with 15 lusty rahs for 'Aunt Lizzie.'"

The team then walked to K.C.W. where the girls were holding a dance in the gymnasium, again festooned in gold and white everywhere, in honor of "their boys."

The Centre "5" was too exhausted to play, but the girls found other musicians, and everyone danced into the night.

Centre had beaten Harvard.

How far from North Side High in Fort Worth, from Somerset, Owensboro, Springfield, Harrodsburg, Mayfield, Newport, and Louisville in Kentucky, from Fort Smith, Arkansas, Amarillo, Gatesville and Dallas in Texas, from Pittsburgh, Pennsylvania and Middletown and Columbus in Ohio, from Abbeville in Louisiana—how far this remarkable group of young men had traveled, because—Centre had beaten Harvard.

NATIONAL COVERAGE OF THE GAME

Headlines all over the country appeared in Sunday newspapers on the morning of October 30, and for days afterward, announcing the totally "amazing" fact that Centre College in Danville, Kentucky, had defeated the mighty Harvard Crimson.

Boston "Sunday Post"—CENTRE TRIUMPHS OVER HARVARD 6-0
Boston "Sunday Post"—SAW NOTHING BUT VICTORY
New York "Herald"—CENTRE BLANKS HARVARD BY 6-0
Louisville "Herald"—NOTHING SANCTIMONOUS IN PLAY OF
"PRAYING COLONELS"

The "Courier-Journal" ran a large, all-column, wide-angle photograph of the Centre campus, with Old Main in the middle, and superimposed on the photo was a large C E N T RE spelled out. Filling out the inside of the letters were students. It was really quite a remarkable effort, as there were over 100 students in each of the letters, or nearly half the student body. The whole rendition was under the heading:

WHERE "BO" McMILLIN AND KENTUCKY COHORTS
LEARNED TO PLAY FOOTBALL

Louisville "Courier-Journal"—HARVARD COACH PAYS TRIBUTE TO
CENTRE COLLEGE COLONELS

In Hanover, New Hampshire, a young man named Russell Sanborn Harmon, Dartmouth class of 1922, clipped the headlines out of his Sunday Boston "Globe" and carefully pasted them in his scrapbook.

STADIUM VICTORY
OUTPLAYED HARVARD MOST OF TIME IN WINNING 6-0
McMILLIN AND ROBERTS STARS OF TEAM, SAYS W.D. SULLIVAN

The Associated Press and NEA wire services provided their subscribers with coverage of the game.

Denver "Post"—CENTRE, THE PREYING, NOT PRAYING COLONELS
Chicago "Tribune"—BO McMILLIN OF CENTRE TOPPLES HARVARD 6-0
Philadelphia "Inquirer"—CENTRE PLAYED "POSSUM"—ACCOMPLISHED
WHAT YALE, PRINCETON, PENN STATE COULDN'T
Des Moines "Sunday Register"—CENTRE GIVES HARVARD FIRST DEFEAT
IN YEARS

The M.I.T. newspaper, the "Tech," rather gleefully covered the game and reported under a similar heading:

CENTRE'S COLONELS GIVE HARVARD FIRST DEFEAT IN YEARS
The New York "Herald"—HARVARD BOWS TO CENTRE;
"BO" McMILLIN'S TOUCHDOWN IS TRIUMPH FOR DIXIE, 6-0

Louisville "Herald"—"FIGHTINGEST SQUAD I EVER SAW"
PRINCETON COACH ROPER
Louisville "Evening Post"—CENTRE'S LINE OUTCHARGED THE
HARVARD FORWARD WALL
Philadelphia "Public Ledger"—CENTRE'S VICTORY OVER HARVARD
WILL HAVE HEALTHY EFFECT ON SPORT

Howard Reynolds wrote his impressions of the game in the Boston "Post" under the heading:

CONFIDENCE AND ABILITY AND WONDERFUL SPIRIT
CARRIED CENTRE THRU

The Washington "Post"—McMILLIN SHINES IN COLONELS' TRIUMPH
Oakland "Tribune"—HARVARD MEETS FIRST DEFEAT IN YEARS
Charleston (W. Va.) "Daily Mail"—HARVARD MEETS HER WATERLOO IN
LITTLE CENTER COLLEGE
(One would have thought that after Centre beat West Virginia in Charleston in 1919, the correct spelling of Centre would have been known, but "Center" it was.)

Syracuse "Herald"—CENTRE BEATS PROUD HARVARD 6-0
Ogden "Standard-Examiner"—CENTRE DOWNS HARVARD
KENTUCKY COLONELS OUTPLAY CRIMSON
Galveston "Daily Herald"—CENTRE WINS FROM HARVARD
KENTUCKIANS BREAK 40 YEAR INTERSECTIONAL RECORD OF
HARVARD
(The Galveston story was on the front page and continued into the sports section. The paper was absolutely correct in pointing out the fact that Harvard had never lost an intersectional game, which would have been defined as having been played against a team outside of the East. It was another of the "amazing " facts which sports fans across the country were finding out as they drank their coffee and read their Sunday papers that October 30 morning, so many years ago.)

And so it went, as an enormous amount of newsprint was devoted to the Centre-Harvard game of 1921. Finally, it seems appropriate to share one more headline which demonstrates how much pride there was in the South in learning of Centre's win.

The Augusta, Georgia "Herald" ran a two inch high, all-column headline in big, bold, black letters across the top of its front page. It read:

The key was that the editors wanted the readers to know that it was a SOUTHERN football team that slew the Eastern giant. In smaller letters, more details were provided.

CRIMSON SUFFERS DEFEAT AT HANDS OF CENTRE'S "PRAYING COLONELS"

MORE RECOGNITION

Army received a telegram from Joe Hunt, a student at Oxford University, congratulating the team on its victory.

Dr. Ganfield read a wire from Prentiss M. Terry, the American Relief Administrator who was based in Vienna, Austria, who wasn't even a Centre graduate: *Vienna received most important news emanated from America last seven years. Centre beat Harvard!*

The Colonels seemed to bring out the poetry, or at least the attempt, in some people. Duke Ridgley, in the Huntington (W.Va.) "Herald-Dispatch," wrote;

> *The sun shines bright 'round the old Kentucky home,*
> *'Tis autumn, the students are gay.*
> *The football star wears a crown around his dome,*
> *And the rah rahs make music all the day.*

Joe Ward in the Pittsburgh " Dispatch" satisfied his muse as follows:

> *Red-old head,*
> *You're there, that's all!*
> *I'll say a bear, and call*
> *On fifty thousand more*
> *To say I'm right.*
> *Red-old head,*
> *That was some fight*
> *You gave fair Harvard.*
> *Yea, Bo, some show*
> *And so—*
> *Where'er you go,*
> *You and your Centre crew—*
> *Good luck to you!*

Telegrams continued pouring in from across the state and nation. The Chief posted them on a bulletin board on the first floor of Old Main so that they could be read by the faculty and students, and after a few days, he had them taken to K.C.W. and pinned on a corkboard there.

On Monday, October 31, the day that the team returned to Danville, Dr. Rainey was contacted by the University of Detroit's Charles Bruce, who sent a proposal that

Centre travel to Detroit and play his team on Thanksgiving. There was to be a guarantee of $7,500 and an offer to split the gate receipts. It was felt that Centre would take home $15,000, half again what had been the payout from Harvard.

Centre had to turn down the offer even though it was tempting. Georgetown was wavering about being the sacrificial turkey for the annual, traditional Thanksgiving game, and the Chief and Dr. Rainey were already near to firming up a game with another opponent, even though they weren't ready yet to make an announcement.

On Tuesday, things were settling down. Classes were again being held, and the day began with the usual chapel service. Several faculty members and various student leaders spoke to express their gratitude and admiration for what the team had achieved for the school through their success on the gridiron.

Bo made a plea to the packed First Presbyterian Church audience after first thanking everyone for their support and the warm welcome that the team had received the day before.

"Sometimes, your best friends can become your worse enemies without meaning to. If we hear all of the time about how great we are, we may begin to believe it. We still have several games left, and we need to concentrate on what is coming up, and not on what has gone before."

Kentucky was coming up next, and it was Homecoming.

ABOUT THAT OFFSIDES PLAY AT HARVARD

The story about the famous Centre-Harvard game wouldn't be complete without relating something that happened nearly 20 years later.

Haskell Short wrote the following story which appeared in the now merged Danville "Advocate-Messenger" on August 20, 1941.

Startled, we'll say we were when a man walked into the office this morning and said he was a former Harvard football player—the man who was responsible for Centre beating Harvard twenty years ago this fall.

Now we have always believed it was Bo McMillin, Army Armstrong, Ed Kubale, Red Roberts and others who were responsible for the 6-0 victory by the Colonels which was played up by papers all over the world, but after listening to the former player, we are inclined to believe he did have something to do with that history-making performance for the boys who wore the Gold and White.

Before we tell you the story, let us introduce the man. He is Richard Fields who played end for Harvard in 1921 and is now living in Cincinnati. At present, he and Mrs. Fields are vacationing at Ashley's Camp on Lake Herrington.

Mr. Fields said that late in the final quarter of the game, he made a desperate tackle of McMillin, but that Bo hit him so hard he was addled.

Then minutes later, Harvard was in possession of the ball and making a determined effort to get the ball across the Centre goal line and had moved the ball down to near the Colonels' 30 yard stripe.

As the game faded into its final moments, Buell of Harvard threw a beautiful pass to Churchill who was downed on Centre's three yard line. But poor, addled Dick Fields was called offsides, and the ball had to be brought back.

Dick didn't know about that until the next day when he woke up in the hospital where he was taken following an injury that he suffered on the play.

Mr. Fields said the game was one of the hardest he had ever taken part in or witnessed.

"But despite all the intense rivalry and hard playing by the two teams, I have never seen a more sportsmanlike athletic event of any kind," said Mr. Fields. "One side would tear down the field like all heck to encounter the other, but after the whistle blew, you would see the boys picking each other up," he added.

Since coming to Cincinnati, Mr. Fields had a chance to know Bo McMillin and Red Roberts better. He remembered them from the game well enough, but since then has seen them at various places and they have become warm friends. He said the three of them had often discussed the game and the offsides play which probably saved the game for the Colonels.

And now you know the reason that Dick Fields tells his wife that, "Kentucky owes me a lot," each summer when he packs up his fishing equipment and heads for Herrington Lake for his annual fishing trip.

CHAPTER 14:
HOMECOMING 1921
CENTRE-KENTUCKY

Centre and Kentucky were true rivals, but the feeling of respect that each had for the other was certainly boosted by the way that the Wildcats and citizens of Lexington had gotten behind the Colonels and been so supportive regarding the Harvard game in 1920, and the one just finished.

The Kentucky contest was going to be the last one played in Danville during the season, and this fact made it all the more imperative for the supporters of the Gold and White to be in attendance. Not only did fans want to see the team that had just defeated Harvard, but it was to be the last home appearance of three of the stars who had contributed so much to the team's success over the last five years.

Bo, Army and Bill James would be playing their last game on Cheek field. They had put on the Centre uniform 36 times through the Harvard game and had been major parts of 33 wins against three losses, for a winning percentage of 91.6.

Also, during that period, the three had helped to totally turn the tables on Kentucky. They were 3-0, and Centre had outscored the Wildcats, 108-0.

1917	Centre	3	Kentucky	0
1918	No game			
1919	Centre	56	Kentucky	0
1920	Centre	49	Kentucky	0

Coach Juneau, the Kentucky mentor, felt that his team had a reasonable chance against the Colonels. They were 3-2 at the time, with the following results:

Kentucky	68	Kentucky Wesleyan	0
Kentucky	28	Marshall	0
Kentucky	14	Vanderbilt	21
Kentucky	33	Georgetown (Ky.)	0
Kentucky	0	Sewanee	6

(Vanderbilt was playing excellent football during the early 20's. The Commodores won their last two in 1920, were 7-0-1 in 1921, the tie being with Georgia. In 1922, their record was 8-0-1. The tie was with Michigan.)

Kentucky had lost its last game to Sewanee, 6-0, in a game played at Louisville's Eclipse Field while Centre was playing Harvard. There was as much, if not more, interest, in what was going on at Harvard Stadium as there was at Eclipse Field. One of Louisville brokerage houses was "carrying" the Centre game and had a stream of couriers who would bicycle the few blocks to Kentucky Avenue and 7th Street and stand in the bleachers hollering out the results of the play in the East. There were oddly occurring great cheers which would come from the stands which had no relationship to what was happening between Kentucky and Sewanee on the field.

Danville was still decorated in gold and white, but now even more so than on the Monday that the team returned from Boston. C6 H0 adorned even more windows and storefronts. If a site was available for the team colors and pennants to be displayed, someone would quickly get to work and wrap or hang or do whatever was necessary to get it decorated.

Tickets sold out quickly, and it was obvious that people were going to be turned away. Uncle Charlie used this fact to begin discussions again regarding getting a new stadium for Centre. He pointed out that anytime a team was so popular that fans couldn't be accommodated, it was time to take action. He had a sympathetic audience wherever and whenever he brought up the subject, and his efforts in 1921 would pay off starting the 1923 season.

As Centre was preparing for Kentucky, the attention was still on the prior week's game with Harvard. In class after the game, the Centre chemistry professor, Dr. W.H. Coolidge, said he had discovered a new formula, one which would kill the fondest hopes of anything crimson in color. It was C-6 H-0.

On November 4, an ad appeared in the "Messenger," with the headline:

VICTORS

Napoleon met his Waterloo; Centre met Harvard; Piggly Wiggly met the high prices of foodstuff. Centre's "Wonder Team" has dragged Harvard's pride down into the dust; so in like manner, Piggly Wiggy has brought the high cost of living down, down to the lowest possible margin. Like Centre, Piggly Wiggly has won fame "all-over the world" by making prices, not meeting them.

During the week, Bo was talking to a group of admirers on the street when a young boy raced up to him and grabbed his hand.

"Bo," he cried excitedly, "I had a little brother come to my house today, and we've named him Bo after you."

According to a reporter, Bo was as excited over the announcement as he was from scoring against Harvard, and said he was going over the next day to visit his "offspring."

Shortly afterward, the "Messenger" announced:

Mr. and Mrs. Clel Upton of Shelbyville, formerly of Danville, have named a fine, 10 pound boy, Norris McMillin, in honor of Centre's team captain, Norris "Army" Armstrong, and Bo. It is hoped by all that he will live up to his name.

Another poem, this one appearing in the "Advocate."

There was a young man from Fort Worth
In whose mouth was a spoon at his birth
He touched up old Harvard for a touchdown.
He has shown all there is of fame and renown—
And Danville will give him the earth!

A telegram was received from William Weatherford, a native Kentuckian, who was a cotton broker in Houston.

Am proud of Centre, like every other Kentuckian. Arrange banquet for team. Spare no expense. Send me the bill.

Telegrams continued to pour in. L.W. Roberts, athletic director at Georgia Tech, and the mayor of Indianapolis, Charles W. Jewett, both sent messages to Bo.

Roberts: *The Georgia Tech team congratulates you and your team on its wonderful victory over Harvard on Saturday.*
Jewett: *Congratulations. Certainly your great desire expressed to me last year has been accomplished. Your victory ranks second to none on the gridiron.*

It would have been quite natural to have a letdown against Kentucky after the Harvard game, despite the fact that the Wildcats were the Colonels' main rival. Certainly, Kentucky was fired up. The Lexington "Herald" set the tone in the week leading up to the game.

The Wildcats are not underestimating the strength of the Centre eleven; they know that the Danville team is the best in the South if not the country this season and that the Colonels are capable of even better ball than they played against Harvard. The facts are not worrying the Wildcats much, however, for they know that despite the reputation of the Centre collegians, only an every-minute fight can stem off defeat by an overwhelming score.
Arrangements are underway for taking the largest crowd of rooters that ever went from Lexington to witness the game at Danville. A special Southern Railroad train will be run, leaving Lexington at 12:30 in the afternoon and returning after the contest is finished. An automobile special, similar to that which took the boys to Louisville for the Sewanee game, will be run by local

people. Those who go in the automobile caravan will be able to stay for the dance which will be given in honor of the Kentucky-Centre classic. In additions, hundreds of former Centre and University of Kentucky students from throughout the state will make the trip by either train or automobile.

The annual Kentucky classic is attracting more attention than ever before, and the largest crowd that ever witnessed a football game in this state is assured.

The Danville "Advocate" ran a summary of the series since its inception in 1893. Of the 25 games, the Colonels had won 15, lost eight, and there had been two ties. Overall, Centre had outscored Kentucky, 399-307.

Just before the Kentucky game, there was a report in the "Messenger," under the heading, OFF TO THE COAST, that it seemed like a certainty that the Colonels would be heading to the West during the post-season.

Whether they will play in the big Tournament of Roses, or the stellar East verses West contest at San Diego has not been decided. R.C. Barlow, manager of the Tournament of Roses, wired Chief Myers that the committee was giving Centre serious consideration. W.I. Aimes, Chairman of the East verses West game, also wired the Chief that the committee was interested in Centre playing in their game.

Had it been just over two and a half years that the Centre athletic department was having trouble lining up games with the more notable teams? It seemed continually amazing to all involved that Centre College of Kentucky was being sought out by schools and committees, and that now it was a matter of picking and choosing rather than hoping to attract notice and being squeezed into some slot on a preferred team's schedule.

KENTUCKY—NOVEMBER 5, 1921

The Saturday of the Kentucky game was a perfect, cloudless afternoon with a bit of a chill in the air-ideal football weather. The attendance was estimated at over 9,000, the largest crowd yet to assemble for an athletic event in Kentucky. There weren't close to 9,000 seats, but fans were congregated literally everywhere near the field. They were hanging from trees and phone poles, standing on roofs of cars, peering out of the windows of Breck and Young Halls and Old Main. There were people under the stands who were trying to watch between the legs of those who were in the bleachers. In addition, the field was lined with hundreds of "standing room only" enthusiasts who were several rows deep wherever there was space available.

The highlight of the afternoon was the cheer and recognition for Captain Army, Bo and Bill James. The Colonels ran out to the 50 yard line and waved to the standing crowd which was trying to smile, wave, whistle and clap all at once. Even every wearer of Kentucky's blue and white was on their feet, adding their appreciative recognition to what the trio had not only accomplished for Centre, but also for the entire state, over the past five seasons. There was no doubt which was the superior team as pointed out by Bruce Dudley of the Louisville "Herald."

The question of victory by Kentucky never came into the fray. This was taken for granted by everyone except the Centre players who rushed into the battle with only one object and that was to win. But the crowd of over 9,000, with 7,500 wearing gold and white and 1,500 equally enthusiastic Wildcat fans decked out in the school colors of blue and white, were interested in the margin of victory.

The hope of the Kentucky portion of the crowd was to have their team score at least once, and to keep from losing by as many as 50 points.

Such had the tide turned.

The "dope" on the game was that Centre would win by at least the 50 points that Dudley had mentioned, and backers of the Gold and White had to give that many points in order to get any Wildcat fans to take them up on a bet.

The game started slowly, and after seven minutes, there was no score. Wildcat fans began to have a glimmer of hope.

Finally, Centre began a drive at midfield. A 20 yard Bo to Snowday pass took it to the 30. Snowday then ripped off 15, and Tom Bartlett and Red alternated runs until the redhead bulled over for the last yard. Bo kicked the extra point, and it was 7-0 as the 1st quarter ended. Kentucky's fans were feeling pretty good about their bets.

In the 2nd quarter, Bo scored on a 49 yard dash, Herb Covington streaked for a 38 yard TD, one extra point was converted, and the half ended, 20-0.

Wildcat bettors were feeling fairly confidant. Centre was substituting freely, and it seemed like the 50 point margin was pretty secure.

Bo threw three touchdown passes in the 3rd quarter, one each to Snowday, Red and Clifton "Hennie" Lemon from Mayfield. The whistle blew with the Colonels holding a commanding 41-0 lead.

Uncle Charlie continued to run men in and out, seeming determined to get all of his squad into the game. Even though their team was far behind, Kentucky's partisans felt somewhat optimistic going into the final 15 minutes of play. Centre would need to score and kick both an extra point and a field goal to reach the margin needed to cover the spread.

Early in the final period, Bo tossed a 25 yarder to Red who was standing unguarded in the end zone. The kick was good, and it was 48-0.

It was getting dark. The Kentucky fans were cheering for their team continuously, not for victory—the game was long lost—but for solvency. Centre was having trouble getting its offense going during the period due to the frequent substitutions, and had several penalties and fumbles.

With less than two minutes to play, Kentucky's Fuller punted to Covington who returned it to midfield. It was difficult to distinguish the players due to the darkness. Centre had time for one more attempt to score.

Bo ran for 19 to take it to the Wildcats' 31. On 1st and 10, he circled around in his backfield for what seemed forever, his front wall providing him all of the time that he needed. Bo was standing on the 40 when he fired a long, perfect spiral to Hennie

Lemon, who was literally loitering around in the end zone. The big-handed Lemon pulled in the pass and with the completion, Kentucky fans began to reach into their pockets to pay off their bets. The extra point made it 55-0 as the game ended.

Centre's win ran its record to 6-0. Since the loss to Georgia Tech, the Colonels had won 11 straight, outscoring their opponents, 492-13, an average margin of 45-1.

During the last three games against the Wildcats, Centre had put 160 points on the board to exactly 0 by Kentucky.

1919	Centre	56	Kentucky	0
1920	Centre	49	Kentucky	0
1921	Centre	55	Kentucky	0

The analysis of the 1921 game was indicative of Centre's superiority during this period. Uncle Charlie played 32 men, Kentucky, 16.

Centre never punted, not even once. The ineffective offense of the Wildcats (or overwhelming defense of the Colonels) resulted in 10 punts by the boys from Lexington.

Centre racked up 38 first downs while Kentucky had but seven, and the majority of those were against Centre's subs. But the most amazing statistic was that Centre picked up 204 yards in the air on 12 out of 16 passes, and 804 yards on the ground in 96 carries. Overall, the Colonels gained 1008 yards on 112 plays, averaging exactly nine yards every time they called a play.

Teams just don't gain over 1000 yards! Teams just don't average nine yards every time they call a signal! But as unbelievable as it may seem, that's just what Centre College did on that afternoon of the first Saturday in November, 1921. How far the Colonels had come since that 68-0 drubbing in 1916.

Now it wasn't even close.

CHAPTER 15:
KNUTE ROCKNE COMES TO DANVILLE
THE COLONELS KEEP ON ROLLING

Jop wrote in his column in the "Messenger" on November 8 that Uncle Charlie had received a letter the day before from the sports editor of a "leading New York newspaper" asking if Centre would come to New York to play either Yale or Princeton in the Polo Grounds on December 3, "to settle the country's football title."

Jop related that the team was due to vote about going to New Orleans to play Tulane on Thanksgiving. Since Georgetown, the Colonels' traditional turkey day opponent, had wisely opted out of providing "the holiday feast," the Chief and Uncle Charlie were considering accepting an invitation from Tulane if the players were willing to travel that far south, which would cut into their Thanksgiving vacation considerably.

If the Colonels were to go to New Orleans, then turn around a couple of days later and head to New York to play in the Polo Grounds, it would mean they would spend almost a week on the train.

Considering the trip the team later undertook, a Danville to New Orleans round trip, followed by a similar journey to New York, wasn't such a lengthy undertaking, but it looked daunting at the time. The team voted to go to New Orleans. The "leading New York newspaper" received a "thanks, but no thanks," regarding the game proposed for the Polo Grounds.

There were three efforts to try to get Centre to come to Chicago to play Notre Dame. On November 8, Floyd Fitzsimmons of Benton Harbor, Michigan, promoter of the Dempsey-Brennan fight and other big-time fights of note, arrived in Danville with a contract which he wanted to get signed and notarized for Centre to come to the Windy City the week after Thanksgiving for a December 3 game against the Irish.

The "Advocate" reported:

Chances are very remote as the faculty and students don't look upon a match of this sort with much favor.

Chicago wouldn't give up so easily after Centre turned down the offer.

John Russell, the business manager of the Chicago "Herald-Examiner," came to Danville. Russell was also pitching a proposed Notre Dame game, but he brought a considerably sweetened offer. First, he announced that Chicago White Sox owner Charles Cominsky had offered his ballpark for the game and wouldn't charge a cent for its use.

The "Herald-Examiner" was owned by the newspaper mogul, William Randolph Hearst, then at the absolute pinnacle of his power due to controlling newspapers from coast to coast with millions of subscribers. Russell said that the Hearst papers would get behind a drive to help Centre build a much needed new stadium, and would guarantee $50,000 toward the amount needed to begin construction.

On November 17, it was announced by Centre that a final decision, "irrespective of other offers," had been made. Centre was heading south to play Tulane in New Orleans on Thanksgiving, November 24, and didn't plan on an early December game.

The Chicago proposal must have been hard to turn down. Getting the powerful Hearst organization behind the little school would have been a real boost in putting up a stadium unequaled for a college the size of Centre.

Even after Centre announced its plans to play Tulane, the proponents of the game with Notre Dame simply refused to take "no" for an answer. Now they pulled out their biggest gun and enlisted his help.

Knute Rockne, the Notre Dame coach, was intrigued with Centre. The "Rock" desperately wanted to pit his team against the Colonels. He felt that if the Irish could meet, and possibly beat, the conqueror of Harvard, it would be a major step in his quest to place Notre Dame at the absolute pinnacle of the football world.

Rockne joined with the "Herald-Examiner's" John Russell for a trip to Louisville to confer with Major Forrest Braden, an old friend, who in turn set up a meeting with influential Centre alumni in the city who were felt to have enough pull with Centre to get the school to reverse its decision. After receiving encouragement in Louisville, Russell and Rockne drove to Danville to meet with the Centre athletic committee at the Busy Bee Restaurant.

The offer that they took to Danville was sweetened even more. There was still Cominsky's offer of his ballpark for free. There was still the $50,000 toward getting a stadium built in Danville. Rockne said he would also give up half of Notre Dame's guarantee of $10,000 from the gate, so that Centre would get $15,000 and his school would only receive $5,000. (Anything over $20,000 taken in on ticket sales was to go to a Christmas charity to buy baskets for disadvantaged children which the "Herald-Examiner" sponsored each year.)

Certainly, Rockne felt his being willing to make an arduous 750 mile round trip to Danville, Kentucky to personally make the case would impress Centre. Certainly, Centre would be swayed by his offer to increase the guarantee. Certainly, Centre would agree, now, to come to Chicago to take on his team.

Again, the "Advocate" published a short announcement.

The athletic management of Centre College turned down the proposition.

Why? First, there was the contract which had been signed with Tulane. Centre felt honor-bound to live up to the agreement. Tulane was making a lot of plans, and Centre didn't want to back out of the game.

Another reason, just as important, was that Centre was working on a big venture to go out West after the regular season. While the exact arrangements were still being fleshed out, the plans were fermenting, and the Centre officials felt that one post-season happening was all that they should take on.

Turn down the "Rock" and Notre Dame? Turn down $50,000 for the new stadium? Turn down $15,000, an offer that exceeded the Harvard payout of $10,000? As the Chief and Dr. Ganfield had said so often after the telegram had arrived in Chicago inviting Centre to play Harvard in 1920, "Who would have ever believed it!"

"HERE'S TO YOU OLD CENTRE" and "THEY HELD THE LINE"

Here's to you Old Centre, the best of them all;
You've put Centre squarely on the map of football.
At Harvard they said you had not a chance;
Wonder how they felt when they saw Bo advance?
You did what had not been done for years;
And you won by clean sportsmanship, prayers and tears.
We can review Kentucky's history with pride, not sorrow,
From Daniel Boone on down to Governor Morrow.
She's won many victories, for which we are proud,
And we'll sing her praises, both long and loud.
When we think of the triumphant battles she's fought—
Our hearts beat the quickest at—
Centre, six; Harvard, naught.

"Here's to You, Old Centre" was written by Howard Camnitz and published in the Louisville "Herald." Young Howard was the son of a Louisvillian named Samuel Howard Camnitz who had a 12 year pitching career in the National League, compiling an overall record of 133-104 from 1904-15. It may be that Howard, Jr. had a bit of help with his offering, as he was but a fifth grader at Louisville's Emmet Field School.

I've saved the poem, "Centre Held the Line," for last, because it is my favorite. Imagine the emotion that the great Centre victory over Harvard stirred in people which compelled them to write poetry in homage to their heroes. It was truly a more innocent time, and a time which we won't see again.

Up from the line they came that day,
Old Centre's boast and pride;
Sinews of steel and thews of stone
By many a battle tried.
The will to win in each strong heart,

Their eyes with hope a-shine;
And Harvard gave the best she had,
But Centre held the line.

Fair the day and massed the throng
Who came to watch them play,
And wonder crept to every mind
When the Colonels stood at bay.
Wonder that such a thing could be
Spread out before their sight.
For when the second quarter closed
They'd matched the Crimson might.

And then the miracle came to pass
While fifty thousand stared;
Bo was flying down the field
To do the thing he dared.
Twisting, turning, dodging, fleet,
His good old soul aflame,
He bought the pigskin to the goal—
And won the Harvard game.

But still they fought as men will fight
For all they hold most dear;
Man after man the Crimson brought,
Urged by despair and fear.
Their bravest and their best they gave,
Aye, gave their very all;
But it was all in vain for none could pass
Beyond that golden wall.

Why call the roster of that band
Who journeyed north that day,
And in that Eastern stadium
Were victors in the fray?
On every heart Kentucky holds
Their names are graven deep;
And in our souls throughout all time
Their valor we will keep.

No pomp and pageantry were theirs,
But quietly and with calm,

They donned their moleskins and their gear
With never a coward's qualm.
They fought the fight and kept the faith
There in the sweet sunshine.
And Harvard's pride is stained with dust—
For Centre held the line.

Edwin Carlisle Litsey

(Edwin Carlisle Litsey was the assistant cashier in the Marion National Bank in Lebanon, Kentucky and developed into a writer of short stories and poetry. He was beginning to develop a reputation when he wrote "They Held the Line" in 1921, and by 1954, had achieved enough renown that he became Kentucky's fourth Poet Laureate.)

AUBURN—NOVEMBER 12, 1921

The Auburn Tigers (4-1-0) were next for the Colonels. The schools had never met. Two games were of significance when comparing the two programs. (Auburn has had, and still has, several nicknames. The use of "Plainsmen" came from a poem by Oliver Goldsmith who wrote, "Sweet Auburn, loveliest village on the plain…." which the citizens of Auburn just knew must refer to their town. The fact that Goldsmith was born in Ireland, later lived in England, and died nearly 70 years prior to the incorporation of Auburn, didn't seem to be of overriding importance. Also, Auburn's teams were referred to as the "War Eagles." There are so many stories about the origin of the "Eagle" that is probably best to just Google "War Eagle" and pick the one which seems most plausible, or perhaps, the least implausible. Since Auburn's teams are currently most often called the "Tigers," we'll use that nickname.)

The Colonels had beaten Clemson, 14-0. Auburn crushed Clemson two weeks later, 56-0. Also, the Alabamians had lost to Georgia by only 7-0 in a game played in Columbus, Ga. That same Georgia team had gone up to Harvard and lost by just 10-7, which further demonstrated that the Tigers were indeed a team of significance.

Auburn	35	Samford	3
Auburn	44	Spring Hill	0
Auburn	55	Clemson	0
Auburn	14	Fort Benning	7
Auburn	0	Georgia	7

When one added in the fact that the game was to be played in Birmingham, virtually a home game for Auburn, sports writers and fans felt the contest was a toss-up. The Tigers had fared well in the city. Since 1900, they had played 30 games there and compiled a 17-11-2 record.

However, while the crowd would be overwhelmingly cheering for the in-state team, Centre planned to be well represented. Special Pullmans were to be hooked onto a Southern train which would stop in Danville on Thursday afternoon and carry the team and fans to Birmingham, arriving the next morning.

There was no way I was going to miss the Auburn game. Everybody was really excited about our beating Harvard, and about our having just run all over Kentucky. The special cars were going to be packed, so I started making plans. My parents sent me a check each month for expenses, and I decided that I'd "borrow" a little of my expense money. Even if I didn't have any money left over after going to Birmingham, there was no way I was going to miss the game.

Howard and I decided to get a ticket just to ride in a coach, not to pay extra for a Pullman berth. We knew Crep Hays, a childhood friend from Elizabethtown, had a ticket for a sleeper car, and we thought that late at night, we could sneak into his car and climb up in his upper berth and get a little sleep on the way. I only had $5.00 when I got on the train, but as things worked out, it was enough, thanks to Red Roberts.

The faculty had gotten so much criticism about the Harvard game and lack of excuses that they said we could miss classes, but would have to make up the work when we got back. That was all I needed to hear.

Rickwood Field was the site of the game. Auburn had played there twice in 1920 with great success, beating Vandy, 56-6, and W&L, 77-0.

Like all venues during Centre's great seasons after World War I, it was recognized that the demand for tickets was greater than Rickwood's capacity, and temporary bleachers were hastily thrown up, increasing the seating to 18,000, and still there were those who were going to be turned away.

We managed to get into Crep's Pullman and all three of us shared an upper bunk. It was awfully crowded, but better than sitting up all night. I had a little box camera and we took pictures of each other boarding the train, and I still have mine.

We rode all night and when we arrived, there were a lot of photographers and reporters at the station. Of course, the big news and what everyone was asking about was Harvard. Not only were the newspaper people there, but there were a lot of other people who wanted to see the players and take their pictures.

What impressed me was not only how many people were there to greet the team, but how the team handled the situation. If someone wanted to have their picture with Army, or Bo or Red, or any team member, they were smiling and gracious when asked. The guys must have shaken hands and signed autographs until their hands nearly fell off.

It took a long time to get away from the Birmingham station, but we finally got to the Tutwiler Hotel, and four of us chipped in for a room, and all slept in one big bed. You did what you had to do in those days, and when you're 17 like I was, it's was all just an adventure, anyway.

Just as the Colonels had been able to upgrade in Boston from the adequate but unpretentious Arlington Hotel to the Lenox, now the team found itself staying in the best that Birmingham had to offer. The Tutwiler was a 343 room, 13 story luxury hotel at the corner of Park Place and 21st Street, easily the top-drawer facility in the city.

The Colonels workout Friday afternoon at Rickwood was open to the public, and a large crowd congregated in the stands and around the field. There was no contact, but it was a full-dress affair, running through plays and further refining the timing which was such an integral part of the offense.

The coaches didn't give any secrets away. They didn't have to introduce any new plays. The team was now so in harmony that it was like a well-oiled machine, needing no tweaking, purring along on all cylinders without a hitch.

Uncle Charlie and Tiny could only say, "Great workout, boys," as they closed out the session. It was rare for the coaches to not have recognized some flaws, no matter how minor, to point out and work on. Now, there were none.

There were no injuries of significance. Tom Bartlett had an infected knee and was doubtful, but it was a testament to the depth of Centre's backfield that even if "Long Tom" didn't start, it wouldn't hamper the offense in any way. Hump and Red Roberts could fill in at fullback and not slow the attack one bit.

The Centre alumni in Birmingham were led by S.L. Yerkes, a partner with F.A. Grider in the Grider Coal Company, which specialized in high grade coal used in railroad steam engines. Yerkes had made all of the social arrangements which had become such a part of the Colonels' activities wherever they appeared.

Meals were to be served at the Birmingham Country Club, and special buses were made available to transport the team back and forth from the Tutwiler. A dance was held at the club Friday night, attended by the team and "thirty of Birmingham's most beautiful girls," debutantes all. Red Roberts was the hit at the dance. Red was not only an excellent dancer, but his genuine surprise that he was appealing to the ladies made him all the more so. Red was quoted as saying, "Tear my sox. Can you imagine them calling me cute? What have I done to earn such an accusation? Me, a big sap like me, cute? Me, a big ham and egger, cute? Well, tear my socks!"

The team had breakfast at the club Saturday morning, returned to the hotel for a quick skull session, and headed to Rickwood which was already beginning to fill by the time their bus pulled up.

I had seen Red in the lobby before they went out to the country club for breakfast. He asked me something about where I'd had breakfast and what did I think about the hotel, and I told him I was saving my money for a big victory dinner after the game.

Red said, "So you're a little short of money?" I told him maybe you could say that. So he said, "No son of mine is going to go hungry!"

Red told me to be in the lobby when the team came back from breakfast, and so I was. And he brought this big napkin, it almost looked like a tablecloth,

filled with biscuits and bacon and sausages, so much food that Howard and Crep and I together couldn't eat it.

We certainly didn't go the game hungry, I'll tell you that.

Auburn was coached by a Yale graduate, Mike Donahue who had been at the helm since 1904, missing the 1907 season. Donahue had compiled a record of 91-31-5. Excluding ties, he had an excellent 75% winning percentage.

Auburn was known for having big linemen, and Centre had a decided weight disadvantage, but the Colonels felt confidant their speed would win the day.

The Auburn squad came to Birmingham the morning of the game, boarding a regularly scheduled Southern train at Opelika and traveling on the single track spur to east of Birmingham, where they merged onto the main, double-tracked, east-west route into the city.

It was another of those perfect fall football afternoons. It was another of those perfectly colorful events which so typified football during the era. The crowd all dressed for the game, the men in suits and ties with overcoats if they didn't have on a vest, and the ladies in the more mannish styles of the early 20's, with loose fitting waists, flattened chests, and full length coats. Cloche hats covered close-cropped hair. Whatever the fashion, every spectator's allegiance could be determined by the chrysanthemums worn, the gold and white of Centre, or orange of Auburn.

If there was ever a game where the score didn't begin to reflect the skill levels of the teams involved, it was Centre-Auburn in 1921. Bruce Dudley filed a story after the game for his paper, the Louisville "Herald."

Tonight the Centre boys are saying, "Fine, ok. Fine, ok"

This afternoon they beat Auburn and they beat Auburn as decisively as Auburn has ever been beaten. Mike Donahue, former Yale star and Auburn coach since 1904, is convinced that Centre has the most remarkable team in the United States. Mike thought his team was one of exceptional merit until he witnessed their efforts against Centre, and this afternoon, those efforts seemed feeble.

The game was one of the prettiest ever played in the South, and it was one of the cleanest. Good sportsmanship, in contrast to the Georgia Tech contest last year, was evidenced on almost every play.

Eighteen thousand people, forming the greatest crowd that ever gathered in Birmingham for any event, saw the game, and every fan left the game an enthused admirer of the Kentucky eleven.

One of the surprises to the Auburn fans and local sportswriters was how the Centre line so totally outclassed the heavier front wall of Auburn.

Bruce Dudley continued his report:

The Centre line far outplayed the Auburn line. On the offense, the freshman, Kubale, stood head and shoulders above the All-Southern Caton, but Caton played a whale of a game on defense.

"Baby" Pearce, the 210 pound tackle, lived up to every pleasing thing that could be said of him, but he didn't outshine "Baldy" Cregor one little glimmer.

Bill James right-ended his way to All-Southern fame, and Rubarth, Shadoan, Gibson, Jones, and Gordy, showed the Auburn linesmen tricks they didn't know.

Red Roberts played end, tackle and fullback, excelling in whatever spot he played. Red would tell another Colonel in the huddle that he wanted to trade positions.

"Humpty, I feel I can take it over the left side for a first down. You hop up in my position and I'll carry the mail."

The amazing thing was that Auburn knew Red had jumped in the backfield and was going to run the ball, but they couldn't stop him. After long drives in the 1st and 2nd quarters, Red scored both times on short plunges, Bo converted the extra points, and Centre led at the half, 14-0, after being on the Auburn two yard line and threatening as the clock ran out. The 3rd quarter was scoreless, but Centre moved the ball at will, simply being unable to punch it in.

Bo scored in the final period on a three yard run, finalizing a drive that had begun on the Colonels' 39. The extra point made it 21-0. Centre was threatening again near the end of the game, but a pass from the seven resulted in a touchback.

The real measure of the domination, absolute domination, of the Colonels, was that the Gold and White picked up 29 first downs. Auburn was helpless to stop Centre's relentless attack. The Tigers picked up exactly two first downs in 60 minutes of play, one in the 2nd quarter and one in the 3rd.

Auburn got across the midfield stripe only once, to Centre's 48 yard line, and this was made possible only due to an intercepted pass. Bruce Dudley wanted his readers to be able to absorb the magnitude of Centre's superiority.

Centre, against the vaulted line of Auburn, made twenty-nine first downs. Auburn made but two. Think of this, Centre with twenty-nine and Auburn with two!

The game was played almost entirely on the Auburn side of the field. The Colonels had three or more men in on every tackle. A good Auburn team was helpless against a great Centre team.

During the 1st half alone, Centre picked up 265 yards. Auburn's total was 18.

Dudley also wanted the people back home to appreciate the sportsmanship displayed on the field. It was Dudley who had been so incensed at the conduct of Georgia Tech the year before, and he always appreciated, and mentioned, good, clean play in his reporting.

Red Roberts spent much time administering to injuries of the Tigers. Whenever an opponent was hurt, Red would bathe his face with water, help lift him to his feet, and help support him in unlimbering walks. Red never lost an opportunity to help a stricken opponent, and before the half was up, fans were referring to him as "Red Cross" Roberts. The Auburn rooters gave him quite a cheer in the last period when he was caring for Ollinger, who was severely injured, and had to be removed from the field.

The Colonels were now 7-0 for the season and had won 12 straight since the loss to Georgia Tech. There were two games left in the regular season, and everyone waited with great interest to see how the trip to the West was going to shape up.

Back in Cincinnati, after hearing about the results of the game, the sports editor of the Cincinnati "Post" decided to run a photograph of the St. Xavier halfback, Herb Davis. The caption mentioned that Davis had scored the only touchdown against "the famous Centre College team thus far during the 1921 season." The "Post" felt young Davis should be given recognition, even if his score had been the result of fumble recovery in the end zone.

THE POST-GAME RECEPTION

After the game, the Centre alumni joined Mr. and Mrs. Yerkes in hosting a dinner and reception for the team and Kentuckians at the Tutwiler.

You know, in my later life, I went through reception lines all over the world. I met the Queen when there was a reception that Helen and I attended at Buckingham Palace for recipients of the Order of the British Empire.

We were in Rome and attended a party at the American Embassy. There were many formal affairs at medical meetings in London and Paris and Edinburgh. We attended quite an affair in Tokyo. One great event was a formal reception on the Queen Elizabeth in the 1950's when the members of the American Medical Association took the great Cunard liner to England where we meet in Leeds, Yorkshire with members of the Royal College of Surgeons. And of course, we were always going to the Homestead, the Greenbrier, Boca Raton, the Breakers, the Broadmoor, the Waldorf, the great hotels of San Francisco like the Fairmont and St. Francis. In each of these elegant settings, I've been part of, and gone through, innumerable reception lines.

I don't bring this up to brag, even though it brings back great memories to think of all of the places Helen and I have been privileged to visit.

I mention all of these places where there were wonderful receptions because none ever impressed me like the affair that was held for the team at the Tutwiler after the Auburn game.

The team stood along the wall and shook hands with everyone who came in, and there was a huge crowd. I didn't think the line would ever end, and that was not only because there were so many people, but because everyone wanted to not only shake hands, but the men wanted to pat the players on the back, and the ladies wanted to hug each of the guys as they moved along, and everyone wanted to have a few words with each member of the team.

Of course, I was just standing around watching, but I was close enough that I heard, "We love you," and, "We're so proud of you," and, "That was the best game I've ever seen!" Everyone was just in awe of each member of the team. And the other thing I remember was how well the guys handled the situation, just like at the railroad station when we arrived. They must have said, "Thanks, it is a pleasure to meet you," and, "Appreciate your being here," a thousand times. But they never seemed to get tired of hearing the compliments, and they always smiled and looked people right in the eye.

After the line finally got through, and after dinner, Red got a great kick out of taking me around and introducing me as his son.

"Yes, that's who I am. I'm Red Robertson."

I was really fortunate to have my name because I know it got me a lot of attention that I'd never have received otherwise.

The Colonels were allowed to sleep in the next day as the overnight train didn't leave until 7:30 p.m. The free time allowed them to leisurely read the Sunday morning Birmingham papers. Auburn's Coach Donahue was quoted extensively.

Centre has a great team and has everything it takes to make one. They have age, weight, experience, power and dazzling speed. They play real football, and it was one big game in which Auburn, playing its traditionally clean game, was matched by another just as clean.

The train rolled into Danville on Monday morning at 5:30 a.m., in time for the team and students to make it to chapel. Amazingly, even though it was still dark, there were over 500 cheering fans at the station to welcome the Colonels back home.

It was truly a love affair. Harvard notified Centre after the Auburn game that it wanted a return engagement in October, 1922. The offer was accompanied by a generous increase in the guarantee that would be paid. Harvard could well afford to up the payout. Centre was a huge draw.

Fred Moore, the Harvard graduate manager, told the Chief that he wanted the game to be earlier in October as, "Centre and Princeton are too much for Harvard on successive Saturdays."

Meanwhile, John McGee, the student manager working under the Chief, reported that he was receiving daily wires seeking a game with the Colonels in 1922. The most recent inquiries were from Indiana, Northwestern, Fordham and the University of Pennsylvania. McGee told the "Advocate," We could play 50 teams next year if we wanted to. There's hardly a college in the country which hasn't contacted us."

WASHINGTON & LEE—NOVEMBER 21, 1921

The Louisville games in 1919 with DePauw, and 1920 with Virginia Tech, were each so successful that Centre decided to reserve a date for the city each year.

The 1921 opponent was Washington & Lee, from Lexington, Virginia, the ninth oldest institutions of higher learning in the country, tracing its founding to 1749.

There were several reasons that Centre and W&L were an attractive match-up for Louisville. They were both liberal arts schools, founded by Scots-Irish pioneers. They were situated in similar little towns which were much more sophisticated than their size would have indicated. They both had relatively large alumni organizations in Louisville. (W&L had long been a favorite college where Louisvillians sent their sons.) Both schools were small, but W&L had 749 students in the fall of 1921, making the college nearly three times larger than Centre. (Both were all male.) Both were admired for their willingness to take on the "big boys," and to do so successfully.

Coming into the Centre game, W&L was 5-2 with the following record:

W&L	41	Randolph Macon	0
W&L	27	Emory and Henry	0
W&L	13	Rutgers	14
W&L	33	Morris-Harvey	0
W&L	3	Virginia Tech	0
W&L	7	West Virginia	28
W&L	41	Roanoke	0

The two schools had one common opponent in Virginia Tech, with Centre beating Tech 14-0 in Danville, while W&L won in Blacksburg, 3-0. If the home field is worth a touchdown, then the game would have seemed to be an even match. However, the Colonels were certainly playing at a much higher level than they were earlier in the season.

In the week leading up to the game, a faculty member at W&L decided to do a little research on slang expressions used on his campus and in Danville. He wrote James Hewlett, English professor at Centre, and asked him to help.

Hewlett had his students write down their favorites, compiled them, and sent them over to Lexington.

JELLY BEAN—one who does nothing but rush girls
CHISELING—edging in on a party
STICK—an unpopular person
SAP—a person with no brains
BEANERY—a place to eat
KNOCKED ME FOR A PLENTY—flunked me
BURN MY CLOTHES—exclamation of surprise
TEAR MY SOCKS—can't believe it (Red Roberts' favorite.)
TIGHT—drunk
OIL CAN—a poor sport
SPANISH ATHLETE—a user of bull
JILLIN—a large number
DOUGHPOP—a knockout

SQUIRRIL—one who attends all dances
FLING A PARTY—act as host
FUSSING—pay attention to the fair sex
JAZZ PUPPY—one who likes jazz
TO HEEL—to trick somebody
KNOWS HIS EGGS—efficient and well-informed
HOT AS A FIRECRACKER—efficient socially
FLAT TIRE—a person of low estimation
DEAD LAY—a sure thing
CERT—yes, of course
PUT THE WEIGHT TO HIM—get the best of him
TAP YOU—I'll bet you all you have
PASS OUT—to be overcome by something

For W&L, to have a shot at Centre was the highlight of its season. Prior to embarking for Danville, there was a huge pep rally which filled the rather modest stadium at Wilson Field. The coach, W.C. Raftery, told the students that his team understood Centre's offense well enough that he felt the Generals could adequately shut down the Colonels. He also said that he felt that Herb Covington was more of a threat than Bo. Why, was never explained, and whether the comment made its way back to Danville isn't known.

The team and student body then moved en mass to continue the rally at the railroad station. The "Ring-Tum Phi," the W&L student newspaper, reported:

The send-off at the station showed even more spirit than the rally on the field, and left no room in the minds of the men that they were all backing them to the limit. The band added harmony to the unholy din, and rousing cheers were given for all members of the team. The train pulled out with the team full of "old fight" as the crowd sang the swing.

Centre came over to Louisville on Thursday night, November 17, and went directly to the Seelbach Hotel, team headquarters also in 1919 and '20. The W&L team arrived Friday morning and headquartered a block down on Walnut from the Seelbach at the Watterson.

Once again, the downtown merchants had turned Fourth Street and all of the areas around the hotel into a sea of gold and white, with phone poles wrapped, banners and pennants hung on stores and over intersections, and team member's photographs decorating storefront windows.

On Friday, the Centre Louisville alumni hosted a luncheon attended by over 100 people for the Colonels at the Pendennis Club. A highlight was to introduce the four Colonels who were certain not to return in 1922—Bo, Army, Tom Moran, and Bill James. Chick Murphy and Ben Cregor were also introduced as "two who may not return, but hopefully will."

Bo had a difficult time when he was asked to speak. He was overcome with emotion, realizing that now, six years after his arrival from North Side High in Fort Worth, "To think that tomorrow will be the last time I will play football on Kentucky soil...."

In the evening, the Colonels walked up Fourth Street and attended a movie at the recently opened, art deco-inspired Kentucky Theater, and after the movie, spent some time with the W&L players at the Watterson before heading back to the Seelbach.

There had been a considerable amount of rain during the week leading up to the game. Despite the weather, the goal posts were decorated in Centre's gold and white, with the phone poles outside the stadium wrapped like candy canes. The W&L alumni had only the remaining goal post to wrap, but they had roped off a small area of the stands in their school's blue and white which they would occupy.

It was an enthusiastic capacity crowd (something to which the Colonels had become accustomed) of 18,000 fans which flooded into Eclipse Park for the 2:00 game. The sun was out, and the band that the Centre alumni had hired added a festive air.

Red Roberts raised donkeys on a friend's farm outside of Danville. Roscoe, as usual, did all of the work. Red had decided to bring one of his jennies (a female donkey) to Louisville and had Roscoe accompany it in the baggage car on the train. When they arrived in Louisville, another friend of Red's met them at the Seventh Street station with a truck, and the animal was taken to a backyard at Belgravia Court near Eclipse Field and stashed in a fenced-in back yard. Roscoe looked after the needs of the donkey.

Now, on the afternoon of the game, the jenny was again put in the truck and brought to Eclipse Field. Red had a blanket which he put over the back of the animal with "C6 H0" sewn on each side. He met Roscoe at an outfield gate and walked the donkey onto the field and paraded her around in front of the stands. It brought down the house as everyone stood and cheered wildly, the W&L fans as enthused as those of Centre. (Uncle Charlie kept an album of photographs taken during his years of coaching at Centre. A photograph of the jenny, Red, and team members, was passed on to the author by Ann McCurry, grand-daughter of Uncle Charlie.)

I still have the program of the game. Howard and I went over on Saturday morning and were met by the chauffeur of Uncle Theo and Aunt Mary. He drove us through the downtown to see all of the decorations and then took us to the game. Believe it or not, he parked and waited for the game to be over so he could take us back out to their home on Cherokee Parkway for dinner that night.

I wrote in pencil, "McMillin-6," and after the "6," there's a "1" for the extra point.

Then there is, "Roberts-6," then "Snowday-6," and finally, "Armstrong-6." I added it up to be "25."

In the section of the program where you were supposed to put the Washington and Lee scoring, there is nothing.

That's the way the game ended. We won, 25-0.

The muddy field conditions somewhat negated the Colonels' offensive superiority, at least in regard to running up a big scoring margin, but the statistics told the tale.

Centre gained 551 yards overall. W&L picked up but 103. The Colonels ran 98 plays and had 27 first downs. The Generals were able to get off only 34 plays, and were able to move the ball for a first down but three times.

The 1st quarter was scoreless. Centre put 13 points on the board during the 2nd quarter to lead 13-0 at the half. During the break, the Louisville Retail Merchants Association made a presentation to Centre of a huge banner to commemorate the victory over Harvard. Prominent Louisvillian, Judge Arthur Peter, handed over the felt cloth which was one half in white with a gold "C-6", while the other half had a white "H-0" on a red background. The Colonels added scores in both of the last two quarters for the final margin of 25-0.

Only once was Bo thrown for a loss. He was attempting to skirt his left end when a young man named Tucker managed to bring him down four yards behind the line.

Bo was heard to say, "Nice tackle, boy. It was a beaut!"

Coach Raftery may have wanted to rethink his comment made over in Virginia about Bo. The Centre star gained more than the entire W&L team did on the ground, 107 yards to 103. He also connected on 13 of 25 passes for 152 yards.

The Colonels were stopped once on the one yard line, and five other times they were within the 10 yard line without scoring. The never-say-die spirit and clean play of the Generals gained the respect of not only the Colonels, but of everyone who witnessed the game. Even as the two teams were walking off the field, plans were being discussed for a return of Washington & Lee to the Derby City.

Judge Robert W. Bingham, newspaper baron, owner of the Louisville "Courier-Journal" and its sister paper, the evening Louisville "Times," gave a dinner and dance at the Pendennis Club for the two teams on Saturday night after the game. The menu had at top, "Let's Eat and be Merry!" Besides the teams and coaches, there were over 100 guests including "some of the prettiest girls in these United States."

The "Courier-Journal" printed a lengthy article about the gala.

One of the features of the banquet was the "Pigskin" edition of the two local papers which was placed at every plate, containing the menu, the dance program, and various "quips and quirls" of the two football teams which were the honored guests.

You would never believe it if you did not see the way the members of these two teams fraternized. It was just as if the great Centre College Colonels had not given Washington and Lee a severe drubbing, rubbing them into the mire of Eclipse Park. If the participants have any say in the matter, the Generals and Colonels will meet again next year, even if they have to argue it out on a soaked field with the mercury frozen stiff, after the party they enjoyed last night.

An added highlight of the event was reading the account in Judge Bingham's "Times" about the results of the Yale-Harvard game. Bingham had copies trucked right off the press over to the Pendennis.

The Crimson had beaten Yale, 10-3, at the same time that the Colonels were playing W&L. The Elis had gone into the Harvard game undefeated at 8-0, and had just come off a 13-7 victory over Princeton. (The win by Harvard over Yale made the fact that the Colonels had beaten the Crimson all the more significant, since Yale beat Princeton, Harvard beat Yale, and Centre beat Harvard. It was obvious from comparable scores that Centre could play competitively, and most probably beat, each member of the "Big 3.")

Centre stood at 8-0, and had a 13 game winning streak. The Gold and White had recorded another shutout and had now given up only six points, that aberrancy against St. Xavier, during the entire season.

Centre had allowed their opposition only 12 first downs in the last three games. Kentucky got seven, mainly against reserves, Auburn picked up but two, and now W&L had gotten only three. Thus, in 12 quarters, 180 minutes of play, the Colonels defense had been virtually impregnable.

Army and I were friends for a long time. He was in his last year at Centre when I was a freshman, but we became close when we both served on the Centre Board of Trustees.

Often, I'd come up the night before a meeting at the college and stay with Army and his wife, Porter. We would talk about affairs of the school, but after a couple of highballs, it seemed that we always ended up talking about football, often far into the night.

Army said that the team felt they could score on anyone, and the figures certainly bear that out. Other than the 1917 DePauw and 1920 Georgia Tech games, no team held us scoreless during Army's five years at Centre.

So Army said that the fellows dedicated themselves to playing the toughest defense that anyone had ever played. It was to be literally all eleven men on pursuit every play. The guys would literally swarm, and most of the times there would be two or three or even more in on every tackle.

He told me that his last year, the 1921 season, the team started the season with the goal of shutting out every opponent.

And you know, they came pretty close to doing just that. They were the hardest hitting group that you'll ever see.

The Cincinnati "Times-Star" published an editorial after the Colonels beat W&L.

Last Saturday, Bo McMillin played his last game on the "dark and bloody ground" of Kentucky.

For many years, Centre turned out men who won national distinction in their later lives. Bo decided not to wait for greatness, so he thrust greatness on himself and his college. Centre suddenly became a name to conjure from Bangor to San Diego, from Duluth to Laredo. From its academic groves it issued strong men who invaded the East, who invaded the South, to return from each journey as conquering heroes. The supreme moment came when Centre preyed on Harvard, the incomparable Bo threading his way among Crimson warriors to a touchdown and victory.

Yes, Kentucky's greatest son! Ask the man in Butte, Montana, who are the senators from Kentucky, and you'll get a blank stare for your answer. But ask the man from Butte who is the Centre quarterback, nay, who is Centre College itself, and you will provoke an enthusiastic reaction and a quick response. And greater than Henry Clay, too, for Henry was only the "Great Compromiser," whereas this later Kentuckian is a "Great Conqueror," who knows no compromise. Yea, Bo!

This great Colonel just defeated the boys from Washington and Lee who were pretty good Generals in their day.

THANKSGIVING—1921

The Thanksgiving date had been in a state of flux all season. The traditional opponent, at least for the past five years, was Georgetown. The Colonels and Tigers first played in 1898, and the Thanksgiving date was adopted in 1916. Even in the war-shortened 1918 season, the two teams had met on the last Thursday of November.

However, Centre received word that Georgetown was considering calling off the game as the season progressed. It was obvious that the two schools, so recently at parity, had gone their separate ways regarding skill levels on the gridiron.

Therefore, the backup plan was to play DePauw in Indianapolis. The 1920 game there with the Tigers had been a big success even though DePauw had lost to the Colonels, 34-0. To their surprise, Centre received communications from DePauw that there was worry about the game generating enough revenue to cover the expenses which would be incurred.

This made no sense to the Chief. The previous year's contest had been a sellout, and the 1921 game would generate the same type of revenue. Nonetheless, for whatever reason, DePauw wanted out, Tulane heard about it, and an offer came up from New Orleans that Centre found satisfactory. So it was off to New Orleans to play the Tulane "Green Wave."

It was just as well, Centre figured. New Orleans in late November was better than Indianapolis, and it would be a new experience to visit the Crescent City. Other than Minos Gordy from Abbeville, Louisiana, none of the Colonels had been to New Orleans before. The Chief and Uncle Charlie had always felt that football was a great way to allow the players on their teams to see the country. Many of the Kentuckians had never been out of the state before their travels with the squad. (A good example was George Chinn. George was from a prominent family from Harrodsburg, Kentucky and first left the state when the train taking the team to the 1920 Harvard game crossed the Ohio River and entered Cincinnati.)

The trip to New Orleans was going to require a quick turnaround. The team didn't arrive back from Louisville until Sunday afternoon on November 20, and was to pull out of Danville and head south at 10:55 a.m. on Tuesday, the 22nd.

The Southern left two Pullmans on the siding in Danville, one for the team and one for the fans. They were hooked onto the regularly scheduled Cincinnati-New Orleans

Limited. The route south required the big steamer to go to and through Chattanooga, on to Birmingham, through Tuscaloosa, and then cross over the Mississippi state line to Meridian.

From Meridian, it was another six and a half hours before the Limited braked to a halt at the New Orleans Union Station, the only railroad station ever designed by Louis Sullivan, the famous Chicago architect, considered to be the "father of modernism," and creator of the skyscraper.

It was a pleasant journey for the team, watching the scenery flash by, playing cards, eating meals in the dining car, sleeping overnight, and arriving fresh and ready to go, nearly 24 hours later, at 9:55 Wednesday morning in a city where the temperature was hovering around 70 degrees.

As always, the Colonels were met by a warm reception. After meeting with the welcoming committee and reporters, they were quickly on their way to Heinemann Park, also known as Pelican Park, home of the New Orleans Pelicans, a Southern Association AA minor league baseball team.

F. Edward Hebert was a Tulane student who was the sports editor of the school's newspaper, the "Hullabaloo." He also covered the college's sports for the New Orleans "Times-Picayune."

The young reporter filed a story for the city newspaper after attending the Colonels' workout, and it is one of the most descriptive in pointing out exactly what made the team's offense so effective, and so hard to defend against.

The "Wonder Team," as the Centre College outfit has often been described, is certainly well named after what we saw yesterday at Heinemann Park. To the mere casual onlooker, the Centre team seems nothing more than a bunch of men dressed up in some gold sweaters striped in white. They do not seem an extraordinary group of players, nor do they appear to be greater than the average run of football teams.

But what a change when those boys get into action in signal practice! If they play just one half as well against a team as they run signals, then a real football game is going to be the order of the day. We never have seen such a marvelous squad as the Centre team of yesterday afternoon.

One has often heard tell of magicians who claim that the hand is quicker than the eye. And from what we saw yesterday, we are of the opinion that the whole Centre outfit is composed of a bunch of magicians. The plays of the Colonels are absolutely the most baffling and dazzling ever seen on a New Orleans gridiron. It is a treat to stand on the sidelines and watch the Kentuckians run through their drills.

On some formations (and they have them to the nth degree) one cannot see just who is carrying the oval. The interference is wonderful, and it is going to take a mighty good team to stop the boys from the Bluegrass.

Bo McMillin and Red Roberts, the two real big stars of the team, are perhaps the most unconcerned men on the entire squad. The average fan would pick neither of these players as stars. But what a change comes over them when they start calling out signals and warming up. The sound of a signal seems to awaken them as a bugle does a soldier, and then some real football starts.

Tulane's campus is all astir over the approaching contest. While no one says openly that Tulane is going to defeat the greatest team in America, some students believe that Tulane will score on Centre, which seems to be placing a lot of confidence in the members of the Olive and Blue.

The Colonels were now causing speculation about whether a team could even score on them. Defeating them seemed not to enter the equation.

The same day's "Times-Picayune" had a large composite picture taken at Heinemann Park under the heading:

THE MIGHT AND BRAIN OF THE PRAYING COLONELS

The "Might" was represented by Bo, Red, Army, Louisiana's Minos Gordy, and Terry Snowday. The "Brain" was represented by, "The two in citizen's clothes," Uncle Charlie and Tiny Thornhill. The caption under the entire photograph read, "The Praying Colonels are perhaps the greatest collection of football players in the entire country."

Tulane came into the game with a 4-4 record.

Tulane	0	Mississippi College	14
Tulane	26	Mississippi	0
Tulane	7	Rice	6
Tulane	7	Mississippi State	0
Tulane	10	University of Detroit	14
Tulane	0	Auburn	14
Tulane	6	Washington U. (Mo.)	14
Tulane	21	LSU	0

The key to the strength of Tulane was the shutout they put on a strong LSU team. The Tigers had an excellent season, going 6-1-1, with their only defeat being against Tulane. LSU had beaten a strong Texas A&M team, 6-0. (The tie was with Alabama.)

Auburn was a common opponent of Tulane and Centre, and comparable scores would indicate that Centre was the better team. Centre beat Auburn 21-0 and Tulane lost to the Tigers, 14-0.

The game was to be played in Tulane Stadium, a reinforced concrete structure, covered with stucco, built in 1917. (Tulane's stadiums are known as Tulane I, II, and III. The first was a wooden structure, built in 1909, but it was soon outgrown. Tulane II was on McAlister Drive, and dedicated on October 27, 1917. Tulane III was built in 1926 and was the stadium which eventually was known as the Sugar Bowl, and had a capacity of 80,000. Sadly, it was demolished in 1980.)

It was 70 degrees at game time. There were over 10,000 fans who had come from all over the South to see the famous Colonels. A band had been hired by Tulane to sit in the Kentucky section to play "Kentucky music" for Centre's team and fans.

In an unusual display for an opposing team, the entire crowd stood and cheered lustily when the Colonels came onto the field, and their greeting was only intensified as the band blared out "Dixie." It was for the South they were cheering. Centre had taken on the mighty Easterners and been victorious. Centre had represented everyone below the Mason-Dixon Line, and the whole region had exploded with pride when the news was heard.

"Centre beat Harvard! Did you hear? Centre beat Harvard!"

"The South will rise again!"

When the band played "My Old Kentucky Home," everyone again stood and cheered, rebel yells and all.

The Tulane game was a virtual replay of the Auburn and W&L contests. The outcome was never in doubt. No one wanted to belittle the Colonels' opponents. The reporters friendly to Centre always made a point of writing about the "courage" of those who lined up against Uncle Charlie's warriors.

The players always complimented their opponents, and were very humble about their superiority. But there was no getting around the story that the figures, when the analyses were made, told about the skill levels of the Colonels and the teams they played against during this era.

A "special dispatch" to the "Courier-Journal" was printed under the headline:

MORAN'S MEN OUTCLASS TULANE GRIDDERS IN HOT WEATHER

New Orleans, La., Nov. 24—Centre triumphed over two opponents today, Tulane and the torpid weather. The final score was 21–0. The weather was 70 degrees at the kickoff.

The Colonels, playing in their usual fashion, outclassed the Green Wave in every department, gaining 477 yards to Tulane's 135. Centre registered 24 first downs while the local outfit could gain but two.

So now in the last four games against Kentucky, Auburn, W&L, and Tulane, Centre's opponents had only 14 first downs in 16 quarters of play.

"Unbelievable!" is what the sports columnists of the day declared. Bo and the Colonels completed 14 of 18 passes for 183 yards, an average of 13 yards per successful toss, with no interceptions. Tulane only attempted three passes. Two were intercepted and the other fell incomplete.

The first touchdown came on the initial possession by the Colonels. The long gainers were a 22 yard pass to Army, a nine yard end around by Bo, and a 16 yard touchdown pass to Tom Bartlett. Tulane made one of its first downs to start the 2nd quarter. During the period, Centre racked up 161 yards to the Green Wave's 33.

Centre's 2nd score came on a pass from Bo to Terry Snowday which was described as, *Bo hurled a 15 yard pass to Snowday. Taking the ball on the 15 yard line, Snowday twisted out of the grasps of two tacklers and did a somersault over a stack of players, landing beyond the goal.*

Bo's second successful kick made it 14–0 at the half.

Herb Covington made several long runs in the 1st half and picked up some big yardage on punt returns.

As the players retired to the dressing rooms at the half, the crowd stood and cheered the play of the Colonels. A local fan was quoted as saying that he normally attended the opening day of the horse races at Jefferson Park, as was the tradition in New Orleans amongst the "sporting set," but, "I can go to the track any day. But this is my only chance to see the greatest group of athletes ever to play football in the history of the game. I wouldn't have missed being here for anything." Many in the crowd expressed the same sentiment.

Centre couldn't punch it in during the 3rd quarter despite several long and sustained drives. In the last period, Bo put on a passing exhibition and then capped off the effort by faking a pass and twisting through the line from the three. His extra point ended the scoring.

After the game, the Tulane alumni hosted a party for the team at a theater in the French Quarter, followed by a banquet at the famous la Louisiane Restaurant on Iberville Street, known for its French-Creole cooking.

THE RACE TO COLUMBUS

Not every Colonel was able to go to the entire post-game affair in New Orleans. Bo, Red, Bill James and Chick Murphy had agreed to play in an All-Star charity game on Saturday afternoon, November 26, in Columbus, Ohio. Bo had been offered $2,000 to play in a similar game in New York but declined, not wanting to forfeit his amateur status with the pending trip to the West still being planned.

The quartet boarded the "New Orleans-Cincinnati Limited" at 8:10 in the evening after the game for the long ride to Cincinnati, arriving in the Queen City at 9:15 Friday evening. They then transferred to a New York Central train for the trip up to Columbus, arriving the morning of the game.

The Centre players' team was comprised of present and past All-Stars from colleges all across the country, including former Harvard great, All-American Eddie Casey, plus the incomparable Jim Thorpe, now playing professionally, who had been such a force when he played with the Carlisle Indians. They were called, fittingly enough, the "Rainbow" team.

The opposing team was called the "Starbuck" team, and was made up of former and present Ohio State players. The venue was Ohio Field, capacity 14,000, the Buckeyes home field prior to the opening of their magnificent Ohio Stadium the following year.

Bo's team won 16-0. Eddie Casey scored on a 37 yard pass from Bo in the 1st quarter, there were an additional two points gained from a safety, and the highlight of the game was described as follows, when writing about Bo:

The little quarterback, his goal in danger, circled the end, wiggled his way thru opposing tacklers across the field, and in an 86 yard dash, planted the oval across the goal.

Red Roberts made a huge impression with his play.

He spoiled more plays than any other man on the field. His football intuition seemed to put him in the right spot to break up Ohio plays and to make those of his own team on offense successful.

At the half, Red and Jim Thorpe put on a show.

Between halves, Roberts and Thorpe gave Columbus fans the greatest exhibition of the sort ever seen. Thorpe was punting from 60 to 70 yards, and dropkicking from 40 to 50. At the same time, Roberts was throwing forward passes to Bailey of West Virginia, and on each he was averaging 40 yards, while some of his tosses were for 50 yards. At no time did Bailey have to move more than a foot to catch the ball.

Bo had guided Centre to a victory over W&L in Louisville on November 19, quarterbacked his team to a win over Tulane in New Orleans on the 24th, and gone all the way to Columbus on the 26th to lead his All-Star team to a win. (Of course, Red and Bill James had been integral parts of all three games. Bo often got the glory because of his incredible talent. But the other two Colonels, while not as widely acclaimed, were vital cogs that helped make it all possible.)

In seven days, three games, three shutout victories, and well over 2,000 miles traveled by train. It had been a big week for the young man from North Side High in Fort Worth.

On the same day that the game was being played in Columbus, Governor Morrow issued a proclamation from Frankfort that he was making Howard Reynolds, Centre's great supporter, a Kentucky Colonel—*in appreciation of his spirit of clean, fair sportsmanship, as evidenced by his kindness, consideration, and splendid treatment of the Centre College football team in his writings for the Boston "Post."*

Certainly, no one had done more to promote the little college, in Danville, Kentucky, than Howard Reynolds.

A LITTLE ABOUT THE "SHOP PERFECT"

One damper on an otherwise perfect 1921 college year in Danville was the announcement of the closing of the Shop Perfect on November 28, just after Thanksgiving. Every college had a favorite student hangout. In Cambridge, it was the venerable Leavitt and Peirce Tobacco and Specialty Shop on Harvard Square, established well before the turn of the twentieth century. It's smoke-filled, second floor chess and game room was a preferred gathering place for students from Harvard, as the campus was just across Massachusetts Avenue.

The "Cento" published a student's feelings about the closing of the "Shop" which paints a vivid picture of life in those more simple and wonderful days in Danville.

THE PASSING OF THE "SHOP"

Alas! The Shop Perfect is no more. This week the students of Centre College and K.C.W. are sadly mourning the demise of that famous establishment which for years has so closely and vitally been connected to those two institutions.

The "Shop" has come to play an important part in the daily lives of the college boys and girls who have come from the four points of the compass to Danville, as their Mecca, where they might worship at the shrine of knowledge. The outsider can have little feeling when reading, "Shop Perfect changes hands. Confectionery will be made into up-to-date drug store. No fountain installed for thirsty students." But these terse words have brought sorrow to many of us.

The "Shop" has always been more than an ordinary confectionery. Not only has it served food and drink to the thousands which have passed through its doors during its period of existence, but it has served many other purposes as well.

It has been a true assembling place for the gathering of the clans. Thither the fair of K.C.W. have come, and gazing demurely over their sodas and sundies, have sought to attract the attention of proud youths of Centre shamelessly strutting in front of the building. (For many a time, they have succeeded.)

There, has every football game in which Centre has participated been fought over a score of times; there, have been hundreds of freshmen, so soon to find their true station in life, been figuratively "wined and dined" in the mad rush for fraternity pledges.

Behind the fountain on the mirrors have been inscribed the stories of Centre's victories, Centre's defeats, eloquent inscriptions, all of them.

To the "Shop" we have gone for tickets for athletic events and dramatic productions. During Homecoming and the Carnival, the old grads sit around the "Shop" and tell how things were done when they were young and spry. When the banks closed, the "Shop" has cashed student checks galore. It has served as the depository of books until the faculty has given it the title of the "traveling library."

Whether to meet a buddy or a rushie, to fill a date or assemble for a feed, it has always been, "I'll see you at the 'Shop.'" A fond father who has sought an offspring in every classroom is told by authorities, "Go to the Shop Perfect, corner of Third and Main. You will probably find him there." And nine cases out of ten, Willy has been there.

Wars, politics, religion, fraternities, dances, automobiles, girls, pranks, love, and a jillin other things, have all come in for their share of discussion at the "Shop."

To be sure, there are other establishments in Danville which will in great measure fill up the vacancy which the Shop Perfect has left, but it will be many years before any establishment will mean as much as the "Shop" has meant.

Alas! The Shop Perfect is no more. This week the students of Centre College and K.C.W. are sadly mourning the demise of that famous establishment which has been so closely connected with these two institutions.

Those indeed, were the days.

CHAPTER 16:
THE 1921 REGULAR SEASON ENDS

The regular football season was over for Centre as it was for most teams across the country. Many colleges shut down after their Saturday, November 19 game. For others, the Thanksgiving contest with a traditional rival signaled the end of the year.

Writers and football analysts were comparing teams and sorting through the statistics for the year to try to determine the best team in the country. There were no weekly polls as we now have. No computerized rating systems were available in the pre-computer age. There was no playoff system then, just as there is none now in major college football.

Post-season games were in their infancy. There was a Rose Bowl on January 1, 1902, and then there was a 14-year gap until another Rose Bowl was held on January 1, 1916. Another Rose Bowl followed in 1917 between college teams, and then the Pasadena contest pitted service teams against each other during the games played on January 1, 1918 and 1919.

ROSE BOWL HISTORY (January 1)

1902	Michigan	49	Stanford	0
1916	Washington State	14	Brown	0
1917	Oregon	14	Penn.	0
1918	Mare Isle. Marines	19	Camp Lewis	7
1919	Great Lakes Naval	17	Mare Isle. Marines	0
1920	Harvard	7	Oregon	6
1921	California	28	Ohio State	0

The only other bowl game that had ever been held was the January 1, 1921, Fort Worth Classic, in which Centre smashed TCU, 63-7. So there had been five college meetings in the Rose Bowl, the one Fort Worth Classic, and that was that. It can be easily seen why the statement was made that bowl games were in their infancy.

Uncle Charlie's initial reaction on coming back from New Orleans was to shut things down, head to Horse Cave and his farm, do a little hunting, tend to his cattle, and get some rest prior to spring training ushering in another baseball season.

He knew that offers had been pouring in for Centre to appear all over the country. The Chief had been handling things, along with the athletic committee members, but Uncle Charlie felt that a dominating season in which his boys had gone 9-0, and outscored their opponents 282-6, meant there was really nothing left to prove, especially since one of the wins had been over mighty Harvard.

Also, Uncle Charlie had seriously considered retiring. His initial reason for being in Danville was to help with the team that had his son, Tom, as a member. Tom was graduating, and for that reason, the coach felt that he just might move on. He had actually expressed that he would probably retire at the end of the season while talking to reporters in his room at the Lenox after the Harvard game.

On the other hand, Uncle Charlie knew that a trip to the West would be a great opportunity for his young men to see much of the country, and he let the Chief and the committee know that if a trip could be "first class," he'd get behind it .

"Let me know the details. Please make certain that they realize that this is a special group of young men. If they want us to come out to play, we want to show our boys the country in the best of possible circumstances."

Later, he again made the point that any trip, "should be seen as a reward, and an unforgettable experience that my boys will remember the rest of their lives."

So the Chief, the student manager, Johnnie McGee, and the athletic committee continued fielding offers, all being of like mind to come up with not only a post-season game, but a great adventure as well. They succeeded beyond their wildest dreams, as we shall see.

THE BEST TEAMS OF 1921

There were six undefeated teams in 1921, and two which were undefeated but tied.

UNDEFEATED

Washington and Jefferson	10-0
Centre	9-0
California	9-0
Lafayette	9-0
Cornell	8-0
Iowa	7-0

UNDEFEATED, BUT TIED

Vanderbilt	7-0-1 (tied Georgia, 7-7)
Penn State	8-0-2 (tied Harvard, 21-21, and Pitt, 0-0)

Washington and Jefferson was a small school which, like Centre, W&L, and Sewanee, played a big-time schedule. The Presidents had victories of significance over Syracuse, West Virginia, Pittsburgh and a tough Detroit team.

California had a suspect schedule early on, including games with St. Mary's, Olympic Club, Nevada, and Pacific Club, but then the Bears went on to beat Oregon, Washington State, Southern California, Washington and Stanford.

Lafayette had a season highlighted by a 6-0 win over Pitt. But the Leopards were little known outside of their area, as they only played teams close to their campus in Easton, Pennsylvania.

Cornell beat Penn and Columbia, but both had off seasons. Its 59-7 win over Dartmouth was impressive, but the schedule was riddled with weak programs including St. Bonaventure, Rochester, Western Reserve and Springfield.

Iowa was the only team to beat Notre Dame, 10-7, when the Irish were riding a 22 game undefeated streak. The Hawkeyes had wins over Illinois, Purdue, Minnesota, Indiana and Northwestern, but the combined record for these teams was only 11-24.

Vandy? The Commodores just squeezed by Kentucky, 21-14, while Centre slaughtered the 'Cats, 55-0. Penn State? The Nittany Lions were tough, but they tied Harvard and Centre beat the Crimson.

So which was the best team in the *regular* season? You can debate it, but Centre would certainly be a good pick, and its defensive prowess could be the decisive factor.

Again, as in 1919, there was no ambivalence in Danville, Kentucky.

CENTRE CONTINUES TO FASCINATE

The Baton Rouge "Star-Times" weighed in on why Centre had enjoyed such success in a story after the regular season had concluded.

MYSTERY OF FOOTBALL SOLVED SAYS WRITER... SUCCESS OF CENTRE TEAM DUE TO ENVIRONMENT OF DANVILLE

Every newspaper from the East to the West and from the North to South has sung the praises of the Centre College football team.

The secret is out! The all-absorbing mystery that has been agitating the football world for the last three years has been solved. It is not because they kneel in prayer before each game, nor is it due to the cunning and strategy of Coach Charlie Moran, that the Centre College team has proved an unbeatable combination on the gridiron this year.

The reason for the remarkable career of the Centre team is solely due to the environment. In a letter received by the "States-Times," in which our attention is called to the fact that Danville, Kentucky is not in the mountains—as this paper had inadvertently stated—but in the Bluegrass of Kentucky, a Danville man describes this environment as follows: "In the fall, the hills are aglow with red and gold, when the morning sun slants its rays through a mist of silver and purple, and the air has the tang of new wine, when home-killed meat, apple cider and pumpkin pie are the order of the day; or else, when May clothes the cliffs in red trumpet vines, and white dogwood blossoms and pink buds, and the streams are divinely serene between the tall gray cliffs and the peach trees and the cheery trees are in bloom, and May apples are ripe."

The letter ends with an invitation to the editor of the "States-Times" to visit Danville, stating that, "We can say with confidence that when your visit is over, you will leave with an 'honest to God reluctance,' and the feeling that you have been amongst people whose hospitality is sincere."

Along with his letter, our correspondent sent a booklet entitled, "Danville in the Bluegrass," which is beautifully illustrated with fine old residences, modern business houses, the stately buildings of Centre College, the Kentucky College for Women, the Kentucky School for the Deaf, and picturesque views of the surrounding country.

"Everyone has heard of the Bluegrass," the booklet says, "and most folk of Danville. To those who know us, we send our loving greetings; to those who do not, a cordial invitation to come and see—not a big city—but a little one with big ideals."

Thus the mystery is explained. A little city, a little college—but one with big ideals. We shall no longer wonder at the feat performed by the football warriors, trained in such an atmosphere, blazing a triumphant trail across gridirons all the way from Harvard Stadium on the Charles to that of our own Tulane on the Mississippi.

Someday, we hope to accept the kind invitation extended to us to visit Danville. We believe we would profit from it.

On December 2, Bo was back in Columbus playing in another All-Star game. The press was laudatory in describing the talent on the field.

The players represent the greatest assemblage of gridiron stars ever gotten together. In all, nineteen men whose names have appeared on various All-American teams played on the two teams.

Bo, one of those All-Americans, was captain of the West team, and his squad won when another All-American, Harold "Brick" Muller of California, blocked a punt, scooped it up, and ran 60 yards for the only score of the game.

CHAPTER 17:
POST-SEASON BOWL GAMES
AND THE TRIP OUT WEST

Even though everyone, including Uncle Charlie, had come around to being in favor of a post-season excursion, things were getting complicated in regard to just where, and when, the Colonels would go.

George Joplin, writing for the "Messenger," light-heartedly summed up the current state of indecision.

There has been confusion on Wall Street. Smart financiers are refusing to buy rail stocks. They are whittling their pencils to see which roads will profit when the Colonels' travel plans are announced.

Centre had decided not to go to Chicago to meet Notre Dame, or to go to New York to meet the Irish in the Polo Grounds, though the offer was there. Neither city, in December, was seen as being an "attractive" destination which would reward the players.

Fort Worth wanted to hold a second "Fort Worth Classic" after the success of the game between TCU and Centre. Of course, the Rose Bowl, on secure footing, had become a fixture and would remain so to this day.

Civic leaders in San Diego saw what the Rose Bowl had done for the Los Angeles area, and decided that hosting a bowl game in their city would bring favorable publicity, and could also be a financial windfall for hotels, restaurants and retail merchants. They had the perfect facility in Balboa Stadium just north of the downtown area, a classical facility built for use during the 1915 Panama-California Exposition.

San Diego decided to dub its bowl the "East vs. West Bowl." Centre was such a draw and had so captured the attention of sports fans all over the country that as soon as San Diego decided to definitely get in the bowl business, the first school that was contacted was Centre.

"We get Centre and our future is assured," was the comment of one of the organizers.

Naturally, Centre was flattered.

Meanwhile, the Rose Bowl contacted the Chief and asked that Centre not sign anything, as there was a good possibility that the Colonels were going to be invited to Pasadena. The Chief thought he had a solution as to where Centre should go.

"We'll play in both bowls," he told Jop. "It won't be a problem. We can play in San Diego on the 26th, travel by train up to Los Angeles, and play in the Rose Bowl on January 1."

There was only one problem. California had definitely signed for the Rose Bowl, but the Bears had an understanding that they were to play an undefeated, untied team, like themselves. The feeling was that it would basically be a "National Championship" game, and therefore both participants would have to have an unblemished record on January 1. If the Colonels were to lose in San Diego, then California could back out, and of course, no one in Pasadena wanted that to happen.

Negotiations went back and forth. Centre kept hearing that the Rose Bowl committee was sending out feelers to other schools. Meanwhile, San Diego's offer was firm. Centre was their team. So Centre signed a contract which guaranteed the school $16,000 to play in the "East vs. West Bowl."

The old saying that, "A bird in the hand is worth two in the bush," must have entered the Chief's mind. The Rose Bowl had wavered. San Diego was firm. Then, to complicate matters, the Chief received a signed contract from the Rose Bowl inviting Centre to play California, but a stipulation was written in that the game in San Diego was to be cancelled. Centre felt honor-bound to live up to the contract with the San Diego organizing committee, and that is why when you look back over the storied history of the oldest and most famous of post-season bowl games, there is no mention of Centre College.

Many people felt it was a shame, and do so to this day. So how did things finally work out? Since California insisted on an undefeated, untied opponent, the pool of teams was extremely limited. Centre was out. Iowa had hung up its gear and had no interest. That left just Lafayette, Cornell and Washington and Jefferson. There was a little problem, however, with W&J. It had committed to play Texas A&M on January 2 in Dallas.

Here's what happened. W&J was told it could back out of the Dallas game if it could find someone to take its place. Centre had agreed to go to Fort Worth after leaving San Diego and play in two bowl games by taking on TCU in a second Fort Worth Classic, but Fort Worth let Centre off the hook, and Centre agreed to play in Dallas in the place of W&J, and there was no bowl game in Fort Worth. It was nice of Fort Worth, but in reality, the cancellation spared the TCU Horned Toads of another pasting.

So, Washington and Jefferson got the nod for the Rose Bowl. The little school from Washington, PA, 30 miles south of Pittsburgh, proved to be an excellent choice. Bo was asked about the Presidents when the announcement was made.

"California will be meeting one of the great teams of the country, a team which will surprise a lot of the folks on the West coast."

Bo proved to be as good a prophet as he was a quarterback.

W&J entered the game a decided underdog. The California Bears had outscored their opponents during a 9-0 season by a whopping 312-33, and had crushed an undefeated Ohio State team the year before in the Rose Bowl by 28-0.

The Presidents and Bears played to a 0-0 tie.

The performance of W&J was all the more amazing when California's record is analyzed for the five year period, 1920-24.

1920	(9-0-0)	
1921	(9-0-1)	*The tie with W&J is included in 1921 record.
1922	(9-0-0)	
1923	(9-0-1)	Tied Nevada.
1924	(8-0-2)	Tied Washington and Stanford.

California was 44-0-4 during those years, and Washington and Jefferson's performance has to rank right up there with Centre's great win over Harvard in the David vs. Goliath category.

With the Rose Bowl match-up locked in, an opponent had to be found for Centre in San Diego. California was by far the best team on the coast, but which team was the second best?

With the Bears going to Pasadena, the organizing committee started looking around to see who was available. Someone threw out the fact that Notre Dame-Centre would be a great pairing.

"But we're the 'East vs. West Bowl.'"

Anyone with just a rudimentary bit of geographical knowledge knew that it was perhaps a bit of a stretch to have even designated Centre as being from the East, but at least the college was located "east of the Mississippi," as someone pointed out.

But a school from northern Indiana, in South Bend? How could Notre Dame be the "West" part of the game? It's amazing how quickly one can change course when they are flying by the seat of their pants.

"Let's call our game the 'Christmas Bowl.'"

"But it's on December 26."

It was decided that "The Day after Christmas Bowl" was a bit cumbersome, and a vote was taken, and a compromise reached. It would be the "San Diego East-West Christmas Classic." If someone wanted to quibble about two teams coming from the East, it could just be called the "Christmas Classic," and the press referred to the game as the "Christmas Bowl."

All of the worry about the name proved to be unimportant, because for various reasons, Notre Dame and the committee couldn't come to an understanding, even though it was announced that the Irish were going to play Centre. There were monetary considerations which couldn't be worked out. Also, there was a question about some players, particularly star halfback, Johnny Mohardt, having played in a professional game with the Racine team against Green Bay. Notre Dame's season was over on November

24, and Mohardt didn't realize that his team was even considering a post-season game when he suited up with Racine on December 4. So Notre Dame was out and it was back to the drawing board.

The Pacific Coast Conference was made up of California, Stanford, Washington, Washington State, Oregon and Oregon State. (Southern Cal and Idaho joined the next year.)

Washington State was the second best team in the conference, but the Cougars got blown out by Southern Cal, 28-7. Scratch Washington State.

The problem with the possibility of inviting Southern Cal was even though it was 10-1, the opponents had included two submarine bases (or two games with one submarine base, it isn't clear), the battleships Arizona and New York , Pomona, Cal Tech, and—the Trojans had been buried by California in their only loss, 38-7. Scratch Southern Cal. Oregon was 5-1-2. Not bad. But in their conference games, they were 0-1-2. Scratch Oregon.

Finally, the committee began to look somewhat inland and realized that the University of Arizona would make an attractive opponent. Its schedule may have been a bit suspect, but the Wildcats were 7-1, and their only defeat had been against a strong Texas A&M team in College Station, 17-13.

It took a few days of negotiations to get Arizona on board, but a deal was struck and the announcement was made in the December 13th papers.

SOUTHWESTERN CHAMPS TO OPPOSE COLONELS

The announcement was nearly lost due to the really big news.

McMILLIN ACCEPTS BIG OFFER— TO COACH AT CENTENARY IN LOUISIANA

Bo had several offers to coach, and the position that he mentioned to the team back in 1920 regarding the professional Canton Bulldogs was still his for the taking. He had received a firm offer of $7,000 annually to coach Howard College, now part of Samford University, in Birmingham.

The University of Dallas was also trying to sign Bo, but the Centenary offer of $10,000 was so attractive that he turned down the prospect of returning to his home state.

The offering and acceptance of the Centenary head coaching football job finally allowed Bo to firm up his wedding plans. Bo had dated his high school sweetheart, Maude Marie Miers, ever since they met just after Bo had entered North Side High in 1912. She was the love of his life, and he'd never seriously courted any other girl since falling for Marie.

Bo's long range plans had always been to achieve success on the gridiron and then parlay that success into a football coaching career. After securing the financial freedom that a head coaching career would bring, he planned to marry Marie.

The trip to the Southwest was timed perfectly in order to allow Bo and Marie to finally walk down the aisle. Bo had his job. Centre was going to be playing in nearby Dallas, so it was a natural to include a wedding in Fort Worth when the Colonels arrived for the scheduled game with Texas A&M.

Marie and her family would make the plans. Bo and his teammates would arrive from the game in San Diego, and it would be the ultimate "killing of two birds with one stone." Football and a wedding. For Bo, it couldn't get any better than that.

POST-SEASON HONORS AND RECOGNITION

All-American teams were being announced. Of course, a Walter Camp selection was the most prestigious. For 1921, Camp put Red Roberts on his first team at an end position, and Bo made the second team at quarterback. With Red's selection, Centre had three Walter Camp first team All-Americans, Bo and Red Weaver in 1919, and now Red Roberts, the smallest school to ever be so honored. Terry Snowday received honorable mention in Camp's selections.

There were other All-American teams announced. Walter Turnbull of the New York "Herald" had Red Roberts on his first team at end and Bo on his third team at quarterback. Fred Haynor of the Chicago "Daily News" picked Bo on his first team as a halfback and Bill James on his second team at end. Haynor left Red Roberts off his selections altogether. It sometimes hurt Red when selections were made because it was hard to categorize him. Was he a fullback, tackle or end?

Second to Walter Camp's teams, as far as prestige, was that picked by Lawrence Perry, "noted authority on college sports." Perry put Bo in a first team slot at halfback. Perry said of Bo, "McMillin's merits are too well known to require commendation. In the words of Dr. Johnson—it is vain to praise him and useless to blame him. He lacks none of the equipment that goes to make up a great back."

Charles Brinkley, a Camp All-American in 1912 and 1913 as a back at Harvard, put Bo and Red on his first team, Bo at halfback and Red at end. The United Press placed Bo and Red on its second team at quarterback and end.

Finally, one of the most respected All-American squads was that selected by 267 football coaches across the country and published in "Football World," based in Columbus, Ohio. Bo was picked as the first team quarterback and Red was placed on the second team, this time as a guard.

George Owen, Harvard's great junior fullback, joined Red on the second team.

Bo had become so famous nationally that a horse was named for him which would later run in the Kentucky Derby, "Bo McMillin."

A.E. Hundley and Sons, thoroughbred breeders, sold a yearling to Tom Pendergast, the Kansas City, Missouri politician who controlled the Democratic Party in the city for a quarter of a century.

Pendergast's horse was considered to be Derby material after finishing first in the Sanford Memorial at Saratoga in 1922, and won the Bluegrass Stakes, run before the Derby, in 1923.

Unfortunately, the Bo on the track wasn't as swift as the Bo on the gridiron on

Derby day. Jockey Danny Connelly rode his mount to a 12th place finish in a field of 21. Zev won the 49th running in 2:05 2/5 on a fast track.

An additional honor came Bo's way when it was announced that Centre's Louisville Alumni Club had commissioned an oil portrait of him to be painted by the noted artist, Charles Snead Williams. At the unveiling it was stated that the likeness was to hang in Old Centre so that, "students in years to come may look at it and hear tales of the star's prowess on the gridiron."

Unfortunately, the portrait is hanging somewhere other than on the Centre campus if it is hanging at all. Hopefully, some member of Bo's family has it, but no one knows for certain if it still exists.

IT'S TIME FOR THE 1921 BANQUET

The team banquet was held at K.C.W. on the evening of December 9, hosted by the Danville Chamber of Commerce. There were 44 players listed in the program who were honored. Many had been but scrubs, having rarely been in an actual game, or possibly having never even suited up. However, their contribution was recognized and appreciated for what they had helped the team become, as George Joplin had written about with such feeling in the "Messenger" just before the Transylvania game.

Out on Cheek Field every afternoon the spectators will see a crowd of red-jerseyed youths fight for all they are worth to check the dynamic assaults of the first and second teams. The first team will have their turn smashing into the mass of red. Then the second team, all fresh, will open up their guns. When the powder has cleared away, and the scrimmage is over, one will find a battered, bleeding, weary, heavy-footed gang still holding the fort. Their goal line may have been crossed a dozen times during the afternoon, but they have battled and are inwardly proud of their showing.

The feast started with oysters, celery hearts and stuffed olives, with the entrees being Kentucky country ham and chicken a la king. Vegetables were potatoes au gratin, and asparagus tips on toast. There were various breads, and dessert was frozen pudding on egg kisses. After dessert, cigars were passed around to guests (but not the team) who wished to fire up and smoke with their coffee.

Then the speeches began. The keynote speaker was Judge E.V. Puryear of Danville, and it was no surprise that his topic was, "The Harvard Game."

Back of every great and good thing stands the greater thing that produces it; behind the Centre College football team stands the great spirit of Centre College, and back of that, the members of the team in their right thinking and clean playing.

Judge Puryear went on for some time in that vein, and then reached into his coat pocket and pulled out a hand-written poem which he must have labored over for several days.

Have you ever heard the story of Old Centre's glory?
How her team made things hum in the big stadium,
And on a Saturday laid Harvard away,
Along with VPI and those who die,
When they meet the might of a Centre Fight?

How with Arm who was strong and Bo who was mighty
She shocked them all and made them look flighty,
With Bill James behaving like Jesse James Uster,
And Uncle Charlie directing with Roscoe as booster?

Did you hear how Chapin, like he had a strong toddy,
Went down right now when tackled by Snoddy?
How the line of old Harvard was made to look meager,
By Gordy and Jones and Gibson and Cregor?

Did you hear about Kubale, Centre's hot tamale—
Too hot to handle, he held them quite jolly,
With the help of the line and the lengthy Shadoan, and
Whenever they started, the boys stopped them a-going?

Never, they say, was such football yet
Displayed in a game as was shown by Bartlett,
And in skill in stopping the forward pass,
And in all that makes football, Centre showed class.

'Twas all the boys that did it—they're heroes every one,
The whole darn line and Rubarth and Covington.
The score looked fine, they wrote it, "Centre is now 6,"
And underneath they added, "Harvard, she is nix."

We tanned them good and proper in a satisfactory manner,
We had the team to do it, and we took along our Tanner.
I expect, maybe, that you got the word, 'Twas a little talked about,
And several persons heard it, including Dr. Stout.

But then, if you know it all, there's no more to be said,
Except, of course, to mention, 'Twas a whole lot due to Red.

The judge managed to get all of the 16 players who appeared in the Harvard game included in his poem, if you made the "Centre showed class" account for young Ray Class, who was in for one play, the missed field goal. The word "Uster" must rhyme with "booster," but "Jesse James Uster?" The meaning is unclear, but must have had some contemporary reference.

After the poem, Tiny Thornhill spoke on, "The line, God bless the line."

Each of the players gave a short talk. Lefty Whitnell once again sang his rendition of "The World is Round, but it's Crooked, too."

Letter winners were announced. Those awarded the coveted gold "C" included:

Army Armstrong	George Jones
Tom Bartlett	Ed Kubale
Don Beane	Clifton Lemon
George Chinn	Bo McMillin
Ray Class	Chick Murphy
Herb Covington	Red Roberts
Ben Cregor	Frank Rubarth
Royce Flippin	Bill Shadoan
Dick Gibson	Terry Snowday
Minos Gordy	Hump Tanner
Bill James	Case Thomasson
	John McGee—(team manager)

The last event of the evening was to have the letter winners move out of the banquet for a private meeting to elect next year's captain. The voting didn't take but a few minutes. The 1921 leader, Captain Armstrong, brought the attendees back to order and announced that he had the pleasure of introducing, "the captain of the 1922 Centre College Colonels, James "Red" Roberts."

Red stood up to speak. Normally the big guy was good on his feet, but his election had left him in somewhat of an emotional state.

"People, we must have the same coaching system that we have had for the past few years. This is the greatest question before the minds of the American people at the present time."

There were cheers and laughter. "I am coming back here next year to play football, and if the boys will stand by me, we will clean the map off the United States."

There was prolonged laughter.

"But, really now, talking serious, and so forth and so on."

As Red mopped his forehead, time had to be taken out for several minutes to allow the members of the audience to recover from their laughter, many nearly literally rolling on the floor.

George Joplin was in attendance.

Red attempted to thank his mates for the captaincy, but, arising for the speech, words failed him. After trying out a dozen choice adjectives, and finding that they were leading him to nowhere in particular, he sat down with the remark, "Gus King is right. I don't know ten words."

TROUBLE ON THE HORIZON

Dr. Frank Rainey, faculty athletic advisor, had to miss the banquet due to traveling south to represent Centre at the Southern Intercollegiate Athletic Association's annual meeting. On the agenda was an issue which was of critical importance to Centre.

Each year, the issue of the "one-year rule" had been brought up, and it had been defeated by the narrowest of margins at the previous meeting. The rule, if adopted, would have made freshmen ineligible to participate in any intercollegiate sports until 12 months after their enrollment.

Centre had grown a bit each year, and the entering freshman class contained the largest number of first year men to ever enroll in the college. The excitement and publicity surrounding the great success of the football team was credited with being the driving force behind the record number of new entrants.

STUDENT BODY	1921-22
Seniors	32
Juniors	33
Sophomores	72
Freshmen	125
Total	262

Freshmen made up 48% of the students on campus. If they were declared ineligible, Centre would have had but 137 men to choose from in order to compete with colleges who would have had many more in their pool of possible athletes.

Half of the 16 men who played in the Harvard game were freshmen: Ed Kubale, Minos Gordy, Bill Shadoan, George Jones, Dick Gibson, Frank Rubarth, Herb Covington, and Ray Class.

Of the 28 players who made the trip to Boston, 14 were freshmen. In addition to those who got in the game, Don Beane, Hope Hudgins, Clifton "Hennie" Lemon, Case Thomasson, Les Combs and Weldon Bradley were all first year men.

"If you pass this rule, it will kill us," Dr. Rainey argued. "We'll be alright next year because we have such a strong freshman class this year, and most will be back. But in the future, it will place great hardship on Centre, and to other small schools our size."

Of the 27 member schools represented at the conference, 18 voted in favor of implementing the "one year rule."

As a consolation to the smaller colleges, the conference attendees passed the "migratory rule," which meant that once a young man had enrolled in a school and participated in a sport, he couldn't transfer later, prohibiting athletes from starting their careers at one institution and then transferring to a larger school where they may garner more fame.

"That's not a problem with us," Dr. Rainey declared. "But the 'one year rule' will make it impossible for the smaller school to compete in the future."

Dr. Rainey's words were prophetic.

HEADING WEST—THE GAME PLAN FOR THE TRIP

Centre was firming up its plans for the long trip to the West. The games with Arizona in San Diego on December 26, and with Texas A&M in Dallas on January 2, were the kingpins around which the trip would be mapped out. It had taken a lot of detailed planning to pull it off.

Howard King, the Southern Railroad district agent, based in Lexington, spent days traveling between his office and Danville in working out every moment of the travel. Finally, he held a press conference and released a schedule, carefully typed out on the railroad's letterhead in bold letters.

CENTRE COLLEGE FOOTBALL TEAM REQUIRING ONE 14 SECTION, DRAWING ROOM, PULLMAN SLEEPING CAR, TO BE HANDLED ON CHARTERED BASIS TO SAN DIEGO AND RETURN AS FOLLOWS:

LEAVE DANVILLE, KY-SOUTHERN RAILROAD, 5:30 PM, DEC. 16
ARRIVE ST. LOUIS, MO-SOUTHERN RAILROAD, 7:10 AM, DEC. 17
LEAVE ST. LOUIS, MO-WABASH RAILROAD, 9:03 AM, DEC. 17
ARRIVE KANSAS CITY, MO-WABASH RAILROAD, 5:30 PM, DEC. 17
LEAVE KANSAS CITY, MO-UNION PACIFIC RAILROAD, 6:15 PM, DEC. 17
ARRIVE DENVER, CO-UNION PACIFIC RAILROAD, 12:50 PM, DEC. 18
LEAVE DENVER, CO-DENVER & RIO GRANDE RAILROAD, 8:15 AM, DEC. 19
ARRIVE OGDEN, UT-DENVER & RIO GRANDE RAILROAD, 1:40 PM, DEC. 20
LEAVE OGDEN, UT-SOUTHERN PACIFIC RAILROAD, 2:20 PM, DEC. 20
ARRIVE SAN FRANCISCO, CA-SOUTHERN PACIFIC, 2:30 PM, DEC, 21
    (ALLOWING FOR THE THREE HOUR TIME DIFFERENTIAL, THE TRIP FROM DANVILLE TO SAN FRANCISCO WOULD HAVE TAKEN EXACTLY FIVE DAYS).
LEAVE SAN FRANCISCO, CA-SOUTHERN PACIFIC, 8:00 PM, DEC. 21
ARRIVE LOS ANGELES, CA-SOUTHERN PACIFIC, 8:00 AM, DEC. 22
LEAVE LOS ANGELES, CA-SOUTHERN PACIFIC, 1:30 AM, DEC. 23
ARRIVE SAN DIEGO, CA-SOUTHERN PACIFIC, 8:00 AM, DEC. 23
LEAVE SAN DIEGO, CA-SANTA FE RAILROAD, 12:01 AM, DEC. 27
ARRIVE LOS ANGELES, CA-SANTA FE, 6:00 AM, DEC. 27
LEAVE LOS ANGELES, CA-SOUTHERN PACIFIC, 8:30 AM, DEC. 27
ARRIVE EL PASO, TX-SOUTHERN PACIFIC, 8:30 AM, DEC. 28
LEAVE EL PASO, TX-TEXAS & PACIFIC RAILROAD, 6:00 PM, DEC. 28
ARRIVE DALLAS, TX-TEXAS & PACIFIC RAILROAD, 1:10 PM, DEC. 29
LEAVE DALLAS, TX-MISSOURI, KANSAS & TEXAS RR, 8:00 PM, JAN. 2
ARRIVE ST. LOUIS, MO-MISSOURI, KANSAS & TEXAS RR, 11:55 AM, JAN. 3

LEAVE ST. LOUIS, MO-SOUTHERN RAILROAD, 9:20 PM, JAN. 3
ARRIVE DANVILLE, KY-SOUTHERN RAILROAD, 10:55 AM, JAN. 4
(SIGNIFICANT STOPOVERS IN ST. LOUIS, DENVER, SAN FRANCISCO,
LOS ANGELES, SAN DIEGO, EL PASO, DALLAS, AND, ON THE RETURN,
ST. LOUIS.)
    THE CHARTERED PULLMAN WOULD GO OVER THE TRACKS
OF EIGHT LINES.
    (1) SOUTHERN RAILROAD
    (2) WABASH RAILROAD
    (3) UNION PACIFIC
    (4) DENVER AND RIO GRANDE
    (5) SOUTHERN PACIFIC
    (6) SANTA FE-(ATCHISON, TOPEKA AND SANTA FE)
    (7) TEXAS AND PACIFIC
    (8) MISSOURI, KANSAS AND TEXAS

King stated at the conference that he had been meeting with representatives of all the railroads to make the trip as smooth and enjoyable as it could possibly be. There had been personnel from each of the lines who met with the Centre representatives to even formalize the meals that would be offered on the trip and to address any dietary restrictions which any of the players may have.

We need to understand in a little more detail exactly what the logistics of the venture were to entail. The Southern would provide a private Pullman which would be the Colonels' traveling hotel, a "home on wheels," for the entire duration. Centre would pay a flat fee for the car, and the railroad would in turn pay the Pullman Company, the actual owner of the sleeper. It didn't matter which railroad's tracks were to be the "road," the Pullman would simply be hooked onto another regularly scheduled passenger train of the line which owned the tracks. The Pullman Company also provided a porter, part of the rental arrangement. The same porter accompanied the team on the entire trip, and the individual assigned to the car was the same gentleman who accompanied the team on their 1921 trips to Boston and to New Orleans.

The Colonels would have the full use of any train onto which they were hooked. If they wanted to use the observation car, or sit in a day coach, if such were part of the consist, they were free to do so. Their baggage would be transferred to the baggage car of their present conveyance, and they would take their meals in the dining car of the train onto which they were connected, unless they were on a "stopover."

The arrangement was that Centre's Pullman would be connected as the last car on any of the trains. That way, they truly had a "private" car, as the rest of the passengers could walk back and forth on the train, but couldn't use the Colonels' car as a "pathway."

Each night, the porter would convert the seats into beds, there being two beds, an upper and lower, in each of the 14 "sections." The next morning, while the team had breakfast, he would convert the beds back into seats for the daytime travel.

The Pullman had a drawing room, and there were toilets and basins on the ends of the cars, one each for males and females. Of course, since there were all males on the trip to the West, both facilities could be used.

Travel in this era meant that often hotels were part of the train stations in various cities, especially in the larger terminals. Passengers would often stay over and "freshen up" en route. The Centre entourage had several layovers scheduled to break up the trip, but there were no plans to stay at the terminal hotels. Rather, layovers would find the Centre entourage at the finest establishments in each city where they stopped for the night—Denver, San Diego and Dallas. The team would also make several daytime jaunts along the way.

The itinerary was to go from Danville to Louisville and then to St. Louis. From St. Louis, the team would head due west through Kansas City to Denver, and then wind over the Rockies, through Salt Lake City, to Ogden, Utah, and then to San Francisco.

From San Francisco, they would go to Los Angeles, then to San Diego. After the "Christmas Bowl," they'd go back to LA, and then go southeast to Fort Worth and Dallas.

After the January 2 game in Dallas, they'd return to St. Louis, and then retrace the journey on the same tracks that had carried them from Danville to St. Louis.

The trip would take 20 days! It was to be certainly the most memorable adventure in which any of the participants had even been involved. The Chief and everyone who had been part of the planning had as their constant goal that the journey be "first class," that it be "fun," and that it should always be understood that the whole endeavor was to reward the team for, as had been expressed at the team banquet, "a job well done."

Danville was euphoric, as was much of Kentucky. Just a few short years ago, the little town had basked in the knowledge that it hosted a respectable center of learning, and took pride in the fact that young men who had spent some years there had achieved prominence across the country.

But now? Reporters came to Danville from all over the country to see exactly what was going on. Arizona? People in Kentucky started getting out their maps.

Arizona had only become a state nine years earlier, joining the union as the 48th state on February 14, 1912. The state school, the University of Arizona, had been founded in Tucson in 1885, but it was six years later when the first classes were held.

Tucson? Where was that? It was spotted on the map as being in the south part of the state, not far, 40 miles, from...Mexico!

If someone had an older map, one printed 10 years or more ago, Arizona was shown as, "Arizona Territory."

"Goodness, are there still wild Indians out there? Will our boys be safe?"

By 1920, Arizona had a population of 334,162, but the state, with 114,006 square miles, had a population density of only 2.9 per square mile, so that each person could have had slightly over 225 acres of land if it had been divided up proportionally.

Tucson had slightly over 20,000 residents. During the school year, 1921-22, the University of Arizona had an enrollment of 1369 students and 107 faculty members on a campus of 41 acres, on which sat 21 buildings.

The "Wildcat" was adopted as the school mascot in 1915.

ALL ABOARD!

It was necessary to include clothes for varying climates which would be encountered along the way. December temperatures could be well below freezing in Denver and the Rockies, to balmy and warm in California. The week before the trip had been spent in packing, trying to prepare for all contingencies, including the fact that invitations had been coming in from alumni groups, civic organizations, and people who were just fans, all along the route, hoping to host functions for the team while they were in town. Proper attire was going to be necessary.

Hump Tanner told one reporter that Terry Snowday was packing enough clothes to outfit the entire cast of a D.W. Griffith movie, and if you look at many of the photographs taken on the trip, you'll see that Terry was indeed a very dapper guy.

Centre had decided that those who would be included on the journey were the letter winners who had been announced at the recent banquet. There were 22 players and the team manager who had received the gold "C." The five additional spots on the 14 section Pullman, with its 28 berths, were occupied by Uncle Charlie, Tiny Thornhill, Carl "Swede" Anderson, trainer, George Joplin, reporter and great booster, who was going along not only to report for his paper, but also to handle press relations for the team, and faculty athletic representative, Albert Eugene Porter. Business obligations kept Chief Myers in Chicago, much to his regret.

The send-off for the team on the evening of December 16 was greater even than the rousing celebration that occurred when the Colonels left for the Harvard game.

It was like they going on a Grand Tour of Europe, or something like that. They were going to be gone nearly three weeks, and everyone wanted to see them off. They all had leather suitcases with stickers on them that were from so many of the trips where they had been—from hotels and trains and places like Niagara Falls.

Some Louisville friends of the team shipped steamer trucks over to Danville for the team to use. Steamer trunks were big leather and wooden trunks which opened up and were like a closet and wardrobe combined. You could hang clothes in them, and they had drawers where you could put shirts and underwear. They also had shelves on the bottom to put shoes.

You dressed when you traveled back then. Now, people just dress casually or worse, but not back then. You dressed for the occasion, and the guys always looked great whenever they went anywhere.

The team left when Christmas vacation began, on a late Friday afternoon, so any students who lived in Lexington or Louisville, or even west toward St. Louis, anywhere that the train was going, had tickets to go to their homes for Christmas vacation.

Howard and I couldn't go because in order to get to Elizabethtown, we had to take the L&N home instead of the Southern.

The Danville brass band played, George Swinebroad led cheers, there was a lot of hugging and wishing the team well, and then, I'll never forget, the whistle blew and blew and the team waved from the windows, and slowly, they pulled

339

away, and they left with every person at the station so proud that our school was going on this great adventure.

The Pullman car that the team traveled in was named the "Cowdray," named for Lord Cowdray, the British-born engineer who had built the Hudson River Tunnel which connected New York and New Jersey.

The train stopped in Lexington for a brief layover where a crowd once again was at the station to cheer on the team. Then it was west to Louisville where they were met again by a large, enthusiastic group of supporters, this time at the Seventh Street Station. After getting off briefly to meet with the fans, the players headed for their berths, prepared by the porter while they mingled on the platform.

Next stop—St. Louis. Time of arrival—7:10 a.m., on December 17.

The St. Louis University athletic officials had organized a breakfast for the team during the two hour layover while the "Cowdray" was to be hooked onto a westbound train.

The meal was to be served in the massive St. Louis Union Station. The terminal, built in 1894, had a restaurant open to passengers and the public operated by the famous Fred Harvey organization, staffed by attractive young ladies called "Harvey Girls," and catered meals in an adjacent private room. The "Girls" were a hit with the team, and, it was said that the squad made an equally favorable impression on the pretty waitresses.

Before going to the breakfast, each of the team members had to experience a phenomenon in the huge Grand Lobby where a towering arch, 40 feet wide at its base, allowed a person to whisper while facing the wall, and another individual, facing the opposite wall, could clearly hear what was said.

"Hey, Terry," Army barely whispered. The startled Snowday turned around, certain that the captain was standing just behind him, not way across the lobby.

Of course, everyone had to experience the "Whispering Arch."

"Nothing like that in Danville," Bill James said to Jop, who sent news about everything that happened on the trip back to the "Messenger" in Danville.

Ward Goodloe, representing a group known as the "Kentucky Society of St. Louis," had wired Danville just before the team left for the West Coast, offering to also host a breakfast. When his organization received a return wire that the Colonels were already committed, the members came to the station and met with the team when they left the dining room, and walked them back through the train shed to the "Cowdray," sending them off with loud cheers as the train pulled out just after 9:00 a.m. on the next leg of the trip.

Over the Wabash Railroad they traveled all day, heading west on the 250 miles of track to Kansas City. In the afternoon, the "Cowdray" was switched to a Union Pacific train to make the 400 mile jaunt through Kansas, mainly traversed while the Colonels slept for their second night.

After breakfast, they crossed the Kansas border and entered the plains of Colorado. There was a mid-morning stop in Hugo, elevation 4,943 feet, to allow the big engine to take on coal and water, and the Colonels disembarked in order to run a few wind sprints.

It was 1:30 in the afternoon, Sunday, December 18, when they pulled into Denver's beautiful Beaux-Arts style, Union Station, rebuilt in 1894 after the previous terminal was destroyed by fire. When the Colonels reached the interior of the massive lobby, they were overwhelmed to see more than 400 people waiting, each crowding in trying to personally greet them.

The "Rocky Mountain News" had a reporter assigned to spend the day with the team.

The famous yell of the Colorado mines, "Rip 'em up, tear 'em up, give them h... Centre," was transposed to fit the occasion, and the Centre College booster's cheers thundered in the ears of the visitors as they were pushed, pulled, and shoved by the admiring crowd, swelled to several hundred, to the station exit.

Following their arrival, the Kentuckians were guests of the sports editor of this paper in an automobile tour of Denver. In the big enclosed limousines of the Denver Cab Company, the Southerners visited the Civic Center, City and Chessman Parks, and the residential and other scenic districts of the city.

After the tour of the city, the limousines returned to the heart of the city and let the team out at the ornate Denver Athletic Club where they would stay for the night. The athletes changed into workout clothes, did some exercising, had a welcomed shower, and returned to their rooms to get ready for the evening.

Once again, limousines were lined up outside the Club to transport the Colonels to the Albany Hotel at the corner of Stout and 17th Street. The official reception included many of Denver's dignitaries along with friends and alumni of Centre, reporters and photographers.

"Here's to Uncle Charlie..."
"Here's to the Gold and White..."
"Here's to the Centre spirit..."

As soon as the toasts ended, the team again piled into the limousines for a night at the Orpheum Theater.

The performance was interrupted by the crowd standing and cheering the Kentuckians before the actors could continue.

The next morning, the "Cowdray" was connected to a Denver and Rio Grande passenger train for the trip over the Rockies to Ogden, Utah. For this part of the trip, the Colonels' car was placed in front of the observation car so that the team and other passengers could enjoy the scenery from the rear of the train as it slowly wound its way up from the flatness of Denver through the towering peaks. Most of the team had never been in the mountains, and some hadn't seen any significant snow which began to become more evident as they reached a higher elevation.

Some 25 miles west of Denver, the conductor came into the car and told everyone to watch for water running along the side of the train. "You'll see water running one way, and then water running the other way. You're going over the Continental Divide. Water going that way," and he pointed to his left, "will eventually end up in the Pacific Ocean, and water running the other way," and he pointed out a stream on the right, "will end up in the Gulf of Mexico, or Atlantic Ocean."

There was a lot of discussion about that fact, and more than a little disbelief, but Uncle Charlie confirmed what the conductor had told them.

"Well, if you say so, Unc…"

The train took the Royal Gorge route, going over the highest mainline track in the country at the 10,240 foot Tennessee Pass. It was a slow, twisting, wonderful ride, punctuated by another overnight segment, and the "Cowdray" didn't reach its next goal, Ogden, Utah, until 1:30 in the afternoon on Tuesday, December 20, over 29 hours after pulling out of Denver.

Ogden was the end of the line for the Rio Grande, and there was a 40 minute layover awaiting the Southern Pacific's crack train, the "Overland Limited" which had originated in Chicago.

The railroads had opened up the West with the meeting of the Central Pacific, originating in Omaha, and the Union Pacific, originating in Sacramento, at Promontory Summit, northwest of Ogden. The "Golden Spike" which joined the two lines was driven on May 10, 1869.

The original transcontinental route skirted around the northern boundary of the Great Salt Lake. However, under the leadership of E.H. Harriman, plans were drawn up for the railroad to actually cross the lake, and in 1904, 103 miles of new track were completed which included 15 miles of fill and an incredible 23 miles of wooden trestle, and this is the route which the team took after having pulled out of Ogden.

The "Overland Limited" entered Nevada nine miles west of Lucin, Utah, and continued across the state throughout the afternoon and evening. Once across the state line into California, the train journeyed through the Donner Pass, in the northern Sierra Nevada, and then began the descent to Sacramento, going down a grade of 7,000 feet in 100 miles.

After a short stop in California's capital, the final leg of slightly over 100 miles found the "Limited" in Oakland, where the "Cowdray" was uncoupled and placed on a siding, with the rest of the train being pulled onto a Southern Pacific ferry, the "Solano," for transport across the Bay into San Francisco. (Until 1930, the Southern Pacific brought passenger trains into San Francisco via large ferries, and the "Solano" was the largest of all. It was 410' X 110' and had four tracks. Not only could it convey two entire passenger trains, but a switch engine as well. Freight trains went around the Bay on a land line.)

The Colonels rode the ferry across the Bay, marveling at the skyline of San Francisco which lined the opposite shore. When they stepped on land again, it was 2:30 in the afternoon, December 21. Allowing for the three hour time differential, they had been gone exactly five days since leaving Danville, and they were still over 500 miles from San Diego.

At the pier awaiting Uncle Charlie and the squad was the athletic director of Stanford University, Walter B. Powell, the secretary of the Pacific Coast Football Association, J.R. Klawans, and the former coach of the Owensboro High School team back in Kentucky, who had been Stanford's coach in 1919, Bob Evans.

The three were going to be the hosts of the Kentuckians while they were in the Bay Area. Evans was particularly interested in greeting Owensboro natives, Hump Tanner, Tom Bartlett and Terry Snowday. Accompanying the official committee was a large group of transplanted Kentuckians including Centre graduates, and the usual reporters and photographers who met the Colonels wherever they went.

Photographers from the San Francisco "Call and Post" clicked away, and the morning edition, on December 22, published a picture under the large heading and caption:

CENTRE COLLEGE VISITS SAN FRANCISCO
The "Praying Colonels" lingered in town long enough to pose for a few pictures before proceeding to Palo Alto. Bob Evans, former Stanford football coach, who gave three Centre stars their first instruction in high school, was on hand to greet the team. At top, from left, Tanner, Evans, Bartlett and Snowday. The inset is Bo McMillin, left, sensational quarterback, and Red Roberts, All-American end.

The San Francisco "Chronicle" had a four column wide, large photograph in its morning issue also.

CENTRE COLLEGE COLONELS

The photo had the entire team and those who greeted them, and the inset identified, "Bud" Jones, All-American, Red Roberts and the, "famed quarterback, Bo McMillin."
Local reporter Fred E. Farmer filed a story under the heading:

FAMOUS CENTRE FOOTBALLERS, COACH,
COME TO SAN FRANCISCO
COLONELS FROM KENTUCKY
MOST IMPRESSIVE LOOKING BUNCH OF HUSKIES
The Colonels from Centre College, with Coach Charlie Moran, arrived in San Francisco yesterday on the "Overland Limited" of the Southern Pacific. A fine, husky bunch of football men are these sons of Kentucky—the kind who can be singled out in a crowd at once.

A person is impressed with them, but not in the manner to consider them the team that went to Cambridge and conquered Harvard. They look more of the freshwater college variety, but their football record is their credential. And it is some hardy credential.

Bo McMillin, perhaps the most talked about football player today, is a quiet chap, speaks with a typical Southern drawl, and wears gloves. He is not that tall, but a peek at the width of his shoulders speaks of the tremendous driving power for which he is noted.

Bo is built rather close to the ground, and in street clothes looks almost meek. But according to his teammates and his record, this mien of meekness is left in the dressing room, and Bo is a regular "eat-'em-up" man on the football field.

The majority of the Centre men are short and husky. Jones, a guard, looks to weigh about 150, but lays claim to 185. It was that way all along the line. Snowday, the great Centre halfback, is long and rather thin, but according to his teammates, hits the line like a ton of bricks.

Red Roberts, an end of the Colonels, picked by Walter Camp for the first All-American team, is a giant of a man. Red weighed 235 pounds when he left Kentucky, and he certainly looks like it. He resembles his brother All-American end, Brick Muller of California. Both are red-headed, freckle-faced, and husky enough to tear a backfield man in two.

All of the boys are extremely mild-mannered. And perhaps the most quiet of the bunch is the captain of the team, Norris "Army" Armstrong. And then there is Uncle Charlie Moran himself. Charlie is a National League umpire in the baseball season, and when asked to pose for a photograph, jokingly said umpires are not accustomed to having their pictures taken. He is always on the lookout for his team, and every man on the Centre team swears by him.

After satisfying the press and thanking the fans who came to greet them, the Colonels boarded buses for a tour of the downtown area. It had only been 15 years since the devastating San Francisco earthquake, but the city had been rebuilt even more beautifully than it had appeared before the catastrophe.

The buses wound up Nob Hill so that the mansions, rebuilt after the earthquake, could be appreciated, and the players got out and walked around, taking in the grandeur that even exceeded what they had experienced in touring the Back Bay of Boston. Then it was 35 miles south to the campus of Stanford, in Palo Alto.

Stanford had been founded by Leland Stanford, railroad magnate and former California governor, and his wife Jane, in honor of their son, Leland, Junior, who died from typhoid fever at age 16. The first classes were held in 1891.

Stanford's initial bequest was $5,000,000 and after his death in 1893, his wife donated another $11,000,000, assuring the ability of the school to grow into one of the great educational institutions in the country.

The University had just completed a new football stadium when Centre arrived on the campus for a workout. The facility had been completed in just 132 days, held 60,000, and cost $573,470. The inaugural game had been played five weeks previously, a rather unhappy affair with the Cardinal losing badly to the California Bears, 42-7. The tuft on the practice field was in better condition that that of the new stadium, so the Colonels worked out there.

George Joplin, ever present, filed a story for his readers in Danville's "Messenger," and for the Louisville "Herald."

Did you ever see a band of youngsters at play after having been penned up in a house for several days? Well, the Centre College football warriors resembled a bunch of frolicsome kiddies after a quarantine in their workout at Leland Stanford University. The drill was the first thorough one in several days, and the boys reveled in it to the fullest. They had begun to get mighty tired of the train, and welcomed with eagerness the feel of moleskins once again. Muscles stiffened by the tedious but pleasurable ride here were flexed in the snappy drill Coach Moran gave his charges at Palo Alto.

The boys were in uniform at 3:30 in the afternoon. They were a bit slow in getting warmed up, and had some difficulty hanging onto the slippery ball as there was a slight drizzle. Near the close of the practice session, they found their footing and were working true to form.

A large crowd of students and other spectators turned out and applauded the work of the squad. Tonight, the athletic officials of Stanford gave a dinner in honor of the Colonels. Nothing that would add to the comfort of the members of the party was overlooked by the University officials. After the practice, the team was shown about the new stadium which greatly resembles the Harvard horseshoe. After their showers, the men were taken on a motor tour around the college's 9,000 acre campus, which seems about the size of Danville.

The party was led through the library and the $2,000,000 church and chapel. A.E. Roth, college treasurer, described the points of special interest to the Colonels while in the chapel building. He announced that chapel attendance was non-compulsory. George Chinn announced that "any student who would cut chapel ought to be hung."

After a wonderful dinner, the squad was taken back to San Francisco and took the ferry back to Oakland. They entertained themselves by feeding the gulls which would fly in low and eat right out of their hands.

Swede Anderson, the trainer, insisted that he wanted to go through the "Golden Gate" before it closed and invited "Old Nero," Red Roberts, to come with him. "It may be your only chance."

The "Cowdray" was coupled to the Southern Pacific "Lark" and is scheduled to pull out later tonight.

At the station, a reporter asked Bo what he thought about California playing Washington and Jefferson rather than Centre in the Rose Bowl. Bo diplomatically side-stepped the question about why Centre was heading to San Diego rather than Pasadena.

The Centre great said that W&J is one of the trickiest teams on the Eastern fields, and one which can never be taken lightly.

A DAY IN LOS ANGELES

When the Colonels awakened on Thursday morning, December 22, they were still north of Los Angeles, being hauled along behind the Southern Pacific "Lark," an overnight, all-Pullman consist which traveled between San Francisco and Los Angeles.

It was a popular train for taking Californians between the state's two major cities. You went to the station and boarded for an evening departure, perhaps headed to the lounge car and had a cocktail or two if you had a flask (due to prohibition) and then turned in for the night. The next morning you awakened, went to the dining car for breakfast, and rolled into LA or San Francisco, depending upon which way you were traveling, and disembarked at 9:00 a.m., rested, fed, and ready to spend your day doing whatever.

The Colonels had a "Lark" experience, except for having their own private "Cowdray," when they climbed down the steps to head to the Los Angeles Southern Pacific Terminal. (The Los Angeles Union Station, constructed to service the Southern Pacific, Union Pacific, and Santa Fe, wasn't built until 1939.)

The usual large number of press representatives was at the station, and the Los Angeles "Evening Herald" published a picture of the team standing on the platform. Each of the squad was dressed in suits, ties and overcoats, as usual. An inset photo showed Uncle Charlie, Army, Bo and Red, all looking very dapper.

In addition to the press, alumni and fans, there was a special person on the platform awaiting the team's arrival. Jack Dempsey, the "Manassa Mauler," heavyweight champion since 1919, and arguably the most famous and popular boxer of all time, came up to Uncle Charlie and introduced himself. He asked if he could spend the day with the Colonels, and indeed he did. Dempsey seemed to be as in awe of the Centre team as each member of the squad was impressed with him.

"Can you believe it? Jack Dempsey!"

Dempsey playfully shadow-boxed with Red and said, "Come on big fellow. Let's see what you have." Red was nonplussed and smiled.

"Mr. Dempsey, I really wouldn't want to hurt you," which received an appreciative laugh from all who stood around.

The alumni had arranged transportation to take the Colonels to Bovard Field, home stadium of the University of Southern California. Inside the stadium, Uncle Charlie and the team were met by the athletic director, coaching staff, and student manager who welcomed them to USC.

"Whatever you need and we can provide, just say the word." It was typical of the courtesies shown everywhere that Centre went.

After donning their gear, it was time for more photographs. The San Diego "Tribune," the afternoon partner of the morning San Diego "Union," had sent a photographer and reporter up by train to cover the team for both of the papers. The evening paper published a picture showing 13 Colonels in uniform along with Coaches Moran and Thornhill.

After the workout, again on a somewhat wet field like that in San Francisco, the squad showered and then headed to the Famous Players-Lasky Studio, created in 1916 by the merger of the two companies, located on Vine Street from Selma Avenue to Sunset Boulevard.

The actors and actresses shut down production on the various big stages when the Colonels would walk in, fascinated and pleased that they were having an opportunity to meet the celebrated Kentuckians.

"Ladies and gentlemen, I have the pleasure of introducing the famous team from Centre College back in Kentucky, the team that beat Harvard this past October." Applause would erupt from performers and stagehands as each of the buildings was toured.

There was a production in progress starring a 22 year old actress named Gloria Swanson. Despite her young age, Swanson had already appeared in over 20 films, working with, amongst others, the legendary director, Cecil B. DeMille. Swanson appeared in five movies released in 1922, all under the direction of Sam Wood.

When the Colonels entered the stage where Swanson was involved in a scene, Wood shouted "CUT!" and all action ceased. After introductions, Bo was asked to show the actress how a tackle was made. A quick dash to the prop department uncovered a football which was handed to Swanson who dutifully followed her director's instructions.

The resulting photograph was a classic, and was carried in newspapers all across the country. Bo is bent over, smiling into the camera, with his hands behind Swanson's knees. Army and an actress named May McAvoy have their hands on Bo's shoulder. Swanson holds the football under her left arm, her expression one of minimal amusement at best. Sam Wood is shown "directing" the shoot. On the left margin are Uncle Charlie, team manager, John McGee, and an unknown man.

After the studio tour, the buses took the Colonels on a tour of Los Angeles, already a sprawling city of 575,000. The alumni and friends of Centre hosted a dinner in the evening at the recently opened (January 1, 1921) Ambassador Hotel on Wilshire Boulevard, designed by the renowned Myron Hunt, also the architect of the Rose Bowl which was under construction at the time in Pasadena.

The team was accompanied all day by Eddie Orcutt of the San Diego "Union" who wired a story back to his paper which would appear in the next morning's edition. He described the workout at Bovard Field.

By far the greatest part of the workout was given to passing, fake passes and line plays from passing formations, and it was the passing exhibition of the team that furnished both the spectacular and puzzling part of their showing. Apparently the Centre backs pass from any angle, at will and without any premeditation—on the spur of the moment. They pass with a nonchalance that sometimes amounts to obvious carelessness, and yesterday, amazing passes alternated with fumbles. It was this particular carelessness—call it virtuosity—that puzzled the crowd that watched.

Bo McMillin is, of course, the star performer in this department. Sometimes, Bo runs a step with the ball before throwing it—sometimes he calmly turns his back on that stonewall line and walks back toward his goal. Most often though, he zig-zags back, eluding imaginary tacklers, looking in one direction and shooting the ball in another. The receiving units also executed a criss-cross behind the opposing line so that in most cases, there were at least three men on either wing, ready to receive the throw.

McMillin's ability to shake off opposition and take his own sweet time to throw is said by his teammates to have been a feature of his phenomenal career this year. While in practice, some of his passing feats looked impossible for actual playing conditions, any Colonel will tell you that Bo has "pulled" them time and time again.

Orcutt had a bylined second story in that same issue of the paper in which he gave his impression of Uncle Charlie and the coach's approach to his team.

While the Centre College Colonels were doing their stuff yesterday on the marshy wastes of Bovard Field, a sturdy middle-aged man in a flapping raincoat paddled nonchalantly through the puddles and whipped them on with a line of talk which kept them moving all the time.

He didn't raise his voice, particularly—this man in the floppy raincoat—but everybody heard him. The man was Uncle Charlie Moran, head coach of Centre College. The voice that he used was the same that he employs every spring and summer in the major league ball parks, calling balls and strikes.

Sarcasm, entreaty, disgust—every inflection of Uncle Charlie's voice reached its mark very emphatically, and the boys of the Gold and White had no difficulty in getting his meaning.

Coach Moran has a "line" all his own, and a big part of the show on Bovard Field was listening to it.

"Yah!!" sang Uncle Charlie, turning the single syllable to the nth power of I-told-you-so disgust.

Someone didn't move fast enough.

"Come out of that—don't start growing in the mud—you cranberry!"

Or, again—

"Well, you're a nice boy. I'll give you one more chance."

A man just sent into the lineup failed to catch a signal.

"All right, Flip. Fine stuff. I ought to snatch you right back out of there."

"Well! Well! If you're going no place, stand aside and let the rest of 'em move on."

"Terrible Terry" Snowday kicked it high, but it went out of bounds.

"Well, isn't that just fine?" Moran beamed. "Can't kick beyond your own 10 yard line. Honest, I know a little tyke in kindergarten who can beat that."

Three times in succession, forward passes were incomplete because of the "thrower" not leading the runner far enough. The last time the runner twisted to make the catch and fell with a splash into one of the many lagoons.

"Oh—ouch! Say, I'm sorry. I forgot to tell you boys the field was muddy. On a muddy field, always lead the runner. Throw it up above his knees. Also, on a dry field—or any kind of field. I've only told you 50 times. Sorry I forgot to tell you again."

"Well, well, what are you standing around for? Can't swim?"

Somehow, it didn't make anybody sore. The men dug into the muddy grass all the harder. The unfortunate "mermaid" who had taken the spill grinned through his mask of mud and jumped to his place in the lineup.

Occasionally, when the boys pulled a circus play that seemed impossible, they got a dram of praise.

"Well!" Uncle Charlie would exclaim in an umpire's whisper that would shake the goalposts. "Well!"

SAN DIEGO, FINALLY!

The team's plans were to stay in the great resort, the del Coronado outside of San Diego, across the San Diego Bay from the city.

The Coronado was built in 1888 and was situated on the island of Coronado, directly on, and facing the Pacific Ocean. The authorities back in Danville, in planning

348

the great trip to the West, had as a constant the desire to make the excursion "first class," and "fun." The Del met both criteria, and then some.

The organizers of the Christmas Bowl (let's just call it that) were so determined to be the perfect hosts for Centre that they had the manager of The Del, W.A. Truquand, take the train up to Los Angeles so that he could meet with the team late on Thursday evening, after they had re-boarded the "Cowdray." Truquand's purpose was to introduce the players to his hotel, and to make certain that any special requests were met by the staff.

The manager wanted to make certain that everyone knew how much of an honor it was for the team to have picked The Del, and "please feel free to use our facility in any way that you may wish. Your pleasure is our constant goal."

"Darn nice of you," was Red's reply, and everyone nodded in agreement.

After the meeting with Truquand, the Colonels turned in for the last segment of the journey to San Diego, an overnight run to their host city, arrival time, 8:00 a.m. on December 23. It would have been, again allowing for the time differential, just over six hours short of a week since they left Danville.

Robert E. Hughes, head of the San Diego Chamber of Commerce, led the delegation which lined up at the station to meet and cheer the Colonels. There was a caravan of cars which would carry the team to the wharf for the trip on a ferry across the Bay. (Until 1969, the only way to get to Coronado Island was by water. In August of that year, a beautiful and impressive, arching bridge was opened to traffic.)

Jop sent a report back to Louisville and Danville to keep the fans of the team up to date on how the trip was progressing.

The players have been given the most spacious and preferred rooms on the ground floor, and many of the biggest battleships are anchored at the great San Diego Naval Base and may be seen from the verandas and guest room windows.

The San Diego "Union," the morning paper here, turned out a Centre College edition today. The entire front page and three pages of the sports were devoted to the Colonels with attractive layouts and interesting narratives. Southern California has gone wild over the coming game, and with Centre the first to arrive, many neutrals have already announced they are pulling for the Colonels.

During registration at The Del, each member of the team was given a packet, an indication that their hosts were "pulling out all of the stops," as Jop reported. Then it was off to a great breakfast in the dining room.

"Well tear my sox!" Red exclaimed as he opened the envelope which he'd been given at the front desk, trying to look at the contents between bites of food.

"Wait until they see this back in Somerset! I've been made a member of the Coronado Country Club, the San Diego Country Club, the University Club and the C-u-y-some other club, whatever it is."

It was the Cuyamaca Club, a social club founded in 1887, and situated atop the Union Building downtown since 1909. It wasn't exactly that the Colonels were going to be able to take advantage of their memberships, but it a wonderful gesture on the part of the San Diego committee, and many of the players proudly showed off their membership cards upon their return home, and several still had them in their wallets decades later, as a reminder of when they were so appreciated and ruled the world of college football.

After breakfast, the team gathered out on the lush green lawn overlooking the Pacific. The wind was picking up a bit, and there were some clouds, dark clouds, out on the horizon. There was a wonderful view of the Naval Base to the northwest of the hotel, home not only to several of the dreadnaughts, the generic name derived from the first all-big gun battleship, the British H.M.S. Dreadnaught (1906), but over 60 destroyers which had been built in the run-up to the Great War. George Joplin wrote that there were 6,000 officers and 20,000 enlisted men stationed at the base.

By 10:00 in the morning, the team was in uniform and on the manicured turf of the Coronado Polo Field, home every March to the California Polo Championships. Several hundred appreciative fans, people who had come over by the ferry, plus guests of the hotel, turned out to witness what was a festive affair. The Colonels realized that they were on display, and made their best effort to "strut their stuff," as one reporter stated.

After the practice, the players dressed in casual clothes for a boat ride around the Bay in the "Virginia," a launch owned and skippered by the manager of the Coronado, Mr. Truquand. George Joplin went along and worried about the "sea legs" of the team, most of whom had spent very little time on the water, especially of the choppy variety.

The boys stood their trip at sea well, none evidencing the slightest indications of sea sickness, but the captain was warned not to battle the breakers, and to stick close to the shore.

After the tour of the Bay, the team dressed for dinner. The "Kentucky State Society" was in charge of the meal and reception, and it was another tribute to the great accomplishments of the Colonels. Naturally, much was made over the Harvard victory. San Diegans had received the news with the same appreciation that had been generated all over the country.

Army thanked the hosts for a wonderful event, and it was left to Uncle Charlie to give a few closing remarks. During the dinner, a messenger had come to the head table and handed the coach a telegram.

Uncle Charlie opened it again as he spoke, then read it aloud.

"The University of California would like to extend an invitation for Centre College to play our team on Thanksgiving, 1922, in the dedicatory game of our new stadium."

It was from Luther C. Nichols, graduate manager of the California Bears.

Uncle Charlie said that he didn't know if Centre could accept the invitation.

"But isn't it wonderful that my boys are so appreciated that a big school like California wants them to come out and help dedicate their new stadium?" (The University of California Memorial Stadium was originally to have a capacity of 60,000, but as Stanford was going to equal that total, and the city of Los Angeles (for Southern California) was building a stadium, Los Angeles Memorial Coliseum, of even greater capacity, Cal upped its seating to close to 80,000, which delayed opening its facility until the "Big Game" against Stanford on Thanksgiving, 1923. Cal prevailed, 9-0.)

ARIZONA GETS EXCITED

Meanwhile, people back in Arizona were getting pumped up about the game, the biggest that the Wildcats had ever had. Coming into the Christmas Bowl, Arizona was 7-1 with the following record:

Arizona	84	Bisbee Legion	13
Arizona	75	Phoenix Indians	0
Arizona	13	Texas A&M	17
Arizona	74	Texas El Paso	0
Arizona	31	New Mexico State	0
Arizona	24	New Mexico	0
Arizona	114	New Mexico Military	0
Arizona	7	Whittier	0

Admittedly there had been some weak sisters on the schedule, but the key game, when analyzing the strength of the boys from Tucson, was the contest with Texas A&M.

A&M was tough. They had quite a program going on after World War I, led by Coach Dana Xenophon (D.X.) Bible. (Xenophon wasn't a musical instrument, but rather an ancient Greek writer and historian.)

Arizona had taken an all day and overnight train to College Station from Tucson on October 22, gotten off and gone right to the game, and came close to beating the Aggies. A&M was 18-2-1 since the beginning of the 1919 season at the time of the Arizona game, and the two losses were close, 7-3 to Texas, and 6-0 to LSU. LSU was also the team that played the Aggies to a 0-0 tie.

The San Diego "Union" asked a reporter in Tucson to send a story to the paper so that its readers might see how the Centre-Arizona game was shaping up from the perspective of the Arizonians. The story was penned by "Cross Buck," obviously a pseudonym.

The article appeared on the morning of December 23, under the headline:

FOOTBALL ONLY TOPIC HEARD ON TUCSON STREETS. ARIZONA 'CATS CONFIDENT THEY'LL BEAT ELEVEN THAT HUMBLED HARVARD

This town has stopped talking about irrigation projects, sunshine, poor cattle markets, and tourists who have failed to come to the West, and for the moment is deeply agitated over the prospects of its football team which meets the undefeated Centre College of Kentucky eleven on Monday in San Diego.

It is considered by everyone to be the chance of a lifetime for the University of Arizona, and if the Wildcats win—well, Nogales is only a few hours over the border, and they still sell bottled in the bond stuff there, right over the bar.

A widespread feeling may exist elsewhere that the college cowboys are in for a bad day, but this town thinks it will be a fight to the finish. With a team that has scored 422 points to but 30 for their opponents—and among those turned back was Whittier College, champions of the Southern California Conference, Arizona can't see where it should shiver in its boots over the prospect of meeting a football team that doesn't even swear. These Colonels may be a power in Kentucky, but in the West, they wouldn't even make good buck privates to listen to Tucson tell it.

And so, with that kind of talk ringing in their ears, the Wildcats left tonight on the trip that may mean a big day for the local college. Once before they invaded California and fought with such frenzy that there was nothing for the opposition to do but to call them "Wildcats," and that name has stuck ever since.

(The "opposition" was Occidental in 1914. Arizona lost to Occidental 27-0 in Tucson in 1913 and then traveled to Los Angeles in 1914 and lost 14-0, but Los Angeles "Times" columnist, Bill Henry, wrote that "the Arizona men fought like wildcats." The name caught on and was officially adopted in the fall of 1915.)

You can't scare these babies about what Centre has done among the gridiron elite since the Colonels first crashed into the football drawing room three years ago.

"Harvard?" echoed and old-timer who has followed the fortunes of Arizona for several years. "What do we care what they did to Harvard? They are playing us."

"McMillin? Say, what are you trying to do, scare us with a lot of names? We have a little 140 pound quarterback with as much brains as Bo McMillin, and maybe he will show the All-American wonder how to skirt end, too. He is a fine triple-threat man. Well, you saw what he did in the Whittier game—Slonaker, I'm referring to. You may recall that 40 yard pass he made to Captain Wofford for the only touchdown of the game. Well, that was this boy at his worse. He was suffering from pinkeye that day. When he's right, nothing west of the Rockies, except perhaps Brick Muller of California, can throw a pass more accurately."

"And we have a swell line-plunger in Hobbs. They say Armstrong, Snowday and McMillin form a wonderful secondary defense. They'll have a lot of work stopping this baby. He and a bullet are twins."

"We do not claim to have any ends as good as Red Roberts, but we have a mighty good pair of wings in Wofford and McClellan. We'll give them a fight, I'll tell you that."

This Arizona team has probably done more traveling during its regular season this year than any team in the United States. Washington and Jefferson, when it comes to Pasadena, will no doubt throw Arizona's mileage out, but in the regular season, no one has ridden the rails more.

As a matter of fact, the only defeat was to Texas A&M when the Wildcats had been on the train for two days, and they played the game the day they got there.

The Colonels, from their record, not only have combined piety and punch rather effectively, but they seem to be a team of remarkable defensive strength. It is this side of Charlie Moran's team that is worrying Arizona. Can the Wildcats penetrate that line? The answer to that is the answer to the chances that Arizona has for victory.

Arizona is a typical Western team. It believes the best defense is a good offense, and it plays to score all the while. It wants to get all the traffic will bear. By this method, it won the Southwestern Conference title, and then defeated the Southern California champion, Whittier, in a post-season game. But overcoming Centre by the same tactics is, as Abe used to say to Mawruss, "something else again."

PREGAME ACTIVITIES

The Colonels awakened on Saturday morning on December 24, with plans to go to the stadium where the Christmas Bowl was going to be played.

Balboa Stadium had opened in 1914, and when it was built, was the largest municipally owned stadium in the country. It was conveniently located, just minutes north of downtown, and the team took the ferry across the Bay to be motored to Balboa. From the outside, the concrete stadium looked impressive, but when the players ran out onto the field, they felt someone had trucked in a hunk of desert and poured water on it.

Bo was asked what he thought about the turf.

"Turf? Haven't seen any, yet." He added, "It's the worse I've ever seen, but we'll play on it, and do the best we can. After all, Arizona has to play on it also."

The field was "heavy," as the papers described it, from the recent rains, and the forecast didn't look like things were going to get any better soon. The locals were calling the weather, "Rather usual, I'd say. Rather unusual."

Wet field or not, Uncle Charlie and Tiny Thornhill put the squad through a brisk, two hour workout, mainly concentrating on the running game, as a wide open passing attack looked rather doubtful if the field conditions didn't improve. The coaches had the second team line up in what they felt would be Arizona defensive positions. They admitted, however, that they didn't know much about their upcoming opponent, and what little they knew had come from D.X. Bible, the coach at Uncle Charlie's old school, Texas A&M.

The University of Arizona got into San Diego in the evening of Saturday, December 24, having arrived too late to get in any practice. They had traveled over 600 miles in what seemed a circuitous way, but was the route which the trains took at the time.

From Tucson, they journeyed through Casa Grande and then Maricopa, south of Phoenix. Then they headed to Wellton, and west of Wellton, they entered California, after passing through Yuma.

From Yuma, their train pointed northwest and cruised through sleepy little Palm Springs, at the time the home to only 75 permanent residents, but already beginning to establish a reputation as a winter playground for the stars. Then it was on to Los Angeles where they boarded a southbound train to San Diego.

While the Arizona Wildcats were en route, the Colonels returned to The Del and washed the mud off, had lunch, and returned to the ferry landing to go back across the Bay where they were met by members of the "Kentucky State Society," under the leadership of W.B. Fritts, for a sightseeing tour of the San Diego area.

The team visited La Jolla, Mission Cliff Gardens, Balboa Park, and then the highlight was an excursion to Rockwell Air Depot at the Naval Air Station on North Island, the point just above and west to the hotel where the Colonels were staying.

Captain Randolph, one of Uncle Charlie's players at Texas A&M, was the host for a tour of the base. The white uniformed, career flyer, lead the Colonels around the base, explaining the features of the planes on the tarmac and in the hangers, and how they would be used in combat, if needed. Several of the more intrepid Colonels went on short rides with the pilots who did some upside down flying and loops. Hump was rubber-legged when he got out and kissed the ground. He said he'd never fly again. Uncle Charlie said it was a thrill to see one of his former players become so successful, and "what an outstanding career he has had."

"But then, all of my young men here are outstanding, and will be equally successful in their lives," the coach said to one of the many accompanying reporters.

Uncle Charlie could appear somewhat gruff, "but that's when we know he really cares. If Unc never got on us, we'd really be worried then," explained Minos Gordy.

At 5:00 p.m., Christmas Eve, the group once again ferried back to The Del. It had sprinkled off and on, and clouds from the west were looking more ominous, but the weather hadn't put a damper on the great day that the Colonels had experienced thus far. That evening, it got even better.

The Louisville "Herald" carried one of Jop's dispatches which its readers read on Christmas morning.

The Kentuckians in San Diego, under the chairmanship of Thomas N. Faulconer, gave a real Christmas party tonight in the famous Coronado ballroom.

Santa Claus had decorated a 20 foot tree for the Centre crowd. The branches of the mighty cedar were weighed down with presents for the Colonels. These gifts, representative of the products of Southern California, were there for every member of the Danville party. There were bottles of ripe olives, tins of tuna fish, the "everlasting Japanese flowers," handsome descriptive booklets, dates, candies, confections, and fresh fruit, in addition to the many gifts which had been sent out to the team from cities all over Kentucky.

A 10 piece orchestra furnished Christmas music, and then two memorable hours of dancing rounded out a wonderfully memorable evening.

The members of the team requested this correspondent to send the folks back home their best wishes for a merry, merry Christmas.

Most of the Centre team awakened for their first Christmas morning away from their homes and families. Bill Shadoan had been overseas on a December 25, but for the others, being removed from family and friends left them somewhat homesick, with a feeling of nostalgia.

Uncle Charlie had recognized that very fact at the Christmas party the night before, and had spoken to the team privately before his boys turned in for the night.

"I want each of you to know how very proud I am of you, and how I have only heard compliments about you everywhere we have gone. I know it is somewhat difficult to be away on the holidays, but someday, you'll be sitting around the fire with your children or grandchildren visiting you for Christmas, and you'll tell them about the great adventure out West in 1921, and you'll tell them about how you went to the horse races on Christmas, in....Mexico!"

Uncle Charlie had saved the Christmas afternoon outing as a surprise.

"What do you mean, Unc?"

"I mean, we're going to church in the morning, and then we've been invited to go across the border to Tijuana where the owner of this beautiful hotel, who just happens to also own the race track there, Mr. John D. Spreckels, has arranged an afternoon in our honor."

Christmas day, 1921, indeed proved to be a day for the Colonels to remember and to talk about for all of their remaining days. Everyone was up early on the morning of the 25th. There was a pianist playing Christmas songs in the lobby which you could hear into the dining room. The Colonels were literally dressed in their "Sunday best." Hotel manager Truquand had his staff go to each of the player's rooms before they turned in after the party and collect clothes which were returned early the next morning, suits steamed, shirts washed, starched and on hangers.

As usual, the day's activities began with another ferry ride. The team was beginning to know each of the crew members and greeted them by name.

Once again, the "Kentucky Society" members chauffeured the team, this time to the First Presbyterian Church on Date Street, between 3rd and 4th. The red brick building had been dedicated in November, 1914, and sat on a sage-surrounded hill somewhat on the periphery of the downtown area.

The Colonels were getting used to be recognized everywhere that they went, and this time was no different. The minister gestured to the team and told the congregation that they were in the presence of "young men who are from Kentucky and are known all over the country as the 'Praying Colonels.'"

Outside the sanctuary, those "Praying Colonels" shook hundreds of hands and were wished "Merry Christmas," "Welcome," and "Good Luck," by the parishioners. Then it was off to the races, again courtesy of the "Society" members.

A formal invitation had been sent to Uncle Charlie by the president of the Tijuana Jockey Club, James Wood Coffroth. The town of Tijuana had a population of only 1028 in 1921 and would have seemed an unlikely site for a race track, but its location, right on the easily traversed border between San Diego and Baja California, made it an ideal location for one simple reason.

Betting was illegal in California, but quite the opposite was true in Mexico. The Spreckels brothers, John and Adolph, took over the Jockey Club in 1916 and encouraged guests at the Coronado to frequent the track.

The acceptance by Uncle Charlie to bring his team to the track had prompted publicity in the "Union," and it was announced that two races would be run in honor of the Colonels, the "Centre College Handicap," and the "Bluegrass Stakes," in honor of the "Kentucky Thoroughbreds."

Before the "Handicap," the members of the team were brought out on the track and were introduced to the crowd. Due to all of the press coverage since their arrival, they were well-known to most of the crowd, and received a standing ovation. Throughout the racing card, a steady stream of fans came by and sought out the players.

"Just wanted to welcome you and shake your hand."

"Bo McMillin! Why honey, I never thought I'd get to meet you. Can I have just one little hug?"

Again, Red was heard to utter his favorite expression after he'd been seized by yet another adoring female fan. "Tear my sox! Just tear my sox!"

After a memorable day, the Colonels were again transported back to the ferry landing, but this time, the trip across the Bay was much different. There had been a major downpour across the border in San Diego while the team was at the races, and gusts were creating white caps on the normally placid waters. By the time they reached the big white hotel, it was raining so hard that the building could hardly be seen until they were literally upon it.

"Yes," the front desk clerk said, when asked if there was any forecast. "There does seem to be a severe storm predicted, which is quite unusual, I must say. Quite unusual, yes."

"QUITE UNUSUAL WEATHER, YES"

Historically, San Diego received little precipitation in December, at least normally. The citizens were more concerned about keeping the reservoirs full than about flooding.

YEAR	DECEMBER RAIN/INCHES
1910	.15
1911	1.39
1912	.03
1913	.72
1914	2.21
1915	2.60
1916	1.14
1917	0 (This is not a typo.)
1918	0 (Nor is this.)
1919	.48
1920	.54

Since 1910, the total rainfall was only 9.26 inches, for an average of .84 inches in the eleven Decembers. Statistically, it looked like a pretty safe bet to schedule an outside event in December in San Diego.

There had been an unusual amount of precipitation during the first two weeks of the month. A light rain had then begun on December 18, five days before the Colonels arrived in San Diego. All of the West Coast had intermittent showers, and the team worked out on a wet field in Palo Alto, and an even wetter field in Los Angeles.

The Polo Field at the Coronado had been blessed with such thick tuft, periodically irrigated during the year, that the moisture on the grass wasn't really a factor.

Things began to look more mucky when the Colonels practiced on the wet, sandy soil which was considered a playing field, at Balboa Stadium. Now, the situation was beginning to get serious. As the players looked out of the seaside windows of their rooms, the ocean could be heard, but certainly not seen. There was a full-blown storm, locked in right over Southern California, and what was going to happen tomorrow, game day, really couldn't be imagined.

Ticket sales to the game had been robust. There were 115,000 people in San Diego County in 1921, and there was an enormous interest locally, but what promised to swell the crowd to full capacity was the number of people who were planning to come down from as far away as San Francisco, and even more were planning to attend from the Los Angeles area.

There were several factors that had generated such enthusiasm for the game throughout the state. First, the fact that Centre had beaten Harvard made the "Wonder Team" known nationally. Secondly, there had been many articles written prior to the final Rose Bowl pairing about the possibility of Centre playing the University of California in Pasadena. When that match-up didn't materialize, many football fans decided the next best thing would be to spend the day after Christmas in San Diego watching Centre play there.

The third reason was the coverage that the team was given in the San Francisco and Los Angeles papers when the Colonels spent a day in each city. The Centre team just made good press, and the public was hungry for any information about the college and its wonderful group of football players. Additionally, the organizing committee had placed ads in the Los Angeles papers about the game.

Both the Southern Pacific and the Atchison, Topeka and Santa Fe, better known as just the Santa Fe, ran regular passenger trains from Los Angeles to San Diego. Thousands of fans planned to come down to San Diego on the December 26 early morning runs south, so many that both railroads had additional coaches added to their consists to accommodate the numbers.

The last passenger train able to travel from Los Angeles to San Diego arrived at 6:35 p.m. on December 25. It carried a large number of fans who planned to stay overnight in the city, and to attend the game the next afternoon. No other rail traffic was possible after the arrival of that train, as the track between the two cities was covered with more than two feet of water in the Sorrento Valley north of San Diego. Further compromising travel were the tons of mud that obliterated the lines in the San Juan Capistrano area.

It had hardly rained in Tijuana while the Colonels were at the track, but it was a different story across the border. In the 24 hour period from 2:30 a.m. on the 25th until 2:30 a.m. on the 26th, three inches of rain had fallen, surpassing the old 24 hour record of 2.75 inches. It was still pouring when the team awakened on the morning of the scheduled game.

The total rainfall for December now stood at 9.18 inches, and by the time the downpour finally stopped, the accumulation was at 9.26 inches, exactly the total for the eleven previous Decembers, combined!

The storm wrecked havoc on the highways between Los Angeles and San Diego as well. On the coastal route, the bridge at Cardiff—by the Sea, south of Encinitas, was swept away. Further inland, Escondido was cut off from San Diego by damage to the bridge at Lakeside. And in the Imperial Valley, traffic was stopped at Dulzura, blocking passage into San Diego from the southwest.

The organizers of the Christmas Bowl were faced with a very tough decision. Should they go ahead? Postpone? Cancel?

The two coaches, Uncle Charlie and "Pop" McKale, were consulted, and both said they would rather play on the scheduled date, but if necessary, could stay over another day and play on the 27th. However, there wasn't any guarantee that conditions would improve in 24 hours due to the vast amount of rain, and conditions may actually worsen even more.

The papers delivered on Christmas morning had run stories that the game was on, no matter what. This fact had a bearing on whatever decision the committee would make. But the major factor regarding playing or postponing, or even cancelling, was the matter of insurance.

Who would have thought that it would be necessary to insure against rain in December in San Diego? It seemed like money poorly spent. After all, December was typically dry. Seven of the last eleven years had a total December rain of less that an inch. Two years had no rain at all. Who would have ever thought of taking out insurance?

The organizing committee was composed of good businessmen, men who wanted to put San Diego on the map by the publicity that a prestigious post-season game could generate. They had seen how Pasadena and the Los Angeles area had benefited by the Rose Bowl. They envisioned the same for their city. But they were leery about guaranteeing money to the participating teams without some assurance that there would be funds available to pay out those guarantees.

Centre alone had been promised $16,000, equivalent to $160,000 in today's valuation of money. By the time Arizona was paid, and other expenses were covered, the committee felt it would need to take in over $30,000 just to break even.

So they went shopping and found an insurer who would pay up to $25,000 if it rained at least one inch on the day of the game. The wording of the policy was critical. Rain "on the day of the game" meant just that. It was obvious that at least an inch would accumulate on the 26th because at midnight on the 25th, there was no lessening of the intensity of the storm.

If the game were to be postponed and played the next day, and the rain ceased, there would be no payout, even if the crowd had been drastically reduced because of the weather.

"We've got to play. We have no choice. The whole enterprise could be a big money loser. It would guarantee that we don't have a game next year."

The committee's vote was unanimous. The members were determined that the game would take place, as one participant later related, "come hell or high water."

"And we realized that may well describe the conditions."

THE CHRISTMAS BOWL

Uncle Charlie had the foresight to bring extra long cleats along in the equipment trunk that accompanied the team, and he got several of the players and team manager Johnnie McGee to help him screw them onto the black leather high-tops which every Colonel wore.

There was a light breakfast and a skull session before the Centre entourage once again headed to the ferry landing. The rain was coming down in sheets, blown by a strong wind coming in from the southwest. The ferry rolled from side to side, and several members of the team felt nauseous from the motion, but arrived at the opposite shore with their breakfasts still being digested.

The faithful "Kentucky Society" members met the team and transported them to Balboa Stadium. There was no let-up in the storm, and the wind, even away from the Bay, was just as brisk inland.

The Wildcats from Arizona arrived shortly after the Colonels and the two head coaches met with the officials to discuss the playing conditions. The four officials had been announced Saturday. Mourney Pfefferkorn, a local banker, was going to be the head linesman. J.R. Klawans, of the Pacific Coast Football Association, would be the field judge. The umpire was Dr. Boles Rosenthal, a University of Minnesota graduate who had played center for the Gophers, and was the team's captain in 1914. The referee was to be the same Bob Evans who had coached some of the Colonels back in Owensboro. Coach McKale had no problem with that.

The officials and coaches examined the field and, as they later stated, "It was a sea of mud."

The chalk marks which had designated the dimensions of the playing field were for the most part, long gone, so it was agreed that volunteers would stand along the sidelines, where the markers had been, so the players could try to stay within the boundaries.

Warm-ups were held to a minimum due to the weather. There was absolutely no let-up in the intensity of the rain.

Hump Tanner ran over to Red and hollered, "Look out big guy. Duck ! Duck!"

When Red instinctively ducked, Hump began to laugh.

"It's raining cat and dogs. I just kept you from getting hit!"

Red burst out laughing.

"Hump, you little rascal. Wait till you need a block from me."

At 2:15, the captains, William Wofford for Arizona, and Army for Centre, were called to the 50 yard line for the coin toss.

Years later, Army and I were talking about the trip out West, and he said that the field conditions for the Arizona game were so bad, and there was so much mud and water, the official said, "Boys, I'm not going to flip this silver dollar and let it land on the ground like I usually do. I'm just going to close my hand around it. I'm afraid if I flip it, we'll never find it."

Arizona won the toss and elected to kick.

Amazingly, with such atrocious weather, a respectable crowd was gathering. All of those who braved the conditions were totally covered with rain slicks, and there was hardly a soul who wasn't hunkered down under an open umbrella.

Contemporary accounts placed the crowd at anywhere from 5,000 to 7,000 which was truly remarkable, especially considering that those thousands who planned to come down by train were stymied by the storm, as were the many locals who decided to not brave the rain.

Several wire photos taken during the game emphasize the way the Wildcats and Colonels found the field. There are reflections in the pictures which make it appear like the players were running around on a mirror. They aren't shadows. There wasn't any sun to cast shadows. They are true reflections, and it's hard to imagine that any game requiring movement could have been attempted.

The first kick-off by Arizona's Smith resulted in a "foozle," according to a report, and the slick ball went sideways and out of bounds. The second attempt by Smith rolled and slid all of the way to the Colonels' 15 yard line. Army finally ran it down and returned it 25 yards, and Centre had a first and 10 on its own 40.

The first drive was typical of the whole game, so let's recount it play by play. Bo failed to gain on the opening play, slipping down as he tried to cut around his left end. Hump barreled ahead for 10 and picked up a 1st down, and Centre had the ball at midfield.

Bo picked up five, Terry Snowday got another five, and it was 1st and 10 on the Wildcats' 40. Bo went around his right end for seven, Hump picked up another six, and it was 1st down on the 27.

Bo carefully headed around his left end and got another 12, being brought down when an Arizona back literally ripped off his jersey when he threw the Colonels' quarterback to the mud. Time was called while Bo replaced his jersey.

When play resumed, Centre had 1st and 10 on the 15. Three line plunges took the ball to the three. It was 1st and goal for the Gold and White. Red Roberts shifted to fullback and powered over for the score. The wet ball scooted off Bo's foot and was far wide to the left on the extra point attempt.

The opening series summed up the game. Centre could move the ball at will, even with the horrible field conditions, and would continue to do so throughout the contest. There was no need to pass, but when Arizona stacked its defense expecting the Colonels to run, Bo wasn't hesitant to go to the air even with the ball so slick and slippery.

Arizona chose a very unique strategy. The team which was scored on had the choice of either kicking or receiving. Arizona chose to kick!

That was another point that Army and I talked about. He said it was the strangest strategy. How do you score if you don't have the ball? Army said that the only thing they could figure was that Arizona had so little confidence in its offense that it kicked, hoping we'd fumble the slick ball deep in our own territory.

There just didn't seem to be any other explanation.

After Arizona kicked, Centre repeated the pattern of the initial possession except that Bo mixed up the attack a bit by completing two passes to Red, one for 10 yards and the other for 12. Bo picked up the final three yards to complete the drive.

Again, the point after attempt was wide, and it was Centre 12-0.

Arizona kicked off again! All that the Centre players could do was shake their heads and be thankful for the gift of the ball. "Cross Buck" had written that Arizona felt that the best defense was a good offense. But how did a team display that "good offense" if it never had possession of the ball? The initial quarter ended with the Colonels up 12-0.

Four minutes into the 2nd quarter, Army finished off a long drive by going in from the four yard line. The kick was missed again, and it stood at 18-0.

Arizona chose to kick—again! It was getting weird!

The 4th possession was highlighted by a 40 yard pass from Army to Snowday, but Chick Murphy replaced Snowday after the completion and fumbled the slippery ball away on the Wildcats' 20 yard line.

Except for the Arizona kicker holding the ball before he kicked off, it was the first time that a Wildcat had touched the ball, and it was well into the 2nd quarter.

The Arizona quarterback, little Slonaker, attempted a pass which fell incomplete. The Wildcats ran into the line for no gain, and of course, punted!

After one of Bo's passes was intercepted, Arizona's halfback, Manzo, picked up two and on second down, the Wildcats punted again!

Centre ran two plays and the half ended with the Colonels up, 18-0. It had been a strange half, to say the least. Arizona had run a total of three offensive plays in 30 minutes of football. The Wildcats gained a total of two yards, had no 1st downs, and had kicked off four times, and punted twice.

Meanwhile, despite competing on the worse surface they'd ever encountered, the Colonels played as always. The fumble and interception were certainly understandable under the conditions. Otherwise, it had been a flawless 1st half.

Everyone in the press box wondered, "What in the world is Arizona trying to prove?" A non-bylined story appeared in the San Diego "Union."

YOU TAKE IT, CENTRE!

Arizona chose strange tactics. They elected to let Centre have the ball during all of the first half. In the first period, not a Wildcat claw touched the oval in the entire 15 minutes of play. Centre received the kickoffs and never gave up the egg save when they scored a touchdown, and again and again, Arizona chose to kick!

Centre made fine use of the Wildcats' generosity. They were only too willing to take the offensive, and charge they did with vigor and determination which left nothing to the imagination.

Just when things seemed like they couldn't get worse, they did. It was one of those "good news, bad news" situations. While the players were breaking for the half, the torrential rain began to slacken, reaching just a drizzle when the teams returned to the field. But as the downpour eased up, fog began to roll in off the bay which was a little over a mile to the west. Soon, it was hard to follow the action on the field, and the fans moved back and forth in the stands, trying to stay as close to where the ball was marked as possible.

Arizona displayed a little offense in the second half. The Wildcats came out in dry jerseys, but other than Bo removing his socks and pads, the Colonels entered the second half in their mud-smeared, soaked uniforms.

Red kicked off and nearly fell down as he approached the ball. The result was a spinning effort which barely made it past midfield, and Arizona recovered it on its own 45. For the first time, the Wildcats' fans had something to cheer about, because it looked like their team was actually going to try to move the ball!

Hobbs ran for 10 and Arizona was on Centre's side of the field! Suddenly, the Wildcats' bench and fans seemed to awaken and get into the game. Slonaker then completed a 10 yard toss to the team captain, William Wofford, and it was 1st and 10 on the Colonels' 35. Slonaker went to the air again, and hit Broderick for nine, and Hobbs picked up the additional yard and Arizona was moving!

"Go Wildcats!"

Centre hadn't given up a point since that fluke scored by St. Xavier in the 3rd game of the season. The Colonels didn't plan on giving up a point in San Diego. Army called timeout and gathered the team around him. It was a typical Army moment, calm but firm.

"Boys, we vowed at the start of the season that we wouldn't let anybody score on us. We have come close to our goal. Now, I want you to toughen it up. There is no way that this group should be able to score. Get tough. Remember, we are Centre!"

Hobbs gained five and then two. It was 3rd and three on the 18.

Slonaker tried another pass and Hump raced over and batted it down. Another pass fell incomplete in the end zone. It was a touchback, and Centre had it 1st and 10 on its own 20.

"We are Centre!"

The Colonels went to work immediately. Bo picked up 10, Red crashed through for five and the wind seemed to go out of Arizona's sails as Bo zig-zagged down the field for a 35 yard gain. Just like that, Centre had the ball on the Wildcats' 30 yard line.

Army picked up 10 on two carries, Snowday ripped around right end for 17, and then Snowday got the call again and ran over tackle, untouched.

Centre had marched 80 yards in seven plays with machine-like precision. Bo got the first extra point. Centre 25-0, which was how it stood as the 3rd quarter ended. Uncle Charlie substituted freely in the last period, eventually getting 20 men into the game.

The Colonels scored twice in the last quarter. Herb Covington fielded a punt on his 50, faked left and then cut back down the right sideline, water flying off his shoes, and crossed the goal without a Wildcat anywhere near.

Red put the extra point through the crossbar for a 32-0 lead.

For whatever reason, down 32-0 and with the last period half over, Arizona chose to kick! If the Wildcats were going to make a gift of the ball, the Colonels figured they might as well just play their own game, and well they did.

Bo returned the kick 20 yards, hit Red for 15, swept around end for another 22, and let Tom Bartlett and Red alternate at fullback while they marched it to the three.

"Bo called out to Red Roberts to take it in, then changed his mind and asked Bartlett if he'd scored yet, and Bartlett said he hadn't."

"So Bo told Red that he should get back in the line because it was Bartlett's turn to score. He hollered to Red to take out the left side of the Arizona line, because that was where Bartlett was going to carry the ball."

"Bartlett made it. Arizona knew he was coming—they clearly heard Bo tell him where to run—and they couldn't stop it. It was that easy! They took turns scoring a touchdown. One each for Bo, Roberts, Armstrong, Covington, Snowday and Bartlett."

It was hard to get a handle on the contest. Centre was obviously the far better team, and the sportswriters covering the game felt that on a dry field the Colonels could have scored as many points as they had wished.

Arizona had only surrendered 30 points all season. Centre scored 38 on an absolutely terrible field.

No one could understand Arizona's tactics, and Coach McKale never offered an explanation. The boys from Tucson picked up six 1st downs, but after getting to the Centre 18 early in the 3rd quarter, never remotely threatened again.

Probably the best "feel" for the game can be gained by what the "Union" said in its next morning edition.

BO AND MATES TAKE WILDNESS OUT OF WILDCATS

Centre won 38-0. Field sloppy. Weather raining. On a fast gridiron, in my humble estimation, Centre could have made it 75-0.

Arizona had no business in the same park with the famous Kentucky Colonels. They were outclassed from the start. Of all the Western champions, only California could have stood toe to toe with Centre yesterday. So closely would they have been matched that the breaks of luck may have decided the battle.

Sockless for the reason that wet woolens may have cut down on his speed, Bo McMillin packed the ball the majority of times that it was in the Colonels' possession, and he lived up to all of his advance notices. He was one Eastern satellite brought West who lived up to predictions.

Bo skidded all over the soggy field in a manner that dazzled. He broke loose continuously for 20 and 30 yard runs. His slippery clothing made him even more elusive and difficult to tackle. Like an eel was Bo. There was no stopping the stalwart Kentuckian. He snapped out his signals and then executed deeds of daring back of the stone wall of his line. His passing was brilliant, and he was successful even though he was throwing a slippery ball.

The teaming of McMillin with Red Roberts leading the way provided a force that Arizona was unable to stop. Red served as a Roman shield for McMillin. Roberts roved around the field, first playing end, then tackle and then at full when brought into the backfield to serve as a battering ram for Bo, or to carry the ball when a sure gain was needed.

Red would plough through with such strength that there was no stopping his charge. He smote the Wildcat line and rent it asunder, leaving a huge path for the speedy McMillin, who made every use of the open channel. The red-haired behemoth, doubly noticeable by the white band he wore in place of a helmet, made Roberts stand out like a beacon light in a fog. And there was fog, too—no foolin.' A genuine Portland afternoon it was—with a heavy drizzle pouring steadily, while a low mist moved in from the Bay, making the players scarcely discernable, and giving them an appearance of spectres running around in the night.

Centre showed speed and dash in the attack, before which Arizona was helpless. The Kentuckians marched down the field almost at will. Through tackle and around ends, the heavy Centre men assaulted their lighter foes for consistent gains. Generally it was McMillin you found breaking loose. Sometimes Bartlett, Armstrong, Tanner, Snowday, Murphy, or Covington. Centre just had too many horses, too much talent.

Covington, inserted into the line-up in the second half, was the author of the most spectacular stunt of the day. On an Arizona punt to midfield, "Covey" snared it on a bounce and followed his perfect interference down the sideline 50 yards to a touchdown.

The writer ended his story by expressing a sentiment that nearly every football fan on the West Coast shared.

Centre is unquestionably the greatest college football team to ever come out of the East to play the West. The businesslike way in which they went about their work under the field generalship of Bo McMillin—one of the greatest players the gridiron has ever known—made a deep impression on the Western experts.

It is actually a crime to athletics that the University of California didn't oppose the brilliant array of Kentuckians which yesterday displayed their sterling worth on our watery, slippery, skiddy stadium, a place where almost any other team would have tried straight football and line smashing—but where Centre revealed an amazing speed and power which the West can never forget.

A front page story in the "Union" added facts about the sportsmanship which had been displayed in the Christmas Bowl.

The final shot signaled the end of the game, and the mud-covered boys from far-off Kentucky and nearby Arizona gathered in little groups to cheer each other with a final yell, a yell which was a tribute to prowess and grit from each.

And just as the echoes of the yells died away, the setting sun ran a rosy shaft almost through the clouds of mist which a few minutes before had nearly hidden the players from view. And in that way, San Diego's first big football game had come to an end.

There was nobody in the crowd who was not ready for another one every year.

Centre was now 10-0 for the year. The Colonels had scored 320 points and only given up six. They had not only played in Danville, but Cincinnati, Lexington, Cambridge, Birmingham, Louisville, New Orleans and now San Diego. A writer for the Boston "Globe" pointed out that since Cincinnati was in Ohio which bordered Lake Erie, Boston was on the Atlantic, New Orleans, near the Gulf of Mexico, and San Diego was on the Pacific, Centre was the only college football team in the country which could claim the championship of "all four quadrants of this immense country."

And furthermore, the "Globe" stated that Bo alone had outscored the teams that Centre had played in those four quadrants. Bo got 14 in Cincinnati on two touchdowns and two extra points, six against Harvard, nine points on a TD and three extra points in New Orleans, and in San Diego, seven points on a TD and extra point.

The team had been away from home for eleven days, living out of steamer trunks and suitcases, being entertained everywhere they went, and providing entertainment for their adoring fans in each location they visited. And just as importantly, the way that the Colonels conducted themselves assured that they had made lifelong friends for their little beloved school back in Danville, Kentucky.

It was a happy but tired group that made its way once again across the Bay, and the sanctuary of the Coronado.

While the weather had made the play on the field more difficult, it had an even greater effect on Southern Californians regarding their mobility. Attendance at the game had certainly been curtailed by the roads, bridges and tracks which were buried or swept away. Those who had gotten into San Diego on that last train, or had driven down before the highways had been interrupted, now found themselves stranded. The hotels and restaurants filled with visitors, and one of the reasons for staging the Christmas Bowl inadvertently materialized, because a lot of money was being spent by those who couldn't get home.

Centre's plan was to get ready for yet another party hosted by the "Kentucky Society" in the big ballroom of the Coronado. After taking part, the team was to pack and make one last journey back into San Diego to catch a Santa Fe northbound train at midnight, and head back to Los Angeles.

Word was received when the Colonels got back to the hotel that the passenger representative at the station had called and said there was no way any train was going to be leaving on schedule. There were repairs that had to be made. The rain had lightened, but the fog was thicker than ever. The team was socked in.

The players really didn't care. They were in one of the nicest places they'd ever known. The food was great, there was a wonderful orchestra, and they knew that they had a week before the January 2 game in Dallas with Texas A&M.

Many of the guests staying at the hotel wandered in and out of the ballroom, wanting to greet the players, and have photographs made and get menus and programs from the game autographed. When they asked for Bo, they received a surprising answer.

"You're looking for Bo? Bo McMillin?"

They'd then point to one of the large windows facing the Pacific. "If that fog would let up out there, you may be able to see him. He's on his way to Los Angeles."

When that answer was met with an incredulous look, and the comment that, "No boat would be out in that fog," they were told, "You should never underestimate the United States Navy."

The fact that no trains could get out of San Diego, and there was no assurance when they would start rolling again, was a serious matter to Bo. There were wedding parties in Fort Worth that he was supposed to attend. The plan, before the tracks were washed out, was for the team to arrive in his home town for a short layover on the 29th, during which time Bo would hop off and join his fiancée, Marie. There was a big party scheduled for that night, and affairs the next three nights, leading up to the wedding. How could he start off a marriage to his long-time love without even attending his own parties?

Bo remembered Captain Randolph at the Naval Air Base, the individual who had played for Uncle Charlie at A&M.

"Unc, would you call him? See if he can get me on the base. Maybe the weather will clear and I could catch a flight in one of those planes if someone's going up to Los Angeles."

"Bo, I've told you for years that you've always had big ideas, and you've always been able to pull them off. But this is the dumbest thing you've ever...."

"Unc, I'm desperate."

"Look, I'll try to get through. Probably can't do it. But, if I can, I'm not going to be asking any such dang nonsense sort of question. If I get through, I'm handing you the phone."

Uncle Charlie finally got connected to the base, and to his surprise, was put through by the switchboard operator to his former player.

"Captain, I've got someone here who wants to ask you a question."

Bo explained the bind he was in. Uncle Charlie looked puzzled when he heard Bo say, "Really? Really? I'll be right over."

Everyone found it hard to believe later when Bo told how he'd gotten to Los Angeles in time to catch the train heading east, but it was absolutely true.

It was only about 125 miles up the coast to L.A. A fast destroyer, cruising at 30 knots, could easily make the trip in four hours, arriving in plenty of time to allow Bo to catch the scheduled 8:30 a.m. Southern Pacific departure.

Bo McMillin, Jack Dempsey, Babe Ruth. Probably only those three great sports figures, and the president of the United States, could have gotten a U.S. Navy destroyer to run them up the Pacific Coast in order to be on time to catch a train. Hard to believe, granted, but absolutely true.

The party at the Coronado lasted until 2:30 in the morning. The players slept in late. By early afternoon, the weather had finally cleared and the Bay was completely smooth as the big ferry transported the Colonels once again back to the San Diego wharf.

It was 4:30 in the afternoon, 16 ½ hours past the scheduled departure, before the train pulled out of the San Diego station, the faithful "Cowdray" trailing along on the end of the train which had extra cars to accommodate the fans who had been stranded.

The conductor told the Colonels that the engineers weren't certain how long it would take to get to Los Angeles, as the track had only been temporarily repaired in some sections.

Despite the weather, it had been an exciting time in San Diego. The hospitality had been almost overwhelming. Time after time, the players had marveled at how nice everyone had been over the years when they went on the road. It was the same everywhere they had traveled. They were met with smiles and treated royally, whether in Boston or Birmingham, Charlottesville or Charleston, Lexington or Louisville, Fort Worth, Denver, San Francisco or Los Angeles, everywhere!—and now in San Diego.

One of the last things that Hump said as he boarded the train and was thanking the members of the "Kentucky Society" who had been so supportive, was, "Thanks for all you've done. And now I know why they chose your town for that Navy base. You folks certainly don't lack for water!"

TRAVELING TOWARD DALLAS

After the team finally reached Los Angeles, the "Cowdray" was removed from the Santa Fe train and switched to a Southern Pacific regularly scheduled passenger train with El Paso being the next goal, at the end of the SP's tracks.

The route went down the center of Southern California and crossed over into Arizona at Yuma. Halfway across Southern Arizona was Tucson, a scheduled stop for coaling and taking on water for the big steamer.

It was early evening, and darkness was just settling in as the train braked to a halt at the depot on Toole Street. As the Colonels looked out of their Pullman's windows, they saw a throng of people, estimated to be over 500, many carrying lighted torches, coming toward the "Cowdray."

Suddenly they heard, "Hail! Hail! The gang's all here!"

It was members of the Arizona team, who had arrived in Tucson before the Colonels' train, and all of the students still in town, along with a group of townspeople, accompanied by the town band.

Cheers followed, and then there was a spontaneous song belted out by the band with everyone joining in.

> *For they are jolly good fellows,*
> *For they are jolly good fellows,*
> *For they are jolly good fellows,*
> *These boys of the Gold and White.*
> *These boys in Gold and White,*
> *These boys in Gold and White,*
> *For they are jolly good fellows,*
> *These boys of the Gold and White.*

Army stood at the door of the "Cowdray" and thanked everyone on behalf of the team. "Arizona has a peach of a team, and a wonderful group of players. We were honored to play such good sports, and I know that you must be proud to have such fellows represent your school."

There wasn't a dry eye in the "Cowdray" as the train churned out of the station.

On the 28th, as the Colonels were traveling toward El Paso, a story was printed in a College Station newspaper (home of Texas A&M) which demonstrated how Uncle Charlie's legacy still lived on at A&M.

The great respect that tradition has kept alive in the minds of Aggie athletes for Charlie Moran, because of his glorious work with athletes at the A&M college of Texas, will be to stimulate their stamina and provoke them to a superhuman use of their strength when they meet his Danville team of Praying Colonels at the Dallas Fair Stadium on January 2.

There is an actual love in the hearts of the Aggies for the man whom they know only as the unknown quality, responsible for a great achievement that was made in athletics at the college earlier in the twentieth century.

In the presence of Charlie Moran, supporters as well as players will be stirred to exert the greatest demonstration of Aggie spirit through the inherent force that was implanted by him many years ago, making them always do their best on the field of battle. It would be shameful to player and supporter alike to make a bad showing in the contest in Dallas, for we are all determined that his teachings were lasting.

This loyalty to the principles of Moran, and the desire to vindicate themselves before his eyes as true disciples of his teachings, will make the Aggies a dangerous opponent for the Praying Colonels.

Uncle Charlie's overall record during his six years at A&M was 38-8-4. His winning percentage, to this day, excluding ties, is higher, at 82.6%, than any coach who has ever held the position more than two years.

(Dana Bible, 1917, 1919-28, was at 79.1% and R.C. Slocum, 1989-2002, had the 3rd best percentage of 72.4.)

A STOPOVER IN EL PASO

The original plan, before the delay in getting out of San Diego, was to arrive in El Paso on Wednesday morning, December 28, at 8:30 a.m. Arrangements had been made to spend the whole day in the border town of some 100,000 population.

Instead, the train arrived a full day late, at 8:30 on the morning of the 29th. It was decided to just delay getting to Dallas, and go through with the activities which the local committee had worked so hard to put together for the Colonels.

Everywhere along the route, the Chief's request that events be arranged which were "first class and fun" was forefront in the various host's minds. El Paso was certainly no different.

The Colonels disembarked at the El Paso Union Depot at 700 San Francisco Street. The station, built in a neo-classical style, was the terminal for all of the railroads serving the city and over 20 passenger trains arrived daily, making the Depot one of the busiest sites in town. The "Cowdray" was uncoupled and placed on a siding as the team walked into the beautiful interior of the station where they were met by reporters and photographers, par for any place that the Colonels visited.

There was a Kentucky contingent even in El Paso, plus Uncle Charlie had a lot of admirers who had appreciated what he had accomplished at A&M, and many of them went to the Depot to welcome him.

"We can't wait to read the papers on Sunday and see what you and your boys did the previous afternoon."

"You know Charlie, ever since you left A&M, the papers down here have followed your career, but after you beat Harvard, your name is everywhere, and everyone down here is mighty proud of you and your team."

The Kentuckians drove the team out to the El Paso College of Minerals and Metallurgy where arrangements had been made to have a workout, and a spirited two hour session was held. It was the first perfectly dry field that the Colonels had stepped foot on since they left Danville, but after breathing the dust from the almost barren soil, some felt that a wet field didn't seem so bad after all.

After showers, the caravan traveled out to Grande Park for a typical Southwestern cookout, and to attend the "Annual Rodeo." There were slabs of beef ribs, a whole hog, and corn on the cob boiled in a big vat. A wooden bowl of butter was surrounded with various breads, and sweet tea had been prepared in metal pitchers especially for the Colonels. If you liked pie, you could choose from pecan, apple, chess or cherry. Several of the team took one of each.

Then it was over to the rodeo. The events included a race around fixed poles where a penalty was handed out if a pole was toppled, straight quarter horse races, bronco riding, both saddled and bareback, calf roping, bull dodging, trick riding, musical chairs on horses—if there was an event that belonged in a rodeo, it was included the afternoon that the Colonels spent outside of El Paso.

Someone dared Red to try calf roping and Red went over to a rider and asked if he could "borrow that horse of yours. I'm from Kentucky, and everyone in Kentucky knows how to ride."

Uncle Charlie quickly intervened.

"Carrot Top, sometimes I believe that red hair just sucks all of the sense right out of you when you get too much sun."

"Aw, Unc, geez louise."

It was late in the afternoon when the team was hustled back to Union Depot. It had been a great and memorable afternoon, and other than the Texans on the team, it was the first such affair which they'd ever attended.

"Yahoo," Hump hollered when he got back to the Depot. He had a red bandana around his neck, and a cowboy hat which a fan had given him.

"Got to get me some spurs. Some boots and spurs, and some of those leather pants." Texan Frank Rubarth said, "Chaps, Hump, you don't call them pants. You could get shot."

"Chaps, and some of those cowboy boots."

Red Roberts looked over at the barely 5'5" Hump.

"Get some with real high heels on them Humpty, and you might be able to see over a fireplug."

"I'm going to hurt you one day, Somerset. Hurt you bad."

And so it went, the bantering continuing as they walked to the back of the train to reach their Pullman.

"Track's pretty high, Humpty. Let me help you get over it."

"Like I said, Somerset, hurt you really, really bad."

The "Cowdray" was the trailing Pullman , hooked onto a Texas and Pacific train for the 600 mile run into Fort Worth, and then to Dallas. Due to the delay, it was December 29 at 6:00 p.m., when they eased out of the Union Depot, the Kentuckians and fans waving from the platform. They had been gone 13 days, and had 19 hours of travel ahead.

Back in the East, New Yorkers were reading an editorial on the day that the Colonels spent in El Paso. It was published in the New York "Herald" and praised, *the Centre College football team which is characterized by power, speed, intelligence and dazzling brilliance.*

The Texas and Pacific Railroad ran parallel to the southern border of New Mexico from El Paso toward the north central part of Texas.Once it got past the New Mexico border, it began a slightly more northern course as it headed east through the heart of the state toward Fort Worth.

The team slept as the train steamed through the Texas night. After breakfast, they watched the plains of the giant state flash by as they continued on their journey. It was 1:30 in the afternoon of December 30 when they reached Fort Worth, just a few hours short of two weeks since they'd pulled out of the Southern terminal in Danville. There was the usual greeting at the station, a large crowd along with the press. The Fort Worth connection, starting with the players from North Side who went to Kentucky in the fall of 1916, had kept Centre and the Texas natives in the press for the past six years. And of course, Bill James and Bo were still a big part of the Colonels' football team. Everyone wanted to know any and everything about "our boys and the Praying Colonels."

Bo met the train and brought along his fiancée Marie. Another interested participant at the terminal was Sully Montgomery, the large tackle who hadn't returned for the 1921 season due to having "taken myself a wife." Sully was pursuing a professional boxing career, but had lost his last fight to a fireman from Pueblo named Jim Flynn.

The big former Colonel raced up to Chick Murphy and lifted him off his feet with a bear hug. The two had been known as the "Cow and Calf" back in Kentucky, and when their photograph was taken together that afternoon, it wasn't difficult to see how the nicknames evolved.

After the brief layover in Fort Worth, the team re-boarded the "Cowdray" for the short ride east to Dallas. Gus King, the recent Centre grad and Dallas native, was at the Dallas Union Terminal with a "fleet of high-powered cars." Gus was a take-charge type of guy who had always been a wonderful organizer back in his days in Danville, and he was developing the same reputation now in his home town. He had made certain that all of the Dallas newspapers were at the station, and had contacted anyone who had even a remote connection to Kentucky to "give the boys a rousing reception."

The Colonels were delighted to see that each car was decorated in gold and white, with ribbons through the spokes of the wheels, Centre pennants hanging from the side-mounted spare tires, and signs attached to the passenger's and driver's side doors which announced:

CENTRE COLLEGE COLONELS
DANVILLE, KENTUCKY

Gus wanted there to be no doubt that the famous Kentuckians were in town.

The parade of cars drove the few blocks from the station to the wonderful Adolphus Hotel, the most luxurious facility that the Colonels had ever stayed in. The Lenox in Boston was a great hotel, as was the Tutwiler in Birmingham, the Seelback in Louisville, and of course, the Coronado which they'd recently left. But the Adolphus was in a class all by itself.

The hotel was a 21 story, French Renaissance masterpiece constructed by the St. Louis beer baron, Adolphus Busch, who sold a lot of beer in Dallas. When the Colonels entered, they saw Flemish tapestries, and a Victorian Steinway once owned by the Guggenheims. They made not have appreciated the significance of the individual treasures, but they knew that they were in the presence of splendor, and they came up to Uncle Charlie as they were checking in and told him as a group how magnificent it was to travel with the Centre College Colonels.

Uncle Charlie beamed, and turned to the manager who had come out of his office to welcome the team.

"Nothing is too fine for my young men."

The Adolphus had an interesting history. As Dallas was growing in size and importance from a dusty cattle town to the financial and cultural center of Texas, the local civic leaders lamented the fact that there wasn't a significant world class hotel to host important visitors who came to the city.

Adolphus Busch (1839-1913) co-founder, with his father-in-law, Eberhard Anheuser of the Anheuser-Busch Brewery, agreed. He decided to build one of the great hotels of the world, and succeeded. Unfortunately, he didn't live to actually see what he had accomplished. The hotel opened its doors in October 1912, and Adolphus died the following year in Germany while vacationing.

After getting their bags to their rooms, Uncle Charlie and Tiny Thornhill hustled the team out to Fairgrounds Stadium, two and a half miles from the Adolphus. It was getting late but there was still time to get in a workout at the stadium where the game was to be played.

Conspicuously absent was Bo. He had stayed behind in Fort Worth to be with Marie and her family. There were still pre-wedding functions to attend. In Bo's absence, the quarterback position was taken over by freshman, Herb Covington.

Friday night the 30th, the Texas A&M alumni held a reception downtown for both teams and any students from the schools who may be in town. The grads had hired a jazz band and the party was just gearing up to full tempo when the Colonels had to walk back to the Adolphus due to Uncle Charlie's 10:00 curfew.

Saturday, the last day of 1921, the Colonels conducted another workout at Fairgrounds Stadium, this time behind closed doors. Herb Covington again ran the offense due to Bo being late. Bo had suited up back in Fort Worth and hopped on an interurban train which he thought would take him to where the workout was being held, but he had the wrong location, and ended up at Gardiner Park, where a game was being held to determine the best team in the local Independent Football League.

The Dallas "Morning News" reported:

"BO" NEARLY BROKE UP SCHEPPS VS. ALL-STAR GAME

"Bo" McMillin, in football togs, completely faded the Schepps Bakery vs. All-Star game at Gardiner Park yesterday. The Kentucky leader dropped off an interurban at the Park, thinking practice would be staged there. The crowd found greater interest in the famous quarterback of the Centre eleven than the game, and proceeded to gather around "Bo" until he discovered that he was at the wrong location. (It was again notable that "Bo" was all that was needed in the headline to identify Bo McMillin. During the heyday of the Colonels, "Bo" was all that was required.)

MEANWHILE, TEXAS A&M.........

It wasn't like Uncle Charlie and Tiny weren't preparing their team for the upcoming January 2 game. After all, there had been a curfew, and there had been two workouts. But while the Colonels were taking things somewhat seriously, there was a totally different attitude in the other camp, the camp, literally, that Texas A&M was occupying on the campus of the University of Dallas.

The University of Dallas? What and where was that? While the name would seem to have designated some big, municipal institution, the University only dated back to 1910 when the Vincentian Fathers had appropriated that name for what they had formerly called Holy Trinity College, which they had founded a few years earlier.

Aggie coach, D.X. Bible, had brought his team to the rather isolated campus so that they could concentrate on football. They had been holed up in dormitories for several days while the Colonels were traveling. Their day began after breakfast with a two hour skull session, and then exercise. After lunch and a period of rest, there was a two hour, full-scrimmage session devoted to defense. Coach Bible had a good idea of what Centre's offensive schemes were like from talking to coaches around the country who had met Uncle Charlie's team on the gridiron.

In the modern era, teams obtain game films of their opponents, and scout other teams. For the Centre game, Bible contacted coaches, and it was part of the profession to extend the courtesy of cooperating if one was asked. After all, the coach asking for help today may be the coach being asked to provide information tomorrow.

Texas A&M kept up the two-a-day routine through December 31, drilling, drilling and then drilling some more. There were no temptations. The team was virtually locked up in the former Catholic seminary, and except for the Aggies attending the alumni-sponsored reception along with the Colonels during the evening of the 30th, from which they also left early due to a curfew, it was—football, football, and more football.

The upcoming game was tremendously important to Texas A&M for several reasons. The paper back in College Station had published that story which stated:

The great respect that tradition has kept alive in the minds of Aggie athletes for Charlie Moran, because of his glorious work with athletes at the A&M college of Texas, will be to stimulate their stamina and provoke them to a superhuman use of their strength when they meet his Danville team of Praying Colonels at the Dallas Fair Stadium on January 2.

Certainly that was true. It was almost that Uncle Charlie was coaching against himself! He was so well respected and fondly remembered that it was imperative that A&M make the ultimate effort—to honor him!

It was, "We can't let Uncle Charlie down. We must beat him! Then he will know that we have absorbed and upheld his ideals and standards!"

Also, Texas A&M was looking for respect outside of the South and Southwest. It wasn't that the school didn't have a good program going. D.X. Bible had things really rolling. His first team, in 1917, set the tone at 8-0-0. He missed the next year due to flying in the Army Air Force in France, but then resumed his winning ways when he returned to the campus for the 1919 season.

1917	8-0-0
1918	6-1-0 (Bible missed due to Army service.)
1919	10-0-0
1920	6-1-1
1921	5-1-2 (Prior to Centre game.)

The 35-3-3 record was impressive, especially when considering that the only losses were to Texas in 1918 and 1920 (Texas was undefeated both years) and LSU in 1921 (the Tigers were 6-1-1.) The ties were with LSU in 1920 and with Rice and Texas in 1921.

Obviously the Aggies were no pushover. However, Texas A&M wanted to receive recognition outside of the area where they played. Other than the game with Arizona, nearly all of their games had been with teams in Texas, and nearby Oklahoma and Louisiana.

Centre had developed such a national following that a victory over the Colonels would be front page news in newspapers from coast and coast.

Both teams spent New Year's Day resting. The Colonels had been kept up late by the revelers welcoming 1922 in at the Adolphus. There was no such distraction out on the secluded University of Dallas campus.

MONDAY, JANUARY 2, 1922   A WEDDING AND A GAME

Monday, January 2, was to be a busy day for the Centre team. When they awoke, they were entering the 18th day of their trip. Every member of the team, along with the coaches, John McGee, the manager, and any present or past students of the school who were staying at the Adolphus, had gotten up, dressed in their best, and headed to Union Terminal to take a very early train west to Fort Worth.

It was Bo's wedding day. The man of the hour, the bridegroom, Alvin Nugent McMillin, had been granted marriage license #50,973 at the Tarrant County courthouse on December 30, having barely arrived before the office closed on Friday afternoon.

"Man, I don't know what I would have done if I'd been just a few minutes later getting to that courthouse. I don't think even the U.S. Navy could have bailed me out," Bo said later.

Thad McDonnell was in Fort Worth to serve as Bo's best man. Thad had known Bo since they had been students together at North Side, and he gave a reporter some background on Bo and his love, Marie Miers.

Bo had never dated anyone other than Marie, Thad stated. He recounted how many times Bo had nearly hopped a freight train back to Fort Worth during the 1916-17 school year that he, Bo, and Red Weaver spent in Somerset, prepping for entrance to Centre.

"I don't think anyone ever loved somebody as much as Bo loved Marie. Red and I used to listen to him pine away, talking about how much he missed her and how he was heading to the tracks to jump on a freight train and hobo back to Fort Worth."

"We could usually talk him out of it, but once the Chief had to come down on the train. We'd had somebody call the Chief and tell him that it was looking serious this time, and the Chief sent back word for us to sit on him if we had to, and he'd be there as soon as possible."

"And?"

"And, you know what we did? Bo had two pairs of shoes, some school shoes and his good shoes that he was really proud of. We jumped him and got his shoes off and had already hidden his good shoes, and it was cold as it could be, and even Bo, as much as he missed Marie, wasn't about to go hopping on a train in freezing weather with no shoes, because we put them out in a shed, and he couldn't find them."

McDonnell laughed. "Bo went around in his socks until the Chief got there and had him promise that he'd stick it out. We knew that if Bo told the Chief something, he'd keep his word. So we gave him his shoes back, and you know, Bo thanked us later for caring enough about him to steal his shoes! That's the kind of guy Bo is. None finer."

The wedding was scheduled for 9:00 a.m. Marie's mother had helped her send out the invitations, and they went out to locations all over the country. Naturally, a large percentage went to family and friends in Fort Worth, but Mrs. Miers was astonished that so many were being sent not only to Danville, but cities all over Kentucky, and elsewhere.

"Who is Howard Reynolds in Boston? And Mr. Edward W. Mahan, also from Boston?"

"Mother, Bo knows people all over the country. Mr. Reynolds is a sportswriter, and

Eddie Mahan was an All-American at Harvard who came to Danville with Mr. Reynolds."

"The governor of Kentucky? Edwin P. Morrow? Isn't Jim Thorpe that Indian player?"

"The governor and Bo are friends. He's taken Bo to dinner and made Bo a Kentucky Colonel. Plus his son is at Centre. Bo played football with Jim Thorpe in that All-Star game in Columbus and they really liked each other."

"Judge Robert Worth Bingham?"

"Bo said he owned the two most influential papers in Louisville. He met Bo when the team played those games in Louisville and said he'd heard Bo was getting married, and he'd have his papers write bad things about Bo if he weren't invited to the wedding!"

"Maude Marie, your Bo is something else again."

"Why do you think I waited all of these years, mother dear?"

The day began for Bo at a breakfast in his family home. He told reporters who had arrived almost as the sun came up that his only regret was that his mother couldn't be there. Pearl McMillin, Bo's sister, supplied coffee and sweet rolls for the press. Bo always got favorable publicity, because he never failed to be courteous and considerate in his relations with writers and photographers, no matter if they were with the major city publications, or some little rural weekly.

All Saints was the church in which Bo, a devout Catholic, had been raised, but it was too small for the anticipated crowd, and the larger St. Patrick Cathedral on Thockmorton Street was the site where he would walk Marie down the aisle and she would become Mrs. Alvin Nugent McMillin. The church began to fill well before the ceremony.

The fact that Bo, one of the most famous people in the country, and the coaches and the players of Centre College, the most famous football team in the country, were going to be there, prompted many curious uninvited spectators to show up and line the sidewalks outside of the church, because the newspapers in Fort Worth and Dallas had published the time and place.

In addition to old friend Thad McDonnell as his best man, Bo chose Army, Red Roberts, Bill James, Ben Cregor and Tom Moran to be his groomsmen. Pearl, Bo's sister, was maid of honor. Marie's sister, Mrs. G.E. Melton, was matron of honor. Bridesmaids were Edna Christian, Kathleen Kelly, and Rebecca Walton, all of Fort Worth, Mildred Beaty of Waco, and Lorena Reilly from Dallas.

The Miers and Bo's family members had put a lot of effort into making certain that Marie and Bo had a proper union. The organist was Mrs. R. Cox of Fort Worth. Catherine McMillin Sherrod, Bo's youngest sister, sang the always popular, "Because," and a violinist helped add to the beauty and solemnity of the affair. The actual ceremony was a traditional wedding performed by the Very Reverend Robert N. Nolan, followed by a Nuptial High Mass.

It was a beaming, happy couple who marched back down the aisle, arm in arm, got pelted with rice, shook a lot of hands outside the church, and then raced to Dallas, courtesy of Gus King, who had again rounded up the group of drivers who had met the team earlier in Dallas. The long row of gold and white decorated cars was led by one with white ribbons streaming along its sides and from its rear spare, with signs on the front doors announcing:

MARIE and BO...JUST MARRIED

There was a post-wedding brunch at the Adolphus which was held for the wedding party and the team and coaches. Again, detailed planning had assured that it was a successful affair. Mrs. Miers had taken charge and met with the catering manager to make certain that everything was just right.

Uncle Charlie kept circulating, reminding the players, "Slow down on the eating, fellows. We've got a game in a few hours," but wasn't too successful. It was a party not only in honor of the newlyweds, but for the Colonels as well, as Marie's mother kept reminding the team.

"Eat up, boys. Look at all that food we've had prepared for you. And save space for the wedding cake which is going to be just sumptuous!"

After the Adolphus, it was off to the Texas State Fairgrounds for the game. It had been a whirlwind day thus far, hardly proper as a pre-game routine, but after all, the whole trip was as a reward for a season well done. Bo's wedding had been factored in from the onset. What else was a coach to do, thought Uncle Charlie.

While the Colonels were partying, Texas A&M was following a much more traditional ritual for a morning before a contest. The Aggies had been allowed to sleep in until breakfast in the college dining room at 9:00. Then it was an extensive skull session, followed by actually going out on the field where they had been practicing and once again lining up in the defensive positions which they were planning on employing to hopefully shut down the Colonels' high-powered offense.

It was a solemn and determined group of Texans who boarded two buses and headed to go into combat. While the Aggies were traveling quietly toward Fair Park, it was a different story for the Colonels. Gus King's caravan raced through the city streets, weaving in and out of traffic, packed with Colonels who were stuffed with Mrs. Miers' brunch selections and "sumptuous" wedding cake.

The Fairgrounds dated to 1886 when a group of local businessmen and ranchers from outside the city decided that Dallas needed a proper site for an annual Texas State Fair. A wooden stadium was constructed in the spring of 1921, capacity 15,000, and the availability of this facility was one of the deciding factors in putting together the Centre-Texas A&M pairing. The game was a total sellout, as was expected. A&M had quite a following in the area, and of course, Centre packed them in wherever the Colonels appeared.

In the dressing room before the team went out on the field, Army called everyone to attention and said he had an announcement. He said that Red Roberts had been elected captain for 1922, and it was January 2, 1922.

"Like I did after our banquet last month, I want to introduce you again to Captain James B. "Red" Roberts who will be your captain for the game."

It was typical Army, a great leader and team player.

As the kickoff neared, fans of the Aggies in Bryan, Texas who couldn't get to Dallas, began to assemble at the Wallace Building where a telegraph line had been installed to receive the play-by-play. Additionally, telegraph lines were opened up between Dallas and Boston and Cambridge, Louisville, Lexington and Danville for "play-by-play."

We need to review the history and evolution of college football post-season games again.

Why? Because, Centre was a participant in the 2nd, 3rd and 4th bowl game venues ever played. It is just another absolutely amazing fact that few know, but hopefully, the publication of the "Wonder Team" will bring even more of an appreciation of what the little college accomplished in the years after the Great War.

The January 2, 1922 game was called the Dixie Classic. It was the 4th bowl venue ever played in the history of college football. Of course, the Rose Bowl was the original post-season affair. The first Rose Bowl was January 1, 1902. The Fort Worth Classic between Centre and TCU on January 1, 1921, was the 2nd bowl venue. The East vs. West, or Christmas Bowl, contested in San Diego between Centre and Arizona, on December 26, 1921 was the 3rd bowl of all-time. Now, the 4th bowl ever played, the Dixie Classic between Centre and Texas A&M, was about to commence.

BOWL HISTORY

BOWL	DATE	TEAMS AND SCORES
Rose	Jan. 1, 1902	Michigan-49 Stanford-0
Rose	Jan. 1, 1916	Washington State-14 Brown-0
Rose	Jan. 1, 1917	Oregon-14 Pennsylvania-0
Rose	Jan. 1, 1918	Mare Island Marines-19 Camp Lewis-0
Rose	Jan. 1, 1919	Great Lakes-17 Mare Island Marines-0
Rose	Jan. 1, 1920	Harvard-7 Oregon-6
Rose	Jan. 1, 1921	California-28 Ohio State-0
Fort Worth Classic	Jan. 1, 1921	**Centre**-63 TCU-7
Christmas Bowl	Dec. 26 1921	**Centre**-38 Arizona-0
Dixie Classic	Jan. 2, 1922	**Centre** vs. Texas A&M
Rose	Jan. 2, 1922	California-0 Washington & Jefferson-0

Not only did Centre College of Kentucky play in the 2nd, 3rd and 4th bowls ever played, but Centre had received a signed contract to appear in the Rose Bowl but turned it down due to having committed to the Christmas Bowl in San Diego. As the Centre athletic officials said after the invitation to play Harvard, "Who would ever have believed it!"

The two team captains, "Hennie" Weir and Red, met at midfield for the toss which was won by A&M, and the Dixie Classic was ready to begin. Red put the ball near the Aggies' goal, Sammy Sander returned it 40 yards, and A&M went on the attack. Centre played tough, gave up no yardage, and A&M had to punt.

Tom Bartlett fielded the ball on the two yard line and tried to evade the on rushing defenders by moving laterally, and as he stepped just behind his goal line, a diving Aggie tripped him up and he fell just behind the marker.

An official raced over and declared that it was a safety since Bartlett had been downed in his own end zone. With just a couple of minutes run off the clock, it was Texas A&M up 2-0, much to the delight of the partisan crowd.

The points were the first surrendered by the Colonels since the St. Xavier game on October 15, slightly over two and a half months and eight games ago. While the points were obviously a disappointment, the concern wasn't about being down by two, but was about seeing Red limping. The captain had taken out a maroon and white clad Texan and gone for a second block when he cut sharply and fell to the ground in obvious discomfort.

Red got up and continued to play, but it was obvious from that moment on that he wouldn't be able to be as effective as normally. It wasn't particularly a good start. Down by two, and Red with a hurt knee.

Army told me later, and Hump did too, that despite Red being hurt, they weren't too worried. I guess it's human nature to sometimes underestimate an opponent. Our guys realized that they had just toyed with Arizona and still won, 38-0. They couldn't help but realize that Texas A&M had been hard pressed to beat Arizona, 17-13, even on its home field. The papers had mentioned that fact in story after story, and the betting had us as 4-1 favorites. But of course, games are won on the field, and not in the papers.

Centre dominated play the rest of the first half. There were three series when the Colonels had great field position and should have scored.

After a Centre punt, Sammy Sanders caught the ball, juggled it, and the ball hit the ground. As he tried to pick it up he was hit by Bill Shadoan who was running at full speed. Sanders was knocked totally unconscious, "the ball dropping from his nerveless fingers." Shadoan pounced on the ball on the Aggie 28.

Three plunges gained seven, then A&M was whistled for holding and the penalty resulted in the ball being marched to the Aggies' six, and it was 1st and goal. First Bo, then Snowday, then Army hit the line, and the ball rested on the six inch line.

On the 4th play, Bo fumbled the snap and the delay caused him to just get back to the line of scrimmage. Texas A&M took over and decided to punt it away.

Herb Covington was in the game and caught the punt and couldn't advance, but the Colonels were starting on the Aggies' 40 yard line.

Bo hit Covington for 15 and the little speedster picked up another 10, and it was 1st down Centre on the 15. Centre moved to the nine, and Bo fumbled and A&M recovered.

It was the 2nd time that it appeared the Colonels were going to put points on the board and they had nothing to show for their efforts. The offense that Uncle Charlie had installed depended on split timing. He had his team run signal drills over and over, perfecting the precision of the offense which the young reporter in New Orleans had been so awed by.

The lack of practice time on the long trip, and Bo having missed much of the sessions in Dallas, was beginning to show. The Colonels simply weren't sharp.

Still, Centre was paying its usual tenacious defense. After the Aggies recovery of Bo's second fumble, they couldn't move the ball and had to punt again, and Herb Covington returned the ball to the A&M 28. Great field position again.

Bo went to the air. Two passes were incomplete. The 3rd picked up five. On the 4th straight aerial attempt, Bo's pass was picked off as he tried to pick up the 1st down.

Two fumbles and an interception after three possessions begun well into A&M territory. There was an exchange of punts and the half, the very frustrating half in which nearly the entire action had taken place in A&M territory, ended with the safety being the only score. It was 2-0. As the two teams left the field for the break, the Texas A&M Cadet Band, 30 strong, marched onto the field and formed a "T" and played the school song.

The "Aggie War Hymn" had been written by J. V. "Pinky" Wilson while he was standing guard with the American Expeditionary Force on the Rhine right after the Great War.

"THE AGGIE WAR HYMN"
All hail to dear old Texas A&M!
Rally around Maroon and White.
Good luck to the dear old Texas Aggies.
They are the boys who show the real old fight.
That good old Aggie spirit thrills us
And makes us yell and yell and yell.
So let's fight for dear old Texas A&M.
We're goin' to beat you all to—
Chig-gar-roo-gar-rem!
Chig-gar-roo-gar-rem!
Rough Tough! Real Stuff! Texas A&M!

(Chorus)

Hullabaloo, Caneck! Caneck!
Hullabaloo, Caneck! Caneck!

Then the full dress-uniformed Cadets played "My Old Kentucky Home" in honor of the Colonels and their fans.

Red Roberts had hardly been a factor in the 1st half. Unless a run came right over his position, he seemed to be unable to move toward the play, and his interference was lacking on offense. It wasn't from lack of effort of the big redhead. No one could ever say Red didn't have heart. But the fact that his knee was so swollen from the injury early in the game severely limited his mobility.

It was like in the Harvard and Georgia Tech games of 1920. The Colonels weren't able to play up to their expected level without a fully functional Red. He continued to play the entire game, never going to the sidelines, but he and Centre were tremendously handicapped by his swollen, painful knee.

Texas A&M had its own share of injuries. Two starting backs hadn't even suited up due to injuries suffered during earlier games, and their captain, fullback "Hennie" Weir, was carried off the field during the 1st quarter with what was discovered later to be a broken leg. The lack of manpower on the part of the Aggies resulted in one of the most endearing, and enduring traditions in all of college football. Coach Bible began to worry about having anyone to substitute as the injuries kept piling up. It was a hard-hitting game. Thus was born the fabled "Twelfth Man" tradition.

E. King Gill was a former Aggie football player who had decided to concentrate full time on basketball. He was in the press box helping to identify players for the writers covering the game. Coach Bible sent someone up to the press box who told Gill that the coach wanted him to hustle down to the dressing room and get suited up. He may be needed. As a matter of fact, the messenger said, if there were any more injuries, he would indeed be needed, and sent into the game.

Gill was later quoted as saying, "I wish I could say that I went in and ran for the winning touchdown. But I did not. I simply stood by in case my team needed me."

This gesture, by Gill, was more than enough for the Aggie team. Although Gill didn't play in the game, he had accepted the call to help in any way possible. He came to be known as the Twelfth Man, because he stood ready to help in the event that the eleven men on the gridiron needed assistance. That spirit helped kindle a flame of devotion among the whole student body that lives to this day. The entire A&M student body now is the Twelfth Man, and stands throughout the entire football game to show their support. King Gill is immortalized by a bronze statue presented to Texas A&M University by the class of 1980 which stands outside of Kyle Field.

The game resumed with the crowd amazed that Centre, the number one team in the country, the team which had defeated Harvard, the team that had given up only six points all year, was coming back onto the field trailing, even if it was only by 2-0.

The 3rd quarter was a defensive contest featuring exchanges of punts, neither team giving ground. With five minutes left in the period, Centre got a break when the Aggies' Miller fumbled, and Hump Tanner scooped up the ball on the 32 yard line and lugged it down to the three before being bumped out of bounds.

Centre lined up, determined not to blow another chance, and Snowday literally went through the air, leaping over the mass of Texans defending their goal. Red kicked the extra point and Centre finally had broken through. It was 7-2.

The Centre College Colonels were just a little over 19 minutes from an 11-0 perfect season and a sure claim for a national championship. Then disaster. Coach Bible decided to kickoff. His team hadn't been able to move the ball on the Colonels who had been displaying their customary, impregnable defense. It was a wise coaching call. The kick wasn't deep and went to Bill James who brought it to the 33 and fumbled when he was hit by the same Miller whose bobble set up the Colonels' score. It seemed to be poetic justice, a way for the young Aggie to redeem himself.

On the 2nd play from scrimmage, the Texans lined up and ran a triple pass play when their halfback, somewhat confusingly named McMillan, passed to Wilson, who passed to Miller, who put the ball in the air, 40 yards to Evans, who scored. The extra point made it 9-7, Texas A&M. The Colonels held the lead less than a minute.

The second Aggie touchdown came with equal suddenness. Herb Covington received the kickoff and returned it to his own 24. Two plunges went nowhere against the fired-up A&M defense, and then "Covey" fumbled and it was recovered by the Aggies. Four plays later, Wilson raced around Red who simply couldn't move laterally and dashed into the end zone. The extra point made it 16-7, which is how the 3rd quarter ended.

The momentum had definitely shifted, and things were looking serious. Early in the 4th quarter, Bo had his team on the Aggies 40 yard line. He knew that if his team could score, kick the extra point, and then put three points on the board with a field goal, they could pull it out, 17-16. It certainly wasn't beyond what the Colonels were capable of doing if their offense was clicking.

Bo decided to go to the air. His line gave him perfect protection and he raced back and forth, getting further and further back behind the line of scrimmage when he finally fired a desperation pass which was picked off by a maroon and white-clad Ted Winn, who returned it 45 yards for a touchdown. The extra point was no good, but Centre was down 22-7, and things were looking more than serious for the Gold and White. They were looking bad. The Colonels fought back, refusing to go down without giving it everything they had.

The kickoff was returned to the Colonels' 30. Bo hit Red for 20 and then 16. Bo called six straight ground plays with freshman "Case" Thomasson, who had replaced Terry Snowday, carrying the ball each time. With the ball on the 18, Bo hit Snowday, who had checked back in, for the final 18, and Red's kick made it 22-14. In the few minutes remaining, Bo fired passes left and right, long and short, but couldn't connect on a score, and the final margin was 22-14.

The Kentuckians picked up 14 first downs to but five for the Aggies. The Colonels gained 314 yards, usually sufficient for a win. Herb Covington picked up 137 yards on 22 carries and was easily the best man on the field on January 2, 1922, accounting for over 40% of Centre's yardage. The combination of Centre's fumbles and intercepted passes proved fatal. Statistically, the Colonels were the better team, but games are settled on the scoreboard. The Texas Aggies never had a sustained drive, but they won, and the Colonels accepted the loss in the manner in which they had accepted their victories. They were never arrogant or bragged when they won. The rare times when they lost, they offered no excuses. The Colonels stood at midfield after the final whistle and gave a "Hip, Hip, Hooray for the Aggies. Hip, Hip, Hooray for the Aggies." It was an appropriate way to end the Dixie Classic.

THE AFTERMATH

When the results came in over the wires, there was skepticism everywhere.

"Some wise guy said the final score came in and Centre lost. That can't be true. When the right score comes in, let me know."

Meanwhile, in the Centre locker room, Bo asked that the reporters listen to what he had to say.

"I have been credited many times for winning games for Centre. I want to take credit again, but this time for losing one. It was all my fault. Certainly Texas A&M played well, and we want to give them all of the credit that they deserve. But the simple fact is that it was my play which lost this game, and I accept the responsibility."

Was Bo correct? While not one player offered any excuses, in analyzing the loss, George Joplin wrote a story for the Louisville "Herald" which tried to make some sense about what everyone considered a great upset.

It was obvious that playing a big game on the 18th day of a road trip was a factor. Nothing tires a person like living out of a suitcase, often cooped up in a Pullman for days on end.

The lack of regular workouts was also a contributor.

The Colonels' offense depended on perfect timing, and perfect timing depended on constantly running drills that kept refining the plays until there was no margin for error.

Staying at the Adolphus may have been a mistake, especially with all of the celebrations ushering in the New Year. Certainly the almost monastic existence of the Aggies contrasted with the surroundings in which the Colonels found themselves. However, it must be remembered that the trip to the West was a reward for an excellent season, and the Centre staff felt that the team deserved to be maintained in wonderful hotels like the Coronado and Adolphus.

Bo's wedding was a contributor. His mind obviously had to be pre-occupied with more than football, and his play seemed to reflect that.

There was the matter of over-confidence. Any team naturally looks at what their opponents have done in prior games, in order to gauge their strength. The Colonels wouldn't have been human if they hadn't underestimated Texas A&M. The Aggies had struggled to beat Arizona on their own field in College Station.

Centre had so overwhelmed the Arizonians that the Colonels had to take into consideration the Aggies' close call when they were mentally preparing for the game.

Jop, in his article wired back home, failed to bring up another factor, and that was the injury early in the game to Red Roberts. Anytime the big fellow was less than totally fit, it became obvious just how important he was to his team's success. It was not only "As goes Bo, so goes Centre," but is was true of Red, also.

There was the issue of the crowd. Most of the times that the Colonels had played on the road, at least early on, they were embraced by their opponent's fans because everyone loves an underdog, or everyone loves the little, smaller school, even if "David," or the underdog, is playing their own team. The Colonels were no longer underdogs. Unlike at Cambridge or even New Orleans, in Dallas there was no sentiment other than the desire for the home team to win, and fully 99% of the spectators were pulling for the boys from Texas A&M. Fan support is important, and the Texans were great fans.

But in the final analysis, the reason that the Aggies beat the Colonels, is that they played hard, they took advantage of the breaks they were given like a good team should, and they deserved to win because they were a talented group of dedicated young men. Coach Bible had done an excellent job. His was no weak team, as proven by its record over the past few years.

The Aggie coach, when interviewed after the game, said, "The men went into the game with the spirit of self-sacrifice and won. They played a wonderful game, and I am proud of their showing."

Uncle Charlie was gracious in defeat. He told the reporters that, "A&M played a great game and deserved to win." And he added, quite sincerely, "If my team had to lose, I would rather lose to Texas A&M than any team in the country."

After the game, the team attended a banquet at the Oriental Hotel given by the A&M Alumni Association for the Cadet Corps and the two teams. Hump Tanner spoke for the Colonels when he stood and told the large crowd how much his team respected the Aggies, "for their hard play, for their sportsmanship, and we appreciate the alumni of the school for their kindness, and lastly, we thank the citizens of Dallas for all of the hospitality shown to each of us during our stay here in Texas."

It was three cheers for Texas A&M, three cheers for Centre, and finally, three cheers for Dallas. Then it was off to the Union Terminal for an 8:00 p.m. departure, heading back to Kentucky.

HEADING HOME

Once again the faithful "Cowdray" was waiting for the team. It was connected to the back of the regularly scheduled Missouri, Kansas and Texas passenger train which pulled out of Dallas each night for the run to St. Louis, arriving in the big Union Station there before noon, so that anyone needing some time day in the city would arrive with the whole afternoon still available.

The railroad, known as the Katy, went north out of Dallas, crossed over into and through Oklahoma, running north, and then cut through the southeast tip of Kansas before entering Missouri. Once in Missouri, the route went northeast until reaching Central Missouri where it veered off onto a true eastern direction to St. Louis.

With the addition of Oklahoma on the return from Dallas, the Colonels would have traveled through their 13th state on the trip—Kentucky, Indiana, Illinois, Missouri, Kansas, Colorado, Utah, Nevada, California, Arizona, New Mexico, Texas and Oklahoma. When the additional 11 states are included which were traveled to, or through, on prior journeys since the Chief and Uncle Charlie arrived in Danville—Ohio, Pennsylvania, New York, Massachusetts, Tennessee, Virginia, West Virginia, Georgia, Alabama, Mississippi and Louisiana, the young men of the Gold and White would have been to 24 of the 48 states which then made up the United States. It would have been a rare person who would have said, in the early 1920's, that they had been in half the states in the country, but the Colonels, from little Centre and Danville, could. Also, they had crossed the border into Mexico.

The Katy train was delayed six hours on the way to St. Louis. The original plan was to have a big luncheon when the team arrived and to spend the afternoon touring the city, but the delay obviously made that impossible. It was just as well. The team was anxious, terribly anxious, to get back to Danville, and was relieved that they didn't have to once again dress and make another appearance.

The "Cowdray" finally arrived early in the evening on January 4. It had been 20 days almost to the hour since the wild Danville send off. Despite the loss to Texas A&M, and despite the arrival of the train being off schedule, there was the usual, large enthusiastic crowd at the little Southern station to welcome "our boys" back home. From Danville to Louisville, to St. Louis, and across Missouri to Kansas City. They had steamed through the Great Plains of Kansas and Colorado to Denver, at the foot of the Rockies, and wound up and over the great mountains to Salt Lake City, and then to Ogden, Utah and across the Great Salt Lake. The "Cowdray" had been pulled on the Overland Route to Oakland, and then it was into San Francisco on a Southern Pacific ferry. Down the West Coast they'd gone, spending a day in Los Angeles, and then on to San Diego and the record setting storm.

There had been rain delays out of San Diego, but then there was the wonderful, torchlight welcome in Tucson. A day in El Paso, a Southwest cookout and rodeo, had followed. Finally it was to Fort Worth to be welcomed by old friends before the short hop to Dallas.

They'd slept through the night going from Dallas to St. Louis and been switched back onto the Southern tracks for the ride back through Louisville, to Lexington, and finally home to Danville.

It was a weary group of young men who climbed into their own beds on Wednesday night, January 4, 1922. There is truly no place like home, especially when you love it so.

Bo left Dallas and he and Marie headed to a banquet held in Shreveport, Louisiana, where he was introduced as the new football coach at Centenary.

The rest of the team went back to classes, and things returned to normal on the campus of the little college in the Bluegrass.

TWO POST-SEASON AFFAIRS

It was time for the recognition on the campuses in Danville and College Station.

The Texas cotton broker, William Weatherford, who had wired Danville that he wanted to pay for a banquet, "with no expenses spared," again sent word that he was waiting for the tab so that he could make good his offer.

In College Station, a huge cake was being assembled under the supervision of the culinary department as part of a luncheon for the entire A&M Cadet Corps and faculty to celebrate the great victory over Centre.

The monstrous dessert contained 340 pounds of baked dough, 40 pounds of jelly between the layers, and 50 pounds of 8-color icing, the majority being in the maroon and white, team colors of the Aggies.

A tape measure was put to the creation. The base was 85 inches in length, and the layers were built in a pyramid configuration to a height of 37 inches. On top was a replica of a football molded from brown icing.

Inscribed on the sides were, "Greetings Farmers, Welcome, 100%, A&M, and Jan 2, 1922." There were little footballs, the score, 22-14, and "other letters, emblems and signs further recalling the great victory."

It took seven men working eight, non-stop hours, to complete what was to be a surprise, as only those involved were allowed into a room which was locked and off-limits to even others in the food-service department.

Finally, after all of the student body and faculty had assembled in the dining hall, the huge confectionary was rolled out and met by cheers and expressions of wonderment. Over 1,000 pieces were cut, served, and enjoyed.

Later, little gold footballs with a red "A" and "1921" were awarded to letter winners in honor of the great season of 1921, capped off by the January 2 win over Centre.

The Centre banquet didn't feature anything as spectacular as the gigantic cake constructed in Texas, but it was a wonderful fete. Mrs. Jones, who was in charge of preparing the meal, took Mr. Weatherford at his word. The banquet was held in the dining room of K.C.W. on the night of January 6, just two days after the team returned from the momentous trip. The girls from the school were the servers.

The menu included fruit salad, several aged, sliced Kentucky country hams, chicken croquets with mushroom sauce, a specialty of Mrs. Jones, peas, sweet breads in pastry shells, creamed potatoes, asparagus tips on toast with cream sauce, various fresh baked breads, butter and jams and jellies, congealed salad, sweet and dill pickles, olives, sweet tea, chocolate covered mints, mince pie a la mode, and cigars for everyone who wished to smoke with their coffee, now that training was over.

A lot of talk at the banquet was about the fact that Centre didn't have a president, and it was hoped that the college would hire someone like Dr Ganfield who had been so supportive of the athletic programs. Also, a topic for discussion was the newly adopted "freshman rule." It was simply a fact that a little school like Centre was going to be tremendously handicapped in the future since freshmen couldn't compete.

Army got up and suggested that Centre withdraw and become "independent." Chick Murphy gave a strong speech supporting Army. While many in attendance agreed, it was pointed out that no significant school could be scheduled if Centre tried to go its own way.

"Look what happened when Pitt wouldn't play Georgia Tech. Some said it was because Tech plays so dirty, but Pitt said it cancelled because Tech wanted to play freshmen."

For Centre, the "freshman rule" was a "lose-lose" proposition. Either Centre wouldn't be able to compete due to the loss of eligibility of first-year men, or it wouldn't be able to compete because of the unwillingness of schools to put them on the schedule if they played freshmen.

Everyone agreed that once the wonderful group of athletes sitting in the K.C.W. dining hall began to graduate, there would be an inevitable and irreversible decline in Centre's athletic fortunes.

Uncle Charlie was the last speaker. Through the haze of cigar smoke, he talked about the game in Texas. He complimented the Aggies and the way they had played. But he also spoke about how proud he was of the team and their season.

"We traveled too far, and we weren't able to keep our game sharp. We make no excuses, but we simply played one game too many."

Then Uncle Charlie related what he had told the A&M coach, D.X. Bible, after the game.

"I told Coach Bible that after we beat Harvard, Eddie Mahan and Coach Fisher came into our locker room, and they said to me, "Charlie, this win will do you a world of good, and it won't hurt Harvard."

"And I said the same—your win will do Texas A&M a world of good, but we won't be hurt. We'll come back just as strong next year."

Then, Uncle Charlie flashed a big smile and took a long puff off his cigar.

"You know, I have signed a contract for the next two years to stay on as coach here at Centre. We will come back, and we'll continue on what we have built. I want you boys to know just how proud I have been to be called the coach of the Centre College Praying Colonels, the greatest team, with the greatest players, at the greatest college, at anytime, and anywhere."

There were cheers which could be heard echoing throughout the long halls of the gorgeous old buildings that were K.C.W.

"Of course, with Unc coming back, we'll be alright!"

LOOKING BACK ON 1921

The post-season scrambled the picture for the best team of 1921. Three undefeated and untied teams had played in bowls, and none emerged unblemished. California and Washington and Jefferson both went into the Rose Bowl with perfect records and tied 0-0. Centre went West at 9-0-0 and split in two bowls to end 10-1-0.

There were three undefeated, untied teams:
Lafayette   9-0-0
Cornell   8-0-0
Iowa   7-0-0

There were also three who were undefeated but once tied:
Washington and Jefferson   10-0-1
California   9-0-1
Vanderbilt   7-0-1

Eight teams had one loss:
Centre   10-1-0
Notre Dame   10-1-0
Yale   8-1-0
Georgia Tech   8-1-0
Utah State   7-1-0
Nebraska   7-1-0
Navy   6-1-0
Chicago   6-1-0

Which was the best team in 1921?

Centre would have been a lock if it had beaten Texas A&M, but it didn't, and the loss hurt the school's certainty of being selected by sportswriters and "experts."

The undefeated Iowa Hawkeyes had a reasonable claim.

Iowa	52	Knox College	0
Iowa	10	Notre Dame	7
Iowa	14	Illinois	2
Iowa	13	Purdue	6
Iowa	41	Minnesota	7
Iowa	41	Indiana	0
Iowa	14	Northwestern	0

Certainly the win over Notre Dame was big, as it was the only loss that the Irish had for three years, having gone 9-0 in both 1919 and 1920.

Knox College was weak, and, as stated earlier, of the Hawkeyes' opponents, none had a winning record, and combined, Illinois, Indiana, Minnesota, Northwestern and Purdue were a woeful, 11-24.

Still, that Notre Dame win was important.

Cornell had a good year, of that there is no doubt. The Big Red only surrendered 21 points during the year, but their schedule included Saint Bonaventure, Rochester, Western Reserve and Springfield.

Cornell	41	St. Bonaventure	0
Cornell	35	Rochester	0
Cornell	10	Western Reserve	0
Cornell	31	Colgate	7
Cornell	59	Dartmouth	7
Cornell	41	Columbia	7
Cornell	14	Springfield	0
Cornell	41	Pennsylvania	0

Cornell's decisive victory over a 6-2-1-Dartmouth team was impressive. However, the combined record of Colgate, Columbia and Penn was only 10-11-5.

Still, Cornell should be given consideration.

Lafayette?

Lafayette	48	Muhlenberg	0
Lafayette	6	Pittsburgh	0
Lafayette	27	Dickenson	0
Lafayette	20	Bucknell	0
Lafayette	28	Fordham	7
Lafayette	35	Rutgers	0
Lafayette	38	Pennsylvania	6
Lafayette	44	Delaware	0
Lafayette	28	Lehigh	0

Undefeated, weak schedule, tough defense, big win over a good Pitt team, virtually unknown outside of their area because they didn't venture far from Easton, Pennsylvania. That's about as good a summary of Lafayette as can be given.

However, Lafayette was one of the three teams in 1921 with a perfect record.

So who was the best?

Certainly Centre would merit a place in the top four or five, and Mr. Howell's computer rating system, which we've referred to in the past, and will again, put the Colonels in the number two slot.

CHAPTER 18:
THE 1922 SEASON

While everyone knew that the "freshman rule" would eventually harm Centre and similar schools, things still looked rosy in Danville. The Colonels would definitely lose only four players, each of whom had significantly contributed to bringing such glory to Centre College during the past five, glorious years.

Bo, Army, Tom Moran and Bill James had suited up for the last time. Red Roberts, Ben Cregor and Chick Murphy could have graduated but had another year of eligibility due to the war year of 1918 being negated. Red and Ben decided to return. Chick, now relegated to a reserve role due to the abundance of backfield talent, chose to take his diploma and move on.

Certainly the loss of the four great Colonels and Chick would be felt. While the incomparable Bo would be hard to replace, Herb Covington had been well tutored by Uncle Charlie and had gotten enough playing time to be ready to take over at quarterback. You don't actually replace a Bo. You simply try to find the next best person available, and Herb Covington more than filled the role. He became a star in his own right.

Army had provided not only consistent, steady play for five years, but quiet leadership. He had been an inspiration to the other players and helped set the tone which contributed much to the Colonels being so admired in every city they visited.

It was often said of the much loved Army that he was the quintessential Colonel, a gentle man, and a gentleman, but as tough on the gridiron as they came. People who mistook his subdued demeanor for lack of desire, or thought he wouldn't put a hit on them, did so at their own peril.

Bill James never sought the spotlight. He was simply there when needed. He had matured over the years until Tiny Thornhill looked to James to be the steadying influence amongst a group of freshmen who went to Cambridge and outplayed the front wall of the mighty Harvard Crimson. Nobody worked harder. No one played so consistently up to, and beyond, his ability.

Like Bo, and Army, Bill James would be missed. When prognosticators began to size up Centre for 1922, here's what they saw.

The backfield was set. Covey would be the quarterback. Hump could step in and relieve him if needed. At half, Terry Snowday and Tom Bartlett were experienced and talented. Tom could also play fullback if needed. Hump would be the regular fullback, and of course, Red could slip into the position if needed. Case Thomasson, a freshman from Newport, Kentucky, who had played well in the backfield against A&M, was coming back. Case could also play end. Hope Hudgins, another freshman, from Amarillo, Texas, could literally fly and even though he was small, he was expected to get significant action at halfback.

So even with the loss of Bo and Army, the Centre machine would continue to run a high-powered offense, and the prospects looked good.

The starters in the line against Harvard were:

POSITION	STARTER	WEIGHT
Left end	Bill James	180
Left tackle	Minos Gordy	182
Left guard	Bill Shadoan	196
Center	Ed Kubale	177
Right guard	George "Buck" Jones	213
Right tackle	Ben Cregor	180
Right end	Red Roberts	225

Everyone except Bill James was coming back. The freshmen, Gordy, Shadoan, Kubale, and Jones, would all have another year of experience. Red Roberts and Ben Cregor were coming back for a 5th year. In addition to the returning regulars, the following had contributed in the line during the 1921 season and could be expected to be factors in 1922.

Clifton "Hennie" Lemon	165
Howard Lynch	180
Dick Gibson	180
Frank Rubarth	175
Clarence Jones	176

THE ANTICIPATED ROSTER FOR 1922

(SENIORS)
BEN CREGOR

	SPRINGFIELD, KY	23	5'11"	180	TACKLE

RED ROBERTS

	SOMERSET, KY	23	6'1"	235	END/FULL

TERRY SNOWDAY

	OWENSBORO, KY	23	5'10"	175	END/HALF

DEWEY KIMBELL
         LOUISVILLE, KY   23   5'10"   134   HALF
CHARLES CECIL
         DANVILLE, KY   20   5'8"   160   END

(JUNIORS)

TOM BARTLETT
         OWENSBORO, KY   22   5'10"   160   FULL/HALF
JAMES GREEN
         LOUISVILLE, KY   20   5'9"   145   HALF
CLARENCE JONES
         LOUISVILLE, KY   21   5'10"   176   GUARD
JAMES LIGGETT
         PITTSBURGH, PA   23   5'9"   167   HALF
HOWARD ROBERTSON
         ELIZABETHTOWN, KY   20   5'8"   145   HALF
HUMP TANNER
         OWENSBORO, KY   22   5'5"   165   FULL

(SOPHOMORES)

EDWIN ALEXANDER
         JACKSONVILLE. IL   20   5'10"   163   HALF
LESLIE COMBS
         LEXINGTON, KY   20   5'11"   156   END
HERB COVINGTON
         MAYFIELD, KY   20   5'5"   158   QUARTER
RICHARD GIBSON
         LOUISVILLE, KY   21   6'1"   180   TACKLE
MINOS GORDY
         ABBEVILLE, LA   21   5'10"   182   TACKLE/END
HOPE HUDGINS
         AMARILLO, TX   21   5'7"   160   HALF
JOHN HUNTER
         DETROIT, MI   21   5'8"   155   HALF
TED JOHNSON
         LAWRENCEBURG, KY   21   6'1"   186   GUARD
GEORGE JONES
         DALLAS, TX   19   5'8"   213   GUARD
ED KUBALE
         FORT SMITH, AR   22   6'   177   CENTER
CLIFTON LEMON
         MAYFIELD, KY   20   5'10"   165   END

HOWARD LYNCH				
AMARILLO, TX	20	5'10"	180	TACKLE
JACK ROWLAND				
RACINE, WI	20	5'8"	150	HALF
FRANK RUBARTH				
GATESVILLE, TX	22	5'11"	175	GUARD
WILLIAM SHADOAN				
SOMERSET, KY	27	6'1"	196	GUARD
CASE THOMASSON				
NEWPORT, KY	19	6'	175	FULL/END
PROCTOR WOOD				
MILLERSBURG, KY	22	5'8"	170	CENTER

There would be five seniors, six juniors, and 17 sophomores on the anticipated 1922 roster. The new "freshman rule" would have severely handicapped the 1921 team, as there were 18 first year men on that team, 17 of whom were returning to compete in their sophomore year.

One person who wasn't returning in 1922 was the line coach, Tiny Thornhill. Tiny had developed such a reputation with his line's play against Harvard that he became a "person of interest" to programs across the country. While the team was visiting Stanford in Palo Alto in December, the coaches there received Uncle Charlie's permission to talk to Tiny. Soon after the first of the year, Tiny was signed, sealed and ready to be delivered to Stanford as an assistant to the famous Glenn "Pop" Warner. To replace Tiny, Centre hired another Pitt graduate, Jim Bond. (After being on "Pop" Warner's staff for nine years, Tiny became the head coach at Stanford in1933 and compiled a 35-25-7 record in seven years. Interestingly, Tiny's 1935 squad went 7-1 during the regular season and beat SMU, coached by Centre graduate Matty Bell, in the Rose Bowl, 7-0. Tiny took his 1933 and '34 teams to the Rose Bowl also, losing to Columbia and Alabama.)

Since freshmen couldn't play on the varsity, Centre decided to field a first year team and hired Chick Murphy as freshman coach.

As always, Dr. Rainey, the Chief, and Uncle Charlie worked on the schedule together. The Danvillians had a much easier time in 1922 than they had five years earlier when they almost had to go hat-in-hand to be included in a team's lineup. Now they dealt from strength.

"Centre wants to play us? Just ask them where and when, and book it!"

California again sent word in early January that the Bears wanted a game. There was a feeling on the West Coast, even after the tie with W&J, that the two best teams in the country in 1921 hadn't met, but had come so close. California didn't want to leave it up to the uncertainties of hoping for a post-season pairing in a bowl. The college wanted to add an early December game following its November 25 match with Stanford. Cal requested that Centre agree to a contract and date between two mighty programs.

Centre reluctantly declined. There was some sentiment on campus amongst the professors that another "barn-storming" tour wasn't advisable, even if it was only for a "tacked on" regular season game. They worried about the college becoming known only because of its football team, and not its academics. Additionally, the S.I.A.A. sent word that post-season games weren't going to be allowed, and the Southern Conference frowned on them as well, and it was not until the January 1, 1925 Rose Bowl, three years later, that Alabama represented the Southern Conference in a bowl game.

Harvard was the team that was a "certain" for 1922. Centre decided to open with a "breather," and then play some more significant teams in preparing for a return to Cambridge. Significantly absent from the schedule were two old rivals. Transylvania and Georgetown sensibly sent word that they wouldn't be available, understandably. (Transy reappeared on the schedule in 1924, and Georgetown in 1925.)

Centre was determined to play at least four games at home, and firmed up the card for 1922 prior to the end of January.

SCHEDULE FOR 1922

DATE	OPPONENT	LOCATION
Sept. 23	Carson-Newman	Danville
Sept. 30	Clemson	Clemson, S.C.
Oct. 7	Mississippi	Danville
Oct. 14	Virginia Tech	Richmond, Va.
Oct. 21	Harvard	Cambridge
Oct. 28	Louisville	Danville
Nov. 4	Kentucky	Lexington
Nov. 11	Washington & Lee	Louisville
Nov. 18	Auburn	Birmingham
Nov. 30	South Carolina	Danville

The last official function of each school year was the annual Centre College Carnival. In what was becoming a routine, another football player, so admired on campus, was elected King of the Carnival.

"Well, team my sox!" Red exclaimed when told of his selection.

And so the 1921-22 year was over. The Old Centre yearbook for 1922 contained full pages and summaries of 32 seniors. As a class, they had made their mark, and each in his own way had done much for putting Centre on the map.

An article carried by a Louisville paper, and picked up by the Associated Press, was dated June 12.

The class of 1922, which will be graduated June 14, 1922, is the largest in numbers to be graduated from the little college in many years. Only two previous classes in the 103 years' history of the school have been larger than that which graduates this year. Those were the classes of 1903 and 1904, due to the consolidation of Central University, then located in Richmond, Kentucky, into the Centre College of Kentucky.

Of the 32 featured in the yearbook, 29 earned degrees. Ben Cregor, Joe Murphy, Tom Moran, Red Roberts and team manager John McGee all received their diplomas. (Army and Bill James had actually graduated the pervious year, but returned for their extra year of eligibility.)

Bo didn't have enough credits to walk across the stage. However, a degree from Centre was extremely important to him, and he took courses after leaving Danville and came back in 1937 and received not only his sheepskin, but a long, appreciative ovation from students, faculty and guests who were as delighted as he at his accomplishment.

There was one damper on an otherwise wonderful period. Tiny Maxwell, the rotund official who worked both the 1920 and 1921 Harvard games, the same Tiny Maxwell who came up to Bo after the great victory and said, "Mr. McMillin, here is your ball," was involved in an automobile accident, and died June 30, 1922, at age 38. (Maxwell had also refereed the Centre-Texas A&M game.)

My first year at Centre during 1921 and 1922 had been wonderful. I'd gotten to see the team play in Danville, against Clemson, Virginia Poly, and of course, the great win over Kentucky at Homecoming.

I'd gone over on the day train to see the Transy game in Lexington. The Auburn game in Birmingham and staying at the Tutwiler was a trip to always remember, plus we played such a perfect game that afternoon. I was at the W&L game in Louisville, the game where Red Roberts brought his donkey.

My only regret was that I hadn't gotten to the Harvard game, but at least Howard did, and he told me so many stories about it that I almost felt I'd been there. I joined Howard's fraternity. Phi Delta Theta.

Howard, Red Roberts, Tom Bartlett, Hump Tanner, Terry Snowday, Bill Shadoan, Les Combs, Hope Hudgins, Charles Cecil, and Ed Alexander were all members of the football team and were Phi Delts. One reason that I remember so much about what was going on with the team was that if the guys weren't talking about girls, they were talking about football.

Also, George Swinebroad, the head cheerleader, was a Phi Delt, and he always had stories to tell. The same was true of team manager Johnnie McGee.

In the spring of 1922, I was a scrub on the baseball team. Didn't get to play much, but with Red, Army, Ben Cregor, Herb Covington, Les Combs, Hennie Lemon and Chick Murphy on the squad, I certainly was on the inside as far as what was going on with the football program.

When I was in high school back in Elizabethtown, I never wanted the summer vacation to end and have classes start up again. But when I was at Centre, it was just the opposite. I couldn't wait for summer to end so that I could get back to school!

One more thing. I wasn't the greatest student, but I always made my grades, and one of the reasons that I passed my courses was that I was determined to come back to school and be able to follow the team.

I'm sure that I wasn't the only one who made sure that he passed so he could come back.

Centre football certainly was an incentive.

SEPTEMBER 23   CARSON-NEWMAN

After the great and exciting season of 1921, everyone who followed football was anxious to see if the Centre College Colonels could continue in their winning ways. Those who were really in the know regarding the trends that were developing recognized that the "freshman rule" had to eventually catch up with the smaller schools like Centre. It was the old adage, "not if, but when."

Nonetheless, things looked good in the fall of 1922. Centre had a talented core of players coming back, and it looked like the Colonels could still play in the "big time," at least for awhile.

Tom Moran, Uncle Charlie's son, had been hired to coach the Carson-Newman Eagles. The little Southern Baptist college in Jefferson City, Tennessee, some 25 miles northeast of Knoxville, had a very sparse schedule the past three seasons, playing only 14 games, winning six and losing 8.

Hiring the son of one of the most famous and successful coaches in the nation seemed like a good move. Carson-Newman had the hope of gaining the recognition that Centre had garnered over the last five years by pumping up its football program.

Uncle Charlie couldn't be on the sidelines to coach against his son due to his umpiring duties. The Chief came down from Chicago and joined new assistant Jim Bond on the sidelines. Two anticipated starters couldn't even dress for the game. The S.I.A.A. had heard that Bill Shadoan and Minos Gordy had played in a professional baseball game over the summer. Shadoan and Gordy said it wasn't true.

"Guilty until proven innocent," was the verdict, and the two were prohibited from playing until an investigation was completed. When it would be over wasn't known.

It didn't matter against Carson-Newman, but certainly the two big linemen were going to be needed in the future.

Howard Lynch started in place of Shadoan. Terry Snowday was moved to end in place of Gordy. Ben Cregor was held out due to a minor injury, and Frank Rubarth started in place of "Baldy." Clifton "Hennie" Lemon started in the backfield, along with Hope Hudgins, Bartlett and Covington.

POSITION	PLAYER	WEIGHT	CLASS
Left end	Red Roberts	235	Sr.
Left tackle	Howard Lynch	180	Soph.
Left guard	Buck Jones	213	Soph.
Center	Ed Kubale	177	Soph.
Right guard	Frank Rubarth	175	Soph.
Right tackle	Dick Gibson	180	Soph.
Right end	Terry Snowday	178	Sr.

395

Quarterback	Herb Covington	155	Soph.
Left half	Hope Hudgins	150	Soph.
Right half	Hennie Lemon	165	Soph.
Fullback	Tom Bartlett	160	Jr.

The Colonels put an awfully young team on Cheek Field. There were two seniors, a junior, and eight sophomores. The two who were ineligible, Shadoan and Gordy, were sophomores.

Young team or not, it really didn't matter. The Colonels picked up 27 first downs to but two for the Eagles, and won, 72-0.

A highlight of the game for the team was that Jimmy Green, a junior from Louisville who was a favorite of the team, scored twice.

Green had been a faithful member of the squad but hadn't gotten many minutes over the last couple of years.

"Way to go, Jimbo!!"

SEPTEMBER 30, 1922   CLEMSON

Clemson was next, at Clemson. The Colonels had beaten the Tigers in 1921 in a game played in Danville by a 14-0 score.

Centre took a chartered Pullman which was connected to a Southern passenger train through Chattanooga and then to Clemson.

The old saying, "If it weren't for misfortune, he'd have no fortune at all," seemed to fit Uncle Charlie and the Colonels.

Red Roberts' sister had been ill for some time and died while receiving treatment in Louisville. Naturally, Red chose not to go to Clemson but went to Somerset for the funeral. In addition, John Hunter received word that his mother had died, and he left the team to go home to be with his family.

Centre still hadn't heard from the S.I.A.A. about Bill Shadoan and Minos Gordy, and they couldn't play against Clemson.

Depleted but undeterred, the Colonels moved on.

The was an overflow crowd announced at more than 10,000 for the game, boosted by not only the fact that it was Centre playing, but also by the beautiful, Saturday afternoon. "Shirtsleeves weather," it was called. The papers stated that it was the greatest attendance at a football game in the history of the sport in South Carolina, a feature which seemed to accompany Centre's team during the era. Clemson had designated its opening game of the season as Homecoming, a bit of strange scheduling. However, the South Carolinians knew that Centre would pack them in, and decided that the game would be the attraction needed to encourage record numbers of the old grads to come back to their alma mater.

There were numerous scouts in the stands. Harvard sent two, E.J. Weatherford and Buster Dewey. Mississippi, Virginia Tech, Auburn and W&L also had representatives taking notes.

In a speech which long preceded Knute Rockne's famous 1928 , "Win one for the Gipper," Uncle Charlie made an appeal to, "Win one for our captain, the redhead. Win one for your teammate, John Hunter. Win one for Old Centre. Win one for the people back home. Win one for all of Kentucky!"

It was an emotional team of Gold and White which ran out of the dressing room determined to indeed, "Win one!!" The fired up Colonels dominated.

Herb Covington was easily the most effective player on the field. The little quarterback made several long runs during the first half and scored the only touchdown when he took it in just after the 2nd quarter began. Hennie Lemon was perfect on the extra point, and the half ended 7-0.

The score wasn't truly indicative of the play during the first two periods, as Centre had a first down margin of 11-2.

The Colonels continued to demonstrate their superiority in the 2nd half. Terry Snowday and Tom Bartlett both scored, Lemon kicked two more goals, and the final score was 21-0.

Again, even though Centre won easily, the score didn't tell the whole story. In the second half, Covey and his teammates continued their offensive onslaught as indicated by their racking up first downs at will, 13 to but three for the Tigers, to end up with 24 for the game to Clemson's 5.

"Not bad," was the opinion when Uncle Charlie was asked by a reporter after the game how he felt his team had played.

It indeed was a great performance, considering that Centre had played very conservatively due to all of the scouts present, and due to the fact that three starters were out of the lineup.

After the game, the players showered and dressed and headed to their Pullman. The Clemson student body followed them to the station and the Tigers' cheerleaders led them in cheers for the Colonels. It was, after all, the team that had beaten the Easterners, no matter that they had also just thoroughly defeated their own squad.

The Colonels' Pullman was pulled onto a siding in Greenville where the team slept. The next morning, they were hooked onto the back of a westbound Southern train, and journeyed back to Danville.

Centre was 2-0, not tested, and things were looking good for the season. Of course, "the season" was Harvard in three weeks. Again, as before, it was always Harvard.

OCTOBER 7, 1922   MISSISSIPPI

Centre and the University of Mississippi had never met before. It was one of the home games for the Colonels, and there were several reasons that the Rebels were penciled in during 1922.

Mississippi was one of the colleges which had been spun out of the S.I.A.A to form the Southern Conference. Even though Centre was left behind when the new conference was formed, it was still felt in Danville that the school could claim the "Championship of the South" if the Colonels played and beat the teams which had joined together to form the new organization.

On the 1922 Centre schedule were seven members of the Southern Conference: Clemson, Mississippi, Virginia Tech, Kentucky, Washington and Lee, Auburn, and South Carolina. Run the string and Centre could certainly claim to be the premiere team in the South.

Other considerations in scheduling Ole Miss were the Rebels willingness to come to Danville, and the fact that the team qualified as a good "warm-up" opponent prior to the Harvard game.

Carson-Newman was cannon fodder. Clemson was a little tougher. Mississippi was thought to be about like Clemson. The 4th game, Virginia Tech, would provide sufficient competition to get the Colonels "battle-hardened." And then it was Harvard. The schedule was made out very precisely to prepare the team for the trip to the East on October 21.

Mississippi had opened with a weak showing against a weak opponent, Union College, from Jackson, Tennessee. Neither team could score a point in what had been a rather listless performance.

Ole Miss lived up to its lack of prowess and reputation by being wiped out by Centre, 55-0.

In the weeks leading up to the game, Red Roberts had worked hard to get his weight down. He had ballooned up to 248 pounds during the summer. By the first week of October, he weighed in at 225. Parallel to his loss of 23 pounds was his gain in speed. On the Thursday prior to the Ole Miss game, Uncle Charlie lined up the entire team for a 100 yard dash. When the linemen complained, he let them have a 10 yard lead and then blew the whistle.

Tackle Howard Lynch came in first, followed by Tom Bartlett. Ed Kubale barely nipped Red for 3rd. The fact that the big All-American could come in a close 4th showed how hard he had trained in getting ready for Harvard, and he looked trim and quick against Ole Miss.

In the Mississippi game, Herb Covington again demonstrated his wizardry. Time after time, Covey ripped off long gainers, averaging an amazing 25 yards every time he ran the ball, and returned a kickoff 55 yards for a score.

Hope Hudgins ran for 80 yards and a touchdown, the longest run of the game.

Centre subbed freely, with the entire 27 man squad seeing action, and in the last quarter, 10 subs played the entire 15 minutes. The only Colonel to play the entire 60 minutes was Ben Cregor, and it was old Baldy who supplied some unwitting fun for Uncle Charlie and the team.

Red and Covey consulted with Uncle Charlie on the sideline and the coach laughed and said, "Do it!"

In the huddle, Red said, "Baldy, you're playing your usual great game. I want you to score a touchdown now that we're close to the goal. You take over the fullback slot and we'll open some holes and you can get some points."

The ball was on the Mississippi eight yard line when the Colonels lined up, 1st and goal. Kubale centered the ball to Cregor and the Centre front wall let the Ole Miss linemen charge forward untouched. Baldy lost eight. It was 2nd down and 16 to score.

"Come on, you can do better than that! Take it in!"

Again, Cregor cleanly fielded the center, the linemen stepped aside, and the loss was seven yards. It was 3rd and 23 yards to the goal.

Everybody but Baldy was in on the scheme. The Centre bench screamed for Cregor to "get serious!"

"Baldy, this is your chance. Don't keep losing yardage. The goal is the other way!" Red offered encouragement.

"Baldy, you can do it! You're looking good! You have great style. You just need to head that way," and Red pointed to the Colonels' goal, barely able to keep a straight face.

Red lined up the team for another "effort." He told Cregor to line up 10 yards behind Kubale and run it around the left end.

"Kube will lead you with his center pass so you can get a running start."

"Baldy" caught the ball on a dead run laterally, no one blocked, and he was brought down on the 33. Three plays ands a loss of 25 yards!

As Cregor later recounted, "Red then told me we had to punt, and since I'd gotten us so far back, I would have to make the kick. I'd never punted the ball in my life, but I think the ball carried about 10 yards, and I felt like I'd done a pretty good job!"

Hump Tanner was back in fine form and scored twice, as did Red. Other TD's were by Covington, Hope Hudgins, Bartlett and Snowday. Covey kicked a field goal, and Red and Lemon both were good on two extra points.

One reason that the Colonels could have some fun with Ben Cregor was that they were so clearly superior to the Ole Miss Rebels. The Mississippians were so stymied by Centre that they failed to register a first down all day. Not even one! Centre was 3-0 and had outscored its opponents, 148-0.

In the last three years, during which they'd taken the field 24 times, little Centre College had blanked its opponents 19 times. The Colonels were on a roll, again.

OCTOBER 14, 1922   VIRGINIA TECH

As Centre was getting ready for the Virginia Tech game, the S.I.A.A was contacted to check on the status of Bill Shadoan and Minos Gordy. No decision was yet forthcoming.

"You're aware that our players have absolutely denied receiving any payments over the summer? You're aware that we're playing Harvard on October 21? You're aware that we'll be representing the S.I.A.A. and the South? You're aware how important these two men are to us, that they started the game last year in Cambridge?"

Uncle Charlie and Jim Bond continued to have Shadoan and Gordy work out with the team, hoping to hear any day from the S.I.A.A. However, the preparations for the Tech game were made with the realization that the two linemen probably wouldn't be available.

The game was to be played in Richmond, Virginia. It would be the 3rd straight year that the two schools had met. The 1920 game in Louisville resulted in Centre winning, 28-0. The teams met in Danville in 1921, and the Colonels ground out a tough 14-0 win.

This year's game was to be played at Richmond's Tate Field, home of the Colts, a minor league baseball team. The stadium was located on Mayo's Island in the James River. Major league teams stopped at Richmond on the way back from training in Florida, and Babe Ruth hit the longest homer ever recorded, according to local lore, when he belted one during the previous spring.

The "Bambino" powered a pitch over the fence toward a railroad track, landing the ball in a passing coal car, "and it hasn't been found to this day!"

Centre had second thoughts about the VPI game. It was going to be a long ride to Richmond, leaving on Thursday and not arriving back in Danville until Sunday evening, and then the team would have to head to Boston on the following Wednesday. The coaches remembered what had happened in Dallas against A&M. Too much time on a train seemed to dull the team's sharpness. Richmond had gone all out in preparation for the game and there wasn't any way to call it off or switch it to another date.

So Centre had a plan. The team would go to Richmond, actually stay over Saturday night for a function planned by their hosts at the team's headquarters, Murphy's Hotel, and then head out Sunday morning to Mansfield, Massachusetts, west of Boston, and stay at a hotel and restaurant called The Tavern, and prepare there for Harvard. That way, a lot of time on the train spent going back to Danville and then heading East wouldn't be necessary. The squad would only be 20 miles from Boston at Mansfield. A fleet of cars driven by Centre alumni and other Kentuckians had been arranged to take the team into Boston and the Lenox after a Thursday morning practice.

It seemed like a sensible solution and would let the Colonels arrive in great shape for the Harvard game. All of the travel plans and reservations had been completed. The best laid plans are often made impossible to implement by events beyond ones control.

Howard Reynolds, the staunch Centre supporter, had spent the week on Princeton's campus covering the Tigers' football team, and then came to Richmond to take in the Centre-VPI game in order to report back to his Boston "Post" paper on Harvard's upcoming opponent.

Reynolds said that while he was in Princeton, the college's coach, Bill Roper, asked him, "What's going on with Centre? Do they go to school just so they can play football?"

Reynolds also said that an Eastern writer had written a column in which he asked, "Why doesn't Centre send its football team to the Orient, and award them diplomas when they return?"

Roper had also said that there were comments being circulated in the East that Centre was, "just a football factory." Howard Reynolds considered Uncle Charlie a friend, not just a source of a good story, and he was concerned. Uncle Charlie was incredulous.

"I don't understand, Howard? It's true, yes, that we plan to go to Massachusetts after the game here in Richmond, but we have a professor from the school traveling with us. We've gotten the faculty's permission. We've packed the boy's books, and they will have two hours of instructions every day."

Reynolds was empathetic. He'd been on Centre's campus. He knew that the team members were responsible for keeping up their grade averages. He and Eddie Mahan had left Danville completely convinced that Centre had an honorable, clean program, or else they would never have advocated that Harvard put Centre on its schedule.

"But I just wanted you to know what is being said, Charlie"

"Did you hear that Harvard was saying such things?"

"Not a word from Harvard," Reynolds said. "I'll guarantee it."

"That's all that is really important, what Harvard thinks," Uncle Charlie said.

Then the Centre mentor pointed out that Centre had to travel more than any team in the country.

"Harvard plays nearly all of its games at home. Princeton and Yale do the same. The only way we can schedule colleges with reputations is to play on their turf, or at a neutral place like here in Richmond. You've seen our stadium, and you know how hard it is to even get a place to stay overnight in Danville. We have to travel all over the country in order to play decent teams."

Uncle Charlie was certainly correct. In 1919, Harvard only played Princeton on the road until going to Pasadena to play in the Rose Bowl. In 1920, the Crimson traveled only to Yale. In 1921, the only trip was again to Princeton. Thus far in 1922, the three games had been played in the friendly confines of the big horseshoe on the Charles. Thus, during that period, Harvard had played 32 games, and 28 were at home. Princeton had taken the field at their Palmer Stadium 20 times since 1919. They had traveled to Yale twice, Harvard once, and to Annapolis one time to play Navy. Yale had played 29 games since 1919, and 26 had been in their big bowl. Overall, the "Big 3" had contested 81 out of 92 games at home, nearly 90%, and when they traveled, except for Harvard's trip to Pasadena, it wasn't far.

By contrast, Centre had played 34 games, and 22, or approximately 65%, had been road games.

"We have to travel. They don't. How can they criticize us?" Reynolds said he understood.

"But you know how it is, Charlie. The perception becomes reality for folks, and the perception is that Centre is emphasizing sports at the expense of studies."

Uncle Charlie wasn't going to allow that to happen, no matter that Centre had to compete in a way which was different from the Eastern schools, especially the "Big 3." He immediately got busy and cancelled the plan to head to Mansfield from Richmond and made arrangements for the Colonels to return to Danville after the game.

"Howard, I wouldn't do anything, not one thing, to tarnish the reputation of Centre College. We'll go back to Danville. I'm not going to allow anyone, anywhere, to make accusations like you have reported. I know they aren't true. Sure, we play hard, but we play fair and clean, and we run an honorable program."

Howard Reynolds said he agreed.

"But I also agree with what you are doing. I think it is best for Centre College."

Of course, had Centre not been so dominating on the gridiron, such sentiments would never have been expressed. Success had its price, and came with the territory.

Meanwhile, there was an important football game, a game which the Colonels had to win in order to go to Cambridge undefeated. Virginia Tech was playing good football. The Blacksburg college was 7-3 in 1921, having lost to Centre, Maryland by 10-7, and W&L by 3-0.

Thus far in 1922, the Hokies were 3-0.

VPI	38	Hampden-Sydney	0
VPI	25	King College (Tn.)	0
VPI	20	William and Mary	0

Centre's game with VPI was one of the most colorful contests in which the Colonels ever participated.

Tech contracted to bring the entire Corps of Cadets over to Richmond on a specially chartered train, and 700 students, in full uniform, disembarked at the station and lined up in formation behind the school's band. The local John Marshall High School band got in position behind the Cadets, and then the entire throng marched through downtown Richmond with cheering spectators lining the route, clapping and waving and then falling in behind to go to Tate Field and the game.

The Richmond "News Leader" described the scene, printing 46,669 copies of a "Special Edition" right after the game.

The largest crowd of football fans in the history of sporting events in Richmond witnessed the game.

Every available point of vantage, where even a partial view of the field could be obtained, was crowded with spectators.

The framework of the railroad viaduct and points on the bridge and roofs of the nearby factories were filled with people, some of them keeping their eyes on the game with field glasses.

The crowd was estimated at over 15,000, and the gate receipts are placed at $25,000.

By 2:00, there wasn't an empty seat to be had. Hundreds were standing in the promenades around the gridiron.

The Tech and John Marshall bands took turns in rendering popular airs.

The Tech team entered the field at 2:20 and drew an immense outburst of applause. The squad immediately began to go through its formations.

Centre took the field after Tech had entered, led by Red Roberts. Its entry was the cause of another swell of applause, the John Marshall band greeting them. The "Praying Colonels" then went through a short signal drill.

In addition to not having Bill Shadoan and Minos Gordy available, the Colonels were minus another lineman who was a vital part of the team. Dick Gibson, a tackle who weighed in at 180 pounds, had been summoned home to Louisville due to the death of his father. The streak of unfortunate events continued.

The VPI game was tough, just what Centre needed to get ready for Harvard, and then some.

The Hokies scored the first points. Red hauled in a Covey pass but fumbled at midfield and VPI recovered. It took 11 plays, but the Virginians methodically moved down the field and finally took it in. The extra point was missed, and it was 6-0, the touchdown being the first points that Centre had surrendered during 1922.

Centre moved the ball fairly well during the rest of the 1st quarter, getting three first downs. VPI had four, all coming on the scoring drive.

The 2nd quarter began with the Colonels in possession of the ball on the Hokies 35. After failing to convert a first down, Covey tried a long field goal, kicking from the 45, but it fell short. The rest of the period was played back and forth, neither team really threatening. The half ended with Centre finding itself in the unusual situation of having VPI hold a considerable advantage in first downs, nine to four. Centre had been outplayed. There was no other way to describe it. The crowd stood and cheered as the purple and white clad Virginians left the field after a great 30 minutes of football.

Both the VPI and John Marshall High bands put on a spirited halftime show, playing separately, and then lined up together for the VPI fight song, "Tech Triumph," which ended,

So give a Hokie, Hokie, Hokie, Hi,
Rae, Ri, old VPI.

The crowd smelled a possible upset, but except for the diehard Hokie fans, feelings were somewhat ambivalent. Sure, many thought, we'd like to see a team from Virginia win, but Centre had gone up to that bastion of the Yankees, Boston, and beaten their best. There was no more "South" than Richmond, Virginia, the Confederate States' capital, and the Colonels were going back "North" in a week to once again do battle in "enemy territory." There was no small number of actual Civil War veterans in the crowd, men now well up into their 70's, and old loyalties are a tremendously strong bond.

It was later said that much of the capacity crowd wanted Tech to do well, to make a "good showing," but for Centre to actually win.

Red boomed a kick deep to start the 2nd half. VPI ran it back to the 20 but had to punt. The entire quarter was a defensive standoff. Centre picked up two first downs, VPI but one, and the 3rd period ended with the Hokies still up, 6-0. There were four punts during the quarter. Centre intercepted a pass and recovered a fumble.

Before the last period began, Red called the team around him. The Colonels were going to start the 4th quarter with good field position. As the teams changed ends of the field, Centre had the ball, 2nd and nine on the VPI 23.

"We score now, we win," Red said. "We want to go to Harvard undefeated. Give it your all. We are Centre! We are Centre!"

Covey took the pass from center on the initial play of the last period and failed to gain. The Hokies were playing tough. It was 3rd and nine. Terry Snowday took a hard hit on the next play and got only a single yard. Now, 4th and 8.

Covey then hit Tom Bartlett on what was probably the most important play of the game. The pass covered 15 yards before Bartlett was brought down. 1st and goal on the Hokies' seven.

Everyone was on their feet. The Cadet Corps was chanting, "Hold! Hold! Hold! Hold!"

On the first play after the yard marker was moved, Covington followed Red around his left end. The Centre captain literally swept the defenders away, knocking them off balance and onto the turf. Covey dashed into end zone untouched.

Hennie Lemon kicked the important extra point. It was 7-6, Centre. Colonels' fans were breathing a bit easier, but there was still a lot of time left.

After the kickoff, VPI put together an excellent drive and moved the ball downfield to the Centre 17. The Hokies were within field goal range and looked like they may wrestle the lead back. On 4th and two, it appeared that they had a 1st down when Wallace gained four, but there was a holding penalty which moved the ball back to the Centre 32. Now, a field goal would be improbable, but VPI made the attempt, and the kick was short.

Centre took over on the 20, could only pick up eight yards on three plays and punted to the Tech 35. The ball was juggled and Lemon recovered it. The Colonels picked up two first downs, moving it to the 15. After VPI hung tough, Covey split the uprights with a field goal. Centre 10-6.

VPI had no choice, as time wound down, but to go to the air. The Colonels intercepted and were able to run out the clock. The first down margin ended with the Hokies up 13-10, the first time in a long streak when Centre had come up short.

Herb Covington proved to be the difference in the game. The little quarterback had taken over Bo's position and was beginning to make people realize that life went on without the famous McMillin. Few people could have stepped into such a pressure filled spot and performed so creditably. Covey gained 149 yards in 28 attempts, averaging 5.3 yards per carry, and he accounted for nine of the Colonels' points.

The two teams met at midfield and gave cheers for each other's efforts.

Hokies, Hokies, rah, rah, rah!
Colonels, Colonels, rah, rah, rah!

It had been a hard-fought, cleanly played game. Uncle Charlie and VPI's coach, Ben Cubbage, met out on the field and gave each other a warm hug. Cubbage wished Centre success in the upcoming game in Cambridge.

The Centre coach left the field feeling that his team had dodged a bullet. He had only used six plays, not wanting to give away any of his plans to eyes in the stands, two of which belonged to the starting quarterback for Harvard, Charles Chauncey Buell.

The Crimson were playing Bowdoin while Centre and VPI went at it, and Coach Fisher felt that his team could win with a second string quarterback. It was a measure of the importance that Harvard placed on the upcoming rubber match with

Centre that Buell was sent to Richmond to scout the Colonels.

Howard Reynolds accompanied the team back to Danville after the game. He typed out his story and hopped off in Lexington to hand it to a Western Union operator. Reynolds said that Uncle Charlie was happy to escape from Richmond with a win, and that the Colonels had suffered no significant injuries.

However, he reported there was now a new worry. Several players were complaining of sore throats. Tom Bartlett, Hump Tanner, Hennie Lemon, Terry Snowday, Ed Kubale and Howard Lynch all felt ill, with Bartlett having rather severe symptoms.

First two starters had been declared ineligible. Red's sister, and the fathers of John Hunter and Dick Gibson, had died. Now, six starters were ill. What else could possibly occur?

VPI proved during the rest of their season that the strength displayed against Centre was no fluke. The week following the game in Richmond, the Hokies traveled to North Carolina and tied Davidson. Then they reeled off five straight wins, beating Catholic University, Maryland, North Carolina State, W&L and VMI to finish at 8-1-1.

The two colleges played again twice after the three games of 1920-22, with VPI winning 28-0 in 1939, and 10-6 in 1940, long after the Colonels' days of glory were but memories.

CHAPTER 19:
THE THIRD HARVARD GAME

The third game with Harvard was next. Centre was 4-0 and Harvard, 3-0.

Harvard	20	Middlebury	0
Harvard	20	Holy Cross	0
Harvard	15	Bowdoin	0

I know that the 1920 and '21 games drew a lot of interest. But I feel that the '22 game was even bigger, because we had won the previous year, and now it seemed like everyone all over the country wanted to know even more about Centre and Danville.

The week leading up to the game, there were reporters from papers all over who were on the campus. It seemed like every time you turned around, there was some reporter wanting to interview not only the coaches and players, but us students, too. They wanted to get some idea of the sort of person who went to school at Centre.

There was a funny incident when somehow, a sports writer from the East started interviewing me, thinking I was Red Roberts. He looked confused, and I just answered his questions like I thought Red would.

He asked me what I weighed and I said 135. He said he thought I weighed 235, and I told him someone must have made an error. I said it wasn't how big a person was, but how determined he was to play tough.

He didn't catch on until some other student gave me away.

I'd have loved to see his story, "135 pounds, and how he can crash the line!"

On the return from Richmond, a very welcome telegram arrived in Danville, sent by the president of the S.I.A.A., Dr. David R. Phillips, announcing that the investigation into the "Shadoan-Gordy affair" had determined that the two young men had not done anything that would jeopardize their amateur status, and "they are thereby deemed eligible for intercollegiate play."

While the ruling about Shadoan and Gordy was welcome, the report from the local doctor who looked after the team wasn't.

Tom Bartlett was really sick. The others who had complained on the way back from Richmond seemed to be improving, but Bartlett could hardly swallow due to his tonsils being so swollen. Then to compound things, Hump developed a boil on his leg, and for a while, he looked iffy for the Harvard game. In the pre-antibiotic age, tonsillitis and a significant boil were not so easily treated.

Hump's boil was drained, and it appeared he was going to be available. Tom was gargling a lot of salt water, but wasn't progressing at all.

We all went down to the station to meet the team when they came back from Virginia. Every time the guys went on a trip, or returned, it seemed that everyone in town was down at the station, and even though they got back late Sunday night from Richmond, we were all there to cheer them when they got off the platform.

They were like royalty to us.

That night, I decided I was going to the Harvard game. I wasn't exactly sure how I was going to pull it off. I just knew that there was no way I wouldn't be there.

Howard was on the team. He didn't make the travel squad to go to Boston, but he was a member of what was now called the Centre "Six." He played the banjo and mandolin, and the "Six" was going to be paid to play at a function in Boston, so he was in good shape.

Anyhow, I was going to be at the game, even if I had to hop on a freight train, which I'd never done before. Thank goodness I didn't have to, because I'd have probably ended up in Canada, or someplace, who knows where.

On the train ride back from Richmond, Uncle Charlie and Coach Bond had set up a chalk board in the back of the team's Pullman and began diagramming a new type of play which no one on the team had ever seen, much less run.

The Centre coaches had discussed the new scheme with the officials at the VPI game. They wanted to get an opinion, confidentially of course, as to the legality of what they planned. Two of the game's refs were from Virginia and the other from Michigan.

"Charlie, it may be crazy, but it's legal. We're all pulling for you next week, and won't say a word."

That's all that Uncle Charlie had needed to hear. He hadn't even considered employing the formation against Virginia Tech. That would have removed the important element of surprise.

Uncle Charlie was known everywhere for being an innovator, and had enjoyed that reputation since his earliest days at Texas A&M. However, what he was now planning outstripped anything that he had ever proposed in all of his years of coaching.

"It's called the 'lock-step.' It's legal, and it should be a complete surprise when we put it into action."

The Centre linemen would take their usual positions as would the four backs. Then all seven linemen would stand and either turn left or right, with the last six holding their right arm on the shoulder of the man in front of him. They would march to the left or right, pause, then turn and march back in the opposite direction. This "marching" may take place more than once, back and forth.

Meanwhile, the backs would follow, moving left or right as the linemen had done. As this movement back and forth took place, suddenly one of the linemen would reach down and snap the ball back and off everyone would go.

A contemporary cartoon-diagram illustrated the "lock-step," which was also dubbed the "penitentiary shift," or "chain-gang formation," because the linemen, walking one behind the other, hand on the person in front, resembled a group of convicts being marched along.

On the way back from Virginia, Uncle Charlie drilled the team on how they were to employ the new offensive scheme.

"We'll play conservatively the 1st half, just like we did last year. Then we'll unveil the "lock-step" to start the 2nd half. That way, Harvard won't have time to go in at the half and figure out a way to defense us."

"Crazy, Unc" said one of the Colonels.

"Yeah. But crazy like a fox," offered another.

The plan had been to work in secrecy up in Mansfield, Massachusetts and have four practice days to get the new formation down just right. The comments that Howard Reynolds brought down from Princeton had changed everything. Now, the team had a long train ride to the East, and only two days of practice to get ready.

I scraped together every cent I could. Howard loaned me some money, but I was still short, so I went to see Cousin Ella who gave me two $20.00 gold pieces from this little purse that she kept hidden away. She saw me at the door and said, "Oh Red, I bet I'll need to got get my little sequined bag," and off she went and came back with money. She was wonderful to me.

However, I still didn't have enough money to buy a ticket on the train and to pay for a hotel. But it didn't matter. I told several people that I was going to get to Boston one way or the other, and word got to Red Roberts that I may stow away on a freight train, and all of a sudden, everything changed. I was up in my room in Breck Hall and heard a lot of shouting. People were saying, "Red. What's happening? Red. It's Red Roberts!"

It was a big deal when Red came into the dorm, because everyone looked up to him so.

I went out to the hall and looked down the stairs and heard Red ask, "Which room does my son live in?" It was number 314.

So Red came up the stairs and said, "Son, I hear you're going to hobo your way to Boston," and I said I was if I couldn't come up with enough money, and he said, "Here's what we'll do. We'll pack you in a ball bag, and I'll carry you into our

Pullman. I'll tell the porter that the bag contains my lucky footballs, and I never let them out of my sight. Then when we get you on, you can just hide under the seat anytime the porter comes around, and you can ride to Boston in the team's Pullman."

Ride in the team's Pullman? I couldn't believe what I was hearing. So I asked Red what would happen if I got caught. I didn't want to get anybody in trouble, and I didn't want to kicked off the train maybe out in the middle of nowhere, either.

Red said, "Just leave it up to me. I'll take care of everything."

So I decided to do just that. I'd leave it up to Red, and I'd get to Boston, riding in the team's Pullman!

Can you beat that?

Centre practiced the "lock-step" on Monday and Tuesday before the Wednesday departure. Howard Reynolds filed stories from Danville which described "intense workouts," but of course, didn't reveal any of Uncle Charlie's new plans. Reynolds reported, *The team was full of spirit and confidence, bolstered by the return of Bill Shadoan and Minos Gordy, two of the standout linemen who played so well in last year's victory.*

The Boston pundits were confident that Harvard would win the third game. Coach Fisher was bringing his team along in the traditional Harvard manner, having scheduled and beaten the weaker teams before getting into the meat of the season. After Centre, it was Dartmouth, Florida, Princeton, Brown and Yale.

Centre again had a private Pullman for the trip to Boston. The plan was the same as the previous year. The regularly scheduled Southern train which came through would stop long enough in Danville to allow the Colonels' car to be hooked on, with departure out of Danville for the 103 mile trip to Cincinnati, through Lexington, at 8:30 a.m. Then it would be the responsibility of the New York Central system to complete the haul into Boston.

Everything seemed on schedule. Classes had been cancelled at both Centre and K.C.W. Businesses didn't plan on opening until the Colonels were off, and the usual huge crowd, including Governor Morrow, was at the station ready to stage a boisterous and enthusiastic sendoff.

There was just one problem. In a season when it seemed if something could go wrong, it did, the Colonels were once again the victims of misfortune. There was no train to connect to. Just south of Danville, a freight train had derailed, blocking the track. Time was critical, because if the Colonels didn't arrive close to right on time in Cincinnati, they'd miss being hooked onto the northbound train to Cleveland.

Red had me get in this duffle bag in the bathroom of the station, and he packed me over his shoulder and several team members gathered around him as he walked through the crowd toward the Pullman. Everyone wanted to greet Red and wish him well, so he put me down and I just laid there like some clump while he mingled with the crowd. Finally, I heard him say, "Let me put my gear on board and I'll be back."

So Red packed me on his shoulder again, and I heard him talking to the porter and tell him that he wanted to stow his gear, me, and then go back to tell everybody goodbye.

Red put me down on the floor in one of the sections, right by a vent where heat was coming out, because they were keeping the car warm for the team as it was pretty chilly outside.

I waited and waited. I didn't know that the train had been delayed by a wreck. I had my wool suit on, and the duffle bag was tied closed at the top, and the heat was just pouring out and I thought I was going to die.

Finally, even if I got caught, I had to get out of that bag, or I really felt I would have suffocated.

So I managed to get the drawstring untied and slipped out of the bag and moved down to another section which didn't have a heating vent. Then I heard the porter talking to someone about the wreck and the delay of up to several hours.

I just laid on the floor with my legs in the duffle bag, and anytime I heard footsteps and felt anyone was heading my way, I pulled the duffle bag up around me, and I was real still.

It was a long wait, and I wondered if the whole thing was a good idea after all.

Uncle Charlie tried everything to get to Cincinnati on time. He got the faculty members on the athletic committee, Dr. Allen and Dr. Rainey, to try hiring an engine to get the Pullman to Cincinnati. Governor Morrow joined Allen and Rainey. An offer was made.

"We don't have a fireman available."

"You see that young, strapping fellow over there?"

The governor pointed to Red. "He stoked engines all one summer, on this very railroad. He can shovel the coal."

"We don't have permission to let him do that," was the answer.

"Is there an engine and Pullman available in Lexington if we get a caravan of cars to drive us over there?"

Word came back by telegraph to the station master.

"No Pullman available."

The team waited, some sitting on the stranded Pullman, others milling around the station. One member waited, bundled up in his bed which the porter had prepared. Tom Bartlett was so sick from his infected tonsils that he didn't even feel like sitting up. Uncle Charlie knew it would take a miracle for him to even be able to suit up, much less play in the game.

"He has been a large part of our team in the past, and if he wants to go, even if he never gets to the stadium, he is one of us, and he'll be on the train, even if we have to carry him on."

Four hours after the scheduled departure, at 12:30 in the early afternoon, a whistle was heard and smoke was sighted south of the station, and the train which was to carry the Colonels to Cincinnati finally rolled into Danville.

The delay had thrown everything off. There would be no seamless trip to Boston. The New York Central in Cincinnati couldn't wait, and when the Colonels crossed the Ohio River, they discovered that their Pullman was going to be shunted onto a siding, because there wasn't another northbound train for over five and a half hours.

The team had planned on arriving in Boston on Thursday morning around 9:30, checking into the Lenox, and going to Harvard Stadium for a workout after lunch. Now, with connections being missed, they wouldn't make it to Boston until Thursday evening, with the predicted arrival time being 8:30 p.m., 36 hours after they should have left Danville.

The second that the train stopped in Cincinnati, Uncle Charlie hopped off and trotted into the station and was back out and on the team's Pullman in minutes.

"Ok, boys. Grab your gear. We're going to Redland Field to work out." (What later became Crosley Field was called Redland Field until bought by Powel Crosley, manufacturer of refrigerators, radios and the Crosley automobile, in 1934.)

Howard Reynolds quickly completed a dispatch and telegraphed it back to Boston.

Coach Charlie Moran did everything to try and move those in charge of the Southern Railroad in Danville to come to his aid, and to get his team through, so that it would be possible to take the much needed workout in the Stadium tomorrow afternoon, but it was to no avail.

Moran and Danville must feel that this is but another handicap that the Colonels have had to face this year in presenting the best team possible to meet Harvard on Saturday.

As it was, the boys got here in Cincinnati hours late, and had to wait until 6:05 p.m. for the next fast train heading east. Uncle Charlie did not waste time, for he quickly made arrangements to use the National League park for practice, and sent his eleven through a stiff, two hour drill.

This practice will not have the same effect that one tomorrow afternoon at Cambridge would have had. Besides, it means that the boys will be cooped up on the train for a full night and most of the next day before reaching Boston, and will not, in all probability, get to bed at the accustomed hour.

The utter neglect of the railroad to help out on a delicate situation, together with the long trip back to Danville from Richmond and the epidemic of sore throats, will not tend to bring the Centre team into Boston in the best mental attitude for its big game of the year.

When Howard Reynolds had brought the news from Princeton to Richmond about the comments being made that Centre was a school which apparently placed football above the classroom, he was reporting on an attitude that wasn't based on any similar, practical experience by those who were complaining.

Traveling was physically tiring. Playing on the road, in hostile territory, was emotionally challenging. The fact that Centre had to compete under these circumstances, and was able to compete successfully, made the little school's record during its glory years all the more outstanding.

The third trip to Boston was just another example of the hardships that the Colonels sometimes faced in order to play in the upper echelons of college football.

As Centre was trying to get to Boston, a columnist wrote an article about what a great draw the Colonels were. Few teams could pack Harvard Stadium, or any stadium in the country, like the boys from Danville.

The first three games that Harvard played in 1922 attracted decent, but hardly capacity, crowds.

Harvard—Middlebury	16,000
Harvard—Holy Cross	30,000
Harvard—Bowdoin	18,000

A 1922 "season ticket" could be purchased for Middlebury, Holy Cross, Bowdoin, Centre, Florida and Brown for $6.00, or $1.00 per game. Separate tickets would be sold at $2.00 for Dartmouth, and $3.00 for Princeton. Yale was being played in New Haven in 1922.

If a person didn't have a "season ticket," the Centre game could be attended for $2.00 if one was an alumnus of Harvard, as alumni had the first chance to buy, and if any tickets remained, the general public could then also purchase one for $2.00.

The wooden, end zone bleachers had been expanded for the 1922 season, with the intent to have more seats available for Centre, Princeton and Dartmouth. The other games wouldn't need the extra capacity, as the crowds could easily be accommodated in the original, concrete horseshoe.

The additional seats in the end zone bleachers, and the admissions sold atop the roof over the colonnade which rimmed the Stadium, meant that 52,000 spectators could be squeezed into Harvard stadium, an all-time record crowd.

The final 5,000 seats were sold at 9:00 a.m. on the 20th, the morning before the game, at Wright and Ditson's in downtown Boston, and Leavitt and Peirce's on Harvard Square in Cambridge. The previous evening papers had announced the sale, and lines were stretched for blocks when the doors at both businesses opened on Friday morning. It was felt that well over 70,000 tickets could have been sold, such was the interest in the game, just as they could have been sold the year before.

The gross receipts for the game can be calculated. There were 52,000 seats sold. Of those, 37,000 were held by the "season ticket" package of $6.00. Therefore, at $1.00 per game, $37,000 could be credited to Centre's game. Each of the additional 15,000 seats sold for $2.00, which added an additional $30,000.

The gate would have been $67,000, or $670,000 in today's money.

Centre's payment of $17,000 in 1922 would mean that Harvard cleared $50,000 before expenses, big money in the era, and the reason that programs all over the country were trying to get the little school from Danville, Kentucky, "wherever that is," to come to their facilities and help fill their stadiums, and coffers.

THE FIRST FOOTBALL GAME BROADCAST ON RADIO?

There will always be some confusion and debate about which was the first college football game ever broadcast on the radio. However, the Centre-Harvard game of October 21, 1922, certainly has a valid claim. Here are the facts as known.

Radio broadcasts were relatively new at the time. It is well accepted that station KDKA in Pittsburgh, a Westinghouse-owned entity, had begun commercial transmissions on November 2, 1920. That KDKA was first to get on the air is not in dispute, but the station never claimed to broadcast the first football game, just to be the first to broadcast at all.

A group of radio buffs, amateur but licensed, "broadcast" the November 24, 1921 season-ending game between Texas A&M and Texas which was played at Kyle Field in College Station. (The game ended in a scoreless tie.)

The method of "broadcasting" the game in Texas was described as follows.:

The Gray brothers, Clark, and Endress, manned the transmitter and receiver positions. They copied the messages received from the Kyle Field press box and occasionally communicated back to Harry M. Saunders there. They then passed the slips of paper on which the messages were written to Matejka. He relayed the decoded messages over a horn speaker through an open window to the crowd of UT students gathered outside. These play–by–play descriptions were reported seconds after the conclusion of each play. A listener in Austin noted that the broadcast "was just like seeing the game, and lots more comfortable."

The October 21, 1922 Centre-Harvard game was a true broadcast across a wide geographical area, with listeners able to sit in their homes and tune in. The effort in Texas, while commendable, was basically somewhat like the recreations of games via messages sent by wire, with a "broadcaster" shouting out the messages received, and the listeners had to cluster around the location where the messages were sent.

WIR was a station operated by persons associated with Tufts University. A "rehearsal" at Harvard Stadium to check out the equipment to be used was held during the October 14 game with Bowdoin. When all seemed to go according to plan, WIR notified the press, and the press in turn notified the public that the Centre-Harvard game was going to be broadcast by radio.

It is felt that the WIR claim has been lost in the fog of history because the station's records were destroyed in a 1925 fire. However, the broadcast was well publicized at the time.

Over half a million will "listen in" as Harvard and Centre play in the Stadium Saturday. A radio report of the game, play by play, will be broadcast throughout the East, and football fans sitting in their own homes will hear of every move of the players almost at the exact instant that each play is made. The report will be sent from the press stand on top of the Stadium.

A full page banner headline in the Boston "Post" read:

PROGRAMS FOR TODAY

STATION WGI, MEDFORD HILLSIDE

7 A M Radio health school.
10 A M—Musical program.
10 30 A M—Official weather forecast (485 meters).
1 30 P M—Weather forecast (485 meters) Produce market report.
2 30 P M—Harvard-Centre football returns
5 P M—Market reports.
6 30 P M—Police reports, early sports, late news
8 P M—Evening program, "Science up to date"; concert by male quartet.

Anyone researching the issue has to come to the conclusion that the Centre-Harvard game of October 21, 1922 was the first college football game ever truly broadcast by radio as we understand broadcasting today. Such was the importance of the Centre-Harvard game of 1922. (In the history written about Franklin Field, home of the University of Pennsylvania's football team, it is claimed that the first football game ever broadcast on the radio was by station WIP on November 30, 1922, the date of a game between Penn and Cornell, won by Cornell, 9-0. In actuality, the Centre-Harvard broadcast preceded that contest by nearly six weeks.)

WHAS in Louisville announced that it was going to carry the game also, but its coverage was going to be a recreation by an announcer who had received the results of the action over the telegraph lines. (An interesting aside is that Ronald Reagan got his start in show business by recreating Chicago Cubs' baseball games after receiving the results via a telegraph line coming into his station, WOC, in Davenport, Iowa.)

NEWS REPORTS WHILE THE COLONELS WERE EN ROUTE

Centre dominated the Eastern newspaper's sports sections the week prior to the game. Of course, Howard Reynolds was sending his reports from stops along the way. But there was a lot of other coverage as excitement and speculation built concerning the big game.

It was recognized that the Centre-Harvard game would be the last between the two schools. The presidents of the "Big 3" had gotten together and decided to ban any future intersectional games after the 1922 season.

During the current year, Harvard was taking on Centre and Florida. Princeton traveled to the Windy City to play Alonzo Stagg's University of Chicago team. Yale hosted Iowa. The presidents even went so far as to agree they would consult each other prior to making out their schedules each year. Since it was obvious that Centre wouldn't be coming back to Cambridge in 1923, the week was rife with rumors about which Eastern schools could land the Colonels.

Brown, Dartmouth, Boston College, Pennsylvania and Columbia all sent out feelers. The proposals were for Centre to either come to their stadiums, or for a game to be set up in New York City.

And why not? Centre was the most popular, most attractive team that anyone could hope to play. You want publicity? Centre is your key to the press. You want a big payday? Centre is your ticket.

David J. Walsh, a New York sports writer, got into the act. He wrote that the logical next trip East for Centre should be to New York because the team had a huge following there, mainly because of all the coverage that the press had devoted to the Colonels over the past couple of years.

Quite a sizable amount of money is to be made from doing business with the Colonels, as Harvard will attest.

If Centre can draw more than 50,000 to Harvard Stadium, it would certainly fill the new field of the New York Yankees which could be configured to a capacity of 80,000, and a rich, golden harvest for all concerned would be the gratifying result.

A New York promoter is figuring on bringing Centre College here in 1923 to play the leading Eastern team of the present season. New York, which patronizes anything from street fights to sword swallowing, would riot at the gates for the first view of the Kentucky team.

Seemingly, Centre College has become a permanent institution as a box office boon.

Howard Reynolds filed a report before boarding the train in Cincinnati.

The accommodating management at Redland Field tried to do everything possible for Uncle Charlie's team. They had the heat turned on in the clubhouse, the hot water turned on for showers, soap and towels in abundance, but no amount of kindnesses shown could obscure the fact that the Colonels' trip has gotten off to a bad start. The train is to pull out heading north at 6:05 p.m., and nearly 10 hours after we should have left Danville, we are only 103 miles into a long journey.

HEADING OUT FROM CINCINNATI

There was a porter who was going to stay with the Pullman all of the way to Boston, and he was then going to be on the car on the way back to Danville, too. There just wasn't any way I could keep avoiding him, because he was constantly going around checking to see if anyone needed something.

So Red gave him a couple of dollars and everything was ok with the porter. However, it was the conductor we worried about. Whenever there was a stop and people came onto the car to greet someone on the team, the conductor would come back to make sure they got off, and for awhile, he'd even check tickets, and of course, I didn't have one, so back in the duffle bag I'd go and some of the players would sit with their legs covering me while I was under a seat.

Red set up a system where whoever was sitting closest to the door of the car would holler out, "Beat Harvard!" if the conductor was coming through, and I'd jump in the bag. I got where I could disappear really fast. The trouble was that Hump thought it was really funny to see me jump into the bag and roll over under a seat, so he'd call out "Beat Harvard!" even when there was no conductor coming, but Red told him to stop after everyone had some good laughs at my expense.

The team went to the dining car not long after we left Cincinnati and several guys brought me back a little food, and when it all added up, I had a pretty decent dinner. I was feeling great, riding along to the Harvard game, feeling awfully lucky to be traveling with the greatest group of guys I'd ever known, or ever would know, as a matter of fact.

But then it got late, and the porter came through to convert the seats into beds. He'd take the two seats which faced each other and flatten them into a bed, and pull down the bed tucked in the wall above that made a top bunk, and there was a curtain which he'd pull out that would close off the sleeping area, and that's where the guys would bed down. The seniors and juniors had first call on the lower bunks.

The problem was that I was odd man out. There was nowhere for me to sleep. So Red did the only thing I guess he could do. He said, "Let's go son, back in the bag."

And he packed me to the baggage car and told the conductor that he wanted to store his footballs, and that's where I spent the night. Red left me his heavy overcoat and I had mine, and I slept pretty well, even though it was cold that night. The good news was that we were pretty far along, and I hadn't gotten caught.

Bill Cunningham was a sportswriter for the Boston "Post." (There was another Cunningham, Ed, who wrote for the Boston "Herald.") As the team was speeding toward Boston, Cunningham wrote an article about the previous year's Centre victory over Harvard, and about Uncle Charlie. It was a very timely remembrance based on what was to transpire regarding the Centre coach's new plays soon to be unveiled.

Saturday night, October 29 of last year, this writer was one of a small group of visitors seated in rickety, cane bottomed chairs in the back room of a newspaper office of a town down in Arkansas. It was a miserable night, with a driving rain chattering on a low corrugated roof of the place, and the unpaved street outside a swirling river. The one telegraph instrument that the office boasted was singing off the Eastern football scores, and we eagerly watched the operator's typewriter list them through the gray-blue haze of cigar smoke.

Yale	*45*	*Brown*	*7*
Pitt	*28*	*Penn*	*0*
Penn State	*28*	*Georgia Tech*	*7*
Cornell	*59*	*Dartmouth*	*7*
Princeton	*34*	*Virginia*	*0*

The wire tolled them off with exasperating nonchalance and deliberation.
Then a break—

Centre 6   Harvard 0

"I'll be, are you sure that's straight?"
"Absolutely," the operator said with his ear still against the tobacco tin he was using as a resonator after the fashion of all dyed-in-the-wool newspaper telegraphers.
"Well, Uncle Charlie has kicked through. I wish I were there to shake his hand."
The speaker was Choctaw Kelley, the famous open field flash of the old-time Carlisle Indians, Charlie Moran's quarterback at Texas A&M, and later Uncle Charlie's colleague at Carlisle.

Choctaw Kelley went on to tell stories about how he had taken over from "Pop" Warner at the famous Indian school, Carlisle, when Warner moved on to the University of Pittsburgh.

"Meanwhile, Uncle Charlie had left Texas A&M and I asked him to come up to Carlisle and help me coach the Indians, because I knew there was no better trainer or motivator in the country."
"We carried on "Pop" Warner's way of coaching, and you know "Pop" had a lot of trick plays. One time he painted exact replicas of footballs on the front of his player's jerseys in a game against Harvard, so it seemed like every player was carrying the ball!"
"I wouldn't be surprised if Uncle Charlie pulled something like that in beating Harvard."

Uncle Charlie hadn't introduced any such trickery in the 1921 win over Harvard, sticking to a very conservative game plan. But as Bostonians were reading Bill Cunningham's story in the morning's "Post," the Colonels were staring intently at a chalk board in the rear of the Pullman, going over repeatedly just how and when they were going to run the "lock-step" in Harvard Stadium.

Red came to the baggage car in the morning and carried me back to the team's Pullman, stuffed in the duffle bag. I got to sit through the skull session that they were having about this new formation. It seemed really complicated, but Uncle Charlie kept saying that it was that very fact which should make it be effective.

I hadn't had any breakfast but Red and Hump took care of that by bringing me something from the dining car. For some of the day, I sat by Howard Reynolds from the Boston newspaper which had done so much to get Harvard to play Centre. I heard him say that he had gotten a wire when he got off somewhere to send in a story that every seat to the game had been sold and that people were offering $50.00 or more to get a ticket.

I remember thinking, "Uh-oh."

What if I got all of the way to Boston and couldn't get in to see the game? I not only didn't have a ticket for the train, but I didn't have one for the game, either.

Wouldn't that be something, to get all the way to Boston and have to stand outside wondering what was going on when people cheered?

So I asked if there were any tickets, not one?

"Not one ticket," Reynolds said. "Why do you ask?"

I told him my problem. I didn't have $50.00 to spare, even if I could locate some scalper to sell me a ticket.

Reynolds thought for a moment and then he said, "I can take an assistant in with me. I have a pass in order to cover the game from the press box for my paper. I can get another press pass when I get to my office at the paper and put your name on it, and you can sit in the press box and be my assistant. How would you like that, Red Roberts' son?"

How would I like it? Not only was I riding with the team, but I'd have one of the best seats in the whole Harvard Stadium, sitting up in the press box as Howard Reynolds' assistant.

Things were looking good!

HARVARD ANNOUNCES ITS LINEUP

Harvard was a team of stars. After all, Harvard was Harvard. Three players stood out. The team captain and quarterback was senior Charles Chauncey Buell, the young man who had missed the prior week's Bowdoin game in order to scout the Colonels in Richmond.

Buell was the typical Harvard man. He was born on January 21, 1900 in Hartford, Connecticut, and prepped at the Pomfret School in Pomfret, Connecticut, some 40 miles east of his home. Buell was the captain of the freshman baseball team, and was on the varsity team during his sophomore and junior years. His senior year marked his 3rd season on the varsity football team.

In addition to his athletic activities, Buell was a member of the student council his sophomore and junior years, was elected sophomore class president, served on the athletic committee in 1922-23, and was Second Marshall his senior year. Buell was a member of the A.D. Club, Institute of 1770, the S.K. Club, and his fraternity was Delta Kappa Epsilon.

George Owen, another senior, was the starting fullback, weighed 185 pounds, and was considered by many to be Harvard's greatest athlete. Owen was born in Hamilton, Ontario, and moved to Massachusetts as a teenager.

Owen was a nine-letter winner, supreme in three years of stardom in football, hockey and baseball. In football he helped beat Yale three times, scoring a touchdown and kicking a field goal in the 10-3 triumph in 1921, and the only touchdown in the 1922 victory by the same score. Owen twice captained hockey, never lost to Yale, scoring nine goals in eight games against the Elis, including one in overtime to win a 1923 game. In baseball, he was the only player in history to win the Wingate Memorial Trophy three times. Owen also won the Wendell Bat. He went on to lead the Boston Bruins to the Stanley Cup, emblematic of the world's professional hockey championship.

Charles Hubbard was a 195 lb. junior guard who was playing at an All-American caliber. Hubbard was from Milton, Massachusetts and prepped at Milton Academy. Hubbard was in fact placed on Walter Camp's 1922 and 1923 teams. He lettered in crew his junior year, rowing #5.

THE STARTING LINEUP THAT COACH FISHER PLANNED TO SEND ON TO THE FIELD AGAINST CENTRE WAS:

NAME	POSITION	HT.	WT.	CLASS
J.M. Hartley	Lt. end	5'8"	165	Sr.
C.A.C. Eastman	Lt. tackle	6'	200	Jr.
H.S. Grew	Lt. guard	5'11"	209	Jr.
H.S. Clark	Center	6'	175	Sr.
C.J. Hubbard	Rt. guard	6'2"	195	Jr.
H.T. Dunker	Rt. tackle	6'1"	187	Soph.
R.W. Fitts	Rt. end	5'11"	180	Sr.
C.C. Buell	Quarterback	5'9"	160	Sr.
Vinton Chapin	Rt. half	5'10"	165	Sr.
Edwin Gehrke	Lt. half	5'11"	182	Jr.
George Owen	Fullback	5'11"	185	Sr.

It was an experienced team with six seniors, four juniors and only one sophomore. The line would average 187 lbs., the backs 173 lbs., and the team 182 lbs.

Some had accused Coach Fisher of holding back in 1921, saving his team for later engagements, even though there is no evidence that he in fact did. However, in 1922 there was going to be no possible way that anyone could claim that Harvard wasn't entering the Centre game with all guns firing to the maximum. Going into the Centre contest, Harvard hadn't lost two straight games to a team since the Percy Haughton era began in 1908. Bob Fisher didn't plan to do anything other than keep that record intact.

STILL ON THE TRAIN, AND NOT YET IN MASSACHUSETTS

When the team got to Albany, there was a delay for an hour while their Pullman was disconnected and attached to a Boston and Albany passenger train. It seemed they'd been gone forever and they hadn't gotten to Massachusetts yet. Then when they finally got underway, there was another delay in Springfield, Massachusetts, this time for an hour and a half. The team was tired but rose to the occasion in order to accommodate the large number of photographers who had come west to Springfield from Boston in order to get material for their papers.

The members of the press piled into the Colonels' Pullman for the 100 mile ride into Boston. Uncle Charlie, Coach Bond and Red fielded questions, and the Centre coach, not normally a complainer, couldn't help but mention how disappointed he had been when he heard the comments about Centre's plan to go to Mansfield, Massachusetts from Richmond.

"We got up at 6:30 in the morning in order to grab some breakfast and make sure we had everything at the station that we needed for the trip. We're going to arrive some 38 hours after we got up. We heard that they're saying we go to school just so we can play football."

"How long does it take for Harvard to get to New Haven to play Yale?"

"Two hours."

"How long does it take for Princeton, where some of the comments came from, to get to Boston?"

"Maybe five, six hours, maximum."

"Princeton to Yale?"

"Probably no more than three hours."

"If we have any luck going home, we'll have been on a train over 60 hours just on this trip. Add in the time it took to get back and forth to Richmond, and my boys will have spent close to 100 hours on a train, many more than the Eastern schools spend in one of their boy's whole career."

Uncle Charlie's voice trailed off as he said again, "They say my boys go to school just so they can play football."

It was an exhausted group of young men who gathered up their equipment and suitcases and carried them to the truck which the Harvard Athletic Association had waiting at the Huntington Street Station. Due to the delay in finally arriving, the team wasn't met by as large a crowd as in the prior two years, but what was lacking in numbers was more than made up in enthusiasm.

Bill Cunningham of the "Post" recounted the scene.

Some newspaper writers, forecasting the arrival of the Colonels, had said that there would be none of the famous Southern beauties on deck to welcome the grid battlers from the old chivalric realm this year. The one bet that the well-intentioned prognosticators overlooked was the fact that a small multitude of the fairest daughters of the Old South are already in New England attending school, and they were on hand, radiant as a June morning, and dancing on their silken toes with excitement as the big locomotive churned past with its breaks streaking fire.

The team shook a lot of hands, hugged the young ladies, and then Hump said, "Follow me boys. I think I remember the way to the Lenox." They walked the short distance, with two of Tom Bartlett's teammates helping him along. Bartlett was so weak that he couldn't stand at the front desk, and the registration card was brought over to where he sat so he could scribble his signature.

There was a lobby full of well wishers at the hotel, but Uncle Charlie made it clear that there needed to be no lingering before everyone made it to their rooms.

"It's been a long and tiring journey. We want you to know how much we appreciate your being here, but my lads need rest, and we're going to try to get ready for why we came here—to represent Old Centre in a way that will make you proud."

It was, "Hip, Hip, Hooray," as the Colonels ascended to their rooms.

Thank goodness for George Cresup Hays, my childhood friend whom Howard and I bunked with on the trip to Birmingham for the Auburn game in 1921. He had gone back to E-town on the L&N to try to get his parent's permission to go to the Harvard game when I left for Boston.

We planned to room together if we got to make the trip, but I didn't have any idea if he had made it or not. If he hadn't, I wasn't sure exactly what my backup plan would be.

When I went to the desk, you can't imagine how happy I was to hear that, "Yes sir. We have a George C. Hays registered here as one of our guests."

So old Crep had made it!

I immediately went over to the Western Union desk and wired my parents that I had arrived safely, that I was rooming with Crep, and I had my warm overcoat. I knew that my mother especially would be concerned about the weather, because she was always worried about my catching a cold.

I'd ridden to Boston with the team, and I was going to be a member of the press on Saturday and sit up in the press box with Howard Reynolds, my new friend.

Not bad for an 18 year old, as I look back on those wonderful days, so long ago.

FRIDAY, OCTOBER 20, 1922—THE DAY BEFORE THE GAME

Uncle Charlie had been met at the station, when the team finally arrived on Thursday night, by a representative from Harvard who said that Centre could use the great Stadium at anytime.

"We're sorry that you had so much difficulty in getting here. Tomorrow, whatever your schedule needs to be, we will accommodate you."

It was appreciated, and by 9:00 Friday morning, the team had finished breakfast at the Lenox, suited up in their uniforms in their rooms, and been bused to Soldiers Field and was on the Stadium tuft, ready to workout. Most of the team had been at the

Field and was on the Stadium tuft, ready to workout. Most of the team had been at the field the year before, but no degree of familiarity could totally erase the sense of awe, the feeling that one was in a special place, that stepping onto the perfectly manicured grass inside the great horseshoe was an experience of a lifetime.

Red saw that I got to go along. Crep couldn't go, but I piled onto one of the buses and we drove through Boston out to the Stadium. When we got close, I saw this beautiful structure in the distance. I'd seen Roman ruins like the Coliseum in some encyclopedias that we had at home, and I'd seem pictures of Harvard Stadium carried in the newspapers, but I guess nothing could prepare you for being there and seeing it in person.

It was beautiful! It was huge, like a cathedral.

I had to think about our wooden stadium out on Cheek Field, how little and primitive it seemed. Even the stadium in Birmingham, and Eclipse Field in Louisville seemed so—I guess you'd say—insignificant, when you compared them to what we were approaching.

I remember thinking, "How in the world did we come up here last year and beat a team that plays in a place like this?"

Then we went through the gate and I climbed to the top of the stands while the team walked around on the grass. The field was covered with photographers with their tripods and cameras and reporters carrying their notepads. There were also people wearing Harvard jackets who were there to take care of anything the team needed.

There was a photo session that had become a familiar part of the Colonels' appearances. The "Post" carried a picture of the starting backfield—Hope Hudgins, Herb Covington, Red Roberts and Terry Snowday.

Tom Bartlett, a starter, had his spot taken by Hudgins. Tom was so ill that he was left back at the hotel, barely able to even get any liquids down. A physician came to the Lenox and determined that Bartlett had a peritonsillar abscess, and that surgery would be required. He was taken to a hospital for care, and was left behind when the team headed back to Danville.

The press asked Uncle Charlie for his starting lineup, and he handed out slips of paper which listed the starters for the game.

PLAYER	POSITION	HT.	WT.	CLASS
Minos Gordy	Lt. end	5'10"	177	Soph.
George "Buck" Jones	Lt. tackle	5'8 1/2"	203	Soph.
Bill Shadoan	Lt. guard	6'1"	184	Soph.
Ed Kubale	Center	6'	176	Soph.
Frank Rubarth*	Rt. guard	5'11"	175	Soph.
Ben Cregor	Rt. tackle	5'11"	180	Sr.
Clifton "Hennie" Lemon	Rt. end	5'10"	165	Soph.

Herb Covington	Quarter	5'5"	158	Soph.
Hope Hudgins	Rt. half	5'7"	150	Soph.
Terry Snowday	Lt. half	5'10"	178	Sr.
James "Red" Roberts	Fullback	6'1"	225	Sr.

*(Frank Rubarth didn't actually start. A last minute change prior to the kickoff was made, and Howard Lynch, another sophomore at 5'10" and 180 lbs., got the call. However, Lynch twisted his knee in the 1st quarter, and Rubarth replaced him.)

Even with eight sophomores starting, Centre had a fairly experienced group of players. Everyone other than Lemon and Hudgins had seen action in the 1921 game, even if some had been substitutes.

Uncle Charlie decided to start Red at fullback due to the absence of Bartlett. He felt he needed the big redhead to lead interference, but also planned on shifting him back into the line and sending in Hump as needed.

While Hudgins was game and had great speed, Tom Bartlett's absence was going to remove a major facet of the Colonels' attack, and increase the pressure on Covington, because Tom had the ability to both throw and receive passes, plus he was a great defensive player. Bartlett was somewhat like Army had been. He didn't run up any spectacular stats, but when a post-game analysis was made, his play would always be seen as critical to the team's success. Tom Bartlett would be missed.

After the press was satisfied, Uncle Charlie asked that everyone leave and the team be allowed to practice for the next two hours unobserved. The coach wanted to perfect the "lock-step," and nearly the whole session was devoted to the new formation.

"Now, Hennie, now, pick up the ball and shovel it back to Covey. Then everyone go right."

At the end of the peppy session, Uncle Charlie had the players sit in the enclosed end zone.

I could see that the practice was winding down so I came down from the stands and followed the guys to the end of the field. I was getting pretty comfortable about being along on the trip and hanging out with the team. After all, Red was the captain, and if he wanted me around, who was to say anything? And nobody ever did.

While we all sat there, Uncle Charlie gave a great speech, and I remember the main points, and it went something like this.

Tomorrow will be the last time that most of you will ever be in this magnificent structure. Centre College has been represented well here, but we won't be back because Harvard has elected not to play any more intersectional games with teams like us.

There will be over 50,000 people watching your every move. The papers say there will be several hundred thousand people listening to the action on the radio. They say that our game will have a greater audience than any sporting event in the history of the world! Think of that, in the history of the world! More than last year's Jack Dempsey-Carpentier fight.

We have played with true Centre spirit in the past. We have won the hearts of many of the fans here and everywhere because of our hard but clean play.

We have been true sportsmen, just as Harvard has. This year we have suffered many hardships. We've had players declared ineligible who had done nothing wrong. We've had deaths of family members. We've had illness strike our team. We've had hard travel and delays that other teams don't have to endure.

But through it all, you have proved to be real Centre men. You have brought pride to your school, to Old Centre. You have made our great state of Kentucky proud, and the whole Southland has embraced Centre College, as have people all over the country.

Tomorrow, when you run out on this field, I want each and every one of you to know that you have also made me proud. You're the finest group of young men, the finest group I have ever known, and whatever the outcome, I want you to know that I love you for what you are.

You are Centre men, through and through, and there is no greater compliment that I can pay each of you.

You are Centre men, through and through.

I know that I had tears in my eyes when Uncle Charlie stopped speaking, and so did the players. Even Uncle Charlie's eyes were glistening, and Uncle Charlie was hardly the type to cry.

I have often wondered back about those times. We were often called the, "The Fighting, Crying, Praying Colonels."

"Crying?" Did real men cry? I think you have to understand the times. Every member of the team so wanted to do well, and every member of the team tried so hard to live up to what was expected of them, that they became really emotional when they thought about going out and representing their team and Centre College.

It's different now. College athletes want to win, sure, but it's not a life-or-death sort of thing for them nowadays.

When the Colonels were playing while I was at Centre, the players felt that they were truly representing each and every one of us who went to school in Danville, that they were not only representing those of us who were on the campus at the time, but they were playing for everyone who ever was enrolled, no matter how long ago. They were playing for K.C.W., they were playing for Danville, they were playing for Kentucky, and they were playing for the South and for everywhere that there were fans who followed them.

And, yes, they were very emotional about it.

Real men do cry, if they feel strongly enough about something, as our guys did.

After the return to the Lenox, lunch and another quick chalkboard session, there was a vote to see how the rest of the afternoon would be spent. Buses could be engaged quickly for a tour of the city and environs. Tickets could be bought for an afternoon vaudeville show down the street. Or, the option was available to anyone who just wanted free time to explore the city on his own.

When the vote was tallied, there was an overwhelming margin to travel to Plymouth Rock, the site of the landing of the first Pilgrims in 1620.

The 300th anniversary of the landing had taken place in 1920, and there had been a significant amount of publicity, magnified by the recent ending of World War I and the tremendous patriotism which had swept the country the last few years.

There was room for me on the bus, and Red said, "I don't go anywhere without my son," so I hopped on and sat in the back, just happy to be going.

We went through Boston and the driver pointed out the sights as we went along, and then headed south toward Plymouth, a place which I was vaguely familiar with, but, of course, I'd never been there.

When we got to Plymouth, we drove to the site where the famous Plymouth Rock was, and to tell you the truth, it didn't seem that special, just a rock sitting inside this little open building with a lot of columns. But when our guide started talking, everyone seemed really interested, because, like he said, this was the very spot that the Pilgrims had supposedly stepped off their boat when they first came to America.

I had to wonder, how did they know it was this particular rock, and not some other rock? But, of course, I didn't say anything.

After listening to the story about the rock, we drove back to Boston so everyone could get ready to go to a reception for the team that night.

There were several Southern Clubs in the Boston area. If Southerners moved to the Northeast, often the first thing they did was to associate with one of the Southern Clubs so they could socialize with people from similar circumstances and backgrounds.

Multiple Clubs banded together to rent the huge Boston Arena, a facility which opened in 1910 near the Back Bay on St. Botolph Street, adjacent to Northeastern University. They planned a Friday night reception before the game to honor the Colonels and any Kentuckians who were in the city for the game.

In addition to the members of the Southern Clubs, the event was also attended by members of many of the college fraternities in the area. Not only was the team an attraction, but it been publicized the "The Famous Centre 'Six'" was going to play, and the whole evening promised to be a gala happening.

Howard played the banjo and mandolin. I still have what is called a "potato bug" mandolin that he played in the Boston Arena. The Centre "Six" was different than the group that called itself the Centre "5" the year before. In addition to Howard,

there were three fellows who played the clarinet and two played the saxophone.

They could play just about anything, depending on what the crowd wanted. They performed popular and novelty songs, and could even get into classical music somewhat. They were so good that the Chief's Chautauqua company booked them in the big hotels all over the South, and they played in New York City and some of the Eastern colleges like Wellesley and at the Harvard Union.

They were very professional and always put on quite a show.

The players came into the packed arena and mingled with the folks. Occasionally a flash would illuminate the cavernous hall as still another photograph was taken of individuals and groups of players. The Centre "Six" was in good form, their up-tempo music creating a lively and festive air. A wooden dance floor was packed with the younger crowd showing off the latest steps, and of course, a pretty young lady grabbed Red and pulled him out to the center of the dancing throng, and soon everyone began to back away and leave the floor to Red and his partner, clapping and cheering as the smiling All-American, always ready when the music started, went through his moves.

The plan had been for the Colonels to only stay for awhile, hoping there would be time for everyone attending to have some contact with the players, but the size of the crowd made it obvious that the members of the team couldn't shake every hand, and reply to every compliment and every wish for success.

There was a platform behind the dance floor and the Colonels were asked to get on it so that they could be introduced. The Centre "Six" played the school song as the team climbed onto makeshift stage.

OLD CENTRE

Old Centre marches ever on,
On to victory, on to glory,
Loud cheers ring out, huzzars resound,
To proclaim the same old story.
Ever bold, as of old, guard her honor;
On the field, never yield, win her fame.
For Centre now be bold,
The Gold and White unfold.
Our heads we bare,
Our pledge renew,
Old Centre we'll be true.

As soon as the "Six" finished, there was huge roar which echoed off the walls of the arena.

"Centre! Centre! Centre! Centre!"—the cheer went on and on.

"Centre! Centre! Centre! Centre!"

It made a chill go over your entire body, just a hair-raising chill.

The crowd kept shouting, "Centre! Centre!"

Finally, Red stepped forward and put his finger over his lips like to try to say, "Shhhhhh," and then they started, "Red! Red! Red!" and I thought they'd never stop.

At last, one of the organizers of the evening got the crowd to quiet down, and the Colonels took turns stepping out of the line and shouting out their names. Of course, each time they did, there was another cheer. Red waited until the last, and when he smiled and waved, he didn't even have to say his name. It was "Red! Red! Red!" until the guys finally stepped back down off the platform and began to make their way out of the arena.

You had to be there. You had to have lived during this period to know exactly how much people thought of our team.

After the guys finally left, the dancing picked up again and went on until at least midnight, or longer.

Howard said that he and the group had played at a lot of events, but that night at the Boston Arena was the best they had ever performed, and that it was the most fun, too.

OCTOBER 21, 1922 —GAME DAY, CENTRE-HARVARD

The Colonels awoke on Saturday morning and raised their windows in the Lenox and found that the weather was going to be perfect for a football game, slightly cool but not uncomfortably so, with clear skies showing not even a hint of a cloud for as far as one could see.

I was about as excited as a person could be. Crep and I got dressed and went down to the lobby, and I asked at the desk if I had a message, but there was nothing in our key box. That sort of worried me, but when I turned around, there was Howard Reynolds standing there with a big smile and he said, "Red, were you looking for something?"

He handed me an envelope and I opened it up and there was a press pass with my name on it, and I felt like he'd handed me the keys to the kingdom! It had, "Press Pass," and "Boston Post" and right under was my name, "Red Robertson." I was set!

There were some Kentuckians who were going to go out to Harvard to tour the campus, and I was able to get in their cab and they let me out near the stadium.

I was early and tried to get in but the gates were locked, and then some guard saw my pass and told me there was a special entrance for "members of the press," and I wondered why he told me that when all of a sudden I realized that I was a "member of the press," or at least that's what it said on my pass.

The press entrance was open and I showed my badge, feeling like a pretty big shot. I climbed up to the press box and couldn't believe how many papers were going to be represented. There were little signs with the papers' name written on them, showing where the different reporters were supposed to sit. Of course, all the Boston papers had spots, but it seemed that there were just as many from New York, and there were places for the wire services, the papers from Louisville and Lexington, and both of the Danville papers, the "Messenger" and "Advocate,"and Hartford and a lot of other cities had signs, too. Syracuse and others, I can't remember all of them.

It made me appreciate all the more how much attention Centre was getting. Could you believe it? All of these reporters were going to write stories about our team!

There was a telegraph machine to send reports back to Danville and cities across Kentucky. And there was the set-up for the radio broadcast that Uncle Charlie had mentioned the day before.

Unbelievable!

Later in the morning, the press box began to fill. Everybody, it seemed, smoked—cigarettes, cigars, pipes—the area was filled with smoke, which I didn't mind, because I loved the smell.

Howard Reynolds came in and everybody greeted him by his first name, and it was obvious that he was respected, and he should have been, because he was the sports editor of the "Post."

He introduced me around and one of the reporters, I think it was Grantland Rice, heard that I was from Centre and he asked me if I knew the players and their numbers, and of course, nobody knew them better than I did.

So he asked me if I'd be the "spotter" for Centre. He said it was hard to watch the game, try to figure out who made a play by checking the program, and type, all at once. He didn't say it, but I thought, and smoke, too.

He told me that they had a "spotter" for Harvard, and he was really important because Harvard's players didn't have numbers. Their coaches felt it was a "team game," and numbers made people concentrate on individuals instead of the team, which didn't make any sense to me, but who was I to say anything?

So, of course, I said I'd be the "spotter," and he told me to stand in the middle of the press box when the game began, and to holler out real loud something like, "Covington ran the ball," or, "Kubale and Jones made the tackle," not to get fancy, just holler out, and the Harvard fellow would do the same.

I must have done a good job, because there was an article in the Boston "Herald" the next day about how Red Roberts' son had made it to Boston on the team's car and been the "spotter" for the press.

As I said earlier, "Unbelievable!"

The morning of the game, the "Harvard Crimson" ran a short story about the game.

Two years ago the daily papers rang with a telegram from the governor of Kentucky to the Centre football team: "Today, every man in Kentucky is thinking of you, and every woman is praying for you. Hit that line! Hit it low! Hit it hard!"

Everyone remembers that game in 1920. And everyone remembers last year's game when the same team came back like eleven men inspired and nosed out the University, 6-0.

The University is far from underestimating its opponent. Centre's record has commanded the admiring respect of every football critic in the country ever since the colorful little college appeared on the athletic horizon. The game this afternoon will be one to remember.

The big stadium began to fill, first with those who didn't have a reserved seat, as people holding just general admission tickets hustled in to find the best spots in the wooden end zone bleachers. Many of the fans felt the very best position to watch a game in the stadium, if they couldn't get a seat that was reserved, was to not have a seat at all, but to arrive early and head to the roof over the colonnade and try to get as close to the 50 yard line as possible.

By 2:00, the Harvard players were on the turf, warming up, and Centre's team came trotting out just moments later, led by Captain Roberts, as usual with no helmet, his flaming red hair wrapped with the customary white scarf.

The officials for the game were Ernest C. Quigley, well known in baseball and football circles, as referee, Elmer Oliphant, a former star at West Point, as field judge, W. R. Crowley of Bowdoin as umpire, and from the University of Kentucky, H. G. Tiggert, head linesman.

At 2:05, the Harvard band was heard playing Crimson songs as they marched across the Charles over the Anderson Memorial Bridge. The smartly dressed musicians came into the Stadium through the entrance between the temporary bleachers and the permanent concrete horseshoe, followed by many members of the student body who had marched along behind them.

There was a big cheer when the Harvard band came onto the field and made its way to their seats. Then there was an even larger uproar and I looked down and it was Howard and the other members of the Centre "Six," marching down the field, playing as loudly as they could.

Before the 2:30 kickoff, the two captains, Charles Chauncey Buell and Red Roberts met for the traditional flip of the coin. Red won the toss and chose to receive. Centre entered the contest realizing that it was going to be a battle, but didn't feel that Harvard should be the favorite to win by two or three touchdowns as the local press was predicting. As they lined up to begin the action, the Colonels felt they could play with the Crimson.

At 2:30, it was time for the last game in the series between Centre and Harvard to begin. Each of the over 50,000 spectators was standing as Edwin Gehrke's powerful boot rolled into the end zone for a touchback, and the Gold and White took over on the 20.

Herb Covington picked up a quick three. Centre planned to stick with the same type of attack during the 1st half that it had in 1921, mainly keeping it on the ground, certainly not giving away the "lock-step."

On 2nd down, Covey called for a cross-buck in which he was to take the center pass and head right before handing off to Terry Snowday who was to sweep around his left end. However, Snowday couldn't get around the Crimson wingman, right end Roscoe Fitts, and had to continue running laterally, trying to get into a position to cut up field.

When Terry tried to shift the ball from his right arm to his left in order to be able to stiff-arm, the ball squirted loose, and in the melee to cover it, the oval was kicked toward the Harvard goal where Fitts smothered it on the Centre four. Not a good start, most definitely.

On the 1st offensive play of the afternoon for Harvard, George Owen, the great fullback, drove across for a score, Buell drop-kicked the extra point, and with less that a minute gone, Centre was down, 7-0.

The Colonels regrouped and moved the ball effectively on the next possession, making consistent gains until they had the ball on the Harvard 31. However, the Crimson stiffened and Covey had to take it to the air and was intercepted.

After an exchange of punts which ended up being much in Harvard's favor, the Crimson had 1st and 10 on the Colonels' 40. From this point, Harvard mounted a sustained drive down the field, first Owen, then Gehrke, then Chapin. After 10 consecutive gainers, Gehrke crashed over, Buell was good again, and it was Harvard, 14-0.

It looked really bad. I heard the writers say things like, "It seems like Harvard's going to totally outclass the Southerners this year," or "Red Roberts looks so slow it seems like he's hardly moving."

I felt terrible for our team. The game was still in the 1st quarter and we were two touchdowns behind. But I was the "spotter," and no matter what, I had to keep hollering out names.

Gehrke kicked off again and Covey brought it back to the 20.

Desperate times called for desperate measures. Centre had planned not to unveil the "lock-set" until the 2nd half, hoping to spring it as a surprise. But now there was no way to hold anything back, or the score was going to be so lopsided that the game would be long lost.

Centre lined up normally. Then the linemen stood up and marched laterally toward the sideline, each holding the shoulder of the man in front of him, and a writer said, "Looks like Centre's had enough. They're leaving the field!"

I knew that we weren't leaving the field. I'd seen that play diagrammed when we were in the Pullman on the way to Boston. Howard Reynolds knew about the formation also, but he didn't let on. He just sat there watching, but I blurted out, "Centre's not quitting! Our team won't ever quit. You just wait and see!"

After walking nearly to the sideline, the linemen, followed by the backs, reversed direction and came back toward the other sideline. Harvard's players seemed in a bit of a daze. They somewhat followed the direction of the Colonels but looked terribly disorganized.

Suddenly Hennie Lemon grabbed the ball and shoveled it back to Covey who gained a quick five yards but then fumbled after being hit hard by George Owen who outweighed him by over 25 pounds. The ball was kicked in the scramble to fall on it and bounced all the way up to the 40 where Harvard recovered. Owen came out to appreciative applause, and his play was over for the day.

On the 1st play after the recovery, Captain Buell fired a pass to Chapin who picked up good downfield blocking and raced across the goal. Buell was good again and it was 21-0 and still in the 1st quarter.

I couldn't believe it. We'd never been down 21-0 in the initial quarter. I couldn't remember when we'd ever been that far behind, at least not since the Georgia Tech game, and that certainly wasn't in the 1st quarter. It looked like we were going to get killed. As a matter of fact, it didn't just look like it, we were getting killed.

Centre had two fumbles and an interception in the 1st quarter, and each miscue led to a Harvard score. Many teams playing away from home in front of greater than 50,000 spectators, and down 21-0, would have folded. Centre didn't fold. Rather, from that moment, the Colonels totally dominated.

Centre huddled before the 2nd quarter began and vowed to fight harder than ever. The Colonels began using the "lock-step" frequently. Every time they executed the new formation, the crowd stood and cheered then on. Using the new scheme, the team started piling up the yardage. The Harvard players tried to follow the Colonels, attempting to line up opposite whichever player they felt was appropriate, but just as they would try to get positioned, a Centre lineman would fire the ball back and a back would shoot around an end, or cut right up the field. Once, Centre even passed off the formation.

The surprise attack allowed Centre to have a concentrated drive, and Harvard was only able to stop the Colonels when they reached the six yard line. Determined to get on the scoreboard, even though down by three touchdowns, Covey kicked a field goal to make it 21-3.

Mistakes continued to plaque Centre, and Harvard got the field goal back after another interception, and the boot made the margin 24-3 at the end of the half.

It had been a discouraging 30 minutes of play for the Colonels, a mistake filled half in which they had fumbled twice, lost the ball two times on interceptions, and each error had resulted in points being scored. The only true drive by the Crimson was the excellent 10 play movement of the ball which resulted in the 2nd score.

Harvard had made 10 substitutions. Centre had removed Howard Lynch when he twisted his knee and replaced him with Frank Rubarth. Hope Hudgins had taken a hard hit on the 4th play of the game. He got up, blood pouring from both nostrils and knew he had broken his nose. Hudgins begged Red not to send him to the sidelines, saying he was ok and wanted to continue. Hope Hudgins played the whole game, broken nose and all.

You know, because we were fraternity brothers and friends, Hump told me more about what was going on with the team than probably anyone except maybe Howard, who was on the team in 1922, but Howard wasn't dressed out for the Harvard game. He was there with the Centre "Six."

Hump told me that at the half, all of the talk was how proud Uncle Charlie was of the team and how they hadn't given up, but had done much better in the 2nd quarter, and all he wanted them to do was go out and play as hard as they could the rest of the game. He said it didn't matter what the score was at the end, he just wanted them to be able to walk off the field knowing that they'd done their very best, to keep trying until the very last play.

He said that they were Centre men, and to remember, as always, that no matter what the score was, Centre played hard, and Centre never quit, but Centre played clean, like the true sportsmen each of them were.

The Colonels played their hearts out the 2nd half. There had rarely been hitting like the spectators witnessed that afternoon. Despite the ferocity of play, the officials said later in a post-game interview that it was as clean a game as they'd ever witnessed. Centre had three penalties for 25 yards, one for holding and two for jumping offsides. Harvard had two for 10 yards, both for being offsides. As in the previous encounters between the two squads, there was always a helping hand to pick up an opponent.

Ten minutes into the 3rd quarter, Centre held the Crimson after three runs had picked up only four yards, and Harvard had to punt to Covey, who returned it 43 yards, being brought down by sophomore M.W. Greenough, who was the last man between the speedy back and the goal.

Covington had electrified the crowd by cutting in and out of defenders, pivoting once when it seemed certain that he would be brought down which caused two Crimson defenders to collide, taking them out of the play.

Red gathered the team around him and urged them on for a maximal effort, shouting as they broke apart, "We are Centre!" Red wasn't known for his motivation like the previous captains, Bo and Army. Bo had led by both emotion and action, Army by his quiet determination and steadying influence. For Red, it was mainly his example on the field. He was a bull amongst boys when he got riled up, and now he was ready to show some people how Centre played football, no matter the circumstances, no matter the score.

It was Red leading the way, and Covey following. Centre ran right over the Harvard right tackle position, nothing fancy, no "lock-step, just Red leading the way, and Herb following right behind him.

3 yards, 2, 2, 5—1st down!

5 yards, 2, 4—1st down!

4 yards, 2, 3, 2—1st and goal on the Crimson one yard line!

The crowd roared its approval. Even the most partisan Harvard supporters were on their feet, urging the Gold and White on. The Centre "Six" had started little bursts of music, time after time, halting for—

"Go! Go! Go! Go!"

Red moved back into the fullback position and crashed into the left side. Harvard held. Covey tried the right side with Red leading the way. Harvard held. Covey off left tackle, again behind Red. Harvard held. On 4th down, Covey asked Red if he wanted to try to take it in. Red, said no, he would lead the way, and for the little quarterback to follow behind.

Red looked over at Bill Shadoan and George Jones, guard and tackle on the left side of the front wall. "Bill, you and "Buck" block your men out. I'm going right between you, and Covey is going to be glued to my moleskins."

The play unfolded perfectly. The two linemen hit their opposite numbers hard, driving them both laterally, and Red barreled behind them with Covey as his shadow. The linebacker was hit by Red and knocked aside, and Herb shot into the end zone, untouched.

I was screaming as loud as I could, trying to be heard above the crowd. I had to run back and forth behind the members of the press so they could hear me.

"Covington scored! Covington scored! Red Roberts led the way! Shadoan and Jones and Red Roberts led the way!"

Then, even though it wasn't part of my job as "spotter," I couldn't help but start jumping up and down and telling anyone who was near, "I told you we wouldn't give up! I told you we'd never quit!"

I remember Howard Reynolds just looking over his shoulder at me and smiling.

Centre lost the game in the 1st quarter, falling behind 21-0. The Colonels won the hearts of the crowd in the 2nd half with their never-say-die play.

Hennie Lemon's kick brought the score to 24-10.

In reality, there wasn't enough time for Centre to win, but the Colonels kept playing with an intensity rarely exhibited by any team on any field at any time in the history of football.

The Colonels got the ball back after Harvard had been forced to punt following the kickoff by Red. The Crimson kick was fielded by Covington on his 30 and he returned it to the 39.

Centre began to drive. Covey got 10 and a 1st down after dashing over tackle and then cutting to the outside. Red then smashed through for another 10. Covey picked up five behind a crunching block by Red. Covey was stopped for no gain, and on 3rd down his pass attempt was knocked down by Winnie Churchill.

Herb then followed behind Red who cleared out several defenders and Covey picked up 21 yards, and Centre had a 1st down on the Crimson 15.

On the next play, Covington, playing against the clock, went to the air but his pass to Lemon was just wide, and the ball went into the end zone for a touchback. Still, the Colonels fought on.

"Hold 'em, guys! We can get it back! Hold 'em!"

Hold they did, and after three short gains, Harvard had to punt it out and Centre started another march.

The crowd was on its feet the entire 4th quarter, cheering every move of the Colonels during one of the most courageous comeback attempts they had ever witnessed. Centre got all of the way to the Harvard 12 yard line before another pass was again incomplete in the end zone. It was another touchback. Still, the Colonels fought, harder and harder, hitting and hitting, cheering each other on.

"Way to go Baldy, great hit!"

"Cajun, watch for a sweep on your side!"

"Great play, Cajun! Great play, Louisiana!"

Harvard once again had three plays and a punt, and the Colonels lined up quickly, desperately trying to score.

A 23 yard pass from Covey to Hennie Lemon brought the ball to the Crimson 17, the 3rd straight drive when the Colonels had gotten inside the Harvard 20.

But it was not to be. The whistle blew, and it was over.

There were a lot of comments in the press box like, "I've never seen any team like these boys from Kentucky. Don't they know when they are beaten?" People were saying that it was a shame that Centre had to lose, because except for the first quarter, we had definitely seemed like the better team.

Of course, I was heartbroken, but I was so proud. I'd heard from Howard about how the year before, the fans had gone out onto the field after we'd won. Now there was what must have been a similar scene. There weren't that many Kentuckians who were at the game, but the entire playing field was covered with fans who had come rushing out of the stands to get to the players and congratulate them about how great they had played.

Harvard made a total of 21 substitutions during the game, playing a total of 28 men.

HARVARD PLAYERS IN 1922 CENTRE-HARVARD GAME

POSITION	STARTER	SUBSTITUTES
Lt. end	Hartley	McGillin, Holder
Lt. tackle	Brocker	Greenough
Lt. guard	Hubbard	Kunhardt, Hubbard

Center	Clark	Kernan, Bradford, Clark
Rt. guard	Grew	Miller
Rt. tackle	Eastman	Tower, Robson
Rt. end	Fitts	Crosby
Quarterback	Buell	Lee, Pfaffman, Akers, Buell
Rt. half	Gehrke	Hammond
Lt. half	Chapin	Churchill, Chapin
Fullback	Owen	Coburn, Rouillard

Only 14 men saw action for the Colonels. Frank Rubarth replaced Howard Lynch in the 1st quarter after Lynch's knee injury. In the 3rd quarter, Case Thomasson subbed for Terry Snowday after he was shaken up, and then Hump came in for Thomasson. Of the backfield starters, Hope Hudgins, Herb Covington and Red, who also played in the line, went the entire 60 minutes in the backfield. Ed Kubale, Ben Cregor, Bill Shadoan, Buck Jones, Minos Gordy and Hennie Lemon played the whole game in the line.

The game stats were very revealing. Harvard had five total first downs, four in the 1st half, and one in the 2nd. Five total! Centre racked up over three times Harvard's, picking up six in the 1st half and 11 in the 2nd, for a total of 17.

Centre literally controlled the clock, running the ball 53 times and passing 10, and therefore had 63 offensive plays. Harvard only ran 28 plays! The Crimson rushed 26 times and passed twice. That statistic is worthy of being repeated. Centre ran 63 plays, Harvard but 28. The Colonels picked up 228 yards rushing for an average of 4.3 yards per attempt, and when adding the 48 yards gained passing, the afternoon's yardage was 276. Harvard picked up 134 yards rushing, completed one pass for 40 yards, and had a total yardage of 174.

How does a team run over twice the plays, gain over 100 yards more, and lose 24-10? It's not hard when you have two fumbles and two interceptions, all of which result in scores.

Having said all of that, however, Harvard had to be given credit. A good team takes advantage of the breaks. A good team takes advantage of its opponent's mistakes. Certainly there is no doubt that Harvard was an excellent team, and certainly Harvard did what good teams should do. Harvard capitalized.

The matter of substitutions has to be considered. After the Crimson jumped out to the 21-0 lead, George Owen, their stellar fullback, was taken out and didn't appear again. It was a wise decision by Coach Fisher.

Did Fisher's running subs in and out all afternoon mean that he was saving some of his starters for future contests? Did it mean that he was determined to wear Centre down with his superior bench? Or, did it reflect on how hard the hitting was by both the Crimson and Colonels? The answer is probably "yes" for all three possibilities.

The Crimson mentor was determined not to drop two straight to Centre. He started his strongest eleven, and even when he subbed, he often sent his starters back in after giving them a rest. But he had Dartmouth, Florida, Princeton, Brown and Yale to face, and having that part of his schedule still ahead had to have some influence on his decisions.

However, an article in the Boston "Globe" on October 23, the Monday after the game, had a headline across the full width of the sports section:

HARVARD WILL HAVE LIGHT WORKOUT FOR A DAY OR TWO AFTER THE HAMMERING IT GOT IN THE CENTRE GAME SEVERAL REGULARS GIVEN HARD BUMPS

For a day or two, the Crimson's workouts will be light, as the team took quite a hammering in the engagement with Centre College, several of the regulars getting their fullest share of the bumps.

George Owen, after his wonderful breaking in the opening period, was withdrawn and did not return. He will therefore be in shape for the Dartmouth game, in which he is likely to be a very necessary asset.

Three of the first string men and two valuable substitutes were severely shaken up in the Centre game. All but one should be in trim again before Saturday. Phil Coburn, hurt again after being out of play the previous two weeks, injured his leg and is likely to be out until the Princeton game on November 11.

Joe Hartley, right end, Esky Clark, center and Erwin Gehrke, halfback, will have to rest most of the week. Kernan, the substitute center, who suffered a bump on the head, will probably be able to scrimmage this week.

The Syracuse "Herald" sent sportswriter David Walsh to cover the game. His summary epitomized not only how those covering the game felt, but also the sentiments of much of the crowd.

The varsity "H" was forced to stand for both Harvard and Horseshoes in an overflowing Stadium yesterday afternoon. Any defeat is heartbreaking to the loser, but the one suffered by Centre College yesterday afternoon was nothing short of tragic.

The Colonels from far-off Kentucky outplayed Harvard, outsmarted her, outrushed her, and did everything but defeat her. Centre literally fumbled the victory into Harvard's lap, but be it said for the Crimson, she was the great opportunist.

Speaking about the performance of Herb Covington, Walsh wrote:

Covington seemed to run the ball on almost every play, and he ran it so well that the gridiron looked like a battlefield strewn with fallen Harvard defenders who had tried to stop the agile young Southerner and failed.

The Harvard games of 1920, '21 and '22, had been the most important events ever for Centre College. They had brought a vast amount of attention to the little school as only encounters with such a great institution as Harvard could. In the contests, Centre had proven its worth.

The first game was a standstill during the initial half, with Centre battling back

437

from a 7-0 deficit to actually lead after two electrifying touchdowns. The half ended, 14-14. Harvard's overwhelming depth and superiority in the line turned the tide for the Crimson in the 2nd half, and resulted in a 31-14 win for the boys from Cambridge.

The second Centre-Harvard pairing lacked the fireworks of the 1920 game, with the Colonels intent on sticking to a conservative attack, confident that the team's improved line play could hold the score down so that one or two touchdowns would suffice. Army and Bo were prescient in advocating this strategy.

Army had said, "Hold them scoreless in the first quarter and we will win."

He was absolutely correct. Centre's defense held, Bo scored early in the 3rd quarter, and the Colonels emerged victorious, 6-0.

While most called the 1921 win an upset, Centre's players didn't feel that way. The Colonels felt they had the manpower and skills, plus the great Centre spirit that characterized the team every time it took the field, so that the better team won.

The third game once again proved that the Colonels could play with any team in the country. They lost, but they competed at a winning level, and they walked off the field at Harvard Stadium with the esteem of the record crowd, the hundreds of thousands who followed the broadcast of the game over station WIR, and the millions who read about the October 21 contest all over the country the next morning in their Sunday newspapers.

Never in the history of college football has a series, the Centre-Harvard games of 1920-22, so captivated the attention of sports fans everywhere, and none has since.

All of us talked about the games the rest of our lives. They were defining moments for each of us, players and students alike.

We loved our team, but you know, we ended up loving Harvard and its traditions and sportsmanship nearly equally.

Those were wonderful days, days that sadly will never be repeated. I know I was made a better person by having lived through and experiencing those times, and I'm certain that everyone associated with Centre felt the same way.

Also, I have to say, I feel that Centre touched Harvard, as well as the people of Boston and the East Coast.

Uncle Charlie had told "Bowman" in "First Down, Kentucky," that the Eastern schools didn't really know about anything west of the New Jersey state line. Now, their horizons had been expanded due to the football games between Centre and Harvard in the early 1920's. It was no longer, Danville, Kentucky, "wherever that is." It was Danville, Kentucky, "home of Centre College."

COACH FISHER INVITES RED
When the team was leaving the locker room to head back to the Lenox, Coach Bob Fisher sought out Red Roberts and told him how much he appreciated the play of Centre, and how proud Red should be that he was the captain of such a wonderful

group of young men.

"Red, I'd consider it an honor to have you as Harvard's guest for our game with Yale down in New Haven on November 25th."

Red checked with Uncle Charlie who was standing nearby.

"We don't play that weekend," Uncle Charlie said, "We don't play until the following Thursday against South Carolina."

Coach Fisher continued, "We'd like you to sit on our bench. There's no better seat in the Yale Bowl!"

Howard Reynolds overheard the conversation.

"Red, the "Post" will pay your expenses if you'll write your impressions of the game for our paper."

Uncle Charlie indicated by a smile and nod that Red should go.

On the morning of November 22nd, the big redhead from Somerset, Kentucky took the train to Boston and joined the Crimson team for the trip to New Haven. He did indeed sit on the bench, and he wrote a bylined article for the "Post."

The Crimson defeated the Elis, 10-3.

The Colonels never had better friends than those they made in Boston.

BACK TO DANVILLE

The team left for Danville late Saturday evening, their spirits raised by another boisterous sendoff from the Southern contingent in Boston, and the hundreds of locals who had grown to admire, even love, the boys from the Bluegrass.

Everybody hated to leave Tom Bartlett behind in a Boston hospital, but they said he was better off in a big city where he could get the care he needed. The only good thing for me was that I got to sleep in the Pullman on the way back, and not in the baggage car. One of the players took Tom's lower berth, and I slept above.

While the guys hated to lose, they were most concerned that Terry Snowday and Herb Covington not feel bad about the fumbles. Red came up to Covey and told him we'd have lost by 30 if it hadn't been for his play, and he was right. Herb Covington was everywhere, especially in the 2nd half, and kept us in the game.

The train went west through the night, crossing Massachusetts and New York and arriving at Niagara Falls in the early afternoon. In what had become a Centre ritual, there was another afternoon spent at the great, natural wonder.

Roscoe had again accompanied the team in 1922, but didn't perform at the half. While on the platform at Niagara's station, he was interviewed and a memorable quote made the next day's papers.

I'm in favoah of doing away with the fust period. Make it only three quatahs. Call the staht in on the second, and my boys will win every game they play.

Roscoe had pretty well summarized the game.

The team spent the day at the Falls, returned to their Pullman and pulled out toward Cleveland at 7:00 p.m. Sunday evening. Once again, as in previous years, they hooked onto another southbound New York Central passenger train at Cleveland, were coupled onto the Southern's Royal Palm in Cincinnati, stopped briefly in Lexington where they were greeted by fans, and arrived back home in Danville, right on schedule, at 10:55 A.M, Monday, October 23.

George Joplin had accompanied the Colonels on the trip in his capacity as a reporter for the "Messenger" and Louisville "Herald."

It was another memorable reception, as wild and boisterous as those of the previous years.

With hearts full of respect and gratitude, one-third of population of Danville met the Centre College Colonels at the Southern Station when they arrived at 10:55 this morning. Business men closed the doors of their stores, public schools closed, Kentucky College for Women and Centre dismissed their classes, and the student bodies moved to the station.

When Captain Roberts stepped from the special Centre sleeper, followed by other Romans of the gridiron, a mighty shout went up from the throng.

It was mighty sweet music to the ears of the players, for down in their hearts, every one of them was feeling blue. They had set their hearts on beating Harvard and had bent every effort in that direction. Fate has played some cruel pranks on the Gold and White this autumn, and thrown Centre for several losses. The fine spirit shown by the home folks paralleled that "never-give-up spirit" exhibited by Captain Roberts' men in Harvard Stadium Saturday. Win or lose, Danville is behind Centre and this fact was convincingly impressed upon the minds of the gridders today.

There was another parade away from the station, the team riding in specially decorated cars, the Centre "Six" playing and leading the throng. The sidewalks for the several blocks to the Main Street were lined with cheering spectators who then joined in behind the cars and moved to the courtyard in front of the old Boyle County Courthouse.

Dr. M.A. Hart, pastor of the Christian Church, spoke on behalf of those who welcomed their heroes home.

Your game this year meant even more than last year's victory. You had to fight with your backs to the wall, and you came through nobly. You displayed the spirit that makes men famous. You have taken your defeat like men, and you have won even greater love and respect. Fumbles may be unfortunate in games or in life, but they are not unforgivable in either.

The crowd cheered for several long minutes after that remark by the minister. As soon as Reverend Hart sat down, Hump rose and spoke.

"We have always played as a team. If we have done well, it is to the team's credit,

440

not to one individual. If we have lost, again it is the team. If we make a long run, all of the team made it possible. And if we fumble, again, it is not an individual who has fumbled, it is the team."

Uncle Charlie stood and surveyed the crowd, and then looked back at his boys, and particularly Hump. It was like the moment when he was holding practice on the wet field in Los Angeles, and the reporter described his action and comments when the team ran a formation to perfection.

Occasionally, when the boys pulled a circus play that seemed impossible, they got a dram of praise.

"Well!" Uncle Charlie would exclaim in an umpire's whisper that would shake the goalposts.

"Well!"

Uncle Charlie, his eyes glistening, stood for the longest time, composing himself. "Well!" he finally said.

"Well!"

CHAPTER 20
THE 1922 SEASON CONTINUES

Centre was now 4-1 on the season and 42-4 since Uncle Charlie took over the program following the loss to DePauw over five years ago, on October 20, 1917. The four losses included two games with Harvard, and one loss each to Georgia Tech and Texas A&M, all formidable foes, and all on the road.

The coaching staff had learned not to schedule any team after the Harvard game which could be much of a challenge, and the University of Louisville fit that bill perfectly.

Louisville dropped football completely from 1917 through the 1920 season. When the University, the second oldest in Kentucky, resumed the sport in 1921, it did so with minimal impact, going 2-2-1 against a lightweight schedule, and thus far was 0-4 in 1922. (U of L was founded in 1792, Transylvania, in 1780.)

Louisville	0	Western Kentucky	6
Louisville	12	Bethel	14
Louisville	0	Kentucky	73
Louisville	6	Franklin	27

When you lose to Bethel (TN) and Franklin (IN) and get blown out by Kentucky, 73-0, your program is in need, big time, and Louisville hoped that the exposure from being placed on Centre's schedule would at least generate some publicity and let the sporting world, and potential players for the school, know that its team was in business again.

Uncle Charlie decided not to run up the score against the Cardinals. The Colonels scored two touchdowns, each followed by a successful extra point. The highlight was Herb Covington's exhibition in kicking field goals. Covey set a national record by booting six dropkicks through the goal posts, with Centre being content to kick whenever it got within range.

In the period of the Colonels' heyday, field goal records were designated by whether the kick was made with the ball being held in place by a holder, or by being dropkicked. The record from field goals using a holder was seven.

Covey was good on six of eight attempts from 40, 30, 32, 30, 30 and 33. He hit the goal post on a 40 yard effort and the ball bounced back. The 8th attempt was just wide.

His six exceeded the old dropkicked record of five set by Harvard's B. W. Trafford in 1890 against Cornell, and tied by Walter Eckersall of the University of Chicago against Illinois in 1905, and against Nebraska in 1906.

The one consolation for Louisville was that it scored the first points on Cheek Field since Georgetown was successful on a field goal on November 28, 1918, which was 12 games ago. The final score was 32-7.

After the game, it was announced that Centre had hired another assistant coach, "in order to give the team the best opportunity of winning the Southern grid title."

Jim Kendrick had played under Uncle Charlie at Texas A&M. With the addition of first Jim Bond and now Kendrick, plus the Chief helping out when possible, and Chick Murphy coaching the freshmen, Centre now had a staff which was at least comparable to some of the mid-sized schools playing football.

HOMECOMING IN LEXINGTON, CENTRE-KENTUCKY
NOVEMBER 4, 1922

There were two ways to approach a Homecoming game. You could schedule a "patsy" and allow the alumni to watch you rack up a certain win, or you could engage a college which was well-known and loved throughout your area and nationally, realizing that even though you may lose, your stadium would be packed.

Kentucky chose the latter, and picked Centre for its Homecoming opponent in 1922.

The Colonels had won the last three games with the Wildcats by a cumulative score of 160-0.

1919	Centre	56	Kentucky	0
1920	Centre	49	Kentucky	0
1921	Centre	55	Kentucky	0

During those games, Centre had scored 23 touchdowns, converted on 22 extra points, and totally dominated the flagship, Kentucky state school.

The Colonels had garnered so much national attention that Fox Films announced it was sending cinematographers to Lexington to film the game. LaRue de Gribble (I promise you that I didn't make that up) and Carl P. Pope first came by Danville to get Centre to sign a release, and of course, it was readily given.

While Centre was getting ready for the Kentucky game, sportswriters were still analyzing the Harvard game. The week after the Colonels left Harvard Stadium, a decent Dartmouth team came to Cambridge and got beaten 12-3. The "Big Green" managed only four first downs all afternoon. "How in the world did Centre get 17 first downs and lose?"

Kentucky had high hopes for 1922. The 'Cats were undefeated and had given up only six points in building a 5-0 record.

Kentucky	16	Marshall	0
Kentucky	15	Cincinnati	0
Kentucky	73	Louisville	0
Kentucky	40	Georgetown (Ky.)	6
Kentucky	7	Sewanee	0

The Louisville score stood out. Kentucky fans thought, "We beat Louisville 73-0. Centre just won by just 32-7. This is the year!" Of course, most weren't aware that the Colonels could have won by any margin Uncle Charlie had wished.

Good news reached Danville that Tom Bartlett was doing well following his tonsillectomy and hoped to be home in a week, and back in uniform for the November 18th game with Auburn. (The "good news" wasn't actually factual. Bartlett continued to have difficulties and had lost so much weight, and was so weak, that his football playing days were over, not just for 1922, but for his career.)

The Kentucky game was a sellout. In addition to the permanent seating, additional bleachers were constructed to increase the capacity to 10,000. The Southern Railroad put together a special day train to carry the Danville fans to Lexington for a $1.88 round trip fare. Special cars were also added to trains coming over from Louisville.

Centre was so popular and guaranteed such a crowd that the usual arrangement of the home team just paying the visitor's expenses, plus a modest, agreed upon amount, was changed to having the two schools split the gate, 50-50. However, some people thought that the admission price of $2.50 was excessive.

Jop pointed out that the Centre-Harvard reserved seats were only $2.00.

And we thought Jesse James was dead!

Centre's football team was now doing so well financially that it was announced the athletic department was contributing $25,000 toward the construction cost of what it hoped would soon be a new stadium on Cheek Field.

A contemporary account in the Lexington "Herald" set the scene for the game.

With its row on row of seats packed with people flaunting blue and white for Kentucky, and gold and white for Centre, Stoll Field presented a picturesque scene approaching perhaps the tournaments of the olden days.

All of the seats in the bleachers and boxes were sold several days in advance, and the temporary bleachers which were erected at the east and west ends of the field failed to care for the crowds that thronged the field. Trees, telephone poles and roofs of houses facing Stoll Field were utilized as observation posts. The fences surrounding the field were literally lined with onlookers.

Beautiful girls from all parts of the state were in the stands and boxes, wearing the colors of their respective schools, and they made many bright splotches of color in the crowds. Blue, gold and white ribbons could be seen as far as the eye could reach, and each fan was loud in praise of their favorites.

I think that every student from Centre, and most from K.C.W., went to the game on the train. We'd had a big pep rally the night before at the courthouse. Howard and the "Six" played the school songs and some of the popular tunes of the day, and we all sang along.

We had sheets with the words of the cheers written on them so that we could all join the cheerleaders when they got started. In those days, cheerleaders led cheers, they didn't just get out and dance around and do flips and things like that, as they do now. They led cheers. I don't know why they still call them cheerleaders now, because they should call them dancers, or acrobats, because they perform, they don't get people involved like we used to get going.

Of course, I didn't need a sheet to holler along with my favorite cheers.

I can still hear one of them, just like I shouted it out so long ago.

Fight—Centre fight!
Fight with all your might!
Fight! Fight! Fight! Fight!
Fight! Fight! Fight!

Of course, it didn't take a genius to remember that cheer. All you had to think about was to stop after seven "fights.

As time for the kickoff approached in Lexington, the spectators noticed a new object on the Centre sideline. A fan had bought the team a sulphur-crested cockatoo. The bird had a yellowish crest which you could call gold if you wished, so it was called gold. The rest of the feathers were appropriately white except for a yellowish "wash" under the wings. The benefactor had requested that the bird be displayed at the football games, and Roscoe was made the handler.

The creature didn't exactly follow in the tradition of other winged mascots such as a "War Eagle" or "Hawk" or "Falcon," but it was a bird, and it had the name "Colonel," and it was going to have to suffice.

"Colonel" was on the sideline at Lexington. There is no report of his ever appearing again. Whether he flew to freedom or ended up confined to a cage somewhere on campus isn't known, but he had his moment, however fleetingly.

GAME TIME

Kentucky came out fired up, determined to show the Homecoming crowd that it deserved its sterling 5-0 record. The 1st half was a real surprise, and the Wildcats played the Colonels more than evenly.

During the initial quarter, Kentucky's quarterback, Turner Gregg, kicked a field goal and the three points were the first that the Wildcats had scored on Centre since 1916, a period covering four games, 16 quarters, and over 240 minutes of play.

The Kentucky fans were astonished, not only from looking at the scoreboard, but from watching the fierce defense that their team was playing in shutting down the Colonels' offense. Centre couldn't mount even a semblance of a drive, and the half ended with Centre down, 3-0.

"This is the year!"

Kentucky had five first downs. Centre had but two. No one could remember Centre being beaten statistically by an in-state team forever.

"This is the year!"

Red Roberts played erratically during the half. I remember thinking that he was making mistakes, not playing his usual game. I realized later what had happened when Hump explained it to me.

Before the game, the Kentucky students had started a song to the tune of, "The Old Gray Mare," but instead of "The old gray mare, she ain't what she used to be," they sang, "The old Red Roberts, he ain't what he used to be," and it made Red furious.

Red was usually the most even tempered person in the world, but this got under his skin, and he went running all over the field on every play trying to take out all of the Kentucky players instead of concentrating on his assignments.

Hump said he was playing hard, but not smart, trying to prove that the students were wrong.

At the half, Uncle Charlie kind of got on Red according to Hump. He said maybe the Kentucky students were right, but he could prove they weren't by settling down and playing smart.

Hump said the Chief came up to Red and said, "Red, you've not had a good first half. You're the best man on the field. Why if I were your size, I'd be the heavyweight champion of the world."

And Red just looked down at the Chief and said sort of seriously, "What's the matter with your being the bantamweight champion?"

In a special dispatch to the "Courier-Journal", the halftime activities were described.

A large part of the student body formed the letters "UK" on the field, and motion pictures were taken while the band played "My Kentucky Home," with the crowd standing up during the entire halftime.

The rest of the students then marched around the field, in and out of the human formation of the big "UK" in a burlesque of the Centre "lock-step," and the crowd went wild. Five moving picture machines took motion pictures, and airplanes hovered over the field, doing stunts. It was one of the most wonderful displays ever seen in Kentucky.

When our team ran back out after the half, the students sang the song about Red again. That proved to be a mistake.

Red really turned it on. He led Herb Covington and the other backs on nearly every play, just taking out the men directly involved, not running around trying to block everybody.

When he ran the ball, there was no stopping him. On defense, it seemed he made every tackle.

The students didn't sing the song again. Red made believers out of them, and he made believers out of the Kentucky team before the afternoon was over.

Kentucky's 3-0 lead held up through the first six minutes of the 3rd quarter, and then the Colonels simply wore down the Wildcats with a relentless attack. Hump, Covey and Red alternated line plunges, moving the ball behind their hard charging line.

Ed Kubale, Bill Shadoan, Ben Cregor, Minos Gordy and Frank Rubarth took absolute control of the line, assisted by Terry Snowday and Hennie Lemon at the ends. Kentucky fought valiantly, but the Wildcats were helpless. At the 'Cats' 31, Covey fired a perfect pass to Lemon, who was tripped up on the one yard line.

Red took it over on the next play. Lemon's kick made it 7-3, Centre.

Kentucky couldn't move the ball on their next possession and the Colonels were off again. Lemon got 25 on an end-around. Line plunge after line plunge forced the Wildcats back on play after play, and again, Red broke through for a short gainer and scored.

Hennie Lemon made it 14-3. The Kentucky partisans were noticeably more subdued as it was apparent that their team was being not outfought, but overwhelmed.

Another long drive in the 4th quarter ended with Hump carrying it in, and after Lemon's 3rd perfect kick, it was Centre 21-3.

"This is the year!" changed to, "Maybe next year."

After Centre kicked off, the Wildcats again hit an impregnable defense, the Colonels simply racking up every Kentucky attempt with vicious gang tackling. After another punt, Covey hit Hope Hudgins, back in action after missing the Louisville game due to his broken nose against Harvard. The little back hauled in the 20 yarder and stepped across the line. Covey missed the extra point, and the score was 27-3.

Centre was driving and was on the Wildcats' four yard line when the final whistle blew.

Red Roberts had dominated during the final 30 minutes, his 225 pounds unmovable on defense. He was either running over Kentucky players when he carried the ball, or brushing them aside or flattening them when running interference for his teammates.

Toward the end of the game, the Centre fans picked up on the Kentucky student's song that had so riled up the big redhead.

Old Red Roberts IS what he used to be,
IS what he used to be—
IS what he used to be.
Old Red Roberts IS what he used to be,
He'll be for many games more.

There was a cheerleader named Yeager who wrote out the words and asked us to pass them around, and after a lot of us had read the lyrics, he signaled and we started singing.

I can hear it to this day.

He'll be for many games more,
He'll be for many games more.
Old Red Roberts IS what he used to be,
He'll be for many games more.

I couldn't sing then and can't now, but I was chiming right in there with everybody else.

Red later said he could hear us singing, and it made him feel awfully good.

The statistics painted the picture about how totally the Colonels controlled the 2nd half. At Harvard, Centre had won the stats and lost the game. There was no such dichotomy in Lexington, Kentucky on November 4, 1922.

Centre had 21 first downs during the 2nd half to Kentucky's three, making the margin for the Colonels 23-8 for the game.

The Colonels completed five of 16 passes for 104 yards. The Wildcats connected on two of eight for 11 yards.

On the ground, Centre rushed for 258 yards, the Wildcats, 139, and the total yardage found the boys from Danville up 362 to 150. It was a measure about how Centre had outpaced their great rival, Kentucky, during the post-World War I years, that Wildcat fans left Stoll Field feeling that their team had made great progress. They were correct in a way. 27-3 was better than 56-0. It was better than 49-0 or 55-0. Kentucky wasn't there yet, but the 'Cats were closing the margin, albeit slowly.

Meanwhile, Centre was 6-1, with Washington and Lee, Auburn and South Carolina left to complete the season.

After the game, a staff photographer for the "Courier-Journal", Charles Betz, raced out to the Lexington airport carrying a valuable cargo. He met Lieutenant Albert M. Woody who was sitting in an airplane owned by A. H. Bowman of Louisville. The engine was running, and Betz jumped in the back seat and put on a leather helmet and goggles. They taxied out onto the grass runway, revved up the engine, and eased into the sky, heading west toward Louisville.

A front had come in after the game. It was drizzling and getting dark. The pilot and photographer were determined, however, to make the flight. Their goal was to have the film which Betz had taken get to Louisville in time to be developed for the evening printing of the Sunday morning "Courier-Journal".

Lt. Woody had to steer by compass. The ceiling was so low that he couldn't pick up any landmarks. After an hour of flying, and a lot of luck, Betz shouted out that he could see the lights of Louisville on the horizon, filtering up through the low hanging clouds. The intrepid pilot brought the plane down as low as he dared, circling in the rain, the open cockpit providing no protection.

"Over there," Betz hollered, while tugging on Woody's shoulder.

A.H Bowman, owner of Bowman Field on Taylorsville Road, had circled his airport with flares, and the bright white lights were visible enough to assure Lt. Moody that he was indeed on the right course. The plane circled and descended toward the flares, the landing area coming slowly into view. After a couple of hard bumps, the plane settled on the grass and came to a stop. A car raced out and the driver beckoned for Betz to hop in.

"We have a deadline. Let's go!"

Betz thanked Lt. Woody and ran to the car, and off they went, racing at full speed to the Courier-Journal building in downtown Louisville.

The photographs of the Centre-Kentucky game were in the first edition of the paper which hit the streets at 9:00 that night, and in the later editions delivered all over the city by the next morning.

None of the many thousands of readers had any idea how perilous the journey had been to allow them to be published in such a timely manner. None except one brave young pilot, and one adventurous photographer. Such was the importance of Centre's football team during that era.

A LITTLE CORRECTION IMPORTANT TO MRS. HENRY MEIER

The Danville "Messenger" carried a "correction" in the November 7 edition. It seemed that the Women's Club had held a pageant and Mrs. Henry Meier was reported to have played "The Spirit of Ignorance," when actually she had filled the role of "The Spirit of Christian Education."

It wasn't divulged exactly how such a grievous error could have been made, especially when the paper had reported that Mrs. Meier "played her part well, and deserved special mention." Apparently Mrs. Meier was not amused.

NOVEMBER 11, 1922   CENTRE-WASHINGTON & LEE

One of the main things I remember about the Washington and Lee game was the decorations all over the downtown in Louisville. Howard and I went over on the train and were picked up again by Uncle Theo and Aunt Mary's chauffeur, and he drove us through the downtown, and just like in the previous years, the areas around the Seelbach and all along Fourth Street and Walnut Street were just covered in gold and white. Of course, we'd played in Louisville the previous three years, and the alumni association seemed like they tried to outdo themselves each time to get our colors hanging from anything they could reach, or wrapped around every pole or column in the area.

The Generals were 4-1-1 on the season.

W&L	85	Emory and Henry	0
W&L	14	North Carolina State	6
W&L	13	Carson-Newman	0
W&L	12	West Virginia	12
W&L	6	Virginia	22

The tie with West Virginia proved what had been known for some time in football circles. W&L, like Centre, could more than hold its own with the large, state schools. The game against the Mountaineers, played in Charleston, W. Va., proved to be the only blemish in an otherwise 10-0-1 season for West Virginia. (Interestingly, the boys from West Virginia capped their season by traveling to San Diego and playing in the same Christmas Bowl as Centre had the year before. The game was actually played on Christmas Day, and West Virginia beat Gonzaga, 21-13.)

The tie in Charleston, and the next week's loss in Charlottesville to Virginia, proved to be costly for the Generals. By the time the team was ready to travel to Louisville, Captain Mattox, the quarterback, four other regulars, and the backup quarterback named Frew, were out with injuries.

Coach Jimmie DeHart was interviewed and quoted in the "Messenger" as saying, "I dislike offering excuses, but in all frankness, I must say my team is in poor shape."

Unlike W&L, Centre came out of the Louisville and Kentucky contests in good shape. The only injury was to Case Thomasson, and Case was injured not in battle on the gridiron, but in combat on an even more dangerous battlefield, the chemistry lab in Young Hall.

We were in the lab, and of course, most of us didn't have any idea what we were doing. Anyway, my station was right across the table from Case, and he was reading the manual we had and trying to follow the instructions. He poured some liquids out of different containers into this beaker and smoke came rushing out which I suppose he thought was ok, so then he put the thing over the flame of our Bunsen burner and there was this big explosion, and to tell you the truth, it nearly scared me to death. It sounded like some bomb had gone off, and I hit the floor, and when I got up, Case was white as a sheet and there was blood dripping from his hand.

Fortunately, he didn't get cut anywhere but his hand, but there were some pretty significant lacerations. We got them wrapped up in a towel and Dr. Coolidge came running in and he called off the lab and rushed Case to the hospital.

The papers reported that Case had been injured so badly that he'd have to miss the W&L game. They underestimated Uncle Charlie who was skilled in developing protective gear for his players, even if the "snorkel" for Bo's nose injury had been less than a great success.

At the W&L game, Case's hand looked something like an Egyptian mummy, but Uncle Charlie had wrapped it so he could use his fingers just enough to be able to hold the ball. Case made the trip, and he and Hump shared time in the backfield.

Speaking of Hump, I've said before that Hump was the class wit. He always had something to say. He was a good speaker, and he was also funny. Anyway, in chemistry lab, Hump would holler out, "Case Alert!" whenever Case got ready to do anything with chemicals, and when Case was through, Hump would holler, "It's safe now. Case closed!"

Centre beat W&L decisively, but the outmanned Generals made it a fight, and earned the appreciation of the overflow crowd of more than 10,000 which jammed Eclipse Field.

I still have my program from the game, and I kept score by pencilling in the points in each quarter. Here's what I wrote.

	1st	2nd	3rd	4th	Final
W&L	6	0	0	0	6
Centre	7	6	7	7	27

Centre scored quickly, with Red leading Covey on a 45 yard dash which a reporter described as "a twisting, stiff-arming, ducking, dodging and side-stepping dash down the field for a score."

W&L made its only concerted drive after receiving the kickoff. There was nothing fancy, just good hard-nosed football. Bruce Dudley was in the press box for the Louisville "Herald."

The shock of the touchdown shook the Colonels quite a bit, and from then on the Generals, despite the courage of their efforts, did not seriously menace the Centre goal.

Quick slants by Covey and Hudgins, a Covey to Lemon 23 yard pass, and three straight line thrusts by Hump made it 13-6 at the half. Hennie Lemon missed his first extra point after being good on 16 straight.

Centre dominated the 2nd quarter, picking up 11 first downs to one for W&L. Bruce Dudley recounted the play after the half.

On the third play after the start of the third period, Hope Hudgins intercepted a pass from Hamilton and as coolly as Eliza picked her way across the ice, he picked his way through the field of Generals for 50 yards, and reposed the ball back of the goal posts. When halfway to the touchdown, Hudgins discovered three Generals waiting for him. Calmly, he reversed his field, then retraced his steps and stoically continued without further heckling. Lemon booted the ball squarely between the posts. (For those readers who aren't totally familiar with "Eliza," she was a character played by Mary Pickford in D.W. Griffith's 1920 production of "Way Down East.")

Covington scored the last touchdown in the 4th quarter on a 30 yard run, Lemon kicked, and the game ended, 27-6.

Uncle Charlie always tried to get any hometown boys in the game if possible. Jimmie Green, who had played at Louisville's Boys High, was given a standing ovation when he replaced Hope Hudgins.

During the game, the crowd kept shouting, "lock-step!"

Centre ran one play from the formation, picking up five yards. Centre gained 393 yards on the ground and completed four of nine passes for 76 yards, resulting in a lopsided margin over W&L of 469 yards to 137. In first downs, it was 21-9.

After the game, the Centre alumni held a dinner and dance for both teams at the Seelbach. The players "acted like brothers, not competitors," according to the wife of one of the sponsors.

Of course, that was the norm. Centre played hard. Centre played to win. But Centre's players handled themselves in a manner which assured that they left the field having won the admiration and friendship of whomever they met along the way.

After all—"We are Centre!"

NOVEMBER 18, 1922 CENTRE-AUBURN IN BIRMINGHAM

During the W&L game in Louisville, Uncle Charlie had allowed J.P. Fitts to sit on the Centre bench, scouting the Colonels for Auburn, the next opponent. It was the way things were done, and only proper because Auburn had allowed Jim Bond, Centre's assistant coach, to sit on its bench on November 4 when the Tigers played and beat Georgia, 7-3, in Columbus, Georgia.

Bond came back to Danville and reported that Centre would have its hands full against Auburn. The Colonels had won the previous year, 21-0, but the Tigers were much improved and were eager to avenge the 1921 defeat.

Auburn was 7-1, the only loss having come at the hands of a strong Army team at West Point, 19-6. Army was a powerhouse in 1922, going 8-0-2, the ties being with Notre Dame (8-1-1) and Yale (6-3-1).

Auburn	61	Marion	0
Auburn	72	Howard	0
Auburn	19	Spring Hill	6
Auburn	6	Army	19
Auburn	50	Mercer	6
Auburn	30	Fort Benning	0
Auburn	7	Georgia	3
Auburn	19	Tulane	0

The game was being billed as the "Championship of Dixie." If the Colonels won, they could reasonably make that claim, having beaten Clemson, Mississippi, Virginia

Tech, Kentucky and W&L, with South Carolina not expected to provide too much opposition in the closing game of the season.

Carson-Newman was definitely in the South, being in Tennessee, and Louisville was also, if barely, but neither figured in the equation regarding the possibility of a Southern championship, as neither was a member of the Southern Conference.

Auburn still had to meet Georgia Tech in its final game, after Centre, and any claim the Tigers may make on the championship had to take Tech into consideration.

Nonetheless, Centre knew that if it got by Auburn, and beat South Carolina, the Colonels would have a legitimate claim as being the best team below the Mason-Dixon Line, as well as being one of the best in the country.

The Southern Railroad once again put a package together for Kentuckians to go to Birmingham. The round trip Pullman fare was priced at $38.50. At the same time, the agent in charge helped with the arrangements for the freshman team to go to Chicago to play Keewatin Academy. It was really quite a weekend. Little Centre College was sending Chick Murphy and 18 freshmen to Chicago, where they would be joined by the Chief, while Uncle Charlie, Jim Bond and Jim Kendrick were taking 25 members of the varsity to Birmingham. When coaches, managers and trainers were added, over 50 people connected to the football program were going to be on the road the weekend of November 17-19.

Was it just a few short years ago that Centre had trouble finding enough young men available to even have a scrimmage?

Well, it was time to once again to go over to Cousin Ella's. I knew that she and her husband were really wealthy, probably worth more than anyone in Boyle County. But dadbummit, it got to be sort of embarrassing always going over to see her with my hand out. But she was always nice, and eventually she'd say, "Now Red, do you need a little money? I see there's football game coming up."

Cousin Ella was quite a fan of the team, like everybody in Danville. So she told me before the trip to Birmingham that she and her husband really wanted to go to the game, but couldn't for some reason. She asked me if I'd go and come back and have dinner with them and tell them everything that happened over the weekend.

I told her that I supposed maybe I could do just that. I didn't even have to ask her, she just went and got that little purse and came back with two $20.00 gold pieces. And she said I was her "personal reporter," and reporters got paid to report.

That's how I got to the Auburn game. I'd been Howard Reynolds' assistant at the Harvard game, and I was going to be Cousin Ella's reporter in Birmingham.

Centre had been treated royally during the previous year's journey to play Auburn in Birmingham, and the 1922 trip was no different. The Colonels were staying at the Tutwiler again, and were to be guests at an affair Friday night at the hotel hosted by Kentuckians living in the Birmingham area.

For Auburn, the Centre game was the biggest on its schedule. The Tigers were somewhat like Centre in playing most of their significant games on the road. In 1922, Auburn played Marion, Mercer and Fort Benning at home, hardly stellar attractions. Army was at West Point, and Howard was an away game on the Howard campus in Birmingham. Spring Hill and Tulane were at Montgomery. Georgia was at Columbus, and Georgia Tech was to be played in Atlanta.

Auburn was treating the Centre game as somewhat of a Homecoming event, since the three actual home games hadn't been sufficient draws to attract the alumni back to the campus.

The Optimist Club of Birmingham was going to take the Tigers to the Roebuck Country Club for lunch Friday, and the team was going to conduct a signal drill on a Roebuck fairway which was open to all fans who wished to attend. The Southern Club was hosting a big dinner and reception for all of the alumni on Friday evening.

Tickets simply weren't available. Each of the 17,000 seats at Rickwood Field was long gone, and a report stated that, "none can be begged, borrowed or stolen." It was another standing room only event for the Colonels, as usual.

Intermittent showers occurred on the day of the game, but nothing could have deterred those who were going to the game. The newspapers reported 20,000 squeezed into and around Rickwood, and the contest "attracted the greatest crowd ever to see a sporting event in Birmingham." The game was beautifully played. There was one five yard penalty against the Colonels. Auburn didn't draw a flag all day. Basically it was a defensive struggle. Auburn's offense never got closer than the Colonels' 40. Centre never got inside the Tigers' 35.

Halfway through the 3rd quarter, Auburn's captain, left half Shirley, boomed a punt which put Centre deep into its own territory. The Colonels ran the ball three times for minimal yardage as the Tigers played great defense. On 4th down, Red lined up to punt and stood on his five yard line. Left tackle Grisham broke through and got his hand on the ball as it left Red's shoe.

"A mad scramble of blue and gold jerseys fought for possession," was how it was reported. The slick ball was like grease, and several times it looked like someone had smothered it when it would shoot back out and both teams would again try to make the claim. Finally, the Tigers' left end, Moulton, fell on the ball in the end zone. Moulton's extra point effort was no good. The blocked kick was the game, as the final score was 6-0. Statistically, it was a dead heat, as both teams picked up eight first downs.

One thing was certain as the soaked players left the field. The game had been a classic between two excellent teams. There was an instant groundswell for a rematch, a rubber game, in 1923, and before Centre even left Birmingham Saturday night for the long ride back to Danville, both schools had agreed to meet again, at Rickwood Field, in Birmingham, on a weekend in November.

Sometimes you lose a game and realize that it was just meant to be. Those of us who were in Birmingham that afternoon were as proud of our team as we could be.

We had fought hard and played with great heart. Of course, we'd have loved to come home as victors, but nobody really lost that game, and everybody agreed that it would have been wonderful if the two teams had tied, they were that close. And that's the way Cousin Ella's reporter described it at dinner one night after I returned.

She said, "Oh, Red. It seems just like I was there! I must send my little reporter to other games."

And again, I told her that perhaps we could work something out.

Centre received a detailed financial report from Auburn after returning back to Danville.

Auburn Polytechnic Institute
Auburn Athletic Association
Auburn, Alabama

Income:	$24, 727.56*

*See later "Additional Ticket Sales Added in."

Expenses:

Park Rent	3,709.10
Centre's Expenses	1,332.78
Auburn's Expenses	627.38
To Birmingham for Placing Tickets	19.77
Ticket Takers	109.76
Ticket Counters	20.00
Advertising	435.20
Thomas, Lineman	75.00
Van Surdam, Referee	203.58
Williams, Umpire	141.98
Total	6,674.55
Net Gate	$18, 053.01

Additional Ticket Sales at Auburn		
240 Tickets at $2.50	600.00	
126 Tickets at $2.00	252.00	
Total	$852.00	
Park Rent —15% of Additional Sales		127.80
Net —Additional Ticket Sales		$724.20
50% of Net Gate		$9,026.50

456

50% of Additional Sales at Auburn	362.10
Adjustment Rate of 1033 Tickets @ $0.25	258.25
Due Centre	$9,646.86
Paid Centre, Expenses	1,332.72
Total to Centre	**$10,979.58**

It was amazing that during this era, Centre could play a game in which all of its expenses were paid and still clear nearly $10,000 for a Saturday afternoon. It would have been close to $100,000 in today's valuation of the dollar. It needs to be pointed out also that many times, expenses for meals, banquets, and receptions were paid by Centre alumni who wanted to have some way to contribute to the team's success and experiences.

After the Auburn game, everyone who had gone to Birmingham headed back to Danville on a Saturday night train. Everybody, that is, except one very important person. Uncle Charlie said he was going to stay over since there was no game for 12 days, until the November 30, season ending, Thanksgiving contest with South Carolina.

"I'm going to give the boys a couple of days off, let them rest a bit. They deserve it."

This made everyone in Danville terribly nervous, because there were rumors. It was well known that representatives from the University of Alabama had been at Rickwood Field.

"Why were they there?"

It was said that Alabama wanted to get Centre on its schedule in 1923.

"Is there some additional reason?"

It was unusual that just Uncle Charlie stayed behind, alone.

"What in the world is going on?"

Alabama actually did want to play Centre during the next season, if possible, and if not, sometime in the future. But the real reason its people were in Birmingham was to try to hire Uncle Charlie to coach its football team.

Xen C. Scott had been the Crimson Tide's coach since 1919, compiling a 27-9-3 record at the time that Uncle Charlie decided to stay behind and hear what the Alabamians had to say. It wasn't that Coach Scott was being let go. Far from it. He was tremendously popular and respected, and had brought stability to a program which had nine coaches since 1900.

Scott was unfortunately losing a bout with throat cancer and would die after the 1922 season. It was obvious that he wasn't going to be able to return, that Alabama was going to need a new mentor, and it was felt that Uncle Charlie, one of the most successful coaches in the history of football, at the absolute peak of his career and popularity, was just the man needed in Tuscaloosa.

The Alabamians couldn't help but be impressed with what Charles. B. Moran had accomplished. His 38-8-4 record at Texas A&M, combined with being 44-5 with Centre at the time, meant that, excluding ties, he won at an 86.3% clip. Uncle Charlie was right at the top when listing the "best of the best" in the college football coaching hierarchy.

The Danville papers were apoplectic. The "Messenger" printed an editorial on November 21 while Uncle Charlie was still in Birmingham.

CAN CENTRE LET MORAN GO?

Is Centre College going to let Charlie Moran leave Danville and sign up with another school as football coach? The Horse Cave wizard, who is recognized as a football authority from coast to coast, has received several offers to go elsewhere next season. Many of these offers call for twice and one for three times the amount he is drawing at the local institution. The University of Alabama is making every effort to land him down there. Representatives of the Southern university have held several conferences with Mr. Moran and are determined to land him.

What are local supporters and alumni doing while all of this is going on? Standing idly by, marking time. Charlie Moran came here in 1917 when victories were as rare as Republican majorities in Boyle County elections.

While Coach Moran has been in charge here, the team has gone up from what one may term "bush" to major league ball. We want to keep in the "big time," and we want and must have Charlie Moran here to keep us in the spotlight. Unless there is someone like Charlie Moran here, we will never again have a "Wonder Team," and can look in the near future when Centre will again be playing Transylvania, Georgetown, and teams of that caliber.

Keep Coach Moran here, and Centre is assured of taking on the leading elevens of the country, and trouncing them.

Will Danville and Centre let Charlie Moran get away? Has Centre seen the golden sunset of athletic achievement? Are dark clouds about to descend over the camp, or will steps be taken to keep Charlie Moran here?

With Moran back on the job, we will enjoy another golden dawn as magnificent as the one that visited Danville on the morning of November 4, 1917, when supporters rubbed their eyes after our Colonels defeated Kentucky, and Centre found that it was again the "Kentucky Champion" in gridiron circles.

Again we cry, "Keep Moran here!"

It was real tense when we didn't know what Uncle Charlie was planning on doing. Uncle Charlie WAS Centre football. Since Howard and I had first followed Centre's team, it was Uncle Charlie who made it happen. We just couldn't imagine his leaving, and nobody else could either. It was all anyone talked about, all over the campus and town.

Then we heard that he was back. And even better, he was talking about the schedule in 1923, and he was talking about a new stadium.

Everybody thought, "This is good. Somebody doesn't start planning for the next year, and somebody doesn't start talking about building something like a stadium, if they're leaving."

It was never inferred that Coach Moran was using a little leverage to get both an increase in salary, and to finally have the administration approve his plans for a new facility. But who would have blamed him?

He'd coached the most successful program in the country for basically nothing. He'd labored under the handicap of not being able to attract the big, established programs to Danville due to the antiquated stadium.

Centre and the great coach came to an understanding. Alabama ended up hiring Wallace Wade away from his assistant coaching job at Vanderbilt. Wade stayed from 1923 through the 1930 season, compiling a 61-13-3 record. He took the Crimson Tide to three Rose Bowls, winning over Washington and Washington State and tying Stanford.

Alabama did indeed get Centre on its schedule, not in 1923, but the following year. Everything settled down, and the townspeople and the Colonels were now able to concentrate on the upcoming game with South Carolina.

THE SEASON ENDS, CENTRE-SOUTH CAROLINA
NOVEMBER 30, 1922

Centre was 7-2. South Carolina was coming to Danville on Thanksgiving, November 30, to close out the season. The traditional turkey day opponent, Georgetown, was still unwilling to place its neck on the chopping block, quite wisely.

It was important to beat South Carolina. An 8-2 team which lost two tough games on the road, against Harvard and Auburn, would be an attractive opponent in 1923. It would have a much easier time firming up a game with a big-time college in the East, than a 7-3 squad which closed with a loss to a just average South Carolina.

Centre planned to beat the Gamecocks, but the college and Danville also wanted to "roll out the red carpet" for the visitors. Everyone reflected on how wonderfully the Colonels and their followers had been treated on their travels over the last several years.

Indianapolis had pulled out all the stops when Centre played DePauw there. Charlottesville had been gracious hosts. The courtesies shown in Fort Worth at the "Classic," and everywhere the team visited on the long Western journey—St. Louis, Denver, San Francisco, Los Angeles, Dallas, and most certainly San Diego and El Paso had been so nice. That's the only way that Centre's administration, coaching staff and team could describe it.

Everybody had been so—nice!

How about the torch light welcome in Tucson?

"For they are jolly good fellows...."

Birmingham, Clemson, Bloomington, Chattanooga, Richmond, Charleston in West Virginia, the people in Louisville and Lexington—everyone had knocked themselves out to make the team feel welcome. Even in Atlanta, where the team was disappointed with the Georgia Tech play, the fans had packed the stadium, and for the most part, treated the Colonels wonderfully.

Cincinnati and New Orleans? Great experiences.

Maryville in Tennessee, and certainly Winchester, Kentucky, and old rivals

Georgetown and Transylvania—all had provided pleasant memories.

Boston and Harvard?

As Uncle Charlie often said, "Salt of the earth. They are peaches, absolute peaches. Salt of the earth."

Centre and Danville hadn't been provided many opportunities to go all out for visitors. There was the matter of accommodations. The two hotels on Main Street, the Gilcher and Henson, filled quickly when there were events in the city. And the several "rooming houses," were usually occupied by "regulars" who were in town for business.

The Danville Chamber of Commerce contacted a representative of the Southern Railroad office in Columbia, South Carolina, and asked to be supplied with the names of "250 of the leading citizens of the state." On the list that came back were prominent residents including the governor and other state politicians, mayors of several of the larger cities, the president of the university, and major figures in business and the professions.

Each received an invitation to "spend the weekend in Danville as our guests," and the response was heartening. W.A. Coleman, the mayor of Columbia, accepted, as did a state senator, Thomas Pearce, who had made a fortune in the wholesale food business. Judge J. Needles and his wife wired that they were coming, and the acceptances kept rolling in until over 100 had signed on to "spend the weekend in Danville."

What about that nickname? Danvillians discovered that the "Gamecocks" had been so named after a 1902 story had reported that the football team, "fought like gamecocks."

In the week leading up to the Thanksgiving game, a novel athletic event was held. Uncle Charlie and the Chief, who had come down from Chicago, decided it was important to get another game for the 23 man freshman squad.

Several calls resulted in no interest, but when the University of Louisville was contacted, the attitude was, "Why not?"

Louisville was eager to get its program to the next level in whatever way it could. Centre proposed that the varsity team of the Cardinals, the same team that Centre met and beat, 32-7, on October 28, come down to Danville for a game on Saturday, November 25. Louisville agreed.

Naturally, the freshmen wanted to beat Louisville by a greater margin than the Centre varsity, and the Lieutenants, as they were called, drilled hard under the tutelage of Chick Murphy, with Uncle Charlie and his assistants helping out.

On game day, each of the varsity except Red, who was watching Harvard and Yale in New Haven, was behind the bench, cheering the first year men on. Centre won 32-0, eclipsing the margin of the varsity, which the freshmen naturally repeated every time they had the opportunity.

"You guys let them score on you? You just beat Louisville by 25 points?"

The good natured ribbing continued all of the school year.

The freshman team finished 3-2, splitting with Kentucky, beating Keewatin Academy and Louisville, and losing to Sewanee.

South Carolina came to Danville with a 5-3 record, the losing margins adding up to only a total of seven points.

South Carolina	13	Erskine	0
South Carolina	7	Presbyterian	0
South Carolina	7	North Carolina	10
South Carolina	20	Wofford	0
South Carolina	0	Clemson	3
South Carolina	6	Sewanee	7
South Carolina	27	Furman	7
South Carolina	13	Citadel	0

Clemson was a common opponent of Centre and Carolina, with the Colonels winning 21-0, and the Gamecocks being blanked, 3-0. While Centre was certainly favored, South Carolina had played a very tough North Carolina squad to a virtual standstill in a game played at Chapel Hill, losing only 10-7. The Tar Heels finished at 9-1, their only loss to Yale in New Haven.

While South Carolina's offense had sputtered, their defense had allowed only 27 points thus far in the season. The school's program had virtually been resurrected by Sol Metzger who took over in 1920 after a dismal 1919 campaign in which the Gamecocks were 1-7-1, scoring only 25 points all season. At the time, attendance was so poor that the football team was a drain on the school's finances. Metzger had turned the situation around after a loyal group of supporters went to the administration and board of the school and promoted him as just what the college needed to become competitive.

Metzger was a known winner, having coached at Baylor, Pennsylvania, Oregon State, West Virginia, and Washington and Jefferson, plus he wrote a nationally syndicated column, "Gridiron Questions and Answers."

The Danville Chamber and Centre lined up a "fleet of cars" to ferry the visiting South Carolinians around town and out to some of the nicer farms when they arrived. There was a dinner for both teams Friday night at K.C.W., and a big reception at the Centre library in honor of the Carolina fans prior to the game. The merchants had paid for sashes and badges for the men, and corsages for the ladies, all composed of the Gamecock's red and black colors.

Jop wrote that while everyone in Danville welcomed the guests, it was hoped that they'd only need the black part of their identifying colors after the game.

The contest was to be the last for four very important members of the Centre College football program. Red Roberts, Ben Cregor, Terry Snowday and Hump Tanner were going to be representing the Gold and White against South Carolina, and then their careers would be over. Red and Ben had been stalwarts since 1918, having stayed the extra year due to not having 1918 count against their eligibility. Terry Snowday, after leaving the University of Kentucky, had been a fixture since the undefeated season of 1919, and Hump since 1920. (Hump was technically only a junior, at least academically. However, he had used up his eligibility since he played at Colorado in 1919.)

It was appropriate that the last game for the four seniors was going to be played in perfect weather, before a crowd which filled every seat at Cheek Field. The spectators were warmed up by the Centre "Six" which had been set up along the 50 yard line. Centre showed wonderful Southern hospitality by first acknowledging the five South Carolina seniors who were also playing their last game.

"Captain Waite, left tackle"
"McMillan, left guard"
"Lindsey, right guard"
"Fulton, quarterback"
"Coker, left end"

Each of the Gamecocks was given a big cheer by the appreciative crowd as they ran out onto the field, waving. Then it was bedlam. Two seniors who had always been there, who hadn't been of the superstar caliber, but were valuable members of the team, were introduced first.

"Dewey Kimbel from Louisville, Kentucky!"
"Charles Cecil from Danville, Kentucky!"

Then—

"Ben Cregor, Springfield, Kentucky. All-Kentucky, All-Southern, right tackle!"
"John Porter "Hump" Tanner, Owensboro, Kentucky. All-Kentucky, All-Southern, fullback!"
"Terry Snowday , Owensboro, Kentucky. All-Kentucky, All-Southern, honorable mention, All-American!"
"Captain James "Red" Roberts, Somerset, Kentucky. All-Kentucky, All-Southern, All-American!"

I thought the game would never get started. People stood and cheered so long that I was afraid it would be dark before the kick-off. The seniors walked around the circumference of the field, and Red, Ben, Hump and Terry circled a second time, waving, and while there were smiles on their faces, there were tears coming down their cheeks, and there was hardly a dry eye in the stands. Even the South Carolina fans were standing and cheering, and the South Carolina team seemed just as pleased as everybody, and finally, they all ran out onto the field and lined up and each of them shook hands with our seniors.

I know that Bo was loved, and so were Red Weaver and Army—as were all of those who had graduated before. But I believe these were the best loved of all. They had played so well, and they had always conducted themselves so perfectly. It was hard to let them go, and I think that everyone felt that the longer they cheered, the longer they'd have Red, Ben, Hump and Terry to remember.

I caught Red's eye as I was whistling. I could always whistle really loudly by putting my index and little fingers in my mouth. I know that I could see Red form the words, "My son," as he waved to me.

Centre never played a more perfect game than it did that Thanksgiving afternoon against a decent South Carolina team. Centre racked up 25 first downs to four for the Gamecocks. In the whole 60 minutes of play, South Carolina only ran 24 plays, and those 24 efforts resulted in but 79 yards. The Colonels hit on 18 of 27 passes for 271 yards. They picked up another 514 yards on the ground in 73 rushes. Of those ground gainers, Covey picked up 385 yards in 40 carries, over nine and a half yards per effort.

Overall, Centre gained 785 yards on an even 100 plays, an average of 7.85 yards every time a member of the Gold and White touched the ball! And this was against a team that all season had surrendered only three touchdowns and two field goals, a team which took great pride in its defensive strength.

Red Roberts, Terry Snowday, Herb Covington, Hope Hudgins, Hump Tanner, and senior Charles Cecil, all scored. Hennie Lemon kicked four extra points and Red got two.

The Colonels tried to let Ben Cregor score, this time for real. Covey lined him up near the goal and handed off the ball. Old "Baldy" crashed into the line and was stopped short. It was about the only failure in the 42-0 victory over the Gamecocks.

Coach Metzger came into the Colonels' dressing room after the game and asked everyone to let him say a few words. He congratulated Ben, Terry, Hump and Red on their sterling careers, and he congratulated the Colonels on their wonderful display of football. Then the veteran coach turned to Uncle Charlie while he continued to speak.

"Charlie, I played on some wonderful teams, and played against some great squads while I was enrolled at Pennsylvania in the early 1900's. I've coached some very talented teams and we played against major colleges all over the country. But Charlie, I want you to know that today I saw the greatest exhibition of football that I've ever seen, or feel I'll ever see in the future. I congratulate you for what you have done here in Danville. My boys were privileged to have been on the same field as yours."

Before the team left the dressing room, there was a short meeting in which Ed Kubale was elected team captain for 1923. The big center, probably the one new-comer who could have come in and replaced an All-American, Red Weaver, was a typical Centre man who led by example both on and off the field.

There was a big dance to be held in the Boyle-Humphrey Gymnasium the night after the game, but first all of the visitors and both teams traveled by automobile out to a pig roast hosted by the Blue Goose Club at the Cliff Dwellers' Club House on the Dix River. Governor Morrow and his wife were in attendance.

Jop reported that Uncle Charlie presided at the party, "as the chief carver, and wielded a wicked knife."

POST-SEASON HAPPENINGS

Immediately after the South Carolina game, the local newspapers started a campaign for the Colonels to go to another post-season game out West. Centre pointed out that the S.I.A.A. frowned on such appearances.

"But why? It's during the Christmas vacation and the players won't miss any classes."

Of course, the papers were correct, and it seemed like a logical argument.

West Virginia and Gonzaga played in San Diego's second, and last, Christmas Bowl game. Southern Cal beat Penn State in the Rose Bowl, and that was it for bowls after the 1922 season. It was felt Centre most certainly could have gotten the invitation to the Rose Bowl if the school had lobbied for it, and been able to travel to California.

As it was, the promoters of the Pasadena New Year's Day event had to settle for a 6-3-1 Penn State team which had lost to Navy, Penn and Pittsburgh, and tied Syracuse.

While Centre stayed at home, several of the former and current players didn't. There was another charity game in Columbus, Ohio. Army, who had been at Centenary assisting his old teammate, came up from Louisiana with Bo. Chick Murphy and Red went up from Danville. It was a reunion of Colonels who had put on the uniform together in so many contests over the years.

Bo captained the West team, and his squad won 6-0 in front of 20,000 spectators.

At the annual football banquet, letters were handed out to:

Tom Bartlett
Charles Cecil
Herb Covington
Ben Cregor
Minos Gordy
Jim Green
Hope Hudgins
Clarence Jones
George Jones
Dewey Kimbel
Ed Kubale
Hennie Lemon
Jim Liggett
Howard Lynch
Red Roberts
Frank Rubarth
Bill Shadoan
Terry Snowday
Hump Tanner
Case Thomasson
Jerome Berryman—manager

After the awarding of the coveted gold "C" to the recipients, Dr. Charles Allen, Chairman of the Athletic Board, held up a white, shawl-collared sweater which had a gold "C" sewn on the left, front side.

"We feel honored to present this letter-sweater to our good friend, Mr. Howard Reynolds of the Boston "Post." Mr. Reynolds has kept the colors of Centre in the hearts of people all over the East. We now feel it proper that he wear our colors as a member of the Gold and White."

When word reached Boston, a large cartoon appeared in the "Post" showing a sweater flying through the air and wrapping its arms around a surprised Reynolds.

The caption: "Oh gosh, just look what happened to our sporting department."

Reynolds was interviewed.

"Not bad that a 44 year old daddy can letter in football!"

He was so genuinely moved that he wired Dr. Allen that he was coming to Danville to accept the award in person.

"You know, I love to come to Danville and see all of my friends there. I'll be down in the spring."

Howard Reynolds, the best friend that Centre College ever had, indeed did take the long train ride down from Boston and was seen around town, beaming, as he greeted folks on the street, sporting his white sweater with the gold "C."

Uncle Charlie headed to his farm at Horse Cave after the banquet to do some serious bird hunting. He invited Herb Covington to come down and the Centre quarterback proved to be as accurate with a shotgun as he was at throwing a pass.

Dr. Allen kept the coach and the Chief informed about offers flooding into Danville wanting to put the Colonels on their schedule for 1923.

Michigan wanted a game in Ann Arbor. Alabama tried again to interest Centre. Georgia sent word, "Come to Athens." Colgate wanted a game in New York and had Grantland Rice intervene on its behalf. Other writers in New York were promoting Centre and Penn in Yankee stadium as had been previously proposed.

There was a suggestion that Centre come to New Haven, but Yale let it be known that it would honor the pledge that it had made with other members of the "Big 3" that the Bulldogs wouldn't schedule any intersectional games. How about Penn State rather than either Colgate or Penn at Yankee Stadium?

Clemson wanted a rematch, as did Auburn. The city of Louisville was lobbying for another visit by the Colonels. Memphis made an attractive offer for the Colonels to come south and play a Tennessee team, either Vandy, Tennessee or Sewanee, whichever could be arranged.

Interest in Centre only intensified when Harvard reported that the Crimson had played in front of record crowds and generated record income during the 1922 season, spurred on by the sell-out with Centre.

Harvard played in front of 338,916 spectators. The Yale game in New Haven drew 74,013. The official paid attendance at the Centre game was 48,842, but it was accepted that there were actually more than 50,000 who were there. Florida attracted 20,017. The other dates for the Middlebury, Holy Cross, Bowdoin, Dartmouth, Princeton and Brown drew a total of 196,044.

Of course, Kentucky, Centre's biggest rival, was going to have to be penned in on the 1923 schedule.

There were two constants which were considered in planning the upcoming season. Centre hoped to have a new stadium in place, and to host teams in its new facility. Also, Uncle Charlie, the Chief and members of the athletic department wanted to have at least one big game in the East. The Harvard games had been such a positive force in building public awareness of the little college that everyone agreed that the publicity gained from playing a strong Eastern squad was essential.

Frank Menke's column in the Washington "Herald," published at the same time that Centre was working on the games for 1923, reinforced how Centre had benefited from its leap into big-time football.

Fully fifty percent of the tremendous increase in college enrollments in the past few years has been directly due to the interest in football. A perfect example is Centre College down in Kentucky. About 109,900,000 of the folks in these United States didn't know three or four years ago that such a place existed, but now, because of Bo McMillin and the other brilliant "Praying Colonels," Centre is one of the best known colleges in all of the land.

Bearing out Menke's assertion, Centre's rise to prominence in the world of college football, and thus in the public's awareness, paralleled its increased enrollment.

CLASS	ENROLLMENT
1918/19	134 (Centre's S.A.T.C. war season)
1919/20	181 (The big win over West Virginia)
1920/21	191 (Harvard-31 Centre-14)
1921/22	262 (Centre-6 Harvard-0)
1922/23	284 (Harvard-24 Centre-10)
1923/24	292 (The new stadium)

Dr. Ganfield and the Chief, if they read Menke's column, must have felt terribly vindicated. It was their original vision, nurtured by Uncle Charlie's brilliant coaching, that had allowed Centre to have the dream, to follow the motto, "credendo vides," that allowed them to first believe, and then to see that belief become reality.

POST SEASON HONORS

Walter Camp's 1922 All-American selections were published in Collier's in December. No Centre player made the first three teams, and Kentuckians were incensed. Only two Southerners gained any recognition. Lynn Bomar of Vanderbilt and Georgia Tech's "Red" Barron made the second team. As upset as the Kentuckians were about Centre being snubbed was the belief that it had been an injustice not to include the Harvard quarterback, Charles Buell, and to put the great Crimson fullback, George Owen, on the second team. Harvard did garner one first team selection, Charles Hubbard, at guard.

Camp put Red, Covey and Ed Kubale in the Honorable Mention grouping.

Heywood Broun, formerly with the New York "Tribune," but currently writing for the New York "World," placed Red at fullback and Covey at quarterback on his first team, greatly influenced by having seen their play against Harvard.

About the time that Camp's selections were appearing, the 214 coaches who voted and selected the team for the nationally distributed "Athletic World," picked Red as a first team tackle, and Covington as the second team quarterback.

"Who knows better than the coaches?" was the sentiment in Danville and around the state.

The "All-Southern," All-Southern team, compiled from the All-Southern teams picked by newspapers all across the South, gave Centre three unanimous selections- Red, Covey and Kubale.

And finally there was the publicity that Red Roberts received by having a large photograph of him printed in the "Police Gazette." The "Gazette" was a nationally distributed tabloid with a circulation of 500,000, and millions of readers. You couldn't go into a barber shop, pool hall, or bar (speakeasy after prohibition), without seeing a copy of the "Police Gazette" lying around.

Shortly after the end of the 1922 season, there was a "splendid likeness of Old Nero, our Red Roberts," in the publication, according to the Danville "Messenger."

CHAPTER 21:
1923

In January, after working through the Christmas vacation, Dr. Allen announced the schedule for 1923.

Oct. 6	Carson-Newman	Danville
Oct. 13	Clemson	Danville
Oct. 20	Oglethorpe (Ga.)	Danville
Oct. 27	Pennsylvania	Philadelphia
Nov. 3	Kentucky	Danville
Nov.10	Sewanee	Memphis
Nov.17	Auburn	Birmingham
Nov.24	Washington and Lee	Louisville
Dec. 1	Georgia	Athens

An important consideration was putting six members of the Southern Conference on the schedule—Clemson, Kentucky, Sewanee, Auburn, W&L and Georgia. Centre again wanted to be in a position of playing enough of the conference's team that if it could defeat them, the little school, left behind in the small college S.I.A.A., could again make the claim of being the "class of the South."

"WE'VE GOT TO HAVE A NEW STADIUM—NOW !"
Centre had long since outgrown its football stadium. Winnie Churchill, the Harvard back who had come to Danville during Christmas vacation in 1920, actually went to Cheek Field and torn off a piece of the stands to take back to Cambridge.

The incident revealed much. You just aren't able to go to many stadiums and rip off a piece to keep as a memento! However, such was the case at Centre. The old wooden stadium had been shorn up, patched, altered, expanded when a huge crowd was expected, shrunk when a segment became too unstable, and was basically just barely holding on until some other structure could be raised and allow it to be put out of its misery. Uncle Charlie was determined to be the executioner of the old, and oversee the birth of the new.

"We've got to have a new stadium—now!"

When Uncle Charlie got into gear, things began to happen. The plans for the stadium, and the plan to finance it, went through an evolutionary process. Uncle Charlie had a friend who did a rendering and then drew up the plans for construction at no cost. It was decided to build the stadium so that the field ran north and south rather than its present east-west configuration. One reason, perhaps the main one, was that with games being played in the afternoon, the present set-up meant that the teams were battling the sun half the time, because as it set, it was directly in the players eyes when they were running their offense in that direction.

Originally, the stands were going to be constructed only between the 25 yard lines, with the ability to stretch them further toward the goal line as financing permitted. However, the revised plan called for the stadium to go the full 100 yards of the playing field.

The west stands were to be the "home" seats and the press box was to sit at the top of that portion of the structure. That side was to be a few rows higher than the east side. A track would circle the playing field, and a baseball diamond would be just west of the football stadium. A fence would circle the entire "athletic complex," and two columned gates were to be constructed at the entrance on the north side.

If Uncle Charlie could pull it off, it was going to be quite a facility, and Centre and the citizens of Danville and Kentucky would be extremely proud of what had been accomplished.

All of us were really interested in what the new stadium would look like. I remember that people were saying that it would eventually be a small Harvard Stadium. Uncle Charlie wanted to build the two sides and then enclose the south end, making it a horseshoe, and eventually put columns around the top like Harvard's. The way he had it planned, it would seat 12,000, and when the end zone part was built, it would have a capacity of over 15,000. That would accommodate any crowd, even Kentucky at Homecoming.

The proceeds from the football program had already jump-started the financing by contributing $25,000. The original scheme by Uncle Charlie was to raise the required funding by selling "pieces" of the stadium. A person could buy an inch or several inches, a foot, a yard, a section, and so forth. However, there was a new proposal defined by the slogan, "Say it with Cement!"

It was calculated that 18,000 barrels of cement would be needed to complete the stadium. A barrel cost $3.15, so approximately $57,000 would need to be raised.

Newspapers were contacted and they agreed to publicize and support the stadium building fund. Typical was sports editor Robert E. Dundon's article in the Louisville "Herald" when the campaign kicked off in March of 1923.

Centre College tomorrow starts a drive which should have the backing of every sport-loving Kentuckian. It is to obtain for this plucky little college in Boyle County, which, like

David proceeding against Goliath, carried the hopes and prayers of Kentucky over the modern Goliath of the gridiron, Harvard, in the never-to-be-forgotten fall of 1921, a modern, complete athletic stadium, a picture of which appears in today's issue of the "Herald."

Boyle Country, home of the Colonels, has started the financial ball rolling. We shall pass the good word along for Charlie Moran's plan, and trust that there shall be no slippage in this campaign to give Old Centre a home field worthy of its success abroad and here.

The stadium drive was going to be concentrated on three main forces.

First, Uncle Charlie was venerated across the state and had also made a lot of friends throughout the country. He would be the engine that propelled the whole endeavor. Secondly, Centre, though small, had prominent alumni sprinkled across the state and nation, and they would be called on to lead the effort in their communities. Lastly, the Colonels' players, past and present, had achieved such recognition, and were held in such high esteem, that they were naturals to participate in the fundraising, not only in Danville, but throughout the state.

On March 3, letters went out to alumni all over the state and nation designating certain individuals to be chairmen who would spearhead the campaign in their area. McBrayer Moore was made the statewide chairman. Louisville was to be a major focus, and the goal was to raise $15,000, slightly over one quarter of the total needed, in the city. Uncle Charlie and McBrayer Moore kicked off the Louisville effort by personally attending the organizing breakfast and "fired up the troops" with speeches.

Local Danville businesses made pledges. The motion picture theaters had designated "stadium movies" in which a percentage of the ticket sales were donated to the drive. A local lumber firm, Bland and Stagg, pledged a new scoreboard which "would be a thing of beauty and would be thoroughly in keeping with the symmetrical proportions of the structure." Joe Stagg also announced that he was sending out 200 letters to friends in the lumber business soliciting donations.

Uncle Charlie spent every available moment traveling and speaking until he had to return to his umpiring job. He'd address the Rotarians at a breakfast in Lexington and hop on a train and meet with the Kiwanis Club in Ashland in the evening. He went to Owensboro with natives, Hump, Tom Bartlett and Terry Snowday. Herb Covington and Hennie Lemon from Mayfield, accompanied their coach to an engagement in that far western part of Kentucky.

Ben Cregor went to Springfield, Kentucky, his home town, with Uncle Charlie. Of course, Red and Uncle Charlie went to Somerset, and then Red toured eastern Kentucky by himself, and "brought home the bacon," which was over $1,500.

Louisville quickly raised $4,000 and Uncle Charlie and McBrayer Moore decided to send a group of students from Louisville, football players and non-players, led by Paul Bickel, who was from a prominent family, to canvas businesses and professional organizations. Uncle Charlie then made a second trip to the city and returned feeling confident that the $15,000 goal would be met.

The "Messenger" started a movement to get non-alumni to pledge.

Get behind the campaign. Support it and "Say it with Cement." Build it for loyalty, for spirit, for grandeur, for strength of Old Centre. Become a member of the class and be called a "Stadium Builder."

The fraternities had fund raisers, and the girls from K.C.W. and the Kentucky School for the Deaf did the same. Local businesses followed Joe Stagg's lead and sent out letters to their suppliers asking for a donation. If a hardware store purchased from Belknap, the big wholesaler in Louisville, one could be certain that when the salesman for the company came into town, he was going to head back to Louisville with a request for a donation to hand to his superiors. All of these efforts helped the city of Danville reach its goal of $8,000.

Alumni in New York, Chicago, Cincinnati, Lexington—cities all across the country—began sending in money.

Henry L. Farrell, the sports editor of the United Press wire service syndicate, sent out a story to several hundred newspapers throughout the country which subscribed to the company's service.

Little Centre College in Kentucky is spectacular in everything it does. That is one reason why Centre is no longer little, but has a spectacular football team that has appeal all over the country.

Centre is going after a new stadium, and the college leaders are getting at it in the same spectacular way. A campaign slogan of "Say it with Cement" was adopted, and friends are asked to "kick in" with a barrel or two.

Uncle Charlie Moran, the football coach who mends the shoes of his boys and sews their uniforms, is going about the stadium project with the same vim and vigor as he coaches. About 18,000 barrels of cement at $3.15 each are going to be needed. The "Praying Colonels" want their friends in the East to, "Say it with Cement!"

Damon Runyon, the famous newspaperman and short story writer, sent a check. Rube Goldberg, a nationally syndicated cartoonist, creator of "Boob" McNutt and "Steve, Himself," contributed 10 barrels and sent a note which said, "I've been saying it with cement for years through my characters. That's what their brains are made of!"

Ring Lardner, writer of humor, sports columnist, a master of the short story, had become a great fan of the Colonels and sent $31.50, good for 10 barrels. He also sent a warm note which described how he was thrilled at the little school's courageous and clean play on football fields all over the country, and his hope that the drive was a big success.

G.B. Woodcock, formerly of Danville but presently living in Newtonville, Massachusetts, a suburb of Boston, sent a check for $400.00. His accompanying letter stated he "had no trouble raising the money, as the people in and around Boston think more of Centre College than any team that has ever played in the Stadium, and the Colonels are admired all over New England for their play and clean sportsmanship."

General of the Armies (a rank reached by no other living officer in the history of the United States) John J. Pershing, leader of the American Expeditionary Force during the Great War, wrote to the fundraising committee endorsing the idea of Centre building a new structure for football. He wrote, "The prowess of Centre's famous football team demands the erection of a stadium appropriate to their achievements."

Army and Thad McDonnell were working the timber business in Pennsylvania after Army finished his coaching duties with Bo at Centenary. The two Centre alumni sent $12.60 with a note that they wished it could be more, but the business was slow due to a huge amount of snow.

Army—"I'll be in Canada for the next 3-4 weeks buying for my company. Can I express a case of Johnnie Walker?" (Canada had not imposed the insanity of prohibition.)

Bo came through Danville on the way to New York "in the interest of a Louisiana royalty concern to which he is connected." He brought a check for $100.00.

And so it went. Money continued to pour into Danville from all points in the country. Finally, a check arrived which, though small, made the papers due to its uniqueness.

Dear Sir,

Please find my check for $3.15 for a barrel of cement. I am not a wealthy man, and at the present an inmate in the state reformatory. I was born one of twelve children in a log cabin and never had a chance to attend college, but I am true Kentuckian and love to see football games, and am certainly proud of the great record Centre has made. I pray that Centre will raise the amount needed for a new stadium.

Frank Reid
Number 9698
Frankfort, Kentucky

CONSTRUCTION BEGINS

By mid-April, satisfied that the campaign was on solid footing, Uncle Charlie headed back to Horse Cave for a short stay and then once again donned his black uniform and returned to his National League umpiring job. Everything was on in place for the actual construction to begin.

The "Messenger" reported on the first day's activity, as the dissembling of the old structure and then excavation and grading began.

Twenty local, colored football enthusiasts have volunteered their services for two days each as work on the stadium gets underway. This is very laudable.

The best timbers from the former stadium were stacked for use in building the baseball facility. Also, planks were saved for possible use in building temporary end zone bleachers if the need arose.

On April 23, Hickman Carter, business manager of the college, announced that seven contractors had been sent specs for the construction, and bids would be opened on May 5. Meanwhile, a notice went out that if cash were paid, literally on the barrelhead when cement arrived, a 10% discount would be given, "so get those pledges in, as cement is on the way."

When the bids were opened, the Blanchford Construction Company of Dayton, Ohio was the low bidder. Work was to begin May 21, and the contractor stated that the project would be finished one and a half months before the October 6 opening game with Carson-Newman.

Twenty five tons of steel were shipped in by the Southern Railroad. Ten carloads, 2300 barrels of cement, were on hand. Excavations for footings were completed, and it was projected that 75 men would soon be employed, many being Centre students who would join the Blanchford Construction regulars as soon as classes were completed.

There was a lot of excitement about the new stadium being built. Everyday we'd walk over to see what had been done. We felt like we were watching history being made. The old stadium had been there so long, constantly being repaired, and now we were going to have the best facility in the whole state of Kentucky.

I really couldn't wait to see it completed, but my problem was that I had to go back to Elizabethtown for the summer. I got reports from fraternity brothers who stayed behind to work on the project. They would even draw pictures to show how things were progressing.

Naturally, Howard and I wanted to help out so we collected money in E-town. Cousin Ella's sister who lived in the biggest house in town gave $50.00. I remember it well because it was the first time I'd ever seen a $50.00 bill. The minister at our church, First Presbyterian, preached a sermon around the "Praying Colonels" and what a great influence they were, and he said that if anyone wanted to help the fund raising drive, "Please see Red or Howard Robertson and they'll be glad to receive any amount you may wish to donate."

Dad was an officer in a bank downtown and he talked to all of the businesses on the square and helped us raise money. Eventually, we had over $400.00 which Dad used to buy a cashier's check to send to Centre.

On May 16, the Chief was back in Chicago working on the upcoming Chautauqua season. He decided to write to the members of the team, and his letter needs to be offered in its entirety to show the type of person the Chief was, and his approach to the players. Also, it is interesting to note the expressions of the time, some of which haven't been passed on to our generation.

Dear old fauna and flora:
It's time for you varmints to come out of your holes and rise and flutter, and this is my coy sweet way of telling you. Tempus is fugiting pretty fast, and before it is too late, I would like to have a few winged words with thee, or thou, as it were, and whisper some feeble remarks into your shell-like ear.

The main thing now is to see that you pass all of your work. You're on the home-stretch now, and every day counts. Knowing of old your general "indisposition to commerce," and unfamiliarity with most forms of mental activity, I come tearing out of the under bush at this point to remind you to get your work in shape right now, in spite of the hot weather or cool, heck or high water, heavy dates or other impediments, if you want to pass time with the Colonels this fall. Don't take anything for granted. Don't try to slip through thinking that the faculty won't notice the difference between male bovine con and honest work. If you think so, you are wrong.

Keen eyesight? Why our faculty could pick fly specks out of pepper. Hang that pool cue on the weeping willow tree. Ram facts into your system with both hands, and get your work in shape, past, present, and future, until the professors cease to view you with alarm but begin to point with pardonable pride. Otherwise, the football world will know you no more, and you shall be cast into the outer darkness by the slack of your raiment, and there shall be weeping and wailing and gnashing of teeth.

Occasionally some freckled-minded genius tells me that since he has done so much for Centre in attending the college and playing on the world's most famous football team, somebody ought to do something big for him, endow him for life, I suppose. He intimates that if it hadn't been for him, the grass-grown walks that now lead to the buildings would carry one only into a howling wilderness where the hoot-owls gather like crows at a grey mule's funeral; but now that he has graced the institution with his presence, the goose hangs high, the students come pouring in like water over the cascades, and the professors stand up to their salaries like Hereford bulls eating prairie hay.

We know, of course, in our heart of hearts, that Centre owes none of us anything. We owe everything to Centre. What greater privilege could we have than to go to Centre and be a Praying Colonel? If you and I lived to be a thousand, we could never repay that debt. Think of the influence of Dr. "Sammy" Cheek, the knightly soul who has just left us. Think how he has touched every boy's life with upward impulse, given courage and character; and kept his eyes on the mountaintop. Repay Dr. Cheek and Centre for that? It would never be possible.

When you come back, bring a good man with you. Some big boy whose socks, perhaps, exist only in the realm of fancy. I mean a rawhide, pig iron lad who growls as he walks, and who could on slight provocation explode with loud report on the football field. Tack a buckskin patch on the gable end of his overalls, throw a half-hitch around his neck, lead him in , and tie him to a stump in back of the gymnasium, and pray that he can pass the entrance requirements.

Brother, we have a mighty big job cut out for us. That schedule of ours puts us out in front. But things look fine, and we'll come through. Just do your college work right, and come back with brotherly love in your heart, and do your best, and we will win. That means glory old fellow, and the things that money can't buy. But fall down in your work now, and you will, in a manner of speaking, have your name carved on a little marble slab out amongst the jimson weeds and pickle bottles where once twixt the gloaming and the shank of the evening, the rank thistle nodded in the wind and the wild fox dug his hole unafraid.

Animal Kingdom, I'll be glad to see you all this fall, and will welcome you with even more spontaneous delight than Miss Woods in welcoming a tuition fee or any of us in greeting

a live five or a spruce deuce up-jumping on the very first gallop.
      Yours in old Centre,

ROBERT L. "CHIEF" MYERS.

END OF SCHOOL YEAR HAPPENINGS

On June 10, Dr. R. Ames Montgomery was installed as the 15th president of Centre College. United States Senator Richard P. Ernest, who had attended the 1921 Harvard game, introduced representatives from 15 colleges and universities who were in attendance. The annual Centre College Carnival was held and the King was Springfield, Kentucky's Ben Cregor, and the Queen, Margaret Cook. During Carnival, Centre students published the first edition of a magazine called the "Centre Colonel." It was a five color, slick publication which was to provide a vehicle for the students to present their offerings of fiction, poetry and humor. Illustrations and the cover art were to be produced by the students, and it met with enthusiastic approval, "for its sophistication and professional appearance."

UNCLE CHARLIE GETS TO SEE HIS CREATION

Work on the stadium progressed through the early summer, and timelines were met. The west side stands were completed during the 3rd week of June and the east side was scheduled to be finished two weeks later. It was announced that there would be enough money to complete the two sides, but the enclosure on the south end would have to wait another year. Temporary bleachers would be put up for the Kentucky game to accommodate the crowd.

The attitude was, "No problem. We'll have another successful year and complete the enclosure after the season." The college wanted to pay as it went, and therefore the decision was to defer, but not forget, the plan for the completion of the horseshoe.

Uncle Charlie was involved with his umpiring duties and Centre couldn't start practice anyway until September 10 due to a ruling by the Southern Intercollegiate Athletic Association. The coach may have not been in Danville as the stadium went up, but he had gotten everything so organized that his presence really wasn't necessary.

Finally, he had an off day after a game in Cincinnati and decided to take a late train down from Cincinnati on September 11. When he arrived, it was dark and he was tired and headed straight to the Gilcher.

Early on the morning of the 12th, he rose early and walked over to the new stadium.

We all had heard that Uncle Charlie was in town and would tour the stadium in the morning. I got up early and raced to the field because I wanted to see what he thought when he saw it.

The gate wasn't locked and there was still dew on the grass which had gotten really thick and beautiful. As I remember, everything was completed, even the cinder

track was laid, and the stadium could have been used, it was that finished.

Suddenly I saw the Chief, Uncle Charlie, Ben Cregor and Coach Kendrick come walking up to the stadium. They all stopped just outside of the fence and just stood there, letting Uncle Charlie take it all in. The sun was barely up, but I could see him clearly, standing there, with his hat on that he always wore, just staring at the stadium, looking one way and then another, and then a big smile came across his face and he walked out onto the field and said, "It's beautiful. Magnificent. Beautiful. Magnificent."

I was out on the field when he walked toward me and he said, "What do you think, Red Roberts' son?"

And I said, "Uncle Charlie, I think it's beautiful and magnificent, too."

And he said, "It is, indeed. Beautiful. Magnificent."

The Danville "Messenger" carried a story the next morning which I still have in one of my scrapbooks about what Uncle Charlie thought when he first saw what his vision had inspired.

Coach Moran saw the Centre stadium for the first time today and he was enthusiastic in expressing his pleasure and pride in the fine memorial to athletics. Since the first day that Uncle Charlie arrived in Danville, it has been his ambition to see a model stadium on Cheek Field. While many thought such a thing impossible, Coach Moran mapped out his plans and had faith that a stadium could be built here.

"It's a fine thing for Centre, Danville, and Kentucky," said Uncle Charlie, "and it was made possible by the contributions of the loyal friends of the college. It is a real testimonial to clean athletics and the Centre spirit, and no one can appreciate it more than I do. Its potentialities for Centre, for Danville and Kentucky, for the entire South and country are beyond any estimate that can be made."

You know, Uncle Charlie got that stadium built. As I got older and looked back on it, I came to realize even more how important Uncle Charlie was to the college, not only as a coach, but as a wonderful role model for his players. You know, many of them later went into coaching, and it is a testament to him that they continued with his philosophy not only in coaching, but in life.

I think it would have been appropriate to name the stadium for Uncle Charlie—Moran Stadium at Cheek Field—something like that. A lot of colleges did that. He was the person who had the idea and was the driving force behind raising the money.

Maybe it's not too late. Maybe the Centre Board of Trustees and the administration could still honor the man who did so much for our little college while he was there.

THE 1923 SEASON

Once again, Centre had to start the season without its head coach. No other

477

"big time" program had to operate in such a manner. Uncle Charlie was able to stay in Danville for two days when he came down to inspect the stadium, and he put the men through drills on September 13 and 14, and then he had to head back north. It was hoped he'd be back by the 24th, but there was no guarantee.

Ben Cregor signed on as an assistant coach. He, the Chief, and Coach Jim Kendrick assumed control of the program in Uncle Charlie's absence.

The football guide that everyone looked forward to each year was put out by A.G. Spalding, the manufacturer of sporting equipment. Walter Camp was the editor, and the book was published in New York by American Sports Publishing.

The 1923 issue had a photograph on page 46 of the Colonels team of 1922, and a summary of the season on page 103.

Centre College, Danville, Kentucky.
Covington at quarterback was highly commended by competent critics for his fine play during the season. In the game with the University of Louisville, he set a record by kicking six straight field goals. Centre has adopted the freshman rule even though it has not many more than 250 students. Kubale, Roberts, Hudgins and Thomasson were players of unusual merit, while Gordy, Shadoan and Cregor were the main strength of the line.

On page 200 was the record of the 1922 season. On page 80 was a picture of Bo's Centenary team. There was no season's summary, but the school's record of 8-1 was listed on the same page as that of Centre.

Centre's jerseys were changed to solid gold with just a small white stripe around the neck. There were three small white stripes around the sleeves. The stripe around the middle was deleted.

Spectators who came out for the early practices couldn't believe how many young men were interested in playing football as a member of the Centre College Colonels. There were 30 varsity players on the opening day, with several yet to arrive on campus. Jop reported that there were 68 men at the September 13th session, including freshmen, and 12 more candidates had sent word that they were on the way. By the end of the first week of practice, 80 young men were on the field, fully a third of the student body!

When Jop interviewed several first year men, it was reported that they were like so many others of their age.

"We want to be a Praying Colonel!" However impressive was the quantity, the quality lagged somewhat behind. Everyone wanted to be a Colonel, but as the future would show, not many were ready to play in the "big time."

Of the 20 players who lettered in 1922, 11 were returning.

Captain Ed Kubale
Herb Covington
George Chinn (Lettered in 1920-21)
Minos Gordy

Jim Green
Hope Hudgins
Hennie Lemon
Jim Liggett
Howard Lynch
Frank Rubarth
Case Thomasson

There were various reasons that certain of the 1922 winners of the gold "C," weren't coming back. Tom Bartlett wasn't able to return to school, much less play football, after his severe bout with a peritonsillar abscess. Red Roberts, Ben Cregor, Terry Snowday, Charles Cecil, Dewey Kimbel and Hump Tanner graduated. George "Buck" Jones decided not to play a third year, and Clarence Jones wasn't able to continue his education at Centre after the death of his father. Bill Shadoan had to drop out due to financial considerations, and secured the head football and basketball coaching positions at Valparaiso University in Indiana.

The Chief agreed to stay in Danville and help out until Uncle Charlie could return. On September 14, he gave a speech in chapel which was covered by the "Messenger."

The talk was given in the Chief's customary, brilliant manner and was one of the best ever delivered in the Centre chapel. He touched upon the traditions of the institution, the fine spirit that exists here, and the great record that has been made by the Centre football team.

Danville is always glad to welcome the Chief and wishes he could be here the whole year. He breathes, sleeps, talks and radiates the Centre spirit and to him the college and community owe much.

Chief was given a tremendous ovation at the end of his speech.

Each year, Ed Danforth, sports editor for the Atlanta "Constitution," made a tour of the South to get a handle on the relative strengths of the region's football teams. He had started dropping by Centre only during the last few years, and now the Colonels were a definite must for his survey. Danforth arrived in Danville on September 18, having just left Lexington where he observed the Wildcats in action.

The sports expert reported that he felt Kentucky was going to be one of the top teams in the South. He said that the major goal over in Lexington was to defeat Centre after coming up short during the last five meetings between the in-state rivals.

Danforth then gave a glowing account of Centre's new stadium.

It's a beauty. Who would have thought it possible a few years ago?

Centre has got to be good this season to live up to the magnificent stadium that has just been finished.

On first viewing Centre's new "buy a barrel of cement" playing field, the author's jaw dropped and waved in the breeze like the bottom of a steam shovel. I remember last March when they started a campaign in Kentucky among alumni to buy a barrel of cement to build the plant. Little more was heard of it along the way.

Now on each side of a well turfed, scientifically drained rectangle, there rise two grandstands of reinforced concrete. The ends of the structure are open and will be closed with wooden stands for the dedicatory game with Kentucky on November 3, for which over 5,000 tickets have already been sold, nearly seven weeks before the two teams square off.

A high wire fence surrounds the athletic complex. The field is circled with a ¼ mile cinder tract with a 120 yard straightaway.

It is a fine plant, perfectly constructed and laid out. To think of this little school of less than 300 students erecting such a structure is absolutely astounding.

Centre's stadium represents in terms of money and concrete the progress of football as an intercollegiate sport in the South.

Suffice it to say that Centre simply HAS to turn out a football team now to live up to its new home.

Uncle Charlie was actually able to get back to Danville on September 24, as scheduled. However, the National League wired him that he would be needed for a series to be played during the first week of October in Cincinnati, and the first game, with Tom Moran's Carson-Newman team, was October 6.

Many teams opened their 1923 season on Saturday, September 29.

Of Centre's opponents (boldface) during the upcoming campaign, **Penn** shut out Franklin and Marshall, 20-0. **Kentucky** beat Marshall, 41-0. **Clemson** and **Auburn** tied, 0-0. **Georgia** beat Mercer, 7-0. Georgia Tech had a surprisingly tough time with **Oglethorpe**, winning 28-13, and Oglethorpe had actually led at one time. **Sewanee** and **Carson-Newman** tied 0-0.

The Carson-Newman score was somewhat concerning to Centre. The 1922 game with the "Fighting Parsons" had been a virtual track meet, with the Colonels winning 72-0. Now, Tom Moran's team looked like it was going to offer a much greater level of opposition, because Sewanee was no pushover. The Tigers were members of the Southern Conference and were much like schools such as Centre and Washington and Lee in that they could take on the larger colleges and play competitively. (The nickname now for Carson-Newman's teams is "Eagles." But in the 1920's, the name was "Fighting Parsons," perhaps an oxymoron, perhaps not, and later it was just, "Parsons.")

Fans began to wonder, "Where are the breathers on the schedule?"

Uncle Charlie was proud of his son and his team's performance, but not to the extent that he wasn't going to go all out to beat Carson-Newman. He called a team meeting after hearing the Sewanee score.

"You all remember Tommy. He was a competitor when he played here, and still is. There's nothing he'd rather do than come up here from Tennessee and spoil our day. There's nothing he'd rather do than beat his father. We may have won last year, 72-0. There's no way we can come close to that score if you guys don't get going out there."

"Now, six laps and you're through for the day."

Despite preparing on the field for Carson-Newman, the talk all over town was about Kentucky. Tickets were going fast. S.A. Boles, the business manager at Kentucky, took the train over from Lexington to discuss arrangements with Centre's Hickman Carter. Boles said he was being swamped with requests for tickets, and had a list of over 3,000 people who had signed applications for tickets and "are clamoring for their pasteboards." Carter gave assurance that the tickets were being printed in Philadelphia and would arrive the first week of October.

Besides the demand in Danville and Lexington, ticket requests were coming in from all over the state. It was quickly determined from the demand that the temporary end zone bleachers would be needed, and seating would be made available for 13,000-14,000.

As locals heard the news, they were truly amazed. "Can you believe it?"

The 1920 census had the population for all of Danville and Boyle County at 14,998!

Besides the public being kept informed about the Homecoming game with Kentucky, they were pleased to hear about a purchase that Centre had made. It was called a "Grid-Graph," and was a technological marvel for the times, to be used when Centre was on the road.

The "Messenger" described how it worked.

A direct wire from the field where the game is being played will be used in operating the scoreboard. A telegraph operator will receive the message and write it down and hand it to the Grid-Graph controller. Every player will have a number, and when a player, Covington for example, is running the ball, a light will flash by his name at the end of the board. A light will also show where he is on the field and the nature of the play and the gain or loss.

It is a wonderful invention. The board will be placed in the middle of the playing field, about 30 feet from the stands. People who have followed a game on the "Grid-Graph" report that it is as thrilling as seeing the real game. All of Centre's away games will be played on the big electric board, assuring fans of "red-hot" information.

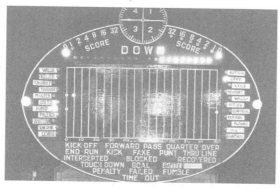

In the age where radio hadn't yet become common, especially in more rural areas, and long before television, this was about as sophisticated as it could get in allowing fans to feel that they had a sense of what was occurring when their team was playing away from home. (Check out the scoring. From the numbers placed above "score," you can tally any score from 0 to 63. Try it if you're skeptical. The numbers would light up and you'd add the numbers to get the score all of the way to 63.)

The "Grid-Graph" made the person hired to holler out the results of the "play-by-play" in former years just as obsolete as Brunswick's automatic pinsetter later made the kids who used to hop down and manually set the pins in bowling alleys. Technology claims its victims indiscriminately.

Jop was amazed, like everyone who followed Centre's team, about how things were changing from previous years.

How far Centre has come! It used to be that Uncle Charlie had to sew up uniforms before games. Now the Colonels have game uniforms, practice uniforms, and sweat suits for light practices, plus the new stadium and the "Grid-Graph." Success sure causes some wonderful things to happen! (It was shortly thereafter reported that Centre had laid in a supply of "moleskins covered with rubber for use on rain-slicked fields." Note was made that the players "squeaked" when they ran down the field, and there was never any mention of the new gear being worn in a game.)

Jop was correct. Now it was time to begin the 1923 season, and to make certain that success continued to cause "wonderful things to happen."

OCTOBER 6, 1923 CENTRE VS. CARSON-NEWMAN

Uncle Charlie's wife and his daughter-in-law, Tom's wife, both came up from Horse Cave to the game. The understanding among those who knew that the father and son were facing each other was that Pearl, Uncle Charlie's wife, wanted Centre to win, "but not by too much."

It was a disappointment to the Centre coach that he couldn't get to Danville from Cincinnati in time for the game. The kickoff was delayed, but even at that, his train arrived after the action was over.

The inaugural game for the new stadium was played on a gorgeous, early fall day. There was a big crowd, anxious not only to see the Colonels in action, but many of the fans arrived early and walked out on the field, around the track, under the stands, climbed to the top of the stadium to "get the view," admired the new scoreboard, and all shared Uncle Charlie's sentiment upon first seeing his creation that it was, "Wonderful. Marvelous. Wonderful. Marvelous."

Centre was going to start nine lettermen, with only two men who had moved into the lineup being from the 1922 freshman team. Albert Spurlock at left half, and Walter Skidmore at left tackle, were the newcomers. George Chinn, the young man who had played so well in 1920 and 1921, but missed much of 1922 due to injuries, was back in good form and playing in the left guard slot. Chinn had filled out to a solid 210 pounds.

Left end	Hennie Lemon	Junior	5'10"	170
Left tackle	Walter Skidmore	Soph.	5'11"	170
Left guard	George Chinn	Senior	5'11"	210
Center	Ed Kubale	Junior	6'	185
Right guard	Frank Rubarth	Junior	5'11"	177
Right tackle	Howard Lynch	Junior	5'10"	195
Right end	Minos Gordy	Junior	5'10"	185
Quarterback	Herb Covington	Junior	5'5"	155
Left half	Albert Spurlock	Soph.	5'10"	185
Fullback	Case Thomasson	Junior	6'	175
Right half	Hope Hudgins	Junior	5'7"	152

The line averaged 185 lbs., the backfield 167 lbs., and the team average was 178 lbs.

The crowd was warmed up by the Centre "Six" which set up along the west side stands and began playing some 30 minutes prior to the 2:30 p.m. kickoff.

Besides the musicians entertaining the crowd, "Rabbit" Abbott, the Carson-Newman right halfback, put on an exhibition which brought a lot of "ooh's" and "aah's" from the crowd. "Rabbit" could pass, punt and dropkick equally well from either his left or right side. He'd fire a pass 30 yards with his left arm, and then another perfect spiral with his right. He'd kick left and right, so effortlessly and naturally that no one could decide if he had a preferred "sidedness," as one spectator expressed it.

Centre had made extra efforts to make Tom Moran and his team and fans feel welcome. Cars were lined up to bring everyone to the new stadium from the Gilcher. The ladies had been given corsages made in the team's colors of orange and blue. Everybody stood and cheered when a smiling Tom, waving to the crowd, led his team onto the field.

The pundits had made Centre the favorite by six touchdowns. Pearl, Uncle Charlie's wife, got her wish that Centre win, "but not by much." Her son's team played tough and intelligently, much as Tom had been taught in playing under and studying his father's way of coaching.

Centre scored once in the 1st quarter when, 10 minutes into the game, Case Thomasson scored on a short plunge after a long drive, Hennie Lemon kicked the extra point, and that was all of the scoring in the first half which ended, 7-0.

Carson-Newman got to the Colonels four yard line late in the 2nd quarter, but Centre dug in and held and ran out the clock. The 3rd quarter was scoreless, and in the last period, Herb Covington scored after another significant drive. Lemon was good again, and the game ended, 14-0.

"Rabbit" Abbott didn't score holding the ball with his left or right arm, didn't throw a pass with either, didn't kick a field goal from starboard or port, but he did punt very effectively. There was no mention with which foot.

Captain Hutchins, the "Fighting Parsons" fullback, played a tremendous game, hurling his 190 lb. body against the Colonels' front wall time after time. It was agreed by all that if he'd had more blocking from his line, he could have been a decisive factor.

The 14-0 win was obviously a far less impressive showing than the 72-0 thrashing of Carson-Newman in 1922. While it was a win, the score left the followers of the Gold and White somewhat concerned about what the future held. It was a statement about how far Centre had come since 1917.

"We only won by 14-0," conveyed a bit of disappointment. Centre's fans had come to expect to win, and to win in a convincing manner. Reading the stats revealed that Centre was more in control than the score may indicate, running up 14 first downs to but five for Carson-Newman.

Centre also played rather conservatively, knowing there was a Clemson scout in the stands. However, the simple fact was that the game was a real contest because Tom Moran had done an excellent job in preparing his team for its game with the Colonels.

TRAGEDY OUT OF CINCINNATI

Shocking news reached Danville on Monday morning, October 8. The University of Kentucky had traveled to Cincinnati for a Saturday afternoon game with the University of Cincinnati, played while Centre and Carson-Newman were squaring off. UK won 14-0.

Prince Innes McLean, a 20 year old center, had suffered a blow to the head during the contest but seemed to be alright and returned to Lexington with the team on Saturday night. Sunday morning he complained of a headache and by noon had lost consciousness. He was rushed to Good Samaritan Hospital where emergency surgery was performed, unsuccessfully.

Looking at the situation in retrospect, it would seem that McLean suffered a traumatic subdural hematoma, or a blood clot on the brain. In today's more sophisticated medical environment, it is often successfully treated if a CT scan is obtained in a timely manner, the clot evacuated and bleeding controlled. However, in 1923, such an injury was most often fatal.

The Centre team sent a large floral arrangement. The following year, the new Kentucky football stadium was named for young Prince Innes McLean, and the Wildcats' facility was known as McLean Stadium at Stoll Field.

OCTOBER 13, 1923   CENTRE-CLEMSON

Clemson was next; the first hurdle in what Centre hoped would be at least a mythical Southern Championship. With Uncle Charlie having missed the game with Carson-Newman, he was gratified to have his son Tom volunteer to stay behind in Danville for a couple of days to help in correcting some deficiencies which Tom had noticed during the previous Saturday's contest. Father and son may be rivals when their two teams met, but all of that was now past history.

Monday afternoon, October 8, the two Morans put the Colonels through a hard scrimmage, with Tom pointing out strengths and weaknesses which he had noticed during the previous Saturday. Tuesday was more of the same, and by the end of the week, the team was a smoothly running machine, and even Uncle Charlie was pleased with his player's progress.

The 1922 game over in South Carolina at Clemson had been an absolute sellout, with people stacked in everywhere to see the famous Colonels play. Centre put on quite a show and didn't disappoint the crowd in winning handily, 21-0.

The 1923 game in Danville wasn't played to a capacity crowd, but the west or "home" side of the stadium was full. Clemson brought only a handful of supporters and the "visitor" side was nearly empty.

The Colonels clearly outclassed the Tigers, winning 28-7. Clemson's points were the first scored on Centre's field since Louisville put across a score against the subs on October 28, 1922.

Statistically, the game was even more of a mismatch than the score would indicate. The Gold and White picked up 21 first downs to eight for Clemson. In yardage gained, the margin was a whopping 702 to 188. Touchdowns were evenly spread with Case Thomasson, Minos Gordy, Albert Spurlock and Covey scoring. Lemon kicked three extra points, and Covey got the 4th. Herb Covington ran at will, picking up 353 yards, half of his team's total, and nearly twice what Clemson gained.

Clemson and Centre had met in each of the past three years, 1921-23, and the Colonels had outscored the South Carolinians by a cumulative, 63-7. The two colleges never again played.

I only had the pleasure of seeing Bo play during the 1921 season. I got to watch him in three games in Danville, against Transy over in Lexington, W&L at Louisville, and I was at the Auburn game in Birmingham. He was undoubtedly one of the greatest backs to ever put on a uniform.

How Bo was better than Herb Covington I don't know. Of course, I got to watch Herb for four seasons, so naturally I knew a lot more about him than Bo.

Herb Covington was the most exciting player I ever saw, at least for breakaway speed and downfield running. Every time he touched the ball, you felt he could score. Not only could he run like a deer, but he could change directions on a dime, letting people overshoot him and then dart off again. He was also a great passer, and he could kick the heck out of the ball.

That Clemson game I'll never forget. Herb ran them ragged, and their players were just worn out by the end of the game from chasing him all over the field. (The win over the South Carolinians was all the more impressive when Clemson's season was analyzed. The Tigers ended up 5-2-1, the only other loss being a road game with Virginia Tech. The tie was with Auburn.)

OCTOBER 20, 1923 CENTRE-OGLETHORPE

Two questions were on everybody's mind leading up to the next game.

"Where is Oglethorpe?"

"What in the bejeesus is a "Stormy Petrel?"

The first was fairly easily solved by going to the library and grabbing an "O" encyclopedia and looking up "Olgethorpe." It told of James Edward Oglethorpe, an Englishman, who came to the New World in 1733 and founded and helped colonize what is now the state of Georgia.

On down under the biography of James would be found a little section which told of a school which had a rather turbulent history. The college was founded in 1835 in Midway, a small town near Milledgeville, then the capital of Georgia. Oglethorpe suffered much during the Civil War as its students went off to fight, its buildings were turned into barracks and a hospital, and its endowment was invested in Confederate bonds which proved to be valuable only for use as wallpaper in the impoverished, post-war South. The administration picked up and moved to Atlanta in 1870, but things got no better, and the doors were closed two years later.

In 1913, Oglethorpe was re-charted, a cornerstone was laid in 1915 for the first building on Peachtree Road in Atlanta, and the college was in its 11th year of its rebirth when the game with Centre was played.

Oglethorpe hoped to quickly gain attention by pushing its athletic programs, and there was no better way to do just that than by scheduling the most famous team in the South, if not the nation—the Praying Colonels of Centre College.

But what about a petrel, and a "stormy" one at that?

Colleges have always seemed to have a preference for using birds for their athletic team's nicknames. There are Eagles, Falcons, Cardinals, Jays, Ducks, Owls, Ospreys, Hens, Herons, Peacocks, Ravens, Sunbirds, Roadrunners, Redbirds, Gamecocks, all kinds of Hawks, including just plain Hawks, Red Hawks, Jay Hawks, Mountain Hawks—bird species rule the roost regarding this sort of thing. However, there is just one team that goes by the "Stormy Petrels," and it would seem to be a safe bet that Oglethorpe will maintain that exclusivity. Incidentally, the petrel is pronounced "pea-trel," and is a bird which can fly at sea against the strongest winds and fiercest storms, thus the "Stormy" part of the name.

Oglethorpe came to Danville with a record of 0-2 record. However, the losses were to good teams and were on the road. Georgia Tech won 28-13, and Georgia, 20-6. Centre not only wanted to win the game, but wished to make a statement regarding its strength when compared to that of Georgia Tech and Georgia.

The Colonels thoroughly beat the Stormy Petrels. Again, Herb Covington dominated the play. Oglethorpe never got close to the Centre goal. The only part of its game which was impressive was in punting yardage, hardly a statistic consistent with a winning attack.

It was 10-0 at the end of the 1st quarter, and 17-0 at the half, with the Colonels threatening to score on the four yard line when the whistle blew. Centre literally ran up and down the field at will, picking up an astonishing 27 first downs to three for the Petrels.

Hope Hudgins from Amarillo, Texas scored twice. Covey and Thomasson each got one TD. Hennie Lemon kicked two extra points and a 30 yard field goal. The final score was 29-0.

After the game, Oglethorpe's coach, Jim Robertson, came into the Colonels' dressing room to congratulate the team on its play. He told Uncle Charlie that his team lost to Georgia Tech and Georgia, but didn't get really beaten, being in both games all of the way. Coach Robertson said that against Centre, his team not only lost, but got beaten in every sense of the word.

Centre was now 3-0, having outscored its first three opponents, 70-7. After the somewhat slow start against Tom Moran's Carson-Newman team, Uncle Charlie's team seemed to be really jelling. Now it was time for the annual excursion to the East.

THE UNIVERSITY OF PENNSYLVANIA

The University of Pennsylvania was a major football power. Just as it is sometimes hard to reconcile the present, modern day programs of the "Big 3" of the day, Harvard, Yale and Princeton, with their dominance of college football in the first 50 years of the sport, so it is with the Penn Quakers.

Pennsylvania began playing intercollegiate football in the Centennial year of 1876 on an informal basis. The first game was on November 1 and the result was a 6-0 loss to Princeton. From that first season until 1885, the students played without a coach and won 20, lost 20, and tied three. Of those 43 contests, 11 were with the Princeton, and Penn lost every time it took the field against the Tigers.

This wasn't acceptable, so Penn got serious enough about the sport to hire its first coach, Frank Dole, for the 1885 season. Dole did fairly well, compiling a 23-19-1 record in three seasons. (During Dole's tenure, Penn played up to 17 games a season, competing three times each year against Princeton.) Even though Dole had some overall success, his teams continued to lose to Princeton, coming up short nine times. That made it 0-20 against the Tigers from New Jersey, located just 40 miles away.

In 1888, E.O. Wagenhurst took over the coaching duties and had a respectable 38-18 record in his four seasons at the helm. However, he was 0-7 against Princeton, and now Penn had lost 27 straight times to its chief rival. The overall points scored in the series found Princeton having run up an embarrassingly decisive margin, 867-46, for an average rounded off score of 32-2. Something had to be done!

In 1892, George Woodruff, a 28 year old former all-around athlete at Yale, took over the Penn football program. Woodruff had a knack for coming up with innovative, unexpected offensive plays, and his arrival began a golden era for Quakers' football. Woodruff's 1892 team compiled a 15-1 record, losing only to Yale in a game played in New York City. Importantly, Penn beat Princeton for the first time, winning 6-4.

In 1893, Princeton edged the Quakers, 4-0. The overall record for Penn that year was 12-3, with the other two losses being to Yale and Harvard.

1894 was the decisive year in the Penn-Princeton rivalry. Woodruff had been perfecting an innovative offensive scheme and saving it just for the Princeton game. The boys from Pennsylvania went to Trenton, New Jersey, where the game was to be played, sporting a perfect 9-0 record. Princeton was 12-0. 12,000 ardent fans turned out to see the battle between the two undefeated teams. For the first time, Coach Woodruff unveiled his carefully kept secret, his "guards-back" offense.

The Penn quarterback, Carl Williams, would call out "guards right!" or "guards left!" The two guards would drop back to either the right or left side of their quarterback, giving the Quakers two extra men to run interference. The play would usually be run toward the side the guards had lined up on, but to keep the defense honest, sometimes it would go in the opposite direction. Princeton simply couldn't adjust to the new offensive formation and remained befuddled all afternoon. Penn won 12-0.

Philadelphia was the home not only of the University of Pennsylvania, but a great number of the Princeton alumni also lived in the perhaps misnamed, "City of Brotherly Love," as mayhem broke out after the game.

On the train ride back from Trenton, the Penn alumni and students began to harass the followers of Princeton. The jeering and what had been good natured razzing got somewhat ugly when a large number of Penn partisans met the train, cheering and singing songs, and then began to get rowdy while streaming away from the terminal and into the streets.

A quick-witted Penn fan wrote a song which was passed out to the revelers and used to taunt the Tiger supporters.

OH MY! OH MY!
HOW WE BLACKED THE TIGER'S EYE.
WHAT'VE YOU DONE? WHAT'VE YOU DONE?
BEAT THE TIGERS TWELVE TO NONE.
HOW DID YOU DO IT? HOW DID YOU DO IT?
EASY! EASY!
WHAT'S THE SCORE?
THREE TIMES FOUR.
PRINCETON'S TIGER'S ON THE FLOOR!

The celebrations continued on into the evening. A theatre performance was interrupted. Wannamaker's department store became the scene of some "unpleasantness" as the crowd raced through "knocking female shoppers to and fro."

A few days after the 1894 game, the Princeton faculty convened and voted to suspend future athletic contests with Penn. Not to be outdone, the Penn faculty decided to meet and voted similarly, prohibiting any contact with Princeton's teams. The two esteemed universities later decided to soften their stances and allowed competition in the "minor sports."

Each school waited for the other to call, but it was over 40 years before the Pennsylvania Quakers and Princeton Tigers met again on the gridiron! Finally, in 1936, there was a truce ("Old boy, tell me now, why is it that we are mad at each other?") and Princeton beat Penn, 7-6, at Palmer Stadium in Princeton, and the two institutions have played most years since.

From the arrival of George Woodruff in 1892 until the October 27, 1923 game with Centre, Penn had won 284, lost 68, and tied 18. Excluding ties, the Quakers had won 80.7% of their games, quite a remarkable record, especially considering that the Philadelphia school played a top-tier schedule.

Teams like Yale, Harvard, Penn State, Michigan, Cornell, Pittsburgh, Alabama, Army, Navy, West Virginia, Dartmouth, Brown, Carlisle, Georgia Tech, along with Chicago and Washington and Jefferson, both powers at the time, appeared frequently in the line-up of programs which the Quakers took on.

In 1922, interest in the Penn football team had reached such a level that the athletic council oversaw the building of a magnificent new Franklin Field which replaced the old wooden stadium of the same name. It held 54,500, nearly doubling the original stadium, and the first game was held in the new facility on September 30, 1922, a 14-0 win over Franklin and Marshall. (Even 54,500 seats weren't enough, and in 1925, a second deck was added, bringing the capacity to slightly over 78,000.)

Penn played all nine of its games at the new Franklin Field in 1922, going 6-3. The schedule for 1923 was again to have all games at home. (Penn played 28 straight home games from 1922-24, finally leaving the friendly confines to travel to Pasadena on January 1, 1925 to participate in the Rose Bowl, which it lost to California, 14-0.)

Centre found Penn to be an excellent fit for its 1923 campaign. While the Quakers weren't one of the "Big 3," if they weren't equal, they were certainly very close. They were from the East, they had a significant following, they had a wonderful new stadium, and perhaps most importantly, a game with Penn would generate an enormous amount of press, and recognition was at the root of what Centre had sought when Dr. Ganfield decided to promote football as a way to put Centre on the map, and keep it there.

During the last few years, the newspapers along the East Coast had provided more publicity for Centre than any advertising agency could have generated with a million dollar budget. The stories flowing out of the Boston and New York metropolitan areas, and from the news syndicates, had been picked up, published and read all across the country. In big cities, small towns, and rural areas, the question asked each Sunday morning in the fall was, "What did Centre do yesterday?"

Centre was "in." Centre was the perfect story—the little school which had become hugely successful, but retained an innocence despite its fame. Centre was determined to remain in the public's eye, and that's why the Colonels were at Danville's Southern station at 5:30 p.m. on Wednesday, October 24, 1923, getting ready to board their specially chartered Pullman for the long ride to Philadelphia.

Waiting on a siding to connect to the regularly scheduled New Orleans-Cincinnati # 42, northbound train, was another Pullman to carry the Centre fans to the game. The fare for an upper berth was $72.00 and a lower, $72.50, for the roundtrip. The Pullman Company had agreed to leave the car in the yard at Philadelphia's Broad Street Station until the return trip Saturday night so that the fans could use their berth for sleep each night in lieu of a hotel.

Centre was taking 28 players to the game, 12 backs and 16 linemen. The Pullman was a 16 section sleeper, and in addition to the players, the Chief, Uncle Charlie, and assistant coaches Ben Cregor and Jim Kendrick were going. The other Pullman had berths for student manager, Elliott McDowell, assistant manager, B.Y. Willis, student trainer, H. Miller, Dudley, the "rubber," or masseur, and Dr. Allen, chairman of the athletic department. It was a far cry from the small numbers from the college who made the trip to Charleston, West Virginia just four years before.

There was one more important person going along, not to perform at the half, but to assist on the sidelines with the water bucket. Jop reported on the scene.

Roscoe, the cake walker, masseur and songster, who follows the team wherever it goes, was at the station far before the time for departure. For fear that someone may mistake his identity, Roscoe toted a large, black leather suitcase. Gaily painted in gold and white on one side was "Roscoe." On the other side, "Centre."

Several hundred people were at the station for the send-off. The rallying cry was, "Go to town, Colonels!" As the team was boarding, Jop reported on an incident which occurred just before the train pulled out.

An old man, a Civil War veteran, his hair snow-white, and his gait unsteady, edged through the crowd and called for Captain Kubale. Taking the Centre chieftain by the arm, he walked a few feet down the platform and pointed to a sign painted on a mill just across the tracks.
"Read, son," he told Kubale.
"Centre 6-Harvard 0. We gave 'em Hell," read the sign. Kubale then pressed the old man's hand and in a choked voice muttered, "We'll battle them," and was on his way. Kubale understood, and he recounted the incident to his teammates as the train steamed out of Danville.

The Colonels and fans were hauled to Cincinnati by the Southern, and disconnected there to be joined to a Pennsylvania Railroad passenger train heading east. The railroad's main east-west line would be met at the Xenia, Ohio junction, and from there the route would be due east across Ohio and then Pennsylvania, with arrival at the Pennsylvania's huge Broad Street Station at 5:00 p.m. Thursday, nearly 24 hours after leaving Danville.

Unlike the last trip to the East, the 1922 "misadventure" to Harvard, the journey to Philadelphia went off without a hitch. The scheduled arrival time was met, and the team was in its hotel, the Rittenhouse at 2126 Chestnut Street, in time to have dinner and still have a couple of hours of leisure in the evening to stroll around historic, downtown Philadelphia, led by a guide supplied by the local Centre alumni. Once again, the Colonels were fulfilling the Chief's goal of having the team's travels serve as a broadening educational experience for "his boys."

On Friday, a practice was held 11 miles southwest of Centre's hotel at Swarthmore College. Frank Fitt's, one of Swarthmore's assistant coaches, had played for the Tulane team that Centre beat in New Orleans on Thanksgiving, 1921. Fitts had kept in contact with some of the Colonels, in particular, Minos Gordy, who was from Abbeville, Louisiana, and had written Centre prior to the departure for Philadelphia offering the school's facility.

The practice was closed to the public because Uncle Charlie had incorporated some new plays into the Colonels' offense which hadn't been shown, or needed, during the first three games. The team was driven to Swarthmore by Centre alumni and friends of the college who lived in Philadelphia. It seemed that wherever Centre traveled, there were always people who were literally waiting in line to help in any way that they could, and the Philadelphia experience was no different than all of the others.

Friday night, the University of Kentucky alumni of Philadelphia joined with Centre's alumni to host a dinner and reception at the elegant Bellevue-Stratford Hotel in the City Center. Comment was made by the UK alumni that when Centre and Kentucky play, "Naturally, we are for our alma mater. But we are Kentuckians, and the rivalry disappears when Centre is playing anybody else. We toast our fellow Kentuckians, and hope you have a great victory at Franklin Field tomorrow."

Hip, Hip, Hooray!
Hip, Hip, Hooray!
Three cheers for Centre,
Hip, Hip, Hooray!

The University of Pennsylvania had been promoting the Centre game for several weeks by placing signs on the Philadelphia buses. The ticket sales had been strong since the initial announcement that the game had been scheduled, and it appeared that the Colonels would draw the biggest crowd yet for the 1923 Penn season. The Quakers were 3-1 with the following record and attendance.

Penn	20	Franklin and Marshall	0	31,000
Penn	0	Maryland	3	38,000
Penn	13	Swarthmore	10	35,000
Penn	19	Columbia	7	38,000

While the attendance figures for the first four games were quite respectable, the fact is that the totals were swelled somewhat by the proximity of Penn's opponents to Philadelphia, allowing fans of the visiting teams to attend with relative ease. Franklin and Marshall was 80 miles west in Lancaster, Pennsylvania. Maryland and Columbia were each approximately 100 miles away, and Swarthmore was a suburb of the city.

Centre's alumni and fans could fill a few seats at Franklin Field, but nearly all of the 42,000 who attended the game were there not only to support Penn, but also to see the famous Colonels, this group of young men who had beaten Harvard. After the game, the officials at Penn stated they were extremely pleased with the numbers when the final tally was released. Centre outplayed Penn in the 1st quarter, moving the ball well and twice getting within field goal range, even if the attempts were at the upper limits of Herb Covington's range. Covey missed both tries, and the quarter ended scoreless.

The 2nd quarter was more of the same, a defensive struggle characterized by hard hitting and great play by both teams. Toward the end of the quarter, Centre looked like it was going to gain good field position and possibly move into range for another field goal effort as the Quakers had 4th down on their own 23. However, Penn's left halfback, Ernest Hamer, got off a booming kick which put the Colonels back on their own 20. A series of runs ended up with the Colonels losing 15 yards in three plays, and Albert Spurlock had to punt while standing deep in his end zone.

Spurlock did a nice job getting the ball fairly deep, and Penn brought it back to the Centre 35 as the clock was running down. The Quakers ran several off-tackle thrusts and moved it to the 11. Just as time was about to expire, Penn sent in its field goal kicker, Hugh King, who was good from the 22, and the half ended with Penn up, 3-0.

Jop reported that he felt Centre had more than held its own during the 1st half. But he said he felt that when the two teams went to their dressing rooms, he was watching a replay of the 1920 Harvard game in which the score had been 14-14 at the break, but Harvard had seemed to be gaining the upper hand as the half wound down.

The Colonels looked like they were getting beaten by the heavier Penn front wall, and toward the end of the 2nd quarter, the Quakers were beginning to control the line of scrimmage, just as Harvard had in '20. Also, it appeared that Penn totally anticipated any new formation or play that Uncle Charlie had inserted into the attack. The players and coaches later said that "it seemed like they had learned about our plays in advance," because Penn was always ready and shifted into effective defensive formations which were able to bottle up Centre's efforts.

Were there "eyes" at Swarthmore when Centre held its "secret" practice? No one ever made that accusation, but there were suspicions.

The 2nd half was all Penn. A McGraw to Dern pass resulted in a 3rd quarter touchdown, and the extra point made it 10-0 at the end of the 3rd quarter. Early in the 4th quarter, Hamer scored, the point after was good, and Penn led 17-0.

Penn's big fullback, Thomas, plowed into the end zone near the end of the game, and the P.A.T. made it 24-0 when time expired.

There were no excuses offered by Centre. Uncle Charlie told the press in interviews after the game that the Quakers had the better team that afternoon. Centre's most ardent supporter, George Joplin, said the same, then added that he didn't think Penn was 24 points superior, "but more like 10."

The night after the game, there was another affair at the Bellevue-Stratford, a dinner dance, attended by the coaches and players for both teams, this time hosted by Penn. Jop wrote that it was a delightful affair, and that Centre had been treated wonderfully during its stay in Philadelphia. The team and fans got to their Pullmans late Saturday night for the long ride back home. It had been a loss, but it had also been a great experience for the young men from Danville.

Despite not returning with a victory, there was a large crowd, even at the late arrival time, waiting at the station. Many felt that they had actually been at the game, as they had "watched" it on the "Grid-Graph" which everyone deemed a great success.

KENTUCKY, HOMECOMING, AND DEDICATING THE NEW STADIUM

Kentucky had grown tired of losing to Centre and had developed a system where alumni in each of the 120 counties of the state were asked to watch out for good athletes in their area and try to steer them to the state university.

Ben Cregor received permission to develop a program for Centre which was hoped would counter the efforts over in Lexington. He would visit various high schools which played football and invite the entire team and coaching staff to come to Danville to watch a game. Of course, there would be no charge for admission, and after the contest, the high school players would get a chance to meet and mingle with the Colonels.

For the Homecoming game, Cregor traveled to Richmond, Kentucky and invited the Richmond Madison team to come over to Danville, and even though tickets were being scalped, Cregor said he would find room to squeeze the visitors into the new stadium for the Kentucky game, or let them stand behind the Colonels' bench.

It was a great recruiting tool. There was no more exciting contest or atmosphere for an impressionable boy in Kentucky to witness than a Homecoming game between Centre College and the University of Kentucky, especially in what was certain to be a stadium packed with an enthusiastic, screaming crowd.

There are traditional football rivalries which are huge. They transcend geographical boundaries and over the years have gained national recognition. Some include: Army-Navy, Texas-Oklahoma, Michigan-Ohio State, Florida-Georgia, Auburn-Alabama, Southern Cal-Notre Dame, California-Stanford, Harvard-Yale.

Centre and Kentucky? Hardly. But in the years after the Great War, at least in the Bluegrass, it was—Centre and Kentucky.

After the 1916 blow out with Kentucky winning 68-0, the series stood 13-9-1 in Centre's favor. Going into the 1923 contest, with Centre having won the last five games by a cumulative score of 194-3, the Colonels held the edge, 18-9-1.

Kentucky had become absolutely obsessed with beating Centre. Likewise, Centre's goal was to continue beating Kentucky. The press played up the rivalry and made the public feel that either team's season was successful, irrespective of other games, if their main, in-state foe was vanquished.

That passion was why so many of the Centre partisans quickly forgot about the defeat at the hands of Pennsylvania. After all, that game was in a faraway place against an unknown team. But now, it was—Kentucky.

Kentucky was playing pretty good football coming into the Centre game. The Wildcats were 4-0-1.

Kentucky	41	Marshall	0
Kentucky	14	Cincinnati	0
Kentucky	6	Washington & Lee	6
Kentucky	28	Maryville	0
Kentucky	35	Georgetown (Ky.)	0

The competition hadn't been especially dazzling, but Washington and Lee ended up tying Vanderbilt for the Southern Conference title in 1923, the Generals' tie with Kentucky being the only blemish in their conference games.

The November 3 game was important to Centre for several reasons. Obviously, the most important was the rivalry between the two schools, and the fact that the winner would be thought of as the best team in Kentucky. Also, Uncle Charlie was anxious to put the Penn game behind the team and get back into the win column. Additionally, the game could possibly be an important part of the claim to at least the "mythical" Southern Championship. And finally, it was the game in which the new stadium would be dedicated.

Lexington had developed "Centre Fever." Again, "This is the year!" was the motto. The Southern Railroad had plans to assemble special trains to bring 3,000 fans to Danville on Saturday, arriving at 1:30 p.m., an hour before the kickoff. In addition, the railroad had lined up multiple Pullmans to bring passengers over from Lexington and Louisville late Friday afternoon for those who wished to take in the Friday evening Homecoming activities. The Pullmans would be left on a siding for the passengers to use as a "hotel" during their stay, departing from Danville early Sunday morning so that the passengers could attend the dance in the Boyle-Humphrey Gymnasium the evening after the game.

Again, as in previous years, all of the rooms at the Gilcher and Henson hotels on Main Street had long been booked. Boarding houses were full, and the citizens of Danville who wanted to accommodate overnight guests contacted the local Chamber of Commerce and let their willingness be known. Special buses were arranged to carry people from the Beaumont Inn in nearby Harrodsburg to Danville and back. Danville literally mobilized for Homecoming!

Every restaurant laid in extra supplies. Florists made certain that they had adequate amounts of flowers in the two team's colors. Again, Spoonamore's and other drug stores did a landslide business in selling crepe paper and pennants until Danville was covered with Centre's gold and white. The local medical community set up a first aid station in the science building, Young Hall, to be staffed all day the Saturday of the game.

Downtown merchants received an appeal from the Chamber to be certain to sweep the sidewalk and gutters "in order that the many visitors will see a pretty and clean town."

Workers took timbers from the old stadium and began the construction of 1,500 temporary seats in the south end zone, assuring that over 13,000 could be seated, and by the time those who would be standing were counted, plus those who would be up phone poles and in trees, and watching from Old Main and other buildings, it was estimated that the total attendance would be 15,000.

There were so many tasks to take care of. How many members of the press will be at the game and are there adequate chairs in the press box? Do we have enough students to sell programs? What about parking and who will be in charge? Who will make certain that the governor's parking spot isn't taken? Will the bath rooms in Old

Main and the gym be adequate? Are they stocked?

The "Courier-Journal" again planned on having photographs available for its "bulldog" edition which hit the streets in Louisville at 9:00 p.m. Saturday night. The paper stated that it would not only have "action photos, but images of the crowd in the new stadium."

It was announced that classes at Centre and K.C.W. were cancelled on the day of the game. All of the merchants had signs printed which they could quickly put on their door or window which announced that they were "Closed for Game." Papers were published all over Kentucky with previews of the upcoming "Harvard-Yale Game of Kentucky."

Each night of the week leading up to the game, pep rallies were held on the Centre campus, including a performance by the Centre "Six" on the steps of Old Centre. There was a final huge rally attended by all of the students from Centre and K.C.W., plus townspeople and out of town guests on Friday evening, just before the smoker and dance in the gym.

Meanwhile, while the town and college were getting ready, Uncle Charlie was similarly getting his team primed for the game. In analyzing the Penn game, it was felt that the line needed extra help, and Red Weaver was contacted and agreed to come to Danville for the week to assist Ben Cregor. Uncle Charlie told friends confidentially that his goal was not only to shut out Kentucky, but to hold the Wildcats offense to under 100 yards.

"We can score against Kentucky, I'm confident of that. We're working this week on defense."

During Thursday's practice, an airplane flew over Cheek Field, banked and came down low and circled the field several times. Uncle Charlie blew his whistle and halted practice until the plane finally gained some altitude and flew toward the direction of Lexington.

"Can you believe that?" Uncle Charlie declared. "They're trying to spy on our practice. Those varmints!"

It was never proven that it was a reconnaissance flight, but Centre always believed that someone had tried to take photographs of the Colonels' formations. At least that was the story, bolstered by the fact that one could go days without seeing a plane circling in the skies above Danville, Kentucky.

Former Colonels' players arrived in Danville on Friday. Bill Shadoan came down from Valparaiso. Terry Snowday was in Ashland and came over through Lexington. (Terry's brother, Roger, was a junior and on the football team. He was also quite a baseball and basketball player, being the captain of the basketball team in 1924.)

Chick Murphy came from Columbus, Ohio. Phil Pigeon, a star halfback some years before, checked into the Gilcher. Tom Moran came up from Jefferson City to see his old teammates, and to lend support to his father.

Herb Covington's parents and Hennie Lemon's mother came from Mayfield. Bo sent a telegram expressing his regret at not being able to attend, but urged the team on.

It was reported that Coach Winn of Kentucky had driven his team hard all week with the slogan, "Beat Centre's line and you beat Centre!"

Jop, on hearing that, wrote in his "Sport Flashes" column:

We believe that Kentucky has as much of a chance of tearing our line to ribbons as an armless man would have in winning a bowling tournament. Any time you see a Centre gridder giving up to a blue-sweatered UK individual, you can believe it's snowing in South Florida.

Centre and Kentucky felt that the game was important enough to warrant four instead of the usual three officials. F.A. Lambert from Ohio State, Don Henry from Missouri, Roger Johnson from Michigan, and Kenyon's Harry Wessling were brought to Danville to call the game.

I think when looking back on my football experiences at Centre that other than going to the 1922 Harvard game, the most exciting and colorful, perfect example of what college football was meant to be, was the week of Homecoming in 1923, my junior year. There was such spirit. We had lost to Pennsylvania, but everybody knew we had a great team, and we all wanted to show our support even more because of that loss. It's easy to back a team when they win. And we nearly always won. But it's even more important to get behind a team that has just lost, and pull them back up by the spirit and support that you show when the guys are maybe a little down.

We had such great pep rallies that even if members of the team were in a skull session, or in their room resting, they could hear the shouting which literally filled the campus. We had a big rally out on the baseball field which I can still visualize, and even smell the smoke which came off a bonfire which we built.

Howard and his group, the "Six," were there performing, and we all clapped and kept rhythm as they played, and then they began these little bursts of music like they had at Harvard. They'd play a few bars and stop suddenly and we'd shout "Fight!" Over and over. They'd play and we'd shout "Fight!" It made chills go down your spine to be out in the cool nighttime air, huddled around a big fire, and just spontaneously be involved in such a wonderful show of love for your school, and love for your team. Everybody was there.

Duh de dum, duh de dum— "Fight!"
Duh de dum, duh de dum— "Fight!"
Over and over.
Duh de dum, duh de dum— "Fight!"

I'm not certain that students do that sort of thing anymore. If they don't, they're missing something. They're missing something they would remember all of their lives.

GAME DAY, NOVEMBER 3, 1923 CENTRE-KENTUCKY

It was an overcast day. The prediction was for rain, but it was still dry, though threatening, as the crowd converged on the stadium. Despite all of the planning, no one

496

had seen the consequences of 3,000 people disembarking from the trains and arriving virtually as one mass. Nor did the Centre authorities realize that many people wouldn't want to immediately go to their seats, but rather just stand at the north end of the field, the open end nearest the gates, in order to stare and admire the magnificent new stadium.

The bottleneck and confusion caused the dedication ceremony to be missed by most of the fans due to the noise, the onset of thunder, and then the final rush to get to their seats. Contemporary accounts stated that Dr. Montgomery gave a nice speech, and the ribbon, which is always part of such proceedings, duly cut, having been held by two Centre cheerleaders, but the impression was given that the whole affair was under appreciated because just as Dr. Montgomery was unwinding, the sky was unleashing, and a real downpour soaked him and every one of the 15,000 people who were squeezing into and around the new stadium.

Despite the less than auspicious start, the crowd remained jovial and excited, anxious to get the game underway, and to cheer on their favorites. Game time was 2:30.

"This is the year!"

After the brief but intense shower, Uncle Charlie decided to make some last minute changes in his line-up. The turf at Cheek Field looked great, but it was deceptive, as the roots of the grass weren't deep, and in the warm-ups, footing seemed slippery and uncertain, and every time someone slid, the grass went shooting off, producing divots.

Uncle Charlie decided to start his heaviest backfield, and that meant switching 185 lb. Minos Gordy to fullback, moving Case Thomasson out of the backfield to Gordy's end position, and replacing the 152 lb. Hope Hudgins with sophomore, Murrell "Jake" Summers, at 177 lbs. The plan was to concentrate the Colonels' attack on running, just pounding the Kentucky line.

KENTUCKY			CENTRE	
Rice, A.T.	185	Left end	Lemon	170
Montgomery	221	Left tackle	Skidmore	175
Ramsey	178	Left guard	Rubarth	170
Sauer	187	Center	Kubale	185
Rice, W.H.	180	Right guard	Lynch	195
Stevenson	209	Right tackle	Chinn	220
King	178	Right end	Thomasson	175
Hughes	155	Quarterback	Covington	160
Kirwan	184	Left half	Spurlock	185
Tracy	155	Right half	Summers	177
Sanders	180	Fullback	Gordy	185

Ed Kubale won the toss and Centre received. Herb Covington returned the kick 37 yards and would have scored except for a last ditch tackle by a diving Wildcat. The Colonels then followed their game plan, running 14 straight ground plays. Hennie Lemon capped the time consuming drive by kicking a field goal from the 20, and

Centre led 3-0. Many of the capacity crowd were still admiring the stadium or trying to get seated when the successful kick was made.

Centre moved the ball at will the rest of the half, and played gang-tackling, inspired defense, spurred on by Uncle Charlie letting the team know in his pre-game speech that his goal was to hold the Kentucky team to less than 100 yards of offense.

Once the Colonels got to the Wildcats' six inch line, but couldn't buck it over. Several times drives stalled within the 'Cats' 20. Twice, after Lemon's first kick, he again attempted field goals, but the field conditions made it hard to make perfect contact, and both efforts were wide.

Centre picked up 11 first downs to Kentucky's two, and one of those was due to a penalty. Despite the overwhelming superiority of the Gold and White, the 1st half ended with the Colonels up by only 3-0.

Halftime saw the Kentucky band try to go through a spirited, precision drill while playing their selections on the field's slick grass.

You know how certain things stand out, so that you later remember them, especially if they're humorous? Kentucky's band had a sort of heavy tuba player—I think that was the instrument. Anyway, it was one of those big, brass horns. He was trying to follow along during the marching, and apparently he was supposed to spin around on his heels and take off in another direction.

As he turned, his feet went out from under him and he fell flat on his back, and his instrument went flying off to the side, and another band member was blowing away, not paying attention, and he tripped over the big horn and landed flat also, but he fell forward, and it looked like he'd nearly impaled himself on his horn, but he eventually got up and shook the mud and grass out of his instrument and tried to keep playing. Several of the members of the band had to quit playing because they were laughing so hard, including both of the guys who had fallen.

It was about that time that they decided to stop trying to march, and just stood around out on the field and finished their songs. The crowd loved it so much that they got a long, standing ovation when they finally walked back off the field.

Several of us decided later that they should have put that routine into every halftime performance. It was like one of those Keystone Cops, slapstick movies which were so popular back then.

The band's performance was the highlight of Kentucky's efforts that day.

Henry Bloom, sports editor of the Louisville "Post," was in the new press box for the game, and wired a story back to his paper.

If Centre can continue to play the kind of football she displayed today against Kentucky, she will probably win the remaining games and capture the Southern crown. The Penn game made Centre. The defeat proved a bitter but beneficial tonic.

Saturday, Centre put the best football team she has ever had on the field. This may sound extravagant to those who recall the days of Red Weaver, Bo McMillin, and Red Roberts.

While it is true the Colonels have no individual stars to measure up to those players, they have the best teamwork that any Centre eleven has ever shown. The line charged compactly, the tackling had ferocity, the interference and blocking were superb, and the generalship by Herb Covington was flawless. Eleven players took part in every play.

Centre was a machine. The plays were run without a hitch, and the thorough drilling the team got was evident in the smoothness of every move.

For Kentucky, it can only be said that the players were courageous and fought with all of the individual skill that they possessed.

After Covington's return of the opening kickoff brought the ball into Kentucky's territory, Centre played the entire first half in Wildcat territory, and Kentucky never crossed midfield.

The 3rd quarter was more of the same. For Kentucky, it was two or three offensive plays and then a punt. For Centre, it was a steady advance all during the period, but each drive was ultimately frustrated by a desperate Kentucky defense.

Jop had some choice comments in his coverage.

Centre's defense was as tight as a window in a Pullman car.

Coach Winn tried to dam the leaks in his defense and moved up replacements like a field general trying to brace a faltering division.

It was one of the cleanest and dirtiest games ever played in Kentucky. The cleanest because of the wonderful sportsmanship displayed by both teams. The dirtiest because of the condition of the field. Enough towels were used in wiping off the ball and player's faces to stock a city hotel.

In the 4th quarter, Covey sent Albert Spurlock and Case Thomasson downfield, one right behind the other. Kentucky had only one back, Al "Ab" Kirwan, defending the area. Case hollered to Spurlock, "You take the pass and I'll block the back."

Case brought Kirwan to the ground by a roll-block, and Covey, because the ball was so slick, took both hands and shot it like a basketball toward Spurlock. The ball arched up in the air and floated without a spiral to "Spur's" outstretched hands, and the halfback pivoted carefully and gingerly ran untouched across the goal.

Jop: *With the score, Centre had a comfortable lead, and Kentucky's hopes perished like a bamboo hut in a fire-swept village.*

Spurlock, known as "Cyclone" to some, got a reserved seat in the Centre "Hall of Fame" by his performance today.

Hope Hudgins, when he replaced Summers, played beautifully, picking up yardage on every play. Ed Kubale, "the battling fool," played wonderful defense and his center passing of the slick ball was unerring.

Covington was master of the situation at all times. He handled the slippery ball like a salty fisherman lassoing his catch.

Danville is making merry, for the Colonels have come back.

When one looks at the final score of 10-0, it seemed like the two programs were reaching parity. It may have been thought that Kentucky was narrowing the gap. It was 56-0 in 1919, 49-0 in 1920, 55-0 in 1921, and the 1922 game ended, 27-3.

However, the statistics and analysis of what happened on the field didn't exactly bear that out. Centre had 17 first downs to Kentucky's three, and one was due to a penalty. In 60 minutes of play, the Wildcats never crossed midfield, not once!

That is domination, whatever the final score.

"Hey Unc, we told you we could hold them to less than 100 yards, didn't we?"

"That you did, boys. That you did. It was a great effort."

A WONDERFUL GESTURE FOR JIMMY GREEN

Toward the very end of the game, when victory seemed certain, Uncle Charlie made only his second substitution of the game. Jimmy Green, the senior from Louisville, was playing in his last game in Danville, as the rest of the schedule would be on the road.

Uncle Charlie called Jimmy over and had him remove his helmet and signaled for Captain Kubale to call time out. Then the Centre mentor walked Jimmy half way out to Centre's position on the field and took off his hat and turned to the home, west side fans, and waved his hat back and forth, as the players on the field and on the bench began to whistle and shout, and then the fans all got on their feet and joined in the cheering. Hope Hudgins came out of the game after hugging Jimmy on the field.

It was a wonderful demonstration for Jimmy Green. I was a scrub on the baseball team and Jimmy was quite a player. Played second base. He didn't have a great career in football, because he had so many fellows who were better than he was playing in the backfield. But he was out there every year, and he was captain of the basketball team one year, and played tennis on our little tennis team, and in addition to that, he was just a prince of a fellow. Everyone stood and cheered when he got in for a few plays, and then Uncle Charlie took him out and let him run back off the field and he got a huge ovation again. It was a great way to end his career on Cheek Field.

ON TO MEMPHIS, NOVEMBER 10, 1923   CENTRE-SEWANEE

The week after the Kentucky game, the Danville "Advocate" received a letter from "its good friend," Colonel Robert E. Burton, who was visiting in Waterloo, Iowa. Colonel Burton reported that he was listening to some men in a restaurant talking about football, and one asked, "Where in the world is Danville, Kentucky?" Another diner, a big husky fellow, looked up, astonished.

"Why you darn fool. Danville is located in Centre College, the place where Uncle Charlie Moran presides, and Bo McMillin and Red Roberts trained."

The "Advocate" added a comment.

That big guy, "shore do know his jargfy."

Centre and the University of the South, located in Tennessee and commonly called Sewanee, for the little mountainous town which is its home, had met in 1917 in Chattanooga, and the Colonels had bottled up the Tigers' star, Eben Wortham, and won 28-0. Now, six years later, the two teams were again going to meet on a "neutral" site, Memphis, the largest city in Tennessee, located on the Mississippi River in the far southwestern part of the state.

Why Memphis? Because the sports fans in the city were much like those in Louisville. They were "mad" for football.

The previous year, the civic leaders of Memphis had contacted Centre and made a very attractive offer for the Colonels to come to their city. They said they'd secure a suitable opponent, one from Tennessee, and Centre sent back word that the offer seemed perfectly suitable, and the school would like to come to Memphis as long as the opponent was a member of the Southern Conference.

The reasoning was that Centre wanted to meet a member of the conference which hopefully could be defeated, and be part of the school's claim to being the best team in the South.

That narrowed the candidates to three possibilities: Tennessee, Vanderbilt or Sewanee. The organizing committee in Memphis was able to get the Tigers to sign on.

Memphis simply hadn't had access to any big-time football. There was a college named West Tennessee Normal College which had been chartered in 1909, and opened its doors in 1912. (This college evolved over the years into West Tennessee State Teacher's College in 1925, Memphis State in 1941, and became known as the University of Memphis in 1994.)

To use the terms "West Tennessee Normal" and "big-time" in the same sentence was actually an oxymoron. In 1922, when plans were fermenting to bring Centre to Memphis, West Tennessee Normal actually was competing at a level where two high schools from Arkansas were on the schedule, and the college just managed to tie both Blytheville High and Wilson High.

If a Memphian wanted to step up to a higher level of college football, it was necessary to travel south 50 miles to Oxford, home of the University of Mississippi. The last game of any real significance in Memphis was in 1915 when Vandy slaughtered Ole Miss by the remarkable score of 91-0.

Centre was a natural for Memphis, the promoters reasoned. Centre had beaten Harvard, Harvard represented the North, and Memphis was about as Southern as it got. Centre would fill any stadium where the game could be scheduled, as folks from Memphis already had developed affection for the slayers of the big, Northern power.

Sewanee was also an ideal opponent due to the significant number of loyal alumni who lived in the river city, and it was a member of the Southern Conference and from Tennessee.

Centre couldn't do anything on the Monday after the Kentucky game but work out in sweat suits. The field had been so muddy that the team changed into their practice uniforms at the half of the Kentucky contest, and the managers were still trying to get the two sets of moleskins scraped off so they could be washed.

Tuesday, things got back to normal, but a surprise arrived in the form of a telegram to Captain Kubale. "Kube" opened the envelope and read with astonishment. Jop was there.

During the past few years, the Centre Colonels have been invited to radio contests, boxing matches, dinner and theatre parties, luncheons, dances and what nots, but the climax came today when Captain Kubale received a telegram from a Southern debutante asking the team to be her guests at a tea Friday afternoon at her home in Memphis.

George Chinn, an A-1 tea hound around Mundy's landing, a popular spot to hang out along the Kentucky River north of Danville, urged Kubale to wire back an acceptance. The captain decided to put the invitation to a vote.

Chinn stood up to make his case.

"There's very little difference between a tea and a weenie roast, except the nourishment served," was Chinn's reasoning.

The vote was 27–1 not to accept. Chinn voted.

The "Grid-Graph" was going to be set up in the gym from now on, starting with the Sewanee game, according to the "Advocate." Spectators said the sun made it too difficult to see, and also, the gym could be heated, and Cheek Field couldn't. The cost to "watch" would be 50 cents.

Centre's freshman team was going to play Sewanee's first year men down in Sewanee while the two school's varsity teams were pairing off in Memphis. The logistics were worked out by agents from the Southern Railroad and the L&N who came and met with the Centre authorities.

The freshmen were to take the Southern to Chattanooga, then transfer at the big Southern station to the Nashville, Chattanooga and St. Louis line to ride up the mountains to Cowan, where they would follow the Mountain Goat route into Sewanee. There would be 20 players on the Lieutenants' squad, and the team was to be coached by Jim Kendrick. Assistant student manager, sophomore Eugene Roemele, was going to take care of the equipment and tape ankles.

The varsity was going to have a skull session and light workout Thursday afternoon, change into their traveling clothes, have dinner and be driven the few miles south to Junction City where the L&N had a small station. The college had chartered a Pullman for the trip which would be left on a siding at the station while the team was in Memphis. The railroad had assigned a ticket agent to accompany the team on the trip, making certain that all of its needs were met.

There were 22 varsity players, coaches Moran and Cregor, faculty representative, Dr. A. E. Porter, two student managers and a student trainer on the 14 section sleeper.

Amazingly, little Centre College was sending 42 players, three coaches, four student managers/trainers and a faculty rep to play football in two locations during the weekend of November 10, 1923, 50 people in all.

To get to Memphis from Danville, one had to take a somewhat indirect route. From Junction City, the Pullman of the Colonels was hooked onto a passenger train heading north to Louisville. The team pulled away on the first leg at 6:30 in the evening, arriving at the L&N's 10th Street Station at 10:00 p.m. The players were able to get off for a few moments and greet well-wishers while their car was joined to a southbound L&N train which was going to and through Bowling Green, Kentucky. They slept through another uncoupling and connection there, being joined to a west bound L&N train which carried them all night toward Memphis, and arrived well rested the next morning.

The trip had taken approximately 15 hours, a relatively short journey when compared to the marathon ventures to Boston and Philadelphia.

The team was transported to the eight story, 400 room Chisca Hotel, built in 1913, located at 272 South Main, and had a hearty breakfast. Then there was free time to explore the downtown which the coaches always tried to find time for the team to do.

"We want you to see the country, and get out and walk and explore when we get into new places," the Chief had said many times. "We travel to play football, but we also travel to broaden our knowledge about different parts of the country."

When one looks back on all of the experiences that Centre's team had, there was arguably no college in the country that gave the members of its football team such a wonderfully broad education through travel. One advantage of not having had a stadium of significance until 1923 was that Centre had to travel, and the team's many journeys took the young players to all corners of the country.

After the sightseeing, the Colonels traveled to Russwood Park, scene of the next day's game. There was a light workout, and the Sewanee team arrived just as Centre was leaving. The players mingled a while, and made small talk about common opponents they had met during the year.

Both of the schools had played Carson-Newman and Oglethorpe, and when comparable scores were analyzed, Centre would have appeared to be the favorite.

Centre-14	Carson-Newman-0
Sewanee-0	Carson-Newman-0
Centre-29	Oglethorpe-0
Sewanee-13	Oglethorpe-0

Overall, Sewanee was 4-2-1 going into the Centre game and had played well against a strong Alabama team (7-2-1), and Texas A&M (5-3-1.) Alabama was played in Birmingham and A&M in Dallas.

Sewanee	0	Carson-Newman	0
Sewanee	3	Howard	2
Sewanee	34	Southwestern	0
Sewanee	0	Texas A&M	14
Sewanee	0	Alabama	7
Sewanee	13	Oglethorpe	0
Sewanee	26	Chattanooga	0

(Alabama was in its first year under Wallace Wade, who took over the Tide's program after Uncle Charlie turned down the offer to coach in Tuscaloosa.)

Friday night, the Memphis Chamber of Commerce arranged a special performance at the Lyric Theatre for both teams. The "Dixie Revue of 1923" was the feature, and special boxes for the Colonels and Tigers were "the best seats in the house."

On Saturday, November 10, the day before the celebration of Armistice Day, and the 5th anniversary of the end of the slaughter that had been the result of the Great War, the Colonels awoke to find a city decked out in red, white and blue.

There were flags all over the hotel, inside and out. The local citizens had also unfurled many a Confederate flag. It was 58 years since the "War of Succession," and many old soldiers who had worn the Blue and Gray of the Rebel Army were still alive and well all over the South.

After a light breakfast, there was a skull session at the Chisca. Uncle Charlie gave a speech at the end of the session, reinforcing the importance of the game.

"We can be the best team in the South. We have defeated Clemson. We have defeated Kentucky. If we win over Sewanee, we have a good shot of running the string out against the rest of the Southern teams on our schedule. If we were to lose today," and Uncle Charlie paused for effect, "it won't make any difference what we do against Auburn, or Washington and Lee, or Georgia. If you play like you did last week against Kentucky, if you play eleven men as one, you can beat any team in the country."

Captain Kubale, in his quiet way, urged his teammates on.

"We are Centre. And Unc, we will play as one. We are ready."

The team picked up on their captain's words.

"We are Centre! We are Centre! We are Centre! We are Centre!"

There were three cheers, and it was off to Russwood Park.

The game was sold out. The 11,500 seats were taken, and a large number who didn't have a ticket paid for standing room. The ballpark was brightly decorated with the Stars and Stripes, Centre's gold and white, and the purple and white of the Sewanee Tigers.

Memphis truly was—"Mad for football!"

The Colonels were met with the enthusiastic applause they were used to when they came out on the field for warm-ups, but the Tigers were even more warmly greeted, which was to be expected, as they were the Tennessee team, even though Sewanee was some 300 miles east of Memphis.

Centre won the toss and received. The Colonels couldn't do anything and Albert Spurlock punted. The sophomore from Mount Cory, Ohio, boomed one of his best ever kicks, with great height and distance. The "hang time" allowed Centre's downfield men to reach the ball just as a Tiger back named Powers fielded it. A hard hit popped the ball loose, and Frank Rubarth covered it on the 13. Hope Hudgins got 11 around end, and on the next play, he popped through the line and scored. Lemon was errant on the extra point, but the Colonels quickly led, 6-0.

It looked like a rout may be in order, but Sewanee was no pushover and fought back, and especially played tough, hard hitting defense. Centre's defense was even more impenetrable. The quarter ended, 6-0.

The second quarter was basically a punting contest between Spurlock and Sewanee's Sanders. The crowd was brought to its feet by an electrifying 50 yard run by Herb Covington, but a holding penalty nullified the great effort by the Colonels' quarterback.

The Tigers never got past midfield during the half, and managed only one first down during the first 30 minutes of play, which ended, 6-0.

At the half, there was a stirring performance by the brass band hired by the Memphis promoters. One patriotic song after another was capped by the traditional, "Dixie," which was met with rebel yells and prolonged cheering, resembling the reception that the Southern "anthem" received in New Orleans in 1921.

Sewanee chose to kick starting the second half, and a most unusual play ensued. The big Tiger fullback, Sanders, placed the ball down, and I.H. Dearing, a reporter covering the game, described what happened.

Sanders, kicking off for Sewanee, furnished a unique sight seldom if ever seen. He braced himself well in order to send the ball far into Centre territory, swung his foot, and missed clean.

Centre gained possession after the officials went to the side of the field and had a long conference. One of the refs later said, "We really were somewhat confused about how to call it because, quite frankly, none of us had ever seen a kicker totally miss the ball. Maybe just squib it, yes, but totally miss it, no. We decided the ball should go over to Centre, and there was no protest from Sewanee, because none of their people had ever seen something as strange as that either."

On the first play after the whiff, as Centre took over on the Tiger's 40, Kubale fired a center pass back but Hope Hudgins had broken the wrong way. "Blood" Miller, Sewanee's left end, scooped up the free ball on the 50 and raced unmolested for a score. The extra point was no good, and it was 6-6. Everyone agreed that it was a weird way to start a half, to say the least.

Uncle Charlie and the Centre bench had remained absolutely calm, much as had been the case after the TCU touchdown in the bowl game of January 1, 1921. As in Fort Worth, Uncle Charlie simply clapped his hands and said, "That's ok boys. Now take it to them."

Centre got to work immediately. Covington directed the offense brilliantly, alternating runs and passes. Hudgins made some timely gains. Near the goal line, Covey squeezed through the line and took it in. The Tigers were fighting furiously and on the score, two of their team didn't get up. Captain Cooper Litton had hit Covey hard as the quarterback fell across the line and remained motionless on the ground, blood gushing from his nose. He was out cold. Another Tiger, George Millard, was writhing on the turf, rocking back and forth and clutching at his arm.

The crowd was absolutely silent as what seemed like every doctor in Memphis rushed out on the field. An ambulance was called, and by the time it got to the field, Litton, though still dazed, was beginning to respond. Both players were placed on stretchers and transported to the Baptist Hospital.

Captain Litton was a Memphis boy and after his nose was straightened and taped, he was discharged to his parents. Millard, with a broken arm, remained in the hospital. Neither returned to Sewanee for several days.

After everything settled down, Lemon kicked the extra point and Centre led 13-6.

Near the end of the 3rd quarter, Covey again directed a drive which culminated with a 25 yard TD pass to Hennie Lemon. The Colonels were somewhat lucky on the play as Powers tipped the ball and it floated over to Lemon who somewhat casually let it drop into his hands and he backed up a step and over the goal. His kick made it 20-6.

That was the final score. Sewanee had heart and never gave up. Once, near the end of the game, the Tigers drove to the one yard line but Frank Rubarth made a stunning hit on the first and goal play, the ball popped loose, and Centre recovered, ending the last threat by Sewanee.

It had been a dogfight, a clean game marked by few penalties. Besides the two injured Tigers, Covey and Hudgins limped off the field. The crowd stood and cheered and waved to the two teams as they congratulated each other and finally left the field, arms over shoulders, with pats on the back, and hands firmly shaken with smiles and best wishes.

It was college football as it should be played, between two small schools which competed in a manner far beyond their size, and everyone felt it a shame that either had to lose. Sewanee and Centre played many times after the Memphis meeting. Both schools faded from the big time, but their sportsmanship and dedication to the game has continued as members of the Division III Southern Collegiate Athletic Conference (SCAC), and the teams now have over 90 years of football experiences and memories, as well as friendships, built around their competition on the gridiron.

Centre retired to the Chisca, had a feast in the dining room, accepted congratulations from their boosters who had come to the hotel, and headed for their scheduled departure and overnight journey back to Danville.

Everyone from Centre was on the train. One didn't get back to Danville.

BROWN YOUNG WILLIS, JR. HAS A SCARY EXPERIENCE

After the game, student manager Brown Young Willis, Jr. was driving a car owned by a Memphis broker, Francis W. Andrews. Jewell F. Thompson, a local salesman, pulled out of a blind alley according to young Willis, and his car was struck. Thompson was thrown out, striking his head on the curb. Willis stopped, called an ambulance, and sent the unconscious salesman to the hospital, and left the scene, according to a later police report, "rapidly."

It was late in the evening before Andrews' car was identified. He was arrested and taken to jail. While there, under questioning, he identified Willis as the driver, said the young Centre student was on a train with the Colonels' team, and he was released on bond.

The police consulted the L&N and determined that the train pulling Centre's Pullman hadn't yet passed through Paris, Tennessee. The police in Paris were contacted and asked to remove Willis when the train made a regular stop in the town, which they did.

Detective Fox arrested the young student and caught a train back to Memphis and turned him over to the Memphis authorities, where he was jailed on a "hit and run" charge. Willis admitted that he had "hit," but denied he had "run."

"I stopped and rendered aid and called an ambulance. That was all I could do, so I left. I didn't speed off. I drove away at a normal speed."

Meanwhile, word was received from the hospital that Thompson was deteriorating and wasn't expected to live. That meant the charge would now be upped to manslaughter, and a jail sentence looked likely.

Prominent local Memphis businessmen Graham Southwick and J.A. Evans immediately came to the jail and posted $2,500 to free the shaken Willis, who proclaimed his innocence. Brown Young Willis, Sr. caught a Southern train to Danville from his home in Nicholasville, met up with President Montgomery of Centre, and together they boarded an L&N train at Junction City and headed to Memphis.

After the dire report from the hospital, the police went to re-arrest Willis, but another $2,500 in bail money was put up which kept him free.

The next morning there was a "whoops" report from the hospital. Thompson was sitting up, asking for breakfast, and wanted to go home. He shortly thereafter walked out of the hospital, none the less for wear other than being somewhat hazy about the whole affair.

Brown Young Willis, Jr. graduated with his class in 1925.

Brown and I were classmates and Phi Delts together. We had heard all kinds of things about how he was in jail and may have to go to prison and no one could believe it. He was the nicest person in the world, and we were really relieved to see him back in Danville.

I remember that he said it would be a long time before he'd ever go back to Memphis, Tennessee!

AUBURN, THE "RUBBER" MATCH   NOVEMBER 17, 1923

Centre was 5-1. Auburn was next, the third game in a series in Birmingham which had been fiercely contested in 1921 and 1922, with Centre winning the first game, 21-0, and the Auburn Tigers prevailing 6-0 the following year when a blocked punt determined the winner.

As Uncle Charlie had said in Memphis, Centre was playing to be crowned the "Southern Champions," even if it was only for bragging rights. The situation was complicated in the Southern Conference because there were so many scenarios, but if Centre beat Auburn, W&L and Georgia, writers and fans would anoint the Colonels as the best of all the teams in the South.

Georgia Tech had tied Alabama and Florida. Alabama had that tie with Georgia

Tech. Georgia hadn't lost in the South, but still had tough games with Vanderbilt and Alabama, plus the season ending game with Centre. Vandy and Mississippi State had tied. Centre was looking good. The Colonels just needed to keep winning.

Even before the 1923 Centre-Auburn game, the civic leaders were talking to Centre about returning in 1924. Centre had developed quite a following in Birmingham, and the two previous games had them hanging from the rafters, total sellouts which had brought a lot of people and a lot of money into the businesses of the city.

During the week leading up to the Auburn game, Centre received an offer to come to Baltimore for a post-season game with the University of Maryland. Promoters had predicted a big payday as interest in the Terrapins' football team had soared after Maryland played powerful, undefeated Yale to a virtual standoff the week before in New Haven, losing 16-14.

Centre had to reluctantly decline, citing the restriction on after season games by both its own S.I.A.A., and the Southern Conference as well. (Yale didn't consider Maryland to be an intersectional game. The "Big 3" agreed that Maryland, the Virginia colleges and Georgia may have been below the Mason-Dixon Line, but they were "Eastern," and therefore scheduling them wasn't prohibited.)

Auburn had a new coach with the memorable name of Boozer Pitts. Pitts had taken over from Mike Donahue, who moved on to LSU after compiling a 95-35-5 record starting in 1904. (Donahue missed the 1907 season.)

Going into the Centre game, the Tigers were 3-2-2, in what most considered a rebuilding year after going 8-2 in 1922. Two of the stars of 1922, John Shirey, who boomed the long punts during the 1922 game, and Ed Sherling, were gone.

Auburn	0	Clemson	0
Auburn	20	Birmingham Southern	0
Auburn	30	Howard	0
Auburn	6	Army	28
Auburn	34	Fort Benning	0
Auburn	0	Georgia	7
Auburn	6	Tulane	6

The only common opponent was Clemson which Auburn tied and Centre beat handily, 28-7. Army beat the Alabamians convincingly at West Point, but it was recognized that this defeat didn't necessarily diminish Auburn as the Cadets had a great year. Army was 6-2-1 during the year, losing to Notre Dame (9-1), and Yale (8-0), and tying Navy in a year in which the Midshipmen went to the Rose Bowl and tied Washington.

Uncle Charlie pointed out that since he had been at Centre, his teams had never lost two straight to an opponent. That was one motivating factor in beating Auburn, and the other was that Centre wanted to win by a greater margin than Georgia's 7-0 win over the Tigers. Sports writers and fans had declared that Georgia had the best team in the South. Centre wanted to make a statement about that.

On Wednesday before the game, Centre held a practice and ran plays with such precision that Uncle Charlie could say nothing except, "Well done," as his players huddled around him before heading to the showers.

Captain Kubale was quoted by Jop to have urged on his teammates by hollering out one of the better comments ever uttered by a player during a football practice.

Come on lads, don't tarry now.

Jop said he didn't know if he was in Danville, Kentucky, or on the playing fields of Eton.

Again, the Colonels had a chartered Pullman to take them down to Birmingham. The car was a 14 section sleeper which would hold 28 people, and the travel group included 23 players, Coaches Moran and Cregor, and three student managers/trainers.

Jop was going on the trip, and he and Pearl, Uncle Charlie's wife, booked a slot on another Pullman which was carrying local Centre supporters.

The Southern had brought the two Pullmans down from Lexington late Thursday afternoon and left them on a siding, staffed, and ready to go. The team practiced in the afternoon, had a big dinner, and went to the station at 9:00. Again, a large crowd consisting of the student body and townspeople was at the station for the send off.

By 10:00, everybody was asleep. The southbound Queen City-Crescent City from Cincinnati, via Lexington, came into Danville at 11:30 and the two awaiting Pullmans were very gently connected to the train for the journey. It was such a smooth coupling that the sleeping Colonels never knew they were moving until the engine picked up enough speed to effect the gentle swaying of the car, and the clickety-clack of wheels on track made sleeping in the moving bedroom pleasurable.

An hour earlier, in Lexington, a similar connection had been made as the train now pulling the Colonels had picked up a Pullman filled with Kentucky Wildcats on their way to play Georgia Tech. The Danville and Lexington additions were the last cars on a long consist that rolled through Central Kentucky toward the state line of Tennessee. The boundary was passed at 3:00 a.m., and by 7:00 in the morning, the train was still north of Chattanooga.

Centre's and Kentucky's players met in the dining car for breakfast as they approached Chattanooga. The rivalry and battle of two weeks earlier was long forgotten as the two teams wished each other well in their upcoming games. At the Southern terminal, the two teams got off and chatted with fans and then the Wildcats' cars were connected to a Southern, Atlanta bound train, while the Colonels' remained hooked onto the Queen City-Crescent City bound for Birmingham, later terminating at New Orleans. (Kentucky tied Georgia Tech , 3-3, lost to Tennessee 18-0 on Thanksgiving, November 29, and finished 4-3-2.)

Birmingham turned out big-time for Centre. At 10:00 a.m. Friday morning, the team stepped off the train at Terminal Station and was greeted by a huge crowd, numerous reporters and photographers, dignitaries, members of the Chamber of Commerce, officials from Auburn, and Centre alumni from the area.

The Tutwiler was headquarters as before, and again, members of the Birmingham Country Club, led by S. L. Yerkes, arranged for practices and meals to be at the facility. By the third visit to Birmingham, the drill had been perfected.

Joe Guyon was at the practice on Friday afternoon. Guyon had been a member of the famous Carlisle Indians football team and went to Georgia Tech where he played on Tech's undefeated 1917 team and was an All-American in 1918. He was presently playing on the Oorang Indians, a National Football League team from Larue, Ohio made up of all native Americans, led by the great Jim Thorpe.

"I just had to see what everybody's been talking about, Charlie. All I hear is Centre, Centre, Centre."

Uncle Charlie invited the great Guyon to sit on the Centre bench for the next day's game.

The 1923 Centre-Auburn was another sellout with 20,000 tickets sold. It was a perfect afternoon for a football game on Saturday, and Centre matched the weather by playing a perfect football game.

The closest that Auburn got to Centre's goal was the 40 yard line. Centre's offense was described as being "like a finely tuned Stutz Bearcat," a sporting and fast roadster of the time. The boys from Danville "never missed a beat and were on key all afternoon. Auburn was helpless."

Centre ran 78 plays and gained 397 yards for an average of slightly over five yards every time a Colonel touched the ball. By contrast, the Auburn Tigers were able to get only 36 plays off all afternoon and gained but 96 yards totally, for an average pickup of slightly over two and a half yards per play.

Herb Covington once again had an outstanding game. The little sparkplug gained 188 yards, nearly doubling Auburn's total offense. Auburn had bottled up Centre's ground game in 1922, and Boozer Pitts had geared his team to watch for passes and end sweeps in 1923, thinking the Colonels wouldn't challenge the Tigers' front wall again.

Boozer made a bad call. Centre decided to ram it down Auburn's throat from the first play. Elmer "Roughy" Rabenstein took over a halfback position in the place of Hope Hudgins, still slowed from an injury against Sewanee.

It was Covey over left tackle. Rabenstein over the right side. Spurlock right up the middle behind Ed Kubale. Covey to the right, Spurlock to the left—play after play—relentlessly, the Colonels picked up yardage on every call.

Despite several excellent drives, Centre wasn't able to get the ball into the end zone during the 1st quarter, but the tone had been set. Auburn would run two or three plays and have to punt. Centre would then gear up its ground game, overwhelming the Tigers once again.

Centre was threatening as the 1st quarter ended, and Covey got six points shortly after the 2nd period began. Lemon was good, and that was all of the scoring for the first half as it ended, Centre 7-0.

One unfortunate event occurred in the 1st half which no one, not even Uncle Charlie, had ever seen before. George Chinn, the big Harrodsburg, Kentucky native, was leading the interference downfield ahead of Covington. He took out an Auburn back and landed, face first, on a yard marker which had been generously laid out with lime. Chinn scooped up a mouthful when he landed and swallowed as his stomach hit the ground. He quickly felt he was ablaze internally.

Time was called and Chinn gulped down water and actually nearly fainted but was revived with ammonia. Finally, Chinn was able to resume play, but after the game stated that, "One thing is certain. I've narrowed my possible jobs when I graduate. I'll never apply to be a fire eater in a side show."

In the 3rd quarter, the Colonels got the ball on the Auburn 40 and Rabenstein took over and ran nearly every play in a drive which culminated with "Roughy" diving over to score. For the afternoon, Rabenstein also out-rushed the entire Auburn team, picking up 106 yards in 25 carries. After the score, the Colonels lined up to kick the extra point and all 11 Tigers rushed. Covey calmly fielded the center and tossed a soft pass to Summers who had stepped into the end zone unmolested.

The 3rd quarter ended with Centre up, 14-0. Lemon kicked a field goal in the last period to end the scoring. Centre won 17-0.

Zip Newman covered the game for the Birmingham "News."

Even the Army's great set of bucking backs failed to dent the Auburn line as Covington, Rabenstein and Spurlock shot through it. Centre's offense moved on a perfect one-two beat, first over the right tackle, then the left, and occasionally slipping around end. Thomasson provided great interference out of the fullback position.

Centre presented a magnificently trained line. It charged as one man, inevitably getting the jump on the Tiger line. Kubale, Rubarth, Lynch, Chinn, Skidmore, Gordy and Lemon simply were superior to the Auburn front wall.

An interested observer at the game was none other than Ty Cobb, the "Georgia Peach," at the time the player/manager with the Detroit Tigers, and considered by many the greatest player ever to put on the spikes. Cobb was interviewed after the game and was very complimentary of the Colonels' play. But the reporter said he seemed even more impressed with Centre's ability to pack stadiums wherever the team played.

A Georgia Tech assistant coach, R.A. Clay, was in the press box scouting Auburn, Tech's next opponent. A reporter with the Atlanta "Georgian" asked him what he thought about the game.

Auburn has a good team. Coach Pitts has done a wonderful job. But Centre isn't just a good team. They are a great team. Auburn will be a tough opponent for us, because they certainly had to learn a lot about the game of football in this battle today. (Coach Clay was correct in his prediction. Tech and Auburn played to a 0-0 tie in their game played in Atlanta on Thanksgiving.)

Centre was 6-1 and was absolutely clicking. The capacity crowd left Rickwood Field knowing that they had seen a special team play as perfect a game as had ever taken place in Birmingham.

There was a festive reception and dance at the Birmingham Country Club the evening after the game. The team and Centre fans who had come down, plus all of the local alumni, partied far into the night. There was no pressure about getting in early as the returning train to Danville didn't pull out until Sunday evening.

It was a great night, well deserved after the way the team had played against the Auburn Tigers.

TO LOUISVILLE AND THE GENERALS OF W&L
NOVEMBER 24, 1923

Washington and Lee and Centre were to play for the third time in Louisville. The 1921 game was the first ever in the two school's history, and Centre won 25-0. The Colonels repeated in 1922, winning 27-6. W&L had become somewhat like Kentucky in that it felt, "This is the year!"

W&L's record when it headed to Louisville was 5-1-1 or 5-2-1. This needs some discussion. Contemporary accounts indicated that the Generals had forfeited a game with Washington and Jefferson, a Pennsylvania powerhouse during the era. However, W&J doesn't even list the game in its records for 1923. What happened was that W&J had a black halfback. W&L wouldn't play if the black half participated, and W&J did the correct thing and sent word that all its players played, or it didn't play at all, so the game was called off. It was cancelled according to W&J, not forfeited, but the all-time records on the W&L website indicate that the game should be carried as a 1-0 forfeit.

Another game on W&L's 1923 schedule also needs some explanation. W&L was shooting for the Southern Conference title. It had a game with non-member West Virginia on November 10, and lost 63-0. It was reported that since the game was meaningless in the race for the conference title, W&L sent some sacrificial 3rd stringers over to Charleston, West Virginia, and held back its regulars for later games with conference members, South Carolina and North Carolina State.

W&L	19	Western Maryland 7
W&L	6	Kentucky 6
W&L	28	St. John's 0
W&L	12	Virginia Tech 0
W&L	7	Virginia 0
W&L	0	West Virginia 63
W&L	13	South Carolina 7

Kentucky was a common opponent for W&L and Centre. The comparable scores would make Centre a favorite, as the Colonels beat the Wildcats much more convincingly than the 10-0 score would indicate, and W&L and Kentucky tied, 6-6.

Centre had played its previous Louisville games from 1920-22 at Eclipse Park, but a fire destroyed the facility and a new baseball park, which could also host a football game, was constructed south of the downtown on Eastern Parkway near the campus of the University of Louisville. Parkway Field was built of steel and concrete and at its completion, was one of the finest minor league parks in the country. It had permanent seating for 11,000, and the addition of some outfield bleachers allowed the promoters of the game to sell 12,500 tickets, which were taken quickly.

The two schools, now meeting for the third time, pretty much knew the routine in Louisville, just as Centre and Auburn had grown comfortable in Birmingham. Centre headed to the Seelbach Hotel and W&L to the Watterson.

Centre's entire student body booked the Southern's $5.04 round-trip fare to Louisville. The Colonels invited the Kentucky team and coaches, who didn't play again until Thanksgiving, to be their guests, and with all of the Danvillians and Lexingtonians going to Louisville, the Southern scrambled to get enough day coaches added to its regular trains to accommodate the huge number of passengers.

People loved to come to Louisville. It was the only metropolitan city in Kentucky, and including the towns just across the Ohio River in Indiana, there were 350,000 people in the area.(Lexington was a distant second with a population of approximately 55,000 in all of Fayette County.)

Louisville had the widest streets, the tallest buildings, the best hotels, the most fashionable stores, the best restaurants, and more theatres and opportunities for cultural advancement. Louisville was a big city with Southern charm, and possessed everything a Kentuckian could want—except a decent football team. Centre had done much to fill that void since its first game there in 1919.

Coming into the W&L game, Bob Dundron of the Louisville "Herald" had some observations about Uncle Charlie.

The season has demonstrated one thing. That is, it was really Moran's cleverness which built up Centre, and not, as many thought, the mere fact that he had the great star, Bo McMillin, on his team. Moran has taken material admittedly inferior to McMillin and Roberts, and has constructed a team that is able to win, and which plays a more varied game than when he had the luminaries mentioned here. We have known Uncle Charlie as a baseball player, an umpire, and a football coach. He is, with it all, a good fellow, but he is a hard driver on the field. That is what it takes to win. One must be relentless to score. Moran is of a natural, kindly disposition, and his men are all for him, but they realize that he will exact all that they can give him in a game.

You know, like I've said, we had several members of the team in our fraternity, the Phi Delts. Red Roberts, Hump, Terry Snowday, Bill Shadoan, Hope Hudgins, Tom Bartlett, Les Combs—they were all on the team.

They'd talk about Uncle Charlie a lot. He could be hard on them, sure, trying to make them the best they could be. But I never heard one player say anything negative about him.

You know, there are some people who you just want to please. You look up to them and want to do your best and get their approval. That's the way the team felt about Uncle Charlie. They didn't want to disappoint him. They wanted to hear his approval. They lived for that approval. I always thought that was a huge factor in what made him and the team so successful. Whatever he said, they'd die trying to do it.

You can't make people respect you. You have to earn that respect. Uncle Charlie was the type who everybody on the campus and in the town loved and respected. He was just that kind of guy.

Centre played almost as perfectly in Louisville against W&L as it had in Birmingham against Auburn. Again, the defensive effort was outstanding. Captain Ed Kubale was constantly urging on his teammates, cheering them to greater and greater effort.

The Centre leader was actually knocked out cold when he made a devastating hit on a W&L runner, but time was called and he was revived and continued playing. (Can you imagine that happening today? At a minimum, a player would have been put on a stretcher, restrained so that he couldn't move about, taken immediately to a hospital, undergone an emergency CAT scan, and probably admitted for observation overnight even if the scan was normal. Kubale was administered "smelling salts" and when he became responsive, he continued to play! But that was then, and now is now, and obviously things have changed, this time for the better.)

Jop was continuing to jazz up his reporting.

The 12,500 fans who witnessed the grid battle were sent into pulsating throbs of ecstatic glee by the thrilling accomplishments of Covington, the Colonel sky rocket, who went cork-screwing, spinning and weaving his way through the Virginian's defense.

The little busy body, who was prying into everything all afternoon, carried the ball four times in the first seven formations clicked off by Centre and gained a total of 57 yards. Three of the plays were end runs off kick formations, his interference forming magnificently on his dashes. After he took it in for the first score, Lemon kicked goal after touchdown.

One of those leading the interference was Frank Rubarth. After returning from the Auburn game, Rubarth had his nose x-rayed as it seemed to sit somewhat askew on his face. It was broken, of course, and that caused Uncle Charlie to swing into action with one of his protective contraptions. Rubarth didn't miss a minute of the W&L game.

The Generals played Centre to a standstill in the second quarter. Their big fullback, Captain Cameron, played heroically just as he had in 1922. Time after time he'd lower his head and rip into Centre's line, but his efforts were mostly in vain as he didn't have blockers in front of him which could overcome the Colonels' defense. The half ended, 7-0.

Watching the game from the Centre bench was big Bill Shadoan, who had come down from Valparaiso. The former Centre lineman was in Louisville not only to cheer on his old teammates, but to discuss the possibility of his Valpo team meeting the Colonels in 1924.

Centre dominated the second half. The Colonels were content to run power plays over the guards and tackles, much as they had done against Auburn. Ben Cregor had heaped praise on his linemen at the half.

"You're controlling the line of scrimmage. As long as you continue driving them back, Uncle Charlie wants the ground game to predominate."

Again, Ed Kubale cheered his "mates" on. "Take it to them, lads!"

George Chinn said, "Captain, you're from Fort Smith, Arkansas. The closet you've been to merry England is Boston in New England for a couple of days."

Twice, Covey led drives which got within field goal range, and twice Hennie Lemon converted, once from the 20, and the second effort, "a kick at a very difficult angle," from the 22. It was 13-0 after three quarters.

Covey had an electrifying run in the 4th quarter when he intercepted a pass at the 50 yard line and through a brilliant display of broken field running, cut back, then reversed, and zigged and zagged down the field for a score, which unfortunately, was nullified when it was determined that he had stepped out of bounds on the 40. From the 40, Covey then led a march, and he took it in from the eight. Lemon missed, and the score ended at 19-0.

Just as Uncle Charlie had been sensitive to the fact that Jimmy Green was playing his last game in Danville, so was the coach aware of the Louisville native appearing for the last time in his home town. Again, Jimmy was put in as the clock wound down and received the same standing ovation that he had gotten near the end of the Kentucky game.

In the three games in Louisville, Centre found W&L to be a worthy opponent. The Generals played hard, and they displayed wonderful sportsmanship. But Centre was a better team during the era, as evidenced by the fact that the Colonels outscored the boys from Lexington, Virginia, by a total of 71-6. (After the 1923 game, Centre and W&L didn't play again until 1933, when the two colleges met in Danville, with Centre winning, 13-0. There was no game in 2007, but through the 2006 meeting, the schools have lined up against each other 58 times, with the Colonels having a 35-21-2 record against the Generals.)

The Colonels stayed overnight in Louisville the Saturday night after the game. There was another of those wonderful parties hosted by the alumni of both of the schools. The rumor was already being circulated that Centre may not return to Louisville in 1924 due to the fact that the college wanted to schedule as many games as possible in the new stadium. It was agreed by all that if the Louisville series ended, everyone from Centre and Danville would always remember the great experiences and hospitality that had been afforded the school during the last five years.

The Colonels had compiled a wonderful record in the city, outscoring their opponents, 155-6.

1919	Centre	56	DePauw	0
1920	Centre	28	Virginia Tech	0
1921	Centre	25	W&L	0

| 1922 | Centre | 27 | W&L | 6 |
| 1923 | Centre | 19 | W&L | 0 |

The little school had competed brilliantly in the five appearances. Equally as important as the player's efforts during the games was their conduct off the field. They had developed lasting friendships and cemented relationships which bonded Centre College and the citizens of the state's principal city, and they were a major influence in creating a special relationship between Centre and Louisville which exists to this day.

ONE MORE GAME— THE GEORGIA BULLDOGS
DECEMBER 1, 1923

Over the years since Centre had begun playing football, the college had played many of the schools which formed the Southern Conference: Kentucky, Vanderbilt, Alabama, Tennessee, Tulane, Mississippi State, Mississippi, Sewanee, Washington and Lee, Virginia, Virginia Tech, Georgia Tech, Clemson, South Carolina, Auburn—15 in all—but Centre and the University of Georgia had never met, and the initial game between the two football teams was being built up because, if Centre won, the Colonels would claim the "Southern Championship."

Centre was now 7-1. Georgia was 5-3, having started with two wins, but then the Bulldogs of Athens had gone on the road on October 13 and been plummeted by the Bulldogs of New Haven, 40-0. After the pounding by Yale, Georgia shut out Tennessee, Auburn and Virginia before falling to Vanderbilt and Alabama by decisive margins.

Georgia	7	Mercer	0
Georgia	20	Oglethorpe	6
Georgia	0	Yale	40
Georgia	17	Tennessee	0
Georgia	7	Auburn	0
Georgia	13	Virginia	0
Georgia	7	Vanderbilt	35
Georgia	0	Alabama	36

Centre and Georgia had common opponents in Oglethorpe and Auburn, with Centre seemingly the slightly better team when comparable scores are factored in. However, Georgia had the home field advantage, so the game was really seen as a toss-up.

Centre	20	Oglethorpe	0
Centre	17	Auburn	0
Georgia	20	Oglethorpe	6
Georgia	7	Auburn	0

Ed Danforth of the Atlanta "Georgian," the same Ed Danforth who toured around the South in comparing how various college football programs stacked up each fall, and who had earlier in the year felt that Kentucky was going to be the class of the region's teams, was having second thoughts. He now had gotten in Centre's corner.

On the face of returns to date, Centre College has a superior eleven to the one that they had last year. Few expected Centre to survive without Red Roberts, yet look what the little S.I.A.A. institution has done to the haughty members of the Southern Conference.

They have defeated Clemson, Kentucky, Auburn, Sewanee and Washington and Lee, all by rather decisive scores. They would not be wrong in claiming the conference championship, even though they don't belong. The conference ought to elect them honorary members, at least their football team.

This was an amazing declaration. A writer in Atlanta, the largest city which had a college in the Southern Conference, was saying that little Centre, a school which hadn't been invited to join when the schools broke away from the S.I.A.A., had outclassed the Conference members. There would be major ramifications after Danforth's column. But while the fallout was still simmering, the issue at hand was Centre's going to Athens, Georgia, to play the Georgia Bulldogs.

You can't write about the University of Georgia without relating a little about the school's nickname. In 1920, a writer for the Atlanta "Journal" proposed that Georgia adopt the bulldog as a mascot since, "there is a certain dignity as well as ferocity" in the animal. Another writer picked up on the idea in reporting on a game later in the season with Virginia, and an English bulldog wearing a spiked collar and red jersey became one of the most identifiable of all college symbols. The mascot has taken on the initials of the University of Georgia, and is called "Uga."

The late humorist, Lewis Grizzard, a die-hard Georgia fan, told a wonderful story about Uga. The mascot was brought out on the field and placed on the 50 yard line during a halftime performance.

Uga began to lick himself in a place where dogs are prone to lick. Two good ol' boys were sitting high in the stands and one leaned over toward the other and said, "Man, I wish I could do that!"

His friend replied, "Hey, if you did, that dog would bite you!"

Of course, when Grizzard told the story, the word "bite" was drawn out with a drawl peculiar to the South.

Centre traditionally played a Thanksgiving game, but 1923 was to be an exception. Georgia wanted to play the Saturday after the holiday, and Centre agreed to December 1.

Georgia Tech was playing Auburn on Thanksgiving in Atlanta. Since there was to be no post-season trip, the administration thought it would a reward for a season well played to have the team go down for the game in Atlanta and then take the train over to Athens, a sort of "long weekend" affair. They'd miss no school as it was closed for the holiday.

The Colonels left on Wednesday, November 28, at 10:45 p.m. on the Southern's Cincinnati-Atlanta Express. Breakfast was next morning in the dining car, and arrival at Atlanta's big Union Station was at 11:25 a.m. Centre alumni met the team with big, 4-door cars and transported the members to a restaurant for a quick lunch, and then it was off to Grant Field and the game. A special section of good seats had been set aside by Tech for the Colonels.

Centre's players were inwardly pulling for Auburn, a team they had beaten rather handily, 17-0. If Auburn beat Tech on Tech's home field, it would follow that Centre was the better team regarding the Georgians. However, they didn't want to display any emotion and appear disrespectful to their hosts.

The game was hard fought, and ended in a scoreless tie. The fact that Centre had racked up 17 points against Auburn, and Tech couldn't score, wasn't lost on the writers covering the game. The comparable scores were another indication that Centre could play with any of the schools in the Southern Conference, and that realization was pouring fuel on a soon to erupt firestorm regarding the Colonels which was being discussed in multiple phone calls across the South, even as the Colonels were spending the weekend in Atlanta and Athens.

After the game, the Colonels went by both dressing rooms to congratulate the teams and then it was back to the station for the 80 miles ride east over to Athens, the last leg being a run down a spur off the main east-west line of the Southern. The team was staying at Athens' most elegant hotel, the Georgian, a five story brick structure of 125 rooms built in 1909. Once again, there was time to tour the downtown and even walk into some of the surrounding residential areas on the mild, Georgian night.

Friday morning, the University of Georgia had guides to show the team around the campus. Of particular interest was a building which dated back to 1806, now called Old College. The building was fashioned after Connecticut Hall at Yale, built in 1752, and just as the building at Yale was the oldest in New Haven, Old College was the oldest building in Athens.

"It was nearly torn down because it became so dilapidated, but the state gave the school $10,000 in 1908 to save it."

Several of the Colonels told the guide about Old Centre, how well it had been maintained, and how, "if Old Centre were to be torn down, I'm not sure there would be a Centre College. It's the symbol of our school."

Georgia had a student body of approximately 1,500 students in 1923, nearly six times the size of Centre, and the numerous classical buildings dwarfed the campus in Danville, but the same sentiment was expressed in Athens as had been when the team walked the grounds of Harvard. "It may be bigger, but we wouldn't trade our little school for any place on this earth."

Friday afternoon, there was a workout at Georgia's Sanford Field. The Bulldogs facility was completed in 1911 along Lumpkin Street and could be used for both baseball and football. (Sanford Field was replaced by Sanford Stadium in 1929. The new stadium originally held 30,000 and has been increased in seating to the present 92,746.)

The Colonels were met before the workout by Coach George Woodruff who was in his first year as the head coach. Woodruff was an interesting fellow. He was from a prominent Columbus, Georgia family, and had been a star and the captain in 1911 of the 7-1-1 Georgia team, then called the Red and Black. Woodruff didn't need the money which the coaching position paid, and had an arrangement in which Georgia gave him $1.00 yearly with the rest of his salary being donated to the athletic department. (Woodruff coached for five years, and his last team in 1927 was 9-1, losing the season final to Georgia Tech 12-0, which knocked Georgia out of a Rose Bowl invitation. The team selected in place of the Bulldogs was Pittsburgh.)

The game was a sellout, as was usual when Centre played. Sanford Field had an "L" shaped section of stands undercover which somewhat wrapped around the playing field, with a significant uncovered stand facing the south end zone. The crowd was swelled by many graduates who were using the Centre game as a Homecoming, plus those who came to Athens because of being fascinated with the Colonels' meteoric rise in the football world.

Centre had to shuffle its lineup due to Elmer Rabenstein and Murrell Summers still being slowed by injuries from the W&L game. The backfield was composed of Case Thomasson, Minos Gordy, Hope Hudgins, who was back at full speed, and Herb Covington. Webster Seeley, a sophomore, was going to be a new starter at end.

As the game began, there were two teams on a mission. Centre was playing for what could be considered the "Southern Championship." Georgia was seeking to show that it was a better team than the one which had been beaten soundly in its last two games by Vanderbilt and Alabama.

Back in Danville, the "Grid-Graph" wasn't utilized due to most of the students being off campus for vacation. Dr. Stout ran a wire into his theatre and set a price which included the game and a later movie.

The Georgia game was a defensive struggle. The Bulldogs scored first on a 28 yard field goal by Joe Bennett in the 1st quarter. Toward the end of the half, Hennie Lemon tied it with a 31 yard effort. That's the way the game ended, 3-3.

Georgia won statistically, running up 14 first downs to Centre's five. Even though the Colonels' were out gained, they nearly won the game when Lemon booted a field goal in the 3rd quarter which hit the crossbar, bounced straight up, and came down just inches on the short side of the goalpost.

But for an inch, Centre would have been the undisputed "Champions of the South."

While the failure to come away with a win was somewhat of a disappointment, the season had been a big success, with the only loss being the game played in Philadelphia. Centre could still claim the mythical "Southern Championship," or at least a part of it.

Of the Southern Conference teams, no school went through 1923 undefeated and untied. Only three colleges had no losses in conference play.

Vanderbilt	4-0-1	(tied Mississippi State)
W&L	4-0-1	(tied Kentucky)
Florida	1-0-2	(tied Georgia Tech and Mississippi State)

Centre's 5-0-1 record against S.I.C. teams looked pretty good when comparing 1923's teams in the South, and the Colonels returned back to Danville confidant in their standing amongst the best teams in Southern football for the year.

CENTRE ELECTS A CAPTAIN AFTER THE GEORGIA GAME

After the Georgia game, while still in the dressing room in Athens, the Colonels had an election to select a captain for 1924. There was really only person who was even considered.

Herb Covington would assume the captaincy. Covey had come a long way since his Danville arrival in September of 1921.

A story was published in the "Messenger" after the election was announced.

Herbert Covington of Mayfield, Ky., brilliant little quarterback of Centre College, was unanimously elected captain of the 1924 Colonels immediately following the Centre-Georgia game. Covey has been one of the Gold and White's mainstays for the past three seasons, and his many friends will be pleased to hear of his election.

Covey can run with the ball, pass or kick. He is also a sterling defensive man and a fine field general. Well does he deserve the honor that has been bestowed upon him by his mates, and congratulations are in order.

POST SEASON—1923

The Chamber of Commerce held a banquet attended by members of the organization and the Colonels and school officials.

Eighteen winners of the gold "C" were announced.

George Chinn
Herb Covington
Franklin Gleim
Minos Gordy
Jimmy Green
Carl Hilker
Hope Hudgins
Ed Kubale
Hennie Lemon
Howard Lynch
Elmer Rabenstein
Frank Rubarth

Webster Seeley
Walter Skidmore
Albert Spurlock
Murrell Summers
Case Thomasson
Robert Wallace

The only senior was Jimmy Green. George Chinn questionably had another year of eligibility due to missing a season but didn't come back in 1924. Hope Hudgins had announced that he couldn't return for his senior year.

Overall, things were looking good for the upcoming season. The just completed campaign had been very successful at 7-1-1. The new stadium was no longer a dream but a fact. The seniors returning promised to provide an experienced core for 1924. The freshmen team had just concluded a good year, beating Kentucky twice, Eastern Kentucky, Stanford High and Kentucky Wesleyan. The lone loss in a 5-1 season was to Sewanee.

Everyone eagerly awaited the 1924 season, because it appeared that Centre would continue on the roll which had begun in 1917 when the Chief, Uncle Charlie, and the boys from North Side High in Fort Worth arrived in Danville, forever changing the face of not only Centre College football, but of college football across the entire country.

Herb Covington again made the consensus All-Southern team. He was a unanimous pick by the 30 sports writers who voted. Ed Kubale won an honor which was much deserved after his play in Philadelphia. Each year, the Quakers' squad selected an All-Franklin Field team designating the outstanding players who had faced off against Penn during the season. Kubale was the only member of the team from outside the East.

CHAPTER 22:
TROUBLES

On December 6, there was a meeting of the Southern Association of Colleges and Preparatory Schools in Richmond, Virginia. The executive committee of the Association submitted a report in which it was recommended that Centre be removed from membership. This organization wasn't concerned with athletics in particular, but in the overall standards of the member schools, which included athletics. It was claimed that Centre "had not me the standards of the Association."

Dr. Montgomery, Centre's president, had heard rumors about what was going to be discussed at the meeting, and he immediately demanded specifics. He stated that he had been told there were accusations about the money Uncle Charlie was being paid, "which some of you have said is greater than that paid me, as president, and some of our professors."

Dr. Montgomery also said, "You are saying we are paying students to come to Centre to play football."

"We are outraged!"

It was shades of 1919 all over again, when West Virginia's Major Earl Smith published an article in his Fairmont "Times" which was the result of his "investigation" which showed "conclusively" that Centre was playing "ringers," and that was how the little school upset mighty West Virginia, conquerors of Princeton. People just had a hard time accepting that Centre, with its small enrollment, could compete, and compete successfully, with colleges so much larger. It didn't make sense.

"They must be cheating! They just have to be cheating!"

Dr. C.E. Allen, faculty chairman of Centre's athletic committee, was with Dr. Montgomery in Richmond, and the two decided to go on the offensive after a professor at Macon College in Georgia stood and urged the Association to "get to the bottom of the present evil in college athletics."

"Let's do just that," Dr. Allen said as he jumped to his feet.

"You accuse us of paying our coach, Charles B. Moran, an excessive salary. Let me give you some facts about that. Coach Moran came to Centre in 1917 and wasn't paid a cent. He received the princely sum of $200.00 in 1918, and $500.00 in 1919, plus a $100.00 bonus if we had a good year."

"Would you gentlemen say that an undefeated season was a good year? Would you gentlemen say that defeating West Virginia, which beat Princeton, served the South well?"

Dr. Allen made eye contact with each of the representatives of the schools. There was silence, then some affirmative nods.

"Our athletic director, Robert L. Myers, has worked in that capacity since 1917 and has never accepted any salary—not a farthing—since coming to Danville. Would you say that he has been overpaid?"

Silence again, then a few negative shakes of heads.

"After the 1922 season, the University of Alabama tried to hire our coach, Charles B. Moran, by offering him $9,000.00. Only then did we offer him a decent salary. We paid him $5,500.00 or we would have lost him to Alabama. Has anyone accused Alabama of offering to pay Coach Moran an excessive salary—$3,500.00 more than we pay him?"

"Here are salaries being paid to some of the coaches in the Southern Conference."

Vanderbilt	$12,000.00
Tulane	$14,400.00
Washington and Lee	$12,100.00
South Carolina	$24,000.00

"Has the Southern Association of Colleges and Preparatory Schools accused these fine institutions of overpaying their coaches?"

Silence again. Dr. Allen was just warming up.

"How many of you had an All-American who couldn't return due to finances? Who didn't return because he didn't have the money to buy his books? "

"None? We had Red Weaver. Do we pay our athletes?"

Dr. Allen mentioned Sully Montgomery, a starter against Harvard in 1920 who didn't return the next year, "because of finances."

"How many of you had a young man catch a touchdown pass against Harvard who couldn't play the next year because of grades?"

"None? We had Ed Whitnell. Do we not have grade standards? "

Dr. Allen then very deliberately reached in his nearby briefcase and pulled out a letter which was typed on the letterhead of Vanderbilt's athletic department.

He held it up and then read it aloud. The letter had offered financial assistance to Minos Gordy if he would enroll at Vandy and play football for the Commodores, "after he had stated that he intended to enroll at Centre."

"Has Vanderbilt, which we understand to be one of our chief accusers, been threatened with expulsion from the Association because of this offer, the offer clearly proffered in this letter?"

Again, silence, as the letter was passed around the room and deemed authentic. Dr. Montgomery then stood.

"If Centre College has an athletic program which is so rotten, as you have not just implied, but have actually circulated rumors about us in trying to make your case, why do so many honored institutions seek football games with us? Here is the list of some of the many who have actually sought games with us in 1924 alone: Indiana, Kentucky, Washington and Jefferson, Washington and Lee, Colgate, Drake, West Virginia, Auburn, Alabama, Furman, South Carolina, Florida, Tulane, Texas A&M, Sewanee, Georgetown in D.C, Tennessee, Georgia, Notre Dame, Columbia—and others have sent word and asked if we have any slots open. Ten of these schools are members of the Southern Conference, members of the Southern Association. Why do they seek games with Centre College? I'll tell you why. Because they know that our team plays a clean, fine game, full of pep, science, and sportsmanship."

Dr. Allen then took over.

"Our records are open to you, but I want it to go on record that not one of you has come to Danville to look them over. We challenge you to come to Centre and either make your case, or close up."

There was an awkward silence. Finally, the president of Johns Hopkins stood and spoke.

"Perhaps the executive committee of the Association should have the matter referred back for further consideration."

Just like after the accusations which came out of West Virginia in 1919, charges were easy to make, and landed on the front pages, while the refutations were buried somewhere in the depths of the paper, if carried at all.

However, several organizations and individuals stepped up to the plate in defense of Centre.

Ed Danforth of the Atlanta "Georgian," praised Dr. Montgomery for his solid defense of his school, and said that he had come as near as a college president can come to saying, "Put up, or shut up!"

The University of Kentucky issued a statement that it felt, "Centre has represented the state honorably on the gridirons across the country. Since coming to the front in football, Centre has kept at the top and no doubt there is envy at the small college's success."

Robert Dundon of the Louisville "Herald" had the same feeling as UK.

The controversy reached all of the way to New York, and the "Times" weighed in, speculating with tongue in cheek that since the Colonels prayed before games, perhaps the Southern school's administrators regarded Centre's offense to be that it invoked the Divine, which was "against the amateur spirit."

More seriously, the "Times" pointed out that Harvard had totally cleared Centre of any misdeeds before playing the Colonels for three straight years.

The meeting in Richmond broke up with the vow that next year, when the Southern Association met in Memphis, charges and countercharges would be investigated further. Dr. Montgomery and Dr. Allen went on record as welcoming any further discussion in the future. Their tone was basically a pronouncement that those who were without sin should be the ones to come forward in the future and cast the first stone.

There were no stone throwers in Memphis. Centre was fully accredited by the Southern Association, and it was apparent that those who had accused Centre didn't want their own programs opened to scrutiny.

When Dr. Montgomery and Dr. Allen returned to Danville, they were pleased to read a letter in the "Cento" written about the matter by George Chinn, which ended by thanking the Centre president.

Well Prexy, we took them on one at a time on the gridiron, but your carrying the ball in Richmond took them on not only one at a time, but you took them all on together, tearing through them like the "Royal Palm Limited" goes through Wilmore, and have won from all of us unlimited admiration.

As 1923 ended, and the students began to scatter home for the Christmas vacation, all looked well in Danville. The Southern Association situation had been defused. The schedule for 1924 was being firmed up. It looked like the players returning and those moving up from the freshman team were going to keep the Centre College football machine humming along smoothly.

However:

When we came back on campus after Christmas, everything seemed just fine with the school and the football program. We all felt that we'd have a wonderful year in 1924.

And then everything just got turned upside down about a week after classes began when we heard that Uncle Charlie was resigning! No one could believe it. Centre football was Uncle Charlie. The Chief was loved and he was a wonderful man, the man we knew had gotten everything started. But Uncle Charlie made it all happen on the field, and he was leaving. We all took it mighty hard, and we didn't understand.

I talked to a lot of the players, and they just didn't know what had happened. All they knew was that he was going to Bucknell.

Where in the world was Bucknell?

Not only the players didn't understand, no one did. Certainly the popular and successful coach hadn't been fired. He'd recently signed a five year contract. Centre had felt he'd coach the Colonels until he decided to retire, hopefully years into the future.

Was it the accusations thrown at Centre in Richmond? Perhaps. But Centre had refuted the charges effectively, and no one felt that anything would happen to the detriment of the college and football program when the Southern Association met in Memphis the next year.

Years later, family members related what they had been told by Uncle Charlie about his leaving Centre. There was never any definite proof, but Uncle Charlie had friends everywhere, especially in the college football world, and he told his wife Pearl and granddaughter Ann that he felt there was a campaign going on which was designed to get him out of Danville.

Centre had literally owned the University of Kentucky since Uncle Charlie arrived at Centre. His record against the Wildcats was 6-0, and his teams had outscored UK by an incredible, 200-3. In 24 quarters, 360 minutes of football, Kentucky had managed exactly one field goal!

Kentucky was the state university. It was the largest school in the Commonwealth. The flagship state university should dominate, not be dominated within the boundaries of Kentucky, or so went the feelings amongst the alumni of the school.

Uncle Charlie felt that pressure was being exerted after the Southern Association meeting in Richmond by Kentucky's supporters, in a backdoor manner, and the goal was to force him out as Centre's coach. He remembered well what had happened at Texas A&M. Texas had severed relations with A&M after Uncle Charlie's teams started beating the Longhorns, and wouldn't play the Aggies again until Uncle Charlie left the school.

He was now hearing rumors coming out of Lexington that Kentucky was going to do the same, to sever relations, if he remained at the helm, and the Kentucky supporters were trying to use the meeting in Richmond as ammunition even though Centre and the team had not been formally charged with doing anything wrong.

Uncle Charlie was in the prime of his life at age 44. He was a successful National League umpire. He and Pearl had their farm, their cattle, their tobacco, their dairy. He had proven himself at Texas A&M, having a record of 38-8-4, and was 52-6-1 at Centre for an overall record of 90-14-5. His winning percentage, excluding ties, was a remarkable 86.5.

One of Uncle Charlie's major goals was to get a stadium built. It was completed. He had originally come to Danville because his son Tom was at Centre and on the team. Tom was gone. The program was in excellent shape. Bucknell had made a good offer.

Uncle Charlie's family felt that with the campaign being started in Lexington, he simply reasoned, "Who needs the aggravation?" It was as simple as that. But it wasn't so simple in Danville, Kentucky.

You know, sometimes you feel that things are never going to change. Your old church was there long before you were born and you felt it would always be there. And then it burns down, and you can't believe what you had so taken for granted suddenly isn't there anymore. It's just gone.

It was like that with Uncle Charlie. From the first time that Howard and I started following Centre's football team, Uncle Charlie Moran was the coach. When Howard enrolled in 1920, Uncle Charlie was there. He was the coach during the three seasons I'd been on campus starting in 1921.

Like everybody said, Centre football was Uncle Charlie, and Uncle Charlie was Centre football. It was like we lost our father and teacher, our role model and our cornerstone. We just couldn't believe he wasn't going to be part of Centre, and everyone wondered what would become of our football program.

Would the players come back? Would they follow Uncle Charlie? Would they just transfer to another school?

Uncle Charlie's leaving was all that anybody talked about.

Centre's administration immediately got busy in searching for a new coach. The committee that was appointed was sensitive about the Richmond meeting. If they offered too high a salary, the college may be criticized by the Southern Association. But at the same time, if they offered too little, they may not be able to land a coach of significance.

A group of citizens in Danville started lobbying for Centre to hire Bo. In 1921, he had arguably been the most famous athlete in the country after Jack Dempsey and Babe Ruth, and he still had name recognition everywhere. No matter where you were, people knew who you were talking about if you just said, "Bo." The past May, the horse he had named for him ran in the Kentucky Derby.

"Who you gonna bet on?"

"Probably put a couple of bucks on Bo."

In Danville, and throughout Kentucky, it was, "Bo can keep the program going. We'll be ok if we can get Bo."

But Bo had another year on his contract with Centenary. What about Red Roberts? Red had been on the staff the past year at Waynesburg College in Pennsylvania and Centre had already locked him in to coach the freshman team in 1924, as Coach Kendrick had resigned.

"We already have Red. Can you imagine if we get Red and Bo?"

Things got so serious about trying to attract Bo that the people of Danville put signs in all of the downtown businesses supporting Bo, and pin-on buttons with "BO!" were worn by nearly everybody. Bo actually came to Danville to discuss the possibility of coaching the team, but he wanted to be able to honor his contract with Centenary and come to Centre the following year. The committee wouldn't consent to that stipulation, and when Bo got back to Louisiana, he announced he was staying put.

Meetings were held throughout the next week after it became apparent that Bo wasn't coming. No decision was forthcoming. Finally, the word got out that the committee was going to make a recommendation to President Montgomery.

I guess that only in a small school like Centre would the choice of a new coach be of such importance. Certainly it was forefront in everybody's mind.

Then something unexpected happened. Some of my fraternity brothers who were on the team let me in on the fact that the players had an idea about who they wanted to be their coach.

There were seven juniors who had been on the team the past three years, who'd played regularly, even as freshmen, and they'd be the main strength of the 1924 squad. They'd been part of the team in 1921 when we beat Harvard. They knew what glory had come to the college, and they had been a big part of the building of Centre's reputation. They wanted to go out the same way they'd come

in—as winners. They worried that bringing in a new coach who didn't understand the Centre spirit and system of play would hamper their last year.

The seven were Herb Covington, Ed Kubale, Hennie Lemon, Minos Gordy, Howard Lynch, Frank Rubarth, and Case Thomasson. They got the team together and came up with a petition which they took to the committee, and then met with Dr. Montgomery.

There had been some concern from both the administration and within the team about which players would return. None of them would be going to Bucknell. Uncle Charlie had done the honorable thing and announced that he wasn't going to accept any transfers from Centre. He didn't want to harm the program he had worked so hard to build.

But would they transfer somewhere else? Would they come back but not play football? The seven juniors came up with the idea that everyone would make a pledge that they'd be back and play, if they could have a say in naming the new coach. Thirty-three players signed a simple typed statement.

CHAPTER 23:
1924—THE CHIEF RETURNS

In October of 1917, over six years before, Robert L. Myers realized his long held dream of becoming the coach at his alma mater. During his short tenure, he coached Centre College to an October 6 rout of hapless Kentucky Military Institute and a loss on October 20 to DePauw. After that defeat, the Chief decided that the school he loved so much could attain greater glory if he turned the program over to a more experienced and skilled coach, and Bob Myers stepped aside, still devoted to Centre, and still helping guide the football program as Director of Athletics, never receiving, as was said in Richmond, Virginia, "a farthing" for his efforts.

Now he was coming back as the head coach, because the declaration by the players stated that those who had signed would return for the 1924 school year and football season, and would continue the proud traditions of Centre College, "if Chief Myers is appointed to be the head football coach."

The search committee and administration enthusiastically approved the Chief's appointment. The citizens of Danville and Kentucky were equally positive. Everybody loved Chief Myers. The return of the Chief set in motion one of the great chapters in the story of Centre's football greatness—the unbelievable season of 1924.

CHIEF MYERS GEARS UP FOR 1924

The first thing that the Chief did was to complete his coaching staff for 1924. While Uncle Charlie let it be known that he wouldn't imperil Centre's future by going after its players, he felt no such reluctance about hiring Ben Cregor to become one of his assistants. "Baldy" was going to Bucknell, and Jim Kendrick had resigned his position as freshman coach. Even before Uncle Charlie's resignation, Centre had lined up Red Roberts as coach of the first year men, and to replace Cregor, the Chief hired Harold Ofstie, a University of Wisconsin star in 1911-13, who had been in coaching since his graduation from the Madison school in 1914. Ofstie's last position had been as coach of the Great Lakes Naval Station where he led his team to the championship of the service league in 1923.

With Red and Ofstie on board, the Chief turned his attention to firming up the schedule and recruiting young men to come to Centre. It must be remembered that there were no scholarships for athletics, but all schools tried to entice graduating high school students not only to attend their institution, but to participate in sports if possible.

The schedule was announced and sent out to the media.

Oct.	4	Valparaiso	Danville
Oct.	11	Carson-Newman	Danville
Oct.	18	Transylvania	Danville
Oct.	25	West Virginia	New York
Nov.	1	Kentucky	Lexington
Nov.	8	Tennessee	Knoxville
Nov.	15	Alabama	Birmingham
Nov.	29	Georgia	Danville

At the time the schedule was announced, it was thought that a 9th game would be penned in as negotiations were once again going on with Notre Dame for a contest in Chicago. However, Notre Dame was booked weekly from October 4 to November 29. Centre had an open date November 22, but Notre Dame was locked into a game with Northwestern on that date. The only possibility for the Irish and Colonels to meet would be on the first Saturday in December. Neither school wanted to extend its regular season into December, even though Notre Dame later went to the Rose Bowl on January 1, beating Stanford, 27-10. (Notre Dame didn't go to another post-season game until January 1, 1970, when the Irish lost to Texas in the Cotton Bowl. It wasn't because the school didn't have eligible, worthy teams, but because the university discouraged any such appearances.)

The Chief sent out another one of his folksy letters on May 24, 1924. It went out under the letterhead listing him as coach, and Harold F. Ofstie as assistant coach.

CENTRE COLLEGE OF KENTUCKY
ATHLETIC BOARD OF CONTROL

Robert. L. Myers, Head Coach   Harold F. Ofstie, Assistant Coach

Dear Friend:

Have you had a chance to talk over at home about going to Centre next year? Better write to President R.A. Montgomery, at Danville, Kentucky, pretty soon for a catalogue so you can look over the courses. Decide as quickly as possible so you can reserve your room at Breckinridge Hall. Every year, we have a large number of applicants, and it has to be a case of first come, first served.

On the square, wouldn't you like to be seen prancing around in our big new stadium right now, kicking the dirt up on your back and maybe getting the gable end of your pants smacked around in front? By the way, we have a practice field for the varsity, another for the

freshmen, the regular game field in the enclosure, all with plenty of grass. We have an "up-town" gym about forty yards from the gate. We have a houseful of equipment with plenty of new stuff coming on. We use only the best. Some of the gang look all dressed like a mule in a buggy harness, but just the same, they step high, wide, and handsome. You bet I'll be glad to crack down on the old boys again. I'll be so full of pep, I'll sound like someone tearing shingles off a roof.

You'll get the same coaching as the varsity gets. Besides your own coach, there is a separate freshman schedule. Say, you ought to have seen our "fish" mop last fall (twice on Kentucky State last year.) They felt their oats so strong they gave the varsity the "heebie jeebies" every time they tangled up. Big boy, our freshmen are game enough to climb naked up a honey-locust tree with a wildcat under each arm; they'd fight a shark on the bottom of the ocean with an anvil in each arm, or get a hair singe in a gasoline shower. It's gotten so we've almost had to wrap burglar-proof safes around our varsity men to keep the frosh from crippling them. I'll guarantee you'll have the time of your life on Centre's yearling football team.

The Chief then typed in the upcoming varsity schedule for 1924, and continued his letter.

I've got a lot of things to talk to you about besides football about the grandest old college of them all. Meanwhile, get all set to be with us for there are wonderful things ahead of you.
Yours in Old Centre,
Robert L. Myers, head coach

In July, Chief Myers sent out another letter which closed with the following.

It's no wonder that we're feeling fine and "sittin pretty" at Centre. The old gang will all be back, the old rootin', tootin', fightin', bunch of brothers which will keep on mowin' 'em down in the future, just as they've been doing in the past, and don't let any one-hitch guy with a bee in his pants tell you any differently.

We'll be looking for you old timer. The latchstring will be on the outside, and we'll be proud to have you with us on the square. What better luck could you wish for than to be a Centre Colonel?

Finally, on August 22, the Chief sent out one more letter, this time speaking about the qualities which he felt made Centre so perfect for a young man's education. He spoke about Centre's physical plant being up to date, how the college had the best equipment, a modern science building, a "splendid" library, and a distinguished faculty.

And then the Chief spoke from his heart, with none of the light-heartedness and clichés of his previous offerings.

Centre has the ability to fill her halls with picked men from many sections; to give them noble ideas and to send them out trained to lead in the battle of life.

Old Centre's traditions run back over a hundred years. She has had an illustrious history. Because Centre is a small college, she can teach you more of the things that you ought to know. The influence of the fine men on our faculty on your character will be pretty near the biggest thing in your life, really bigger, better, truer, than your books, your social life, or your sports.

The older I get, and the more I see of other institutions, the better I appreciate Centre. When you become a Centre man, you in a way confer knighthood upon yourself. We want you to come and be one of us and keep Old Centre's name out in front, and when you do come, we want you to keep your eye on the main things, and resolve to get everything that is good.

Hoping to welcome you to Old Centre in September, I am

Sincerely,

Robert L. Myers

Head Coach

As usual, the school year ended with the Centre College Carnival. Again, one of the Colonels reigned as King-Minos Gordy from Abbeville, Louisiana. The queen was Porter Hudson, a local beauty who would become the wife of Army Armstrong.

THE 1924 SEASON BEGINS

The NCAA rules committee met during the winter after the 1923 season and decided that the "man in motion" would no longer be allowed. Previously, a member of the backfield could start running before the ball was centered. This gave him a jump on the defense as he had momentum before the defense could adjust.

Centre's offense had a great number of its plays designed around one or more of the backs being "in motion." That was why first center Red Weaver, and following Red, Ed Kubale, had been such vital parts of the Colonels' attack.

Now, Centre would have to revamp its offense. Of course, other teams would have to do the same, but everyone who knew football realized that much of Centre's offensive potency came from the precision of its "man in motion" plays. The team had spent hours each week just working on timing. Now, it would take some time to adapt. The Chief was fortunate to have Covey and several experienced backs returning, but even with the veterans, it was going to take awhile to "unlearn" past habits.

The Chief was able to be on campus when practice began, having simply put his Chautauqua duties aside. He knew now that he was the head coach, he could no longer be a "part-timer" in Danville, as before. When the players returned, they found that the "Sloganmeister," as German professor, Dr. Max Diez, sometimes called the Chief, had been at work in the dressing room.

There were still the words that had first been used back at Fort Worth North Side:

BELIEVE!
ACHIEVE!
SUCCEED!

But now there were additional motivational messages painted on boards and placed around the locker room.

YOU CAN'T FIGHT LIKE A MAN WITH LESS THAN 100%
LOYALTY AND TEAM SPIRIT

YOU CAN'T DO YOURSELF JUSTICE
UNLESS YOU GET AND STAY IN CONDITION

OFFENSE MEANS GO HARD AND BLOCK—
DEFENSE MEANS CHARGE AND FIGHT

YOU BETRAY A TRUST WHEN YOU FAIL TO GIVE IT YOUR ALL
WHETHER IN PRACTICE OR IN THE GAME

REMEMBER, IF YOU FIGHT AS BROTHERS, NOTHING CAN BEAT YOU

REMEMBER, YOU WIN GAMES ON THE OTHER SIDE OF THE
LINE OF SCRIMMAGE, NOT ON YOURS

The seniors read the Chief's slogans and drilled into the newly arrived freshmen that these weren't mere words painted on placards, but were the very reason that Centre had become a power in college football.

"The Chief has always been a winner. If you want to succeed, you read these signs every day until you dream about nothing else, and you—freshman—you'll be a winner! You are now—Centre!!"

They truly believed, as the unfolding of the season would prove so conclusively.

CENTRE-VALPARAISO   OCTOBER 4, 1924

The season opener was with Bill Shadoan's Valparaiso (Indiana) team. Shad had taken over the Valpo program, which was sinking, after having been a star lineman at Centre during the 1921-22 seasons, leaving Centre due to financial strains. He had quickly turned the situation around, going 4-2-1 in 1923. He also had been extremely successful as the school's basketball coach, even though he didn't play basketball at Centre. During the 1923-24 round ball campaign, his team had won 22 straight in going 24-4 for the season.

Shadoan was but one of many Colonels who had gotten into coaching. Matty Bell went to TCU where he was joined by Bill James. Bo signed on at Centenary and brought Army in to assist him. Tom Moran was hired by Carson-Newman. Ed Diddle went to Western Kentucky. Red Weaver was coaching in West Virginia and Red Roberts had spent a year in Pennsylvania, and now was coming back to Centre as freshman coach. Ben Cregor had put in time at Centre and was following Uncle Charlie to Bucknell.

Shadoan's 1924 Valparaiso team was such an unknown to the Colonels that the local Danville papers referred to the Crusaders as "the mystery team." The local publisher for the game's programs was also in the dark and didn't know how to print the Valpo lineup for the game because no roster was provided. The "Advocate" and "Messenger" both stated that they regretted they couldn't give a "preview" of the season opener because they didn't have any information to pass on except, "Centre's coaches know that Bill Shadoan will bring a team to Danville which will give the Colonels a real fight."

Valparaiso opened the 1924 campaign against Elmhurst College, a liberal arts school in metropolitan Chicago which was only in its 5th year of competing on the gridiron. Shad's team won easily, 33-0.

Just before the game with Valpo, the Chief received an urgent message by telegram from Chicago regarding his Chautauqua business that demanded his attention, "immediately." He had to rush back to his office and turned the team over to his assistant, Coach Ofstie. Complicating things for Centre also was the fact that two starters, Case Thomasson and Elmer Rabenstein, had injuries which would prevent them from seeing any action. The starters for the Valparaiso game were:

POSITION	NAME	WEIGHT	CLASS
Left end	Clifton "Hennie" Lemon	175	Sr.
Left tackle	Walter Skidmore	175	Jr.
Left guard	Frank Rubarth	170	Sr.
Center	Ed Kubale	180	Sr.
Right guard	Alex Bush	175	Soph.
Right tackle	Howard Lynch	180	Sr.
Right end	George McClure	180	Soph.
Quarterback	Herb Covington	160	Sr.
Left half	Reginald Wilson	154	Soph.
Right half	Robert Wallace	160	Jr.
Fullback	Minos Gordy	190	Sr.

Centre's officials were pleased with the attendance for the season opener. Valpo was too far away to bring any fans and certainly wasn't a big name which would attract Centre's alumni from out in the state. The 4,000 who witnessed the game were primarily composed of locals and students from Centre and K.C.W.

What they saw was a hard fought game in which Centre dominated but couldn't score. Valpo never got closer that the Colonels' 35, and picked up only five first downs, two due to penalties on Centre.

The Colonels were able to pick up eight first downs, none by penalty, and got close enough for Hennie Lemon to attempt four field goals. Two missed badly. Two missed barely. The game ended, 0-0.

It wasn't exactly an auspicious start, but Bill Shadoan had prepared his "mystery team" well, and the Crusaders went on to post a 4-3-2 record for the season.

THE GAME THAT WASN'T, OCTOBER 11, 1924
CARSON-NEWMAN

The archives for Carson-Newman list Tom Moran as the coach for 1924, but he wasn't. According to Tom's daughter Ann, he had been replaced by a recent graduate of the school named Lake Russell, who was related in some way to the college's president.

During the week after the Valpo game, Centre received a letter from an alumnus who lived in Syracuse. It contained a clipping from the Syracuse "Journal" stating that four young men from the city were playing football down in the South at a small college named Carson-Newman. The article pointed out that three of them had played for the Syracuse Orange the previous year.

Carson-Newman was asked by Centre to wire a list of players who were eligible to play football and would be coming to Danville. When the dean, Dr. John D. Everett, responded, there were no players listed as being from Syracuse, and a follow-up phone call to the dean established that there weren't even any students enrolled who were from Syracuse, playing football or not. Centre became suspicious that something strange was going on.

When the Carson-Newman team got to Danville on the Friday before the game, a Centre supporter checked the registration cards at the Gilcher Hotel and found no one had listed Syracuse as their home town. Coach Russell was asked to meet with Dr. Montgomery and members of the Centre athletic board.

"Do you have players on your team who are from Syracuse?"

"Yes, we have three players from that city."

"Are they students who are enrolled in classes?"

"My understanding is they are, yes sir."

"Did you know that your dean, John D. Everett, says that there are no students from Syracuse enrolled in classes at Carson-Newman?"

Coach Russell had no answer. It was apparent to Centre that the Fighting Parsons were bringing in "ringers" to try to register a win which could put their program on the map.

Centre cancelled the game. October 11 is listed as an open date. It was 1948 before the two colleges played again.

TRANSYLVANIA STEPS BACK INTO THE PICTURE
OCTOBER 18, 1924

Centre's next game was with old in-state rival, Transylvania. It was 45 years ago that the two colleges had first met, and the 1924 contest was the first since the 98-0 pasting in 1921 which caused Transy's administration to have its football team take a breather for a couple of years after five straight defeats by a combined 302-3 score.

The schedule had been made out so that the Colonels would have three relatively easy games prior to going to New York to take on West Virginia on October 25. Things hadn't exactly worked out as planned. Valparaiso proved tougher than expected. The Carson-Newman game was cancelled. At least Transy should play the role that had allowed it to be penciled in for the October 18 game in Danville.

"Roundy" Rabenstein and Case Thomasson were healthy again and back in the lineup. Centre won easily, 43-0. A reporter apparently felt that by "only" losing 43-0, Transy had scored a moral victory.

Fighting gallantly against a much superior team, Transylvania held the Centre College football team to six touchdowns and a field goal in a game played Saturday afternoon. Things have changed a lot since 1921. Then, Centre ran over a hapless Crimson crew, running the score up to 98 points, and devoted the later part of the game to practicing drop kicks and not attempting to make touchdowns.

The Chief played each of the 25 men who had dressed for the game. Covington scored three times, with one being on a pass from Rabenstein. Lemon, Rabenstein and Gordy also scored. Lemon kicked a field goal and he and Covey each kicked two extra points.

Centre was 1-0-1. The coaching staff had concern about taking on the Mountaineers of West Virginia with only two games having been played. However, the Transy game had given the subs some experience, and the team came out of the contest with no injuries.

THE CENTRE COLLEGE "CENTO" WEIGHS IN

The Centre College "Cento" was a weekly paper put out by the students. It cost $1.00 annually. The paper was very supportive of the college as there was no adversarial relationship in the least. Nonetheless, the "Cento" sometimes used satire to point out conditions at the school which it felt should be addressed.

One week, during the October football season, it got unseasonably cold. The First Presbyterian Church was neglectful in warming the sanctuary sufficiently for the morning chapel session, prompting a story from one of the "Cento's" reporters.

TERRIBLE TRAGEDY OCCURS FRIDAY
WELL LOVED CENTRE BOY MEETS UNTIMELY DEATH
MOURNED BY ALL

A pall was cast over the entire student body of Centre College Friday morning following the announcement of the death of one of the best loved boys in the entire school, Rodney Pifflick McNutt.

McNutt came to school on the morning of his death in the best of health, but the frigid atmosphere in the chapel was too much for the frail lad, and he slipped into a doze from which he never awoke. Jack Rowland, who was sitting next to the late McNutt in chapel, stated that he himself was asleep as was his usual habit, but well wrapped in three overcoats, and thus did not notice the cold so much. He is suffering from a nervous breakdown caused by the shock of awakening and finding McNutt stone cold dead at the close of the chapel service.

Rodney McNutt was born at Avenstone, Kentucky, just eighteen years ago and came from the famous Kentucky McNutts. His career at Centre, though short, was brilliant, enhanced by his ability to shoot craps.

There was a statement issued by Centre's dean of students which concluded by saying, "At least he didn't die of starvation."

Young McNutt has three brothers who plan to come to Centre in the future and see if they too can die from freezing. It looks likely that they will be successful in their endeavor.

GOING EAST AGAIN—
TO NEW YORK CITY AND THE POLO GROUNDS

For the fifth straight year, the Centre College football team was heading to the East; this time to New York City to play the West Virginia Mountaineers. When the plans were announced, Centre's fans couldn't help but be proud of how far the little school had gone since it last met West Virginia, five years before.

In 1919, the team had taken a train over to Charleston, West Virginia, slept on the way, and after playing an afternoon game, returned back home after the conclusion of what had been the breakthrough victory, 14-6, which sent Centre on its road to national fame.

Now the team was able to travel in a first class manner. The Colonels always had a specially chartered Pullman and stayed in the best facilities in whatever city they visited. It was to be no different on the 5th trip to the East. The hotel chosen for the team was the wonderful Waldorf=Astoria, a combination of two luxury hotels built by William Waldorf Astor and his cousin, John Jacob Astor IV. The 13 story Waldorf, built in 1893, and the 17 story Astoria, constructed four years later, were joined by a corridor which became the "=" symbol in the name of the merged Waldorf=Astoria.

Besides the Colonels' Pullman, two additional sleepers were chartered to take Centre's supporters to the game. The trip was to begin at 7:25 in the morning on Thursday, October 23. The Pullmans would be connected to the Southern Railroad's regularly scheduled "Carolina Special," go through Lexington where some additional fans would board, and arrive in Cincinnati at 11:00 a.m. There would be a layover of slightly over two hours before the Pullmans would leave Cincinnati connected to the New York Central's "Ohio State Limited."

The route to New York City was exactly the same as that taken during the three trips to Boston until the train reached Albany. It was northeast through Columbus, Ohio to Cleveland on the "Big Four's" tracks, and then due east along the south shore of Lake Erie to Buffalo. From Buffalo, the 4-track NYC line continued east to Albany. When the team had gone to Boston to play Harvard, its Pullman was transferred at Albany to a Boston and Albany Railroad train for the trip across Massachusetts.

There was no reconnection in Albany this time, as the Colonels' train continued south from Albany on the double-tracked last leg, directly into New York, with the "Ohio State Limited" arriving at the grand Beaux-Arts, Grand Central Terminal in New York at 9:40 A.M on Friday, approximately 26 hours after leaving Danville.

The roundtrip fare was $81.00 for a lower birth and $78.00 for an upper. A two person drawing room could be had for $95.00 each, and a three person for $85.00 per passenger. Once arriving in New York, the travelers would be responsible for their own lodging at a hotel on Friday night, but could board Saturday evening at 10:00 p.m. after the game and sleep in their Pullman. The train would then pull out of New York at 8:45 a.m. Sunday.

New Yorkers had been trying to entice Centre to come to their city for the last couple of years. However, Centre was committed in 1922 to Harvard. The school only wanted to make one trip to the East each season, and Penn and Philadelphia had won out in 1923.

The promoters of the game rented the Polo Grounds for the contest. The stadium, built in 1911 and located in Manhattan, was originally the home of both the New York Giants and the Yankees, but after a dispute with the Giants' ownership, the Yankees bought land from William Waldorf Astor and built their new Yankee Stadium in the Bronx, opening it in 1923. Appropriately, the stadium which came to be known as "The House that Ruth Built," was christened by the "Bambino" hitting a three run homer in the 3rd inning, powering the Yanks to a 4-1 win.

The Polo Grounds had an odd configuration, being essentially a horseshoe after it was enclosed, except for the center field area. The right and left field fences were only 258 and 277 feet from the plate, and the center field wall was a deep 485 feet away. The layout made sense in the "dead ball" era. A line drive in the gap could roll deep and result in an "inside the park homer," which added excitement to the game. However, after the ball was "juiced," there were many "cheap" homers at the Polo Grounds, the most memorable being Bobby Thompson's 1951, "Shot heard round the world," which cleared the fence at the 315 foot mark, and won the pennant for the Giants in a dramatic comeback against their hated rival, the Brooklyn Dodgers.

The virtual horseshoe made the ballpark ideal for a football game, and hundreds of college football games were held in the stadium. One of the most famous was Notre Dame's upset of Army, 13-7, on October 18, 1924, one week before the Colonels and Mountaineers were to meet. It was the game that resulted in Grantland Rice writing about the Irish backfield and dubbing the players the "Four Horsemen."

When the "Ohio State Limited" braked at the Grand Central terminal, the Colonels once again enjoyed the reception which had become part of their travels over the last several years. The press turned out in large numbers representing the many newspapers in the city. The New York alumni had arranged to have buses lined up to take the team and fans to the Waldorf=Astoria. After everyone got checked in and stowed their baggage in their rooms, the same buses took everyone on a tour of Manhattan. The Colonels, most from smaller cities, had been impressed with the buildings in Louisville, with the skyline of San Francisco when they came across the bay from Oakland, with the Custom House Tower in Boston, but nothing could prepare them for the skyscrapers of Manhattan.

As the guide on the bus would point out different landmarks, there were necks craned trying to see the tops of the towering buildings. The Neo-Gothic, Woolworth Building in lower Manhattan had been finished in 1913 and topped off at 792 feet. F.W. Woolworth had paid the construction cost of $13,500,000 in cash, which was met with amazement by the Colonels.

"Do you mean that he was able to build that with sales of five and 10 cent items?"

"All 57 stories."

It was another world, hard to fathom. But it was part of the education of the Colonels as has been envisioned by the Chief from the start.

The tour was continued from the Woolworth Building to Battery Park where everyone got out and walked past Castle Clinton, a fort dating back to the War of 1812, to get a good view of the Statue of Liberty.

As the guide was telling the story of the Statue, he quite proudly began to recite the poem by Emma Lazarus, "The New Colossus," which is cut on a tablet within the pedestal on which the great copper edifice stands.

When he got to the line, "Give me your tired, your poor, your huddled masses yearning to breath free," one of the Colonels whispered, "Your hungry masses, yearning to eat free," which brought a chuckle from the players and an arched eyebrow from the Chief.

From Battery Park, it was over the Brooklyn Bridge, "Everybody has to go over the most famous bridge in the world," and a return back over the Manhattan Bridge for the long return to midtown and the Waldorf and lunch in the elegant dining room of the hotel.

Friday afternoon was spent in running through plays at the Polo Grounds. The stadium was as near to sacred ground as existed in baseball. Babe Ruth had hit 148 homers in three years playing in the Polo Grounds and had established himself as the premiere long ball hitter in the game. Frankie Frisch had just finished his 6th season. Lefty O'Doul and Carl Mays had pitched off the mound which had been near the end of the field, as it was laid out for football. Everybody knew of the greatness of the New York Giants as the team had gone to the World Series eight of the last 14 seasons.

There were photographers and reporters huddled around the Chief and Red Roberts, scribbling notes and taking pictures. Particular interest was paid to Red, as many of the reporters had covered the games in Harvard and were familiar with the big guy. Also, note was made that the only two who were at the 1924 West Virginia game and had also been in Charleston, West Virginia on November 8, 1919, were Red and the Chief.

Uncle Charlie had moved on. Dr. Ganfield was in Wisconsin. All of the rest who were there, other than Roscoe, who hadn't come to New York, were gone.

One of the reporters asked Red if he could still get out on the field and "mix it up with younger guys." Red took off his coat, tossed his cap onto the ground, got down in a crouch and lunged forward, picking the reporter up and holding him over his shoulder, smiling all the while. The reporter's hat fell off and he was kicking his feet up and down, hollering, "That's a 'yes,' isn't it Red? Now put me down. I'm going to say that's a 'yes!'"

Friday night was spent at a reception in the Waldorf which was hosted by Centre alumni and friends of the college.

Saturday morning found the Colonels getting ready for the game with West

Virginia. The New York papers, in writing about the teams, painted a rosy picture about the boys from Morgantown, West Virginia, and printed the team's record from past years.

The Mountaineers were playing excellent football. In 1922, they had gone 10-0-1, outscoring their opponents, 267-34, and won the East-West (Christmas) Bowl in San Diego.

1922 WEST VIRGINIA (10-0-1)

West Virginia 20	West Virginia Wesleyan	3
West Virginia 55	Marietta	0
West Virginia 9	Pittsburgh	6
West Virginia 12	Washington and Lee	12
West Virginia 28	Rutgers	0
West Virginia 34	Cincinnati	0
West Virginia 33	Indiana	0
West Virginia 13	Virginia	0
West Virginia 28	Ohio University	0
West Virginia 14	Washington and Jefferson	0

EAST-WEST (CHRISTMAS) BOWL

West Virginia 21	Gonzaga	13

The following year, the Mountaineers had a 7-1-1 record, and were just seven points away from a perfect season.

1923 WEST VIRGINIA (7-1-1)

West Virginia 21	West Virginia Wesleyan	7
West Virginia 28	Allegheny	0
West Virginia 13	Pittsburgh	7
West Virginia 81	Marshall	0
West Virginia 13	Penn State	13
West Virginia 27	Rutgers	7
West Virginia 63	Washington and Lee	0
West Virginia 49	St. Louis University	0
West Virginia 2	Washington and Jefferson	7

The scoring average was bolstered by the game with W&L in which the Generals sent their 3rd team over to save their starters, and the thrashing of Marshall. However, again the team played tough defense, yielding only 41 points all season.

In 1924, going into the game in New York City, the team was 3-1.

1924 WEST VIRGINIA (3-1)

West Virginia 21	West Virginia Wesleyan	6
West Virginia 35	Allegheny	6
West Virginia 7	Pittsburgh	14
West Virginia 55	Geneva	0

Centre was entering into a game with a team that was 20-2-2 over the past three seasons, allowing only 101 points in those 24 contests, and had shut out the opposition exactly half the time, having played 12 games where it hadn't allowed a score.

Centre had to be given credit for facing tough teams on its trips to the East, meeting Harvard three times, Pennsylvania, and now an excellent West Virginia Mountaineer squad.

The crowd for the game wasn't what had been anticipated. There were several reasons. The Colonels had been tied by Valparaiso, and that took off some of the bloom. Also, people seemed to remember the score of the 1923 Penn game, and didn't realize that 24-0 didn't represent the true strengths of the Colonels and Quakers. Centre had played Penn evenly the 1st half, trailing only 3-0 due to a last minute field goal. Then there was the fact that West Virginia had no following of significance in New York. If Columbia had been scheduled, or any of several nearby teams in the East, those schools would have brought their fans.

There was the matter of Notre Dame, which had just beaten Army the week before, playing Princeton at Princeton. Many true followers of college football had chosen to travel to Princeton to see what the Irish could do with the Tigers.(Notre Dame did quite well, winning 12-0 on its way to a 10-0 record, capped by beating Stanford in the Rose Bowl.)

And finally, perhaps most importantly, when Centre had been the little school which no one had heard of, and which continuously bumped off the bigger fellows, it was natural to turn out and to cheer on the underdog.

Centre's continued success over the years had removed the "novelty factor." It was a simple fact that over a period of time, an underdog which keeps winning loses that distinction.

The crowd was under 5,000, which in a 55,000 seat ballpark, looked pretty meager. The game was an even match. Centre scored first when Hennie Lemon booted a 40 yard field goal from what was described as a "difficult angle." The 1st quarter ended, 3-0. In the 2nd quarter, West Virginia scored on a double pass, missed the extra point, and it was 6-3 at the half. Herb Covington kicked an 18 yard field goal in the 3rd period, and at the end of the quarter, it was 6-6.

It looked like the game was going to end as a tie. It had been a hard-hitting standoff, continuing that way as 10 minutes ticked off in the last quarter. However, as the clock wound down, the Mountaineers sent in a little 130 pound speedster named "Skeet" Farley who had fresh legs. "Skeet" began to make consistant gains against the weary Colonels who simply couldn't keep him from picking up yardage each time he was given the ball. Five times he got the signal. His 30 yards during the drive were the difference in the game, and West Virginia scored, got the extra point, and edged the Colonels, 13-6.

The game was a draw statistically. The Colonels had a total yardage of 218 while West Virginia had 234. Centre only subbed twice, a pattern which was going to continue. The Mountaineers sent in six replacements.

West Virginia finished the 1924 season at 8-1. In 1925, it was again 8-1, losing to Pittsburgh 15-7. For the seasons 1922-25, West Virginia had a record of 33-3-2, which makes the Centre close loss in 1924 understandable. West Virginia was tough!

The Centre alumni had arranged for a night at the Ziegfeld Follies for the team after the game. They had purchased the tickets far in advance for $6.03 each. The headliner at the show was Will Rogers, the famous humorist from Oklahoma.

Notre Dame had come to New York for the night after its game with Princeton and was also staying at the Waldorf and taking in the Follies. Rogers came out on the stage and was wearing a Notre Dame sweater. He paid a fine tribute to the Irish and asked Coach Rockne to stand, and then turned to Centre and did the same, introducing the Chief and then having the players stand. There was a capacity crowd which loved seeing the two famous teams and gave them both great cheers.

Will Rogers then made some comments.

"Notre Dame has it on Centre as far as substitutes. For many years, Centre had great baseball teams. That was when it had nine students enrolled in the college. A few years ago, two more students enrolled and Centre proceeded to win the football championship of the country. I want to make a plea that they don't invent any games with more than eleven players, for that would cut Centre out."

Rogers then wished both teams success and he was given a rousing cheer by both teams. Then the Irish and Colonels turned and gave a yell for each other.

A reporter was at the Follies.

It was a typical college affair, and the audience seemed to enjoy it as much as the gridders.

The team left on schedule the next morning at 8:45, rolled into Cincinnati Monday morning at 6:55, and reached Danville at 11:35 a.m. The trip had taken just 10 minutes less than 27 hours.

There were over 400 people at the station to meet the team. Even in defeat, the boys who wore the Gold and White were idolized. After all, they were the Centre College Colonels, pride of the school, pride of Danville and Boyle County, and the pride of Kentucky.

Centre went out into the country carrying the banner. Win, lose or draw, they were-Centre College.

UP NEXT—
FOUR GAMES WITH SOUTHERN CONFERENCE MEMBERS
The Colonels found themselves in totally unfamiliar territory. Not since 1917 when they lost the second game of the season had they failed to have a winning record. Now, the team was 1-1-1. There were four games left, all with big flagship state schools, each of which was a member of the Southern Conference.

The schedule after West Virginia and the return from New York was:

Nov.	1	Kentucky at Lexington
Nov.	8	Tennessee at Knoxville
Nov.	15	Alabama at Birmingham
Nov.	29	Georgia at Danville

I was manager of the freshman team in 1924. Red Roberts came back on campus to coach the Lieutenants and as soon as he got in Danville, he looked me up and said he wanted his "son" to help with the first year team. Of course, I jumped at the chance.

There is a photograph that I have—a picture of the freshman team—and on the back row sit Red and me. His head looks about twice the size of mine. That's probably because it was.

As student manager of the Lieutenants, I knew pretty much everything that was going on, not only with the freshmen, but since Red also was helping with the varsity, I was involved with everything going on there, too. Naturally, Red sat in on all of the meetings, and since I was Red's shadow, I was right there in the middle of everything.

There were some really intense meetings after the West Virginia game. The seven senior starters led by Herb Covington made a vow that they were going to go out winners, just like they'd been all during their careers.

Later, the Chief began to call them "The Seven Immortals." The seven were Herb Covington, Ed Kubale, Minos Gordy, Cliff Lemon, whom we called Hennie, Case Thomasson, the boy from Newport who blew up the beaker in our chemistry lab, Frank Rubarth, and Howard Lynch. They deserved to be called "The Immortals" for all that they accomplished while they were at Centre.

I was at Centre during the great seasons of 1921 through 1924. I'd seen some wonderful football games, but what happened during the rest of the '24 season, after the loss in New York, is what I believe was Centre's finest moment.

The seniors made a simple declaration. They would not lose another game, and they would not give up a point. They'd have to be carried off the field if they weren't able to play every minute left in the season.

It was like the determination that Howard had seen in Boston just before the 1921 game when we beat Harvard. The seven senior starters said they had represented Centre with the pride that only putting on the gold and white jerseys of Centre could produce. They had spent four years helping build what the Chief, Uncle Charlie, Bo, Red Weaver, Red Roberts, Army, Bill James, Ben Cregor, Hump, Terry Snowday, and all of the great players who'd gone before them had accomplished.

They had been winners, and they were going out winners. They made that vow in a meeting.

And then they began that cheer which the players sometimes started to reinforce just who and what they were.

"We are Centre!"
"We are Centre!"
Over and over.
"We are Centre!"
"We are Centre!"
They truly were.

The seven starting seniors, "The Seven Immortals," and their hometowns and nicknames, were:

Herbert Hunt Covington—Mayfield, Ky. "Covey"
Edwin Kubale—Fort Smith, Ar. "Kube"
Minos Thomas Gordy—Abbeville, La. "Cajun"
Clifton Wilson Lemon—Mayfield, Ky. "Hennie"
Howard W. Lynch—Amarillo, Tx. "Bull"
Robert Frank Rubarth—Gatesville, Tx. "Rube"
Robert L. Thomasson—Newport, Ky. "Case"

HOMECOMING AT KENTUCKY, NOVEMBER 1, 1924

Centre was continuing to win against Kentucky, its greatest rival, but there was a trend developing which even the most partisan fans of the Colonels had to recognize. The days of winning by 50 or so points were past, though Centre had maintained it dominance statistically even as the margins narrowed.

1917	Centre	3	Kentucky	0
1918	No game			
1919	Centre	56	Kentucky	0
1920	Centre	49	Kentucky	0
1921	Centre	55	Kentucky	0
1922	Centre	27	Kentucky	3
1923	Centre	10	Kentucky	0

One may have felt that after uttering, "This is the year!" the past two seasons, and having their team come up short both times, perhaps a new slogan would have been in order, but on the campus and wherever UK fans were found, it was again, "This is the year!"

Kentucky had a new coach, Fred J. Murphy, a tough customer and standout at Yale where he lettered four years and was a Walter Camp, All-American in 1895 and '96.

In the 1894 game with Harvard, Murphy was knocked so groggy that he had to be helped to the line for the next play. Later, during an official's conference, Murphy backhanded Harvard's Bob Hallowell, crushing his nose into a bloody mess. He also poked Hallowell's eye, drawing blood. The Crimson players grabbed Murphy and literally beat him to a pulp, and he crumpled unresponsive onto the field. A stretcher was brought and Murphy "was unceremoniously dumped onto a pile of blankets so that the medical personnel could get back to watching the game."

The rumor was that Murphy died, but he came around in a few hours, and later continued his football career. His coaching experience had been at Missouri, just after the turn of the century, and Northwestern from 1914 through 1918.

Kentucky got its new stadium up a year after Centre's and named it McLean Stadium on Stoll Field. The "McLean" was in memory of the Kentucky football player, Prince Innes McLean, who died from a head injury suffered during the Cincinnati game of 1923. The "Stoll" was in honor of Richard C. Stoll, longtime Kentucky trustee.

The stadium was built of concrete and held 15,000. Kentucky had opened the season with four straight games in the new facility, but waited until Centre came to Lexington to hold both the school's Homecoming, and the dedication ceremony of the new structure. Coming into the Centre game, the Wildcats were 3-1.

Kentucky	29	Louisville	0
Kentucky	42	Georgetown (Ky.)	0
Kentucky	7	Washington & Lee	10
Kentucky	7	Sewanee	0

The city of Lexington was consumed by the upcoming game. Contests were held to determine which store and office could decorate most effectively in the Wildcats' blue and white. Every hotel and boarding house was booked to capacity by the influx of out of town alumni and Centre supporters coming to the weekend festivities.

A large contingent of UK and Centre fans planned to come over from Louisville, many by train. For those driving to Lexington, the Louisville papers printed the best route "for those who plan to go over by motorcar." Drivers were advised to go to Lexington via Georgetown rather than Versailles, as "there is freshly poured oil on the Versailles to Lexington road, certain to be splashed up on any cars using the highway."

Both Kentucky and Centre closed their practices to the public. Coach Murphy had the Wildcats on the field so late into the afternoon and early evening that he had a ball painted white so it could be seen better.

The Chief had two players injured in the West Virginia who hadn't been diagnosed until the return on Monday. Frank Rubarth had a broken collar bone and Robert Wallace had a fracture in his hand. Both had continued to play in New York.

Rubarth suited up for the no-contact practice on Monday and vowed he was going to play against the Wildcats. Wallace had to sit out.

One spectator who was allowed to watch the Colonels was Lefty Whitnell who came to Danville from Fulton, Kentucky. It was Lefty who caught the long pass from Bo in the 1920 Harvard game.

Local reporters caught up with Lefty who solemnly declared that he'd give up five years of his life if he could "just get into the Kentucky contest for one minute." (Lefty could have perhaps afforded to give up some of his life. In 1978, as he approached 80 years of age, he was living in Florida where he owned a resort, and wrote George Chinn, his old teammate, saying, "I sit around 80% of the time, occasionally swim in the Gulf, play golf about three times weekly, and try to have relations with my girlfriend twice weekly, weakly.")

Once again, Howard King of the Southern organized a special train for the Centre-Kentucky game, this time to originate in Danville. A coach-only day train would leave Danville at 11:00 a.m. on Saturday morning and arrive in Lexington by noon, plenty of time to get to the game. There were 500 tickets available, and all were gone the day they were put on sale.

The Colonels were going over earlier. The school had chartered a coach to be hooked onto the northbound "Carolina Special" with arrival in Lexington at 8:25 a.m. The players had rooms booked at the Lafayette Hotel on Main Street. They were going to have a short skull session in the ballroom and then get naps in their rooms until going to the stadium.

There were no tickets available from anyone at any price. The 15,000 seats were gone, and plans were to sell 2,000 standing room only admissions on the day of the game which would swell the attendance to 17,000, exceeding the crowd of 15,000 at the 1923 stadium dedication game in Danville between the Colonels and Wildcats.

Rain had been predicted which would be to Kentucky's advantage. The Wildcats were larger but didn't have the Colonels' speed. A wet field would be beneficial to their more ponderous line, and the forecast affected the wagering on the game. Originally, Kentucky's bettors wanted 12 points, but when the prediction for rain was publicized, the odds got closer to even money. Bettors who factored in rain ended up factoring in the weather incorrectly, as it was dry all day.

Bruce Dudley, now with the "Courier-Journal", came over from Louisville on an early train Friday morning in order to soak up the atmosphere as preparations were being made for what he designated "the state's premiere sporting event of the year." (Many considered the Kentucky Derby "the state's premiere sporting event of the year." Dudley apparently didn't, or differentiated between the human animal and other species.)

Alumni from Centre and Kentucky have come from all points of the state and from widely divergent sections in the United States to cheer their college on to victory tomorrow, and dazzling visions of triumph are being generated by every dynamic partisan, and all are partisans. There are but few towns in the state that haven't sent a student to Centre or Kentucky, and there are few towns that are not represented here in the rousing reunion of worshipers.

They are here from Rabbit Hash, Boone County on the North, straight through to Fidelity, McCreary County in the South. They are from Bugg, Hickman County in the far West, to Jamboree, Pike County in the East. They are here from Good Luck, Metcalf County, to Good Night, in Barren County.

All of the male members of the buzzing groups are composed of boys. Some, carrying gray in their hair, lean perceptibly on canes beribboned in blue or gold, but they are boys tonight, as robust in spirit as those who call them "Grandpa."

Friday night, there was a UK pep rally in the brand new 3,500 seat Alumni Gymnasium. The crowd of 2,000 sat in the bleachers as the Wildcat cheerleaders dressed in white flannel slacks, white shoes, and blue sweaters, led the yells.

Rah, Rah, Rah, Rah, U-K, U-K!
Rah, Rah, Rah, Rah, U-K, U-K!
Rah, Rah, Rah, Rah, U-K, U-K!
Rah, Rah, Rah, Rah, U-K, U-K!
Team! Team! Team!

G-r-r-r-o,o,o,o, OO,O,O,O,O,O
Kentucky! Kentucky! Kentucky!
G-r-r-r-o,o,o,o, OO,O,O,O,O,O
Kentucky! Kentucky! Kentucky!

Meow! Meow! Meow!
P-st! P-st! P-st!
Wildcats! Wildcats! Wildcats!

Fight Blue and White!
Fight Blue and White!
Fight Blue and White!
Fight! Fight! Fight! Fight!

The University of Kentucky asked the Boy Scouts to come out in uniform to help with traffic, particularly to keep any of the crowd from parking in nearby home's driveways.

"No one is going to question a fresh-faced young Scout in uniform when they are told they can't park someplace."

Programs were being sold for 25 cents to fans who began arriving for the planned 1:30 dedication ceremony. There was a somewhat strange choice of a photograph of a bygone Wildcat team in the program. A group of Kentucky players dressed in a variety of uniforms was featured with the caption, "The mighty team of 1894, George Carey, captain. This team suffered only one defeat."

Further into the program, there was a list of "The Results of Previous Kentucky-Centre Games."

The score of that 1894 Centre-Kentucky game showed that the Colonels beat the Wildcats, 67-0.

Centre's fans laughed when they saw the photo and score. Wildcat supporters said Kentucky's "mighty team of 1894" perhaps "had an off day," but then they confided to friends from Danville that, "It was obvious that the left hand didn't know what the right hand was doing...."

Blue and white was everywhere. The phone poles were wrapped and bunting decorated the buildings around Stoll Field. At various locations around the stadium, vendors sold flowers with the blue of Kentucky or the gold of Centre. There were pennants, arm bands, medallions, ribbons of the team's colors with little gold footballs dangling, and a booth was set up where 8 X 10 glossies of the stars of both teams could be purchased.

At 1:00, the snappy Kentucky Wildcats' Marching band came onto the field playing the school's fight song.

On, on, U of K.
We are right for the fight today.
Hold that ball and hit that line,
Every Wildcat star will shine.
We'll fight, fight, fight for the
Blue and White.
We will roll to the goal, varsity,
And will kick, roll and run
Till the battle is won,
And we'll bring home the victory.

Just as the year before at Danville, the dedication ceremony, beginning as scheduled at 1:30, wasn't appreciated except by those sitting nearby due to the din of the crowd.

Everyone stood as the band played, "My Old Kentucky Home," the speeches were made, Judge Stoll accepted the stadium on behalf of the University, everyone popped up again as the band then played "The Star Spangled Banner," and it was game time.

Bruce Dudley sat in the press box after the game and completed his story which he handed over to be wired back to the "Courier-Journal".

The Wildcats will have to wait at least one more year.
The armor of the Centre College Colonels has withstood for the seventh successive season the clawing of the Kentucky Wildcats for penetration and football supremacy.

Only a thin shield now seems to protect the state championship for Centre. The margin of resistance today was seven points, all of the points that were achieved in the battle.

In 1917, the margin was 3-0. In 1919, 56-0. In 1920, 49-0. In 1921, 55-0. The tide seemed to turn a bit in 1922 as Kentucky held the Colonels to a 27-3 victory. Last year it was even closer, 10-0.

The 'Cats were wildly eager for victory, as another marker for this memorable day, on which Stoll Field was dedicated before some 17,000 radiant sons and daughters of the state. Of the crowd, at least 3,000 were homecoming brothers and sisters of the University. Defeat did not ruin their day, nor lessen one whit their pride in their team and their glory in their stadium. For them the defeat will make victory, when victory comes over Centre, all the sweeter.

Gems, in Centre's rosary of joy, were dazzling dashes by Covington, vicious thrusts by Gordy, and the point after touchdown by Lemon.

Centre's touchdown came early in the 2nd quarter. A Kentucky punt as the 1st quarter ended resulted in a 15 yard penalty due to the Wildcats' "Ab" Kirwan inadvertently tacking Herb Covington before he had fielded the ball.

After the whistle and switching over ends of the field, Centre found itself in good position with 1st and 10 on the Kentucky 40. The Colonels stuck to the ground. It was Covey, Gordy, Rabenstein, Covey, Gordy—each play picking up 3-5 yards. Finally near the goal, Minos Gordy, running with his head low, lunged forward and crashed over the goal. Lemon made it 7-0.

Even though the score was close, and everyone conceded that Kentucky had come a long way since its crushing defeats in the past, again Centre won big when the stats were analyzed. Kentucky never got closer than Centre's 45 yard line. The Wildcats didn't get one first down in the 1st half while Centre got eight, and Centre had a 13-5 margin for the game. The Colonels picked up 189 yards on the ground and 17 through the air for a total of 206. The Wildcats got 91 yards on running plays and completed one pass for 11 yards, for a total gain of 102. Kentucky was closing the gap, but the gap was still there.

A highlight of the afternoon for both schools was the halftime performance of the Kentucky Marching Band, 62 members strong, "led by Ed Gans, the band's bewitching drum major from Louisville." Whether one was a Wildcat fan or not, there was no denying the excitement generated when the band began the stirring UK fight song, "On, On, U of K."

Frank Rubarth started, broken collar bone and all.

I was in the dressing room at Kentucky, helping out. Red brought me along so I could go out with the team and sit on the bench during the game. I actually rode over on the train with the team and just hung out in downtown Lexington before we went to the new stadium.

I had watched Frank Rubarth in practice the week before. There seemed no way he could play at Kentucky because it was obvious that just running caused a lot of pain, and he couldn't raise his arm. But he was one of "The Immortals"

who had vowed to play every minute during the rest of the season.

Before the game, Frank begged Coach Ofstie and the Chief to let him play. He said it was his last season and he had pledged with the other seniors that he would play just as they were. He actually had tears in his eyes, and he kept saying, "I can play. Just let me start and you'll see I can play."

The Chief looked over at Red and he saw Red nod his head, yes. I don't know if Frank even knew it, but it was because of Red that he started.

Frank played with one arm down at his side and obviously favored his shoulder. But he played hard, and the coaches left him in the game for as long as he was able to be effective.

Rubarth finally had to come out in the 2nd quarter, replaced by Jim "Judas" Priest. Unbelievably, he re-entered the game in the 3rd quarter, relieving Walter Skidmore. But after a few plays, he had to come back out and Bill Kagin replaced him. Those were the only substitutions in the game.

Centre and the "Seven Immortals" had won the first of the four games against the Southern Conference teams, and they again had a winning record, as they'd been accustomed.

The day after the game, "Matador" wrote his impressions of the afternoon. He said he overheard "a fair maiden complaining about the officiating."

"On my, did you see that? Centre made a first down in less than four downs and the referee didn't even notice it!"

"Matador" also made note of some of the Colonels' players.

It is too bad Covington can't play another year. When they take Covington away from Centre, it will be like taking the Leaning Tower away from Pisa. And when they take Gordy and Kubale away, it'll be like taking the props out from under that tower. Covington was harder to stop than an ingrown toenail. He and Gordy did more things to the Kentucky line than a Chinese laundry can do to a silk shirt.

Next it was a trip to Knoxville to play the Volunteers of the University of Tennessee.

CENTRE VS. TENNESSEE NOVEMBER 8, 1924

Centre and Tennessee had played seven times over the years, with the first game in 1905. Tennessee held the edge, 3-2-2. The last two games the two teams had played were held in the pre-Uncle Charlie era and resulted in Centre being smashed, 67-0 in 1912, and 80-0 in 1915.

Centre beat Tennessee in 1910, 17-0 in an undefeated 9-0 season. It was a great year in which the Colonels gave up only 11 points.

1910 CENTRE SEASON RECORD

Centre	17	Tennessee	0
Centre	12	Miami (Oh.)	2
Centre	19	Sewanee	0
Centre	33	Hanover	0
Centre	35	Tulane	0
Centre	27	Transylvania	0
Centre	12	Cincinnati	3
Centre	78	Georgetown (Ky.)	0
Centre	12	Kentucky	6

The Volunteers were coached by M.B. Banks who had played at Syracuse and had previously been at Duke as an assistant before moving up to the head coaching job at Drake from 1918-1920. He came to Knoxville to take over the program there in 1921, and had compiled a respectable 22-10-2 record going into the game with Centre.

Banks squad was 3-2 and hadn't fared well in its last game, a 33-0 loss to Georgia.

Tennessee	27	Emory and Henry	0
Tennessee	28	Maryville	10
Tennessee	13	Carson-Newman	0
Tennessee	2	Mississippi A&M (State)	7
Tennessee	0	Georgia	33

Home games were played at Shields-Watkins Field on 15th Street which was located along the Tennessee River. The stadium was concrete and had seating for only 3,200 spectators, but several more thousand could be accommodated by purchasing standing room tickets and lining the field, as was the habit when an attractive opponent was in town such as Centre.

Centre arranged for a chartered Pullman to be picked up by a passenger train originating in St. Louis which didn't come through Danville until 11:30 p.m. The advantage of having a chartered sleeper was that since the train hit Knoxville very early in the morning, the Colonels' car could be left on a siding and the players could sleep until a civilized hour.

They would return after the Saturday game, connected to a northbound Southern train which came straight through Knoxville in the early evening.

The late departure meant that for the first time that anyone could remember, there wasn't a boisterous sendoff at the station. It was nearing midnight, and only a few of the most ardent fans made it down to the station, understandably.

Centre didn't expect Tennessee to present much of a challenge. The Chief got Red Roberts to talk to Frank Rubarth and Bob Wallace about their not going to the game.

Red and I went together to talk to Frank. Bob Wallace had his hand in a big cast and there was no way that he could play, and he understood. But Frank was different. He felt it was a matter of honor to go and to play. He'd made a pledge.

But Red was great. He explained that the team really needed him for Alabama and Georgia. He said, "Frank, do you love this team?"

And Frank said, "Of course Red. How could you even ask something like that?"

Red said, "If you love the team, you'll get healed and be ready for the games when your teammates really need you. By the Alabama game, it will be three weeks since you broke your collar bone against West Virginia. I'll guarantee you'll be fine by then. But if you go to Tennessee and re-injure your shoulder, you'll let the team down."

So Frank said he understood, and he and Bob didn't even go and take up a berth on the train. They said that a couple of the other guys who didn't normally get to go on the trips should be taken along.

Everything worked out for the best. The Chief was a great man, and everybody just loved him. And they all liked Coach Ofstie. But it seemed like if there was ever a problem, like Frank not playing, Red would be asked to see what he could do, and always, Red worked things out.

Not that there were many problems, or a lot of things to work out.

The morning of the Tennessee game found the Colonels in Knoxville with several hours before needing to get to the game. The team had reserved a dining room at the Atkin Hotel across from the Knoxville Southern Station. After they had placed their orders, Hennie Lemon stood and got the attention of everyone by clanging his water glass with a spoon.

"Chief, we want to bring up a very serious and important subject."

The Chief was caught a bit off guard, but said, "You have the floor, Mr. Lemon."

Hennie pulled the November 6 issue of the Danville "Advocate" out of his coat pocket and began to unfold it.

"Would you say, Chief, that Coach Knute Rockne has done an excellent job at the University of Notre Dame over the past several seasons?"

"Yes indeed, Hennie."

"I think we all would agree, Chief. Do you know what has made him so successful?"

The Chief was getting into the spirit as he saw several of the players begin to smile. He didn't know just what was coming, but he knew it must be amusing.

"I'm certain you're going to tell me, Hennie."

Lemon glanced at the newspaper and then held it up.

"Chief, it says here that—just let me read it, and I quote—Knute Rocke, the coach of the Notre Dame team which has had much success, is said to have taken members of the team to a musical comedy to watch the cooperation of the kickers in the chorus. He declares a team's members must work together with a harmony approaching the rhythm of chorus girls—end quote."

Herb Covington stood. "Chief, as the captain of the team, I must state that I felt we were a little out of rhythm at the Kentucky game. I think we need to work on our rhythm, and we're willing to go to Lexington or Louisville or even back to New York to watch some chorus girls. We'll go anywhere to take rhythm lessons."

Carl Hilker, a substitute end, hopped up.

"Chief, I've never felt so bad about anything in my life about how little rhythm us subs had on the bench during the Kentucky game. Why, if any of us had been sent in, I don't know if we could have ever gotten into the rhythm of the game."

By now, everyone was beginning to break out laughing, the Chief included. Then he got a real stern look and said, "You want rhythm? You want rhythm? Everybody on your feet!"

"Now. Left leg up, right leg up, turn-a-round. Come on, Hennie. Come on Covey. Let's see it Carl. Left leg up, right leg up, turn-a-round."

The Chief couldn't keep a straight face as he began to kick his legs up. "Left leg up, right leg up. Turn-a-round. Left leg up. Right leg up. Turn-a-round."

The waitresses almost dropped their trays as they came through the swinging kitchen doors. Some of the Colonels were trying to do little pirouettes on their toes, hands clasped over their heads. Others were doing leg kicks. All were laughing so hard that they had tears coming down their cheeks. If anyone ever let the ladies in on the joke, it isn't recorded. One can only hope someone did.

The game was played on a Saturday afternoon which wasn't atypical for November along the Tennessee River. The field was wet but the rain had stopped. A haze and finally overt fog had rolled in off the river. The conditions weren't a bother for the Colonels. They won easily, beating Tennessee by one less point, 32-0, than Georgia had in Athens a week earlier.

Herb Covington primarily stuck to the ground. Elmer Rabenstein carried the load the majority of times. The Knoxville papers declared that "Roundy" was "the greatest back who had ever played on Tennessee soil." Rabenstein capped off a great afternoon by scoring the final touchdown on a 67 yard run, his second score of the game. Minos Gordy bulled for two scores, Covey took it in once, Lemon kicked two extra points.

Centre played only 13 men. James Priest started in the place of Rubarth and shared time at the guard slot with Bill Kagin. Carl Hilker spelled Lemon late in the game.

As Hennie trotted off, he came over to the sideline smiling and said to the Chief, "I think we got our rhythm down this afternoon. No more exercises!"

It had been a very business-like win over an outclassed but game foe.

Centre was 3-1-1. The team, and especially "The Immortals," was halfway to its goal of being recognized as the class of the South.

However, two big challenges stood in the way—the University of Alabama and the University of Georgia.

I was out on the field every day at practice. We all recognized that beating the Southern schools had become an obsession. The practices were as intense, or even more so, than the games. It wasn't that the coaches were driving the team so hard. It was the team that was driving itself almost brutally.

After the hardest of practices, all of the players would be out on the field running extra laps until they'd almost drop. They were led by the "Immortals." Covey would spur them on, but it didn't take much spurring, because they all wanted to outwork each other and prove by their work that they could literally will themselves to win.

That's what Red and I decided. They were going to will themselves to win. We'd stand on the sidelines and marvel at how hard they practiced.

Red told me that he thought that this team was as good as any Centre had ever put together. Certainly they were as dedicated.

THE UNDEFEATED "TIDE", CENTRE-ALABAMA
NOVEMBER 15, 1924

Alabama was next. Two down. Two to go.

Centre and the Crimson Tide had played twice before with 'Bama winning a 1905 game in Tuscaloosa, 21-0, and defeating the Colonels in Birmingham, 12-0, in 1907.

Once again, Centre was taking on a much larger school. The Alabama student newspaper, the "Crimson-White," reported in its September 19, 1924 issue that there were 2,250 students on campus. Centre had less than 300 enrolled.

Centre loved to play in Birmingham. The Tutwiler Hotel was glamorous. The alumni of the school bent over backwards to make each year's journey to the city pleasurable, and the fans had treated the Colonels wonderfully in the last three games against Auburn at Rickwood Field.

Centre would have played Auburn again except that the Tigers had committed to a game with Georgia in Columbus, Georgia on November 15, and there was no way to switch dates. It was perhaps fortunate, because Auburn wasn't having a great season, and Alabama was. A win over the Tide would gain more recognition than one over Auburn.

Alabama was on a roll. After Uncle Charlie had turned down the 1923 offer to coach in Tuscaloosa, Wallace Wade had come in and done a great job. His team was 7-2-1 in 1923 with the losses being to an 8-1 Syracuse, and to Florida, which had an excellent 6-1-2 record. The tie was with always tough Georgia Tech.

The Tide was undefeated in 1924 with seven straight victories to give Wade a record of 14-2-1 thus far at the helm of the program.

Alabama	55	Union	0
Alabama	20	Furman	0
Alabama	55	Mississippi College	0
Alabama	14	Sewanee	0
Alabama	14	Georgia Tech	0

| Alabama | 61 | Mississippi | 0 |
| Alabama | 42 | Kentucky | 7 |

Obviously, Alabama had a powerful defense, only giving up seven points, but the team's offense was just as formidable, having scored at an average clip of over 37 points per game.

The Kentucky game stood out when comparing Alabama and Centre. Even though the Colonels won statistically by a greater margin than the 7-0 score would indicate, everyone had to think that 'Bama would be the big favorite as it had rolled over the Wildcats by 42-7.

"Centre could only score once against Kentucky? Look what our boys did!"

There were three excellent backs who led the Tide's attack. "Rosey" Rosenfield, "Pooley" Hubert, and Mack Brown, who had a big game against Kentucky, were considered by many to be the best backfield combination in the South. They would be running behind a line which outweighed Centre's front wall by 15 pounds per man. (Mack Brown led Alabama to an undefeated season in 1925 and a Rose Bowl win over Washington. His play earned him a spot on a "Wheaties" box, and propelled him to a 40 year career in the movies, beginning in 1927. He was best known as Johnny Mack Brown and became a household name appearing in "B" movies as a cowboy, being right up there with Gene Autry and Roy Rogers, also "B" stars, in the 1940's and 50's.)

Alabama planned to wrap up the title as the best Southern team. Even though Centre was a member of the small college S.I.A.A. and couldn't influence the official standings of the Southern Conference, it followed that if the Tide lost to the Colonels, it would diminish any claim of 'Bama as being the premier squad in the South. Even if Alabama followed the Centre game with a win in the season ending game with Georgia, its season would be tarnished.

"They claim to be the best Southern team and couldn't even beat little Centre?"

However if Alabama beat both Centre and Georgia, it would finish 9-0 and have a legitimate shot at being declared not only the Southern champs, but the national champions as well. A lot was riding on the game for the boys from Tuscaloosa.

The "Crimson-Tide" ran weekly predictions by the newspaper's resident prognosticator, "The Campus Prophet," in which the "Prophet" picked not only the winner of the upcoming football game, but the score. He had "divined" Alabama as the winner every week, and since the Tide was undefeated, he was looking to be infallible. For the Centre game, it was an easy 20-0 win for 'Bama, or so said the "Prof."

The "Crimson-Tide," besides printing the prediction, began a drive to get the entire student body to Birmingham, certainly a familiar venue for Alabama. In the last 25 years, the college had played 60 games in the friendly atmosphere of the city. It was actually a stretch to consider playing in Birmingham to be a road game. In the current season, Alabama was playing three games at home in Tuscaloosa and three in Birmingham, one in Montgomery, and two truly on the road, at Furman and Georgia Tech.

The newspaper pointed out that there were multiple trains running between

Tuscaloosa and Birmingham, a mere 60 mile, hour and a quarter run. There were late afternoon and night trains on Friday, and two were regularly scheduled on Saturday morning at 4:55 and 8:50, but most students planned on coming over on a specially designed consist of day coaches, leaving at 8:30, which would include no stops, and carried a roundtrip tariff of $2.20.

Alabama planned on having a big parade through downtown Birmingham as soon as the "Special" arrived at 9:45. The band would assemble at 20th Street and the student body would fall in behind. When everyone was lined up, the throng would wind through the main downtown thoroughfares. After marching and cheering, they would scatter to various restaurants and then head to Rickwood Field.

Centre had its usual chartered Pullman and hooked onto a Southern train for the overnight ride to Birmingham, arriving at 11:30 a.m. on Friday. The trip and reception were mirrors of what the Colonels had experienced the past three years. There was a big reception at the station, transportation to the Tutwiler, and a lunch and workout at the Birmingham Country Club, again organized by S.L. Yerkes. Friday night, there was a dinner at the Club, and then the team took in the second performance of a vaudeville show before turning in for the evening.

Hennie Lemon and I were talking one night some years later when he was visiting me in Paducah. We were sitting out on our porch swing, shooting the breeze, listening to the Cardinals and Harry Carey on the radio, and as always, Centre football came up.

I asked Hennie about the Alabama game, and did the team feel it could win against what was obviously a heavily favored team. Hennie always called me "Red Robbie," and he said, "Red Robbie, we never considered that we'd lose in the four years that I was on the team. We felt it was an upset if we lost, not that it was ever an upset if we won."

Hennie said that the team entered the Alabama game with that attitude. They were going to win, no matter that Alabama was favored. He said Centre was Centre, and Centre never went onto the field without the feeling that it would walk off that field with a victory.

Birmingham had been in a dry spell. There had been a little rain the night before the game, but the field was in good shape, and a "fast" field favored the speedy Colonels more than their heavier foes.

Herb Covington and George Joplin were talking on the trip down. Covey told Jop that Centre planned to come out with all guns firing from the onset and jump into the lead. He said that since Alabama had never trailed all season, he was confidant that an initial score would unnerve the Tide, and the Colonels could win if they drew first blood. It was a measure of the little quarterback's confidence that he was planning to take his team in for "an initial score" against a much bigger team that had given up only one touchdown in seven games.

Last minute bets found Alabama fans having to give 14 points. The Colonels' backers found plenty of takers, such was the certainty of the Tide's superiority.

A conference in the dressing room at Rickwood ended with the agreement that Frank Rubarth would start.

"I have only two games! Let me start. If I can't get the job done, take me out."

Hennie told me that each of the seniors came up to the Chief and told him that they wanted Frank to start. They felt that after all he had done for the team over the years, and the fact that he had been willing to stay home when the game was held in Knoxville, he deserved to be out there. And the Chief agreed, but told Frank not to hesitate if he felt he needed to be spelled.

Centre ran out onto the field first. Writers in the press box agreed that the Colonels seemed small when compared to the Alabama team which jogged out shortly afterward. Several commented that giving 14 points seemed like a sure thing. After all, the Tide was undefeated, they were virtually playing a home game, they clearly outweighed Centre, and they had killed a Kentucky Wildcats' team which Centre had beaten by just 7-0.

"It should be a long afternoon for the Kentuckians," one writer said. None disagreed, and the capacity crowd of 17,000 sat back, confidant that they would see Alabama roll to its 8th straight win.

Meanwhile, in the packed Boyle-Humphrey Gymnasium, hundreds thought differently as they sat in the bleachers and awaited the start of the game which they would "watch" on the "Grid-Graph."

THE ALABAMA GAME

The time in Chapel on the Monday after the Colonels had returned from Birmingham was turned over to the Chief and members of the team. Chief Myers wasn't one to hand out praise unless it was earned, but on this day, praise was all he could offer.

"There were no outstanding stars because there were eleven men who starred. There were no long, breathtaking gains. Every man did his part to help make the consistent, short, telling gains count when they were needed most. The game Saturday was as perfect a football game as I have ever witnessed. This is a great confession on my part, because as you all know, something has to be done awfully well before I'll say it was perfect."

Centre had taken the fight to Alabama from the opening play. The Colonels started "The Seven Immortals" who were joined by Elmer Rabenstein and Reginald "Mutt" Wilson in the backfield, and Alex Bush and Walter Skidmore in the line.

The Gold and White had come out of the dressing room wiping away tears after the pre-game prayer. They were literally the "Crying, Praying Colonels" on November 15, 1924.

Herb Covington received the opening kickoff, and from that moment, the Colonels absolutely dominated Alabama. Centre achieved control of the line of scrimmage from the first. The smaller Colonels began to knock the heavier Tide linemen back on every play, going in low and literally driving the 'Bama defenders up and then back. The smacking of leather could be heard all over Rickwood Field, as well as the grunts and groans of the players as they made contact.

Case Thomasson and Hennie Lemon drew a line in the sand and dared Alabama to try to sweep their end positions. That line was impregnable. On 15 end sweeps, the Tide had a net loss of 19 yards.

Ed Kubale played with intensity, as did Howard Lynch. Frank Rubarth, who acted like he'd never suffered a recent fracture of his collar bone, was in the middle of every play that came anywhere near his position. Walter Skidmore and Alex Bush, despite being considerably outweighed, seemed always able to break through the Tide's line when on defense and smother any effort of Alabama to get its offense going.

To understand how magnificently Centre played, and how totally it controlled the game, one statistic speaks volumes.

Alabama only got into Centre's territory once, and that was just to the Colonels' 48! No one in the stands could believe what they were watching. A team that had averaged over 37 points a game could do absolutely nothing against Centre's spirited play.

Centre ran 84 plays and picked up 15 first downs. Alabama ran 54 plays and picked up five first downs. Centre gained 155 yards on the ground and completed six of eight passes for 102 yards, good for a total yardage of 257, averaging just slightly over three yards per play. Alabama got just 42 yards rushing, 36 passing, and the Tide's total for the afternoon was a meager 78 yards, for an average of less that 1½ yards per effort. If you run three plays and pick up less than five yards—then what? You punt, which is what Alabama did all afternoon.

Herb Covington and Minos Gordy led the ground attack for the Colonels. Each nearly equaled the whole afternoon's offensive total for 'Bama. Covey gained 68 yards, and the hard charging Gordy, running out of the fullback position, picked up 67.

Hennie Lemon, besides his great tackling, recovered two Alabama fumbles and intercepted a pass, and the big-handed Mayfield, Kentucky native caught five of the eight completed passes for 85 yards.

Centre scored in the 2nd quarter on a short run by Covington. The Colonels lined up and everybody broke left. Alabama followed the direction that the play appeared to be headed. Covey went the other way, around his right end, and scored unmolested. After Lemon's kick, the half ended, 7-0.

The Colonels had so completely outclassed the Crimson Tide that the score would have been greater had Centre been able to convert on field goal attempts. Two relatively short tries were missed in the initial half, but it was indicative of how the game was going that at least Centre was able to get within field goal range. Alabama never got close enough to even consider a kick.

Centre finally did get a field goal in the 3rd quarter when Lemon booted true from 30 yards out. The quarter ended 10-0.

Coach Wallace kept running in replacements in the second half trying to get something started. He subbed twice in the backfield, and five times in the line, but nothing he did made any difference in his team's level of play, or perhaps more accurately, in Centre's.

Centre missed a field goal attempt early in the 4th quarter. The 38 yarder was long enough, but just wide.

The Chief stayed with his starting lineup until there were two minutes left. Walter Skidmore twisted his ankle running down the field and had to reluctantly come out. Jim Priest replaced him and was in the game when Herb Covington hit Hennie Lemon on a beautiful 20 yard pass for a score. Lemon's kick was good. The game ended with Centre up, 17-0. Frank Rubarth played the full 60 minures.

Sports writers from all over the South, nearly all of whom had come to Birmingham to be part of the coronation of Alabama on the throne of Southern football, tried to convey to their readers just how Centre had so totally outplayed what was supposed to be a superior team. There were terms like Centre "out-charged them," Centre "out-fought Alabama," Covington "out-generaled 'Bama," the Colonels "out-kicked" and "out-tackled" their opponent.

Finally, it was up to reporter Charles Brown, formerly the head coach at Birmingham Southern, to come up with an adequate description of the game.

You might say that Centre simply, totally, "out-outed" Alabama.

The Alabama "Crimson-White" paid homage to the Colonels' play.

The Centre team was fast, the backs being very quick on their line bucks. Their passes were also executed very rapidly, as well as their end plays. They had a dash and zip, never letting down in the least.
The Centre linemen were in fast on every play, leaving the 'Bama backs bewildered. Alabama was whipped and whipped good, by a fast, hard running, brainy team from Centre College.
The Colonels deserved their victory.

Centre had once again established itself as being in the upper tier of college football teams. The Valpo tie and close loss to West Virginia now seemed in the distant past. The dominating win over Alabama had surprised the sporting world, but not the Colonels. They felt they were a team of destiny, and indeed they were.

Now it was only Georgia between "The Seven Immortals" and their supporting cast to be called the "Champions of the Southland."

The guys on the team had never really been down after the less than successful start of the season, but following the Alabama game, there was a different way that they acted.

561

They weren't conceited or went around bragging. It was something different.

I guess it could best be described as being that they had this air of confidence about them. They were now like a machine, and each man knew that he could count on his teammates to play to win, or to nearly literally die trying.

I've said it before. I think that the play of the 1924 team, my senior year, was the most inspired of any group which had ever represented our college.

The Colonels returned to one of the wildest celebrations of all the wild celebrations which had ever been seen in Danville. It wasn't planned like those following the Harvard games. This one was simply a spontaneous outpouring of pure joy. There was such a crowd at the station that many didn't even try to get down to the tracks but waited up on Walnut across from Breck Hall. When the train steamed in and braked, even those who were hundreds of yards away could hear the cheering from all around the little brick terminal.

The students from Centre and K.C.W., with the cheerleaders out front holding the great gold and white banner, led the team up the street toward the campus, clasping hands and weaving back and forth in a snake dance which marched to the rhythm of the town's brass band, blowing as hard as cheeks could blow.

There were no formal speeches, just hugs, kisses, pats on the back, shaking of hands, arms wrapped around shoulders, fists pumped, jumping, whistling, clapping, laughing, crying, and above all, there was a great pride in this wonderful group of young men who were truly living up to the Chief's designation of them as, "The Immortals."

It was a wonderful time, a really wonderful time, and I don't think there has been another like it, or ever will be.

CENTRE-GEORGIA NOVEMBER 29, 1924

Centre was now 4-1-1 and had won three of the four games scheduled with the Southern Conference members. Georgia was the last challenge. The Bulldogs felt that they had outplayed Centre the year before when the two teams tied 3-3 in Athens. Georgia had a point, as it won statistically. However, Centre would have been victorious had Hennie Lemon's field goal attempt, which hit the goalpost's crossbar, gone a few inches further before it came down.

After Centre's big win over Alabama, interest in the Colonels, always great, now intensified. Centre had designated the Georgia game as Homecoming. The other two games played in Danville, against Valparaiso and Transylvania, hadn't really been considered attractions suitable to bring the graduates home. Georgia most certainly was.

Requests for tickets came in from six states. Many of the major newspapers from the South were sending reporters in to cover the game. Ed Danforth of the Atlanta "Georgian," the Atlanta "Journal's" Morgan Blake, Zip Newman of the Birmingham "Herald," Lawrence Perry of the Consolidated Press out of New York, and Walter

Schwan of the Shreveport "Times," were coming. Macon and Athens papers were sending their representatives. All of the Louisville and Lexington papers, along with the two from Danville, and many of the weekly papers in Central Kentucky, were also going to have their men in the pressbox.

Georgia had been unwise in its scheduling for 1924. The athletic department had signed a contact for home and away games with Centre in 1923 and '24, and had an agreement to play Alabama in Montgomery in 1923 and Birmingham in 1924. There was just one problem with the 1924 arrangement. Alabama wanted to play the 1924 game on Thanksgiving, which fell on November 27, and the Centre game was scheduled just two days later, on Saturday, November 29. Georgia, somewhat incomprehensibly, agreed to both dates, which meant that the team would meet Alabama on Thursday afternoon, stay over in Birmingham, and spend Friday on the train coming to Danville. It wasn't an impossible situation, but it meant that the Bulldogs would be taking on two formidable teams within 48 hours.

Adding to Georgia's problem was the fact that it was meeting an Alabama team which had been humiliated by Centre on November 15. The Tide was determined to make a comeback and show the football world that it was still a team to be reckoned with. The Southern Conference title was still in play, and since the Centre loss didn't count as a conference game, beating Georgia meant that 'Bama could claim the championship.

On November 27, Alabama destroyed Georgia 33-0 on the same Rickwood Field where it had met Centre, and finished at 8-1. The Tide surrendered only 24 points all season, 17 of which were put on the board by the Colonels. (Let's take a moment to reflect on how big the Centre win over Alabama was. As noted, after 'Bama smashed Georgia, the team stood at 8-1 and had outscored its opponents 294-24. The following year, 1925, Alabama was undefeated at 10-0 which included a Rose Bowl win over Washington, 20-19. In 1926, its record was 9-0-1, with the tie being 7-7 with another Rose Bowl opponent, Stanford. For the three years, 1924-26, Alabama had a 27-1-1 record, and won and tied in the only bowl game, the Rose, played in the post-season after 1925-26. It outscored its opponents during that run, 840-77, averaging winning by a rounded off, 29-3. The only loss was to Centre College, and the loss was no fluke. Centre destroyed a team that many felt was the best eleven of the era.)

Georgia was having a great year until running into the fired-up Alabama team. Coming into the game in Danville, it was 7-2. The only defeat other than the one that 'Bama put on them was a 7-6 loss to Yale in New Haven on October 11. (Yale was undefeated in 1924 with a record of 6-0-2. It tied Dartmouth and an Army team which only lost to Notre Dame, which was undefeated. The one point loss to the Yale Bulldogs, on the road, was an indication of the strength of the Georgia squad.)

Georgia	26	Mercer	7
Georgia	18	South Carolina	0
Georgia	6	Yale	7
Georgia	22	Furman	0

Georgia	3	Vanderbilt	0
Georgia	33	Tennessee	0
Georgia	7	Virginia	0
Georgia	6	Auburn	0
Georgia	0	Alabama	33

Other than the Alabama drubbing, Georgia had been stingy on defense, giving up only 14 points in the other eight games.

The Colonels and Bulldogs had two common opponents. Both beat Tennessee by similar scores, with Centre winning 32-0 and Georgia, 33-0. Alabama routed the Bulldogs and Centre soundly beat Alabama.

Chief Myers invited the Kentucky Wildcats' team to come to Danville and be guests of Centre. He also requested that the Captain Sanders sit on the bench.

Several coaches wired the Centre athletic board that they were going to be in attendance. William Alexander, Georgia Tech's coach since 1920, was coming from Atlanta. Fred Murphy of Kentucky was coming. Bob Peck, an All-American at Pittsburgh in 1914, and now head coach at Culver Military Academy, sent word that he needed a room and asked for assistance. Former Colonels and now coaches, Bill Shadoan from Valpo and Ed Diddle from Western Kentucky, planned on attending. Ashel "Bum" Day, a Walter Camp All-American at Georgia Tech in 1918, was coming to watch his brother, Rose Day, who played in the center position at Georgia.

Despite all of the reporters and other notables who were going to be in Danville on November 29, the really big news and attraction was that Bo was going to be on the sideline, cheering on his former teammates, the seniors now known as "The Immortals."

Everybody was really thrilled that Bo was coming back to Danville for the Georgia game. He was still the biggest thing to ever happen at Centre. Of course, as freshman team manager, I was in the dressing room when he came in to greet and speak to the team. Bo said that the great victory over Harvard was something that he would always remember and feel great pride in having taken part, but he said when he heard of the equally great victory over Alabama, he thought he was just as happy as he was in 1921 when he heard "Tiny" Maxwell tell him that the game was over, and Centre had beaten Harvard.

It was, "Once a Centre man, always a Centre man."

The week leading up to the Georgia game was filled with Homecoming events. Classes weren't held on Thursday and Friday due to Thanksgiving, but most of the student body decided to stay in Danville and attend the game and participate in Homecoming.

Wednesday morning there was a big pep rally after chapel and a dance in the gym that night. Thursday evening, the freshman team had a banquet at the Gilcher. Friday morning, there was a "Get Together" at the First Presbyterian Church. That evening, there was an alumni smoker at the Boyle-Humphrey Gymnasium. All fraternities had open houses, and then there was a huge bonfire and pep rally out on the football practice field. Saturday morning, there was an event called "Freshman Stunt Day," and of course, in the afternoon, there was the matter of a football game. Just after the game, the election of a football captain for 1925 would take place and be announced at the big alumni dance in the gym that evening.

Centre dedicated the contest to the seven seniors who would be running out onto Cheek Field for the last time. As the game day approached, the weather began to turn cold. On the day that the "Southern Championship" was to be determined, it started to snow, and then came the wind. The temperature was recorded at 25 degrees, but felt more like it was in the low teens. One reporter wrote that the windblown snow and sleet "made ones face feel like it was being peppered with buckshot."

What had been foreseen as a sellout from advance tickets sold turned out to have only 5,000 in the stands who braved the weather. Those who attended felt they had certainly gotten their money's worth as it was a smashing, hard fought, excellently played game.

The Centre partisans stood and cheered when the "Seven Immortals" were introduced. They appreciated that they had the opportunity and privilege of watching seven unique and talented individuals over the last four years.

The "Immortals" ran out onto the 50 yard line for pictures to be taken as applause rocked through the stadium. From left to right, it was Gordy, Covington, Lemon, Thomasson, Rubarth, Lynch and Kubale. Covey still had his warmup over his jersey. Thomasson and Kubale were bareheaded while the others wore their gold helmets.

Going into the Georgia game, they had taken the field 36 times and their team had been victorious in 29 of those contests, with two games ending in ties. They had traveled all over the country representing Centre from coast to coast. The home crowd had the opportunity to watch them compete 13 times in Danville before the game with the Bulldogs. Now, after 60 more minutes of play, they would be gone.

Junior Walter Skidmore, who had to be taken out of the Alabama game during the last two minutes due to a foot injury, was diagnosed after returning to Danville with what was called "a fracture in his arch."

"But, I can play, and will," he announced.

Frank Rubarth was still having some pain from his broken collar bone, and had swelling in his right ankle due to a sprain which he had sustained in the Alabama contest.

Now, he too announced, "I can play, and I will play."

Everyone else was healthy.

Centre started the same lineup as had started against Alabama, with the "Immortals" designated by *:

Left end —Hennie Lemon*
Left tackle —Walter Skidmore
Left guard —Frank Rubarth*
Center —Ed Kubale*

Right guard —Alex Bush
Right tackle —Howard Lynch*
Right end —Case Thomasson*
Quarterback —Herb Covington*
Left halfback —Elmer Rabenstein
Right halfback —Reginald "Mutt" Wilson
Fullback —Minos Gordy*

Centre won the toss and elected to receive. What followed was a dogfight, a clean, hard-fought game between two dedicated teams giving their all on every play. It was a shame that one had to lose. Bruce Dudley of the Louisville "Courier-Journal" captured that afternoon of November 29, 1924, perfectly.

> *The team of Bob Myers has emerged from the crash of Southern football without a blemish.*
>
> *It stands supreme, majestic among the bent, battered and bruised battlers for the coveted crown.*
>
> *Georgia, the last and deadliest threat, goaded to outraged fury by the humiliation heaped upon by Alabama, slashed into Centre today and swooned back, crumpled by 14–7, but only after a fight worthy of the name of Georgia.*
>
> *Georgia is the team that lost by only one point to Yale, which beat Princeton 10–0 after Princeton had badly beaten Harvard.*
>
> *Centre consecrated itself to Covington, Kubale, Lemon, Lynch, Rubarth, Gordy and Thomasson, waging their farewell fight for the Gold and White, and no team in the world could have hammered back its will to climax the luster of their service in victory.*
>
> *Victory for the sake of them was an obligaton. It had to be fulfilled.*

All of the scoring was in the second quarter. Late in the first period, Moore of Georgia punted to Covington who returned the ball close to midfield.

Rabenstein picked up nine, and two, and it was 1st down on the Bulldogs' 40.

Covey then took the center from Kubale and faked a run to the left but pulled up and fired a perfect pass to Hennie Lemon and Lemon carried it to the 13 before being tripped up.

Gordy, Covey, and Rabenstein picked up 11 yards on three line plungers and it was 1st and goal at the two. Rabenstein fired into the line and was hit hard and driven back after having gotten a yard on his initial forward motion. The whistle blew and the teams marched the length of the field to take up action again with Centre on the one yard line.

Georgia was playing for keeps. Rabenstein got the call again and didn't get an inch. It was 3rd and goal, still on the 1, when Covington barely squeezed it in. The officials had to unstack the big pile of players before finally signaling that Covey had scored. Lemon was good on the extra point and it was 7–0.

Hennie Lemon then got off a great kick, aided by the wind at his back and the ball sailed into and bounced out of the end zone for a touchback. Georgia had the ball on its own 20.

A vicious tackle by big Minos Gordy dropped the Bulldogs' right half, Kirkpatrick, for a five yard loss. Weihers got the five back on the next play, but on 3rd and 10, Georgia decided to punt. The same wind which had aided Lemon now hindered Georgia, and the kick seemed to actually hit a wall as it shot into the air and went only 12 yards before taking a bounce toward the sideline, out of bounds.

Covington, Gordy, and Gordy again, picked up 10 yards. It was 1st down on the 22. Covey sliced through the line for seven, Minos Gordy ran on two line plunges and it was 1st and goal just inside the 10.

Rabenstein was called on next and faked a run to the left and then cut back sharply over the right tackle, with Alex Bush and Howard Lynch clearing the way. The Centre right half burst across the goal untouched. Lemon was perfect, and it looked like the Colonels were going to have their way during the afternoon, as it now stood at 14-0.

Late in the 2nd quarter, a fine Georgia punt, kicked on a low line drive so as to negate the force of the wind, put Centre back on its own 11. Covington decided to try a little trickery, thinking he could catch the Bulldogs off balance as they figured Centre would try to just run out the clock with line plunges and take a safe 14-0 lead into the half time break.

The play was designed so that Gordy was to start walking back to Covey as if to ask what the signal was, and as he moved back, it was hoped the Georgia players would be distracted. Ed Kubale was then to fire the ball to Covey and the quarterback would circle Georgia's right end, hopefully for a long gainer.

The play looked good in practice, but failed in execution, as Kubale's center pass struck Gordy on the shoulder and fell to the ground where it was smothered by an alert Bulldog right at the line of scrimmage. It took three plays, but Georgia's Nelson scored on a seven yard run, getting great interference. Hollis was good on the point after, and the half ended at 14-7.

The Colonels had dedicated themselves to not giving up a point during the final four games of the season. They had really felt they had the defense, aided by the nearly fanatical drive to succeed, and they could meet their goal. Only a breakdown on an offensive play had caused them to surrender a point.

As the Gold and White jogged through the snow and sleet, the fans shouted, "30 more minutes! 30 more minutes!"

It was true. Two more quarters, 30 more minutes, and the Colonels would wear the crown as the best team in the South.

The 2nd half was a defensive struggle. Centre felt it could keep the Bulldogs out of the end zone, and played conservatively, determined not to make another error and give up the ball deep in its territory as had happened toward the end of the 1st half.

THOMASSON BEAT US—THAT THOMASSON BOY BEAT US

Bruce Dudley's story in the Sunday "Courier-Journal" pointed out that the Georgia coach, GeorgeWoodruff, had said that Case Thomasson, "that Thomasson boy," had been the cause of the Bulldogs' defeat. Twice, Case had come running, "appearing to fly," after a Georgia back had broken through and seemed certain to score. Both times, he made a dive and brought the runner down.

George "Kid" Woodruff is right, and Centre knows it. Thomasson did beat him and his Bulldogs by making two of the most extraordinary tackles ever achieved in any football game. Failure of Thomasson to arise to such superhuman speed essential for the registration of the tackles would have cost Centre two touchdowns and victory.

Thomasson was the last man between the Centre goal and the runner. No. The runner in each superlative play was actually between the Centre goal and Thomasson. At the start of each play, Thomasson could not be distinguished from the mass of men at the line of scrimmage, and as the Georgia Bulldog sped by the last Centre safety man with a clear field ahead for the goal, Thomasson did not seem to be near. Both plays started around the other end from him, and he was compelled to cover more ground than anybody to become a possibility in the play.

Three minutes after the game started, Moore, beginning from his own 49 yard line, threaded his way around left end, shifting through three Centre tacklers and side-stepping the last safety man. Coming like a wild man obliquely across the field, Thomasson gave chase. The hearts of the Centre enthusiasts stopped beating for an instant. It was Thomasson or a touchdown. And if Georgia got that touchdown with such ease three minutes after play began, its effect would be damaging far more than the six points it would grant.

The long legs of Thomasson scissored away at the fleeing Moore, and then by a stupendous effort, he crashed Moore to earth by a plunging tackle six yards from the Centre goal after Moore had dashed for a gain of 45 yards. And then the Colonels, made anew by the supreme deed of Thomasson, wrestled the ball from the Georgians on downs.

In the third quarter, Georgia held Centre on the Bulldogs' 10 yard line, snatching the ball after the Colonels couldn't make a first down. Nelson made six yards and Randall a first down on a seven yard gain.

On the 23 yard line, Nelson pulled down a pass from Kirkpatrick, evaded the Centre safety men, and again the Georgians had a runner loose for the goal with no Centre defender ahead.

Thomasson came with the speed of a frenzied ostrich, obliquely across the field, and taking up the task after his mates had failed, tore on and on for Nelson. Ten feet from the speeding runner and forty yards from the start of the test, Thomasson sprang for him, like a tiger going after his prey. He did not miss, and those cheering for the Gold and White again slumped back onto their seats, limp through another heart-stopping struggle with the lure of the victory giving speed to the foe, and the horror of defeat charging Thomasson with an even greater speed.

"That Thomasson boy beat us," said Coach Woodruff.

Mr. Woodruff is right, and Centre knows it.

In a scene reminiscent of Tiny Maxwell handing the ball to Bo at the end of the 1921 Harvard game, and declaring, "Mr. McMillin, here is your ball," referee Ernest Quigley picked up the ball as the final whistle blew and walked over to Captain Herb Covington.

"Your team played a wonderful, clean game. I am honored to present you the ball. You are truly the Southern Champions."

Herb was surrounded by his teammates, and they then all ran to the bench and formed a circle around the Chief, Coach Ofstie, and Red Roberts and gave "three cheers" for their mentors. Standing on the sideline were Bo, Bill Shadoan and Ed Diddle, smiling and cheering as loudly as the team.

Bruce Dudley had always been a great admirer of the Chief.

Back of every Centre advance was the motivating spirit of Bob Myers, the Chief, the soft-spoken Christian gentleman who has made Centre what it is today. The Chief, who always preached that if one could but believe, any dreams imaginable could come true, is the heartbeat of Centre College, and has been for years.

Centre played only the eleven starters for the entire game. There wasn't a single substitution. Frank Rubarth, nursing a broken collar bone and twisted ankle, played the entire game. Walter Skidmore, with the fracture in the arch of his foot, played the entire game. Howard "Bull" Lynch twisted his knee and ended the game with a noticeable limp. Howard Lynch played the entire game.

Georgia ran in 10 subs during the contest. The Bulldogs had made a determined effort and played excellently. They had played to win. It was just that on that last Saturday of November, 1924, the Centre College Colonels weren't to be denied.

Bruce Dudley had said it best.

Centre consecrated itself today to Covington, Kubale, Lemon, Lynch, Rubarth, Gordy and Thomasson. Victory for the sake of them was a sacred obligation. It had to be fulfilled.

The statistics were as close as the score. Centre picked up 14 first downs to Georgia's 13. Centre gained 270 yards. Georgia, 238.

Besides Case Thomasson's heroics, the outstanding performance for the Colonels was that of their captain and quarterback, Herb Covington. Covey handled the ball 33 times and gained 155 yards in playing flawlessly.

Centre ended the 1924 season at 5-1-1. What had started in such an unspectacular manner—the tie with Valparaiso—had ended in a story book fashion.

Kentucky, Tennessee, Alabama and Georgia. The total score in those four wonderful November victories was 70-7. Many felt the 1924 season was Centre's finest hour.

Of course, no one knew it at the moment, but winning the "Southern Championship" ended the "Golden Age" of Centre football. The little college would play on, but the days when the Colonels stepped on the field expecting to win, or were expected to win, were coming to a close.

But, what a wonderful run it had been!

I left the stadium after the Georgia game with mixed feelings. Of course, everybody was happy about our great win. The four straight victories over the Southern Conference teams were wonderful. It meant we truly had the best team in the South, and the way we were playing, I felt we had to have one of the best teams in the entire country.

But at the end of the game, I also realized that this would be the last time I'd see our team play. I'd traveled all over to watch them. For four years, my life had literally revolved around the team and the players.

I stood on the field and watched our boys cheer the Georgia team, and then they began to walk slowly toward the dressing room and began to fade in the distance as the snow continued to fall, and finally they were a blur, and then I couldn't see them at all, and I felt a tremendous sadness.

What would it be like not to have a team to follow and to love?

I really didn't know, and I remember walking back to the dorm with a lump in my throat, and tears in my eyes.

I simply couldn't imagine not having the Centre College football team being part of my life.

I got over it, of course. Life goes on, and there are always new experiences and adventures. But if you had lived in Danville, Kentucky, and gone to Centre College back in the early 20's like I did, you would understand how a young boy from a small place like Elizabethtown would have felt that he had lived in a magical era, a time when there was a group of young men who were known as the "Wonder Team" of college football, who had captured the hearts of people all over the United States.

I have always considered that I was fortunate to have been a part of what happened during that period, and I think back on those days often, and still see the guys and hear the shouts and cheers, and feel the pride. And I'm certain I'll continue to do so as long as I live.

It was a wonderful time, and there's never been a finer group of guys. They truly were, in every sense of the word, the "Wonder Team."

At the end of the 1924-25 school year, I attended my last Carnival. It seemed appropriate that the Colonel everyone felt had won the last game, the victory over Georgia, was the King. Of course, it was Case Thomasson. He was a popular choice and there was prolonged applause when he was introduced.

CHAPTER 24:
CENTRE'S OVERALL RANKING
1919-1924

Let's summarize what Centre accomplished in the eight years, 1917-1924. Overall, the college won 58, lost eight, and tied two games.

1917	7-1-0
1918	4-0-0
1919	9-0-0
1920	8-2-0
1921	10-1-0
1922	8-2-0
1923	7-1-1
1924	5-1-1
TOTAL	58-8-2

During those 68 games, Centre had scored 2320 points while giving up only 242. The average score was 34.1 to 3.6. The Colonels shut out their opponents 43 times. Only six times did they allow a team to score in double figures. Of the 68 games, 28 were played in Danville. The other 40 were played in 26 cities in 15 states.

SITES OF CENTRE'S GAMES 1917-1924
Danville, Ky.—28
Lexington, Ky.—6
Louisville, Ky. —5
Birmingham, Al.—4
Cambridge, Ma.—3
Greencastle, In.
Maryville, Tn.
Winchester, Ky.

Chattanooga, Tn.
Bloomington, In.
Charlottesville, Va.
Charleston, W.Va.
Georgetown, Ky.
Atlanta, Ga.
Indianapolis, In.
Fort Worth, Tx.
Cincinnati, Oh.
New Orleans, La.
San Diego, Ca.
Dallas, Tx.
Clemson, S.C.
Richmond, Va.
Philadelphia, Pa.
Memphis, Tn.
Athens, Ga.
New York, N.Y.
Knoxville, Tn.

Bo McMillin, Red Weaver and Red Roberts were Walter Camp, first team All-American selections, and their designation began to establish in the public's mind that even "minor," or small schools, had talent that needed to be recognized. Numerous Colonels had been consensus, All-Southern team members.

Despite unfounded accusations, Centre's players had excelled not only on the gridiron, but also in the classroom. Of the 18 members of the Omicron Delta Kappa honorary leadership society listed in the 1925 Old Centre yearbook, seven had played football: Herb Covington, Minos Gordy, Howard Lynch, Howard Robertson, Walter Skidmore, Case Thomasson, and Robert Wallace. The "Seven Immortals" all graduated with their class.

The comment was made in the beginning of this book that from 1919 through 1924, the years following the Great War, Centre had the top football program in the country. Naturally, it is time to make the case for that claim.

James Howell of Baltimore, Maryland, has devised a method to establish "Power Ratings" for college football programs dating back to 1869, the year of the first football game between Princeton and Rutgers. To see how Mr. Howells' system works, you can log onto: *http//www.jhowell.net* and then click on "College Football Power Ratings."

Mr. Howell ranked the teams for each of the years, and we are concerned with the 1919-24 rankings. If Centre had the 7th strongest power ranking for 1919, as it had, then we would consider that according to this computerized system, Centre was the 7th best team in the country for that year.

Below, you'll see how Centre ranked during the six years in question, 1919-24.

1919	CENTRE	# 7
1920	CENTRE	# 13
1921	CENTRE	# 2
1922	CENTRE	# 6
1923	CENTRE	# 7
1924	CENTRE	# 8

The average for the period is 7.17.

Notre Dame had the following rank based on power ratings:

1919	NOTRE DAME	# 11
1920	NOTRE DAME	# 11
1921	NOTRE DAME	# 11
1922	NOTRE DAME	# 9
1923	NOTRE DAME	# 10
1924	NOTRE DAME	# 1

The average for the period is 8.83.

The lower the numerical power rating was, the higher the ranking for the team. Centre College, the little school in Danville, Kentucky, edges out Knute Rockne's Notre Dame Irish by a slight margin.

The top 30 teams during 1919-1924, determined by their rounded off, average power ratings, were:

(1)	CENTRE	7.2
(2)	NOTRE DAME	8.8
(3)	VANDERBILT	14.1
(4)	CALIFORNIA	15.3
(5)	SYRACUSE	15.8
(6)	GEORGIA TECH	16.3
(7)	ALABAMA	16.3
(8)	PENN STATE	16.8
(9)	GEORGIA	17.5
(10)	WEST VIRGINIA	19.2
(11)	YALE	20.7
(12)	PITTSBURGH	20.7
(13)	TEXAS	22.6
(14)	DARTMOUTH	24.2
(15)	NEBRASKA	24.8
(16)	AUBURN	25.5

(17) FURMAN	26.3
(18) TEXAS A&M	27.0
(19) WASH. & JEFF.	27.8
(20) VMI	29.0
(21) W & L	30.3
(22) IOWA	32.8
(23) HARVARD	33.3
(24) PENN	34.5
(25) VPI	37.5
(26) MISSOURI	38.0
(27) ILLINOIS	38.0
(28) CHICAGO	39.5
(29) TULANE	39.7
(30) NAVY	39.8

In order to be ranked, a team had to have a power rating for all six years. Army, Southern Cal, Lafayette and Georgetown, D.C. didn't meet the criteria, but even if they had, they didn't have the records to bump Centre out of the number one ranking.

During the 1919-24 time frame, Centre played 11 teams in the "Top 30," power ratings a total of 21 games, winning 13, losing seven, and tying one.

TEAM PLAYED	TIMES PLAYED	RECORD
Harvard	3	1-2
Auburn	3	2-1
VPI	3	3-0
W&L	3	3-0
Georgia	2	1-0-1
West Virginia	2	1-1
Georgia Tech	1	0-1
Pennsylvania	1	0-1
Texas A&M	1	0-1
Tulane	1	1-0
Alabama	1	1-0
Totals	21	13-7-1

Of Centre's 21 games, only two were played in Danville (VPI and Georgia), proving once again that in order to play teams with football prowess, the Colonels had to go on the road.

Notre Dame played 10 games against teams in the "Top 30," and compiled a 7-3 record. Of the 10 games, six were with Nebraska. Four of the 10 games were in South Bend.

TEAM PLAYED	TIMES PLAYED	RECORD
Nebraska	6	4-2
Georgia Tech	3	3-0
Iowa	1	0-1
Totals	10	7-3

Any rating system is bound to provoke controversy. However in averaging the yearly power ratings from 1919-24, Centre was the top team in the country during the six year span.

You can argue far into the night about the "best team" in college football during the period of the post-World War I years. No matter. It would seem to be without dispute that the Centre College "Crying, Praying Colonels" were the most unlikely and most colorful group of young men to ever reach the pinnacle of the great game of college football.

Of that, there should be no argument.

POSTSCRIPT—HARVARD

So what happened with Centre and Harvard's football programs?

Harvard finished the 1922 season with a 7-2 record. After beating Centre, the Crimson beat Dartmouth and Florida, lost to Princeton and Brown by a total of 10 points, and finished successfully by defeating arch-rival Yale, 10-3.

Coach Bob Fisher at that time had a very impressive 31-4-3 record during his tenure, 1919-22, including a Rose Bowl victory with the January 1, 1920 defeat of Oregon, 7-6.

Harvard began a steady decline after 1922. It wasn't by accident, but rather by design. Basically, Harvard decided to begin to deemphasize football, as did Princeton and Yale. The "Big 3" got together and decided to take the following measures.

(1) No football practice before the formal opening of school.

(2) No intersectional games. (This restriction was followed rather loosely.)

(3) A signed agreement regarding eligibility of players which shall include the player signing a statement signifying his amateur status.

(4) No transfer to be eligible until passing entrance exams of the respective schools.

(5) No coaching from the sidelines during play, and no communication with players on the bench.

(6) No organized scouting of the opposition.

Harvard and Yale cut their schedule to eight games. Princeton cut to seven. During the next three years, Harvard had a cumulative record of 12-10-2. The 10 losses in three years equaled the total losses for the 10 years of 1907-1916 when Harvard ruled and compiled a record of 78-10-5.

Coach Fisher resigned after the 1925 season, and Arnold Horween took over, the same Arnold Horween who offered the ball which Bo refused after the 1920 Centre.

Horween coached five years. His record was 21-17-3. His 1926 team went 3-5. It was only the second losing record in the history of the football program. (The 1878 team was 1-2.)

Interestingly, in the opening game of the '26 season, Bo was coaching at Geneva

College and brought his team to Harvard Stadium and beat the Crimson, 16-7, in the first game that Arnold Horween coached.

After Horween resigned following the 1930 season, Harvard barely had a winning record until the formation of the Ivy League in 1956. During the 25 years from 1931 through 1955, the overall record was 99-90-12. The schedule during this period was heavily weighed with the future members of the Ivy League: Brown, Columbia, Cornell, Dartmouth, Pennsylvania, Princeton and Yale.

Since 1956 and the formation of the Ivy League, Harvard has comfortably confined its schedule to fellow League members and with games against such as Massachusetts, Holy Cross, Bucknell, Northeastern, Tufts, Amherst, Lafayette, Lehigh, and other colleges of similar athletic ambition. (An exception would be the seven games with Army, 1980-84, 1989 and 1991. Harvard went 2-5 against the Cadets.)

Despite the lesser strength of the Crimson's opponents, there has been no diminution of the magnificence of Harvard Stadium, a National Historic Landmark. A $6,500,000 donor-paid renovation was undertaken in 2006 which included replacement of the natural turf with a state-of-the-art artificial surface, and the addition of lighting which was situated so as to maintain the original classical character of the wonderful structure. A "bubble" was installed which can be inflated in order to make the facility usable during the cold, New England winters.

Harvard Stadium on Soldiers Field, still evokes awe, just as it did when the "Praying Colonels" of Centre College first walked into the great concrete horseshoe during October, 1920, many, many decades ago.

POSTSCRIPT—CENTRE

It really wasn't a good sign for the future of Centre football that the school depended so heavily on "The Seven Immortals" and a few others during the 1924 season, and rarely substituted. This pattern was especially noticeable during the game in New York with West Virginia, and the final four games against the Southern Conference teams.

During the West Virginia game, there were but two substitutions. During the Kentucky game, there were also just two subs, Jim Priest and William Kagin. Down in Knoxville against Tennessee, Jim Priest started for the injured Frank Rubarth who didn't make the trip. The only subs were Kagin and Carl Hilker.

During the Alabama game, all eleven starters played the entire 60 minutes except Walter Skidmore, who came out due to an injured foot, which later proved to be a fracture in his instep. The only replacement was Jim Priest who relieved Skidmore with just two minutes of play remaining.

There were no subs at all during the Georgia game. None. Basically, Centre just played 15 men in 1924, and only 13 regularly. Certainly that didn't speak well for the team's depth, or for 1925. Centre had excellent starters and a few adequate subs, but talent and experience fell off sharply as the coaches looked down the bench for available help.

The 13 who earned the gold "C" were:
Alexander Bush
Herb Covington
Minos Gordy
Ed Kubale
Clifton "Hennie" Lemon
Howard Lynch
George McClure
Jim Priest
Elmer Rabenstein
Frank Rubarth
Walter Skidmore
Robert "Case" Thomasson
Robert Wallace

Added to the lack of manpower in the varsity line-up was the situation with the freshman team. Red Roberts actually took the Lieutenents to Lexington to play UK's first year men, the Kittens, and only had his 11 starters. There were no replacements. Had there been an injury, he would have had to throw in the towel, or perhaps borrow a player from Kentucky.

Analysts could see what was happening. Centre had brought in a core group of young men from Texas who, along with several others, had taken the college to the top of the football mountaintop. But the talent hadn't been adequately replaced over the years. With "The Seven Immortals" graduating, and so little help due to come from the freshman team, things were beginning to look bleak for 1925.

Of course, it's easier to see what the future holds once one has lived through it. While there were definite worries after the successful—actually spectacular—finish of the 1924 season, many felt that Centre was destined to continue on, playing the "big boys" and continuing to have winning campaigns. It wasn't to be.

One factor was that after Centre's enrollment nearly reached 300 during the 1923-24 academic year, it began to decline, and lesser numbers on campus were reflected in lesser numbers on the gridiron.

CLASS	ENROLLMENT
1918/19	134 (Centre's S.A.T.C. war season)
1919/20	181 (The big win over West Virginia)
1920/21	191 (Harvard-31 Centre-14)
1921/22	257 (Centre-6 Harvard-0)
1922/23	284 (Harvard-24 Centre-10)
1923/24	292 (The new stadium to be built)
1924/25	223 ("The Seven Immortals" graduate)
1925/26	241 (The Chief's last year)

While a loss of 69 students wouldn't cause even a ripple at a large state college, the drop-off from 1923/24 to 1924/25 of that number of enrollees equated to a 23% decline.

Especially telling was that during the 1925/26 school year, there were only 130 young men in the upper three classes who were eligible to play football. The "freshman rule" was beginning to literally rule.

Even with the small student body, a college the size of Centre could compete if the will was there to make recruitment and winning a priority of the school. When Dr.Ganfield was president, he indeed encouraged that such a policy be implemented. That determination was no longer part of the Centre mission. The underlying sentiment of much of the faculty was that athletics had somewhat replaced academics as a focus of the college. They wanted to restore the emphasis at Centre to the classroom.

The Chief came back for another year. Harold Ofstie stayed on as assistant coach and Red Roberts was replaced by Bill Shadoan who departed from Valparaiso after the college developed some serious financial challenges. (The Lutheran University

Association came to the rescue, but Shadoan had no assurance that the school could continue with its athletic programs and left.)

The 1926 "Old Centre" yearbook summarized the 1925 football season quite nicely.

In scoring points and winning games, Centre experienced a most unsuccessful season; but in showing fight and winning honor, it compares with the great teams of the past. Possessing but few experienced men and composed to a great extent of green material, Centre put on the field a team that, win or lose, demanded the respect of all its opponents.

The 1925 Colonels went 3-6. For the first time since 1916, the University of Kentucky was able to beat the boys from Danville. Centre's three wins were against in-state teams with little reputation.

Centre	10	Kentucky Wesleyan	0
Centre	0	Oglethorpe	20
Centre	13	Michigan State	15
Centre	13	Western Kentucky	0
Centre	0	Kentucky	16
Centre	0	Tennessee	12
Centre	3	Georgetown (DC)	41
Centre	34	Georgetown (Ky)	6
Centre	0	South Carolina	20

The Michigan State game, played in East Lansing, was a fine effort, and Centre almost won. The Colonels were down at the half, 12-0, came back to lead 13-12, and seemingly had the victory. State had the ball on the Centre 46 with a minute to play and faced a 4th down. The "Old Centre" summary of the season described what transpired.

With the wind against him and from a difficult angle, Smith kicked a beautiful and seemingly impossible goal. A few seconds later the game ended, 15-13, in favor of Michigan State. (Michigan State had a 3-5 record in 1925. The losses were to Lake Forest, Michigan, Penn State, Colgate and Wisconsin. Besides Centre, wins were over Adrian College, a little liberal arts school in Michigan, and Toledo.)

Georgetown, in the District of Columbia, was the destination of the annual "trip East" in 1925. While Georgetown was 8-1 for the year, with the only loss being 3-2 to Uncle Charlie's Bucknell team, the Hoyas weren't exactly up there in the stratosphere of the football heavens. Their opponents in 1925 included Drexel, Mount St. Mary, Lebanon Valley, King College of Tennessee, and the Quantico Marines. Nonetheless, Centre was easily dispatched, 41-3.

Elmer Rabenstein was hurt and couldn't play in the Kentucky game. Centre had virtually no offense during the contest, and the 16-0 loss finally made good the perennial cry over in Lexington, "This is the year!"

Centre managed to beat Kentucky in 1926, 7-0. The members of the team were given little gold footballs with a white, enameled "C" and the score, "Centre 7, State 0" and "State Champions" engraved.

Centre got blown out by the Wildcats 53-0 in 1927, played competitively in 1928, losing 8-0, and was outclassed in 1929, 33-0.

After the 1929 game, Kentucky sent word that it no longer wanted to play the Colonels. Centre couldn't believe it, and protested vehemently.

"When we had the upper hand against Kentucky, we never even considered dropping the Wildcats from our schedule, as well we could have."

Kentucky put out a press release that it was going to concentrate on Southern Conference opponents, as well it could. There were 23 members. There was a significant protest throughout the state. Centre threatened to sever all relationships. Kentucky held firm, and the two colleges never again met on the gridiron. Like Penn and Princeton, the schools later met in the "minor sports."

Kentucky would never have ended the series without first gaining the upper hand. It would have been taken as surrendering. But after winning three of four, the state school thought it could move on, having finally become the top program in Kentucky. (The series, begun in 1891, ended with Centre coming out on top, 20-13-2. Remember that the 1901-05 games, when Centre was called Central University and had a 2-2-1 record against the Wildcats, should be part of the series. Kentucky's "Media Guide" doesn't include the games, and has the record at 18-11-1. It is incorrect.)

Harold Ofstie, assistant coach, took over when the Chief didn't return in 1926. He was 6-10-2 during his two seasons. The days of pouncing on the big schools were over.

During Ofstie's tenure, Centre lost to Tennessee, 30-0, Michigan State, 42-14, West Virginia, 21-0, and Vanderbilt, 54-6. Centre's fans realized that the sun was not only setting, but had disappeared over the horizon, when the University of Louisville, which Centre's freshman team had beaten in 1922, plastered the Gold and White in 1927, 40-7.

Just three years after the wonderful 1924 season, the Associated Press sent out a story in December of 1927 which appeared in newspapers all over the country. Centre had completed the last three campaigns with a combined 9-16-2 record.

Fickle fate is quick to forget the stellar accomplishments of the past for those of the present.

Little Centre College probably offers as fitting example of fleeting fame as any in the realm of football. A few years ago, Centre sprang into the spotlight with a sterling eleven. It swept aside all before it. The "Praying Colonels," as the team was known, because it always knelt in prayer just before starting a game, soon got to be the talk of the gridiron world.

Coached by Charlie Moran, veteran National League umpire, Centre turned out such twinklers as Bo McMillin, Red Weaver, Red Roberts, Army Armstrong, Herb Covington, and others. Some gained All-American recognition.

It wasn't long before little Centre College, situated in the Bluegrass of Kentucky, was the most sought after school in the game. Offers came from far and wide. Centre was the biggest attraction in football.

Even Harvard asked Centre to come to Cambridge. Centre accepted; in fact, met the Crimson at its Soldiers Field enclosure several times. In 1921, Centre chalked up one of its greatest feats in defeating Harvard, 6-0.

Centre's reign at the top was short-lived, however. The shining McMillin, Weaver and Roberts and others were graduated, leaving the Kentucky school nothing much save memories of other campaigns.

During the last years, Centre has done little in football. Its teams have met defeat with too much regularity and mostly at the hands of schools the Colonels would have considered hardly more than set-ups in the winning days. Only recently, Vanderbilt swamped Centre, 54-6.

In a word, Centre has slipped out of the limelight about as fast as it reached the purple heights seven or eight years ago.

No longer does the little hamlet close up shop and turn out en mass to welcome home the conquering heroes. No longer does the band play triumphant airs to lead Centre's mere handful of students in a snake dance throughout the main section of town.

Uncle Charlie is no longer guiding the Danville school's destinies

Centre College is just a little Kentucky school now.

In 1929, Centre reached back into the past and hired Ed Kubale as its head football coach. "Kube," captain of the 1923 squad, certainly had the heritage. He had played every game from 1921 through the 1924 season, 37 in all, and during those years as the team's center, the Colonels had rolled to 30-5-2 record.

Ed Kubale was the coach for nine seasons, and his record was a respectable 51-32-4. However, during his reign, Centre was beginning to downgrade the schedule, and when the Colonels took on one of the more powerful programs, the result was becoming predictable.

Notable losses were:

1929	Centre	6	Tennessee	40
	Centre	0	Kentucky	33
1930	Centre	0	Tennessee	18
	Centre	7	Northwestern	45
	Centre	0	Kansas State	27

From 1931 on, Centre was playing teams like Wittenburg (OH), Washington University of St. Louis, Mercer, old Kentucky rivals Georgetown and Transylvania, Chattanooga, Murray (KY), Birmingham-Southern, John Carroll, Morehead (KY), Marquette, Marshall, and Southwestern (now Rhodes.)

When the Colonels tried to step it up, the picture was less than pretty.

1933	Centre	0	Pittsburgh	37
1934	Centre	0	Tennessee	32
1935	Centre	13	Temple	25
	Centre	0	Indiana	14
	Centre	14	Tennessee	25
	Centre	0	Mississippi	26
1936	Centre	7	Temple	50
	Centre	0	Indiana	38
	Centre	13	West Virginia	26
1937	Centre	0	Indiana	12
1938	Centre	6	Villanova	35

Quinn Decker took over in 1938 and compiled a 14-17-2 record. A memorable effort by the Colonels occurred in 1939 when Centre traveled to West Point and lost a very close game to Army, 9-6. The Cadets were a decent squad, having tied a good Penn State team and played well against tough Notre Dame, losing 14-0.

However, the Army game didn't thrust the Colonels back into the upper echelons. The following year, the season opened with Boston College having its way, 40-0.

The final attempts at playing with the major colleges came in 1941 and 1942. In '41, Centre went down to Atlanta, making its first appearance in the city since the game with Georgia Tech in 1920 when the Colonels felt they had been the victims of poor sportsmanship. This time, in a clean game, they just got thumped. The University of Georgia won, 47-6.

In 1942, in one last try to play with the big schools, even the most partisan supporters of the Gold and White must have realized that David could no longer run out on the fields where the Goliaths of the game roamed.

On October 17, little Milligan College, a faith-based liberal arts school in Tennessee, lying on the banks of Buffalo Creek in the Northeastern part of the state, was invited to travel up to Danville to play Centre. The "Buffs" won, 7-6.

Perhaps that contest should have been fair warning of what was to follow the next Saturday. In the last game ever with the "big boys," Centre went down to Nashville and was slaughtered by a Vanderbilt team which just the week before been handled rather easily by Mississippi State, 33-0. The Commodores won, 66-0.

Centre shut down its program totally during the war years, 1943-45. The pads stayed in the lockers, and attention was paid to classes and a two-front war in Europe and the Pacific.

Carl "Swede" Anderson, the head trainer during the Colonels' "Golden Years," was asked to get the program back up and running so that the college could field a team in 1946.

The schedule was modest. The results weren't so great, but at least Centre was back on the gridiron, even if the school was blanked during its first post-war effort, and had a record of 0-7.

Centre	0	Maryville (Tn.)	19
Centre	6	Mississippi College	26
Centre	0	Wabash	16
Centre	20	Hanover	27
Centre	18	Middle Tennessee	19
Centre	7	Sewanee	52
Centre	0	Arkansas State	14

"Swede" had a 14-23-2 record in five seasons, and went out on a winning note, having gone 6-1-1 in 1950, with the following record:

Centre	26	Tusculum	0
Centre	14	Maryville	7
Centre	7	Anderson (In.)	7
Centre	9	Wabash	7
Centre	24	Hanover	14
Centre	24	Southwestern (Rhodes)	0
Centre	16	Sewanee	8
Centre	3	Georgetown College	7

A memorable season was 1955. Briscoe Inman was the coach from 1952-56 and 1963-65. Inman had an overall record of 38-24-2 in his eight years directing the program.

In 1955, the Colonels were 8-0 and hardly challenged. Herb Covington, little Covey, one of the "Seven Immortals," had a son, George, on the team. The team outscored its opponents, 245-53.

Centre	28	Otterbein (Oh.)	13
Centre	17	Maryville	0
Centre	24	Washington & Lee	7
Centre	28	Southwestern (Rhodes)	13
Centre	53	Georgetown College	0
Centre	27	Hanover	13
Centre	28	Sewanee	0
Centre	40	Washington and Jefferson	7

The Tangerine Bowl, in Orlando, was established in 1947 as a post-season affair for small colleges. It later evolved into one of the premiere big-time, major college bowls, and of this writing, is called the Capital One Bowl. Early on, the Tangerine Bowl was called, the "Little Bowl with the Big Heart," because all of the proceeds went to charity.

Centre was invited to play in the January 1, 1956 game due to its great season, and everyone at the school and Danville was fired up about the possibility of going down to Florida over the holidays.

The college turned down the invitation. Coach Inman later stated his team wouldn't play because he coached a group of young men who were first class, who played for a first class college, and they were offered second class accommodations and second class transportation and expenses. Apparently, Coach Inman didn't think that the Tangerine Bowl was the "Little Bowl with the Big Heart."

The game was played before 10,000 fans, and Juniata College from Huntington, Pa. and Missouri Valley College from Marshall, Mo. tied, 6-6.

In 1970, there was a drive by some Centre alumni to try to put Harvard and Centre back on the field at Harvard Stadium for a 1971 game which would have celebrated the 50th anniversary of Centre's win in 1921. The idea caught on in Cambridge. Even though the game wasn't played, alumni at Harvard campaigned for the next few years to have Centre return.

The feeling was that the game could once again fill the great horseshoe on the Charles. Harvard's attendance had fallen off to such a degree that it was felt that the publicity generated by recounting the Centre-Harvard games of 1920-22, when Harvard and other members of the "Big 3" ruled, could be the spark needed to regenerate fan interest.

Wouldn't it be wonderful to stage another game? Put the Colonels up at the Lenox, not much changed from the early 20's. Send the team to a performance at the Colonial Theatre, still thriving down Boylston across from the Boston Common. Have a jazz band play at a dance in the Boston Garden and invite all of the fraternities and sororities and clubs to try to recreate the dance steps of the day. See if the members of the University Club would have the Colonels for dinner the evening prior to the game. Purchase "retro" uniforms to try to duplicate the look of the equipment of the day. Dress the cheerleaders as they were at the game, and the officials. Cheer the same cheers, with megaphones. Wave the same pennants. Play the same songs. Try to get as many owners of cars from the era to bring them to the game. Find a couple of period buses to take the Colonels from the Lenox to Harvard Stadium. Have a modern Roscoe, dressed as before, take a Centre pennant and "do the cakewalk, and pigeon wing." Give prizes for the most authentic period clothing worn to the game. Print the program for the game as it was printed before. Could the tickets have a "retro" look? Serve drinks out of the same type cups. Get the Boston "Herald" and "Globe" to print an edition with the type of the times, with coverage as before.

Just flat out, do everything possible to recreate the atmosphere of the wonderful, early 20's! Wouldn't it be wonderful to stage another game?

A REUNION IN DANVILLE, JUNE 1950

In 1950, the Chief, now the alumni secretary at Centre, invited members of the teams from 1917-24 to come to a reunion on the campus. There was to be the annual Centre Carnival, the dedication of a new addition to the Boyle-Humphrey Gymnasium, and various functions to honor the old Colonel veterans who were coming back to the scene of so many happy memories.

The featured speaker at the dedication of the gym addition on June 10 was Fred M. Vinson, Centre Class of 1909, Chief Justice of the United States Supreme Court.

The previous evening there had been a smoker to honor those members of the team who had returned.

Those attending were:

Army Armstrong	Clarence Jones
Walter Skidmore	Tom Bartlett
George Jones	Terry Snowday
Alexander Bush	Ed Kubale
Hump Tanner	George Chinn
Hennie Lemon	Bracken Tate
Herb Covington	Herman Lowenthal
Case Thomasson	Ben Cregor
Howard Lynch	Bob Waddle
Ed Diddle	George McClure
Red Weaver	Dick Gibson
Bo McMillin	Lefty Whitnell
Minos Gordy	Joe Murphy
Reginald Wilson	Carl Hilker
Jim Priest	Hope Hudgins
Elmer Rabenstein	Chief Myers
Bill James	Marshall Shearer
John McGee	"Swede"Anderson

John McGee was a student manager and "Swede" Anderson was the head trainer during the "Wonder Team" era, and became head coach in 1946-50.

The team trainer and "rubber," Dudley Doneghy, was also there. Dudley had become associated with the team as a 24 year old in 1919, the year that Centre was undefeated and claimed the National Championship. He ended his career in 1955, a year that the Colonels were also undefeated. It was Dudley on whom Uncle Charlie and all of the subsequent coaches relied so heavily. He was a constant over the years. Coaches and players came and went, but Dudley was always there. He died suddenly on November 28, 1962. Army spoke on behalf of the Centre Board of Trustees and said, "Centre lost a devoted friend. He was always popular with the Centre athletes and other students and was a high-type person."

Team captains who attended were:

1917	Bracken Tate
1919-20	Bo McMillin
1921	Army Armstrong
1923	Ed Kubale
1924	Herb Covington

Matty Bell, captain of the 1918 team, was the athletic director at SMU and sent his regrets. Red Roberts, captain of 1922, had tragically been killed in a hotel fire in Middlesboro, Kentucky in1945. (Walter Skidmore was the captain of the 1925 team. He was also a valuable team member during 1923-24, having lettered during those years, and his service as captain of the '25 team deserves mention.)

Besides Matty Bell, also sending a letter and having to decline the invitation, was Bob Mathias, president of a Chicago bank, who couldn't get out of a prior commitment, and Sully Montgomery, who was in a hot race for sheriff in Fort Worth and couldn't break away.

Despite all of the accomplishments of the men in attendance who had been members of the Gold and White, the man commanding the most attention was presiding over the smoker, Robert L. "Chief" Myers.

The Colonels stood and told story after story about how the Chief had influenced their lives. It was an evening devoted to pouring out their feelings of admiration, gratitude, and love for their mentor, a man they had always also considered their great friend. Over and over, they gave him credit for helping them in their later lives by instilling the "spirit of Old Centre, and the will to try just a little harder when the going was the hardest."

Bo told the story about when he was in Somerset and so homesick and lovesick that he was going to hop a freight and return to Fort Worth. "Thad and Red hid my shoes and called the Chief who came down on a train from Danville and talked me into staying and getting my credits. I don't know what I would be doing today if Chief Myers hadn't talked some sense into me. I do know one thing—everything I have ever done, and everything I have ever become, I owe to the Chief."

Many a tribute was also paid to Uncle Charlie who had died just the year before at age 71. It was Uncle Charlie, a great teacher, who taught them to play "manly football," hard but clean, always representing Centre in a way which would earn the respect of their opponents.

The Chief very emotionally closed out the evening by praising each of "my boys."

"You have truly believed, and those beliefs allowed you to achieve your dreams. As I look out upon each of you, I know that your days at Old Centre molded your lives so that you were provided the knowledge and will to succeed, just as we had so much success during those years which are so near and dear in our memories, but now so far away."

ONE LAST REUNION

There was one more reunion, at another homecoming, just one day short of 40 years after the great 1921 victory over Harvard.

On October 28, 1961, during the halftime of a game with old rival Sewanee, the attendees were honored. My father and I were at the game. Because of his stories and introductions through the years, I recognized the Colonels who were there that afternoon. I knew what they had accomplished, much of which was on the very field on which they stood.

It was amazing that nine of the 16 young men who had gotten into the Harvard game, along with George Chinn, Les Combs, and head cheerleader, George Swinebroad, were once again lined up on the playing field. (George Chinn had started in the 1920 Harvard game and played well until getting hurt. He was in uniform for the 1921 game, as was Les Combs, but neither saw action. George Swinebroad saw a lot of action, leading the small contingent of Colonels' fans in cheers throughout the game.)

They were all now well into their middle years, but were still ramrod straight, and carried themselves like the athletes they had been.

Of the seven missing, three had died; Red Roberts in the hotel fire, Bo of complications from stomach cancer in 1952 at age 57, and Minos Gordy, suddenly from a heart attack, just two months previously.

Bill Shadoan, Frank Rubarth, Buck Jones and Ray Class, the young man who got in on one play, the missed field goal attempt, sent word that for various reasons they couldn't make it to Danville.

Lined up on the turf were Bill James, Fort Worth; Ben Cregor, Springfield, Kentucky; Richard Gibson, Louisville; Ed Kubale, Fort Smith, Arkansas; George Chinn, Harrodsburg; Les Combs, Lexington; George Swinebroad, Lancaster, Kentucky; Army Armstrong, Fort Smith, Arkansas; Herb Covington, Mayfield, Kentucky; and the three from Owensboro—Hump Tanner, Tom Bartlett and Terry Snowday.

Many of the students in attendance had seen the C6 H0 still painted around the Boyle-Humphrey Gymnasium door every time they entered the old building. Most knew only vaguely the history behind why the figures were there.

"Was that the score of some game way back when?"

"Did it have something to do with Harvard?"

The old timers in the crowd, especially the many from Danville, knew exactly what C6 H0 signified, and as they cheered the old Colonels who were smiling and waving to the crowd, they tried to explain.

"It was when these few were young men, and had believed that they could accomplish anything, anything they could dream. They were known all over the country as the 'Wonder Team.'"

"Yes, C6 H0 was the score when they beat Harvard. But they did more than just beat Harvard, as wonderful as that was. They provided the inspiration for a generation of young people, people like you, that if you can imagine it, and if you are dedicated, you can make your dreams come true. That was their greatest accomplishment."

My father turned to a group of students and picked up on the thought.

I was here at Centre when the "Wonder Team" played. They lived by a motto that was always on the wall in the locker room.

"Believe. Achieve. Succeed."

They had that great belief, instilled in them by their coaches. They worked hard, dedicated to achieving, to making their dreams come true. And they succeeded not only on the playing field, but throughout their lives.

I consider myself blessed by having known them. They truly were the "Wonder Team."

CENTRE COLLEGE FOOTBALL SCHEDULES
1917-1924

DATE	CENTRE	OPPONENT		LOCATION

1917 (Won 7 — Lost 1 — Tied 0)

Oct. 6	104	KY Military Institute	0	Danville, KY
Oct. 20	0	DePauw	6	Greencastle, IN
Oct. 27	34	Maryville	0	Maryville, TN
Nov. 3	3	Kentucky	0	Danville, KY
Nov. 9	37	Kentucky Wesleyan	0	Winchester, KY
Nov. 17	28	Sewanee	0	Chattanooga, TN
Nov. 24	28	Transylvania	0	Lexington, KY
Nov. 29	13	Georgetown	0	Danville, KY

1918 (Won 4 — Lost 0 — Tied 0)

Nov. 2	52	Transylvania	3	Danville, KY
Nov. 9	38	Great Lakes NTS	0	Danville, KY
Nov. 22	10	Camp Zachary Taylor	7	Danville, KY
Nov. 28	83	Georgetown	3	Danville, KY

1919 (Won 9 — Lost 0 — Tied 0)

Sept. 27	95	Hanover	0	Danville, KY
Oct. 4	12	Indiana	3	Bloomington, IN
Oct. 18	57	St. Xavier	0	Danville, KY
Oct. 25	69	Transylvania	0	Lexington, KY
Nov. 1	49	Virginia	7	Charlottesville, VA
Nov. 8	14	West Virginia	6	Charleston, WV
Nov. 15	56	Kentucky	0	Danville, KY
Nov. 22	56	DePauw	0	Louisville, KY
Nov. 27	77	Georgetown	7	Georgetown KY

1920 (Won 8 — Lost 2 — Tied 0)

Oct. 2	66	Morris Harvey	0	Danville, KY
Oct. 9	120	Howard	0	Danville, KY
Oct. 16	55	Transylvania	0	Danville, KY
Oct. 23	14	Harvard	31	Cambridge, MA
Oct. 30	0	Georgia Tech	24	Atlanta, GA
Nov. 6	34	DePauw	0	Indianapolis, IN
Nov. 13	49	Kentucky	0	Lexington, KY
Nov. 20	28	VPI	0	Louisville, KY
Nov. 25	103	Georgetown	0	Danville, KY
Jan. 1	63	Texas Christian	7	Ft. Worth, TX

1921 (Won 10 — Lost 1 — Tied 0)

Oct. 1	14	Clemson	0	Danville, KY
Oct. 8	14	VPI	0	Danville, KY
Oct. 15	28	St. Xavier	6	Cincinnati, OH
Oct. 22	98	Transylvania	0	Lexington, KY
Oct. 29	6	Harvard	0	Cambridge, MA
Nov. 5	55	Kentucky	0	Danville, KY
Nov. 12	21	Auburn	0	Birmingham, AL
Nov. 19	25	Washington & Lee	0	Louisville, KY
Nov. 24	21	Tulane	0	New Orleans, LA
Dec. 26	38	Arizona	0	San Diego, CA
Jan. 2	14	Texas A & M	22	Dallas, TX

1922 (Won 8 — Lost 2 — Tied 0)

Sept. 23	72	Carson-Newman	0	Danville, KY
Sept. 30	21	Clemson	0	Clemson
Oct. 7	55	Mississippi	0	Danville, KY
Oct. 14	10	VPI	6	Richmond, VA
Oct. 21	10	Harvard	24	Cambridge, MA
Oct. 28	32	Louisville	7	Danville, KY
Nov. 4	27	Kentucky	3	Lexington, KY
Nov. 11	27	Washington & Lee	6	Louisville, KY
Nov. 18	0	Auburn	6	Birmingham, AL
Nov. 30	42	South Carolina	0	Danville, KY

1923 (Won 7 — Lost 1 — Tied 1)

Oct. 6	14	Carson-Newman	0	Danville, KY
Oct. 13	28	Clemson	7	Danville, KY
Oct. 20	29	Oglethorpe	0	Danville, KY
Oct. 27	0	Pennsylvania	24	Philadelphia, PA
Nov. 3	10	Kentucky	0	Danville, KY
Nov. 10	20	Sewanee	6	Memphis, TN
Nov. 17	17	Auburn	0	Birmingham, AL
Nov. 24	19	Washington & Lee	0	Louisville, KY
Dec. 1	3	Georgia	3	Athens, GA

1924 (Won 5 — Lost 1 — Tied 1)

Oct. 4	0	Valparaiso University	0	Danville, KY
Oct. 18	43	Transylvania	0	Danville, KY
Oct. 25	6	West Virginia	13	New York, NY
Nov. 1	7	Kentucky	0	Lexington, KY
Nov. 8	32	Tennessee	0	Knoxville, TN
Nov. 15	17	Alabama	0	Birmingham, AL
Nov. 29	14	Georgia	7	Danville, KY

INDEX

505, 506, 510, 516, 517, 521, 525, 547, 553, 556, 585, 589, 591, 592.

See Christmas Bowl

University of Virginia 32, 39–43, 49, 55, 66, 67

University of West Virginia 32, 39, 40, 45–47, 50–54, 59, 63, 66, 70, 71, 73, 74

V

Van Antwerp, Howard 18, 20, 21, 31, 34, 43, 49, 55, 69, 71, 73, 83, 84, 89

Vanderbilt 24, 27, 30, 58, 67, 82, 93, 137, 148, 176, 177, 191, 196, 203, 293, 294, 304, 324, 325, 386, 459, 465, 466, 493, 501, 507, 516, 519, 524, 563, 582, 583, 584

Virginia Polytechnic Institute 78, 79, 135, 143, 149, 150, 151, 152, 153, 154, 183, 195, 196, 197, 198, 199, 200, 201, 206, 225, 309, 310, 333, 393, 396, 398, 399, 400, 402, 403, 404, 405, 408, 453, 485, 512, 515, 516, 574, 591, 592

W

Wachter, Edward A. 176

Wagenhurst, E.O. 487

Walden, William Julian "Judy" 175, 177

Walker, Bob 28

Walton, Rebecca 375

Warner, Glenn "Pop" 12, 392, 418

Washington & Lee 183, 196, 304, 310, 313, 393, 493, 547, 585, 592

Washington and Jefferson 83, 137, 324, 328–329, 345, 352, 377, 386, 461, 489, 512, 525, 542, 585

Washington, George 152

Washington State 172, 323, 325, 330, 377, 459

Washington University in St. Louis 26, 583

Wayland, Poolie 28

Weatherford, E.J. 396

Weaver, James R. "Red" 13–15, 16, 18, 20, 21, 25, 27, 28, 31, 34, 35, 39, 42, 43, 48, 49, 50, 51, 53, 58, 61, 65, 68, 70, 73, 75, 80, 82, 83, 92, 93, 94, 99, 103, 106, 112, 119, 121, 122, 124, 125, 127, 130, 136, 137, 139, 141, 145, 146, 148, 149, 154, 155, 156, 159, 160, 161, 164, 166, 168, 169, 170, 171, 182, 184, 186, 188, 191, 195, 197, 206, 232, 234, 273, 331, 374, 462, 463, 495, 498, 524, 534, 535, 545, 572, 582, 587

Webb, Melville 214

Weir, "Hennie" 377, 380

Weisinger, M.G. 145

Welsh, Ella and George 32, 33, 82, 191, 409, 454, 456, 474

West Tennessee Normal College 501

Wharton, Bayard 207, 208

WHAS, Louisville 415

Whitnell, Lefty 28, 31, 34, 62, 65, 69, 73, 84, 89, 95, 111, 120, 121, 124, 136, 145, 146, 149, 154, 160, 218, 220, 334, 547, 587

Wilderness Road 9

William and Mary 152, 196, 402

Williams, Arthur 132

Williams, Carl 487

Williams, Charles Snead 332

Williams, C.L. 28

Y

Z